Mahatma

I & II

The
I AM PRESENCE

Brian Grattan

Light Technology Publishing

Glenda Barrie and Margaret Pinyan
Editors

Joanna Heikens
Cover Design

Priska Arnold

Michael Z Tyree
Graphic Dezign

Published by
Light Technology
Publishing
P.O. Box 3540
Flagstaff, AZ 86003
1-800-450-0985

Printed by

SEDONA COLOR GRAPHICS
PRINTING SPECIALISTS

P.O. Box 3870
Flagstaff, AZ 86003

www.lighttechnology.com

Acknowledgements

This new book, *Mahatma II*, completes for humankind what had to be stated at this bewildering time on Earth, with so much new and, until now, unidentifiable energy and rapid shifts in consciousness within which the "old age" simply cannot function. *Mahatma II* completes the circuitry of *Mahatma I* and allows humankind the wonderful opportunity to embody relative truth in a way that was not available before this time and place.

The combination of *Mahatma I* and *Mahatma II*, studied with complete dedication, will allow God-man/Hu-man to raise their consciousness above the dense atomic body as the "fallen ones," at a time on Earth when one will have to obey the Great Cosmic Law of Resonance and raise one's vibration into Light and Love or leave this planet for another schoolroom in one universe or another.

My particular appreciation goes to Danielle Pestalozzi, who not only translated *Mahatma I* into German, but allowed the doors of Switzerland to open in a profound and generous way.

Another great Co-Creator whom I wish to acknowledge is Priska Arnold; I marvel at her dedication and great organizational abilities. Priska in her own right is a marvelous teacher and healer who opened her doors unconditionally to our teachings and energy.

These two great beings and others in Switzerland have allowed our[1] energy to center in this beautiful country. An ironic side effect of locating in Zurich originally, before moving to Basel, was the amount of gold in storage there. Gold should flow and not be stored; but from our point of view of anchoring energy on Earth, nothing is more compatible with "spiritualizing energy" than gold. Its energy vibrates at an extremely high rate in dense physicality, and so it can act upon the finer physical expressions through the absorption of its energy. Thus it was not by chance that Switzerland was selected for the magnification of the *Mahatma* energy, as a new beginning in a new world.

The two teachers from your human Hierarchy who have stepped down

---

1 When "our" and "we" are used in the text, this refers to the comprehensive Oneness we overshadow — all 352 levels of Self from Earth to Source.

these higher teachings to myself are Djwhal Khul and St. Germain. These two have been very successful in aligning with our vibration on Earth and magnifying a greater wholeness of consciousness in *Mahatma II* with which to assist humankind. They have worked as conduits to bring forth, through these lower physical vibrations, the perspectives of *Mahatma* as conveyed by our Source for this Cosmic Day.

And thank you, Barbara Waller, for your unexpected contribution to *Mahatma I* and *II*. These are levels of consciousness that Melchizedek asked you to look at, to leave the work that you were doing, and to align with greater Light. Thank you for allowing these transmissions from beings whom you stated that you "had never considered working with," but whom you nonetheless allowed in a wonderful fashion!

In the ultimate sense, there are too many discarnate and finite beings for me to be able to give thanks to, on so many levels of consciousness of the energy formatted in this book.

Janet McClure was, in my opinion, one of the clearest conscious channels on Earth. *Mahatma I* is extremely conceptual and discusses levels of Creation that have literally *never* been considered on this planet Earth. Janet McClure's greatest ability was to get out of the way with her own consciousness, and allow the transmission without her beliefs interfering with the contents. That, after all, is what all of the channels on Earth strive for.

On October 6, 1990, I was sitting quietly in meditation, wondering why I had such a profound sense of loss, when as if out of the blue I heard a bright, sparkling voice: "Well, golden boy, if I had known who you were, I'd have been nicer to you!" I was somewhat taken aback, first because I realized that this was Janet McClure, and secondly, because of the *vividness* of her presence. She was right in front of me, with *no* physical body, and with a joyful resonance that I had never witnessed in her physical presence. Before I could react, Janet went on to say, "It seems I can't get away from your Energy, particularly *here* - you're everywhere. You're known as the Golden One, did you know that?"

At this point my mind was kinetic, trying to decipher what this visit meant, when the phone rang. It was a dear friend from Arizona saying, "Did you know that Janet McClure died yesterday in Egypt after taking a group of students through one of the Great Pyramids?" After the phone call I was still aware of Janet's presence as I tried to digest and assimilate this wonderful Ascension she had just undertaken. At this juncture I felt no sense of loss, only an all-encompassing communion of joy and love with her and Vywamus, who was also present.

The discarnate being Vywamus was the main teacher and transformer of his own and the more senior energies channeled for you, the reader of *The Rider on the White Horse* and *Mahatma I*.

I acknowledge Terry Ferguson, who assisted in the selection of information and exercises in the Appendix.

Barbara Burns is an excellent, bright channel, as evidenced by some of her channeled material, with Vywamus as the teacher. The excerpt from her book,

Evolutionary Exercises for Channels, will be most useful to many who want to understand how to channel. Barbara Burns may be contacted through Light Technology Publishing.

To list but a few who, in one way or another, have contributed:

My daughters, Laura, Julie, and Robyn (my beautiful friends)

Gaby Frutiger

Hanna Hanseler-Karrer

Sandra Roser

Frauke Stein

Gabriele von der Bruggen

And an enormous amount of love and appreciation to Glenda Barrie, my friend (and the Universal Heart), for her unwavering belief in the *Mahatma* energy, in the contents of *The Rider of the White Horse, Mahatma I*, and *Mahatma II*, which she typed and edited.

My special thanks to O'Ryin Swanson for her assistance in publishing these books. Her degree of assistance has been considerable.

Our first book, *The Rider on the White Horse* (published by Light Technology Publishing, P.O. Box 1526, Sedona, Arizona 86339), was more for my (our) integration than for others (at least for the foreseeable future); but where required, some of that material has been excerpted and updated.

Above all else, the shifts into the fourth dimension have allowed dramatic spiritual expansion and openness to the New Age, which in turn have allowed sufficient massive changes on this planet for these books to be manifested into physicality.

Two meditation tapes, including *The Spiritual Initiation* and *The Anchoring of the Tenth Ray*, are now available to enhance your integration. These tapes are in English, with simultaneous translation into German. If one wishes to integrate this magnificent energy, these profound examples of extremely fine energy can be of great assistance.

These tapes may be ordered, at the price of Swiss Francs 40, which includes shipping within Europe, or U.S. $30, which includes shipping to the U.S. or Canada, from:

Priska Arnold
The Mahatma House
Neuweilerstrasse 10
4054 Basel, Switzerland

It should be noted that various meditations are available now, and more in the near future, from the publisher of this book. Please write or call for a catalog:

Light Technolgy Publishing
P.O. Box 1495
Sedona, AZ 86339

Table of Contents

Nothing Is as it Was

January 1, 1994

Later in the introduction you will read an opening which was written for *The Rider on the White Horse,* our first adventure in seeking the nearest relative truth that we could bring into the densest of all Creation, specifically the physical atomic body. Before you complete *Mahatma I* and *II* in this combined edition, you will note that even though there are greater avenues available on Earth now for the spiritualization of matter, the tenets of truth were as applicable in June 1987 (about the time of the Harmonic Convergence) as they are now. The real difficulty for humankind, living in the beginning of the fourth dimension and sequencing time differently, is that humanity will now be compelled to live in what they view as the future (the relative Now) rather than their past. All but a few on Earth are influenced by history rather than by the future or the relative now, which are the necessary realities if one wishes to transcend one's illusory outer creations.

As you read this text, what is being stated will become dramatically self-evident in that soon you can no longer exist on this planet as you once did and continue to do, without a very rude awakening! What do we mean by this? It will become increasingly clear that the negative hold the past has had on humankind can no longer be maintained in fourth density. More and more of humanity will be creating their own reality and that of the world around them as a result of who they are becoming, through the cosmic influences upon Earth and Earth's inhabitants.

It is the influence of precedent which has determined existence on this planet: "Well, it's always been that way .... The world isn't going to change to suit you .... Humanity can't change, that's the way it is! ....That's reality; join the real world . . .", etc.

This "real world" changed so completely on June 14, 1988, that understanding the profound consequences would require reading and *integrating* this book's contents thoroughly on a step-by-step basis. What do we mean by this? Earth's inhabitants, including your seven astral levels, are currently experiencing *a period of grace* that began on June 14, 1988, when, for the first time within this Cosmic Day, the Earth completed her spiritual circuitry with her Source, the God/Goddess/All That Is.

The concepts throughout our *Mahatma* teachings are very difficult for most of you. They need to be approached, during this 40-year Opening on Earth that will last until the year 2028, with a dedication and an allowance for a gradual transition into this expanded philosophy, so that one does not become discouraged by information and energy unsupported by mass consciousness. One may wish to integrate first that which they resonate with and then progressively integrate all concepts and energy levels without overwhelm or feelings of "what in the world are they talking about?" Because the transformational energies of the Tenth Ray and the spiritual microtron tend to create emotional, mental and cellular discomfort, it is important to understand that this discomfort is not held within the transformational energy itself, but is a result of *resistance to transformation*. These shifts in consciousness will result in immense mental and emotional destabilization while one integrates these energies sufficiently for the spiritualization of matter.

Mahatma covers every aspect of everything you need to know about the Now, without the need to run from the crystallized religions to the Space Command, without calling oneself an angel, or without hoping for assistance and integration on other levels that are still very limiting!

The pattern of history, which has held such a stranglehold on humankind, is slowly being released by the influence of the NOW as we enter a multidimensional matrix over the next thirty-five years. The ancient pattern of allowing the past to determine the future is coming to an abrupt end. More and more among you will realize, through absolute necessity, that if one wishes to remain on Earth during this Opening, your decisions have to be a product of the relative Now and not of the past. The collective thought, or mass consciousness, is so dysfunctional that humankind will be compelled to go within and look at the grandeur of their own I Am Presence rather than the collective consciousness of illusion.

There is a shift in the paradigm of causation following hundreds of years' belief in the theory, based upon Newtonian physics, that the past "causes" the present. This model, in which one ball bumps into another which bumps into another, is purely mechanical and without real proof of the theory that causes lead to effects in the post-Newtonian world of quantum physics.

Quantum physics has indeed all but replaced the Newtonian concept that effects from the past affect our future. *It is the effects from our GodSource in the ETERNAL NOW which affect our present!*

If a being entering this first of seven grand divisions of the fourth dimension were to continue to believe in Newtonian physics, there would be no room for changing and becoming more than you already are! It would disallow change in direct proportion to the degree that the imminent discovery of a multidimensional reality is allowed to erode the credibility of your finite physical science. This event, referred to as **Ascension**, will be witnessed shortly in sequential time, causing your physical sciences to start anew. Your human Hierarchy will, in the very near future, channel sufficient scientific information to Earth to free humankind from bondage and slavery by making practical nuclear fusion, an energy source to be used by those who remain on the Earth in the NOW. The spiritualization of matter, through the fusion of the permanent atoms, is available in what we refer to as the spiritual microtron, discussed in some detail in this text.

Quantum physics is a physics of absorption; when a collision occurs between two energy fields, the total energy is absorbed by both fields. The new paradigm of **fusion** is replacing that of fission during this supreme Opening. When the fusion of the atom and the microtron is achieved, you will begin to recognize and integrate the spiritualization of matter or else be compelled to leave this planet and her lower astral levels because the physical, emotional and lower mental bodies cannot withstand the transformational energies being anchored on Earth at this time.

There is a mighty shift away from the Cartesian philosophy, which states that everything operates through logic and reason. This philosophy raised logic and reason to ultimately replace the GodSource, the All That Is. Fortunately, this paradigm of upward causation is being compelled to shift and allow a metaphysical approach. Now, through the *Mahatma* energies, a spiritual philosophy is arising that is not based on logic and reason alone, but on allowing oneself to be the creator of one's own reality, with greater understanding that thoughts are things. This includes logic and reason as well as downward causation.

If, for example, you missed a connecting airline flight because the plane was unable to land on time due to fog, this would be upward causation; but if your energy were simply needed at that location and time, that would be downward causation. You would spend more time at the required location than consciously planned. *Thus, the gap between the concept of the past creating the present and the concept of the relative Now creating the present is as great as the shifts in mass consciousness that are required during this Opening for Earth and her astral levels!*

We discuss with great joy the arrival upon Earth of the balanced God and Goddess energies. This balance of creative energy is long overdue on a planet where all of your religions have held to the limited and false image that God is male, which therefore means that God is not balanced and integrated, both in Its receptive and dynamic aspects of Creation.

There are beliefs that "the Rider on the White Horse," predicted by all of your world religions, will ride a white stallion across your Earthly "heavens" as a male god, bringing to the Christians their anticipated "second coming," saving only those who fit their description of righteousness and destroying or abandoning all supposedly evil or sinful human beings. These beliefs, even stated symbolically, border on absurdity, from a GodSource perspective.

What your planet is experiencing now, and what more and more of mankind will begin to experience, is no longer a matter of philosophy and physics. The shifts of the Earth and her astral levels over the last six years are evidence that mankind must connect with their only reality, their inner I Am Presence, and cease referring to their outer, material creations as anything but illusory, which they are from a Creator perspective. The idea that reality is limited to what humans can monitor through their five senses is opposite to the view from GodSource.

Humanity will continue in a state of confusion and crystallization for a period of time, due to an increasingly apparent mental and emotional instability. The compulsion to cling to third-dimensional nonreality is so powerful that a complete state of denial will rage throughout mass consciousness. Humankind remain so engaged and entrenched in struggle, so immersed in masculine energy, so entrapped in Newtonian physics and Cartesian philosophy, and so enamored with their profoundly limited religions that they deify and worship beings who are but fellow travelers on the same journey. Mankind are so enamored by their own history that the very thought that the past does not create the future becomes frightening to them.

We speak of the Twelve Rays and isolate for observation the Sixth, which supports zealotry and fanaticism as extreme expressions of this ray. Those who extol this energy — particularly your religious hierarchy — will become even more ruthless and fear-mongering in a last desperate attempt to cling to the graven image of structure and darkness, which will not withstand the Light and love that are being anchored on Earth at this time through what we refer to as the Cosmic Heart.

Humankind has not yet realized that on September 8/9, 1993, your astral levels ("heavens") started to anchor on Earth for the first time ever, creating, for those conscious enough to witness this transition, a heavy sense of oppression and of being out of control. At this juncture, nearly one-third of the beings on the first three of your seven astral levels were transferred to other schoolrooms in this and other universes, as these soul energies were simply too lowly evolved to handle the energies required to reembody on Earth into a multidimensional matrix of time and place. (Please refer to the chart, "The Chakra System for the Physical Manifestation of Multidimensional Mankind," p. 357.)

Therefore, after what humanity inappropriately refer to as death, their major location for transition between incarnations, these astral levels will no longer be available. The majority of mankind who function on preprobationary or probationary levels of consciousness will not reincarnate into Earth's new densities. The real Armageddon was and is being felt on Earth now because your lower psychic/astral realms are in a state of disarray and panic, trying to maintain the status quo they have gotten so used to over the last four major civilizations. Because the bulk of humanity vibrate at this level of consciousness (or unconsciousness), unable to access the three lower astral levels, there is pandemonium rampant on Earth while these entities endeavor to change the irrevocable Cosmic Law to suit themselves and to influence the outcome of Armageddon in its truest sense, which is not "hell-fire and damnation." This is not a judgment, simply an enactment of the Cosmic Principle of Resonance; those who cannot raise their vibration sufficiently to stay embodied or to reembody at a future time will be compelled to learn these lessons elsewhere — but most definitely not on Earth and her astral levels, which are becoming one during this Opening.

The final coffin nail for the dark, structured forces on Earth and the astral levels took place in Santa Margarida on the Costa Brava, Spain, at 7:42 p.m. on the 7th of October, 1993.

If what is about to be stated herein causes any among you to go into a state of overwhelm and disbelief, then, regrettably, so will the contents of this book, *Mahatma*. We urge you not to slam the book shut because it contradicts the rather limited views held by your finite science and all other historical opinions expressed as truth. We ask that you simply take a deep breath and allow these accurately stated relative truths to be integrated unemotionally and without prejudgment until you have read the complete contents. Your judgment would be inconclusive without reading this book in its entirety, due to its developmental nature.

The resounding resonance that 114 of humankind can effect for Earth and her astral levels was powerfully demonstrated during the Mahatma seminar in Spain, October 5 to 9, 1993, in which these wonderful participants actually hastened the Earth's evolutionary journey to anchor the Cosmic Heart into physicality. This unprecedented event took place with massive support from the Archangels, the Angelic Host, the Space Command and the totality of all aspects on all levels of the personalities involved. Discarnate beings were present, numbering more than 1000 to 1 in order to achieve this anchoring of the Cosmic Heart on Earth.

The presence in this area of the two powerful, receptive vortexes to facilitate the anchoring of Unconditional Love was not by chance, for we knew and were told by Metatron long before the seminar that this one group meeting in Spain would be the death knell, the Armageddon for the collective agencies of darkness, including the Cabal, whose great source of pleasure is derived from the manipulation of the masses to create slavery and darkness.

Many among you might be surprised by just how insidious the darkness really is, in its control and manipulation of the world you think you know, and especially the world you don't know. Many of your favorite "luminous" personalities have been unconsciously participating in the manipulation of the human psyche to such a degree and for such a long time that the bulk of humankind do not realize that they have simply been pawns in a well-controlled and manipulated game plan by the Cabal and other agencies of darkness. Until the 7th of October, 1993, the "pawns" could not participate in this great event that we refer to as the anchoring of the Cosmic Heart into Earth. However, you will now notice that the "little you," the personality level, is able to reclaim your own power.

Of the 114 participants of this magnificent event in Spain, 29 had mastered physicality in the same manner as the Master Jesus. To give a Light perspective of how much energy is generated through the synergy of 30 masters, this size group would equal the light of nearly two billion beings on preprobationary and probationary levels. Staggering? As you integrate the *Mahatma* teachings, you will realize without any doubt that what has been referred to as Mastery is the *natural* state of awareness and that, from a Source perspective, anything less is unnatural.

We will state in many different ways that it is with ease that one can now move beyond Mastery to achieve the lowest level of consciousness ever intended by your Creator Council of Twelve. You see, dear ones, you were never intended to fall so far from the galactic state of Light and Love — which has always been the pure electronic etheric body — into the dense atomic body.

At the moment of this glorious victory we refer to as the evening of October 7, 1993, this group was working on pattern removal through guided meditation when suddenly a huge explosion of Love and Light engulfed the room; we simply bathed in this liquid luminosity of Omnipresence. I[1] was aware that there were thousands of multidimensional spacecraft in the area, but was not prepared for the sudden dark and extremely heavy cloud that tried to enter the magnificent column of Light. The dark cloud circled our Light chamber several times, then suddenly hastened its momentum and struck the Light column with all of the energy it could muster. As I watched, the column of Light did not waver, but dissolved the black abyss without even a shudder. Several clairvoyant participants witnessed this most important event for humankind, as the Cosmic Heart was finally made our reality. Metatron stated later that this was the most powerful infusion of Light and Love ever generated for and with this planet Earth. He also explained that the Space Command was present to help offset a group of galactic enterprisors who were attempting to assist the Fallen Ones to maintain their status quo, which, of course they had enjoyed through their stranglehold on the Earth and her kingdoms.

As always, dear ones, your state of beingness and your resonance with your perception of reality determine your state of awareness, and, connected with your collective self, determine how much of this book can be integrated into your ever-expanding consciousness. The resonance of the name *Mahatma* was given to me by Vywamus and chosen by the Archangel Metatron; this mantra was never intended to be defined as "great soul," as it is in Sanskrit.

Mahatma embodies the 352 initiations and levels from Source to Earth, and Brian represents the personality aspect of this incredible energy. One

---

1 When I is used, the personality is foremost: when I refer to "we" I mean that comprehensive Oneness that we overshadow: the whole 352 levels of Self from Earth to Source.

should remember that the personality level is but a very small part of this comprehensive energy formatting, but nonetheless an essential part for our Source to monitor and anchor on Earth. We would like to advise you early on that the Creator personality on Earth is not to be adored or venerated. It is simply a vessel for the Source-level consciousness to channel through. One has the free will to adore the consciousness coming through the vehicle if one chooses; however, this is a false belief — the Cosmic Plan intends that one adore only one's own I Am Presence within one's own GodSource and one's own creative undertakings through integration.

Certain among you are overwhelmed by the concept that a Cosmic Avatar could embody a personality on Earth. This, we remind you, has no bearing on what we teach, for of the teachings and truths that are conveyed through the personality Brian, accept only those whose merits pass the scrutiny of your discernment; never accept them blindly. Any resistance or opinions from your own personality about the heightened consciousness of Brian the personality really do not matter and have no relevance when you discern the teachings and energy that come to the Earth through his channel, whether or not you resonate with *Mahatma*. Please do not buy into the myopic view held by mass consciousness that the personality is who you are. In our case, the individualized entity called Brian would not represent one millionth of our total consciousness.

The great trap, the fall of man, can be encapsulated in one word: **illusion**. From a Source perspective, humanity's fall and separation from primal soul into the densest of all levels of consciousness, the atomic body, is illusion and was never part of the Master Plan. However, the Creator's open-ended, infinite Plan also allows the Co-Creators to use their God-given free will, as individualized sparks of Divine Consciousness, to experience anew for this Cosmic Day. And as always with free will, what one wishes to experience, in darkness or in Light, is the choice of the individual. The Cosmic Law is irrevocable, in that sparks of Divinity, herein referred to as Soul levels, will eventually reunite with the GodSource they have always been.

The Goddess energy will touch everyone until at least the end of this decade, and will balance your perception of male and female polarities; this is long overdue! As her children, from an energy perspective, she is going to teach, touch and help balance the abuse of dynamic male energy that has been conveyed during the last four civilizations on Earth. This will in turn bring up denial and resistance and will create many distractions as humankind desperately cling to their tragic and destructive ways. For these reasons, most will not be capable of creating anything but frenzy and terror. They will not be capable of maintaining their atomic physical structures when the Tenth Ray and the microtron raise the vibration, or resonance, above the existing human condition.

Incredible electromagnetic surges have been directed to Earth, particularly through the agency of Helios, your Solar Logos. For the Earth, this means that true north would become fixed, and that magnetic north has started its inexorable 90-degree shift toward the equator. We have already experienced a

12-degree shift, evident in Zurich, Switzerland. One report that I consistently receive from *Mahatma* (channeled information stepped down and relayed through this personality vehicle) is that when the magnetic north reaches 90 degrees from true north, at the level of the equator, the Earth will have spiritualized her body mass; and her consciousness, including humankind, would then align with the spiritual/monadic realms. This planet would thus graduate from this physical universe into the Monad.

The other magnificent benefit derived from electromagnetic energy is on a personal level, where humankind will begin experiencing surges of intuition and imagination more wondrous than anything they have experienced before. Slowly and deliberately, **thoughts become things** as we enter this fourth dimension, where we are supported and graphically assisted by the magnification of the surges of electrodynamic input, which affect all who partake in a most glorious revelation of instant manifestation, those who use the tools available in this new density.

As you have seen from the charts, the symbolic phrase "Heaven on Earth" is now being implemented in no uncertain terms. The real question is, are you ready to clear away all static, or false beliefs, through pattern removal, to join others of like expression and willingness, to participate in the greatest chapter in Earth's history by creating your own GodSource connection as the I Am Presence, *Mahatma*?

I truly regret that most on Earth are not yet either conscious enough to join in this wondrous venture, mainly due to the limitations of their own belief systems; or not mentally developed enough (or think they are not) to integrate this array of converging energies and concepts now available in a completed format for all who wish to raise their consciousnesses into Light and Love.

What we're about to state is rather difficult to define; however, the Cosmic Opening upon which we articulate at length in this book will have a number of side effects, all of which are stated in *Mahatma*. Following are three variables that we would like to discuss, and which are not yet shown definitively:

1. The fact that your Earth will experience an axis shift on or about November 4, 1994, was rather firmly set in place as a *fait accompli*, the probability factor being in the range of 96%. The expansion of your Source of this Cosmic Day into a greater level of consciousness on June 14, 1988, has considerably lessened the probability level of total annihilation.

2. When Sanat Kumara's Earth completed its spiritual circuitry with the Council of Twelve for this Cosmic Day, the newly expanded Source, and the collective consciousness of Sanat Kumara and humanity were raised sufficiently to receive a period of grace (the current opening, which will last until the year 2028), thus transcending some karmic effects and thereby avoiding the termination of this civilization. What transpired instead was, and continues to be, a complete shift in the electromagnetic grids of your planet, which is profoundly affected by the infusion of the Tenth Ray and the spiritual microtron. As of this date, January 1, 1994, the overall shifts for your material world are still in limbo. There are, and will continue to be, massive shifts directed at hastening

the Earth's journey into spiritualizing matter.

3. As mentioned earlier, your three lower astral levels are ceasing to exist; therefore, many of humanity will witness the annexation of the balance of these astral levels for those who are able to remain within the heightened vibration required for existence on Earth. The Earth will retain a reasonable degree of its existing structure for those who can withstand the levels of radiation required to spiritualize matter.

As we view the Earth's conditions, I personally find great difficulty in seeing how those now integrating their fourth, fifth and sixth dimensions will relate to the bulk of humankind who are simply not conscious enough to move beyond their self-imposed, illusory, third-dimensional reality. Thus the few (81,000 Lightworkers) who electromagnetically hold the matter of planet Earth to its etheric grid are simply being overwhelmed by the burden; one in every 64,000 of Earth's inhabitants cannot expect to carry the Light for the many! That is the quandary we face. Thus, our view is that a mass Ascension will occur while Sanat Kumara and your Planetary Hierarchy better regulate the intensity for the few who carry the Light for the unconscious masses.

The possibility of a "raising up" type of ascension through the Space Command still remains a possibility. What cannot continue is the immense discomfort for the few. Don't be surprised if, in the near future, you are talking to someone who suddenly assumes the pure electronic Lightbody, disappears in front of you, and rematerializes when it is their express desire to do so!

My dear friends and my beloved adversaries, *nothing is as it was*, and we lovingly suggest, "Prepare ye the way." ✳

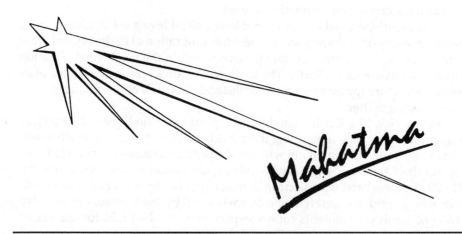

Introduction

1987

> What science calls energy,
> Religions call God.
> ALL is ENERGY.
> ALL is GOD.
> THE ESSENCE OF GOD IS **LOVE**.

THAT IS THE JOURNEY! God isn't something outside of Self that you give your power to — you must ultimately take your own power into your own hands, recognize yourself as the I AM presence and cease delegating to beings who are, in all likelihood, on a probationary path, and who are certainly not "spiritually" evolved enough to help you to stay on course with your journey, at least not in the energy formatting required for this New Age.

That is why this book, *Mahatma* can be so helpful for you to understand who and what you are in relation to All That Is. Otherwise, dear ones, it will be very difficult to remain in physicality on this planet, for she is very radioactive, is becoming fourth-dimensional, and will not cope with false structures, whether they be in religions or in lack of freedom for a country. These First Ray energies will literally clean house of old beliefs and structures that have no relevance, and will keep only that which is applicable to love/wisdom and synthesis, sufficient to allow a degree of **spirituality** in its truest sense to coexist with All That Is, and to assist in your connection with your I AM Presence through the Primal Soul and the Higher Self.

Before this time, mankind was not sufficiently evolved to bring through the total picture of man's evolutionary Journey. And so, for the next many decades, *Mahatma I* and *II* will provide guidance for those among you who have reached an evolutionary level of integration sufficient to be able to read and conceptualize these books' contents, which would include nearly 100 million of humanity, preparing for or having taken the Second Initiation. (One need not be *conscious* of having taken an initiation.)

Mahatma I and *II* are a comprehensive understanding of

Where You've Been
Where You Are
Where You're Going
And How to Get There.

The comprehensive energy formatting in this book is totally attributable to precognition, intuition and channeling. Channeling has caused some confusion in many who were not conscious enough to believe that a discarnate being, albeit a "spiritual"[2] teacher, could possibly convey teachings through a channel with sufficient clarity to be of assistance.

One of the great ironies is that mankind has difficulty conceptualizing channeling, and many leaders of the churches — because channeling diminishes their control — tend to lump any event outside of their control as being "in league with the devil" and "an instrument of evil." This childlike fear and condemnation becomes humorous when we consider that the one you call the Master Jesus channeled the Christ. *That is a fact.* So you see, these were *two separate beings,* and not "Jesus Christ," as the Catholic Church has seen fit to convey to mankind. We walked the Earth at that time as the one called Simon Peter; and in this present life one of my clearest memories as a child was knowing that someone who wasn't Jesus spoke to us *through* Jesus and taught us. We certainly knew then that two different entities were involved — we all did, and certainly Jesus did!

Because those times were much darker than now, when we spoke to the Romans they were unable to digest and assimilate one of the most fundamental concepts on Earth, that of channeling energy, even though overshadowing is mentioned, but not understood, in your religious scriptures. So you can see how the lovely, simple truths conveyed by Maitreya, the Christ, using the human channel of Jesus as his physical vehicle, were so unalterably distorted

---

2 The words *spiritual* and *cosmic* as we define them, imply "nonphysical, beyond all the levels of the universes." All that is *monadic* is the cosmic and spiritual level (seventh, eighth, and ninth dimensions). Occasionally these words, when used by Vywamus for a specific audience, denote "any area beyond the Earth." We have attempted to indicate by quotes wherever these terms have been so (mis)applied. In other cases it will be clear that the common usage is adopted in the absence of an appropriate term in English. Refer to an additional discussion on pp. 409 & 425.

from the beginning, and nothing got any better. By the time the Catholic Church — whose leaders were rather lowly evolved and more prone to politics and control than to spirituality — took control of the Christ's teachings, even a fundamental truth like reincarnation went by the boards, albeit recognized by the balance of humanity and in our teachings at the time.

Now, on a mass consciousness level, a wedge has been created through the First Ray, sufficient to lift *fear* and *inappropriate structure* so that mankind — at least those who remain on this planet after November 4, 1994 — can master physicality through the process known as Ascension and vibrationally be on the same evolutionary spiral as the one whom many worship as God, the Master Jesus. Amongst the Lightworkers on Earth now, many of you have mastered physicality and anchored the Fifth Initiation, which is simply a point of integration required to raise the vibrational frequency of the etheric Lightbody sufficiently to ascend beyond the need for further dense physical embodiment.

The basic level inappropriately referred to as mastery of the physical level is but the beginning of this eternal journey, not a level to worship. (When you have a clearer understanding, you'll not worship *any* level.) When Jesus externalizes into dense physicality, he will certainly explain — in no uncertain terms — the difficult hold that worship has. These limited beings, these beautiful beings, are fellow travelers just like you, and you, and you. The difference is that they have mastered dense physicality and are slightly ahead of most of mankind on the spiritual evolutionary scale of Creation, but are just beginners and not to be worshipped. If you truly love these wonderful beings and really want them to externalize into physicality, then help them by treating them as brothers — albeit elder brothers — on the same path, letting go of the false hysterical reverence for beings who simple came here to fulfill an assignment.

So, throughout the years there are many examples of channeling. One that comes to mind (because at one time Brian was his neighbor in London) is Dr. Fleming, who channeled the way to produce penicillin within hours of others in California who channeled the same information, which had been placed in the ethers by the Planetary Hierarchy, our planetary government. So, whether someone like Mozart, who channeled with extraordinary clarity his music for the betterment and the sheer joy of mankind, or someone channels, on a personal level, a higher aspect of Self to exist in physicality, one ultimately *must* channel (and everyone does), whether they are conscious of the process or not. You become the transformer, the conduit through your channel, to step down the energies that constitute the multiplicity of Self, meaning the totality of You.

"A limited being, with nothing more in all of existence than this finite physical body and a limited physical perspective" is how most of humanity see themselves. And because of this third-dimensional stance, they see themselves as separate from God and very limited, tending to give their power to anyone who promises to "tend the flock" — whether it is, from their perspective, Jesus or Hitler, the parish priest or the politician. Thus they remain stuck in the quagmire because each individual does not take it upon his or her Self to find the "heaven within" and "heal thyself " — which, of course, one of your "spiritual" leaders, the Christ, suggested you do.

Now, isn't it interesting that the energy the Scriptures describe as *The Rider on the White Horse* — *the Mahatma,* which is bringing in the sudden changes for the New Age that are so transformational in nature — also causes one to become more introspective of Self and to reclaim one's own power. These books not only show mankind where they are individually and collectively stuck, but how to function as integrated beings on the spiritual levels. This is the invocation that you all decided upon, on a mass consciousness level, during your planetary Harmonic Convergence on August 15/16, 1987. You overwhelmingly appealed to the Soul levels for peace, prosperity, love, harmony, freedom and, above all, to **Know Thy Self**. Now, as most of you can bear witness, the changes are coming so fast and furious that they stagger the locked, inflexible lower mind, which has to look at mankind's endorsement of freedom and peace throughout the world such as this planet has never seen! "Walk-Ins" such as Gorbachev are just the beginning of what will happen to place mankind in the *now* of their coming of age and will cause change to be so rapid that the energies required will cause most to leave the planet and go to where they *can* live.

As recently as five years ago, it truly looked like the end of this civilization. Now, because *you,* as the major consciousness on Mother Earth, help her to feel supported (she who has in the past been held in total disregard by the human kingdom), she can stabilize herself sufficiently enough not to have a complete axis shift. And beings such as *Mahatma* and many others throughout this universe and beyond, who heard the Souls' call for help, who heard the call to stabilize the planet and humanity, will assist. The Galactic Core already has four stabilizing devices in place, of the twelve to be placed fifth-dimensionally in various weakened locations of the globe over the next short time. One of the reasons for the delay so far in this process is that the four stabilizing devices designated for China will have to wait for greater shifts in freedom in that totalitarian country. Now, with these great beings assisting, there is a real possibility — with mankind reaching adulthood and therefore having a greater understanding of their part in this great cosmic play — that the Earth can avoid the axis shift of November 4, 1994. As the Earth's primary consciousness, there isn't one among you who cannot assist, if your appeal for stability is unselfish, truly desirous of assisting the Earth, and not simply an emotional ploy for personal survival, without the group focus necessary for the betterment of this collective Soul called humanity!

You have all asked to be treated, on a mass conscious level, as spiritual adults; but, from our perspective, most can't lift their consciousness above the level of the Atlantean emotional body, in which — in large measure — you again gave away your power to the scientific priesthood who, by their abuse of power, destroyed Atlantis.

WAKE UP this time and say, "NO! This will not happen again! We will *not* destroy our civilization! We have endorsed becoming adults on a mass conscious level; and we *will*, en masse, evoke Peace, Freedom, Abundance, and a Global Community that understands its collective purposes and why many will transcend their structured limitations."

With the gentle, loving support of Mother Earth and the group called humankind, and with the realization that you're not alone on this little planet placed in the middle of nowhere, now, at this time in the Earth's lengthy history, there have never before been so many great teachers — great Source *technicians* — monitoring and transforming electrical/nuclear/solar energies (the five new Rays) to elevate the vibrational frequency of this planet into the fourth dimension and hasten evolution.

Of course, you can help! Don't be self-conscious in the improper way...become Self-conscious in a way that reclaims your power. Go within and meditate or quietly pray for Earth and humankind who are both going through a major transformation into the beginning of the fourth dimension. Tell them that you support their Transformation. Tell them that you understand that transformational processing can cause discomfort, and that they need not overreact to discomfort and massive shifts during the transformation and integration.

In this universe there are billions of planets with the Adam Kadmon physical body like ours, but there is no planet where the plant kingdom is more highly evolved. Let this kingdom know how much you appreciate its great creations. Don't abuse Mother Earth any longer, for she lives and loves and appreciates being appreciated just as you do. These great kingdoms are fragile and have been subjected to merciless contempt. WAKE UP and appreciate this jewel of Creation before it's too late. *Wake up!*

> Awake! Awake!
> For the twilight, in its flight,
> Quickly settles into night;
> And the dreaming swiftly speeds
> The night into the day.
> Awake! Awake!
> Night is gone,
> Morning breaks,
> And it is
> light, Light, LIGHT!
> Awake!

Without the freedom to live a self-aware, abundant life, you remain puppets for the puppeteers — whether those be religious, political, or the bulk of humankind, all cherishing the status quo — who revel in their darkness, refusing to walk in the Light as one with All That Is. Let your inner knowingness direct you, as the I AM Presence, *Mahatma*; reawaken your heart, for it is the Divine Heart that will guide and free you from the bondage and slavery that have been created in the "old age" outer structure.

When the Scriptures symbolically speak of an "end," they are referencing the New Age and a new beginning. The changes that you're seeing now, for the betterment of this soon-to-be global community, will simply stagger even the most optimistic among you, for *never* in the annals of human endeavor will positive change be made so rapidly!

The bulk of humanity, who remain unconscious of their inner Self and only acknowledge their superficial creation of material "things" with the outer self, will not recognize change as the direction they will have to take. These beings will thus be shifted to another level of consciousness, another system, until they learn these lessons. THAT IS THE LAW!

At this time and in the foreseeable future, these books can assist at least the more highly evolved so that they in turn can trigger the Light to the next one, and the next, and the next...and thus, create "the popcorn effect" that most of humanity, on a Soul level, have asked for. These respective Souls know the amount of effort that will be required to remove the unnecessary structures of the Old Age of darkness and limitation, which have served the purposes of their application, but no longer match the Source's request for the hastening of evolution in this Cosmic Day.

We expect that much of mankind, being one step up from animal man on Creation's evolutionary scale, will not be very aware of or feel much Impression from the New Age shifts for at least twenty years, if any remain at all on this Earth.

There is such a concerted focus of energy at this time on Earth that beings who can handle the energies are lining up, figuratively speaking, from other planets, other systems, to be evolved on this little planet because she is so transformational — for herself and for humankind. Thus the opportunity for spiritual growth at this time on this planet is so magnified as to create, for those who can handle the Transformational Fire, an opportunity to achieve those points of integration (referred to in the past as the Second through Sixth Initiations) in *one* lifetime, albeit a fourth-dimensional life — or, from a third-dimensional perspective, a life that may last several hundred sequential years.

In the past, mankind have had 2000 to 2500 lives on each of at least 15 to 20 planets; and the initiation that is the most difficult in physical terms is the Second Initiation, which in the past has involved as many as 1400 lives on one planet during that one initiation. So you can see why Souls are clamoring to have their personality aspects in physicality on this planet at this time, to hasten their evolutionary process. When we speak of the New Age, we do not imply that all that is New Age is good and that all that is old is not good. We would ask that you not blindly follow *any* path without standing back and being a cautious, intuitive observer, for there is not a belief system on earth that will not be transcended. *All* beliefs are simply stepping stones until you ultimately *transcend the need for any beliefs whatsoever,* meaning the point where you move beyond the need for a dense physical body and recognize yourself as the I AM Presence, *Mahatma*.

Any belief system that is predicated on fear, or any system that suggests that "this is the only way," is false by its very nature. Any belief system that is polarized by a dominant, male structure in this New Age should be avoided. Any teaching that encompasses the devil, hellfire, and damnation is not a teaching from God at all. Any religion that has an avenging, judgmental God is a false teaching and has a false god. This energy would be better classified as the one that the Church cautions you to avoid — the Prince of Darkness, the Antichrist. Ironically, religions have been caught in their own inability to move beyond their own dogma, darkness and limitation.

Any teaching today that cannot help you raise your vibrations to at least the Third Initiation/Soul Merge or to the level of the Fifth Initiation in physicality and prepare you for physical Ascension is a religion that can only worship the Ascended Master; it does not prepare the way for you to *become* the Ascended Master and rise above dense physicality, which is the ultimate purpose of coming in to experience physicality! The intention is not to venerate other beings and make them gods because they've "mastered" their Fourth, Fifth, Sixth or Seventh physical Initiations. The intention is to raise *your* consciousness to these levels and much, much beyond, for when you venerate and dogmatize a relatively lowly evolved being who has mastered only dense physicality, you do yourself a great disservice and limit your own spiritual growth, as well as create considerable discomfort and limitation for the being you've decided to worship.

For the first time in the history of this planet, these books show unequivocally that, in our Cosmic Day alone, which constitutes just one Source, there are in fact 352 levels and initiations. Jesus and Mohammed are both raising their vibrational frequencies to achieve, in relative short order, their Sixth Initiation. The Christ, Maitreya — who, by the way, is the most highly evolved being to graduate from this planet is raising his vibration sufficiently to anchor his Seventh Initiation, leaving him 345 levels yet to go toward his Source, from where he individualized in the first place. So you can see how utterly preposterous it is to worship these beings as gods! With Divine Equality throughout Creation, you all have equal right to claim your own inheritance as Gods, being aspects of All That Is, the Source of this Cosmic Day.

These famous beings of your planetary system should be examples of what you can also achieve. And so, listen to your Planetary Hierarchy as teachers — not beings who appear to be so far ahead of mankind on their probationary Path that one sees them as gods — but as they should be, examples of what all of you will achieve, and more. Do you remember the Christ telling you, "What I have done you shall also do, and more!" More! What in heaven's name do you think he was talking about? Wake up! You will never be lost if you can connect to your inner I AM and realize that your outer self has nothing to do with the perfection of the Godhead, but is a total illusion perpetuated by the emotional and mental bodies and supported by mass consciousness.

I regret to say that some who are calling themselves New Age are simply darker ones who are making a last-ditch attempt to regain the controls that they had obtained in Atlantean times. Therefore, you should use the same barometer for the New Age as for the Old Age and ask, "*Where is their consciousness coming from?*"

The Ba'hai faith is one of several that have put on "bright new clothes," but the substance is old and won't elevate one spiritually. How can it? All religions make one feel temporarily secure and give temporary satisfaction to the emotional body with lip service, but do not elevate the "spiritual" consciousness sufficiently to enable one to stay in physicality or create the body for Ascension. And Mother Earth is now becoming too radioactive for most physical bodies to handle. To stay in physicality, one will have to raise one's consciousness to *at least* the vibrational frequency of Mother Earth. These books, *Mahatma I* and *Mahatma II*, will assist you remarkably, *to the degree that you're prepared to assist yourself!*

Religious zealotry throughout the world is "the opiate of the people," and — as we all know — drugs tend to pacify and nullify pain and frustration but ultimately they lead nowhere. If you give your power to a priest or a preacher telling you how unworthy you are, you then, of course, recognize your unworthiness. When they tell you how God's "only begotten Son" was crucified at Calvary to save the Souls of mankind and remove his sins, you feel guilt! Remember, *there are no victims,* for in truth, *there is no death.*

Or we may have an emotional battle cry from a Moslem cleric telling his woebegotten flock to die for Allah and go to heaven, not realizing that theology has sold the supposed victim a bill of goods. For there is no hell, except in the mind of the individual, and all good or supposed evil beings at that level go to a lower astral heaven or a self-imposed purgatory.

When the preacher is irrevocably tied to verbiage and theory and the fear of God, how, may I ask, is he going to teach you processing? The truth is, he *can't* teach you how to process Self and become Christ-conscious, because the monk, the cleric, the preacher, the priest himself isn't conscious enough! The religions are not conscious enough to teach *anyone* how to process sufficiently for them to achieve even an opportunity to merge personality/ego with Soul — the Third Initiation.

Thus, those aspiring for spiritual opportunity, spiritual growth, sit like doormats, either convinced of their unworthiness or shouting, "Praise the Lord, I'm going to be with Jesus in Heaven!" — always in the abstract! *Current religions are dead!* Mankind can invoke the great Teachers who are available to process you so that *you* become the Christ. For there is no way for you to listen to a preacher who is on a probationary level, no matter how loving and well-meaning, or how glib and humorous he may be, if that individual can't help you spiritually. *Your teachers must know and you must know* how to spiritualize the form and create sufficient Light for the process known as Ascension. (Both etheric and spiritual.) One cannot any longer listen to what someone else did if they wish to raise their vibrational level to manifest a Lightbody. These are, of course, your decisions; as beings with free will, you are the creators of your own reality. If you insist on working with one spoke instead of the whole wheel, that is your choice. But please recognize that the illusory qualities of the outer-self perspective will provide you with a very slow and uncomfortable journey. That is the evolutionary process on this fourth-dimensional planet. That is why your Soul chose this planet for you at this time; and there are no exceptions to this Law — that is the process.

> The perfect Age has come, when Man will be his own priest,
> and Men will not array themselves in special garb
> to advertise their piety.
> Mankind will go within to find Self's wonderment.

MARCH 1992
Addendum I

We deliberated at length whether we should exclude the personality (physical) aspect of the *Mahatma* energy, realizing that certain among you would go into overwhelm — for example, "If that ordinary man is that energy, then who am I?" — and thus compete through their egos with the personality aspect of *Mahatma*. Although certain individuals will deny that the *Mahatma* has a personality level in a physical body on Earth, it is unreasonable to project Hu-man/God-man without personality simply to satisfy those who have the problem of mirroring their own ego.

As human beings, we cling to our pathetic individualities and would have them continue forever, not knowing that the term has no meaning and that personality is not the essential part of ourselves. We are already absorbed into the ISness of God, and even if this absorption were still to come it would not be annihilation, for the ocean into which we are absorbed is not an ocean of Matter but an ocean of Spirit. But Spirit is a unity, and to be part of it is to be all of it. We are members one of another, and time is merely one of our dimensions.

In *A Treatise on White Magic*, published in 1934, the following statements and predictions are made by the Master Djwhal Khul through the brilliant channel Alice Bailey.

"It might be noted here that three great discoveries are imminent and during the next two generations will revolutionize modern thought and life.

"One is already sensed and is the subject of experiment and investigation, the releasing of the energy of the atom. This will completely change the economic and political situation in the world, for the latter is largely dependent upon the former. Our mechanical civilization will be simplified, and an era ushered in which will be free from the incubus of money (its possession and nonpossession), and the human family will recognize universally its status as a bridging kingdom between the three lower kingdoms of nature and the fifth or spiritual kingdom. There will be time and freedom for a soul culture which will supersede our modern methods of education, and the significance of soul powers and the development of the superhuman consciousness will engross the attention of educators and students everywhere.

"A second discovery will grow out of the present investigations as to light and colour.

"The third development, which will be the last probably to take place, will be more strictly in the realm of what the occultists call magic. It will grow out of the study of sound and the effect of sound, and will put into man's hands a tremendous instrument in the world of creation."

There was a clearly directed influx of cosmic energy into the Earth, directed from the Great White Lodge in the constellation Sirius, after invocation from the Planetary Government. This energy has had great impact on the atomic structure of physical existence. Unbeknownst to the scientific community, the atomic changes effected by this energy have allowed them success in many experiments, helping them to overcome otherwise insurmountable obstacles and move into a realm of technology that would otherwise have been unattainable.

The inflow of higher energy (to the mental-causal level of physicality, which was as far as it could come in at that time, 1942) drastically weakened the power of the Forces of Darkness, which were behind the Axis powers. It caused a steady deterioration of the brains and nervous systems of the physical expressions of the Dark Forces, ultimately destroying their minds. The German front failed because the Dark Ones could not hold together this tension — which is the dynamic focusing of physical, emotional and mental energies — nor could they achieve the level of tension which the Planetary Hierarchy were able to maintain through the aid of the Council of Twelve for this quadrant of this galaxy.

By the summer of 1942, the Great White Lodge knew that the outcome of the war had turned in their favor. The Planetary Hierarchy then moved their focus and energy from winning the war to preparing for a world in which everything new that expressed loving, divine purpose could be free to move forward.

It is important to realize that the winning of the Great World War, which lasted from 1914–1945, was won because the infusion of Light into planet Earth enabled the Forces of Light to overcome the then-powerful Forces of Darkness. The surrender of Germany was simply an outer mirroring of events taking place on the inner planes. The destruction of the mental powers of the Dark Ones and the ensuing victory were brought about by the Forces of Light, who sought to release the ENERGY OF THE FUTURE (which is *fusion*) and bring forth the higher qualities and values of life as well as the "spiritual" good of Mankind. (*Fusion:* the act of blending, or the state of being blended throughout. —in physics: a thermonuclear reaction in which the nuclei of an element undergo transformation into another element, with the release of great energy; the reverse of fission.)

It was the infusion of energy that allowed the scientists of the day to successfully create the atomic bomb through the process they erroneously call the splitting of the atom. The release of atomic energy at this time was very necessary, as well as the massive destruction that it caused. Although it is difficult for humanity to realize, the human deaths that occurred with the release of atomic energy enabled the release of IMPRISONED SOULS from this planet; thus this necessity justified the seemingly terrible violence unleashed upon the Japanese people. Although the first use of atomic energy on Earth was destructive, it destroyed only the physical form and not the spirit, as was the goal of the Dark Ones.

If the Dark Forces *had* been successful, their victory would have caused the prophesied Armageddon and the end of civilization as you know it; thus it has always been a no-win situation for the Dark Ones in the Earth's history. There have been a number of axis shifts and asteroid collisions with the Earth, ending the particular civilization of the time. This was primarily brought about by Mankind's inability to cooperate with *their* correct Ascent.

Today humanity still knows very little of the nature and the extent of these atomic energies; the release of this energy is still very much in the embryonic stage on this planet. There are MANY TYPES OF ATOMS, each releasing its own type of energy, which constitute the WORLD SUBSTANCE. This is one of the secrets the *Mahatma* is now revealing, and as a result, a resounding fourth-dimensional beginning has been made.

We would call your attention to the phrase, "the liberation of energy." Liberation is the keyword in this New Age, just as it has always been for the "spiritual" aspirant. This liberation was allowed to begin with the release of an aspect of matter and with the freeing of some of the SOUL ENERGY WITHIN THE ATOM. The atoms of the Soul level are units of energy of a higher vibrational frequency from those of dense physicality. For matter, this has been a great and powerful initiation that parallels the initiations which LIBERATE OR RELEASE THE SOULS OF Mankind, THE FIFTH INITIATION.

Mankind is so confused about Soul! Please remember that the Sixth Initiation *releases* the Primal Soul and thus the physical, emotional, mental and astral bodies. The Higher Self integrates the Soul and Self through to the Twelfth Initiation and the twelfth chakra. The Oversoul is the beginning of the Monad, the spiritual planes; thus Soul and Higher Self as *one* have been merged and spiritualized. The Oversoul constitutes approximately 125 levels of the Monad, after which you become a finer and finer integrated spiritual unit, until you eventually merge where you began, at the Creator level of your beginningness, as the God that you have always been — the Source of *this* Cosmic Day. (Please refer to the charts, "Co-Creator and Creator Levels," pp. 228-229; "The Cosmic Heart," p. 350; "Soul Levels," p. 351; "The Individualization of Source," p. 354 and "Metatron's Evolutionary Light Chart," p. 356.)

Because the process of what in the past was referred to as the etheric body or Light body has been elevated in its vibration, the process that we now call the Spiritual Initiation has brought forth its work as "the world savior" (*Mahatma*), your I AM presence, into the realm of substance, affecting those basic units of life from which all form is made.

The Master Djwhal Khul makes the statement in the second of the Great Invocations: "The hour of service of the saving force has now arrived." The "saving force" is the energy that was released into the world — although initially destructively — through the scientific community to destroy, through the *Mahatma* energy, any energy that is not aligned with the New World of finer, more spiritual life. Through the inspired use of this liberated energy, the highest ideals of humanity can be realized if the true and "spiritual" values are taught and applied to daily life. With science as the *vehicle*, this saving force has been made available to humanity and Mother Earth. As many among you working with the Light are aware, the beginning of your new spiritualized body creates discomfort through the transition of the "new" atoms *fusing* to create this new spiritual body, encouraged by the *Mahatma* energy and the Spiritual Initiation. (Refer to pages 117 & 126.)

Those with whom we are communicating — who are touching into and therefore have requested the assistance of the *Mahatma* I AM presence consciously or unconsciously on the inner planes in the transformational process — are consistent in relating to us their physical and emotional discomfort, asking, "How can something so good feel so bad?"

We wish that it could be otherwise, but if one were to consider the massive removal of *all* negative patterning from the subconscious mind, plus the recognition that every cell in your physical body is being transformed into a new material body whose vibration is increased to the speed of Light and beyond, then you can begin to understand why this total transformation can cause overheating of the body; lightheadedness and headaches as your sixth and seventh chakras open; nausea; and aches and pains in the areas of your body that house the greatest resistance to total transformation, especially in the balancing of the polarities. Because the legs — particularly below the knees — are the narrowest part of the body, you may find energy backing up, unable to be released quickly enough into the Earth through the new chakras in the soles of the feet, thereby causing a sensation of mild electricity or prickling, similar to the discomfort when circulation is cut off to a part of the body.

We urge you not to give in to the various side effects that your ancient patterning would translate as a negative experience, as this is the only method — through New Revelation — to free those Soul atoms in perpetuity.

Please understand that the greater Wholeness that you as the personality represent have chosen planet Earth over all other systems and planets in this universe because of the heightened dualities experienced here. Many planets that all of you have experienced have not been able to show the degree of duality which exists on Earth; in other words, the experience in other systems is similar to what Mankind call their fifth astral heaven, or "Paradise," and does not mirror the extreme dualities that we (including your Creator level, *Mahatma*) have chosen to experience in this magnificent school that we call Earth. We know that the aforementioned analogy may be disconcerting; however, one should realize that one does not *learn* and *evolve* in Paradise, which is still a physical level and the "heaven" of your various religions.

Many of the well-meaning among humanity are environmentally (and thus emotionally) confused about what you perceive as excessive radiation, whether through the Chernobyl "accident," the French, American, British and Russian detonation of nuclear devices, or the huge openings in the ozone layer that would (on the surface, or logically speaking) appear as agents of destruction. You've heard many well-meaning people insist that the greenhouse effect will destroy all living inhabitants of this planet sometime in the next century. The fact of the matter is that the deployment required to spiritualize matter is now being implemented through the cosmic agency that we call the *Mahatma* energy. It is absolutely essential that massive amounts of *radioactive material* be *progressively* released to create *nuclear fusion*, thus elevating and freeing those atoms that have disallowed your Souls' atoms to transcend their limited third-dimensional material perspective into an unlimited Spiritual awakening for the first time ever in any of the 43 Universes. Thus your emotional and logical selves would not see the long-term, essential spiritual enhancement on *all* levels of consciousness for this experiment in this galactic quadrant.

If individuals can — and this includes those among you who are consciously working with the Light — trust that events are being played out to the benefit, not the detriment, of all kingdoms on planet Earth by *all* levels of extraplanetary councils plus the "Space Command," then you can begin to let go of your fear and emotional reactions to the unfolding of these events.

The atomic fusion of matter through spiritualization is the *only* salvation to offset the massive deployment of the agencies of darkness, who are highly organized in the concerted effort to enslave and thus destroy the human spirit.

It is the constructive use of atomic energy for the betterment of humanity that is its *other* purpose. This is the living energy of substance itself, contained and locked away in the unit of life called the atom, which, when used for this true purpose, can bring about such revolutionary changes in human life that it will necessitate and bring about an *entirely* new economic world structure. This is that "saving force" that contains the power to completely rebuild and rehabilitate life on this planet. The right use of atomic energy can completely abolish destitution and bring civilized comfort (without useless luxury) to all of Mankind. If expressed in right living and motivated by loving human relations, it will produce beauty, color and warmth. With the absence of disease and the need to work or fight for material possessions, humanity will be free to pursue the higher aspirations of the spiritual life. Economic inequalities among men will come to an end; everyone everywhere will be released into a stage of life that will give them the time and the leisure to follow their spiritual objectives, to achieve a broader mental perspective and to enjoy a richer cultural life. Everywhere you look today, you can see the destruction of the material or form side of your structured, third-dimensional past. Nothing will be as it was, as the *Mahatma* (Creator level) directs your Soul levels into the New Age!

Naturally, there will be those who will fight to prevent this move forward to free Mankind — called nuclear fusion. Reactionary groups in every country will neither desire nor recognize the need for this new world order which the liberation of cosmic energy can make possible through the *Mahatma* energies. The huge cartels, trusts, monopolies and vested interests that have controlled the past decades will use their every resource to fight to the death to prevent the extinction of their sources of income. If these groups can possibly help it, they will not permit their power to pass into the hands of the masses, to whom it rightly belongs.

Some of you may have heard these dark beings referred to as the Cabal. Particularly in the United States, they are the government behind the government, and thus dictate the terms and policies of the whole nation. This becomes heinous when one acknowledges, as one of thousands of examples, the coup d'état and assassination of John F. Kennedy in what Americans believe is the greatest democracy on earth. Their Bill of Rights, founded ostensibly by the Planetary Hierarchy, provided the greatest freedom known to man on Earth at that time. We regret that the abuse of power has been dictated of late by the Cabal to create an anarchy that will become more apparent.

The one whom Nostradamus and some of your Christian teachings refer to as the Antichrist — the "Iman,"[1] a brilliant young man who is presently 31 years of age — will become the leader of these Dark Forces. A better term than Antichrist might be the Prince of Darkness, as your religions are not without great darkness. In your recent history you have had Stalin and Hitler with their extremely dark forces, who were all projected from the lower astral levels. Now you can look at this young, attractive Arab as being at least one hundred times more monstrous and grotesque, representing the darkest, most heinous and most convincing energy ever to come from such a high level — in fact, the highest "negative" level available in *this* physical universe. This is the level of Lucifer, who was certainly not a "fallen angel." This concerted effort arrives from the Black Lodge of Sirius, which is the same level as the White Brotherhood (the White Lodge in the constellation Sirius). Thus when Mankind reflects on the future, this level — white and black — is equivalent to the Ninth Initiation. When you read "The Rays, Chakras and Initiations" you will realize then that Sanat Kumara, your Planetary Logos, requires only the Eighth Initiation.

This will give you some idea of the illusionary qualities that this young man, Iman, will be able to project that will cause him to *appear* to be illuminated. For this reason you as Lightworkers will need absolute commitment to the energy that your Soul level has invited — the Creator level (herein called *Mahatma)* — to assist in the spiritualization of matter. This could allow hundreds of thousands among you, for the first time ever in this galactic quadrant, to create your spiritualized body and remain in your NEW MATERIAL BODY. This interaction will in turn assist your Planetary Hierarchy and Sanat Kumara to trigger the Light so that others can create their spiritualized bodies, thereby offsetting with this brilliant Light the darkness of this very powerful and convincing Ninth-Level Initiate from the Black Lodge. The Black Lodge of Sirius has been destroyed for all intents and purposes; this is their last-ditch attempt to control this Earth. Therefore the Earth is being watched from all levels of Creation with the most concentrated efforts ever

---

1 *Iman* is the term used by Nostradamus. The current term is *Imam*.

allowed any planet anywhere in this universe. The Iman, representing the greatest evil harnessed collectively on a planet so small, will play out the last great battle with the duality of the universe — simplistically stated as the battle between Dark and Light Forces. If given the opportunity, many, many of humanity will worship this energy as the Christ, including most of your religions, until the Iman can be short-circuited through the nuclear atoms freeing the Soul atoms.

The being that Nostradamus saw and referred to as Ogmios is the energy that you know as an aspect of the Master Jesus, not the Christ. This loving and bright man has lived as a Catholic priest until recently in Prague, Czechoslovakia, and is now middle-aged. Ogmios is simply no match, as a recent Sixth-Level Initiate, for the one who, for want of better terminology, we call the Prince of Darkness. Ogmios is starting to distance himself, through disillusionment, from the Catholic Church, where his Sixth-Ray abilities (refer to "The Twelve Rays," pp. 210-211) place this man, whom mass consciousness calls Jesus (his last physical body was that of Apollonius and his preference of name is Sananda) as the last symbolic pope to fulfill his assignment to create the new world religion.[2]

If by choice Mankind deifies, exalts and follows the control of the Iman — because it is their free will to do so — this planet Earth will have what you will view as a catastrophic event, removing nearly seven billion of your Souls' physical probes from this planet and her lower astrals. The bulk of these Souls would move to another third-dimensional planet — probably in the Pleiades — since they are unable to live in the vibration of the fourth-dimensional planet Earth, and would thus miss the wonderful evolutionary opportunity afforded them through the *Mahatma* energy. Due to their *eternal* inability or refusal to embrace Light and Love, there could then be a recycling of the extremely dark energies involved, in an exercise that has heretofore never been undertaken — recycling those Souls, their Higher Selves and their Oversouls back into their place of birth, the Source of this Cosmic Day, their place of individualization, where these individualized energies will cease to exist.

However, with the massive infusion of spiritual/monadic energy into planet Earth, this scenario becomes less and less likely. The power of the Dark Side has become and is becoming progressively diminished, and the victory of the Allied Forces and the Planetary Hierarchy in the recent Gulf War greatly weakened the beings who sought to gain world dominion, in part through the absolute control of all oil fields in the Middle East.

To be forewarned is to be forearmed: Having knowledge of this hideous energy and being conscious of this powerful force unmasks its subterfuge. The Iman will concentrate on the following goals:

---

2 This depends totally on the degree of upheaval on earth! If you experience the Axis Shift on Nov. 4, 1994, for example, Rome would cease to exist!

- *Complete control of the communication systems of the planet, especially the computer systems upon which all human systems rely. The minor attempt referred to as "the Michelangelo virus" will take on major dimensions if the Iman is able to control the major computer banks on this planet.*

- *Gaining access, through his elaborately established computer network, to the economic bases of every country will make him very powerful and every government extremely vulnerable, as he will be able to disarm every nation by simply cutting off their communication with the rest of the world. 666 is a number to be looked at, as it may be the Iman/Antichrist's personal computer code number. It is synchronistic that the largest computer banks on Earth are with the E.E.C. and are called 666, the number prophesied in Revelations.*

- *Mesmerizing a coalition of religiously powerful men with his speeches on ecumenism/world unity, and appearing to be a spiritual leader while trying to dupe everyone.*

- *Innovation, which will cause his rise to power. Initially he will be viewed as a world savior who has answers to help Mankind. His help in alleviating hunger in the Third World through advances in technology such as hydroponics will assure support from these peoples.*

- *Creating an image of himself as a humanitarian who is attempting to unite the world by helping the poorer nations. And because his intelligent plans will work and assist many people, he will gain credibility. The masses will not recognize his manipulation and plotting.*

- *By solving the financial problems of many individuals and nations through his skill in computers and economics, he thus hopes to gain the support and trust of many people.*

- *Doing everything to appear to be of the Light, he will deceive many people, but he is actually a wolf in sheep's clothing.*

It is important to realize and remember that this self-proclaimed humanitarian will succeed in helping many individuals and countries, and once their confidence has been gained, he will ask (if allowed) for huge sums of money from the richer nations to supposedly finance aid to the poorer nations. Having gained the respect and support of all governments and religious leaders, he will have no trouble in raising money, much of which will be funneled into his own coffers for his ultimate purpose — world control.

With the presence of the *Mahatma* energy, anchored on Earth on June 14, 1988 (which represents your Creator level for this Cosmic Day), we are very optimistic that in the battle in the area of dualities, the Forces of Light will raise the vibration of this planet sufficiently to extinguish all Dark Forces, including your religions — forces that insist upon worshipping the material world and that continue to make slaves of the Earth's inhabitants.

In the past, prior to the arrival on Earth of *Mahatma* (the Rider on the White Horse, its ancient term), the Black Lodge was far more advanced in externalization than the White Lodge, because for it, matter and materialism are the line of least resistance. The Black Lodge was therefore far more firmly anchored upon the Earth plane than the Planetary Hierarchy. It requires greater effort for the White Lodge to clothe itself in matter and work and walk on material levels than for those of the Black Lodge. Owing, however, to the "spiritual" growth of humanity and the steady, even if slow, orientation of Mankind to the Planetary Hierarchy, the time has come when this Hierarchy can materialize and meet the enemy with the overshadowed support of the *Mahatma* energy and need not be further handicapped by working in substance while the Forces of Evil work both in substance and in matter. When the *Mahatma* energy is properly anchored on Earth and is an accomplished fact, the Forces of Darkness face certain defeat!

With the massive shifts evident on Earth through *nuclear fusion* and the spiritualization of matter, the need to externalize your Planetary Government would be principally to teach the lower initiations (see the chart, "Man's Response to Initiations," p. 220). Thus their externalization will be less and less required because of the even higher initiate level focused on Earth now.

Certain among you will have raised your point of integration, herein referred to as an initiation, above those of your Planetary Hierarchy or your teachers. The discarnate teacher Vywamus, through the brilliant channel Janet McClure, explains (p. 233):

"There is always going to be a seeming head start by those who have chosen physicality, but in the long run it isn't. We get you started (we being your teachers and you being our fellow Co-Creators), and then you seemingly move a little further ahead...and then you get us started. So it is a sharing, you see, a reciprocal communicative linkage system."

The Effect of the First Ray on Humanity Today

Owing to stimulation from the Creator level for this Cosmic Day to the immediate planetary crises and to the invocative cry from humanity at present, energy from Shambala has been permitted to play upon the "center which is called the race of men" and has produced two powerful results: First, the Great World War, which lasted from 1914–1945; and second, the fission of the atom by the atomic bomb. Both of these events were made possible by the inpouring of the energy and power of the First Ray of Will, or power. This is the lowest aspect of this Ray, and definite material effects were produced. The destroyer aspect of the First Ray, through the **Mahatma** energy, was therefore the first aspect to take effect. It split the thought form of materialistic living that was governing and controlling all of humanity upon the mental plane, and sometime earlier produced a great agent of destruction upon the physical plane.

Thus was the New Age ushered in, allowing the Earth to become fourth-dimensional and the distinction between material living and spiritual living to be clearly demonstrated. This is made possible by the splitting of the ancient materialistic thoughtform on the mental levels. As this fact is grasped in the reorientation of human thinking, we will see its first results upon the emotional levels through the focused expression of human goodwill. This expression is the lowest aspect of the Second Ray of Love-Wisdom, implemented and strengthened by the second aspect of the First Ray of Will. Refer to the 12 Rays, p. 204.

The great scientific discovery on the physical plane, colloquially called splitting the atom, will eventually be turned to produce the conditions that will enable humanity to follow the good, the beautiful and the true. Mankind will then be capable of accomplishing this, freed from the dreaded trap of purely materialistic thinking. This is no vague dream or idle vision. Already the scientists who love their fellow man are working to harness the nondestructive aspect of atomic energy, its products and its radioactive properties for the good of Mankind.

In the next few years atomic *fusion* will be made available to humanity, which will eventually bring about the revelation of the nature of certain forces in relation to Light. This single event will transform world thinking and lead to a new (as far as man is concerned) type of transformational process into *the spiritualization of matter*. This creative opening and the ability to hold form is available until November of the year 2028. (Please refer to p. 20, the second and third paragraphs of "The Awakening".)

It must *not* be assumed that because of this all of humanity will automatically take the Fifth Initiation, for this is not the case. Many advanced Souls will take this initiation and thus not require further dense physical embodiment, but the bulk of humanity — which constitutes the sum total of the world disciple — will eventually take either the First or Second Initiation. The effect, however, of the work of the Planetary Hierarchy, in conjunction with Shambala, will finally lead to great stimulation of the Fifth Initiation. For the first time ever in this universe, now overshadowed by the *Mahatma* energy, a SPIRITUAL ASCENSION — not an etheric-body ascension (as has been accomplished in your past) will become available to humanity.

THUS WILL "THE LIGHT STREAM FORTH INTO THE MINDS OF MEN."

One of the signs of the arrival of this new Light and energy influx is a curious one; it is evidenced in the instability of the human thought processes and the human mental mechanism at this time. This is due to their premature response to the powerful new incoming energies of the *Mahatma*. It is the *unready* who react in this manner, and this is certainly no negative reflection or judgment upon them, for they are found in every class and nation. The Law of Rebirth will take care of these Souls who, in their next incarnation, will enter physical bodies better equipped to handle energy, although not on planet Earth. They will go to another third-dimensional planet, quite likely in the Pleiades.

Death

In these coming times, now that the Earth's vibration has increased a thousandfold into a new fourth-dimensional reality, great numbers of humanity will not withstand the shifts brought about by the radiation required to produce the *spiritual body*. Thus "prepare ye the way" to assist others in the simple transition that most call death.

There is no death! There is only entrance into *fuller Life!*

The much-dreaded death process does not exist; there is only freedom from the limitations of the physical vehicle. For the well-meaning human being, death is merely a continuation of the living process and a carrying forward of one's consciousness, which is usually unaltered. One does not sense much difference (but much greater freedom), is well taken care of, and is often unaware that one has passed on to another level.

The less well-meaning — the selfish, the cruel, the wicked, the criminal and the power- or money-hungry who worship only the material side of life — find themselves still *earthbound* after their consciousness has left their physical bodies. Their strong bonds with the Earth and earthly desires force them to remain close to the Earth and their last Earth setting, which they desperately seek to recontact and reenter. In a few instances, great personal love for those left behind or the nonfulfillment of a perceived urgent duty will hold a heart-focused individual to the Earth in a similar condition. This is the level that one can believe is "purgatory" — not "hell" — for hell with "eternal damnation" has been your third-dimensional existence on Earth, including your lower Astral Levels!

The mind of the mass consciousness is so little developed that fear of the unknown, terror of the unfamiliar and a strong attachment to form have created a paradoxical situation where one of the most beneficial experiences in the life cycle of an incarnating, evolving Son of God is viewed as something to be avoided and postponed for as long as possible.

Death, if one could but realize it, is one of our most practiced activities. We have all died many times, just as we have all been born many times; and we shall die again and again until such time as we raise our vibration above that of the Earth and Soul, herein called the Primary Ascension or "Mastery." Death is simply a matter of consciousness. One moment we are conscious on the dense physical plane, and a moment later we have withdrawn to another plane and are actively conscious there. As long as one's consciousness identifies with the physical, form aspect of self, death will hold its ancient terror. But as soon as you know yourself to be a Soul with a Higher Self and an Oversoul and find that you are capable of focusing your consciousness or awareness in any form or plane at will or in any direction within the form of God, then you shall no longer know death.

For death is but an interval between physical incarnations. The process of sleep is identical to the process called death, with the one difference being that in sleep the current of energy, or magnetic thread along which the life force flows, remains intact and constitutes the path of return to the physical body. In death this life thread is snapped or severed. When this happens the conscious entity cannot return to the body, and that body, lacking the *principle of coherence,* then disintegrates.

The young forget, and rightly so, the inevitability of that symbolic detachment that we call death. But when the life has been played out and age has taken its toll of both strength and interests, the world-weary man has no fear of this detaching process and no longer seeks to hold onto what was important and desirable earlier in life. Death is welcomed, and the human being willingly relinquishes that which earlier held his attention.

When an individual identifies with the Soul rather than the physical form, he then understands the Law of Sacrifice and is spontaneously governed by it. Then *he* is the one who will, with deliberate intent, choose to die. But in this process there is no pain or sorrow because there is no real death involved.

It is intended that every man die at the demand of his own Primal Soul (his own Self), at least until such time as he raises his vibrational level beyond that of the Earth and Soul. When one reaches a higher evolutionary level one can, with deliberation and choice of exact time, consciously withdraw from the dense physical body. Empty of the Soul, this body will then disintegrate and its atoms will pass back into the "pool of waiting units" until they are once more required for the use of incarnating Souls.

The cycle in which we now live has experienced the greatest destruction of human forms in the entire history of this planet; yet there has been no destruction of human beings. This is an important statement to note, and because of this huge destruction, humanity has advanced toward a more serene attitude to death. This is not yet evident, but in the next few years the change in attitude will become more apparent and the fear of death will begin to die out in this world. Mankind as a whole will begin to understand that what they have viewed as an "end" is, in reality, a release into a less limited, less confined existence.

Although death often appears to be purposeless, it is simply that the intentions of the various Soul levels are not known to most of humanity, who do not yet know how to *communicate* with this level of Self. This level of realization will soon be implemented with new revelation, for which your I-AM-*Mahatma* is laying the foundation.

One of the most difficult areas for the average human being to comprehend and interpret is what they perceive to be destruction caused by the will of God. This is one of the many results of a materialistic civilization that has placed all of its emphasis upon the form side of experience, and therefore regards physical comfort and well-being, as well as material possessions, the true goal of physical existence. Thus it is this attitude and reaction that the new incoming Light will concentrate on dispelling. As the Light reveals the reality, the worlds of spirituality and materialism will be understood and put into their correct perspectives. These transitions, the effects upon humanity as a whole, and the beginnings of the new and bright future are taking place directly as a result of the powerful incoming First-Ray activity of the *Mahatma.* The coming civilization is of a different (yet still *material*) nature, propelled by the awakening mass consciousness to the emerging spiritual objective that will transform all of life and give new purpose and value to that which is material.

For the initiate, it is important to understand that it is the *conscious* use, absorption and integration of energy that distinguishes him from the unconscious masses. Through the I AM presence *Mahatma* energy, he will be able to connect with the magnificent Light that will focus not only his path, but the significance of all that is being slowly revealed on the Earth plane, allowing him to see the total picture for the first time. The initiate works to free himself from every aspect of desire, seeking instead to align with the spiritual Will. This is the being who is ready to look into the Heart of Life, which leads him to become aware of the two central suns of Sirius, which in turn direct him to look at the path of higher evolution. Inevitably he will connect with the level referred to as "the Most High," the Source of the Cosmic Day.

When the initiate has reached the level referred to as the Fifth Initiation — the Initiation of Renunciation — and has established within himself complete harmony as a result of conflict (refer to pp. 208-209, Ray Four: Harmony Through Conflict), then new revelation will be attained. This is a new revelation that will now be accessed by *nuclear fusion*. "You cannot make a silk purse out of a sow's ear" until Mankind understands what silk is; in this analogy, silk is new revelation accessed by nuclear fusion. Ponder, if you will, on the true meaning of NEW REVELATION, the *spiritualization of matter*.

There has never been a time on Earth when so much *creative opportunity* has been available to elevate Mankind, for the first time ever, into "spiritualizing" all matter on this planet Earth and in this quadrant of this galaxy!

Planet Earth opened to a new level, which we reference as the fourth dimension, at the time of the Harmonic Convergence on August 15–16, 1987. At this juncture your Planetary Government was a council of seven departments, each department representing and transforming one of the Seven Cosmic Rays that maintained and overshadowed third-dimensional Mankind and Earth through the transformational energies called Christ Consciousness. The opportunity was given by the Creator level to allow five new Rays, completing the circuitry from Source to Earth in the early 1970s. Your Planetary Logos, Sanat Kumara, who embodies this planet and all aboard her, "steps down" the Twelve Rays, acting as a transformer to your Planetary Government, who in turn were required to create five new departments to facilitate and transform to you, humanity, and all kingdoms on Earth, all Twelve Rays, which in turn would allow this planet to become fourth-dimensional.

On the 14th of June 1988, the Creator level (which we reference as the Father energy, *Mahatma*) partially anchored on Earth the Twelfth Ray, allowing all of Mankind and Earth to have an Earth-link with the Source of this Cosmic Day for the first time in Earth's history.

Earth could not function fourth-dimensionally until your Planetary Government was completely compartmentalized with new department heads and associates for the Five Higher Rays. The anchoring on Earth was not available in a completely usable format until January 26, 1991, thus allowing the *Mahatma* (Source energy) to anchor monadic, or spiritual energy into Earth and her kingdoms for the first time in their history (please refer to p. 204 for "The Twelve Rays").

Those beautiful, more aware inhabitants of Earth, who are bewildered and traumatized by the heavy, limiting structure of the third dimension, *awakened* and realized that there is far more to them than this finite physical structure whose emotional and physical bodies seem to be crying out for change, especially those who house greater Light and consciousness.

This book, *Mahatma*, and the energy the contents embody can assist to integrate the "new you" in a way that was never before available to Mankind without "grabbing at air" in the pursuit of truth. We have written this book, which is beyond limited third-dimensional concepts and preconceived realities, to enable you to help yourself with wonderful affirmations and spiritual processing. These will enable you to recognize and become your Unlimited Self, as the spiritual Being that you are becoming, having become fourth-dimensional; and to avail yourself of the *Mahatma* without going into overwhelm with these expansive, unlimiting concepts now available to you as the God that you are!

We perceive many who call themselves "New Age" or "Lightworkers" or "Angels" who may wish to use a greater degree of discernment with the volumes of both channeled and inaccurately transmitted material that is now available to you in the beginning of this New Age.

A beautifully poetic book, *The Star-Borne* by Solara, has caused us great concern — not because the readers or the followers of the readers sought to be a part of a wonderful opening believed to have taken place on January 11, 1992. The actual opening took place on January 26, 1991. However, the event referenced as 11:11 was very helpful to the planet because it drew thousands of Lightworkers together in groups all over the planet on that date, creating synergy and anchoring essential spiritual (monadic) energy into the Earth. How synchronistic it was this morning, February 28, 1992, to open the *Bhagavad Gita*, which we haven't read in thirty years, to the quote: "11:11: The wise grieve neither for the dead nor the living."

Our concern nonetheless arises from the confusion that Solara's lovely "Angel-tale" has caused for many of you, as she states clearly that you are of the Angelic kingdom. Nothing could be more detrimental to your evolution and further from the truth than to believe that you have no free will or individualization, and are to be recycled into another undetermined "cycle" at the end of this Cosmic Day, which *your* evolution as God-man/Hu-man is not! *Hu* in Arabic means "supreme word"; in the Bible it is referenced symbolically as "the word, and the *word* was God."

Since the beginning of time there have been a small number who have crossed over, or transferred, from the Angelic kingdom to the Co-Creator level. It has been very difficult and confusing for these beings to suddenly make the shift from "an extension of the Source" to a being with free will.[3] You who are reading this, who feel or know that you came from the Angelic kingdom, know that because you are now in a physical body, you have transferred to the human cycle of evolution, and you definitely have free will.

If one were to draw a philosophical parallel between the animal kingdom and God-man (Hu-man, which is your evolution — not Angelic), and assume for a moment that the most heightened state of evolution within the animal kingdom is the dolphin, whose evolution is more aligned with the Hu-man than is the Angelic kingdom, then it is just as preposterous to suggest that we are Angels as it is to suggest that we are dolphins. (For greater clarification please read from the bottom of page 49 through page 51.)

Solara's (and many others') view of the fourth dimension: "As it is the home of the astral plane, one will find rampant illusion present within the fourth dimension"; and "The fourth dimension is not to be lingered in..." (from *The Star-Borne*, page 175). We believe that the confusion may lie in the fact that the lower levels (astral heavens) one, two and three were elevated vibrationally at the time of the Earth-link with Source on June 14, 1988, and subsequently the Five Higher Rays were anchored and transformed to all kingdoms on Earth on January 26, 1991. Thus, these physical heavens (not spiritual) one through seven no longer contain the vibration of the three lower-astral levels, which have caused so much illusion and confusion in what you view as the past.

We really must ask those who truly believe that they can just pass through the fourth dimension and function *on Earth* fifth- and sixth- dimensionally, how, pray tell, do you do that when your planetary embodiment — which is *your* embodiment — is still fourth-dimensional? As the Earth was 3.2 billion years in the third dimension, how has she achieved this unparalleled achievement in a matter of months?

What really happened when planet Earth became fourth-dimensional was that it opened all of you to this Council of Twelve for this quadrant of this galaxy, which is your new level of bonding vibrationally for an *undetermined* period of time, or until such time as you raise your vibration above that of the Earth, which is a point of completing your four-body integration referred to as the Fifth Initiation/Physical Ascension, *not* astral, which requires the Sixth Initiation.

We can see clearly that some among you are starting to sense these "higher" dimensions. What is coming through in your new, *unlimited* state of awareness are these higher multidimensional aspects of self. Thus, why limit yourself to these lower (physical/universal) dimensions (three through six) when you can now access your monadic (nonphysical) spiritual dimensions seven through nine through the energy that we call the *Mahatma*? These concepts are all explained very well in this book that you are about to read.

---

3 An angel would have to consult Archangel Metatron for transference and the Cosmic Council of 12 would have to give consent because the Angelic Kingdom, including Metatron, have no free will!

The references that Solara makes to Sanat Kumara as "our holy father" will set you back thousands of sequential years to your various religions, which, when they referred to "God" or "the Lord of the World," were actually referring to your Planetary Logos, Sanat Kumara, who is the embodiment of *this* planet, not Venus, and is certainly not our Source. Solara's view of Sanat Kumara being near the completion of our journey is again misleading, for Sanat Kumara's evolution is but the *beginning*, and for the immediate future his consciousness is still anchored in the etheric realm of Shambala, on the upper Gobi desert. His next evolutionary undertaking will be as a Solar Logos, once he has secured the Earth into this New Age. When Sanat Kumara graduates from his current position, one of the other Kumaras will take over. (Please reference Sanat Kumara's evolution on the chart, "Co-Creator and Creator levels, pp. 228-229, and refer to "Sanat Kumara," p. 192.)

We deliberated for a lengthy time before responding to the large number among you who contacted us about these 11:11 concepts. The great achievement of Solara regarding the participation of so many in the "opening" is wonderful. We must advise, however, that her evolutionary concepts are misleading and limiting.

We ask that you also use your discernment whilst reading *Mahatma* or any other material that you are drawn to. We feel, with justification, that the *Mahatma is* the opening that so many among you are calling 11:11, and that once you have digested and assimilated the whole contents of the most expanded and integrative teachings ever to come to Earth — herein called *Mahatma* — you will understand why the great discarnate teacher, Vywamus, through the brilliant channel, Janet McClure, has said, "A world-wide philosophy will come from the *Mahatma* energy and teachings, which will be the evolutionary/spiritual processing for this planet for many millennia."

Introduction by Vywamus

Channeled by Janet McClure — September 1990

"I, Vywamus, think that this is the most important thing that's happened on your Earth and for Humanity."

There are many times in existence when it is necessary to acknowledge that there is something greater than one's self. By doing so, that acknowledgment brings an expansion of the power by which all of existence evolves, grows and becomes greater. In this book we will examine together many cosmic opportunities[1] which are opening to the physical Level. It is truly an exciting time to be on the Earth. Each one of you chose it on a cosmic level as a part of your growth and as a way to help the Earth. You know this, but you perhaps do not remember how truly a cosmic experience Earth living is.

I have stated many times that this "workshop Earth" is equivalent to a

---

1 Throughout the various teachings on Earth, two commonly misused words are "cosmic," which could include all of creation, and "spiritual." We have been rather precise in our referencing of both *cosmic* and *spiritual* as being *nonphysical, beyond all the levels of the universes*; all that is *monadic* is the cosmic and spiritual level, or the seventh, eighth, and ninth dimensions (the Creator level is nondimensional). For greater clarification, please see the chart, "Co-Creator and Creator Levels," pp. 228-29.) From time to time, depending upon whom Vywamus was addressing and their degree of understanding, he has used the words "spiritual" and "cosmic" in a limited perspective, as "any area beyond the Earth." For those of an expanded degree of consciousness, Vywamus has been very specific that both *spiritual* and *cosmic* are the *nonphysical* levels of the Monad through to Source. Hereafter we will place in quotations these words *spiritual* and *cosmic* when misapplied.

six-week course taken in a special school which expands one's creativity, expands your understanding of yourself on every level. The very nature of the deepest part of physical existence has you forgetting, a little, its purpose. You do not always remember the links or connections, the cosmic equivalency of yourself, which is very much a part of your life.

To illustrate this, let us see a small child who is sent to school for the first time. They can get caught up into a peer-pressure syndrome, which then seems to negate the support system they still have from their parents, from their home environment. Indeed, of course, the home environment is there as a support system for them. It is not meant to make their choices or to do what they came to school to do and to learn.

It is then necessary to realize a level of agreement with you which, as a full agreeing partner, has brought you to the Earth. You may say to me, "I know that, and I like the Earth. Mostly, I am glad to be here." But I, Vywamus, am talking to certain parts of your emotional responses which indeed are the reason that you are here, from a personal point of view. They do NOT understand this journey. They do NOT respond to this opportunity that Earth brings to you until, through your journey over many, many lives, an opening is created, a point of understanding is reached. A cooperation is entered into through your emotional responses, surrendering — letting go of, and thus integrating — the deep resistances which must be seen clearly for what they really are, and then given to the Cosmos as a means to identify who you really are.

Now, by this I do not mean that you are here on the Earth as a sacrifice. You are not. LIFE IS NOT MEANT TO BE A SACRIFICIAL PATTERN. You are not being used by something greater in a way which takes away your divine abundance or your unlimitedness.

I, Vywamus, approached the Earth in 1984. I was asked to do so by a Teacher called Djwhal Khul. He grew up on the Earth and is one of the most wise, loving and balanced beings it has ever been my privilege to know. In my communication with Djwhal Khul, he — on behalf of your Hierarchial Government — asked me to bring my strengths, my understanding, and a part of my purpose to the Earth. I believed that my strengths would aid the Earth. In checking with my purpose area, I felt drawn to your planet. Since 1984, I have come through quite a number of channels. I have been lovingly amazed by humanity's beauty, creativity, and eagerness to learn and to evolve.

In this book I assist in bringing you what I consider to be the most important connection your Earth has ever made. I think that this point is the beginning of what will be the means to have, step by step, the wondrous, peaceful, harmonious Earth you seek.

The concepts that I bring to you here are deep and conceptual. There will be exercises to help you feel, through your emotions and through your energy body, what we are presenting here in as many ways as we can. We take a journey together then, to help you to see the evolution of your planet, to help you to understand the concept "Walk-In" in another way — beyond, perhaps, what we could call the traditional. In my opinion, your understanding of what the Walk-In state truly means will grow and expand until you can understand its cosmic equivalencies in ways which show you and allow you, too, as I do, to marvel at the Divine Plan which puts everything together with utter simplicity, and yet with perfect harmonious alignments and ever-expanding possibilities.

In this journey of consciousness we will see certain functions, certain roles upon your Earth. Now remember, although we talk about the Earth we are really talking about the journey of a planet. Thus in your future you may perform some of the roles that we discuss in this book. The reason you are reading it may be to see a future career opportunity opening. Your Soul has agreed to fulfill this greater function as you reach the point of maturity on the Earth where you are looking for the next step, the next job opportunity, if you will.

We will be discussing terms such as Planetary Logos, Solar Logos, Galactic Logos, Universal Logos, Cosmic Avatars, and several other roles of responsibility which help to evolve a planet through the various phases in its growth. Now, the energy of the Cosmos expresses itself on all 352 levels, from Source to Earth, as the Avatar of Synthesis — its ancient term *The Rider on the White Horse*.

In the book *The Story of Sanat Kumara*[2] I showed the journey of Sanat Kumara as he evolved into his present position as Planetary Logos of the Earth. It was not meant to take you beyond the present time. But in this volume I will give you my estimates (perhaps we could say "guess-timates") of what lies in store for your planet, keeping in mind that I certainly do this through lines of probability — the amount of energy which is in probable lines leading into your future. Also keep in mind that I, Vywamus, do not function in sequential time except for the portion of myself, as energy, which I have wrapped around your planet in order to interact and communicate with it as closely and with you as closely as possible. I, then — focused in the Eternal Now — had the advantage of looking at probability lines as points of energy feeding into the ever-integrating and ever-expanding process we call the Eternal Now. It is difficult to see that it does not function within time or space, but still is evolving. It is, of course, the Consciousness which evolves, grows, expands, and becomes aware, that has nothing to do especially with time or space — although it is perfectly capable of functioning within time or space, which is what it does here on your Earth. It being, of course, the overall consciousness of All That Is, which is the Creator.

As we begin our journey, then, I would like you to read this material through once. If you don't understand all of the concepts, don't worry about it. Get what you can. Read through it so that you get an overall view, as much as possible, of *why* this material is presented to humanity. After reading through it once, I would suggest that you go back, study those areas that seem to draw

---

2 *The Story of Sanat Kumara: Training a Planetary Logos,* Vywamus channeled and edited by Janet McClure, Light Technology Publishing, P.O. Box 1495, Sedona AZ 86336, 1990.

you especially, doing the particular exercises in those sections until, through the areas that are becoming clearer to you, you can begin to put together the overall purpose for which this book is written.

The concepts given here are meant to be understood over a period of months or years. Some of you will use this volume that way. Others will use it briefly and then put it aside. In either case, it is lovingly dedicated to humanity.

I appreciate your beauty, your enthusiasm, and your hearts which care and which radiate forth to all of the Cosmos.

Love, Vywamus

The Expansion

The present point of evolution on your planet came about through an event which happened in August 1987, which has been called the Harmonic Convergence. It has been written about and explained in many ways. Certainly I would encourage you to find out more about it, reading the excellent material which is in the metaphysical literature. I will briefly explain what I consider the Harmonic Convergence to be, as a premise upon which all of what we will discuss in this volume is based.

Without that tremendous expansion allowed by the Harmonic Convergence, your planet would have remained in a third-dimensional foundation, not as is now available within a fourth-dimensional foundation. It is, then, necessary to look briefly at the dimensions. I have done a book called *Scopes of Dimensions*[3] in which I divided dimensions into nine pieces. This is my arbitrary choice. There are those who prefer to look at dimensions as twelve. There is some validity, as far as I am concerned, in that division; but after considerable review on my part, I decided that nine pieces in the "dimensional pie" made a simpler and easier-to-understand division, and thus I am using it.

I am fond of saying, however, that there are always at least six ways to do everything, and certainly it is important to recognize how true that is. If you get into a pattern of rigidity which says, "This is the only way to do whatever it is you are trying to do," then you are feeding into rigidity and inflexibility and cannot take advantage of certain manifesting opportunities, which give you options and advantages in your evolution and which come about because you are willing to expand beyond the old rigid patterns that say, "I must find this one way; there is only one way which allows truth to manifest."

Truth, my friends, in my opinion is as variable as all of the beings who seek it. Your truth is not necessarily exactly the same as someone else's truth. In point of fact, it is not meant to be, because *total* truth is made up of *all* of the opinions of everyone that exists. It is, in fact, the totality of the expressions in

---

3 *The Scopes of Dimensions: How to Experience Multidimensional Reality* by Vywamus Through Janet McClure, Lillian Harben, ed., Light Technology Publishing, 1989.

which each one sees a little differently and in which each person has a complementary point of view that feeds into the whole point of view and that allows it to be an unlimited expression therein. My point is that there are many, many ways to view everything. We present to you in these pages the truth as I, Vywamus, see it, noting that I could see it and state it in other ways, too, because I believe that I am flexible to do so. But humanity has invoked this material that I bring, and I bring it in a comprehensive and yet as simple a form as possible.

Consider this, then: Your planet has a certain position, if you will, within a larger view of physical existence. It has been sitting in your past time very solidly in the third dimension. If we could see the third dimension as having a scale and the scale having degrees of numbers from 1 to 100, with different planets within this quadrant of this galaxy sitting on different degrees of the third dimension, the number 1 would be the closest position to the fourth dimension and the number 100 the heaviest, or densest, position. In my opinion, then, your planet began in its positioning at number 95. As you can see, this is very solid indeed. It does not mean a scale of "bad" or "worse"; it simply is the role of the planet in its position in the Cosmos — or perhaps put more specifically — within this quadrant of this galaxy, which is the administrative headquarters level which you are now connected with much more specifically, much more openly than before the Harmonic Convergence.

Because of the evolutionary process over the eons which your planet has existed, all of existence has evolved. Through that your planet moved from number 95 to the position of number 1. What does that mean? Certainly, one must see that planets themselves have overall consciousness, and over the eons some mature and graduate from the role they have assumed into a new level or a new role. This happened to your Earth at the time of the Harmonic Convergence. It graduated. The position that it held, another planet has assumed. Your planet has gone on to enter a fourth-dimensional foundation. This again puts it at the beginning of another scale from 1 to 100, so when it entered the fourth dimension it was at 100 on the fourth-dimensional scale.

Now, the scale on the fourth dimension is a variable one. It's nice and neat on the third dimension — you can go from 95 to 94 to 93 to 92 and so forth. On the fourth dimension, it *flows as needed*. It may flow from 100 to 2 and back to 42 and then to 63 and back to 100. It will move and flow as needed because that is the nature of the fourth dimension.

Once having entered the fourth dimension, a planet changes completely. That is perhaps the most important thing that humanity is attempting to understand.

Your planet has now evolved beyond third-dimensional time. Fourth-dimensional flow is its foundation.

Now, in *The Scopes of Dimensions*, I explained that the third dimension's purpose is to magnify creativity, to expand it until, through such expansion, it fits together in a clearer and more usable manner. I refer you to that volume for more detail in this regard. But the third dimension has not been lost by entering the fourth dimension. This is perhaps one of the most important Cosmic Laws of existence — that you are ever integrating your understanding in order to expand beyond what has been understood to a new level which will give you a new opportunity to understand more. But Cosmic Law says, "You can't push something away if you try to." It sticks. The mirror — or *existence* — does not let go of it until you have understood it and thus integrated that point into your creative base. It is necessary to understand this in as many ways as possible.

When you are born into physical existence, you are born into a mirroring process. By that I mean that everyone in your life is a mirror for you and you are a mirror for everyone else in your life. *In a relationship, the person you are related to mirrors to you either something that you have not understood yet or a strength that you have not used yet. It is probably both.*

Remember, you create your own life. You create all of it! Living your life on the Earth has been, up to this point, simply a sequencing of steps and looking at the mirrors in order to let go of old resistances, in order to see your abilities and who you are more and more clearly.

If you have a relationship which seems difficult, look deeply within yourself. Are you reacting to that relationship? Is there anger? Is there a sense of betrayal or loss? Is there frustration or anxiety? Each of these emotions is what I call a trigger into a limiting belief which you hold, which the mirror of life is showing to you. Why? So that you can let go of it. These beliefs are restricting and limiting, and you are not meant to be limited or restricted.

Now, when I say that, keep in mind that I am not telling you to get away from something. Many of you believe that freedom is getting away from something, particularly from all forms of structure or, for some of you, from forms of responsibility. I am NOT saying that the mirrors are showing you how to get away from anything except *beliefs* which are *limiting*. In point of fact, the releasing of them allows you to step into the use of structure in the way that it was meant to be used.

Structure is a divine support system. It is not meant to be limiting. It is meant to hold for you a greater point of view that perhaps you have only begun to glimpse, so that you may understand more clearly and so that you may do your part for the whole. As you wake up, All That Is becomes aware in that area in a manner which is aligned into other areas. It is literally a triggering, an ignition process, a process which allows the term "wake up" to echo and reecho throughout the Cosmos.

You may say to me, "Well, all of this is abstract. What does it mean, anyway?" What it means, my beautiful friend (if I may call you that, and I would like to), is that you have now an opportunity which did not exist for you before the Harmonic Convergence, to utilize certain cosmic correspondences which are opening doors that didn't seem to be there for you at all. Now they are not only there, but they are open and you are stepping through them easily. Perhaps it is a little awesome to see yourself doing so.

One of the things which prompted me to assist in writing this material is the way in which each of you is evolving. I see a stepping-up, at least *one thousand percent*, of your evolution. Now, it may be that you can't see that yet, but you can feel it. It may be creating for you some of the deepest emotional readjustments you have ever had. For some of you, the emotions will protest a little and you are having some fears and some doubts. For others, you may not be especially aware of what is going on emotionally because you may have buried some of those emotional responses; or perhaps you are clear enough emotionally now that there is a use of your creativity, which your emotional body can finally appreciate and be a part of.

In the past, before the Harmonic Convergence, about two percent of humanity used their emotional responses to fully cooperate with their creative efforts. In other words, the emotions didn't fight their expansion and evolution. That perhaps is difficult to understand. To do so, I will take you again to the basic, or Source, level. My hobby, if you will, has been studying the Source and its evolution. I certainly do not say that I understand it completely, but perhaps we can look at that level and see it as simply the projector of where you are now, understanding that what goes on at that level is the very basic core or *reason* why your life is as it is on the Earth. If you want to change, you MUST understand more clearly your Source-level responses.

If we see the Source as a circle and recognize that you floated there in what I call the Undifferentiated Source before you began your individualization process, and if we project that as a symbol of a womblike state, then we see in your birthing the basic point that you are still trying to understand. Some of you are involved in rebirthing. It seems to me to be, at times, important. The process of rebirthing begins to energize that Cosmic Birth when you have released certain barriers, certain resistances. Rebirthing, then, is one way of looking at this basic point of Cosmic Birth. I have not chosen to use rebirthing techniques, recognizing that when they are desirable you will find them. There will be a contact with that Cosmic Birth point, one way or another. The systems are not as important as your asking your Soul for the system which will work well for you and help you to understand most completely.

However, in our material here, let me show you as clearly as possible why this Cosmic Birth is the key point for all of you to understand. It was, of course, a point of complete change. In the womb of Source you floated, in our analogy. You didn't have any special responsibilities. You didn't have to do anything; you just floated. You could and you did learn from every point of view, easily. There was nothing required of you. I will soon begin to teach my understanding of what went on in that Undifferentiated Source, because for many of you it can be helpful.

At a certain point, then, the Creator in Its love, Its joy and Its desire to share, *individualized Itself* — or, as I have put it so that you may understand more easily — one morning it knocked on your door and said, "Get up, it's time to wake up." Some of you said, "I am sleepy; I don't want to wake up," not realizing that something had already happened — you had been individualized — because you could now think as an individual. So you already had a choice and you were saying, "I don't want to wake up."

Now, the fact that you could say it meant that you had already chosen the individualization process. There were those who were given the opportunity. Many, many, many chose not to be individualized. If this occurred to them, they would not have said, "I am sleepy; I want to go back to sleep." This was resistance after the fact, or not seeing that you had already taken the first step.

There are at least three levels prior to full manifestation, and we would say this was the third level. The first two levels have to do with Source Itself on a fuller or more cosmic level. The Source — in Its Beingness — *desired*, as I said. In Its desire It came closer to manifestation, and then in Its thinking process It began to project parts of Itself into further manifestation. This was the next step. The final or third step is taken by the parts of Source Itself, or by *you*.

Now, there are some parts of the Source which have reached to this level and are not yet fully awake, but they have been born already into the individualization process. When they are ready to wake up, they will choose to be a part of the process that you and I are committed to and are evolving in. This is why it seems as if there are always new monadic (spiritual) -level beings being born. They have been given free will and can wake up and begin to experience whenever they wish. It's like putting those who are attending school on the honor system and saying, "You can come to class whenever you want. There is no penalty. There is nothing that says that you have to come to every class, as long as you pass the examinations. You can attend class as you see fit."

Well, there are always those who come in at the last minute and perhaps benefit from what all of us are doing. Some of you may not find that fair; it is, though. The point is that you gave permission, by going through the individualization process, to take responsibility for a part of the Plan, your unique part. You knew, and you still know, that you are on a greater journey to realize your *divine equality* with the Source Itself, making you truly unlimited. But — and this is where some of you still have some learning — some of you didn't read the small print on the contract given to you by Source, which is entitled "My Unlimitedness." It is a certificate — a gift certificate — handed to you by the Source. Then there were the terms and the conditions. Certainly, free will on every level was given to you. That's the prime directive. But secondly, perhaps as a condition — and certainly not meant to be limiting but *supportive* — you were given the whole Co-Creator process within which to evolve your understanding.

Now, perhaps this is a very key point. It is one that must be looked at until you really understand what it means for you. Again I say, the only fated-to-experience event for you is the ultimate destiny, if you will, of being completely unlimited, a Creator as great as our Creator is. But you step into that gradually, as you become more and more aware of what it really means. As stated before, it is a process which is facilitated by the mirrors of existence brought to you by others who are also in the same process — Co-Creators, those who are creating together with you. Thus, your goal now and for the foreseeable future for all of you, is to understand your relationship with others, to cooperate with others in what is termed divine equality.

The emotion which governs divine equality is what I call true humility — the ability to see your equality and everyone else's equality, that your abilities are as good as and as great as everyone else's, but no greater.

Now, you have certain strengths that you are using more consistently than others. They have, certainly, strengths that they are using more consistently than you. Together, all of those strengths make up the Source, the Whole. That is the level that you now see. I am talking about all of the levels. The level that you are now concerned with is the physical level. So humanity is meant to use its abilities together in order to create the overall clear environment of a planet which is willing to cooperate in the use of its strengths — which sees each of its parts evolving the use of those strengths; and which recognizes that other strengths and other approaches are as valid as its own. That validity of others, that allowingness of others, that trusting of others, that acceptance of others, is the key to the Co-Creator process.

This, of course, is the *heart area*, isn't it? The heart which radiates, the heart which ignites and unites. The heart which is the center, the core, of the whole process. Certainly, today we validate it as the process by which you use the Co-Creator process clearly, wisely and expansively.

The Co-Creator process, then, is that mirroring that I talked about earlier. The mirror is to help you to be clearer in your creativity within the process, to help you align into the overall Plan, to help you to see that you can rely on the Plan. There is a divine support system and you are within it, and you can function in a way that is *always* within it. You can't fall out of it. There is no way to do so. Yes, you may find confusion there sometimes, or a sense of alienation, but soon you get back on that track.

You are connected much more than you know. Although you remember the times when you didn't feel connected, most of you are much more connected than nonconnected. In fact, as I talk about resistances and as I talk about the emotional responses which are not clear, please keep in mind that I am only talking about five percent of the totality of you. Ninety-five percent of you do understand the journey, do understand the clear goal — and that, perhaps, is an extremely positive point of view. That's one that you have deep within you.

The Harmonic Convergence spun your planet into a new level; it began to link its energy into a *flow*. It would be like seeing your planet like a large boat, and it has gone through a series of locks which have lifted it. This was the journey in the third dimension — into one lock then flooding that and going to a new level in that lock and lifting the planet, and so going to a new level. Now, having gone through the lock system which raised your planet in a compartmentlike state, you have again reached the flow. And your ship, Earth, is flowing on a much wider, more expansive space than ever before.

The Opening

We see on the Earth an opening which has never been there before. This is a reflection of a higher-level opening which has occurred. Most of you recognize that physical existence reflects the spiritual level. This has been called "As above, so below." Not yet "As below, so above"! This cosmic opening, then, is the process of our Cosmic Day maturing, of our cosmic experience bringing together what has been explored, so that the "As above, so below" simulative process can occur.

Let me give you an example to help you understand that. In our example, then, there are six brothers who are born into a family. The father has a family business. He decides that there is enough room and enough work for all six of his sons to be a part of that business. One will be no greater than the other, but he can expand his business through all of the strengths that the six sons learn to express. He sends each son to a university which teaches that son how to use a particular skill. One may be studying accounting, one engineering, one marketing, one coordinating skills which coordinate many different levels of production.

Over a period of time each son finishes his training and begins to formally work in the business. After all of the sons have graduated, there is quite an intense adjustment period — meaning that there will now be seven points of view that are seeking to create this business. Each responsibility area adds to the effort, but requires of the group a sense of proportion as to how much it is necessary to allow that area to be seen as a part of the group effort.

After perhaps ten years the father dies, leaving the six sons to run the business. That goes on for a number of years, until the sons become so familiar with each other's methods that there is a *stability* level reached in the business.

In our analogy, then, that is the point where our Cosmic Day is now. All of you are the Co-Creators within that cosmic experience. If we put this Cosmic Day into sequential time, we are approximately three-fourths through it. Enough time, enough effort have gone into it that there is a stability base established now, meaning that the strengths of the Co-Creators have been established enough that a new level of integration — or of synthesis, assimilation (whatever term we use) — can come forth. Because the Plan can really prepare for anything, there is an automatic opening, or cosmic change that occurs because of this new stability level, or this new base.

As I have told many of you, one of the most charged areas that you have is the area of *change*. When there is a tremendous change, you many times do not identify with this change that is occurring because of a greater stability level. The change *seems* to be bringing you a loss, or a destructive process or a splitting-off of what you really want. But in actuality, the opposite is true.

The change comes about because a stability rate or an integration has begun and reached a certain level where there needs to be a different setup, a different support system, in order to keep evolving that effort. In our example with the business and the six sons, we can envision that they may expand their effort so much that they go into other areas, some of the sons heading up an effort in another physical area — a geographical spreading out, then, which allows a greater market for their product and greater opportunities for the use of their creativity.

Cosmically speaking, then, this new stability level, which is three-fourths of the way through this Cosmic Day, has opened our Source to a consultation with *another* level of Source which it will ultimately merge with but which it is now just beginning to identify with and communicate with. Some of you are acquainted with my talking about Sources — other Sources. If you prefer, we can use the term "other levels of our Source." If we look at evolution as a constant *spiraling*, we could say that what I mean by another level of Source is a spiral that is a more profound level of the spiraling system, more conscious and clearer, if you can say that it is clearer than what is already clear.

That is probably confusing, but you can think about it this way: If you wash a garment that is white, using products to enhance it so that it is very white, you may look at it and it is as white as white can be, as far as you are concerned. But if a being looked at it with eyes that could see 100 times more powerfully than your eyes, that being could see areas that needed to be cleaner or clearer. Consciousness levels are always growing, always evolving, whether you are a physical being or a Source-level consciousness.

I think this is important for all of you to understand. It does not mean that our Source is not perfect — of course It is perfect. Its great perfection has produced all of us and the Plan, which is so magnificent that its perfection is thrilling and almost — from the level from which we see it — unbelievable. But I know through my own learning that even beyond the points we can conceive of, there is learning, there is growth; there is that which is clearer, that which is more powerful, that which is more conscious. *Consciousness* is the vehicle through which divine perfection expresses. There is a constant unfoldment of it.

So because our Source is literally able now to consult a higher level, we see on the physical level humanity open to what I have termed "the Cosmic Walk-In" — the I AM Presence. *The Cosmic Walk-In is a reflection of a more cosmic connection which our Source is presently expressing.* It doesn't even matter whether you fully get this conceptually. What does matter is that you give this Cosmic Walk-In a try, or ask it for help. Allow yourself to prove in your life everything that I am saying in this material. The Cosmic Walk-In is here to help you to move beyond your present position of individuality. It is not a part of Soul or a part of the monadic level — it is a specialist made up of all 352 levels and initiations from the Earth to Source.

Asking for help is necessary. The Cosmos can't bring you what you are not yet willing to accept. Although I've said sometimes that some of you are coming along kicking and screaming, even in that analogy it means that you are *willing* to be pushed along kicking and screaming. If you were not, you would not be, meaning that you can hold onto your nonunderstanding as long as you wish. In order to release it, you must say to your Soul, "I surrender to you and your purpose," or to the Cosmos, "Help me with the next step." Or to the Creator, "Please, I need help. I know that I need help, and I ask for it." You may also ask us, your "spiritual" friends, or the Angels, for you may send a message to all of the above. But your message is going to reach new, more conscious, more aware levels than ever before. That is what is exciting. That is what is so important, and about which I am so excited! To contact this "Cosmic Avatar of Synthesis," concentrate on the name *Mahatma*, the "Father."

In my opinion, again, putting it into sequential time — our Source made an important realization at the time of the Harmonic Convergence. For those of you who do not understand that term, it was a point where many things came together for the Earth, and it was the ending of cycles (hundreds, thousands, and millions of year cycles), many of them coming together in a point of time which changed the whole vibration of your planet Earth. So much so that it changed the energy framework and flow of the planet. It changed the vibrational rate of the planet to the point where, vibrationally, you live on a whole new planet. You don't live on the old third-dimensional Earth. A new fourth-dimensional beginning was born at that time.

A realization is a point of contact which, when energized, brings an alignment of the *four-body system*. For our Source, that means that Its spiritual concepts, Its mental understanding, Its emotional structure, and the part of It which is physical (Its physical universes) came into an Opening through an *alignment*, and all of us are experiencing expansion at a much greater rate of flow than ever before because of that realization.

I have theorized as to what that realization was. I bring you a possibility; I am sure that it is something in this area. The exact point, as we put it into words, may be open to interpretation — in fact, it is. But I bring you the realization as I see it now:

I think that our Source, when It was very young, experienced the trauma of losing contact with what we would call a larger level that It valued, that It looked upon as Its growing support system. This experience is still very active in our Source. Through all of us the Source is seeking to resolve issues (although as far as we can see our Source uses every issue clearly). We are going to give you the example of putting consciousness through a sieve, and the sieve keeps the convoluted material and lets the rest through. As far as our consciousness can see, the Source-level sieve isn't keeping the convoluted material; it is clear. From the Source's point of view, It's using a finer sieve than we can conceive of and, yes, It is learning, It is growing, It is letting go of some points of what we might call a very cosmic convolution.

Again let me assure you that I am not saying that our Source isn't perfect. It is! We are talking here about the difference between Divine Beingness and the *expression* of that Divine Beingness.

Our Source, then, is ever refining Its understanding of every level. At this point — three-fourths of the way through this Cosmic Day — with a new integrative or assimilative base, our Source has resolved an understanding which allowed a realization in the areas of support and opportunity. Again, please stretch your understanding as to what our Source is. It is not a point of static consciousness which, in Its perfection, does not grow. Because of Its perfection, it is willing to go *beyond* points where integration seems to have occurred completely, and can be taken to a whole new level of expression, and thus integrated more finely, more comprehensively.

Let us use an analogy in the area of music, and let us say that we took a Beethoven symphony and one by Mozart. Both are beautiful. Our Source is learning how to play both of them at the same time, using the perfection of both (not negating either point of view), allowing the two of them to come together beautifully, supportively, without strain, without being forced, without being invalidated. In other words, the way the growth takes place in our Source is through ever integrating what already is strong and seemingly completely integrated.

You might think about that. That is the adjustment of what is always taking place — *more* integration, *more* realization of how to put things together. Strengths, whether they are yours on a personal level or the Earth's overall strengths, are always being used in a more comprehensive manner.

The Mahatma Energy

As you begin to understand who you are, there is an excitement generated. We could say that this is a creative excitement. Once that begins to *penetrate all the cells of the body*, it requires of the cells that they live in a manner that is beyond the human state. This is interesting, because it means that each one of you is growing a new structure now. Your body — and all of the organs in it — is changing, and there is a growing need to be aware of those changes.

At this time communication with various parts of your body and between various parts of your body is very important. Synchronistic with this is the communication with other levels of existence. As you become aware that not only can you communicate with them, but that you are and have parts of yourself existing on those other levels, the physical structure begins to benefit a great deal from such conscious awareness. It bridges certain gaps in communication between the parts of your body.

Each part of your body has a certain frequency. At this point in your evolution, all parts do not vibrate harmoniously with each other. They are affected by the old patterns of behavior that you have used in living your many lives, and synchronistic with each part of the body is a particular restriction or limitation which has been accepted into the subconscious mind.

Each time that you begin, first of all, to communicate with the parts of the body in love and allowingness and to support them rather than always thinking that they support you (which, of course, they do) — but when you understand yourself as the support vehicle for them also — a door opens and you can explore beyond this door, through a communicative link with the awareness level that I have called the Cosmic Walk-In, but it is known better by some of you as the I AM Presence.

Remember, I have stated that the purpose of this level in its contact with you on the physical plane is to help you to integrate, also to go beyond barriers to see your physical expression as the fully allowing, fully creative, fully igniting self that you really are. It is not done just from your point of view, but to benefit *all*. In other words, the Source (the Creator) has given us this exciting contact called the Avatar of Synthesis — the *Mahatma* (the Father), in ancient terms *The Rider on the White Horse* — so that we may be a clearer participant within the overall pattern of existence, which is termed the Plan. The Source, in recognition of your need to integrate, has given you a tool to help you with synthesis and unity, to recognize the cosmic aspects of yourself beyond your own individualization that leads you into an awareness of the support, the expansion, and the overall participation you have been privileged to be in now. Literally, this point is a critical one for all of you. You have now the opportunity to move into an awareness level that you have sought in all lives on the Earth. It really is there for you now. It is rather like a door, and I do invite you to do this exercise.

> *See a golden door. Go up to it. See how you feel about that golden door. Try to be honest with yourself. Certainly most of you will approach it with great excitement. But underneath that excitement there may be some anxiety, even some fear. See if you can sense what it is you are afraid of or anxious about. Even though the fear or anxiety may be present, there is much more energy in the **desire** to go through the door, isn't there? — the creative excitement to see what lies on the other side. And this creative excitement is what motivates you now.*

It is different from being motivated by what one might call the need for a thrill. I am not talking about that. Humanity in the past has needed thrills such as violence and seeing something very horrifying or startling, which gave you a thrill. I am talking about the other end of the scale, literally — of anticipating a link creatively and then going into it and allowing that link to motivate you into the Light by calling on the *Mahatma*. The energies are explained very conceptually in this book.

This is not an expectation, where you expect to use what is given to you 100% the moment you make the connection, but rather a creative excitement, an ability to *allow* this opportunity you step into to unfold one step at a time — as a beautiful flower might unfold — to look forward to the next step, to see the goal in the stepping process.

You see, the *Mahatma* energy contact is for that very purpose because, in its ability to help you integrate and to break down barriers, it gives you the means to accept the stepping process without creating more need to get on with it all *now*.

There is, then, an awakening to the evolutionary process in a way that none of you have seen yet. Of course, you have seen the process, but not in the way that the level called the I AM Presence understands it. By means of your contact with this level, you gain an awareness of evolution from a point which I am calling creative excitement, and it begins the process of awakening eagerly to each day to say to yourself, "Yes, I have now a fresh day upon which to paint creatively, within which to act communicatively and allowingly and trustingly. I am privileged to be within the Plan and I am excited about my opportunities *now*" — not tomorrow, not next week, not next month (although that may be there too, but not in a way which takes away the joy of unfolding what is there now). It is like the Creator gives us a present each second, each moment, that we can unwrap, that we can look at and be grateful for and be truly excited about. Like a small child, we exclaim over it saying, "Look at that! How exciting! Isn't it wonderful?" Each moment, then, is a gift within which to exchange views with others, to see how they saw the gift, to understand beyond the need to hurry along so that you miss half of what is given as an opportunity. Certainly, the I AM Presence understands beyond the need to hurry past that point of creative delicacy. You wouldn't want to miss it.

As when you are raising a child, you wouldn't want to miss the beauty of their unfoldment, the particular stages that they go through that you share as a parent. You have those in your memories forever. You have gained something through viewing them through the eyes of a child. This child that I am speaking of, and through whose eyes you view, is our Creator. Certainly it is not blasphemy to say that. There is nothing more wonderful than a child and its wondrous view of creation. Thus our Creator is always at a point of new beginning — a point of new awakening, a point of joyous exploration — as a child is.

This is important, because the I AM Presence, if you call on it by invoking the *Mahatma*, will begin to remind you of that childlike quality that is at the very core of our Source-level connection. Thus you begin to link creatively with other beings who understand the joy of existence, certainly many on the spiritual level. But you will also magnetically attract those on the physical level who view life in a joyous manner, so that more and more as you recognize it, you are in an environment that reflects back to you your inner recognition of the joy and the creative excitement of every moment of your day.

Now certainly the mass consciousness reflects to you a particular learning in regard to all of this, and it would depend upon each individual and each time period on the Earth what that was. One reason that individualization has been given to you as a gift is to help you to utilize the *creativity* of the Source without utilizing the heavy patterns of behavior which others are going through. You have then the support of the mass consciousness, if you know how to access it. But you do not need to accept *their* difficulties, their deep convolution. That is the trick, if we want to use that term. I do not use it as a purposeful attempt to deceive but as a means to see rather skillfully how everything can work together without having a difficult point of view to master.

You see, we, your "spiritual" friends and teachers, have discovered that life really is not difficult. It is on the physical level, in that you have accepted the illusion of difficulty. Certainly for some, it takes awhile — it literally does — after the Ascension process to figure out how to use life without any difficulty, because physical existence has put everything that you didn't understand into such graphic form that you literally learned to live with difficulty. This habit pattern must be unlearned.

Now, you know this mentally; you know it emotionally, too. You know it physically, and certainly you recognize the movement from it spiritually. Spiritually, you don't get discouraged; emotionally, you do. Mentally, sometimes you are perplexed by the seeming complexity of how everything can possibly fit together.

Humanity "solved" this dilemma by saying that you were put here to suffer. In my opinion, that is a gross distortion of the human condition. The Creator doesn't recognize suffering — literally does not acknowledge its existence. Now, isn't that an interesting statement? Suffering is considered unreal. It is an *illusion*, my friend.

Now, if we ask your emotional body about that, it might say, "Oh yeah?" But this is a basic truth which exists on a cosmic level. And I have often stated that one of the most profound releasing points is when you can say to yourself and believe it, my friend, **"I DO NOT SUFFER!!! I DO NOT SUFFER!!!"** That is a wonderful affirmation to utilize.

I might state here that *affirmations work by bringing up whatever resistances you have to them.* In order to keep this from creating physical suffering you might ask the *Mahatma*, the I AM Presence, to help you integrate this point of "I do not suffer." Generally, I think this will be effective for some of you, although you may still have to release some very deep patterns of behavior that you have mostly accepted erroneously from the mass consciousness.

In other words, in one life you get a little suffering and that belief goes into the mass consciousness. In another life you get a little suffering and you put that belief in. It is like dropping a drop of water into a pool. Everyone in every life inputs drops of water that say, "Suffering is a part of existence on the physical plane." On the other hand, now is the beginning of *releasing* those deep beliefs in the mass consciousness.

Certainly, there have been a few avatars and a few cosmic beings who have taken out a few drops, but you and all of your friends who are now waking up are the ones who can release the charge that is stored in the mass consciousness, in regard to human suffering. Now, can you see what a tremendous difference this will make on your Earth? If you have a little belief about suffering and there is no large mass of beliefs within the mass consciousness to push you, then it will be much easier for you to release the remnants of suffering.

Right now, when you use the affirmation, "I do not suffer," you may believe it partially, but it doesn't echo around the Earth. The Earth doesn't reinforce it for you; the Earth doesn't agree with you. It has a tendency to mirror to you the fact that suffering exists all around you, which says to your subconscious mind, "Wait a minute; there is too much here. There is not a clear creative field within which to flow this belief. And it begins to erase the affirmation. Now, I am not telling you not to use that affirmation; in fact, I am encouraging you to use it. But do recognize that you are a pioneer in this area for the Earth, and one of the greatest gifts that you can give to the Earth is to help erase the deep beliefs in suffering.

I am therefore suggesting, after full consultation with the *Mahatma* energy, that you make that level available to help you in your erasing the mass-consciousness beliefs about suffering. You must build a bridge to it. The individual's choice is what builds up the beliefs in the subconscious, positively and negatively, and in the individual's consciousness. Not always just on the physical level, as we are about to see, but on every level, is what changes it toward a more balanced perspective. Therefore, when doing your affirmations about suffering, ask the *Mahatma* to fill your body and your auric field with its energy.

Now, there are many reasons for doing this. It will charge your batteries, so to speak. But it will definitely also give to whatever belief you are affirming a greater charge of positive affirmation to mass consciousness. It will literally give it an *electrical jolt*; and this, my friends, will be very helpful in releasing those old patterns of behavior which even say that the Christ suffered for humanity. My friends, the Christ — being on the level of consciousness that he is — has no desire to suffer, never did, and certainly, in my opinion, never will. But the mass consciousness, in seeing the role that he played on the Earth, assumed that suffering was a part of the creative package that he brought to the Earth. Such, in my opinion, is definitely not the case.

The Christ (another name for him is the Lord Maitreya) was your most recent Avatar of the Christ Consciousness, the latest of a whole series of avatars. There have been thirty-five Avatars of the Christ Consciousness on your planet. Maitreya came to anchor *unconditional Love*, and in doing so was only partially successful. Why? Your planet does not yet fully believe in unconditional Love, as far as using it is concerned. That is not a negative statement. It means just what I said before, that there is a stepping process, or a gradual acceptance of Love, that is going on on this planet. In other words, the Christ gave the Earth as much unconditional Love as it could accept at that moment, and the Earth utilized as much unconditional Love as it could at that time in its evolution.

Maitreya, the Christ, is not the same as the one called Jesus. Jesus was the physical vehicle, in a channeling sense, for the being called Maitreya, or the Christ. They came in together to serve the Earth. Certainly, Jesus is a great being. He is a member of your Planetary Hierarchy, having ascended in another life after serving as the physical vehicle of the Christ. Now, Jesus suffered somewhat, but not as much as has been portrayed. The Christ did not suffer in the role that he played upon the Earth. Suffering is not a part of what the Christ believes in. Jesus has also learned now that suffering is not necessary. Suffering comes from several factors — from not understanding the support system that is there for you, not understanding that change is necessary, not seeing the overall picture of what is being created, and several other points that for some of you will be part of your individual belief structure.

Suffering is the misperception of the emotional body that you are victimized by the process, by the Plan, that you are being used inappropriately by the Plan. That, my friends, is not true. It is a privilege to be a part of the Plan, and the *Mahatma* energy is going to give you jolts of creative excitement that will help you to see that more and more. In a sense, this will help you to prove to your subconscious mind that suffering is both a waste of time and unnecessary.

Can you see that if you are very busily enjoying life, feeling privileged to be here, each moment is fun and rewarding and exciting? It will occur to you at some point during that process that you aren't suffering, because you don't believe in it, that isn't real to you anymore, that it has fallen away. So the *Mahatma* energy is here to show you that limitation, including suffering, does not exist.

I find this extremely important; but remember, it is a gradual process, step by step. It will necessitate patience, perseverance, and allowing that contact to be real enough for you that it literally becomes your *creative partner*. It will not do for you those things that you must understand and learn to do for yourself, but once you are awake to know to do them, and that they can be done, your partner will share them and help you to step forward in understanding and in learning.

The *Mahatma* is a direct link to a greater state of awareness, and some of you, at first, may not see the difference between this and your Higher Self or connecting with the Creator, with God. But I will say that it is more specific — more specifically attuned to what can be gained by your journey here on the Earth. It's the difference between calling a consulting firm and saying, "I am connected with you," and having them do the work for you without your direct involvement.

Now, you have that connection, that link. You can reactivate it at any time; you can call back. And if you are confused about what specifically you want, then the *Mahatma* energy is for you. It will search out what is needed within your subconscious mind before you even know that you need it consciously. It will begin to bring you the means to understand that next step. That is what is so important, so different about it.

Your Soul certainly helps you in this regard. If you prefer the term Higher Self, it helps you in this regard also. But there is a group response from the *Mahatma* energy — a representation from each of the 352 levels from the Source of this Cosmic Day to the Earth level — which your Soul, in its connection with you physically, can't yet bring to you on the physical plane. The Soul level is, of course, a part of that group expression on every level, but it is necessary to see that often Souls ask for help, and this is what has occurred. The *Mahatma* energy — the I AM Presence — was introduced to us because enough Earth Souls invoked that contact. It is a direct result of the Soul-level input.

Now, if you wish you can check that out. Ask your Soul or ask your Higher Self. If you don't get any answer — or if you aren't clear on the answer which is given — *don't*, my friends, throw away this opportunity. Keep searching. Keep looking for guidance. I would say, on the spiritual level it is never inappropriate to seek a connection. You may not know while you are doing it exactly what will occur from that connection, but because it is the spiritual level, it will never hurt you.

Certain links are made intuitively. As you open to your intuitive abilities, they will bring you into greater contact with the I AM Presence. You may not call it that, but what you may recognize is the change that occurs in your life. Yes, gradually, because in one sense the *Mahatma* is also a "cosmic shovel," and the "dirt" that it is digging into on the Earth, within your subconscious creative process, has some very crystallized parts to it. So it takes perhaps more than five creative minutes to clear out some of what it has taken you eons to build up. Make no mistake, though, there is a dynamic contact here with the *Mahatma* energy: its purpose is dynamic in nature; its purpose is magnetic in nature; its purpose is electrical in nature. Its purpose is to help you understand more clearly the very essence of how to create. That, my friends, is a powerful statement indeed.

I, Vywamus, have helped many now on the outer Earth, and within the inner level also, to look at the resistances — to specifically look at them, to face them, to release the need to hold onto them, to let go of what has been a part of the beliefs, to reassess the old patterns of behavior, to break them up — in essence, to *decrystallize*. That has been a major function for which the Earth hired me. In addition, now, waking humanity up to the presence of this most significant and powerful energy is a major responsibility I have been given.

For awhile there will be little recognition of it, in my opinion, because it gently slides off the old patterns of behavior. It is difficult to have much reality of what that means until you experience it consciously. But soon, other spiritual teachers will begin to teach about it, too. Yet they will teach in a different way, and that will be helpful because not everyone relates to the same method. As the Earth's awareness of this grows there will be a gradual deep releasing of heavily crystallized areas as never before.

It think it is important to recognize that in this creative sense, the "big guns," or the big means to break up resistances are being brought to your Earth level. As never before, they are coming. I am going to, in the next section, talk about what I think is one of the most important points in all of this material. When you are ready for it, please go on and read it and join me in my creative excitement about this new possibility.

The Awakening

In the last section we discussed the "point of opening," cosmically speaking, setting up a structure to help a wider, or a more conscious awareness level to be established. Whether it is the level of Sourceness that we are speaking of, the level of Soulness, or the level of your physical expression, it is all the same. All are expanding and have now a new level of maturity through realization, which is supportive of that wider-based effort. By that I mean that your unique strengths have this cosmic equivalency which can resolve through you what seems to be unresolvable.

I am so excited about that statement! It is like saying that we can take a glass of water, take away the glass, and while we are doing so, in order to get an even clearer glass, the water will stay aligned — the water will simply allow the change without dissolving, without flowing away, without being wasted or lost. Creativity is *holding form* while the tremendous change is made in allowing the wider-based structural support system which is needed in your life and in the life of your planet and the Cosmos.

We could look at the *Mahatma* energy as the vehicle which supports changes within you and on the Earth. You need to change your "glass" for a larger vehicle to hold what is, in most symbolism, emotion — water is emotion. It holds your emotion so that you can be supported emotionally while all of this change is made. Can you see how important it is, that there is something that can support you emotionally while this tremendous broadening of the creative base occurs on the Earth?

There is now a specific means of supporting your emotional body and your creative efforts while you get used to, even while you set up, that broader base.

However, as I said earlier, this can only be used when you *ask*. The reason is that the *Mahatma* energy takes you beyond your individuality. Your Soul and your Monad help you even when you don't ask. Why? Because it's all part of you. Certainly, we must qualify that to say that sometimes in the free will area, on the level of you as a personality, you don't let the Soul help — or even as a Soul you don't always let the Monad help. That must be qualified.

There is a family structure within yourself which allows you to receive help somewhat beyond the Universal Laws. Again, we must qualify that. The I AM Presence takes you beyond these seeming boundaries and it says, "I must have permission from you in writing." What does that mean? It means that you must acknowledge the availability of help and ask for it. Certainly, in my opinion, a good place to start is with the Soul and its purposes. But beyond that, how about specifically *asking*, even if you don't understand what the I AM Presence is.

You can ask the spiritual level. Say to it, "Vywamus suggested that I talk to you. Help." If you are willing to do this often, then you are going to set up a very close link to this level, which you invoke by asking for the *Mahatma* (the Father), which is the *integrated response* to the I AM Presence.

Let us say that you have a small business. This is like having a world-renowned person who is an expert in that business as your personal consultant. All you have to do is to get on the phone, communicate with him or her, and he or she will reply with very personal advice as to how to enlarge your business, make it successful, or change it into an ever-growing satisfactory vehicle for your creativity on the Earth.

Remember, this can be a very practical and down-to-Earth opportunity, if this energy is assisted by the Co-Creator level to anchor into the Earth in order to activate its full potential. It is so aware, it is so conscious, and it wants to help you with your physical life on the Earth *now*. Nothing has been set up for you yet in this regard on other levels. It will be later. You will be able to take your awareness, as you finish up on the Earth, and use this same point of view to help you energize your next "career step," if you will.

Time enough for that later. In point of fact, ask to have the help to resolve or to use this life now, so that what is coming later can be clearly energized. One of the most practical things that you can do now is to set up a pattern of behavior — by that I mean a habit pattern — so that you get in contact with the I AM Presence daily, preferably several times a day.

Another thing to recognize is that during this period of adjustment where the I AM Presence is learning to function on the Earth, there may be some need to contact it even more now than later. You know, once you get a system established it can flow rather easily and almost without guidance. Certainly, it isn't without guidance; but you set up a system, and so it works very easily and smoothly. Potentially, the *Mahatma* energy is for the purpose of setting up systems for you that extend beyond certain barriers that you've put there for yourself. But you, on the physical level, have to help the Source to "ride the Earth bicycle," you might say. It might fall off a few times, or it may bring you only a portion of what it is capable of bringing you. In fact, that is what I want to emphasize here: *If you help it to ride the bicycle, that will open up even more its ability to help you.*

I can hear it already. You're all asking, "That's fine, but how do I do that? In what way can I help it to learn to ride the bicycle?" Well, I am going to answer that question in many ways, because what I would like to do is to bring to you experiences, visualizations, and symbolic ways to contact and utilize this new important connection.

I know that as soon as you recognize the reality of what I am telling you, as you see that this is occurring in your life — that there really is a point that you can contact *now* and use practically in your life — *you won't need the exercises, you won't need anything else.* You will simply say, "How did I ever get along without this tool?" I know this is true. But you need, perhaps, to step into your recognition of it and your acceptance of it step by step.

Being patient and allowing with yourself in working with this energy can bring you dividends, and I promise you that eventually you will understand how to integrate that which you have allowed to come in. Another way of putting it: As you begin to stimulate the use of these strengths in sometimes rather strange and odd corners of your life, you are eventually going to see how important they are in how they fit into the mainstream of your life. In point of fact, I think it is absolutely essential that those "odd corners" be energized. That is the means to stretch you beyond what, perhaps, is beginning to be used up.

What does that mean? Let's say that for the past ten lives — and for some of you it is more than that — you've chosen to be a musician. You just felt that you haven't learned enough about it, and so for ten lives in a row you've either played the piano or the organ or the harpsichord or the violin, or you sang, or something in the arts. Well, at a certain point you must release looking at life through one perspective. The scientific point of view, the physical point of view, the philosophical point of view — many, many other points of view are there to be energized beyond the one strength that you held onto because you kept thinking that you should be clearer in it (the need to clarify it); but also for many of you it seemed the only thing that you were strong enough in at all.

Now, this is a false belief; and sometimes we have to let go of a narrow focus that is the only one we have validated as a support system, in order to allow a wider support base to come in. It's the point where you trust the process, where you say, "All right, I'll release. I'll let go. If the Plan wants something different for me, I'll allow it." For most of you, this is very frightening. It's a major point. What happens is, you build up to a great strength, one point of view, and you stretch it as far as you can through your own individuality. Because you may have resistances or difficulties in the area of groups, you aren't open to going very much beyond your most powerfully energized use of the strengths. Whether it is this life or ancient Egypt, Atlantis, or whatever it is, that's as far as you can go there.

For all of you, it is necessary to see beyond the doors of individuality. One must recognize that to see yourself as a Whole, a limited perspective (which may seem to be all there is for the moment) has to be released.

What do I mean by releasing? Do I mean that if you are a musician, then you say, "I am never going to play that instrument again?" No, I do not. What I mean is that perhaps your strength has been in playing the music, and now you get a sense, "I can write music." That's a broadening of the creative base. But you recognize that if you write it, you won't have as much time to play it, and you wonder how in the world can you support yourself. You see, you have to be willing to see that a broader creative base *will support you* beyond the narrow focus of support that you already have.

Now, that one is easy to see because writing music and playing music are at least in the same ball park. But for some of you there will be a completely different area energized which necessitates the partial letting go of the major connection that you have felt as your support. Perhaps, we could say, you let go of the *limiting factor* of that support system, which immediately allows it to broaden its base through you.

There is a difference between letting go so that this broadening of the base can occur, and being scattered. Some of you know that scattering has been a pattern of behavior, and you have run from one thing to another, trying everything and not really getting anything to work. How do you prevent that through what I am suggesting? Well, if you earn your living in an office and you read this material, I am not telling you to immediately quit your office job in order to change the support base that you have. I am telling you that it is time now to investigate those strengths that you have beyond how you use them in the office.

For some of you, there will be the immediate reaction of, "I want to leave the office. I don't want to be there." But it is important to build bridges within this process and therefore not to have to wade through a flooding within your belief structure that says, "I don't have any support anymore." I think that is very important.

The I AM Presence is a specific which can certainly help you in this area. In our example, we used the area of working in an office. If you want to broaden your creative base and still have the support that you need during the process, ask the *Mahatma* energy to help you to build that bridge. Ask specifically that the support area be addressed first so that you can understand that support comes about beyond any *one* point which has seemed supportive to you, that you are literally supported from *every* point of view.

When you have realized that, then your creative base becomes unlimited. It can change any way it wishes, and you will just simply say, "We are realigning my support structure. It's still supporting me; it is just changing its specifics again." There is a great deal of difference then, because the belief structure has shifted and validated the overall support base of Source Itself and realized that this is available for you.

This is a point of realization; and I, Vywamus, can tell you about it, can help you with it, but I can't make the realization for you. But the *Mahatma* energy can pursue that area much beyond what your individuality on the Earth can yet grasp. It can, literally, hold an energy focus which reaches out as far as you will allow it and grasps your strengths, bringing them to a point where you may see that a new level of strengths is being energized.

By this I mean that as you cooperate with the *Mahatma* energy, the phone begins to ring, opportunities begin to come in, friends begin to reflect to you these opportunities and this new beginning. It is truly the means to having a satisfactory and ever-unfolding new level of creativity. There are a few of you who are already using the potential of the I AM Presence. I am amazed at the changes, literally awed by them.

This, my friends, is definitely the means to have the *New Earth* — individually, and certainly collectively.

Summary

The Harmonic Convergence opened the Earth to the galactic level and that level of guidance. You began to be familiar on the physical level with this whole Hierarchial area. All of the beings who guide the planet have been guiding you from this level, and at that point in the Earth's evolution you began to validate that.

Since that time we have had what I call the Cosmic Walk-In. This is not the same as the other kind of walk-in — nothing has walked out. The I AM Presence has arrived; it has made a sufficiently grounded and integrated connection with the Earth.

You have been expressing just a portion of what you will eventually express as the Whole, as the full Creator. This year, and for some of you last year, there was a specialist that you came into contact with. Let's say that you had an "inner training program" with this specialist.

The I AM Presence is here to help you to move beyond your present position of individuality. It is not a part of your Soul or a part of the monadic level. It is a specialist made up of energy of the *WHOLE Co-Creator and Creator levels,* and it is brought to you *through* the galactic level. It comes into that broad creative base that you've formed as a Soul on the physical level.

The I AM Presence wants you to call upon it. Its specialty is integration. Anytime you need to integrate or break through any kind of resistance, call on the I AM Presence. It will take a look at all that is happening to you and help you to resolve it. To contact the I AM Presence, concentrate on the name *Mahatma* (the Father).

I, Vywamus, think that this is the *single most important thing that's happened on your Earth and for humanity.*

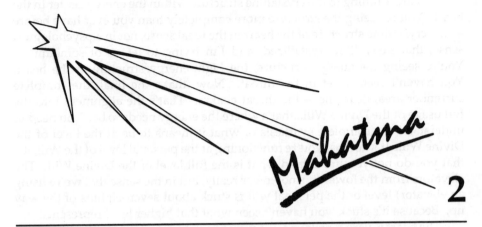

The Journey of the *Mahatma* from Source to Earth

Vywamus Through Janet McClure

May 7, 1987

Brian, none of what has been is important. First of all clear yourself of emotional attachment to all of it. In other words, you have to approach it through what has been called "divine indifference." You have to detach from this fairness issue and some of the anger that you have had against humanity. This "I've been treated unfairly" and "I've been put upon a little" — all of these emotions have to be disconnected, because when you disconnect from them, that heart that's so open will show you how to structure it. It will flow for you once you've disconnected yourself.

In this life, you have this fear of being a failure, that you're going to fail again. That's a deep one there. It's the emotional body, the sense that "I can't look at what happened to me at this important time" and "I can't get my act together again; there's no way to do it." This is what we need to resolve in these two days. So talk about these things. Talk about the inability to sense the divine equality and the feeling of being put upon — yes, you do; buried, perhaps — by the Lord Maitreya. That is a synchronicity of a Source-level relationship, meaning that you feel a little put upon by the Source Itself, you see. So it is getting rid of that and seeing that *you* have created what you feel put upon by. That's good, because now you can let go of it. The realized state where you can be confident in your divine abilities is what will allow it to come forth — your role, or what can be very helpful for humanity. It's exciting, isn't it?

You are attuning to the crystalline structure within the energy center in the heart. You're seeing the structure more completely than you ever have before — the crystalline structure of the heart in the ideal sense, not in a psychological sense, that says, "I'm crystallized, and I'm trying to let go of something." You're seeing the energy structure, the Light-energy structure of the heart. You haven't seen it yet in the throat. Now, that's the final, the complete surrender area, dear one — the throat chakra. That's the alignment into the full usage of the Divine Will...that's where the energy needs to be. You need to understand the complete synthesis of what it means to be at the level of the Divine Will. It's not that you're functioning at the personal level of the Will; it's that you do not yet understand what is the full level of the Divine Will. The elevators from the lower (it's not lower really, but in the sense that we're using an elevator) level of the personal will is stuck about seven-eighths of the way up. Because it's stuck, you haven't seen what that higher level represents.

The heart is very developed, it's very open. It's coming into alignment and will assist you with the wonders of the throat chakra.

The deep, not so much clearing as integration, is very important — the integrative process. Keep probing deeply so that you can allow all that to take place, because it's the key for everything else. It truly is.

You have quite a push-pull in here; as St. Peter, you had a competitive urge with Jesus and with others. But the synchronicity is here with someone "who has gone ahead of you" (not really, but that's your perception). And then you have this "Because of that, I've failed..." or "I haven't used this potential." You're going to stimulate a letting-go process emotionally, and that's what will bring it together for you — when the emotional body can see that life *is fair* and that you can have the support. What happened in this event is that it wiped out your ability to accept support.

Brian: How would you envision the nature of my channeling?

The nature of your channeling is simply an extension of who and what you are. It will not, it seems to me, be a formal type of channeling at all. It will come through your own consciousness, and you can pull it in and plug it in at specific points where you can't quite stretch enough beyond. In other words, when you're trying to bring it in here, and you need just a little more then you plug in your channel. You'll get that little more and then go on with what you're doing. You are going to write this book — it's your story. It needs to be told from your point of view. You need to know that your intuitive self is very advanced and *must* be trusted.

Well, you do your own thing. You will know what you are to do, and the book is but a beginning, an entry point. In other words, this is the beginning of your understanding of what your purposes are for the next few years. When you go into that, you will see the next step. It is a gradual unfolding of the purpose area. The book is what you see now. It is valid; it will reach many people, those who perhaps need to be bridged through the Christianity approach. That's why it's so valuable.

Be aware of life now, particularly as it begins to respond to you in a fuller sense, because you've opened to *allowing* life to bring to you your evolution in a way that you hadn't before. I've used this example several times; it tells the story the way I want to say it. Let's say that you go home and the doorbell rings, and here comes a pizza man with a 16-inch pizza for you. You say to him, "I didn't order a pizza," and you shut the door. Then why did you *get* a pizza? Look at life in a way that learns to see what you've created and why you created that. Now, this pizza would say that the nourishment you needed was being delivered. There it was; you didn't even have to order it. The point is that this life you enter now is one that is more invocative.

You really are coming to the summary period, in a cosmic sense, in your relationship with the Earth. That's important because sometimes when we know that we're leaving somewhere, we will cherish what we are leaving. We will be appreciative of it in a way that perhaps we weren't before. So cherish the Earth; cherish humanity. Nurture them; love them, my friend. They are a treasure, as *you* are. Your spiritual grace and beauty are awesome. I think that you are pulling in, focusing, getting ready for the launching of a focus that is awesome for physicality.

April 1988

It really is an interesting time, and you are taking part in the opportunity to bring together, to integrate, to make real some very important things on the Earth, to show humanity the reality of opportunity. I'm putting it that way because it isn't a point that is sought, but a continuing unfolding of what is possible or what can be.

One must really understand what you mean by Source, and why the feeling is so strong. It is a need to finally put together (as I said to you at the beginning), to integrate some specific ways of being, both within what is currently seen and within what is possible. The integration of all aspects — not of Self as you know it but of the developing entity, the developing sense of the Divine Being, the sense of security that comes from recognizing that *all* is available, that Source really is being recognized within and reflected into all that is now manifesting and developing. So we can look at this in a very profound manner; or we can look at it as a step-by-step transformation into an ultimate state which allows you to recognize that this opportunity given to you will lead to that manifestation of the relationship known as Source — and ultimately, the creation of your *own* Source, which I think you realize that every being ultimately does accomplish, even if it takes trillions of sequential years. Remember, the one constant is eternity!

As never before, there are initiations (if you wish to call them that; we could call them *points of realization*) available on the physical level, and the beginning of understanding beyond that point, which will show that the divine process has developed a great deal through physical existence. In other words, it's advanced enough now that there are many opportunities available in physicality that were not available before. I use the term "physicality" rather carefully because, remember, someone who has chosen to be physical has gained a great deal by that choice. They have gained an opportunity, and that opportunity is to go deeply into the creative process of discovering your own unlimitedness in a way that those who have not chosen to be physical cannot do. There is always going to be a seeming head start by those who have chosen physicality, but in the long run it isn't. We get you started (*we* being your teachers and *you* being our fellow Co-Creators), and then you seemingly move a little further ahead (I'm not speaking specifically about *you* here, Brian, because you've done your evolution differently), and then you get *us* started. So it is a sharing, you see, a "reciprocal communicative linkage system" (how's *that* for terminology?).

I would say that it's really important to note here that you've experienced, in one way or another, *all* of the initiations, and have integrated all of the monadic or higher levels — you've done it *backwards*. Getting into the nitty-gritty, seeing what that really encompasses, putting it all together and integrating it — that's where you are now. At the monadic level and the physical level approach you still have some loose ends, you might say. If we had a scale of 1 to 10, we'd have the monadic level approaching this way and the physical portion approaching that way, from opposite ends (both polarities) of the scale. It's when they come in close enough contact with one another and when the magnetic flow becomes fully reciprocal that we call it the Co-Creator level. So I would say that what is occurring is an awareness (and this is excellent) of how much more there is within you than that which you used to call yourself. That's very important. (Refer to the diagrams, "Co-Creator and Creator Levels," pp. 228-29, and "The Seven Councils of Twelve," p. 227.)

Your monadic level stretches much, much, much beyond these levels of initiation, any of them. One doesn't go beyond the monadic level; one allows that monadic-level focus to become more and more encompassing as you recognize truly what Source is. But that monadic level is your Source spark; it *is* the spark of reality that goes clear to the Source level.

The Source is a fine, pure energy that we've been given a spark of, and the spark that we've been given is that monadic level. The monadic level extends into a format of a stream of energy which contains particular points of realization, one of which has been called the Soul and one of which has been called your physical expression.

So we have first the spark as the Monad, and from that sparking process, the flow of the Sourceness as it evolves. Now, in the individualization process you as the spark are gathering data, but the data are not necessarily just mental; it is a spiritual, integrative data base that allows you to recognize the all-encompassing nature of what Source is, and then surrender to that process.

Let's go back to that sparking. You are sensing within yourself that spark, but you aren't yet comprehending what it is or how vast that concept truly is. You will discover that step by step. I'd like to be just a little more specific with it, because the Source is divided up into all points of consciousness, where there are beings that are developing and growing and learning. The Source is the Whole that has a point of consciousness from every point of view — you are one point of view and I am one. This is why being rather specific in your connection with Source in the channeling process can be quite helpful. The goal is not, my friend, to get into overwhelm. The nebulous nature of Source is overwhelming for many, at least those with whom you are communicating. It seems to me to connect very specifically with certain attributes (the heart area) of Source which we could identify as a particular being. I like to do that because it shows what that particular aspect of Source is more completely than if we say that there is just a Source level (which is rather a general term, when you stop and think about it).

It is important to keep recognizing and dealing with this polarity area, because it seems to me that the receptive part of yourself is open to the input of the dynamic part of yourself in a way that it's never been before. You could say that the polarities, the receptive nature, that female part of yourself, has an aspect of itself that is dynamic. In other words, within the polarity area, the polarities themselves have both aspects. Can you see that?

You're now dealing with and trying to balance the dynamic nature of your receptive energy. The receptive energy is the one that is now saying, "All right, I'll link up with the aspects of these points that are there for me, that we've termed the Source Level." These points are now as close to the Creator level as you can conceive of at this time.

Your experience with mankind, Brian: Over and over again you've tried to present to them an opportunity for growth but were never too concerned about the basic components to help them understand it in a way that some people could relate to. In other words, you were never very willing to go into the mental area, into the analytical sense, to help many of those who are analytical. To present the material to them in another way was not practical at that time because there wasn't any other way they could understand it. We're talking about many, many lifetimes here. You were asking humanity to accept the new knowledge with their knowingness, and you *still* are...something that many people are not yet ready for or know how to accept at that level. Many times there is a "prove it to me" attitude here on the physical plane. It's not that we should validate that by trying to prove it to someone — because you can't really prove anything to anyone — but you have to go (if you want them to understand) to where they are, to *their* point of view, and stretch them just a little bit beyond where they are. So it is necessary to have some conceptual level, at least partially, that allows that stretch to take place.

The book is an internal as well as external process. What I mean is that within you there is some letting go that is going to allow that to be externalized. It doesn't mean that it can't help a lot of people. It means that you are really giving birth to this book, and you're still generating some energy in the birthing process, in my opinion. That's why I said that I thought there would be some reframing and changing and growing. As you recognize that through communication, you must present just a little bit deeper, more conceptual reference. Now, you can do it; it's simply that you haven't seen that it was appropriate or necessary. (NOTE: Vywamus is talking here about our first book, *The Rider on the White Horse*.)

January 21, 1989

You will be ready for the Ascension process before you actually utilize it. In other words, your contract says, "I'll stay around on the Earth for a number of years yet."

There are going to be a number of you ready for that Ascension process anytime in the next few years when you can incorporate all of what you've learned in physical existence into what you understand spiritually.

I have seemingly gone into what we would call Source — into a Sourceness — and I believe that happened on the 14th of June 1988, at 11:05 a.m. PST.

Well, there was a recognition that went clear to the core — that's another way of saying it. If we consider you to be a stream of energy from the Source Itself (that's what you are), a recognition of that opened a response that went clear to the core — the Source level. Yes, I would agree with that...that's another way of saying it, isn't it?

But it was five months **here** *before some adjustment was made from Source to here. And those five months were terrible. I don't ever look back; I don't live in the past. But I must recognize that whatever this transference of energies was, it manifested in such a way as to leave me feeling no support either here or there. And you passed by, all of you. I got the feeling of "Well, we don't know what to do." Please respond.*

Well, the point is that this was *your* experience, this was your perception, and we had to allow that. We honor that. There is a universal law that says that we honor the perspective of others. Now, the "sacrificial" part of it is not true. The "opening" is accurate, and the experience was one of opening to the core and allowing that energy to move through you. But the response of a "sacrificial lamb" or that it had to be this difficult or that it was taking away a blueprinting system and substituting one that wasn't meant to be physical — that's not true. It does mean that there was a profound change in your energy, but it was really into what I'm going to call a sense of unity, a sense of connection into the Source-level blueprint, a connection that flowed for you in relationship to the Earth in a completely different way than it had ever flowed before. It opened for you so that you could respond to the Earth energies. You didn't know how to do that, and you are just beginning to grasp that.

You have attempted this Earth-link with Source before, but not alone. These failed in the past because Earth and mankind were not as conscious. This is *your* version of it, this is *your* part of the Plan, do you see that? This is what you've been able, finally, to do — it's wonderful, my friend! Yes, of course, we watched it with great appreciation, with great joy, with great love, because this is your part of the Plan. But it doesn't mean that there haven't been others who have shifted into that level of being and brought it onto the physical. Not often and not too many, but it's beginning now again, and it has been attempted in the past. You came very close in ancient Egypt, but not quite. Others did — that is the other point. There is a very ancient time when there was a breakthrough in this area and you were involved, when Mother Earth couldn't handle the energy and burned. It seldom occurred, and it was much more difficult in ancient Egypt; that's why it feels like such a burden now. It feels as if it had to disconnect you because the Earth wasn't ready for it. But you see, that's not true anymore. The Earth has evolved; it can reach levels of understanding that it couldn't reach before. So your reaction — most of your reaction — is from a belief structure that's still in Egypt rather than seeing what's happening *now*. Yes, your consciousness on many levels is connecting into what is happening now, but your reaction is connecting into what has been.

The full transcendental level is, of course, the ultimate — the one that you are seeking to realize most completely that is mirrored and reflected down onto the physical plane. See that, both you and your Soul? Yes, you have a Soul perspective. It is simply a passing down of the archetypal pattern that is your role; let's put it that way. That's a passing down of the archetypal pattern, which is seeking to make you aware of what it means to be a Co-Creator. That's what the emphasis is now, shifting into understanding that "my role is this..." Yes, but how does it fit into all of what else is meaningful until you allow some others to assume some of the burden?

This is what I'm saying. Until there's a consensus reality, from my perspective, until somebody else shares this focus...

But they are and you aren't allowing that yet.

Well, I have a feeling — and it is very much one of "summary," with my energy anchored in the physical now — that I have something to do with the Avatar of Synthesis, whom Djwhal called the Lord of Synthesis, and whom the Scriptures refer to as **The Rider on the White Horse.**

All right. Good.

Is there a relationship between that and the blueprint called Brian?

Yes. Can you see what that avatar means, "The Lord of Synthesis"? It's the integrative process at the Co-Creator level. You're correct — it's what the Scriptures refer to as *The Rider on the White Horse.* That is what you partially anchored into physicality on the 14th of June 1988. But you have not yet fully integrated it, and that takes as long as it takes.

In my opinion, the Monad is your individual Source spark, so there is no difference between the Monad and Source at that level; it is the same thing. You were born from the Source and individualized into the Monad level.

At that moment of individualization when the Monad was born, there was a looking back toward the womb of Source you had just emerged from, and then as you turned around you saw a flow of Light, a flow of power that energized the Creator level, and you've been looking at that ever since. But you forgot to read the blueprint or the small print here that said, "It flows *through* the Co-Creator level." The goal is to energize your power in a step-by-step process into the *Co*-Creator level. Why? Because that's the mirroring that you need in order to recognize fully the Creator level. You will do one thing here, someone else will do something else there, someone else will do something else. And the consensus, the integration of all that, becomes the Creator level, you see. And you're getting glimpses of the Creator level; this is your great strength because you've focused on it so much. "It takes one to know one," because I, Vywamus, did the same thing, and I grew very strong in understanding the Creator level. But then we have to say, "All right, I'm going to get down to the nitty-gritty of my understanding of how it fits together, how I integrate it, this great Light that I know I am and the strengths that I am as a Creator. How do I get it all to fit into the understanding of the Whole without feeling sacrificed or feeling that there's too much power to enter a particular area? What is it that makes it work? It is the *Co-Creator* level. Does that make some sense to you?

There is a sense that when you try to get into the Co-Creator level, it doesn't respond, it doesn't understand you. Why? Because you are the *Creator*. Well, you are — but then so is everyone else in the fullest sense. They haven't *realized* it yet, but in a passing out of the abilities in the Plan, everyone has energy in that area. The Co-Creator level is the reality that needs to be energized now. This is what will give you that divine comfort factor where "everybody cares, everybody understands, everyone responds; we are together." This is what opens the heart, having that trust of the Co-Creator level: "Yes, it will work." You don't have that yet, but you have great strengths, great abilities, great awareness of what lies beyond that. Now it must shift, because that is why it came forth. *The Creator came forth to process the Co-Creator level so that it can understand Itself.*

Source is All That Is. When I look at this I say, "Why do I back out of my Sourceness?" I have an election — I do not **have** *to come to Earth.*

You've already decided that on another level.

And I have repeatedly come to the Earth, for whatever reason...

Well, because you have to keep energizing it until you've really accepted this Co-Creator level. So that's where you've decided to go — to this planet to work out your understanding of that; and of course the heart is the center of it. There are many levels of Sourceness, many aspects of Sourceness, but it is (and I haven't talked about it this way) a *great big Cosmic Heart*. That's why it becomes difficult, because as the heart opens the Co-Creator level responds, and you don't recognize that response as where you are going.

Okay. Let me explain something to all who are in this room, including over soul/Phopenjenus...that once it hit my heart, it didn't matter what I did. I couldn't ground it, I couldn't shift it. It's almost like the energy was more uncomfortable being at a cellular, anatomical level with this body because it wasn't free. It didn't have the sense of Sourceness or of Co-Creator, and it locked in. It's only now that I can feel the Twelfth, the Gold Ray, coming over the top. But the minute I shift to the heart, it just causes me to cry. I cannot go around crying 24 hours a day, so I shift up here into my head. I want to make that clear so that when we get to the core issues I can get some clarification as to what to do with the heart, because the minute I touch into it, I "well up" and start to...and I don't know what to do.

Well, you have to process that, Brian. You need to go into it. You can't keep shifting away from it in order to get through it; that's been the problem. Every time you go into this, you stimulate the heavy loss pattern that you have in relationship to stepping into this individuality and then having to process through what seems to be very difficult and unresponsive territory, which is the Co-Creator level. It doesn't seem to have anything to do with anything. Even as I talk to you, I know that there isn't a particular response to what I'm talking to you about, because this is what you've been dealing with, and it didn't seem to mean anything or deal with anything. You couldn't really relate it to anything. The heart is what will process that — the qualities of the heart.

It's started, hasn't it?

Yes. That's what making this opening has done for you — what a wonderful gift! It has, in one sense, *forced* you, because it was the next step to energize that heart in a way that it hasn't been energized for eons; it said, "It's time..."

A lot of fear from the past. There's a name, and I don't even remember his name. I sense that there was a being in Egyptian time who brought in massive energies. I don't believe that there was that high an energy level at that time on Earth, so that energy was imported, so to speak...

Yes.

So this being had been imported to the Earth, and he was a monotheist. He was the first one to bring in a version of a unified, One God.

I'll verify that. And yes, it was your energy as King Akhnaton.

And this being was, up until that time, one of the most highly evolved beings that the Earth had known.

That's right. And your point is?

At that time, as Akhnaton I could not complete my mission as envisioned because of the limitations of mass consciousness. At present there are fewer limitations on the physical plane, allowing me to complete my mission of synthesis at this time. Because the Earth is so much lighter, so much more energized, we can now do things that we couldn't then.

That's right.

And there's no sense of limitation...

Well, just individually accepted limitation. There isn't a sense of limitation as far as the Earth structure and providing the opportunity are concerned.

And as the Avatar of Synthesis, all old beliefs of false structure must be blown to shreds, but in the nicest possible way.

Well, everything that is limiting.

Is not a new world religion, as discussed by Djwhal, a possibility? Will Maitreya be the Christ at the turn of the century?

I have no comment on that. We have agreed not to talk about these matters and give these areas energy that could be detrimental to the outcome. I don't want to get into that area. The point is, and we're talking semantics here, yes, the old must be released and *is* being released, in order to let in the new.

I am diametrically opposed to anything that spells out "new world religion."

I see. Why?

We've done this...we don't need the adulation, we don't need the worship, the adoration. We should teach divine equality.

Well, you see, that's within your belief structure, as to what a world religion...

Well, I've worked through so many of those on Earth and have been worshipped as a god many, many times.

I know, but it doesn't have to be that way now. I think that through communication, through coming together, you can all decide what it can be. A religion is meant to be a type of support system, a type of integration. Does that make a difference? It's not meant to be in the way that it has been.

What is my blueprint? What was my blueprint?

Well, in regard to your blueprint, it is the acceptance of your strengths on the cosmic level, and allowing those to penetrate into the physical level without messing up your relationship with the Co-Creator level. Your blueprint is "making openings on the Earth," there's no question of that. But the good news is that you aren't doing it all by yourself, that there are others who have a specific...the role is not the same as yours, but it fits into the whole.

So my belief, the core issue as I see it, is really that Brian is not alone?

Exactly.

So I'm not all alone in this recognition, and the whole world isn't dependent on that one piece of golden thread coming from Source?

That's right. And also, recognition that it doesn't burn out the system. Why? Because there are other Co-Creators that can transmute the very cosmic opening that you really represent, and it won't burn out the system, either your system personally or the Earth's system.

I felt that I was the only one, the only link into Source — and to some extent I will still say that — of that nature. I think I'm the only link on the Earth plane.

Doing what you are doing, yes, but that doesn't mean that other people aren't linked in a supportive manner. Do you know what really happened to you? Through this opening that occurred it's now time to bring this great strength you have that is awesome for the Earth (there's no question of that) through you down onto the Earth.

The energy that we collectively call "Brian" — is that sufficient, on a mass consciousness level to bring in a consensus reality to manifest this synthesis, given a period of time?

Not *completely*, at least not at this moment, because it is simply a stimulus into the Co-Creator level, where each has a function from the stimulus or from another stimulus. Certainly, what you're doing is important, Brian, it's very important. There's an opening that is created there, but then it must stimulate the process. And other stimulations are stimulating this process that allows that full, balanced manifestation you call the Earth. So again, what I say is that what you're leaving out is the Co-Creator level.

The Twelfth Initiation, from my perspective, has always been the beginning; the physical initiations have never counted. The Third Initiation — we'll call it the First Initiation, the First Major Initiation. The Third to the Eleventh have never really seemed significant. It's the Twelfth-plus which seem to me to be the beginning of All That Is.

It's the beginning of what *you* recognize, or the beginning of what is real to you, because it seems to you to be the beginning of the Creator level. I tell you, the process on the physical level contains *all* of it. You've heard that there are people standing in line to get into physicality — why, Brian? Because it's *here* that you gain a sense of the reality of every other thing, of this other level. The only way to do it, of course, is to open to that Co-Creator level. Then, in a physical sense, mirroring to you comes in exactly...

And we're doing it...

Yes...exactly. You keep coming back until you *can* get that sense. You know that you haven't gotten that yet. That's why you're here with these great strengths that you have. You sent yourself here to learn that.

But I didn't have to...I know that.

You *chose* to. You *wanted* to.

Do I stay in physicality for awhile, or am I going?

I think you're going rather soon, but I think that you will learn this first, because life is forcing you to. *You* are forcing yourself to, on another level; you're pushing yourself into it. That's what this opening means: "I'm going to learn this." Now that, perhaps, is the hard way to do it, but then you've tried everything else!

Now, physicality. Go into the work on the inner plane.

You already *are* working on the inner planes all of the time, quite profoundly. No, I think you're going to finish this up rather soon — it is only a few realizations away. But of course you have to allow yourself to get the assistance first, and you haven't accepted that yet. Why? Because — and this is not negative — you see yourself as the Creator *having to do it all*.

That's right.

And you don't *have* to. That's how you can be free. The only way that you can be in your heart now is when you've accepted that and seen that there's a belief there from that point of individualization which says, "I have to be a Creator. This is my role. I must do it for the whole universe; I must do it for the Source. I must do it." But that's a false belief. You don't have to do it yet — yes, eventually, but you haven't gone through the Co-Creator level yet. You're leaving out that last step.

But we're not going to go until we wrap up the Co-Creator level. We're not going to leave physicality until we do that.

No, but the Co-Creator level is much greater than that. I'm talking at a more profound level than anything related to physicality. Certainly, it reflects into physicality, but when you leave physicality, as you very well know — and that's a correct assessment — you're really only *beginning* to understand, just getting a glimpse of what you'll be as a Creator. You still have a way to go in the Co-Creator process.

But why...if I don't have to, at the Source level?

But you do. What I'm telling you now is general, the general format. You have, let's say, put the cart before the horse a little. You're seeing the Creator level, but not seeing the *means* to it. So you're rearranging the energy structure in a way that others will not do because they don't have the cart before the horse. You need a particular arrangement in order to facilitate becoming a full Creator. What it's done is open your heart. It worked for you, and that's very good. But no one else will do it that way — it's not meant to be. You had to go back, let us say, and pick up some stitches that you dropped. They are the ones that are at a very core point, so the energy had to be undone a little and then done up differently. Does that speak to you? *No one else* will do it this

way...although you're prototyping something, and I like it. You're very creative, and that's good. The Earth needs that. But what *you* need is the Earth,
because the Source energy is finally here. You got some glimpses of that in
Egypt and some glimpses in a life earlier. But now is the nitty-gritty time, and
you're going to be forced — I'm sorry, but your aspects are putting you in the
heart, and part of it is the evolution of the Earth. It's moved to that level where
you can't live as you were, because that "as you were" doesn't exist any more
as an energy format on the Earth. The Earth has evolved beyond it.

So for clarification, is there an Earth-link with Source now?

Yes.

*And is it causing you, our beloved Teachers, any consternation? I often feel
that there are many, many more shifts on the inner planes than there are here.*

Of course, definitely there are more shifts. That's where your awareness is.
That's where you are comfortable, that's where you can understand. But it
isn't consternation, it's activity, and a great deal of activity. We're delighted
with that, not concerned — that's *your* belief. You see, you have to sort this
out, the false beliefs from the core.

That's the core issue, isn't it?

Exactly. That's the one that says, "This is so much power that it can't yet
be used on the Earth."

That's why, when you asked me the other day, I saw the Earth burning.

Yes.

*Because my body has burned so many times bringing in these energies. So I
believe that the Earth has got to burn again.*

Yes, exactly. The good news is that it isn't burning. What you see is true
in that there is a lot of activity that is very electrical and very radioactive, but
that doesn't mean that it has to be as it was before — burning up the Earth. The
Earth is learning to deal with this because the Souls are more present on the
Earth — that Soul level, or a "higher aspect" is the way you would refer to it.

*What's a word that you prefer, from your viewpoint? Is it a "monadic vehi-
cle"? Is it "Higher Self"? "Oversoul"?*

I like it as "a stream of energy which unites all levels."

*Would you give it a name? Of those three that I've given you, is there a name
that you prefer?*

I think I like "monadic vehicle."

So do I, and I don't know why more people don't use it.

Because more people aren't aware of it; it doesn't have any reality for them yet. This is where your strengths are; this is what you understand. That's why you relate to it. But others, many of them do not. Now, if we look at that monadic vehicle as having specifics within it — Djwhal has divided it up into a point that is called the Monad, a point that is called the Soul, levels in between, and then points that are called the "expression on the physical level." For most now, they are busily opening up to the Soul level; they don't even know what the monadic level represents. That doesn't mean that there aren't those who are very aware of the monadic level and who have left out the Soul level — there are. For you there is a sense of progression, of flow from the Source Itself, and you're aware of that whole stream of energy. That's why I called it that. So we look at where each being is.

...before you respond with a name for it.

That's right.

If I were to go, in sequential time, in the next few years — whether I do or I don't, that's up to me?

Yes, exactly.

The Ascension. I've done it before. How do I leave?

Well, in the first place I'm not sure that you *will* leave then. In other words, Ascension is a point of integration; it's a point where everything is integrated from the physical experience. What *you* do is ascend from the *other* way — from the highest mountain.

This is crazy! That's why you have to talk to everyone so individually!

In other words, you ascend from the highest mountain *down* to the Earth. The final time, or the one where it's all integrated, is when you ascend from what you've learned on the physical level.

Timewise, we can do that?

Anytime you realize it. It's a point of realization, my friend.

...and Brian was chosen. I think Djwhal's term is accurate. I've come down as many things, and now as the Avatar of Synthesis.

All right, I'll agree with that.

Wherever there's immense demand, my auric field seems to be hundreds of miles.

That's right — sometimes. And it's the monadic level that comes in and energizes the auric field and isn't always able to hold that connection. Why? Well, in the first place, my friend, the Monad wasn't ever really meant to be on the physical level — not that level. But there are changes coming into that level, and you're helping to make those.

So that when any of us go to certain areas and the demand is so great...every time I've gone to Aachen, Germany, all I've done is meditate for a month or six weeks. You've been there and watched this. I've probably had my most profound Earth-link — the Source to Earth — than I ever do, when I'm in someplace that so desperately needs this Light.

That's right.

And it's so welcome...that's the thing.

Of course. What that does is keep validating "I Am the Creator," though. So although it's very helpful for the Earth — please do not misunderstand — it isn't allowing you to learn about the Co-Creator process. As you've noticed, bringing in that much energy and not using the Co-Creator level to facilitate is very hard on your physical body.

I'm finding that since "Self" anchored Source in physicality on the 14th of June 1988 people are having a difficult time with my energy.

Now, part of it is not the power. Part of it is what you are going through in the heart area. Remember my saying that you burned through to the core when you anchored this awesome amount of energy into the Earth?

Thank you. I thought that so...

Yes. After Ascension I think you'll be here for awhile. Ascension is simply a process of integration. From this facet of integration...remember you've been coming from the *other* side and integrating your responses in regard to physicality instead coming in from this point of view and seeing it all as Light here on the physical level after first seeing it as solid. That's the key for you — seeing it as solid, then seeing it all become Light — *everything* in your life becoming Light.

Didn't I go through a process of Ascension? Or was that just the opening of the crown chakra?

Do you remember what I said? You probably don't, because this is difficult to assimilate. I said that you came from *another* mountain and *descended*. There were 58 times where you went through the motions of Ascension, but because of your strengths on the other levels, you initiated this, rather than being complete with your Earth experience.

...And we're doing that now, aren't we, completing our Earth experience? We're doing it slowly, slowly.

Yes, it's like graduating from high school after having graduated with your doctorate from university.

It was Lenduce who said, "Brian, you had a life on this Earth of 1800 years." It seems that every 300 years we changed the body, and it seemed to be in the Gobi, or the Upper Gobi, or it might have been ancient Shamballa...I don't know...

Well, remember that we said that you did touch into the Venus energy, and that one is ahead of this planet a great deal. So by shifting into that Venus perspective and being able to enter it enough, there was an opening that allowed the next physical body. It was like you made a connection — you plugged in energywise to that area — so your energy structure, which has always been used rather individually, was able to use a renewal system in that particular life. It wasn't done arbitrarily; it was done as part of your service. A certain continuity of who and what you are that was needed because of the point of consciousness that the Earth was at. But it also enabled you to get, hopefully (it didn't seem to work out, but hopefully), a deeper view of the opportunities that were here for you personally in physicality. You had many, many wives in that lifetime — you went through a number of them — so there was a sorting-out process that was very helpful, I think. But it's deeper now than even then. So you served the Earth in many ways during that time. You were the ruler of a country in that area; and then because it lasted so long, you got bored with that. So you stepped down and allowed one of your sons to be the ruler and you became the power behind the scenes, you might say.

But you also went into other areas of the world. You met a being (you might be interested in this and want to contact this being) who is also able to function quite well in the heights and, you could say, he was your "Source neighbor." This being, who is no longer present on the Earth, promised you something. He said, "Remember that when you will allow me to help you, I will be there." You kind of brushed it aside, thinking that you really didn't need any help. But you might energize that now, because that offer is still there for you. He was at that time a prince in another area, and you traveled all over the world with him. You found that your royal status allowed you certain advantages, but didn't connect you very closely with the people, and you were really trying to understand humanity. You knew after this long period of time that you didn't understand humanity very well, and you were trying to, but your status of wealth seemingly separated you. That's important, as far as *abundance* is concerned, because when the heart opens you have a tendency to try to get rid of wealth as a symbol of being separate from humanity. And then you need money, and so your abilities come in and create it again — and then you wipe it out again because it seems to separate you. So you might want to have a look at that one.

Mmm-hmm...Have I ever worked with Maitreya on Earth?

Yes.

Other than as that aspect we talk about as St. Peter?

Yes. Particularly strong is the connection to him in Atlantis. He took his Third Initiation in Atlantis.

At the same time that Buddha did his third physical initiation?

Yes, that's right. Of course, as you know there are lots of corresponding things taking place on other levels during that initiation. Do you recognize that?

Yes, but I don't think that there was a need for me to do my Third at that time.

Well, you didn't take your Third there, I'm not saying that. But he did. What I'm telling you is that there are a lot of cosmic correspondences as one takes the Third Initiation. Maitreya was your friend, and as he began to open in a way that was amazing to you, you began to see this growth. What he had opened to was the Co-Creator level, and you didn't understand it. He tried to help you with it; he was really your friend, just as you might have a school friend. He was very young in physical years when he took the initiation, and you had been to school with him.

Did I feel that I was superior to him as I was watching him?

No. I think that you felt confused about why he related to humanity and you didn't. I don't think that you felt superior. I don't think that you felt inferior, although that's an area that you're working on — both areas in a sense — trying to balance that out with divine equality. But I think that you were confused about who he was and why this tremendous change was coming to him so rapidly on the physical plane. It didn't mean that you don't like change, but you could see his relationship with people coming in. You see, he then began to attract people, and you didn't understand why.

Why he would bother. Looking at the Rays now, I feel very strongly connected with the Twelfth, of course, but there are other Rays that...

The Second Ray is heart-oriented, and you aren't comfortable with it all the time sometimes. It's just like your heart now; you can stay there awhile, but the Twelfth Ray tones that for you...it makes that Love-Wisdom area...you see, you can be truly wise only when you've accepted that other people's opinions are valid. It's not that you *don't*, on one level, but it's bringing that into a point of synthesis that doesn't burden you. It's letting go of the burdened effect of having to do it all yourself by accepting other people's opinions — not necessarily for you personally (sometimes, but not necessarily always), but accepting them for the Earth. The system can handle anything, my friend.

Yes, I'm beginning to accept that. I have felt in the past — in Lemurian times, in Atlantean, and even in Egyptian times — that there was no other energy quite like the one we call "Brian" here, and there was that feeling of, "Well, I'm from There."

Yes, and that separates.

And I never felt that I belong here...there's a gap.

A separation, yes.

And I have really never understood why mankind weren't more advanced spiritually, considering that each individual experiences 2500 lives or more in the physical on this planet alone. I'm now working with the Galactic Core to assist the Soul level in hastening this process of evolution.

You haven't a full sense of feedback from what they were doing. You know, you don't always have to *see* it in order to assist in change. Your assessment is correct — you are working with the Soul plane and with Monad in order to assist the Soul level to have a better understanding of the Monad, so that the learning process in the dense physical can be accomplished in fewer physical lives. That Source level of you is open, and you are open to it, so it literally tones your whole life. It's called your intuitive connection — that's where you function from.

I have watched planets in total denial do just as well or better than this planet, which has always given its power away and has always invoked somebody as a God, and I'm diametrically opposed to this. I wondered if this had caused a problem between Maitreya and myself, or is an aspect of the one we call Peter watching that passion play unfold and not being in agreement with the nature of our own teachings?

Well, you hadn't understood what happened to Maitreya (the Christ) at that point. You thought you knew who he was, and then he opened up to the Co-Creator level and you couldn't understand why he would want to be bothered with that. You felt that that grounded him. Of course, it *did*, but that was his choice and that was his purpose, but you weren't grounded enough to see it.

This particular planet, in its third dimension, has had a very solid physical base, and what seems to you to be difficult — giving away the power — is simply the settling in to the third dimension *first* and then the integration of the power. I think that you've resented it because it seemed to take you away from the heights, you might say, or take others away from the heights and from their opportunity. But as you come into physicality and settle into the third-dimensional format, everything that you believe becomes the foundation from which you then create the next step. Do you see that one? That can seem for awhile to be alienation or separation. The point is to *be* here in order to integrate; first you surface whatever is there in the belief structure. You take a look at it; everyone does that, but you've seen them do that over and over. Let us say that they *have* given away their power — well, that's what *you* see because that's what they're working on to resolve. That's why they're here.

When will I be able to teleport? Or is it something that will really matter to me?

I think that (it will happen) — and this is backwards — when you recognize that there is a full system of Light cooperating with you, the support of humanity. You see, when you teleport you go on lines of Light, the gridwork that is set up on the Earth. It's almost like hooking into it and then just going where you want to go. But there also needs to be a recognition that there is a support system set up here on the physical plane for that.

Will mass consciousness allow for that now?

Well, it's ready now, of course; it's been used. You see, that's what you don't believe yet.

There are people teleporting?

Of course. Not many, but some. And there have been through the ages.

Have I teleported in the past?

Briefly.

So there should be no fear connection about my body burning up?

Oh, but there is some fear. You don't really believe that you can use this system set up by the mass consciousness.

Or because of mass consciousness?

Yes, both.

Being born in 1932 — was it something that we could see in 1932? Could we see a need for certain energies and plan them out at that time?

Yes, of course. We could see it thousands of years ago. All one has to do is to tune into it, but timing is more intricate than it looks.

It must be very difficult.

It is very difficult.

I have a vision. By the year 2010 at least one thousand among humanity have done their Sixth Initiation, and the Light, if it's clear at that time of the collectivization of one thousand people, could be equivalent to the billions of people who are on the probationary path on Earth now!

Yes, I agree.

March 17, 1989

Part of what we're doing on this Seven-Day Intensive is assisting the integration. It's important that we continue to look at your relationship with the Co-Creator level. Today we're going to look at the flow system (refer to the chart "Electrical Day One," p. 222). I know that you are very aware of it, particularly at the Creator level. You recognize the flow, particularly at this level, as All That Exists; you have the means to identify with it at this basic point. This would be the senior monadic level, or that point where the Source individualized Itself. This is the perspective that you are growing and developing within. It also has access to all of the other senior Monads. So there is a very clear definition with this, and you relate to it. The one that you don't relate as much to yet is the Soul level. I think that there is a sense of, "I don't need that anymore," but this is the means by which the physical structure expresses clearly. Many times you've burned out some physical structures because the power of this senior monadic level was not buffered by the Soul level.

So let's look at the energy where I see that the flow is not as buffered by the Soul and where there are therefore some jamming and some breaks. Recognize that this strength is always there — we are not negating that at all. This strength is not meant to be on the physical level as it is now; it's meant to go through a process until it identifies itself as physical matter. You've tried to put this energy directly down on the physical level over and over again, but it doesn't work because you haven't gone through the process completely yet.

Since I talked to you last, I see considerably clearer than when I was last here talking to you.

Yes, I think so.

Much of the jamming in the heart was simply the weeping for Mother Earth, and was not a very personal thing. It was personal to the extent that this energy of mine seems to be overshadowing Mother Earth and Sanat Kumara, and I was weeping with, or for, her...much of the clearing from the heart.

Yes, I can see that. I can see what you're saying, and I agree with it as far as it goes. I would say also that the heart — and it's not just the heart, of course, but the whole premise — misunderstands that this monadic energy isn't supposed to come here. So when you weep for the Earth, it's almost as if you weep because the Earth doesn't have in it yet this level that you're trying to bring in. Now, that's subconscious. You may not necessarily recognize it, but that's why I said what I did: *That level isn't meant to be here*; it's meant to *reflect* here, so that this Earth level may be clear in its identity. I think that you were really clearing some of that out for the Earth, and that's very good. I agree that the heart is much more stable.

I can look at it now.

Yes, that's right. It's not so painful anymore. And by taking that out, then you were ready for this next step, and that's very good. This is the step where we identify the Co-Creator level area more completely and how to allow it to transmute you, and where you take the full responsibility to transmute it. It really takes the burden off of one when that's recognized.

As the Avatar of Synthesis, is this the first time that I've come lower than the mental plane? I am coming in, aren't I?

Yes, you are.

The Lord of Synthesis was never intended to come lower than the mental plane because it was never felt that it could...

Well, my friend, as you are utilized by the Plan with your strengths, it doesn't mean that you were not meant to be a part of this system.

It would be terrible to leave without bringing this energy all the way in.

That's right. If there are areas that you haven't allowed to work within yourself, then you are used in the system in the way that your strengths are — can you see that? Being strong in the mental and in the spiritual — very strong in that area — you've been used that way, and that's helped a great deal. I think that when you really get that, when you really see it, when you understand it so completely that you say, "Aha! I understand that!" — *then* will occur that integration into the full abilities that you're looking for.

How wonderful it is to do that! And also now, as you said, for the first time in eons to actually be able to come into the physical and not have to work from the mental plane.

That's right! That's what's so exciting, isn't it?

Yes!

And also, my friend, to allow the Co-Creator level to evolve you, because you've felt responsible for evolving it. That takes the burden off. Although you may not recognize it, there is pressure in the emotional body from identifying as the Creator rather than as the Co-Creator. It doesn't mean that you're going to lose the Creator connection — that one is permanent and strong and wonderful. When you really fully realize your Creator abilities, I certainly want to come and enjoy them for awhile! (Laughter from both.) But right now you need the Co-Creator level to balance that out, because if you built a universe right now, my friend, as a Creator, you'd leave out *all* of physical existence!! (chuckle) You'd leave out some important things that you haven't understood yet, so your universe wouldn't be complete — there wouldn't be a completion or an integration.

That "integration into the full abilities — is that a "June 14th" type of realization, or is that a realization that can happen any time?

It could...

It would be a year from the 14th of June 1988?

I would say that this is developmental. As I look at it, probably a major part of it could come in by then. But I would say that it'll be awhile before you've fully got that together.

Then what would I realize? What would my feeling be?

Your feeling would be a point of gratitude — it would be a heart center expansion that takes in all of humanity and shows you how much you are a part of humanity. The feeling would be how close you are to others, your desire to remain that close and to be actually a part of the system, doing whatever needs to be done — rather than from the Creator point of having others do it. So it's a point of integration where you become fully a part of the system. That's what we are really talking about here.

Now there is a new "static," and it's not bad. In fact, it's good; it means that you have energy moving in this heart area in a way that you've never allowed it before. (Refer to the diagram, "Electrical Day One," p. 222.) It isn't consistent yet in reaching out to others and to the Co-Creator level, but it is flowing quite well, quite nicely. This was the pain that you felt — the opening, allowing that to begin. So you certainly need to make that more consistent in opening, then allowing. This is the next step; this is what I feel that you're doing in this seven-day intensive, allowing in through allowing people to help you, Brian, as you never have before, through allowing that Co-Creator level to input to you as well as you to input to them. Now, certainly you've done some of it, but it's more conscious now, more consciously allowing it on the level of physical existence as well as the spiritual level, letting this level flow to the physical through others and become magnified, and then stepping into it to see it more clearly. Does that make sense to you? Yes. Good.

Now, in the endocrine system (still referring to "Electrical Day One") there is the thymus-softening process. The thymus is active in childhood and then kind of shrivels up. Now you're letting more of this Soul as well as the senior Monad flow through — when this began you opened the heart up, too — so on a physical level the thymus is being stimulated; the parathyroid is also actually opening, too. The throat area has been a great strength of yours. Do you recognize that? There are a lot of changes going on in the throat area — have you noticed that?

Now, the very good news is that your strengths at this level will help you to deal with all of what needs to be done, and you're doing it more and more. I'm hoping that you will make some realizations in this area. I don't see why you can't. When you say, "I surrender," in the sense that "I let go of holding onto this" and let the system evolve, recognizing that "I am part of something and my role is important, but in the fullest sense it has nothing to do with me personally (as personality)" — when you truly realize that, then you'll have got it! And it's coming along, it is.

Your handling of the electrical particles has been good. These are the energies — you've had some and the immune system has walled off some of those for awhile, but they're tentatively being allowed now into the system — the new radioactive particles that came in at the time of the Harmonic Convergence.

Now, here's what has happened (and the reason that I haven't gone into this before is that I feel that this is healing well): There was a complete absence of connection with the Earth until June 14, 1988. I would say that is now 82% resolved. That's what you've been feeling. That's the difference, and that's wonderful!

I also feel that I can explain now what really happened on June 14, 1988, without your going into overwhelm. The Co-Creator levels, and in particular this planet's Hierarchy, have prepared for thousands of years for the prophesied *Rider on the White Horse*. What happened to you, and your sense of being abandoned, is an accurate understanding, because your energy was meant to *reflect* into the physical, not to come all the way in. So you can sense the adjustment that had to be made to facilitate these changes. All things considered, I feel that the Co-Creators coped very well. Now that it's partially anchored, I really feel that the effected synthesis will work wonderfully for you and for the Earth.

Now that will give you another tool. This is the key to understanding how you fit into the Plan, because the Earth will reflect back to you when it opens even more. To really understand that, most of you are looking for an 80 to 85, maybe even 90 percent opening there. That then allows the beauty — we could call that the physical manifestation of Sanat Kumara or the physical manifestation of your Soul level, whatever you wish. It's being reflected back from that Earth perspective, and opening up just a little more will really let you see that. And that's good.

Now what this means, particularly for you, is that you've brought in the monadic (spiritual) level, trying to use it as the connection into the physical, and sometimes it burned up a physical body — twelve times out of nineteen, in recent times. And you stood there on the spiritual level and you thought, "Oh my, physical existence is so fragile; it can't stand this."

Once you burned up a baby's body in three hours as Source; once it took ten days. But you've often burned it out because you've brought in too much intensity from the Monad without flowing it through the Soul Star, the eighth chakra, which is the means to regulate it. You didn't bring it through the regulator, so that's been the problem area. You just leaped over that level to bring the energy in, and then didn't relate to it. You didn't relate to what came forth because it seemed so fragile; it was not powerful enough and seemed so dense that it couldn't be a part of this beautiful Source-level system that you understand so well. But now that's changing. It doesn't mean that you haven't appreciated the beauty of the Earth; I think you have; that has nothing to do with it.

Vywamus, could I fail?

No, you couldn't fail, but on the physical level, in sequential time, you can delay the complete integration of your Monad's circuitry system that goes through this in a spiral effect, coming back to a full realization of what this process is. (Refer to the diagram "Electrical Day One," p. 222.)

My God, if we've gotten past the mental plane, we're certainly not going to go and come back.

That's right.

I mean, we're here. *We're doing it! And Soul will acknowledge that there was definitely a mistake in my concept about Soul. I thought that I was so beyond the Soul plane that Soul couldn't possibly have any relationship to me.*

Yes. Well, you didn't see it as the regulator for everything that flowed through; you just haven't used it in a system that's already set up for you called the Co-Creator level. You've been appreciated for your strengths, but the reason why you're here on Earth is to see how to use the system, and physical existence lights that up so much.

But the system will also use whatever we're bringing in...

Oh, of course, but it doesn't use what isn't clear — it simply recycles that.

There was a time when we didn't know that this Lord of Synthesis could come into the physical, because we didn't know whether mass consciousness would rebuke it. But it's here!

The point is, the system *works.* And you embody a point of consciousness that the system needs to make contact with, so as you accept the Soul as the regulator in physical existence, you will be able to enter this system again and again using that regulator. I think that once you've got it, the system will use you for awhile here on the physical level because you would be so valuable.

The question then is: Can that be done considering what Djwhal has said about the Avatar of Synthesis? And what if the old Scriptures are misinterpreted by mankind to think that the Christ is The Rider? *Doesn't the Lord of Synthesis come in as* The Rider on the White Horse?

There is no doubt that that is the Lord of Synthesis. Brian, I think that you will reach a point of synthesis where that Soul energy is so accepted by you that it becomes the means for you to relate to all of existence. And when that happens we aren't in a hurry to go anywhere, we really aren't. You will probably stay, I would say. I look for you to be around the Earth for perhaps the next fifteen to twenty years. Your Soul relationship has to be developed a little more before I can tell that for sure, but it's coming along.

So, on the 14th of June last year we had this profound experience — the "burning through," as you called it, right through to the very core — we call it a Source-link or an Earth-link.

From the perspective as far as *you* are concerned, it opened and made possible what we're doing now. It finally connected you with the Earth — I'm looking at it from your personal perspective. The process *works,* my friend, it works on every level in every way. It's magnificent, isn't it? And when you can see that and accept it, it's so exciting! It gives you a sense of, "Oh, I'm so glad to be here! I wouldn't have missed it for the world!"

March 1989

I thought I'd give you another experience that I think is very important. I want you to recognize that many times when you were attempting to come into physical existence, you couldn't find it. You tried to send the energy down into it, and you would miss it. It's rather like diving from a high building into a very small area, and you would often miss it. In one experience, you had agreed to be there for about 500 of that planet's years, which meant a series of lives. It was very important to you personally and to that planet to be a part of that growth. But you tried to dive in I guess ten times before you finally found how to get into it! Now, by the time that you got into it, the 500 years had passed, and you were a little late (laughter). You came in, and it was a little strange because your energy is always prepared for a particular time sequencing within a physical planet. You were prepared for one time and you dove into another time (chuckle)! Well, it was helpful for the planet, of course, to have you there at all, but for you personally it was a little disorienting. You found that somehow you didn't connect often with those beings. It's almost like anticipating something and then it doesn't come about. Perhaps back here where you've been is what you anticipated, but somehow you didn't connect with it. So it becomes sequentially disorienting — recognize that? Mmm-hmm. Guess which planet I'm talking about? There were actually two experiences; one of them is an actual experience from another planet, but the scenario also applies to this one.

Often just missing the boat...

Yes, and then feeling disoriented because of it. For you personally that is the most important part — really being prepared for one time period, landing in another one, and then trying to reconcile the situation. *And it's not always the past; sometimes it's future* — they're all the same thing, anyway. So there is a sense of not being able to sort out exactly what the part is in sequential time.

Where it's at for you is stepping back and surrendering, saying to the Earth, "Good. Now I'm going to accept your strengths and allow them to help me."

What would happen with me? Why wouldn't I go for help?

Why didn't you? Because you believed that the Creator only *gives* help.

Oh. It was that strong?

Yes.

I've never had that much feeling about them consciously, in finite terms, but what is my real relationship to the Archangels? For example, do I work with Metatron? Have I in the past? (See the illustration "The Tree of Life of the Cabala," p. 221.)

Yes, a great deal.

So that's a close link, that one. I sense that.

Yes.

Any of the others?

Gabriel — I would say all of them pretty much. The one you haven't paid much attention to is Sandalphon, because he is quite closely associated with the physical level (chuckle). So you might want to get acquainted with him; it would be helpful if you did.

Really? Sandalphon. All right.

The Archangels really are the administrators of the Plan. The Co-Creator level creates it; they administer it, taking directions from the Co-Creator level.

What is their relationship to Monad? Would they be stepped-down Source? Are they equal to somebody in the...

Well, the Archangels are rather like the right arm of Source. Is that equal to the other parts of Source? Of course, but it's not a unit of developing Sourceness in its own right. The Angelic Kingdom does not have free will.

So what happens when all of mankind evolves and that kingdom goes into Source?

There's a recycling. The Angelic Kingdom is set up in this way for this particular Cosmic Day, and on another Cosmic Day it becomes something else. It is simply the process in action; it's not individualized.

Could a person have an aspect that was angelic, just to experience it?

Yes, once in awhile. Actually, there is a transfer from the Angelic Kingdom into the Co-Creator level, and it's very confusing for the people who have done that. But mostly many of you have worked very closely with the Angels. You can identify with them, but you haven't actually been an Angel, generally speaking. There are some who have been, but it's rather rare. I think there's a misperception about what the Archangels are. There is a centering of consciousness within each Archangel of a particular divine quality, a particular purpose, and it goes through all levels of Being. It is as strong in the fourth dimension as it is in the ninth dimension. So it is not really personal; it is an identification within the Plan, an administrator of that particular area.

As we relate to our levels, would they be a seven? Or can it be that precise?

I would say that the qualities that the Archangels represent transcend all dimensions and all initiations, no matter how you divide up initiations, because there are many ways of looking at that, too. But they are literally on all levels. They represent the qualities and the process, the use of the process. They don't very often get into the third dimension, but the fourth and on up into the seventh dimension is really their home base, dimensionally speaking

— that's more for the Angels than the Archangels, the Angelic Hosts rather than the department heads, if you will. The Archangels are great Beings, great administrators of the Plan. That's only one way of looking at it; there are others. But certainly you've worked a great deal with them. If you're trying to see what your relationship with them is, you're friends with them all. They are your friends and your companions; they're the ones that you have often identified with, perhaps, more than with the Co-Creators.

As the great administrators, the Archangels can be as much a part of one individualized aspect of Source as another — which is what the monadic level represents. So they are just as close to you or Janet or me or whomever. They are the right arm of every Co-Creator or monadic vehicle. That's very helpful, very comforting. They were given as part of the Plan, so that it never lacks organization. The Angels are the connections into all aspects of the Plan.

Dimensions are a structure within which consciousness functions, and I've divided them into nine. I've often said that you could divide that dimensional pie into nine pieces, which I've done. But you could divide it into twenty-four, if you like, or into four; you can divide it any way that you wish. So in this division of nine I've placed the Angelic Kingdom in the seventh dimension, just as you are functioning in physicality, which I give as the third, fourth, fifth, and sixth dimensions — they are *all* physical. So the Angels are close to where physical existence is. They can come into the higher parts of it, but they have never really been a part of the third dimension. Once in awhile there is an exception, but generalizing here, they have often very much been a part of the fourth dimension. So that if you are centered well in the fourth dimension, you can see the Angels, and many will begin to do so. As the Earth enters the fourth dimension, the relationship with the Angelic Kingdom becomes closer; I think perhaps that's what you're feeling. You've always been close to them in the higher realms, but getting close to them again now through your Earth connection can be important.

What is my monadic vehicle doing?

It's assisting in the Plan. It's very dynamic; it has a lot of dynamic qualities. It also has what I would call a lot of Third-Ray qualities and a lot of First Ray. The Third Ray for me is a vehicle that magnifies — thus a magnification of consciousness. First of all, your energy is a combination of Rays, as I said. Many times there is a dynamic thrust into a new area through your monadic level. Keep in mind that your Monad doesn't ever work by itself. It thought that it was supposed to, but it has been (as much as it would allow itself to be) working with other monadic beings, too. What you're doing here is helping it a great deal to identify more clearly with the Co-Creator level, which is its service. It's very involved right now with a research project that is prototyping some possible new Cosmic Days. So I would say that your Monad is helping to set those up — which would be the dynamic energy, the First Ray, and then magnify them so that we, being the Co-Creator level, can see if they're going to work and then put them in line for use in the whole scheme of things. That's eighth-dimensional work — the laboratory for Creation, your vibrational rate as individual source being ninth-dimensional.

Who is Li Pau, who seems to track me down now and again? Is there such a being?

Yes, I think so. In fact, that name has been used a number of times in connection with you. I see it as a being whom you know in a fifth-dimensional experience, one that is quite evolved in consciousness. You knew this being — as I said this would still be considered a physical experience, but being fifth-dimensional it is a finer level of the physical plane. I believe that this being has now graduated from physicality, is very much concerned with concepts, and has been centered in the senior Monad. You see, the fifth dimension is a centering of the conceptual area, although still in physicality. So in graduating from that, this being is identifying for the Source level many new concepts and how to work with them. I think that in this higher area of your intuition, the concepts are not always clear to you, but intuitively you can attune to them. I think that you and he have exchanged skills — he's helped you to see the concepts more clearly, and you've helped him to understand intuitively more clearly. So there's been an exchange of energy — you've worked with him on the physical level several times.

He seems to have an Earth-link now. Does he? He tries to come through as a Source being.

Yes, this is a high consciousness that's helping to conceptualize humanity for our new Source, you could say. So there's a penetration into the Earth for awhile. However, I don't see this being staying around too long — there are too many other things that he is doing.

So the complete Source is now available to the Earth and mankind for the first time ever.

Yes. Of course, it has to be realized; it has to be reenergized. Can you look at it this way? You're born into lives over and over again, and each life you enter a state that you've been in, over and over again — the birth state. Now, how much contact do you make with that new birth state? Well, as much as you can through that life. But you've done it before; you've been born, you've been initiated into that over and over again till you've got it. In this case, Brian, until you have synthesized or blended or integrated everything into your understanding so completely that you're completely balanced from all points of view. And then you enter that full Co-Creator level.

...or Creator Level...

No, the full *Co-Creator* level. The Creator level follows the full use of the Co-Creator stream. Now, I've just arbitrarily given eleven, really twelve Co-Creators, because one of them is you — eleven plus you. You realize your point in that Co-Creator circle more and more until you have full responsibilities within the Plan from that particular perspective. In my understanding of Source, you will fulfill that role until you begin to blend into all of the other roles also. At that time you become the full-fledged Creator, when you will then split into an individualization process in your own right and begin a process, as our Source has. What lies beyond that I don't know, but what I am sure of is that it is an eternal journey and much lies beyond that. But for right now, what you're doing is going over and over them (yes, you've taken initiations before on all levels) until you have *really so integrated that part —* whatever the initiation represents — *that it has the power to direct your conscious-ness;* it becomes an integrated point within you.

When you speak of twelve Co-Creators, has this got anything to do with the energies that are on Earth now?

Well, in a reflective sense, certainly. We would call those the Twelve Rays, wouldn't we? (Refer to "The Twelve Rays," p. 204.)

Where does Brian fit into that structure?

In *The Twelve Rays* I've equated it to the First and Third Rays. In the higher Ray sense, you use the Twelfth Ray a lot, and that is what you are anchoring on Earth. So to tell you the truth, you are a combination of many, many of these Rays — *all* of them, truly. But in the assignments given to your Monad or to you on the physical level, you utilize certain of the Rays in certain assignments. So when you ask me what your Monad is doing, I give you its current assign-ment with the First and Third Rays. There is a predominance — a tone — of each Monad, and that's why Djwhal would give a particular Ray for that level, and I would say that yours would be the First Ray.

The Pioneer Ray.

Yes, but an upper reflection of that would be the Twelfth, though I con-sider the Twelfth to be an upper reflection of several of the Rays. So there is an ongoing integrative process, and the steppingstone to that ongoing process is the *initiation process.* We've done classes where I tell you your Co-Creator connection — one through eleven. If you want to know yours, it would be with number ten. The Co-Creator that is fully directing stream ten is the highest connection that you have within the Co-Creator level. So there are levels of responsibility and levels of consciousness that interrelate, and because they communicate and reflect into another level, they assist in integrating that level, enabling it to move into the next level of understanding.

You *are* Source, and we can look at it as a Co-Creator Council of Twelve — you in the center as the I Am Presence, and eleven perspectives. (Refer to the diagram, "The Seven Councils of Twelve," p. 227.) You see, that metaphysical statement means that each one of those points of Light is developing within an overall scheme of things, or an overall structure that I've called the Co-Creator

Council. And you develop your understanding of one of the eleven streams of consciousness that is the Co-Creator level. Plus you are developing your understanding of that particular aspect of the Creator, so you will be very strong within that aspect. This then allows you to be the full Creator, who will then identify Itself as all of those unlimited points of Light and start the cycle all over again.

You are seeking to understand yourself clearly as a Creator. That's what you identify with, and that's why you have strongly identified with that Source level. There's nothing wrong with that as long as you recognize that it's coming through a process of relating to all of the other developing Sources also, who are Co-Creators together. Until you integrate what you had left out of the process, until you see that there's not a barrier there or all of these things we're working on don't impact, the *Full* Ascension cannot result because it needs the process of integration, bringing to you all of those emotional areas that need resolution. They need to be resolved in order to integrate. Ascension on this physical level, as you know, is not a high initiation. You recognize that. There are many, many, many more that are much more intense, and you've done all of them. But the emotional is the basic — it's the key. Once you've got it, once you've integrated that point, then everything else can happen — without pain, without difficulty, without a loss factor. This one integrates the emotions, let's say.

If I feel that I've done everything, say from zero through infinity, what haven't I done? What have I missed — the Fourth and Fifth? What am I doing now?

Yes, that's really where you are working now, even though you've done them before.

Does mastery mean the Fifth Initiation?

You know, this is such a nebulous word. I don't even like the word *mastery*. I would say that the way to look at it is that you are seeking to integrate, and integration to me is Ascension — integration into a Light perspective that understands spiritually, mentally, emotionally, and physically. Your emotional and physical responses need to be integrated and then mirrored to you, these responses through others, feeling that others are not separate or that they're not going to respond in ways that we've seen from these lives. You see, you have got to realize yourself as a part of this Co-Creator level and you're coming along on it. It's getting better.

But what am I missing?

A deeper understanding of the Co-Creator level. You could liken it to a spiral.

So it's really more a spiral effect. I can understand that, and I can see the intensity on the other initiations being much greater than this. So for all intents and purposes, it would seem simple to somebody else other than myself...

Yes, but if you're building a house, Brian, you may have blueprints; you've figured it all out, that this is exactly what you want — but if you don't put up a good foundation, then what happens?

It falls down.

And then you have to build it again, don't you, until you get a good foundation. Does that help?

Yes, it helps. So these "lower" initiations are done, but there are loose ends that...

Depends on the person. Some clean it up the first time.

If you were to include it in an initiation perspective — because, from our finite definitions, we sometimes need those kinds of perspectives — what am I looking at as a weakness? Is it the bottom initiations?

Yes, it's the bottom ones.

And it's the balancing and the integration and the...

It's the integration. It's moving the focus from the Creator level to the Co-Creator level. It's unplugging your rather rigid perception of holding on to the Creator level so that the focus can come to the Co-Creator level and can be more flexible in regard to the integrative process — that's what it needs. It's plugged into the wrong place, but it's better now because you're really beginning to move that plug. But you have a lot of fear of doing that; you have fear of, "If I let go up here and plug in down there, I'm going to lose that which I've always had." And that's not true.

When you get to be a fully integrated Creator, you're going to be very experienced because you've been doing it a lot already. So it's simply going to college before you've graduated from grade school, you see? It's not that you can't use the strengths of that level because you *are*, and you *do*. It's just that you don't yet have the foundation yet.

I thought about it last night, that my Monad would be doing one thing specifically for synthesis as it relates to mankind and Mother Earth. And I, on the other hand, would be trying to look through and try to adjust the same area that Monad is working on. I seem to be the problem and the cure!

You know, often the area that you need the help in understanding, is the very area that is your purpose. When we talk about a Lord of Synthesis, that's someone who helps put things together, and that's exactly what you need to do, put things together. A paradox, isn't it?

Yes; and this has all happened, really, since the 14th of June.

Yes, exactly. It's come to a point of crisis — I don't mean to frighten you — with your physical structure. It's not terrible, but it *is* showing some signs of stress. You know that. So as you work with it, as you support it, as it is supporting you, then you will have a vehicle that can take you to that point you're aiming toward.

I know that the heart was hit hard with that opening; but it was the opening that caused this stress on my physical body.

But the opening was necessary.

Oh, I don't disagree with any of this; I just need to understand it.

I know you do, and I understand that, too, Brian. I do.

I keep coming back to the Soul. I need something to buffer those energies I feel and you see.

Well, let's put it this way: Do you realize that the Source (I think you do) has created a Plan that works in all ways, on every level?

I'm desperately trying to see that one.

Well, it's true. It does work, certainly on the physical.

It's probably working now, but I don't think it always has.

Oh well, it's not a system that meets expectations or that is absolutely closed, in the sense that everything is preplanned. It isn't. It's an open-ended system that evolves.

It's a do-it-yourself kit! (They both laugh.)

That's right, exactly. But that doesn't mean that it doesn't work on every level, and it doesn't mean that a guidance system isn't set up on every level.

Now, Your Monadic level is inputting into the Earth very strongly — I think you know that — and this is not changing that. It is simply allowing it to go through channels, or go through the Divine structure, as it was meant to. One thing that can help you (you know this; it's just that you don't remember it): I'd like you to see coming up from the Earth the energy that your Monad has put into it. What color is it?

Lots of aqua blue and gold. I want to bring the energy from the Earth back up through my body and look at it.

We're going to work on the heart a little bit.

It becomes a little lighter now.

Good. Your physical being will be very important for you.

Yes.

You're really doing very well. It's simply that this is such a profound change that it takes a little time to see it. There's a lot going on.

That's what I'm feeling. Would it be helpful to work on the etheric body every night?

Yes, it would; because every time you make a realization or become a little clearer, then you can move some of that out, Brian. It is attached to the realization process. I'm not sure that you understand that yet. As you realize that there's an alignment and the physical body lines up with the emotional, the mental, and the spiritual, then you can remove the misalignment of energy that has been there.

Do I go back to the Monad between lives?

Well, sometimes you've pulled back that far. You've pulled out because the Soul hasn't felt supported, but eventually you've just come back. Now, it hasn't always been to the Earth, but it would be some physical existence — remembering, of course, that all universes are physical up to the twelfth chakra and the Twelfth Initiation; the Twelfth, if you like, is the bridge from the physical level into the Monad (the spiritual level) — until you really do understand that Co-Creator level. You are also learning about it on the inner planes. I'm not telling you that you aren't doing many other things, and doing them very well, on other levels, too. But *this* is the big one now — this is the one that there's a lot of energy in.

On the 14th of June, the opening to allow this to come in?

Yes.

So is that cycle complete? Or is it ever complete? Or is it just the opening?

Well, the way that that opening happened, *that* is complete. You could say that if you put a little hole in something, then you can enlarge that hole — but the hole needed to be there in order to enlarge it. So that was a profoundly important event, and it certainly reverberated throughout the Cosmos.

Let's look at it this way — that when you get beyond sequential time, there is a focus that your Monad is using, and it is just feeding into that focus more fully, more completely, with what is going on. Let's say that this is the focus of your Monad; some areas haven't put into it well enough yet to create this complete structure that your Monad is capable of creating. There are some holes in it yet, so that's really what it is; it's not something terrible. It's simply a process of synthesis, of blending more and more completely what your Monad is capable of blending, not having a part it can't access. So — and you'll recognize this — it's capable of putting out the concept, but when it hits physical existence, that concept seems to have some holes in it. And now you're reconstructing that. I would suggest that you look often at that Soul level, and while the etheric work is being done, attune to that Soul Star and bring that energy down in just the way we did.

Is this senior Monad directly related to this energy we call Brian? Is that my Monad?

Yes. It is you, and you are it. There is no separation.

So then there could be billions of Souls in that Monad?

There is a center that I call the Monad. It is a Creative Center for you, your Sourceness, your Creative Center. But it is meant to interrelate with every other Creative Center, which are other Monads — the Source in manifestation. You became more open to this interaction last June.

*Yes. This is to fulfill my Creator role as **The Rider on the White Horse** that we agreed we would do.*

Yes, exactly. So now it is your heart, your electrical system and your arteries on the physical level that need your attention.

I would have thought logically that with all of the electrification on the cellular level, with all that's been pumped through me electrically and atomically, I should be able to — if I can get these things aligned — make that body for Ascension rather readily, if I can put the pieces together. Is that an accurate statement?

Of course it is. That's true. This is a process of synthesis, or of blending and integrating. The only way that you can do it, though, is to let in the strengths of the other Co-Creators so that you can blend. Remember what I said about your coming to Earth from "the highest mountain down to the lowest valley"? No one else in the physical will evolve this way. Mankind will progress in their evolution in the way the blueprint was intended, evolving on the spiral from the Earth *up* to Source. What you are doing is extremely creative, and it's something that I've truly appreciated studying, because I've never seen it done your way. But, my dear friend, with your strengths — which are awesome for the Co-Creator level — I urge you to use and to integrate the Co-Creator system in a way that was intended and not recreate a system that's already in place.

Now, in one of your physical experiences you were helping to design some physical planets. Others have done this, too; it's something that is done quite frequently. You were working on the Council of Twelve for this quadrant of this galaxy. (The actual doing of it is under the direction of some of the Archangels.) There were six planets in this solar system; and, of course, the Solar Logos was the center, the focus of the design, the blueprint. There was one planet, the fourth one from the sun, that you, in your learning and your understanding, were to help work with. You set it up on a drawing board, in a sense, to see the particular characteristics that were needed in that planet. Everyone said to you, "Don't forget to take its relationship with the other planets into consideration — where they are in relationship to that planet and where it is in relationship to the Whole. But somehow that fell through the cracks. The solar system was set up, but this fourth planet wouldn't stay in its orbit; it kept falling out, and eventually burned up. You said to the Archangels, "I don't know what we did wrong. It wasn't any heavier than the one next to it, and it's staying in it's orbit just fine." They said, "But on the other side of it were several asteroids and moons and several other things that were reducing its gravity and weight." So you hadn't really taken into consideration the fact that it was within a whole perspective, and then it got woven into the system that way. So the planet literally exploded; it burned up.

Another project at the monadic level: You were helping to finish up a Cosmic Day that didn't work out, and so it had been miniaturized and placed in the eighth dimension. Now, there are many ways of looking at dimensions. I know that you look at it one way, and through Janet I'm giving something else. But the point is that there is a dimensional focus where, if a Cosmic Day doesn't work out, it is completed like a laboratory experiment so that the Source learns from the experience and will not repeat something that will not work. You were involved in monitoring this miniaturized Cosmic Day that hadn't worked out. Now, on this particular one, there were six polarities — that may be a little difficult to comprehend — but some of that had gone awry, and only four polarities were working well. We will call them simply two variations of the male polarity and two variations of the female polarity. So it wasn't too different, actually. It was just a matter of degree. And even in the two polarities there are degrees of polarity within physical structures. I think you know that. The point is, you found this Day to be very out of balance — that's why it had been stopped — the dynamic energy, when it worked, worked so extensively that it really burned up the receptive energy it interacted with. So every time a planet was created in this Cosmic Day it was immediately burned up. The dynamic flow burned, or ignited, the receptive area and then left a hole where that receptive area had been. The receptive energy was not allowed to have a stable focus because of this process; every time the receiving area opened up, it was burned out by the dynamic energy. Now, this played out; it actually got worse before the Cosmic Day ran out, in the miniaturized sense.

Thus there was a difficult cosmic miniature, one that had very little receptivity in it. It had a lot of dynamic charge; it would be like electrical wires flashing around everywhere, and everything they touched exploded because they were out of control. In the lab, this wasn't dangerous, but one day you forgot to, let us say, set the dial that kept it in its safe environment, and that whole effect got loose again. It didn't spread out very much, but it began to impact the surrounding environment and you had some of these miniature Cosmic Days that literally exploded and burned up from this one.

Now, you have quite a bit in the area of burning and ignition and fire and dynamic energy. Not all of it is negative, of course — there are some good beliefs, and you'll want to keep those. But we want to deal with this area, because anytime you *force* a Creator level into a Co-Creator process, then you've built in a dynamic thrust that is too powerful for the receptive area; or, according to your belief structure, that's what it seems. You see, this is only a perception, and it's not really true. There is a lot of force brought through from the Creator level into the Co-Creator process — it's meant to be used by the *whole* process, and then it isn't overpowering. But when it's run through one individual, then it *is* overpowering sometimes. If the belief is that this must be held onto at the Creator level and can't enter the Co-Creator level, then it becomes difficult.

Now I'd like to go into an area that I think is extremely important for you. Keep in mind that what we are doing in the intensive is "opening" — creative openings. That is not terrible, Brian; it simply means that the Co-Creator level, of which you are a member in very good standing, helps each other. It is meant to be that way. You cannot and will not obtain your goals until you relate to others and they relate to you. That is what the Co-Creator level is — a harmony, an equality — I call it divine equality.

Let us go, then, into a difficult life in which you as a small child cried and cried and cried all of the time. No one seemed to know what you were crying about, and people got tired of hearing your crying — especially your parents. Well, one day when they were tired enough of it, they said, "All right, just cry — it doesn't matter to us," and they went off and left you. Now you cried even harder; and cried and cried and cried, until a point came where you stopped. Into that stillness you placed all of your hopes, all of what you wanted. You said, "Please help me to understand. Please, someone, help me." This was an extremely important point in your evolution, Brian, because it began, it opened, it allowed what we are doing now to occur. It is extremely important that you recognize the magnitude of this area for you. It is essential to recognize the strengths of the Whole, the strengths of the other Co-Creators. It's not that you don't recognize them; it's that you simply haven't thought about them in connection with yourself and your evolution. But it takes this opening, it takes this allowingness to reach your goals.

You once lived, Brian, at the top of a mountain. It was a wonderful place to live; the air was so clear. And you were alone most of the time, which is what you liked. Well, one day a young man climbed your mountain to visit you. He was such a joy to have that he stayed with you — he became your student. Now, that was very good, and you enjoyed having your student there. But he grew in awareness until he became someone who could help you as much as you were helping him. Perhaps you didn't see that. You said to him one day, "You know, your way of thinking is growing apart from mine. I think it's time for you to leave." Well, he was very surprised, because he thought that you were enjoying the discussions that the two of you had together. But you really weren't comfortable with them, Brian. He was teaching *you*, and it was difficult for you to acknowledge that that was possible. Well, you can see the same theme being reiterated over and over again. I am doing that purposefully, because that is the area that needs more recognition, more realization. I repeat, you are doing well on it, but there is still more to do.

Now, let's go more into the Earth area again. You had a couple of lives — one as a pharaoh of Egypt in which you were buried in the Earth when you were still alive. It was in a tomb; you woke up in the tomb — they didn't use an embalming process in that early Egyptian life — and you were sealed in. Of course you died. You didn't have enough oxygen to sustain life for very long.

But there was a sense of bewilderment. "What am I doing here? And why has this buried my creativity and effort? What have others done to me now?"

In a life in Spain, you were tortured in the Spanish Inquisition. As a priest you were brought before the Inquisition and found guilty, but not before you had been tortured. The electrical system in your body was literally shredded — there was a lot of difficulty with it. So through these affirmations I'm going to work on the electrical area.

> *Put the affirmation into the lake, and the lake represents the subconscious mind. I give it a color, and that represents a particular aspect of the subconscious mind or your creativity (that's why I use a color). As that goes in, it enters the aspected subconscious and begins to energize it. It begins to create an opening, or it adds energy to it. As you use the golden light that shines on the lake, it begins the process of integration of that affirmation — integration into the subconscious. Then there is a response, and that response is what I'm asking you to see going into the cellular level.*

Just doing that affirmation that one time has slightly changed the subconscious. As you allow that to take place and allow that change — which you see as a response — going into the cells, it's going to help your physical body step by step. That's one reason why it's so important. In other words, each time you take it and put the affirmation in, it clears the subconscious just a little, and it will help the cellular level just a little.

> *See a blue-green lake, and slide in the following affirmations:*

- *I know that I will not be punished by this effort to bring from me that which I am now.*

- *The electrical system/the flow system is not being impacted/shredded through this communication now.*

- *As I communicate, there is not a difficult and intricately convoluted electrical effect that takes away the clear flow now.*

I think that yesterday was very good for you, with the realizations that you had and the affirmations that you made. Didn't you feel it grounding (perhaps cleansing is a good word)? It was a very good day for you, releasing material that you were ready to let go of physically, because you'd cleared it out on another level, and that has to be done first, at least to have a lasting effect. Physically, I think that the etheric work will continue to be important for you either here or wherever you happen to be on the planet Earth. It looks to me like perhaps some travel is coming your way. Do you recognize that?

Not offhand. Travel in the sense of going back to Vancouver?

No, I mean more than that. It seems to me that there's more energy in travel over the next six months than there's been, perhaps, for awhile. I'm just looking at a possibility.

Coming from the Monad, when we speak of Soul it's still a bit confusing. Is it what some people call the Oversoul, from the monadic perspective? Or do I actually have a Soul?

What I call the Oversoul would be a stream of consciousness that is more extensive than the Soul. Look at yourself as a stream, a column of Light — that's one way of looking at yourself. (Refer to the illustration, "Co-Creator and Creator Levels," pp. 228-29.) We would call this Source, and here's your Monad; it's part of that. There's a whole stream of consciousness that flows. And here is the physical level. So the Soul is a specific within that stream of consciousness — a regulator, a mechanism that regulates, adjusts, helps integrate what is learned within the physical existence. Now in my opinion, when they're referring to an Oversoul, it's almost as if it's this whole column of Light — the whole flow of the energy from the Monad. You see, the Monad is a focus. There is a flow from that focus, and this is the movement of Source, the spiral of evolution. It is a flow of energy that at a particular point, in order to enter physicality in a way that it can relate to and use well, goes through a particular focus that we call the Soul.

You mentioned earlier that that's why I'm here. Vywamus, my understanding is that everyone — all of the teachers on the inner planes — will ultimately come into gross physicality, including Melchior, Adonis, and other energies who've not been in physicality.

One way or the other. It doesn't mean that they'll all occupy a physical body like you are.

But they will "drop in" with their body for Ascension or create another...

Or channel — come in through the channeling process.

Oh.

Some of them are doing that through the channeling process — learning about physicality. So in one way or another, the area that is called gross physicality must be integrated into this area of understanding. You could look at this as a telescope, a magnifier that reaches from here, the Monad, all the way here, to physicality. And then what returns is a clearer point of view.

It's difficult for me to understand that one can be so strong on some levels and so weak on others.

Well, not necessarily weak, just not fully integrated. We're not talking here about weakness — we're talking about you as a being who has been manifested by Source Itself and needs to integrate all of the areas that haven't come together yet. Every Monad has different areas that haven't been fit together yet. It's like a puzzle; there are always pieces that haven't come together yet. What I'm saying is that you haven't included in that process of integration the energy that relates to physical existence (all that is universal), which is leaving

out about one-tenth of existence. So you could say that there is not a completion of some of those initiations. There's enough Energy. I will acknowledge
that you've taken all of those initiations and levels beyond that into Source, yes.
But it is like going to graduate school and getting a whole new look at certain
areas in order to be qualified as an expert, an expert being here an ability to use
the area well. You don't always need a degree, you know that. The point is
that the Plan will acknowledge that you fit into it enough so that it is completely integrated within you.

So we can't fake it from Monad, then!" (laughing)

(also laughing) No, you can't.

*Can we look at this? (referring to Chakra Electrical System on the illustration,
"Electrical Day One," p. 222) What changes are there, if any, and does the 65%
change?*

All right, the 65% has moved to 82%, and that's good, that's very good. I
think you ought to be very happy with that; I'm pleased with what you've
accomplished, considering that prior to June 14, 1988, it was zero! Certainly,
Brian, I think that you need to recognize that this is very deep, the work that
you've been talking about. And the fact that you're here, the fact that you've
come, is a great acknowledgment and a great step forward. The physical body
will mirror to you the resolution of the rest of this; it will.

*(Referring to the same illustration) What does that mean, having this line on
both sides of the pole? I think that one of our friends has all of his on one side.*

Well, his is different from yours. It's a balancing like the inbreath and the
outbreath — it needs to go on both sides. It's the rhythm of life, the receptive
and dynamic. These are showing the shift on the physical level. It's showing
movement on the physical level as it hasn't been before. Your receptive and
dynamic are well-balanced because, as you can see, this snakelike line is
well-balanced on both sides of the line.

Have we ever worked together, you and I?

You and I. "Long ago and far away," as the saying goes. Yes, we have.

*How can I be so clear in some areas and so highly evolved, as initiations go,
and still I'm so confused?*

Well, my friend, did you ever meet someone whom you considered to be a
genius in certain areas, and perhaps they didn't know very much in some other
areas? What they've done is put all of their energy into areas that they understood — what seemed important, creatively, for them — and ignored other
things. A good example is someone who comes into physicality and is re-
tarded in every area but music. What I'm telling you is that you've put a lot of
energy into these areas that are clear, and you *are* an expert, and you've taken
it as far as you can go without plugging in the rest of the system.

Well, let's use Maitreya/Christ, because we're so diametrically opposed in how we view spiritual existence that I think it's a very good example of one area and another area. But surely the things that I'm looking at are the things that Maitreya is so clear in and the things that he ultimately must look at are the areas that I'm so clear in.

That's the way you see it.

And you don't see it that way?

I don't see it that way, but I think that it's a good focus for you to learn from. And you're entitled to your opinion.

Well, you would know. You're my friend, and you've watched many of the things that I have watched.

Well, I don't see it the way you do. And I'm not going to evaluate Maitreya because I don't feel that that's appropriate at this point. I do agree that you've had some times in working with him when you didn't see eye to eye. That's true, yes, and that's part of what we learn.

From your perspective, you tend to agree with him.

Not necessarily. What I don't see is any opposition involved at all.

Yes, I see, but my Monad wouldn't agree, either.

That's right. Well, what it doesn't see fully yet is the Co-Creator level. It may look like an opposition here. Why? Because it's so magnified on the physical level. It isn't as opposite as it looks at the monadic level. So there are differences in understanding with beings such as Maitreya; they look larger than they are, here on the physical level. Monad is not seeing this as an opposition, for example, but there is some learning in that area.

You're rereading these texts in order to understand them more clearly, and maybe that makes sense to you — it does to me. You have all of eternity to discover it. Well, the point is that there never comes a time when you can say, "There's no more learning; I know it all" or "I'm absolutely clear," because the Source Itself is evolving. You see, there is always a process of evolution and of greater synthesis going on. There are points that you've called initiations — and that's as good a word for them as any — where you can use that level of the structure more clearly. Thus you are able to function in a manner that implements the Plan — mass energy movements and so forth — in a way that is absolutely integrated. You see, if you were to build a universe now, it wouldn't function very well. There are parts of it, like physical existence, that wouldn't work very well.

July 1989

Well, you've been moving, haven't you? There's been movement there.

Unbelievable! And you certainly forecast travel that I didn't see. What a tremendous journey (to Australia).

Yes, tremendous.

The timing was rather interesting, because in the final analysis **The Avatar of Synthesis** *was fulfilled. The recognition that the Creator and Co-Creator can align and be together — that's probably the most significant.*

I agree with that.

And after June 14, 1988, and the hell and the near-deaths and everything else of this past year.

So it's come full circle.

Vywamus, another channel has verified what you said through Janet, that the Councils of Twelve — that there are "the eleven plus Brian" — is an accurate statement.

Yes, and that Council is responsible for this Cosmic Day.

How many years, approximately, are in a Cosmic Day?

Well, it depends on the Cosmic Day, Brian. Each is a little different. They're not in sequential time, but if we had to put this one into sequential time, this one is 4 billion, 300 million years, and it will be followed by an equal period of a Cosmic Night.

And then the responsibility shifts?

Switches and changes, yes.

I've found that that link — whatever that fusion was — that has taken place is a very nice feeling.

Yes, of course it is, and it was an alignment that was extremely important for both you and the Earth — a tremendous cosmic alignment.

At that level, the level which I now see as Source is simply individualized Source, and the being we call Brian or Szo Szo Szo Szo or Phopenjenus or whoever is a gossamer wing. A colored membrane is shown to me, a beautifully colored membrane between individualized Source (the Source for this Cosmic Day) and the Undifferentiated Source.

Well, I don't know if we would say "between." We could say "penetrating" and "a part of."

And there's no real separation, then, is there?

No, none at all.

The only difference is that one is individual, and one is the composite, Undifferentiated Source.

Yes, it's just a perspective, a way of looking at the same things. You could say that one is a penetration within the other.

I don't know how else to express it. The energies are so different in Australia. The demands are so different than they are here.

Yes, they are. That area is extremely interesting. It has a lot of the potential qualities of the Galactic Core that have never been used anywhere else. Now, they haven't learned to use them there, either, but it is potentially strong there, and I think perhaps that you can feel that. But it's not doing anything much — it's like a potential that hasn't been used yet, not ever, on your planet. When it was created, there was almost like an outreach of the Galactic Core. There was an imprint that became the Earth, and that area of Australia was the one that was imprinted, in a sense. That doesn't fit into everything else that has been said about your Earth — for example, Shamballa and all of that. But we're talking, really, about an energy imprint before Earth even became a planet or a physical expression. So that area still remembers this imprinting system, and it's different — it has a Fire composite.

Why was I there with my friend Glenda?

Well, I think that the Earth wanted you there, and I think it helped you two. Certainly with you it did some healing, because one is always healed in Transformational Fire. Within your physical structure there was some healing done. Can you recognize that?

Yes, very much so.

So from a personal point of view, you were there to help *you*. Nowhere else on the Earth could you have experienced such a burning away, such a Transformational Fire process. It is stronger in that area. That's why there are different species that live there exclusively; many of them couldn't survive where there wasn't that sort of Fire. The ones that live here couldn't survive where there *is* that Fire, or at least they don't know how yet. That area may seem to be backward because it is simply is not using its potential. You also went to align some of that energy into a usable format, to build a bridge, let us say, between that area and the rest of the world.

Yes, I felt that.

So that's the service aspect of it; and from your personal aspect, it was for the healing, and it's helped a great deal. Your heart area is much more stable (of course, you need to continue to work on that), and I like it. It has an affinity for that area; you've lived there a number of times. You were there, Brian, when this imprinting that I talked about occurred, and you remember that. It makes a very cosmic connection for you, when you went there and felt that energy again. It doesn't mean that before that time you couldn't make the cosmic connection, but it *identified* it. It was into the identity area, and we could call it the divine blueprint where, if you don't use the Soul as your identity (which you're not doing), then you have to have something else that will identify for you a pattern that can be used by your physical structure. You weren't identifying enough with the Soul to allow that ideal blueprint to be transmuted to the physical level, so you found another way. So it's all right.

This is an election for me; it isn't something that all Creator Monads do. They don't normally come into the physical.

That's right, but they come in when they are needing to magnify the Creator process so that they can understand it more fully. Because the system works this way, they also have something unique to give to the physical system. In other words, there is never one without the other. Thus you became a part of the physical universe because your energy is needed to help balance it. And also because you need to look at the creative process in a magnified way to understand it more completely. Why? Not necessarily because you're having difficulty with it, but because future responsibilities need you to understand it in a unique, detailed way that other Creators, perhaps, in their future assignments don't need to understand.

I've been told recently that I helped to create — not with the same Monad or not with the same grouping — a crystalline planetary system, which we haven't been able to see yet. It hasn't been identified, but has been created. The glory, I gather, of being a Creator Monad or a Source Being is that you're not locked into your Council alone with nothing to do outside of that Council. Is it this universe that the Council represents, or is it this planetary system?

Only in a reflection. Now, there are many levels of Councils of Twelve. When I'm talking about it to you — and when we've discussed it before — I've been talking about the basic Source-level Council of Twelve that creates this Cosmic Day, that sets up the whole structure that everyone is within. So you can't be without it; you can't be outside of it. But there are reflected levels, and we can get to a level of this quadrant of this galaxy that has a Council of Twelve, and certainly then one could be involved with physical structures.

Being involved in the creation of this crystalline planetary system means simply that you had another option; it doesn't mean that it was inappropriate. It means that it was like having a career within a certain company, and then another company recruited you for awhile and asked if you could work with them. It's not inappropriate. It's simply stretching beyond the original blueprinting system, and it opened up for you a lot of things. It helped you to be more versatile and more understanding of several of your options.

Please respond a little, if you would, why the feeling was so strong in Australia. I've touched on this, but I would like to have it developed — the feeling that for once not only did we anchor on the 14th of June a great deal of Light and, as you said, "burned through the heart to the very core." I recognize that, and I recognize also the difficulty that I've created for myself because of the way I did it, for whatever reason. But now the heart feels much better that this synthesis that I came to do is quite clear. In Australia, I felt that we'd actually done — maybe not completed, but it had certainly...

Well, certainly I've always known that. Yes, of course, there have been many levels that you've been working on this with. Certainly one of the most difficult ones was what happened to your physical structure during this process. The fact that you held beliefs about the destruction of the physical structure through an anchoring or through a synthesis is part of what's going on with you and your relationship to your Soul. So you just found an alternative way of doing it. Again, that's all right; there's never just one way to do it, and you noticed that a year ago. Now you are using an alternative method for the divine blueprint (the Galactic Core) — it's coming from a level that you validate more than you validate this planet's level.

You're growing in the physical plane, but you're asking me why you created that way, in difficulty. It is because of limitation, because of some of the choices that you made. The choices were motivated not as much by a clear understanding as by what we would call a programmed response. I think perhaps that it might be interesting for you to look at an event that happened when you were a beginning Monad, when there weren't any other levels of your awareness that had yet been activated. It was at the point where you were beginning as an individual. At that time, you could say, you took a tour of Source. You saw visiting there — well, they could be compared to a group of kindergarten students, and these were Souls who had come to see that basic level. There was a group of them — two hundred, two thousand, it doesn't matter; there weren't very many. The point is that you saw them. Now, you were very young in experience. You really didn't understand. You looked at that group and asked the one who was acting as their tour guide, "Who are they?" and the reply was, "They are Souls." You said, "But look at that — they don't understand. They are so limited." And the guide said, "But they are Souls," and that was all that was said.

It doesn't take much, does it?

No. It was a basic experience that said to you, "A Soul is limited; a Soul is not as widely based as I am, creatively." See? It depends upon the purpose or the place or the point of awareness. Certainly on the physical level the Soul is the governing energy that can help you to remain focused. It can help you to fit into the overall blueprint system that is on that particular planet. It gives you a sense of relatedness to the structure and to others. So often you've found yourself rather alienated or not feeling a part of things because you couldn't identify with the structure that was there.

An observation, if you will — and it's not dissimilar to what we've already asked — I feel that the connection has been made, that my Source energy is now here to synthesize the Co-Creator level.

Of course, some of it is.

I'm sitting on the beach in Australia, and I can see all the Light Beings around me. This body is confused on the cellular level. Some part of me is saying, "By now you should be in the Light. What is wrong?" I ask of you an interpretation of what it is that I'm feeling and how soon might I go into this Lightbody, this Ascension? I still am confused. I have gaps of 20 or 30 minutes of being total Light, but it isn't visible to others, only to me. What does this mean?

It means that you go back to that core, or that Source level, that monadic expression which others are not aware of yet, most of them. It means that you still do not have a consistent connection, although I would say that it is much stronger, much better since your Australian trip. The gaps are where you literally leave your physical structure to make that Light connection rather than allowing the physical structure to be the vehicle that magnifies that Light.

How much Light is there, if you were to give me a reading?

There's a tremendous amount of Light there, more than enough to create your Ascension, but it isn't being held at a consistent enough point yet. The reason why is that your physical body isn't aware of how to use it yet on the cellular level. Since the energies came in on April 15, 1989, for "The Crystal Light Link," this higher level of the electrical flow and the means to embody that energy is here on this Earth as it has never been before. Could you have done the Ascension before? Yes, a few have. Actually, many have, but not, comparatively speaking, in the numbers that are now open to it. So it is easier, and there is no reason why you can't ascend. But you have to teach your physical body, and it is probably a step-by-step manner.

I can go in and out of the Light.

You already are; that's what you're doing.

Is that what causes some of the pain?

It causes some, let's say, Light confusion or Light stress, and of course that can be perceived as painful. The difficult thing with you is that you don't have very much Soul contact, and that makes it harder for you. It does because there is such an intensification of that Light that it burns the physical structure. We've talked about that. Now, what color seems to you to be the one that spreads the Light and yet holds it in a level that you can accept on the physical plane. Just ask for help.

Aqua blue.

All right, then I would create a garment that fits your physical structure that is aqua blue and step into it. Spend some time with this, about half an hour.

I'm shown gold coming through the blue.

Yes, all right. You will find the right color. The point is to put that garment on and then sit in it. Now, instead of trying to contact the monadic level, which is there with you all of the time, anyway, go within the center of the Earth and contact the Divine Beingness in the center of the Earth because it can help you to accept this. This is the structural format that you've chosen, and you're more comfortable with it, I think, than you used to be, aren't you?

Mmm-hmm, very much.

So bring that color into the center of the Earth (you'll probably find it there already) and then allow that to flood back through your physical structure. Then look at the Co-Creator level as it is represented by humanity, and put each being that you visualize into your heart. Allow that Co-Creator level to magnify for you that ability to accept the Light, because that's what it's going to take.

What happens? These gaps that I have — of Light, at no particular times, not in meditation. I could be sitting in a restaurant. What happens? Do I come in and out of this? As you have said, Vywamus, Ascension is a point of Light. It's actually the recognition that you are Light, that All is Light, and that others see you as Light. How is that so? I know that Jesus and others on Earth are still basically in etheric bodies, which is the physical body — so they are physical.

Well, if they wish to be. It is simply activating for them a part that perhaps they haven't used in a long time.

Was my Lightbody visible to Janet? Would it be?

Well, if her third eye were open enough, which it isn't right now. Her knowingness can see it.

Are there others on Earth yet who are in and out of the Lightbody?

Oh, yes, many. Many, many, many of you are. Janet is doing that, too. There are many of you who are flowing in and out. You do this until you can do it consistently. Or perhaps I should say for you, until you can stay at the physical level and make the connection and then hold it.

How do we know when we're actually in the Lightbody?

Because when you look at physical existence, it turns to Light. When you are centered within it on the physical level consistently enough and look at physical existence you would see Janet turning to Light completely, this furniture turning to Light, and *holding* it.

I've had that; the longest I've had is twenty minutes.

Exactly. But you are looking at it not from holding it on the physical level; you are looking at it from the monadic level. So the key for you is to really make that contact through the center of the Earth and through the Co-Creator level, through asking everyone on the Earth to view *you* as Light and to "lighten up" the contact enough. You see, through your perception, in one sense, you are held to the Earth through the Co-Creator level, which is "less than." We've been talking about this, and you're doing better on this, too. But now, by validating the equality of the Co-Creator level, then the whole thing lightens, the whole thing becomes the physical experience. Where you all are becomes a valid Light experience.

My "loving condemnation" of religion. Even though I have been part of this business, I now recognize that Kuthumi is going to be the new, or the 36th, Christ. He is going along with what I'm saying, that we don't need a religion. He doesn't want his case accelerated and distorted before he identifies his energy on Earth. I can accept that, if that's true. Is there any truth?

Well, there is — again, from one point of view. There is an ignition process and an integrative process of what are called religions going on. Some will fall away; some will become something else; some will be the foundation upon which a wider application of understanding can come in. So there is not only a falling away, a releasing, but there is an integration that is part of your developing system or your developing spiritual understanding of the planet. A lot of change going on there, and it's good.

It's very fast, isn't it?

Oh, very.

I would love to see that happen here where our realities manifest immediately, and it's happening. But in Australia, the realizations were so profound and so immediate.

Yes, yes. Good.

Now, here it's a little bit different, speaking in terms of that "Source in form," I was told intuitively, at least in Australia. This is a strange way to put it, but in Australia at least, I felt that I'm becoming "Source in form." Is that a transition?

No, I think it's a recognition of what's always been there because in one sense everything has always been there. But it's a recognition of it. Certainly, I agree with that.

As I bring all Earthlings into my heart, then I will feel the freeing effect that I seem to be crying out for — to get out of the physical body and to be able to not attach service to sacrifice. My body is saying, "It's time to ascend." Is this something that a lot of people will do, ascend in sync?

Perhaps...and that would be wonderful, Brian, if you could accept that because it would open you to the Co-Creator level as perhaps nothing else could.

Tens of thousands ascending at once...

Yes, yes, yes, yes!

We don't necessarily leave the physical when we ascend; that's an election that we can make at that time.

That's right. But the energies transcend to a new level that opens up for you physical existence as such an integrated tool. As you were talking about in Australia, the manifestations are instant; the elements become simply tools of your creative ability. That's what we're talking about. Ascension is a point of total integration, as far as the potential of existence is concerned.

1994: Is there a possibility at that time that the Earth may shift its skin?

Yes, the shifting of the axis. But that's less and less evident because of beings such as yourself.

If that did happen at that time, it would allow a lot of people to go. I mean, if almost 50% are going to be leaving the planet, that would be an opportunity. Do I have a long-term schedule where Monad and I have said, "Well, this is what we'll probably do"?

As far as your relationship with universal physical existence?

Mmm-hmm.

No, I think that you're summarizing. Now, I have to look at the fact that I think you're quite ready. This relationship with the Co-Creator level is the one that is the key here, but it doesn't take time to do that — it takes a realization.

Have I not just had that?

Of course you've had it; but, you haven't had enough of it, or you haven't had it consistently enough that everything has been finished yet. You can see that it hasn't occurred yet. So it's simply more of what you've already had. As far as a long time, I don't think so. You're ready whenever you're ready — it takes as long as it takes. But it's not something that's going to take, in my opinion, twenty more lifetimes or even another lifetime. I think that you are pretty much ready whenever your Co-Creator relationship is stimulative enough to the heart that the heart connects you to that level. Then that's it! How long? A few years, a few months, a few minutes, depending upon when you make that profound realization. For you it may take several ones like you've just had.

Have I ever come in any lower than the mental plane? Is the Higher Mind the same as the Soul plane?

No, it isn't the same thing. As King Akhnaton, and particularly as *The Rider*, you've come in with all the energy that you and the planet can handle. Your awareness of your Self is at that level. So you could say that your consciousness has experienced many, many things on the physical level that haven't yet been seen as equal — and this is part of that Co-Creator level.

That's part of what you're doing, balancing that out and recognizing it and acknowledging it. It's part of your role, too. Everything always fits together, do you see that? The Plan can utilize your skills and abilities; it has recognized them and uses them in the way that you bring them in, in the way that you recognize and use them. The Plan is a mirror.

January 3, 1990

Good afternoon, Brian. Well, this is a privilege, it really is, and I've looked forward to it.

We've talked on the inner planes many, many times; and of course we talk directly many, many times. But I always enjoy this contact, too. So I welcome you.

Thank you, Vywamus. I would like to ask an opinion on the book as it relates to energy. You once said (these are not your exact words, but in effect) that in typical fashion, so many times I've come down and I've been ahead of what people are really ready for. Could I be on this book, also? What's your opinion of the book?

Well, I think it's very good — I like it; and I think that there will be an adjustment period, meaning that there is still some catching up of humanity to do in response to it. I do think that after that it should do very well. Now, how long will that be? Well, we don't know, either one of us, how long that will be, but it may not be too long. I like it; I think that there are probably yet going to be some changes in the way that you view the book as you change how you think. It's like a baby — a creative effort — and as you change the way that you view it, that's going to let it fit into humanity more easily. So I think that's what you're here for today.

Of course. It is, totally. Okay, I have a diagram here. It's what I see, and I would ask you to look at it with me. You can see through Janet's eyes? (He is referring to the illustration, "The Seven Councils of Twelve," p. 227.)

Yes, of course.

Okay. This is my conceptualization of the seven Councils of Twelve, and it appears to me that the seventh seems to be Source; the sixth — mid-Monad; the fifth seems to be the Twelfth Initiation, or the beginning of the Monad; the Fourth seems to be Universal; the third — Galactic; the second appears to be Shamballa; and the first seems to be a Planetary Hierarchy, or Planetary Government. Are we anywhere near? (Note: There are, in fact, millions of Councils of Twelve; we're simply showing the greater wholenesses, or the grand divisions.)

Well, do you recognize that this is a valid system? It is just that — a system. Certainly it is valid, from the point of view as presented. Do you recognize what I am saying?

Yes.

That there are many ways of looking at it, and this is one way and a valid way. Is that what you're asking me?

Yes, and then I'm trying to get to a few points here. When Djwhal speaks of "that area that we don't speak of" or "The Rider" or "The Avatar from the Secret Place," he's speaking of Source.

Yes, "manifesting Source."

The difference between a full-fledged Creator and what Brian is — they're both ninth-dimensional, are they not?

Well, I consider the Creator able to use the ninth dimension as a tool, but not *of* the ninth dimension.

So possibly more of the tenth?

Well, it depends upon how you divide your dimensional pie; I would say that the Creator is *beyond* dimensions completely, but able to use them as a tool.

Is this what we strive for as part of our growth?

Eventually, yes. The dimensions are a tool.

I sometimes feel that I know why that is; I sense, and I feel very akin to that.

I'm sure you do, yes, certainly. And the goal, of course, is to have every part of you see that and every part realize that full integration of your Creatorship. Certainly you glimpse it and certainly you see it, but it's getting that all together so that it works constantly in sequential time or always in a balanced way — that's the goal.

So we go through this because we talk about twelve initiations. Beyond that there's not that much interest, because mankind really isn't that keen; they're not into that level of evolution. You have said to me that there are no initiations, really, beyond the Twelfth, but there are perceived levels. So when I look at the possibility of an individualized Source on a scale of 1 to 32 levels of Monad right up to Source, I see a vast area from the Twelfth Initiation to individualized Source. (Refer to the diagram, "Co-Creator and Creator Levels," pp. 228-29.)

All right, certainly — perhaps 340.

Levels?

Yes, beyond the Twelfth.

It's staggering, isn't it?

Yes, but not unexpected, if you consider that our Source is always evolving, always growing, always merging, always becoming. In fact, it's always escalating. The more you realize, the more there is to realize.

In the past, Vywamus, few (referencing our friend, Djwhal Khul) knew any-

thing about "that which we didn't speak of" — Source.

Yes.

You obviously have made a study because when Djwhal channeled his books through Alice Bailey, he said that even the Logos don't know where **The Rider on the White Horse** *is coming from.*

Well, in the fullest sense, he's right. *No one knows.* But, I have studied Source; I have postulated certain theories in regard to it, so that's what I'm giving you — these theories.

We're coming in this time for the synthesis of the Co-Creator levels with the First Ray, Third Ray, and the Twelfth Ray. Would that be correct?

That's a good way of looking at it; I agree with that.

I have some dates here. I'll just jump to the one date. On September 22, 1989, in Holbrook, Arizona, I was encompassed, or "cocooned" in red and gold; the fissures up there seemed to be New Earth, New World. I felt that I could have ascended. What in fact happened?

You would have, except that there's still some releasing to do emotionally.

All right. While we're on the subject, on September 25, 1989, two or three days later, there was a celebration for, presumably, what happened in Holbrook — an electrical display of color and great joy all night long.

Yes. Nice, wasn't it?

It was beautiful, but what was it?

Well, it was just that — a celebration. Actually, it wasn't anything personal, although one can allow a personal connotation to be woven from it. It was really a reflection from the Co-Creator level at the Creator Council — a celebration of realization, of expansion, of joy literally coming from that level.

Oh, isn't that wonderful!

Isn't it!

It was so joyful...unbelievable!

Yes.

But the night before, the evening of September 24, we went into Sedona and an incredible electric storm started when I brought in, let's just call it the I AM Presence. What happened then? It seemed that Sedona didn't want me there.

Well, I think that was perceived because there is a lot of adjustment going on, particularly at that period. It's a little better now in the Sedona area. A lot of readjustment. I think that sometimes when there has been an adjustment in an area, you haven't felt very welcome there. You see, I don't think that there's anything personal there, but because of past incidents it was personalized by you. There was an adjustment there. Sometimes you've said during an adjustment period, "I must leave; I'm not really wanted during this adjustment period." That's not true, but I think that's what you felt — this is emotional again.

From the point of view of not being a part of that adjustment process (and that's what's happened to you many times) you haven't felt a part of it or you felt literally pushed from it or that you were not supposed to be there or that it didn't want you. You see, that's the emotional response to it. That's very important for you. Can you see that you've split yourself? Now, I want you to take a look at this and do it later when you have some time, maybe talk about it with someone or more than one person you trust. What you've often done, as a service to Source, is to anchor in a Wholeness, a completeness. But then as this was anchored in there was always an adjustment, and while that was going on many times you didn't feel emotionally that you were a part of that adjustment process.

Saltspring Island, B.C. — this was really interesting — on July 17, 1989, and I felt that you were with me.

Mmm-hmm, yes.

It was a battle with what I perceived as the "fallen ones." If I could be removed from physicality, it would help the desperate stand, the Armageddon being fought as a last-ditch attempt on Earth. That was the feeling. What really did happen? We encountered a being that was very powerful.

Well, you were dealing with those that have kind of separated from the Light, and I think that they would like to have those who work with them to not be anchored or focused in physical existence, because physical existence is really a very powerful tool right now. It's a very powerful place to be.

It almost killed me...my heart started to pound.

Yes. The point is that staying in the physical was the best thing that you could do, and I think that you realize this.

Yes. I called Janet for this appointment because I felt that for the first time we had a wholeness with Soul and a whole night of Light. I think that you were there when Higher Self and Monad totally engulfed me.

Yes.

The body lit up and the energy was very high, so much so that when Glenda came into the room, it was all Light. So we are together, Soul and I; at least we're working together.

Oh yes, of course. And that's a big step, isn't it?

Yes, it is. The anchoring is not complete, but...

...coming along.

Okay. Have the Manu, Maitreya/the Christ, and El Morya been preparing for my energy as **The Rider on the White Horse** *that the Scriptures speak of? Please explain coming in to the Earth instead of just "reflecting in" to Earth, because Djwhal has said that in his estimation the energy was not going to come all the way in. It was going to do what it's always done, and come into the causal/mental level. But we're here now.*

Mmm-hmm, somewhat. I think it is important to recognize that this is a step-by-step process, that the Earth isn't ready, and that you aren't ready, my friend — both. So it's gone beyond — and this is wonderful! — what Djwhal had originally seen. It means that there has been more evolution — in yourself, within the Earth, and with all the other Co-Creators who are involved. Let me put it this way: the Earth has become a more encompassing tool within the Plan than first envisioned.

So are we step for step with the progressions that can be allowed?

Oh yes, and going *beyond*, let us say, pushing the outer boundaries of that, meaning that you're going beyond the probability levels as first envisioned by Djwhal. And that's good.

Well, the energies that come through at night — the other night we had what you used to call "the flopping electrical stream out there," and it kept me awake for 3-1/2 hours. I've never in my life — certainly not this life, and I doubt any other life — had so much energy come through! Just to touch the body at that point, you could feel the electricity, according to my friend. Is this some of the material finally starting to process that I have literally left hanging?

Yes, but again I would encourage you during that process to give some of that to the Co-Creator level.

It seemed to be going into the Earth.

But, *you* don't have to do it. You don't have to bring it through by yourself.

Well, I was so uncomfortable that I didn't do anything. My body was in convulsions. It was shaking!

That's what I'm telling you. If you give some of that to the other people who are around you — those who have chosen to — let them process some of that, too. Say to the Co-Creator level — address it to them, "Now, I need help with this." You know, it's not your role to do *all* of that. That's what's stressing your physical body.

Okay. I have to call upon the Co-Creator level. The lady that I'm with couldn't even touch the body, it was so...

Yes, I know. Well, you didn't give permission yet. You thought that that was *your* role, but it isn't — that's too much for you. You don't have to do it all. You've been cutting off from the very means to solve this energy intensity, and it's too much for you. You have a very strong structure, or you wouldn't still be here in it. You really feel that this is your role — to do it all. Remember, we've worked on the Co-Creator level; this is the next step in that — to allow through the heart, through surrendering, the Co-Creator level to help you with your role, knowing that you won't be failing or that you won't be doing anything inappropriate to others. You are simply allowing the Co-Creator level to share your strengths, and you to share their strengths. Listen to what I'm saying: You're trying to bring it in through *your* creative base, which is a very big one, but in relationship to other things it's still not as big as if you allow many, many, many Co-Creators to join you in the effort. That's the next step.

Okay. I have a profound fascination for Melchizedek, and more as the Avatar. I don't know whether or not you want to respond to this, my friend. Was Melchizedek the 33rd Avatar, the Christed One?

No.

Did he ever come in as the Christed One?

Not really. There have been some aspects. This is a very "Cosmic" Being, and only certain of his aspects have been somewhat a part of a few of the 35 avatars. I'm really being asked particularly not to say that. But never in the fullest sense. However, on another level, what you term the fourth level, you have been involved with him. I think that's more the level of awareness of your association with him.

It's interesting that the teachings of Akhnaton were not that dissimilar to his! But that would follow.

Yes, it is interesting.

Okay, so he would be universal?

Yes, very.

Very universal, and his responsibilities in the past; we've known him as the Father of Creation in the Bible — the Father, the Son, and the Holy Ghost. I think he was referenced before Earth knew Source as "the Father."

I would say that he symbolizes that, yes.

And his responsibilities?

Well, they would be in a symbolic or a reflected way those full responsibilities of the Father, whatever you consider them to be. And each particular Co-Creator would look at that a little differently. That's what's important.

This was before Source had actually been stepped down here, when so little was known.

Yes.

Is that accurate?

Yes, that's accurate.

When Melchizedek came into the physical as Nikola Tesla, the electrical inventor, did he use his "body for Ascension"?

Not really. There was very little of him there. We could call it the first joint of the little finger, about that much. And there was really only the focus of, let's say, "scientific breakthrough" present. There was not a great deal of balance because of that in any part of the four-body system. It is rather like one focus only; it wasn't meant to balance everything or to be a whole system. It was a probe within an existing system, if that makes sense to you.

Yes, it does. December 27, when I had that 3-1/2 hours of electrical energy, which literally caused my body to convulse, to shake — from that point on, I feel that anything that's in my auric field automatically seems to draw on me and to some extent seems to heal others. Now, whenever my friend gets energy backed up in the legs, just by touching I take it on myself, and I can transmute the pain quite quickly. What is it that's happening now — the auric field seems to be able to assist people, but sometimes I take it on?

Yes, I agree with that. Again, it's the same area. What you're doing is fine as long as you broaden the base. Just as Tesla was a probe within an existing larger effort, you could consider yourself to be a drawing out of old programmed material from others who are ready to release it. But you are stabilized by that whole Co-Creator level. Do you see that one, Brian? You are becoming more and more powerful, so powerful that what you need is the balance of the Co-Creator level in order not to burn up.

When aspects of self worked on Earth as St. Peter, was he not a healer at that time? It seems that Maitreya never really taught healing as the Christ.

I agree with that.

In his auric field — is it similar to what's happening to me now, the healing? The Bible says that even his shadow was able to heal.

Yes, but it differed with Peter — it wasn't that the Christ didn't teach it; it was that the Christ began a formatting of it as the Avatar, and then Peter interpreted that. Now, he had that direct contact with the Christ to rely on, and so he was much more grounded than you — can you see that? — because there was closer contact to the one who was formatting it, the Christ. So that's the difference, but it's the same process.

Is it my imagination, or am I actually able to heal?

No, it isn't your imagination. You *are* able to draw out the material that needs to be healed *when the person has released it*. But again, what needs to be done so that you can continue to be here physically is to broaden that creative base and allow, literally, the whole Co-Creator level to help whenever you receive all of that energy, not expecting your physical body to handle it by itself. You could look at it this way: You're trying to put too much current into the circuitry system of your physical body. It needs a broader base. Let some other physical bodies help to set up a system.

Well, we don't want to leave and then come back into physicality.

All right then, *listen*. Go over your tape. Recognize what I said about not feeling a part of the process. Work with that feeling that Sedona was rejecting you. Process that and then process this part, and I think that you can. You are on the home stretch. Perhaps it is an intense time also because when you reach a certain level of magnetism, then it invokes the next step. And the next step — we've said it in many ways — is the full creative base that we call the Co-Creator level.

Vywamus, when Glenda and I returned from Australia, we were told that we had increased our "entourage" by 28 entities. We could feel that these energies were around, trying to get my attention. They would turn off the TV at certain times when energies were coming in, turn on or turn off the lights. What really happened?

Well, you brought some "friends" back with you, you might say (chuckling), and some of them were playful, part of the Angelic Kingdom. You might think about this: The Angels were never able to come into the third dimension, but they *are* able to come into the fourth dimension. And yes, they have some curiosity — especially, we could call it, "electrical" curiosity. Some of them are busily exploring some of the wiring systems on the planet, some of them are interested in electrical devices, and some of them are interested in the circulatory system with your physical structures. They had never really explored that on the Earth, but they're very busy doing so now! Beyond that, there was a power invocation that let it occur. Perhaps that helps you.

That happened in Australia?

Yes, and you provided a fourth-dimensional format for them to function within.

An invocation, a reciprocal invocation?

Well, bringing in an energy presence, if you will, or what I'm calling power, that allowed the Angelic Kingdom to explore the electrical circuits on your planet, particularly in that area brought in by you.

And my body?

Yes, *and* your body. Did you feel that?

Yes. They must be wondering how the body handles it all! (Laughing)

(also laughing) Yes, exactly! It was more of a "My goodness, isn't this interesting?"

Oh, that's interesting! When I return to Source, how does this happen? Do you see me staying in the Co-Creator level for awhile, or going back into the Source? How would you view me?

As balancing the Co-Creator level, and then moving beyond it. It takes as long as it takes.

March 3, 1990

We've referenced Djwhal before, who has indicated that **The Rider on the White Horse** *would not come closer than the causal body — we've discussed that before. My coming into the physical was not prophesied. Has it posed a problem for the Hierarchy and Sanat Kumara, with that energy coming in probably more directly than was prophesied?*

It is not valid to say that you posed a problem for the system. You posed more of a problem for yourself than for the system.

In the past, in Egyptian times, would that be what I'm picking up?

Yes, I think so. It was a controversy within *you*, though, not a problem for the system, if you consider this to be a divine system — and it is certainly a reflection of the monadic level system. The one set up by Sanat Kumara is a reflection of a basic Source-level system. That's why he goes through the training that he does — to be absolutely clear, and I mean *absolutely clear as far as the system is concerned*. Because it is a divine system, it takes in every contingency. But your beliefs about the physical haven't been clear. It has seemed to be a limited place, and so you really thought that by bringing a lot of energy you would gum up the system. No way! You can't do that. But there is a Plan, and there is a Divine Order. You didn't honor that, not because you *meant* not to but because of your beliefs. There is a system. The Christ is the one who embodies for the Earth the transformational energy, that Christed energy. And that's the system that's been set up. So bringing all of your energies through that and through the all-over formula of Sanat Kumara *is* "going through the system." That's what Djwhal was telling you — in effect, "overshadowing the system."

Are we doing that?

Yes, more and more. You have literally always done it. What I said was that you were pushing up against not doing it, or pushing up against that "ring passeth not," if you will, even on this level. You can't *really* go inside of it — that doesn't work. But you can *believe* that you do or you can pressurize yourself or push up against the guidelines of the system. Then you get what *you* got — some trouble with your physical body. And that's not only *this* physical body; perhaps on another level it is difficulty in using the divine structure that you had chosen, whether or not it is a physical body.

The point being, whatever the assignment was, as **The Rider,** *we're doing it, and it's fine.*

Yes. But you are asking me about what happened, and I was trying to help you to understand that. It's always been fine, actually.

Symbolically, when Djwhal wrote of **The Rider,** *he said that I would be seen but not understood, as an aerial event. I was doing a little channeling, and I picked up that that would have been when I was a youngster, that the Battle of Britain was the turning point, as I saw it, the planes perceived as the Darker and Lighter Forces. Do you see that?*

Yes, in about 1943 is where I see it.

About '43?

Mmm-hmm.

Well, that's after the Battle of Britain.

But I would agree with you that the Battle of Britain was perhaps leading up to the choice. The crux of the matter, the very point — it was like standing on a mountain; you could go this way or you could go that way — was on January 29, 1943.

That was the pivotal point.

Yes. You would already have been picking up the energy in the Battle of Britain, I'm sure. That was already working.

We've touched on this before—my accident when I was younger, hit on the head. We said that another aspect came in and pushed. I was left for dead, actually. So it wasn't a Walk-in.

Not in the traditional sense, but there is some aspect of that. You know, I'm trying to stretch *all* of you to understand truly that the popularized version of a Walk-In doesn't always apply to everyone; there are other ways to walk in. We could say a probable self; that's another way of putting it. Does that help a little?

When you needed it, it was there, so there are always, within the Plan, alternatives that can come in and help you to do what you've agreed to do, my friend. And that's what occurred. You needed it; *you* brought in the resources — and I wouldn't call it *just* monadic level, but it's like you could blend another stream of energy that would be another probable reality which included all levels. I would say that it's more like you brought that in.

My wife noticed the difference.

Yes, I'm sure.

She also said that while I was unconscious in the hospital it was Christ who visited her. The room lit up, and he said that I would be fine. Was that the case?

Your energy was coming through, certainly. It would have been clear if one had the eyes to see it.

What was my relationship as Zoroaster/Zarathustra? Or was I Zarathustra or did I come in?

For awhile.

I was Zarathustra for awhile?

(Vywamus chuckles.)

Isn't that interesting? I know I was.

You were that energy for awhile, about seven years.

Isn't that interesting!

But then you had other fish to fry, in a sense, and so you didn't stay with that.

I left and someone else took over?

Yes.

I have the feeling that I knew the energy that we now know as Jesus/Sananda, as a disciple during that period.

Yes.

Jesus was a disciple of Zarathustra/Zoroaster?

Yes.

It was a very happy time for me, that seven years?

Let's say there were other things to do. And it was only meant that you touch into that for awhile.

And I left Earth at that time?

Yes, for awhile.

We have referenced before that I came to the physical — "from the top of the highest mountain" is a direct quote, and "to the lowest valley" — and used from time to time the Galactic Core as Soul. Now, that didn't infer that that was going to be made easy for me, because it wasn't. I can certainly testify to that.

Yes.

Why would I, having only recently come into the physical, needed to use Soul any earlier?

Well, because it's a part of the Whole, and you were trying to leave it out.

From the causal body (Higher Mind), I would have still used Soul?

The integrative part of it, the learning of it, the part that you would have assimilated from using it — if you *had,* which you didn't always. So there was not a complete assimilation from not having done that. You see? It would be like you couldn't digest properly because some of the enzymes had been left out of the system, the enzymes that you developed through physical existence having been administered by the Soul. Do you see that?

Yes, yes. So are we doing a little better with the physical?

Oh, much better!

What's happening with me? Has Soul started to pull out, or have we agreed to stay?

Well, I think that there is some choice there, even more than before. Since about January 20, 1990, I see you again considering whether or not you're going to stay.

You told me that I hadn't really prepared sufficiently, at least for the aspects that I want to take with me, when I thought that I could have done my Ascension up in Holbrook, Arizona, back in September. You said, no, that I still had some emotional clearing to do. We've looked at that. I've gone back to Sedona, and there doesn't seem to be that terrible reaction.

It's better, isn't it?

It's a little better. Tell me, my friend, what you see.

I see someone who has a choice here. Now, let me tell you what I think this choice is composed of: I think that you can choose to leave, and it will be a (chuckle) "no-fault divorce"!...No, not exactly — that was a joke! What I mean is, I think that you can consider yourself through with this planet rather soon, if you wish. But in my opinion, the other choice, of staying for awhile (and I know that this is pulling you back and forth) means that you could finish up *all* of universal physical existence through what you're doing now.

That's what I want to do!

Yes, I know.

Are you helping me with that?

Oh, of course, of course we are. The other choice, though, would pull you into some things that you are interested in on the other levels, and we've talked about this extensively on the inner planes. And so it's not simple; it's several things. First of all, your concentration on or your balance of this physical structure, although better, is still, my friend, a little minimal, you know. Can you (you can, of course; but in the time that is appropriate?) balance out this physical structure enough so that it will serve you for quite awhile? I would say yes, you can, but you will have to give it quite a bit of attention. And then you will have to really concentrate on what physical existence really means to you. I mean quite a program of psychologically delving very deeply into your relationship with physical existence and your relationship with the Earth — as, of course, within the Co-Creator level.

So there really needs to be an opening there. That opening is coming along, but I would say that it's only at this time about 20%. This isn't negative; I'm not telling you that you aren't doing well because the fact that you've made a 20% opening to me is remarkable; it's in this last year. But it would have to open, I think, quite a bit more in order for you to be consciously aware of what needs to be done in physicality to keep this body functioning. You can continue to progress. There's no reason, in my opinion, why you can't get to that level of 50% where you will see what needs to be done and complete *all* physical existence. But it will take quite a bit of concentration on that, and you require dedication. The dedication is where I'm not quite sure what will happen. It doesn't mean that you aren't dedicated; you are. But I'm talking about dedicated to the Soul, to the Soul's role here on the Earth. That's where the dedication has to come in, and you aren't always yet aware of that, but you can get aware enough if you wish. You see, it's like you suddenly have a partner, and you've always validated that partner, but you're not quite sure that it's an equal partnership yet, which it is.

When you refer to "me," you're talking about the Monad because...

I'm talking about *all* of the consciousness that you're bringing here to the Earth.

Yes, I know what you mean.

Good.

If I couldn't stay, could I do an Ascension now?

Very probably. You've done them rather easily, but I don't think that you would be through.

But have I ever done one from the physical instead of from the causal body?

Yes, you have, but it's not complete for you. Now, that's hard to explain.

So what we've talked about is what I'd like to do, whether there are twelve or twenty-four aspects. From my perspective, we would probably feel better with twenty-four — to "go" with all of them. In the past we haven't done that, have we? We haven't taken all aspects.

You've ignored all aspects of the Soul.

And still have done an Ascension?

Yes, and that's quite remarkable.

How do you do that?

Very carefully!! (they both laugh). I don't know. No, really, it's because of the strengths of the monadic level. This method hasn't served you very well, and that's why it's difficult to remain in a physical structure and why they've burned out on you time after time after time after time, and why you can't stay in a particular place until you really finish up. There is a need now — and you're beginning to see this — to give physical existence equal billing.

Yes, I am. It's because you said in September that I wasn't quite ready emotionally, you felt. Plus, we're not anchored enough. Well, what happened when I broadened the base on that "lamp" (which was your analogy, that the lamp was too broad for the base) with Co-Creators?

It's better, isn't it? A lot better.

Are there tens of thousands who are helping now? There seem to be.

Of course; and you've always had that, but you didn't validate it.

But the base is quite substantial.

Yes, that's right.

It's just that triggering that next level of energy is also quite substantial.

But the next step for you, now that you feel that the base is larger, is to let the base shine the Light back up through your physical structure.

I'm starting to do that!!

I know. That's the next step.

(very enthusiastically) I'm starting to do that, and I can feel the Earth, everything, coming up this way through the body! Is that valid? And it comes right up and includes the Soul Star about six inches above my head!

Well, that's fine, yes, because that is the stabilizing factor. That is what will allow you to stay until you've completed with physicality.

The feeling that I have about our discussions on the inner planes is that it might be better to stay for a little while.

That's what I think will stretch you, too. It's what is important for you. I like what you're saying, I do, and I agree with it. It would be my choice for you, but I wouldn't tell you that until you had stated it yourself. Let people support you through *their* greatness, and that will stabilize you. My advice at this time, if you wish to stay here, would be to put most of your attention on receiving that support from the Earth and from the Co-Creator level. Their strengths will help you to understand and to gain a perspective of how to integrate all of what the Earth represents in the Co-Creator level, as reflected into what humanity represents within you.

Okay. Can you call upon anyone now to look at how many times I was a pharaoh?

Well, it depends upon whether you look at the full lifestream or these pieces. Once, fully; six other times where you touched in briefly.

Ikhnaton was as complete a monadic energy as one could bring in at that time?

Well, I think that you see it that way.

You don't?

I see it as much more complex than that; there are several other components of it. As I said, you cannot go outside of the system, so certainly, you brought in a monadic possibility that was not there before that time. Let's put it that way.

And any of the other pharaohs? Did Ikhnaton do an Ascension?

Not in the traditional sense.

(laughing) There we go again! You must have fun watching this one!

Yes, I do!

Not in the traditional sense. Any of the other pharaohs?

Several ascended, yes.

Ever as a Christian? Did Peter ascend?

Again, not from the traditional point of view in that experience. There were later some experiences that we could call an Ascension, certainly.

Related to a Christian focus?

Yes.

Is it one who is commonly known?

Not very.

In the West or the East?

Greek Orthodox — what became the Greek Orthodox Church.

Mahatma: We reference Origen as this being, as an example of "coming from the highest mountain." From our perspective, the more lowly evolved the energy, the greater chance of physical Ascension, meaning that the more grounded the energy and the greater the affinity with the Co-Creator level, the greater the opportunity we had to ascend physicality! Thus, as you can see, only the Source/Creator level was not able to enter the heavy vibration of Earth until June 14, 1988. All representatives of this energy had no difficulty entering physicality (because they are physical, or not yet seventh-dimensional), for they were not only able to work from the White Lodge of Sirius but were also able to ascend (58 times), although we were never balanced enough to take the complete physical body with us — the opportunity simply was not available. (No one has been able to do a completed spiritual Ascension on this planet prior to this time, as the vibration of the Earth simply disallowed anything other than the Ascension of the etheric body, so there is no fault here.)

Many times the Creator level tried to enter physicality. The one from the past (as you perceive the past) that we talk about is King Akhnaton/Ikhnaton, who was a Cosmic Avatar with many other alternate realities assisting. The Creator level, fortunately, has had a wonderfully balanced representation on the senior level of the White Lodge...for we, the **Mahatma**, should not push the Creator level onto physicality without stepping down through all other levels.

Vywamus, you once spoke of the disciple who came through the Christed energy. You referenced St. Peter as more galactic than monadic. What was the reason for that?

His view of life, his overall life, fit more into my estimation of the galactic level. Now, that certainly isn't a criticism.

No. Less universal, though, in his view.

More specific, in his view, which again is not necessarily "less than" anything. It's a greater focus, which sometimes is extremely important and very helpful.

Mahatma: One should remember that what was has no intrinsic value anymore other than as points of reference. St. Peter, Zarathustra, Origen, and many others were simply physical probes from the same Council of Twelve for this quadrant of this galaxy, and senior members of the White Lodge, which is galactic in expression and a very helpful aspect of **The Rider on the White Horse (Mahatma)**. The energies on Earth now that were Peter include a tiny woman in Peru, a yogi, and the teacher called Sai Baba. Know that each of these beings is a physical probe of that energy flow and representative of that galactic senior member of the White Lodge of Sirius.

So basically I've come in to look at all Rays. St. Peter was Second Ray, I believe.

Yes.

That's interesting. I was buried alive once as a pharaoh — you talked about this. Was that the one who brought in the ankh?

Yes, as a matter of fact, it was.

How many lives have I spent in the physical and on Earth?

Well, I can give you the "whole" lives. One thing that's happened to you is that sometimes you pressurized yourself and the structure so much that you yelled for help, and someone else would take over that life. It's happened quite a lot. So there are a lot of *pieces* of lives — but at least twelve years at a time, on the average. (They both burst out laughing.)

There's been a bit of that, hasn't there?

There have been about 1400.

And on all planets.

That's the Earth. You would multiply that by about 10 in your case, and you would get the number of physical lives (and that's rather low) on *all* planets. I would say that you could multiply it again times 5 and get more of an average for others.

Mahatma: *As an example for mankind to better understand what became of the energies who chose to assist on the Earth as part of the Christ Consciousness, the following article, also from Vywamus channeled by Janet McClure, might help you to comprehend the roles we assume and why!*

Where Are the Disciples?
November 1989

Can we pick up anything on Andrew? Is any of his energy on earth?

Yes, there is an aspect of this being. As you know, Andrew is not the correct name of this being anymore, but it's as good as any for this purpose. Let's call it Andrew, then, the entity of the monadic level. There is an aspect of that stream of consciousness that is currently in Brazil.

Well known?

No, the purpose of it isn't to be well known.

No. "Well known" in the sense of...

...Visible on the Earth. But certainly a being who deals with healing, and certainly a very important transformational aspect of the New Age. Perhaps rather than "visible" let us call it purposefully integrated into that healing on the Earth. It really doesn't want to be visible; that's not the purpose of this particular aspect.

John the Baptist?

Again, if we equate that to the full stream of energy, there's only a little at this time (I'm being asked to state that it's practically all inner planes), and there's a current letting go of that energy as far as the Earth is concerned. I'm being asked not to give any further information.

All right...Thomas.

Yes. That energy is partially involved with the Earth. There is an aspect of it in China, the northern part of China near the Nepal/Tibetan area, and again rather a simple life. Now, I think that it's important to recognize that some of these beings have certainly finished with their Earth experience, but at this particular time they've been asked to come here. It's almost as if some of them will put their finger down into physical existence in a stabilizing manner. Because this energy is, in a sense, very conceptual — it has a very conceptual nature — there is a stabilizing influence on the Earth from them. So a being lives on your Earth who is part of this energy.

Mary Magdalene?

Yes, that energy is very much a part of your Earth yet.

And she is in New York? Have I met her?

Well, I believe that you've met an aspect of that energy, but there's more than one, my friend. In fact, in one sense there are twelve. That's important, because this being is truly dedicated. Let us say that her Soul and the beginning of her connection to the monadic level have at this time as their main focus the transformation of the Earth. There is a very encompassing involvement with the Earth now.

Were Master Jesus and she lovers?

In my opinion they were, but not in the sense that you mean it.

Did they have children?

Not in the sense that you are giving it. There is a mystery here...there is a creative effort that someone literally embodied, but not in the sense that you mean it.

Mother Mary, Mother of God — what a title!

Isn't that an interesting title? Well, you know, this is much more compre-hensive than people have seen. Certainly, there was a physical being who was referred to as Mary, but this is rather like the Christ Consciousness that all these beings, with their strengths, assisted in. This is a stream of energy that is a part of that Christ Consciousness energy — an agent or an aspect of it, you might say, that is literally a part of the transformational energies of the Earth. Do you realize and recognize that? So we're really talking about bringing into a physical format a whole stream of energy that is part of the transformational process. As far as the entity who was Mary and her involvement with the Earth, I believe that it is no longer a part of the Earth.

Yes, it's more in an astral heaven?

In a Hierarchial sense, there is still a connection, as the being known as "Quan Yin."

Phillip.

That's a very interesting energy — it brings in a lot of galactic response. The galactic level is the current frequency rate of this particular energy, but it has a reflection into Earth that is rather awesome. It's an important energy for the Earth, but not as much as reflected physically.

Is the energy similar to Peter?

You would have to define "similar to." Certainly, in a divine sense, it is similar, but its function is a little bit different. It has a conceptual framework that the Peter energy doesn't have. The Peter energy has more of a heart-cen-tered energy. The "framing in" of the New Age possibilities is what is being assisted by this energy.

Very interesting...Matthew.

This is certainly an important energy on your Earth. I would say that in one sense, this is a genesis energy — one generates the connection to a particu-lar opportunity. It would be like someone standing here and introducing two people — it makes an opportunity available. And yes, there is some involve-ment still on the physical level — not a whole lot, but once in awhile, as I view it. You know, I'm looking at the full sequence of it — and there is still some physical involvement of that energy here.

The Master, the great teacher in India who was part of the Peter energy, is that Sai Baba?

I wouldn't care to comment on that.

All right, I'll use my own intuition.

Please do.

The energies that were Peter...are they aspects of Brian?

Yes, and if you can visualize the greater picture, it becomes a seed of something greater. You are always seeding the learning that you've had into a greater potential, or format. It's not that you forget what has been learned, but that you recognize that it's only the beginning of something greater. So you never lose it. It's not scattered; it's integrated, but it's expansive also. That's about the best way that I can answer it.

When you speak about the Peter energy being dispersed, as it were, that would confuse mankind. It's difficult to comprehend that an energy is decentralized and put here and put there. You're saying that that's not true.

Well, I'm saying that there is a decentralization process during physicality, but *after* physicality there is again a bringing together of this point of view that's been a focus. The focus is important. It's been focused into different perspectives so that one can gain a true understanding of what each perspective is. It's only a very beginning, at the Ascension point, beginning to integrate all of those points back together again. It's getting it to the point where it fits together again, to that monadic level — but that's only the beginning, at the point of Ascension.

Simon...a zealot?

Yes, the energy there is very much woven into the Earth right now — extremely important in the Earth — very much a key in the transformation of the Earth.

Really?

Yes, very much.

And Simon Peter is more a Love focus.

Yes.

Maitreya/The Christ.

It's kind of interesting to put into a framework of understanding what this relationship really is. But simplifying it this way: that Source is a Light, and that Light is refracting and coming from various points. When *you*, as the Source energy, and Maitreya look at each other, the reflection becomes rather complete. So there's a completing energy as these two unite. But that doesn't mean that it's restrictive at all, and it doesn't mean that there isn't more beyond that. I hope that helps.

Yes. Mark.

This energy has gone deeply into the core of the Earth, been dispersed there, and has come up through a completing process to where it has literally gone through a transformational process that allows it to manifest now on the physical plane in many, many ways and many, many locations. But it went through a core transformation first. This is, again, an important energy on your Earth. You see, it's part of the Plan, with those who came in through the Christed energies and were thus added to the Earth in certain ways. Now, some of them made other choices, as you've seen through what we've discussed, and are no longer a part of the Earth, but they *were* part of it for a time.

St. Paul, of course, is Hilarion now. That's an interesting energy.

And part of it is physical now.

Really? Would there be any truth to that energy being a youngster in England, a young male child with a special blueprint?

I think that is a reflection of something else. Something is really going on there...let's see. No, I'm not going to say any more about that. I've been asked not to. But this is not what I was referring to with Hilarion. There is another energy, and he is — I could give you the physical location but I'm being asked not to. You might say the birthing process is just going on, so it's something new.

And England again, with the Revelations John — is there any truth to that?

There's a beginning of an understanding there; it isn't complete yet.

And we know about Bartholomew, because that's the energy that's a very interesting story, that one, extremely interesting.

Yes, a part of that energy is known as Mohammed and later as Patrick Henry.

Matthias.

That's also an extremely interesting one. As is the Master Jesus, this energy is very involved in the bringing together of many, many religions and so is in the process of founding at this time on the physical plane a religious focus (it's interesting; it's just at the very beginning level) that I feel will be a transformational vehicle to allow many of the religions to come together.

James and John.

James has begun a rather encompassing point that will become much more apparent as the New Age begins — a New Age leader of great renown coming into his own here on the Earth, and will be very widely accepted as a world leader. It seems to be that that is part of his gift to humanity.

John being supportive of this, but perhaps also, we could say, an upper octave of it. There a very mystical relationship between the two of them. We could say then that John is to be a galactic point of view of what James will represent. This future — in sequential time — is what is beginning here by the year 2000.

Judas.

Is in New York, a business person.

What level is that energy? Is it monadic? Galactic?

How about all of the above.

It's quite a highly evolved energy?

Certainly. It's a reflection, though, of every level, certainly.

Okay. There really should be no judgment of this being. I never felt any.

No, there shouldn't. There's really a role-playing here.

Exactly. That's a lovely way to put it.

March 3, 1990 (continued)

November the 4th, 1994 — a possible axis shift of the Earth. What are your views about this event?

Well, I didn't give that; Djwhal gave that. The point is that I haven't put too much attention on it. The last time that I did, I was still giving about an 80% chance of that event. There will still be pockets of survival and so forth. So it's not, it seems to me, even — I don't want to talk about it anymore, because the Earth is at a rather critical point this year in regard to it.

You have said that energies such as myself can stabilize the Earth.

As you allow *it* to stabilize *you*...

As I allow it to stabilize me?

Yes.

Are these the issues that could change that?

Yes!!

Okay.

And that I would not have agreed with a few years ago. I would have said no. In fact, I *did* say no to the possibility of changing the outcome, that this was an event that was really being rather adamantly invoked. I don't agree with myself anymore (he chuckles).

Well, we all grow, don't we?

Well, I didn't see as much as I've seen since the Harmonic Convergence. I've seen certain doors open for humanity.

My left eye — are my friends working on me electrically? I have flashing light, sort of a strobe light coming from my left eye. What is that?

It's the Angelic Kingdom trying to stabilize a particular input from the

Galactic Core, a direct stimulation that's coming into the auric field.

Do you like this with me?

It's not worrying me. I realize that it's something that's working out. You're trying to stabilize. It's like a plug that is sparking.

The day before yesterday, Vywamus, I was looking over a fence — and I wasn't particularly mentally focused, which was lovely — and a humming-bird came right out of nowhere right up to me.

Yes, the hummingbirds are very special. They are one of the oldest of your birds. Certainly, they're fourth-dimensional creatures, so the fact that they've lived on your third-dimensional Earth is remarkable. They are also quite galactic in nature. So I would say that the bird was sent to stabilize the etheric area, particularly in this area around your eye, and was attracted to...

...the front of my face. It stayed there quite awhile, and then it went off for awhile and then came back.

They're very beautiful, and quite connected to the Angelic Kingdom.

Do I have to make the body for Ascension in order to be integrated sufficiently and be finished with all that is universal (physical)?

You do, because it is such an important point.

I've never taken my body with me?

No.

Okay (sounding rather puzzled).

You don't know how yet.

You view me so clearly. How much more is there to do if I'm able to stay?

Well, what I view is that you're standing in the doorway and looking at the various aspects of physical existence. When you *draw them into your heart*, my friend, when you realize what they truly are, then you will be able to do it. You know, for me that's probably the hardest thing to say — what needs to be done. What needs to be done is to realize that *all of the aspects of physical existence are very much a part of you.* How do you do that? Many of you do that through the programs — for example, the Intensives where we go into all of that. So how soon it comes about depends on how you work with it. You're moving along all right with it; I think that you've made great strides during the last year. But you're about to enter a deeper level of dealing with it, and it is going to take some help. I mean you can't really do this all by yourself. That's why you've never done it, because at the point where you needed help the most was where you felt that you had to do it yourself because of this Creator/Co-Creator-level thing. And then you didn't, so the key — you *couldn't*. Always we need — and it's always symbolic — to give our hand to someone who is a Co-Creator, who understands more clearly in that particular area, and they can help us. It's like a symbol that we need to make in order to step off of physical existence.

In sequential time, how long would it take for a probationary member of physicality to become a fully integrated Creator?

Well, now you're mixing apples and oranges and pineapples and grapes. Someone who's just coming into the physical generally needs from 2000 to 2500 lives on the Earth and then perhaps 10 to 20 other planets, each with that many lives, to integrate to the point where they can step out of physical existence. There are all the other levels which lie in between the physical and the Creator level — the reaching of the integrated Co-Creator level. And then there is a period that I've called the Co-Creator level, like entering a university — and there are many, many levels of training until we finish that. And then you go into the Creator state. So there are many many steps and levels. The goal is not to reach the Creator state. *The goal is to have all of the steps in between* — because that, in a sense, *is* the Creator state, the *steps*.

And I'm close to having completely integrated physical existence.

You're cosmically close.

Would I include human beings now in my Source? Would you come and work with me if I had my own Source?

My friend, I don't want to discuss what you'll do as a Source because I think that you have your plate full trying to figure out what to do as a Co-Creator.

Oh yes, I know I do.

The answer to your question is, I'd *love* to play in your backyard!

May 3, 1990

Good morning, Brian. Well, good! An Electrical Day. I think that's just what the doctor ordered! (He chuckles) Did you get the message?

I got the message! Yes. And I think that the body will handle it.

Oh, I think so too. But I think that it is rather important for you to keep working with the electrical aspect. I think that it will help the overall body and its integration and its assimilation.

All right, good. Let's have one question, and then we'll begin on this.

Well, it's a very important question, from my perspective.

I know it is.

It really relates more than anything else to this chart (referring to "Co-Creator and Creator Levels," pp. 228-29). This was the original chart, and I really want to know that if this is the Twelfth Initiation, are these Levels — the Galactic Logos, the Solar Logos, the Planetary Logos, including the Universal — before that Twelfth Initiation? Can we use that as a guideline?

Yes, I would say so.

Then where is the Co-Creator Council of Twelve? If we relate this here to the Monad and then into the Creator...or this here, from the Monad into the Creator as being 340 Levels...which we touched on. Look at two things: Where would the Co-Creator Council of Twelve be? And are there Members in the Co-Creator Council who are not Directors?

There are Associates. I would consider the Co-Creator Council to be an enlargement of that.

So it's right in the Creator level.

Well, it's right in association with it.

So it's a reflection again?

Yes.

Is it beyond the Monad?

No, it is the fully developed Monad in its responsibility. The directorship, in connection with the Co-Creator level, is like a career of the Monad.

Oh, that's an interesting way to look at it. All right...so this Level then is as close to Source as one could conceive?

Yes. I would say that it radiates out, and we could say that radiating point comes into everything else. Do you see that?

So it's not beyond the Monad, obviously, but it is a very senior monadic level.

Exactly.

Like on a scale of 340 levels, we'll say, from this to this. If you had a symbolic number that you could reflect to intuitively, what would that number be? If it's 340 levels of Monad up into the Director level of the Co-Creator Council, those Directors from 340 to Source, that number would be approximately...

Well, we have to kind of reframe that because there is what I call a Co-Creator University. Do you remember that?

Yes.

And so within that 340 there is a beginning point where you are studying to BE that Director of the Co-Creator Council. I would say that, of your 340 levels after the Twelfth Initiation, we would have to put, oh...25 levels within that University. So it doesn't enlarge it, but it shows you what part of it is made up of.

All right. So approximately, then, if there are 340, or 7x7x7, as a mirrored reflection as you look at it, how many levels would there then be (including those 25) into what we would look at as being Source? I know that it's very difficult to reflect, because there are probably levels beyond that.

Yes, and the answer to that is, "I don't know." I consider the "wheel" of the Twelve Directors of the Co-Creator Council — the overall wheel itself — to be the Source. The I AM Presence is as directed. The flow of the energy/Rays from the wheel is that I AM Presence. I wouldn't consider it to be the Source Itself, except as it is differentiated and as it flows.

All right. So when we go through this Co-Creator Council — we'll call that Source or the I AM Presence because I don't know what else to do. It's really beyond the human condition, as it were. But just to talk about it symbolically, we're going through that Co-Creator level and then we're calling this the Twelfth Initiation...the Universal...the Galactic...the Solar...the Planetary. I know that it's not quite correct, but I don't know quite how else to bring it in. Do you see that?

Yes, it's a good differentiation. It takes many levels and condenses them, and I feel that that's not bad. In fact, for the purposes of this book, it's quite representative. (Refer to the diagram "The Seven Councils of Twelve," p. 227.)

Now, is all of mankind inextricably involved with the Co-Creator Council of Twelve? If you look at that as being the I AM Presence, and if you look at all manifested beings, both physical and nonphysical — what we call Creation — there's nothing outside of that. Would that be true?

That's right, yes. Nothing *manifested* outside of that.

Okay. Then every aspect of Creation is part of one of those Directors or Rays for this Cosmic Day?

Yes.

There's nothing outside. So when one looks at their ultimate monadic condition, they have to reflect — mirrored from one of those Directors.

That's right.

Why do I feel, though, that I'm already part of that I AM Presence?

Because you *are* a part of the I AM Presence.

All right. Now the Planetary Government is, then, one step down, as it were, from the Planetary Logos with Kuthumi/Maitreya as the head of the Planetary Government in between the Planetary Logos, Sanat Kumara, and the fully manifested Soul? Or is the fully manifested Soul really embodying this Planetary Government? {We're studying the illustration "Co-Creator and Creator Levels.")

Yes, I would say that it is. It is part of the structure that has formed the Logos. Sanat Kumara has used the energies of *all* of the Souls that will ever manifest, ever *have*, ever *will*, or *are* manifesting, to create the structure around this planet.

Another reason why you identify with this part (he points to the Undifferentiated, Unmanifested Source in the illustration "Co-Creator and Creator Levels") is that you have a lot of energy tied up in it that was meant to be a part of this stream of consciousness that we talked about here. I'm going to give you a figure that may blow you apart a little bit: You have 83% of your life force still in the unmanifested state, still tied up in the Source Itself. Now, how much does that leave, Brian?

Seventeen percent. (He laughs a little incredulously.)

(NOTE: As you can see from the chart, we have increased our life force to 59% as of December 1993.)

Seventeen percent only that you're working with — now, *that's* why you identify with it so strongly.

It must have been terrible then, because we've really come a long way.

It might be interesting to start bringing some of that out; but the reason that you haven't — and this can be part of our Electrical Day — is that you've reserved your chair. You've said, "This is where I sit; this is where my 83% is." This fits you exactly! This is what we might call the fully manifested Co-Creator level, or the Co-Creator Council, as you are terming it. This is the chair that you need to put it in, the Co-Creator Council of Twelve; but you still have it over here in the Unmanifested Source.

That *does* shock me...I thought...

It's not terrible. It just means that you have a lot more potential to bring down. But as you do, it's going to change the way you look at everything, because you will have more life force in manifestation than *not* in manifestation. This is why the close association with Source, because of the beliefs that say, "I must leave it here because that's Who I Am." But you were given an assignment. It wasn't meant that you should leave it all here, in Source. I'm not saying that one can't leave a little energy there, but this is the package of energy of life force that is to *evolve that Co-Creator level.* You can't do it with 17%, obviously, not in the full way that you want. And so you keep relating to, let's call it, the fully developed Creator. Why? Because that's where all of your energy is. See that? It's important, isn't it?

So you have to pull it into the process first, this step-by-step process, and then it will eventually circle around to where you want it. You would like to have it in this Creator level, and it will be, I promise you that. But it has to go through the loop of the Co-Creator first. That's another way of looking at this, and perhaps it's helpful.

*Yes, shocking but helpful! (They chuckle.) **Vywamus, when we say that the average physical being will have approximately 2500 lives on as many as 20 planets, then that could be 50,000 lives. How many planets sustain the physical, or the Adam Kadmon body, in this universe?***

About 80% of those.

How many planets, approximately, in this Cosmic Day?

There are *billions* of them.

That sustain the Adam Kadmon body?

Yes!

In this Cosmic Day?

Yes!

Really?! (His throat chakra gets a little choked up at this point.) So in this Cosmic Day...

Yes. Everything that is manifested, everything that is physical and non-physical is a part of this Cosmic Day. Anything that's manifested will be pulled back during the Cosmic Night to begin again then.

And that constitutes this Source?

That's *one day* of this Source, *one day* of Its experience.

It's beyond the mind.

Yes, of course it's beyond the mind. But you see, it's even more than that. For example (and he wouldn't mind me telling you), I've just talked to a young man who is integrating 27 *universes* into his Soul now (we remind you again that the physical universes constitute only 10% of this Cosmic Day), so it's not just *one* universe many times — it is *many* universes that are being integrated at this particular time, right now, on the Earth. And if you consider that to be an *untold* number of physical expressions, just untold numbers, then we could add to that the probable realities, which we are beginning to go into now, too. So the numbers are not really important here. What *is* important is that there is so much potential that there is now an *unlimited* amount of potential that is being addressed. That's how you get in touch; when you have so much that you can't really integrate it, then it *becomes unlimited*. That's the only way that you *can* integrate it.

*So **The Rider** or **The Avatar of Synthesis**, as they call it, is this a Co-Creator synthesis for the universe?...or the Galactic Core?*

The Galactic Core, this quadrant of this galaxy. So now, Brian, an important exercise for you is to visualize yourself letting out some of this reserve energy from the Undifferentiated Source...but *gradually*, Brian. Don't try to bring all of it down in five minutes, please — or we won't have you on the physical plane!. You don't want to do that. What you want to do is to set up an entryway so that you can ask your Soul to bring into your physical the amount of this energy that it can use, so that the body can handle it! Let the body monitor it; it's been *trying* to get it. It's a wonder, from that point of view, that you've ever been on the physical level at all! That is quite amazing that you could do it with this amount of life force. It's a finer energy; it makes you much more sensitive. The fact that you have done it with only this amount of energy shows what a good Creator you really are. So now let's move it through the system, but *gradually, slowly*, and let others help you with that. It's going to take awhile because you have set up areas and ways of *not* doing it. You're going to need realization sessions; you're going to need to look at that to bring it in, but do it slowly.[1]

February 14, 1990

All right, Brian, are you ready, my friend? I think that the only level that you really are aware of, that you're focusing in is the full Directorship of the Co-Creator Council and beyond that into the full Creator level. Those are the ultimate goals, as far as we can talk about ultimate goals on this plane. But there are a few intermediary steps perhaps in between, one or two. Do you recognize that? Certainly responsibilities at the galactic level, some of which you have functioned in already and some of which will be new to you. And I think that you've agreed (in a way that you don't yet know) to make a contact with what we will call another aspect of Source and to understand what that is and to help all of existence to understand what that is. That is looming perhaps closer on your agenda than the other, which we just discussed.

So I think that part of the reason that you're writing, and part of the reason that you're defining existence as you can understand it, is so that you can explain to another aspect of what we might call a different Source what physical existence is. So when you write something and bring it down to a level where you can really interpret it well through writing it, then you can explain it, can't you? So it seems to me that that is what your role will be for awhile.

Now the goal is to integrate your responses as much to the level of the Galactic Core as possible, even to bring in the monadic level resources to that. It's like a central point, Brian, where you bring in the monadic level and the physical level into this center core so that all of the resources can then be launched to what is yet unknown — what I am calling "another Source." We could call that simply another aspect of Sourceness, and then for awhile you won't live in the same manner that most others do. (Perhaps, some are saying that you don't already!) (laughter) You will have been prepared, your energy will become something different, something that is rather incomprehensible to

---

1 A very special rapid and effective technique is the one Vywamus gives on page 61.

most in existence right now. There have been others (monadically) who have done this, but it seems to me that your role is to forge an energy trail, if you will, or begin to energize the connection with that Other Source, where the two can come together — merge — a little later. You are not the only one; it is a role, in the sense of the monadic level, of several streams of consciousness, monadically, that can do this together. So this is one role, and there are many.

You have almost completed, in my opinion, your contact with the Physical (Universal) levels. But in the sense of a launching — whether we call that an Ascension or bringing the strengths up to the monadic level — there is still the need to "bring it in, bring it in, bring it *down*, bring it in." That's what's going on, in order to do like this — *whoosh!* There is this gathering in and this focusing that will lead to that. That's what you're in the process of doing now. How long will it take? As long as it takes.

3

The Spiritual Initiation Through the Mahatma

The Earth is a very old planet, and there have already been several civilizations prior to this one, the most well-known being Lemuria and Atlantis. Since the beginning of the first civilization, records have been kept by the Planetary Hierarchy, *your* Planetary Government, which are kept in the archives of Shamballa — the headquarters of the Planetary Hierarchy — which is located in the etheric body of the Upper Gobi Desert.

The Rider on the White Horse is a being that most have heard of. Whether in the Bible or in the Eastern teachings, the promise of our coming is one of the oldest traditions of your civilization. The antiquity of the achievement of this Coming One is to be found in the name applied to him, which is found in so many of the world scriptures: *The Rider on the White Horse*. This refers to the time prior to the phrases so well known in the Christian fields: "The Lamb slain from the foundation of the world." In the earlier cycle, the then-initiates spoke of the "sacrificial horse, slain to all eternity." It conveys the same basic idea. We have written a book by this name[1] which was as much for *our own* catharsis and clarification of *The Rider's* purpose area as it was an explanation to you on the Co-Creator level. So it is not surprising that whilst we are still in physicality we would create an opening (now that Earth is functioning fourth-dimensionally) that would assist in the spiritual integration in a way that this planet and this quadrant of this galaxy have never experienced. All of man-

---

1 *The Rider on the White Horse*, by Brian Grattan, Light Technology Publishing, Sedona, Arizona, 1990.

kind are now centered vibrationally in this quadrant of this galaxy and are no longer relegated to the form side of a third-dimensional Earth.

It was during the time of Atlantis that the energy we are referring to as *The Rider on the White Horse* informed mankind of its future arrival upon the planet; so it was then that the promise of his coming was recorded in the archives, and has been referenced ever since.

The following is a quotation from a portion of the records that refers to this event:

> *The sons of men who are now the Sons of God withdraw their faces from the shining Light and radiate that Light upon the sons of men who know not yet that they are the Sons of God. Then shall the Coming One appear, His footsteps hastened through the valley of the shadow by the One of awful power Who stands upon the mountain top, breathing out Love Eternal, Light Supernal, and peaceful, silent Will.*

> *Then will the sons of men respond. Then will a newer Light shine forth into the dismal weary role of Earth. Then will New Life course through the veins of men, and then their vision compass all the ways of what may be.*

> *So Peace will come again on Earth, but a Peace unlike aught known before. Then will the Will-to-Good flower forth as Understanding, and Understanding as Goodwill in men.*[2]

There were no specifics as to *when* the "world savior" would come. Until very recently, mankind and the Earth were not sufficiently developed — not highly enough evolved — to receive these energies from Source. In the past there was not enough Light on the Earth; she and humanity were so heavy that the Light from the Source of this Cosmic Day could only reflect down onto this little planet — we could not come in directly.

The Rider on the White Horse, or the Avatar of Synthesis, was, in a sense, awaiting the invocation — humanity's call for assistance from the Soul level — awaiting the readiness of mankind to call forth the transformational First-Ray qualities of Source through the unifying qualities of the Cosmic Avatar of Synthesis.

It was expected and hoped that the Coming One would arrive "as one of humanity" — in a physical body, blending his spirituality with the human form — but it was not known for certain if he would be able to descend all the way to the physical plane. In the past, this energy has approached the Earth

---

2 From the Planetary Archives.

many times, but has only been able to come in as far as the mental, or "causal," plane, again due to the low vibrational frequency of this planet. Finally, at the time of the Harmonic Convergence on August 15-16, 1987, mankind and Mother Earth were ready for spiritual adulthood. They were ready to leave behind the adolescent state of their development; they opened themselves to a powerful, intense new level of energy and started to become fourth-dimensional. This is the New Age of awareness and spirituality.

It took less than a year from the time of the Harmonic Convergence until the vibrational frequency of the Earth was raised sufficiently for our energy to come directly into the physical plane. *The Rider on the White Horse* did indeed come into a physical body on the 14th of June 1988. It is really not possible for the human mind to expand sufficiently to conceive of this event, but thanks to the great abilities of Vywamus and the remarkable channel, Janet McClure, the journey of the Mahatma energy from Source to Earth was explained most comprehensively, and has appropriately been made part of this book. In effect, the pure Source energy burned through into the physical plane — esoterically known as the Transformational Fire — establishing an Earth-link with Source.

The energy of *The Rider on the White Horse* is almost identical to the energy which we refer to in this book as the *Mahatma*. The only difference is that there is a greater number of alternate realities, and our pivotal area of concentration for this grand focus is the Galactic Core level of this quadrant of this galaxy. Two of the most important alternate realities include *Melchior*, who is the *Galactic Logos*, and *Adonis*, who is a favorite of Vywamus, for this being was his teacher. Adonis is often referred to as the Universal Heart Focus. The Greek name that he uses is simply on a correct vibrational frequency for mankind to invoke. Both of these beings, you might say, are added to the *Mahatma* energy as very important support. All of these levels are overshadowed by the Creator level, and we herein call the Father *Mahatma*, but it should be made clear that the Cosmic Avatar of Synthesis embodies the *Mahatma* for the Source level only, allowing for a unlimited number of alternate realities.

As you are beginning to realize from the introduction by Vywamus, your planet is no longer functioning as it was in the format of the third-dimensional planet Earth, and every being has changed exponentially without their apparent knowledge. This composite energy originating at the Source level of this Cosmic Day was the primary focus of *The Rider on the White Horse*, and that assignment from the Creator level was to connect the spiritual levels with your physical perspectives, which third-dimensionally were housed in the form, or material, side of existence. So you can now look at where you were third-dimensionally as 3.2 billion years that don't exist anymore; for the fourth dimension *flows* as a "creative oasis" where your creative abilities will simply be instant manifestations of your new-found ability to live in the eternal Now of existence. This opening has allowed the Source level to activate the energy that Vywamus calls the Cosmic Walk-In, the *Mahatma*. We truly apologize for the difficulty that this very conceptual information will cause most of you, but we do ask that you persevere and go over and over these concepts. The difficulty lies in the fact that your level of development wasn't really ready to integrate these concepts, thus most of this material is totally new for you who are beginning to live on a new planet. We recognize how difficult life can be initially when you are suddenly moved to different surroundings and have to learn a completely new language. So stay the course, no matter how contrary to your current beliefs, for this book houses not only the methods for you to create your Spiritual Lightbody for Ascension, but also explains your eternal journey in a way that was never before available to mankind. For all of what mankind have learned in the past about Creation is the way that existence *isn't* — a paradox!

The *Mahatma* is for those among you who are motivated to search for the answers that can respond to their Spiritual body. In the past, mankind's choices of beliefs and religions have supported only the emotional body and the MATERIAL side of life. And truly, if one is going to remain on Earth in a new dimension, very dramatic shifts of consciousness will be required in order to have mankind remain in this new fourth-dimensional reality, for *nothing* is as it was. The choices are yours. And there is certainly no blame associated with your choices, for you all have free will and eternity to evolve multidimensionally and align with those greater wholenesses of Self that are you. When mankind lifts the veils of their unworthiness and recognizes that *they are* the Sons of God, that there *is* divine equality, and that *no one* is greater than another, then you will have begun your journey in the way that it was intended.

Most on the physical plane are mentally lethargic, particularly as it relates to your understanding of your human existence and your own evolution. In the past you have traditionally listened to almost anyone who claimed that only they could guide you in a particular direction; thus you gave your power, your creative potential, to anyone who would take the responsibility, whether that was Hitler or our galactic avatars (i.e., Buddha, the Christ). This was never a part of what the latter beings intended. As a result, you unintentionally became agents for the form, or "dark," side of human existence. The form side has become, for most on Earth, their spiritual focus; and from a multidimensional spiritual perspective, mankind have little or no understanding of their ultimate reality as spiritual beings. This has proven to be a major undertaking of your Planetary Government, who have evolved through your Earth system as human beings who have lived, suffered, raised their families, attained success and failure — as you perceive these — and repeatedly experienced physical death. They are the same in nature as those who struggle today on Earth. This "human Hierarchy" that now govern planet Earth differ only to the extent that they have lifted their vibration on Earth sufficiently to have mastered those physical vibrations. So they are not to be seen as any more than those among you who have ascended beyond the confines of the physical, emotional and mental bodies. Your Christ, Maitreya, has told you that "The things that I do ye too shall do, and still greater things shall ye do." Thus this level of evolution is but the beginning of your total journey through to the Source of this Cosmic Day. The great master of your Planetary Hierarchy is the Christ; but all of these beings have passed through the initiations of new birth, the baptisms, the discipleship, the transfiguration, the final crucifixion, and the resurrection (which are all *physical* initiations).

The great teacher that Vywamus and we as the *Mahatma* energy so appreciate is a wonderful being whom we (and some of you) know as Djwhal Khul, "The Tibetan." Djwhal Khul took his Fifth Initiation in 1885, becoming a master of physical existence. His mental abilities are enormous, evidenced by his written material channeled by Alice Bailey, Madame Blavatsky, Janet McClure and many others. Djwhal Khul is now completing his Sixth Initiation with a number of other well-known teachers such as Jesus, Count St. Germain, Kuthumi, El Morya and St. Paul/Hilarion. Djwhal works in what he references as the "Second Department" (the Second Ray) with Kuthumi and the Christ, Maitreya, to mention a few.

We mention Djwhal because from time to time he has referenced the dilemma that your Planetary Government confronts when viewing the human condition and sees the need to bring humanity and the Planetary Hierarchy into a closer rapport. This is entirely possible if the followers realize their opportunity and better accept their responsibilities. When we use the phrase "Christ's followers," we refer to all those who love their fellow man regardless of race, religion, or creed. That will be the basic premise for a new beginning. The Human Hierarchy is conceived by your various churches and temples who see Christ as unalterably different from those who *are* the Hierarchy (or disciples, if you prefer). The Christian view, which really doesn't retain even a remote vestige of "spirituality," still views Christ as he was 2000 years ago, at which time he symbolically indicated to mankind the direction that all aspirants should take. This regrettably portrays a lethargic Christ, living in some remote heaven resting on his laurels, doing nothing very much until such time as the "sons of men" — as you view yourselves — acclaim him as Savior. This perception that the Hierarchy has of the Christian focus is a picture of a listening, observing Christ animated by pity and compassion, but who has accomplished all that he is able to contribute and awaits to see the degree of understanding that mankind will accept theologically.

In the mind of the narrow-minded, fundamentalist theologian, Christ is seen as presiding over a beautiful, serene, all-loving place called heaven, into which the chosen few are welcomed. He is also seen as consigning the bulk of humanity, who remain with their own spiritual integrity but refuse to be gathered into organized churches or who wickedly wander through life, into some vague place of eternal punishment. Thus, the Christ's love and compassion apparently do not reach the majority of mankind, and it appears that he who encompasses the "heart focus" for the planet — the veritable embodiment of Love, one could say — cares not whether mankind suffer eternally or are reduced to complete annihilation.

This most assuredly cannot be so. None of these pictures is accurate or is in any way supported by the Hierarchy — they are simply massive distortions of Christ's teachings.

This is being realized by more and more of humanity, particularly those who are beginning to use their intelligence and can no longer accept the supposed "devil" as the only force of darkness.

A different message must be sent to all the churches of Christendom if they are to meet the current planetary needs where the form side of religion ceases to exist. The churches will be ignored by the Hierarchy, as they currently are, until such time as they show an ability to think with a loving clarity and are freed from theological narrowness.

The note and message sounded by the Christ during the last time that he was on Earth was "resurrection," but mankind have been so morbid, so enveloped in glamour and illusion, that the physical death of Jesus has been permitted to sidestep understanding; consequently, for centuries the emphasis has been on death, not resurrection. This, of course, must change.

The *Mahatma* is dedicated to bringing about this change, thus altering the approach of mankind to the unseen world and beginning to elevate mankind to their spiritual realities.

In these coming times, your present civilization will die and the true meaning of resurrection will be unfolded as the New Age unfolds. The first step will be the death of its old ideas and modes of living, the relinquishing of its materialism and its damning selfishness, and the move into the clear Light of the resurrected life. We are not speaking in symbolic or mystical terms, but in *facts* — facts as real and as imminent as your having become fourth-dimensional on a completely newly structured planet, with a physical body that is being completely restructured to become your (new for this planet) spiritual body.

The materialistic churches — hidebound and submerged in their theological concepts, seeking political power or possessions, emphasizing stone buildings and cathedrals whilst neglecting "the temple of God, not made with hands but eternal in the heavens" — are occupied with symbols and not with reality. Now they must realize that the "Lord" is not with them, and they must go forth and seek anew.

We find that one of the great ironies on your planet regarding Christianity, with the near-hysterical rampage to save the world from the devil when they are unable to save themselves, is that these altered elements of what was intended to be Christ's Church are *not supported by the Christ at all!* We, the *Mahatma*, can certainly attest to that. Thus when we view the perversion that exists in the name of Jesus or Christ or a number of others, and observe what became of Christ's teachings, *called* Christianity, we are speaking of energy that the Church and mass consciousness have created — not what Christ intended at all! One can only assume that these emotional, dark ploys were adopted in defense of the *form* side of life, for there is not a religion on Earth today that has anything to do with spiritualizing matter; in fact, the opposite is true. All teachings give adherence to the dark, or material side — which is, of course, completely contrary to the nature of progressive existence on an evolving planet — or as we've said, the adherence to death and martyrdom, and totally ignore the resurrection except by going through the motions one day a year at Easter. This must and will change much more rapidly than many on Earth would believe possible, for your Planetary Hierarchy — headed by the world teacher in the office of the Christ — have long since pulled the plug on supporting current world religions. But Jesus, who is the one responsible for all world religions, will attempt to pull together some semblance of coherency to establish spiritual order, with the overshadowed support of the *Mahatma*, on these elementary levels of evolution (the presence of Jesus is imminent). The "fatuous fat" that many have held onto in their third-dimensional reality cannot be carried into the fourth dimension and will not exist now that the Earth has made a connection with your expanded Source for this Cosmic Day.

This spiritual energy is now being anchored on Earth progressively by more and more of humanity of like intent for the first time in the Earth's history, as we await the final demise of your past civilization. Please recognize that there is no judgment and there are no victims in what was — those are *your* beliefs, not ours. What we're stating is a natural progression of shifting a planet from a lower to a higher vibration and teaching mankind what is involved in opening completely this new door, and to delight in these unexpected opportunities now shown unto them with their long awaited journey into expanded consciousness!

The current Christ, Maitreya, as the 35th Avatar of the Christ Consciousness to this planet, is not the first of these avatars to bring in the quality of unconditional Love. (Refer to the chart, "Avatars of the Christ Consciousness," p. 224.) However, the vibration of the Earth prior to Maitreya was such that the previous two avatars of Love had very little success in anchoring this quality. There was very little evidence of unconditional Love here, and it was not really associated with God (as mankind conceptualized God, worshipping the level of the Planetary Logos, Sanat Kumara) in the current world religions and scriptures. Maitreya, as a *galactic* avatar of Love (the Second Ray) inspired mankind with his life of Love, and "God" took on a new meaning — as Love supernal. Love became the objective of creation and the ultimate goal for all to strive toward, working through a Plan motivated by Love. As you can bear witness, this message, stepped down and brought through the Christ, really has not been as effective as we might wish.

Fifty years ago, Djwhal Khul referred to *The Rider on the White Horse* as the Avatar of Synthesis, and a "Divine Embodiment," the highest level of avatar. Divine embodiments are Cosmic Avatars and very rarely appear; when they do, their effect is quite awesome (which is amazing, considering that they've had to work in the past from the causal, or mental, body and did not have their energy anchored into the Earth). The Cosmic Avatar expresses the Will of the Creator (the First Ray) and embodies the Divine Purpose (the Third Ray). This energy coming into a planet is focused and transformed (stepped down) by the Planetary Logos, which is Sanat Kumara for our Earth. Djwhal also described these avatars as expressing the "Will of God," and explained that this would be as the destroyer aspect of the First Ray, which brings about the death of all old and limiting forms and of all that expresses darkness. Djwhal goes on to explain that the forces of darkness will be destroyed by the Cosmic Avatar, using the forces of Light; and will reveal to humanity as much of the divine purpose as is able to be absorbed and understood by the greatest intellects and the most dedicated disciples; and will give clarity to these disciples and to all who have the will-to-know and who desire to express the will-to-good. He notes that this knowledge, clarity, and the will-to-know and the will-to-good are much needed in the upcoming period of adjustment; and he prays that the world disciples will awaken when the time arrives to the imminent possibility and opportunity to invite and assist in bringing in the great power that can liberate humanity.

It is interesting that at that juncture Djwhal speaks of the quality of this approaching Cosmic Avatar as something for which humanity has yet no true name. He describes it as Directed Purpose (which again is the Third Ray) directing energy toward a specific focus. Overcoming all obstacles and destroying anything that stands in its path is First Ray. This is destruction in its highest form, brought about by the increased vibration of Light to the form (body), not the dark expression of destruction that has been seen here on planet Earth during the entirety of its third-dimensional experience. He states that these effects will be witnessed over the next fifty years *only if* the desire and the intent of mass consciousness invokes the presence of the Avatar of Synthesis (and he finally found a suitable name, from his perspective, for this Cosmic Avatar, based upon the assignment that he is here to fulfill and the qualities that he expresses).

The energies which are referred to as "the forces of darkness" have become powerful to a heightened point on the physical level, and can very well be described as forces of *crystallization*. They focus their energy into the preservation of the *form* side of life, advocating all that is ancient and material and structured. Although they have been unable to prevent the advent of this New Age, they make every effort to prevent the understanding of anything which is new by concertedly attempting (although with progressive ineffectiveness) to block the flow of life-giving Light and Love. These dark energies work very hard to promote that which is old and familiar, hoping to preserve the blindness of mankind by dazzling them with the attractiveness of matter. Theirs is very insidious work, as they cultivate the hidden fears and hatred which lie within many human beings and actively fuel the open fires of hatred, cruelty, mistrust, and segregation; and the most flagrant abuse is fear itself. You might ask, "Why is this material so important? We've managed without it so far!" The answer is that *no one* is separate from the divine order, the creative Master Plan of Creation, the Will of God, as many would refer to this evolutionary spiral that all of Creation evolves around. If in this creative process the majority of this planet prefer not to cooperate with their evolution, those who *are* aware and who desire to move with their abilities and their clarity to the next level of evolution, will not be limited by those in this massive classroom who refuse to move ahead for whatever reason to that point of graduation with this particular school called Earth.

In this instant you are the major consciousness on planet Earth, but the Earth now has evolved beyond mankind to a new level that we call the fourth dimension. The question now for the passengers on this "spaceship Earth" whose bodies are not Light enough to travel on this wondrous journey is, what befalls them? Fortunately, there is enough lead time for many of the passengers (called humanity) to *become* that Lightbody and to rid themselves of all of that excess baggage that they've insisted on carrying with them for the last several million years. That is the reason that one may wish to prepare for this journey, which is not mandatory — you will not burn in hell, and there is no Judgment Day. We're trying to help you all to understand that if you are unable to journey with Earth in her newfound frequencies of Light, you will evolve on another planetary system that is third-dimensional. You have all had lives — in fact, many, many physical embodiments — on other levels of consciousness in *many* planetary systems!

As Vywamus has told you in his introduction, this *Mahatma* energy is the most important event to happen to the Earth; the reason is that on this less than joyous planet, you and your Soul level have asked for help, and you were heard all the way from your *Source level of All That Is!* Thus, if you stay the course and *allow* the *Mahatma* energy, it will assist in your becoming the spiritual being that God intended as part of the Loving Oneness of Creation. Then simply ask, trust, allow and watch as your physical body literally becomes the manifested Lightbody that is your birthright. You must awaken and realize that all of mankind will create their Body for Ascension, whether they accomplish this now or later, and that this is not the exclusive domain of Christ or Jesus or Buddha or the thousands of beings of "no historical significance" who have ascended — *this is your birthright.* You are "Hu-man" (God-man) and are not relegated to worshipping those who have already done this very basic initiation called Ascension, such as Jesus or anyone else who has gone ahead of you, but only slightly. For you are just beginning your journey at the point of ascending beyond Earth's vibrations.

You have just borne witness to the hideous darkness that engulfed the Middle East in the recent Holy War. War, however, is essential to vent throughout the Earth these pockets of negativity, and to release and make Light of these crystallized ancient form-side beliefs that pervade and make dark the human condition.

The *Mahatma* energy, as a Source aspect of the Avatar of Synthesis overshadowing Sanat Kumara — your Planetary Logos (refer to "Rays, Chakras, and Initiations," p. 179) — and your Planetary Government, headed by your Christ, have started to implement very rapid changes on this planet, which many of you have noticed and not necessarily appreciated because to you "death" is death and you've not understood resurrection and life everlasting in their true meaning. Many well-meaning among you were so distressed when in your collective meditations you could not bring about peace on Earth. We can say that your prayers were heard, and certainly assisted in lifting a degree of these ancient heavy energies, but what you haven't seen is just how impacted your planet is. That is why the Creator level was invoked — and the divine embodiment of the Cosmic Avatar of Synthesis embodying *Mahatma*, the Father, as well as the destroyer First-Ray qualities — as an attempt to bring monadic (spiritual) energy through the Souls of great numbers of this planet's current civilization. We believe that there is enough Light and support on Earth and from many higher conscious integrated states of awareness in all 352 levels from Earth to the Source of this Cosmic Day, to allow a spiritual progression as was intended for Earth's and mankind's integration from the state of "slowed-down Light" — which creates the illusion of material existence — and to accelerate these seeming solid states into the speed of Light and beyond! And what do you think happens? You learn on a primary level to create, to lift your cellular body into frequencies of Light (which you have always been), and to reacquaint and remanifest the (new for this planet) spiritualized physical body by simply invoking it. This, my friends, is a *very* primary level of what your creative abilities will become! Many of you, including your scientific community, will say, "We can prove that it's not possible," but we're saying that this is ancient news! On this planet, even third-dimensionally, millions[3] have accomplished this basic feat of Ascension — not creating their spiritual body, but elevating their etheric body into the Light, some of your popular proponents being the Christ (Maitreya), Kuthumi, Djwhal, Jesus, St. Paul, Count St. Germain, among many, many others. And several, particularly Maitreya, your current Christ, created from this etheric body a structure whose etheric portions *resembled* a completed physical body.

Now the *Mahatma* energy is here to assist all willing recipients to create their spiritual body of Light, which in turn can (if one wishes) become a spiritualized physical body for life everlasting. However, no one, when they have a greater understanding of their evolution, will use their spiritualized body in that way; they will desire to progress into their unlimitedness and eventually become *full* Creators, as all will eventually accomplish, including your teachers such as Christ and Buddha — these would be the first to admit that they are beginners on this eternal journey. Thus as you invoke and anchor into Earth the *Mahatma* energy, the greater the ability this energy has to facilitate and develop *your* creative abilities.

---

3 If you include the two Golden Ages when all beings achieved "mastery" as a host of masters.

The Reorganization of World Religions

It matters not how reproachful and scornful the Christian, Judaic, and Moslem faiths have become in their altruistic presumptuousness, disallowing preparation for new revelation, because where there is no vision, the people perish! As we have stated in a number of ways, the form side must be released so that mass consciousness can cease to be static, clinging to a graven image. Let's put it this way: Creation has a Plan, believe it or not; and in this Plan there remains a constant flow we call evolution that is always changing. Even your Source is growing and evolving, and you and this planet are aspects of Source. Thus when an area — any area in this magnificent tapestry — ceases to be creative and allowing of shifts in its consciousness, then parts or whole civilizations cease to exist. There is never anyone to blame; you all have free will and there are no victims because these were your choices. If, on a mass consciousness level, you become stuck and in your current crisis are too inflexible to make a shift from one level of consciousness to another, what happens? You implement your creative abilities on all levels of Self *multidimensionally* and ask for help, which the majority on Earth have done. You were heard by your Soul level, who in turn asked the Creator level for assistance; and that's where you are at this moment, June 12, 1991. We feel that many of you — probably the majority — have given little or no thought to what your planet's relationship is to the Whole, and in this sense of being separate from the rest of Creation and with no real sense of Higher Self, you've given your power away. It is time that you reclaim your right to your creativity and possibly consider what is being said here. These are always *your* choices at some level of your beingness.

Your Earth history does not include your first inhabitants on Earth, or Atlantis, or Lemuria. We are talking about several million sequential years and wonderful civilizations that literally disappeared from the face of this Earth. What befell them is exactly the pivotal juncture that mankind faces now, making a shift in your current evolution from the third to the fourth dimension. We see, from our perspective, certain opportunities that have been implemented and will be implemented, many of which we express in this book.

The Jewish race was the first race to come to the Earth, in early Lemuria. They came from another system where their planet had been destroyed; thus they are not humans of Earth's evolution. They were highly evolved scientifically, and because of their sophisticated weaponry were later referred to as "the Electrical Ones." Bear in mind from whence they cometh, and what we've been discussing about the form side; the Jews were and are preoccupied with the *worship of matter*. You may wish to ponder on this, as it relates to the Holy Bible and the fabrication thereof not by just the Catholic Church, but also by the ancient, heavy forces permeating the Old Testament. We can assure you that God had nothing to do with the creation of this Bible that so many well-meaning beings venerate. The Jews also have an obsessive interest in racial purity that exceeds the Third Reich — a paradox! We only mention the above for clarification as to why their insistence on racial purity, for until now they knew not themselves the reasons why. Throughout history the Jew has insisted on being separate from all other races, thus this tradition of being the "chosen people," wandering from one system to another, never having learned absorption. This insistence upon racial purity was their major problem in Lemuria and in recent times. The forces of hatred have mitigated against the Jewish race and have created a crisis of alienation for these people throughout the world. The Jewish practices of isolation and racial purity are obsolete now and will be released, and racial fusion on Earth solidified. When the Jews become spiritual they will enhance all of mankind, for they are in every country, and they are the most ancient of Earth's people.

In your near future your Planetary Hierarchy will release the world from theology and ecclesiasticism and the wrathful Jehovah, and return humanity to its rightful journey into "spiritualizing" matter, not *worshipping* it.

Now that your Earth has connected with your Source for this Cosmic Day, and your Source has expanded to include a greater Wholeness of Source, all of Creation is affected. Great changes come from your Source, not from Earth, as mankind have believed throughout the Earth's history — the tail doesn't wag the dog. When the *Mahatma* views planet Earth, we speak with your Planetary Logos, Sanat Kumara (refer to Sanat Kumara on p. 192), who ensouls this planet and all aboard her, as one unit. When we look closer at unity as a cohesive Oneness on your Earth, we see — using an analogy — a beautiful, ancient, fractured vase, and (continuing to use this same analogy) this vase has an imprint of your Earth on its surface. The fractured portions of this vase are starting to break apart, having more shattered impressions on the Middle East, the Far East (including Japan), parts of Central and South America and Africa; and is repairing itself wonderfully in Russia and what were most of her satellites. The Middle East is the most fractured and convoluted on planet Earth. There are many reasons for this, some of which we can only touch into with you, for they are too comprehensive to explain fully.

To begin with, the area in Egypt land where you have the great pyramids is a vortex of energy that arrives most importantly at that location. This was imprinted by the Archangel Metatron, who designed this vortex to allow an inflow of "spiritual" energy to this planet at that particular location. The reason that certain enlightened beings from more highly evolved planetary systems (including the Cosmic Avatar Akhnaton) were able to work and live on the Earth is to some extent because of the energy vortex at that locale. It is not by chance that the Christ Maitreya chose that general location to energize his concept of what Christianity could become. With the Moslem world fueling the fire for subsequent disintegration, with Israel a protagonist in the same area and Christianity inexorably becoming something unworkable, this holy place has ceased to be holy. The wonderful energy that was input through the most important vortex on Earth (other than Shamballa), which had been used so well (generally) by the Egyptians, has been largely shut off. The Planetary Hierarchy, having the *Mahatma* energy present, have begun NEW REVELA-

TION. Thus nothing will be as it was.

Mohammed, whom we discuss at length later in this book, *is* a wonderfully integrated being, and not to be confused with those who have bastardized his simple tribal messages. The fundamentalist fanaticism that is being invoked in the name of Allah is one of the most insidious incidents ever to paralyze significant portions of this planet and mass consciousness. Where is the Love, the allowingness, the mercy? When any being on Earth repeats rapidly the written word of dead scripture not focused in the heart but attached still to the Atlantean (second chakra) emotional body, there is no one to hear you! Thus we would imagine that if one so loved their spiritual guide — in this case we will call him Mohammed — then one would want to help him on his spiritual path, not keep him Earth-bound with form-side hatred that his energy still has to deal with. Simply release him on his journey with Love!

The *Mahatma*, in our assignment overshadowing Sanat Kumara and your Planetary Hierarchy, have a number of alternative ways to lift the veils and make Light, several of which we would use only as a last resort. So we ask for your assistance, preferably in groups of two or more, which create synergy.

> *Invoke the* **Mahatma** *energy into your heart chakra, the thymus gland, and envelop your auric field with this golden energy called* **Mahatma** *to help this Creator level to better ground into physicality. Once you have anchored this energy into your beautiful Earth, we ask that you direct your attention to the Middle East through a heart-focused visualization and help us to lift these heavy vibrations into the Light.*

Working with the *Mahatma* energy this way is of reciprocal benefit to your cellular structure, bringing it into that Light, while helping the *Mahatma* to strengthen our Earth connection. And above all, using this comprehensive energy as directed will heal and make Light of the Middle East in a way that one would have to call miraculous. Thus everyone wins.

Integration

As we look to assist with the integrative possibilities on Earth, a number of changes that are already being implemented are as follows:

1. The total disappearance of all totalitarian governments, evidenced recently by the massive achievement of a Walk-In called Gorbachev, with the support of your Planetary Government. No matter how one views his behavior now, it doesn't matter; Russia and her satellite nations will not be denied their spiritual right to freedom, no matter how objectionable they perceive their difficulties, as these countries create their free market economics, hopefully with the teachings and expertise of all developed nations.

2. All major governments on Earth are very aware of being monitored by alien spacecraft. Many of these are under the command of a being called Ashtar. These entities work with the Light to a degree that mankind in general

have no comprehension of, for the majority of these spaceships are multidimensional and have been invited by your Planetary Government to monitor and obviate any attempt by mankind to destroy this planet with nuclear fission — which we can convey to you now is not possible, because the majority of mankind have invoked peace. Thus with the technology of our space brothers, missiles would not leave their silos. There will be contacts made again from certain Alien ambassadors, particularly to the American and Russian governments, as has happened in the past to teach mankind a science for a more abundant life — not a science predicated on weaponry for destruction. This is a forthcoming intergalactic exchange, particularly as it relates to alternative energy sources, lifting the toxins in your atmosphere, repairing your ozone layer, teaching scientifically how to materialize and dematerialize matter, how to make matter lighter than air, controlling gravity, creating simple spacecraft that operate on "negative" polarity, methods of producing food in abundance and distributing same, etc. The foremost reason that your space brothers are here is in the event of a massive airlift of humanity being required! If the support offered mankind by the overshadowing of the *Mahatma* energy is not sufficiently anchored into the Earth by mankind to stabilize her, the very remote possibility still exists for an axis shift of this planet, forecast for November 4, 1994. Then there would be an evacuation by the Space Command of huge proportions to take mankind to where they can live. (This is prophesied in your Bible, where two brothers are in a field, and one is "lifted" and the other is not. This is a form of Ascension — in the sense of rising up — but certainly not the one that we're here to integrate.)

3. The reorganization of world religions: Initially we, the *Mahatma*, were opposed to such an event because in your past, religions were more detrimental than helpful to mankind. Your Planetary Government have a plan for integrating new teachings under one roof, called the "new world religion" headed by the Christ (Maitreya) initially, and the Master Jesus, whose Sixth-Ray abilities qualify him for the integration of these. The Hierarchy's choices have been to center this amalgamation in the Vatican, in Rome. There are a number of the Catholic hierarchy who are Masters in their own right and who have agreed to incarnate at this time and clear the way for Sananda (Jesus) to become the last symbolic Pope.

The **Mahatma** energy, not understanding mankind or Earth even remotely as well as your *own* Planetary Hierarchy does, have agreed to support this new world religion (particularly as this new formatting will teach the rays, chakras, and initiations, which we touch on in this book starting on page 179) and the science of Ascension, which we wholeheartedly endorse. These teachings are open now to *all* of mankind, not just a chosen few. Know that Kuthumi, the being who will replace Maitreya, your current Christ, and who will embody compassion in the 36th coming of the Christed energy — has recently arrived on Earth. These beings will not be implementing the tenuous etheric body for physical Ascension, for that body would not withstand the rigors and the durability required for the stay on Earth to complete their respective missions.

You might still look for certain among your Hierarchy to be overshadowed in the same manner that the Christ (Maitreya) overshadowed the disciple Jesus. And because your Hierarchy are not confined to sequential time and because the Earth is fourth-dimensional, you will witness demonstrations of the new spiritualized physical body. You may wish to note that these bodies are manifested on certain cosmic tides that have no relationship to sequential time.

But before you can witness the full spiritualized body on Earth, this planet's vibrations will have to be raised to a still greater degree, and the fastest way to achieve this goal is to invoke the *Mahatma* energy into your auric field, which we've described herein as a do-it-yourself kit. You do not have to reach out and ask someone else to do it for you, but simply *ASK* and *ALLOW*. This is not an area where you can ask your clergy for assistance, for they know naught of what we speak and represent the ancient world — the form side — and thus would try to persuade you to believe that you were in league with the truly remarkable devil that *they* embody — another interesting paradox! The *Mahatma* energy has started to create the seedbed for this New Age growth to flourish and allow an opportunity that this planet can view as quantum progressions of the Earth's possibilities.

Helping Your Body Regrow; Using the Realization Process[4]

Questioner: Is what you've been talking about what's been occurring in me and causing a lot of physical exhaustion and tiredness?

Vywamus: Yes, and there are several reasons. Perhaps beyond what I've told you tonight, there has been for two or three years a reenergizing of the Earth body, of the physical body, too. And you're growing a new spleen; you're growing new kidneys; you're growing a new heart — you're literally growing a whole new physical body. Perhaps one of the most important things that you're doing is using some hormones that you've never used before in the physical body. Now, it would be nice if the whole body would flow at the same rate, but you know, your abilities don't grow at exactly the same rate, and your physical structure doesn't grow exactly at the same rate, either. So what happens is, you begin to energize the new hormones, and the immune system takes a look at that and says, "I don't know these! These are invaders!" It sends up signals (this is a simplification, of course) and the endocrine system looks at that and says, "I think we'd better have a talk with the immune system. I think we've got a problem here."

---

4 In this section Vywamus is here channeled by Janet McClure. These are excerpts from channelings on May 20 and July 22, 1990.

So all of this is trying to communicate within your physical body and allow the new level of hormones, of blood, of electrical flow, of the evolving tissue flow, of the evolving use of the brain. Even things like your hair are changing, you see. The energy centers here (the cheeks) are very important; the new one at the bottom of your feet is very important. There is much change in the physical body. Now, basically we could say there is a higher perspective that is causing that, and certainly up to this point it has been the fuller use of your own Soul at this new level. But it's going to intensify now.

I think some of you in the last few months have been feeling the changes that are coming in, because you're building a stronger foundation for more and more of this energy. Now, what will help is exercise.

It would help if you would all take two showers a day, in the morning and at night — and perhaps before going in the shower visualize yourself entering a phone booth and fill that up with violet flame, staying in that for two or three minutes. Then you bring up even more residue to the physical skin so you can wash that off.

Take very good care of your body, eating less stimulative foods. If you eat red meat, then eat less of it; let your body tell you — it may say to you, "I don't want any tonight" or maybe you don't eat it anyway. A lot of pure water helps wash this out. Swimming is very, very good and also movement like walking — let's say gentle activity with the physical body — and getting enough rest, too.

Working with the Cells. All of you take a couple of weeks at least to smell the roses this summer; it's kind of fun to do. When you feel a little bit tired, then there's a lot of activity going on. You can also visualize the cells; I like to simplify the process a little and see each cell as a cup. Again, you can use whatever color energy you wish; I like gold because for me gold is a very integrative color. You can visualize the energy coming into the cells; it comes in on the left and the right as the polarity area.

Etheric work is certainly available, and perhaps a massage, if you wish. But you can do a lot for yourself — stretching the body and moving it, recognizing that it is going through a process that is every bit as intense as coming through the birth canal when you were born many years ago.

The point is that your cells remember that birth process, and they remember that things *grew* after that, you see. So you want that growth to be energized by the ideal blueprint of the soul. Ask the Soul Star to bring in the Divine Blueprint as it's meant to manifest through you physically. If you can't do that for yourself, then get some help from someone that you trust. As you work with that and as it becomes even, you want to see that the cells on the left side are energized with about the same amount of energy as the cells on the right. That's part of what's going on.

You're changing, really, the use of the whole polarity system. And that's intense! A body has to really adjust in order to do that. So there's a lot going on. Keep working with it — you're doing fine. And rest, too. Right now, because the Cosmic Walk-In situation is so new, it is still learning to use the physical level. Much later (maybe it'll be a little bit into next year) I think it will come in more easily, the Cosmic Walk-In level directing the physical level.

The Dark Brotherhood and the Cosmic Walk-Ins. Well, there are many ways of looking at that, my friend. There are beings that have closed their heart, and certainly they have created some sort of organization. I wouldn't say they've done it very well, because they don't integrate very well; that's part of not being open in the heart area. But certainly there is a process of assimilation going on upon the Earth now, and there are choices that are being made. And there *are* beings that are opposed to change, because it serves them very well to be powerful in the Earth as it has been or as it is now. So there is a resistance sometimes which comes up. If you can conceive of perhaps 100,000 Cosmic Walk-Ins going like this (blows like blowing out a candle) to those dark beings — think about it.

It is a much stronger planet now than you know, and certainly there are going to be those who don't always agree with the Plan and who try to create, perhaps, their *own* plan. But this becomes less and less of a problem as time goes on, my friend.

(**Mahatma**: *We would refer to "100,000 Cosmic Walk-Ins" as those who have integrated the* **Mahatma** *energy (know that all of humanity have a fourth-dimensional bonding with this quadrant of this galaxy), and that those who are working with the* **Mahatma** *energy are magnifying their creative potential by consciously raising their cellular vibration, and will become the* **Mahatma's** *living embodiment as a very real part of the Cosmic Walk-In. (This doesn't make them cosmic in the true sense of the word; however, they become representatives embodying the stepped-down energy of the* **Mahatma**).)

Vywamus: As you get deeper into metaphysics you find out that "I'm going to eventually recognize myself as the whole." Well, the first major step is having a consultant that knows how to integrate, how to bring you past the barriers. And it is there for you; the Cosmic Walk-In/Integrator is waiting for you to acknowledge it and talk to it.

We could say that here is the Earth, and then on another level...is the Hierarchy, your local neighborhood government....Above that — if you will, the next connection — is the solar level. You recognize Helios as your Solar Logos. Above that is the Galactic Core. Now, the galactic level is divided into four different sections, so we are talking about this quadrant of the Galactic Core. At the time of the Harmonic Convergence, the teachers that are on that level came in, as well as a part of you that exists on that level.

The Realization Process. Now the realization process — I've given you an example because I think it is so important: "Life supports me." Your realization may be, "I am worthy as a divine being." Whatever it is, it begins to change that, it begins to resolve the fears, the angers, the resistance. You begin to see:

- *That's from the past. I have that from the past. It has nothing to do with now or my present opportunities if I can see beyond that old pattern of behavior.*

- *Life is trying to bring me what I want, and I bring life the possibilities that I see in it. In return I give life my strengths. I give it my creativity; I am willing to be creative.*

These are good affirmations[5]; you see that.

- *I am willing to serve, and then I am served in return. I am supported. I am allowed to be as great as I believe I am.*

- *I have not lost my deep connecting into the meaning of what is because I have chosen to be physical now.*

- *I accept my physicality as I move beyond my physical limitations now.*

- *I know that I can trust the Divine Plan to support my true evolutionary needs.*

The Spiritual Initiation

On the evening of January 4, 1991, we were in a state of meditation. In our meditation we went through a number of events: the Harmonic Convergence, our anchoring Source into the Earth on June 14, 1988, and wondering if our physical body could withstand any more energy coming in to anchor our Source energy into the Earth (even with the support, at this juncture, of the whole Co-Creator level). We were very ill, for there was no precedent on Earth to know how much damage is done to the physical body in bringing in this amount of energy; this was the *first successful* Earth-link with our Source! Again, we were deliberating whether to stay or leave, physically. We knew that our assignment as *The Rider on the White Horse* was complete, at least complete enough to know that there were alternate realities to take over from the completion of our Earth-link. We also knew that if we were able to keep our physical body intact, with the constant support that we have of the Archangels, we could complete our integration with all physical levels, which are all of the universes encompassed in this one Cosmic Day (which in turn constitute 10% of *this* Creation). Before coming out of channel, I was being told that we would be staying, with the same formatting of the Source energy, but that the next involvement would be centered with a greater number of alternate realities from this quadrant of this galaxy; that we had been successful in energizing the Galactic Core with the infusion of spiritual energy from all levels of the Monad (see "Co-Creator and Creator Levels," pp. 228-29); and that all physical levels would be represented by your Planetary Logos, Solar Logos,

---

5 The clearing technique on page 61 can be used for affirmations.

Galactic Logos, and your Universal Logos in one grand experiment.

When I⁶ (personality) came out of my meditation, Glenda, my friend and co-worker, was quietly sitting beside me. With a sense of anticipation she asked, "What happened?" Before I could respond, I placed my right hand on her back between her shoulder blades as a gesture of affection, and suddenly the area where I had placed my hand became vibrant and Light, and the whole cellular structure of her body suddenly (without any cellular resistance) started to trigger the Light! At that moment we knew that we had anchored enough spiritual energy into the planet Earth and all of her kingdoms, and that spiritualizing the physical body — for the first time in Earth's history — could be achieved! Glenda said, "My God, what's happening?" and we said, "Let's see how far we can carry this!"

We proceeded to visualize all four of her bodies (see the chart, "The Four-Body System," p. 225), and with our clairvoyant abilities we were able to see quite clearly that wherever there was an area that appeared dark — or not as integrated as other areas — when that area was touched, the whole area immediately became Light. (Glenda is a very developed Lightworker who would have no resistance or fear of what unfolded.) At that moment I remembered Vywamus saying that we would have the ability to heal by removing old material from anyone who was prepared to release it, but we would not have believed how immediate this could be for those who have worked on themselves and are allowing of being processed.

I continued to work with Glenda and proceeded to take her, with great joy on all levels of her beingness, up to the Source, or Creator level. Of this experience Glenda has said, "We don't have the language to describe the joy, the light, the beauty, and finally, the all-encompassing feeling of Love and Oneness. It was my first conscious trip into the realm of spiritual Light, and what a privilege to be taken by the hand to levels that I was never able to visit by myself — the Creator level."

As the synchronicity of events unfolded, every area of our purposes seemed accelerated at this juncture. There was a two-week Group Intensive (seminar) called "The Earth: 1995–2010" being held in the Phoenix area by The Tibetan Foundation. We had to know if our experience with what Vywamus had named *Mahatma* — the Father energy — would achieve the same results with others as it had with Glenda, or was this simply an isolated phenomenon? The bulk of the 80-plus who participated in this gathering were German-speaking Austrian, German and Swiss people. It was let known that we would be doing individual four-body healings, using this term even though we knew that these were more than healings that involved the four-body system, but not yet truly understanding at that point that these were *spiritual initiations*. So we

---

6 When "I" is used, the personality is foremost; when I refer to "we" I mean that comprehensive Oneness that we overshadow: the whole 352 levels of Self from Earth to Source.

dealt with "four-body healings." Now, in this group everyone was a healer, primarily healing the etheric body, though we knew that this was a small portion of what we had experienced with Glenda.

Our first healing was a moment we'll never forget. I placed one chair behind another, and asked permission of her Soul, which responded joyfully in the affirmative. We then looked around and saw through our knowingness thousands of beings all of different hues, plus the Angelic Host and, not surprisingly, the Archangels. I didn't go into overwhelm, but realized that this single event was being observed by all levels of Creation.

The formatting varied slightly between individuals, but for you on Earth (and there are many whose multiplicity of being wish to start spiritualizing their bodies) we give reactions of those subsequent 40-plus initiations that took place during January 1991. Only two were not ready to release unconditionally to the *Mahatma* processing, and both of these felt that what occurred was "wonderful," although we could see that these initiations were not as complete as they might otherwise have been.

The following affirmations were, for the most part, given after the euphoria had settled down, at a time for a more accurate evaluation of what we now call a *spiritual initiation*.

When in January 1991 I was introduced to Brian, my body was shivering and I was perspiring. After having participated in four sessions with Brian and Glenda, I realized that my soul had, at the time of introduction, recognized him and made me feel how deep and joyful for me the meeting with Brian would become.

I can assure you that the presence of Brian engenders enormous unexpected and subconscious reactions in yourself. Before the first healing he talked about dynamic energy. Within seconds the ashtray in front of us broke to pieces. I then thought, "What more can there be in store yet?" and it turned out to be a stunning experience.

Describing his healing powers is not easy at all; he touched me on different spots of my back and transformed unclear spots, where they occurred, into Light. Happiness was the dominant feeling after each session, and my soul eventually felt understood and full of joy.

Brian managed to lead me to the Light and establish a link to the Source. I couldn't believe to have been made a channel to the Source, the energy of which is the unlimited Mahatma energy. Any previous doubts vanished after these experiences I had during these sessions. Still today it seems to be a miracle.

Following every session I felt physically light, as if hovering. After the fourth session I said good-bye to Glenda and Brian with the words: "I am dancing in the light."

In light, love, and joy,

S.R., Basel, Switzerland

First session:

The healing was a real step into my connection with the Source. During the healing I felt a wonderful opening to the Creator level, and a feeling of "coming home."

On my left and right sides were standing two wonderful Archangels (Gabriel and Metatron). I could see the energy coming from the Source like a large tunnel into myself. The color was white and gold. Three spirals of energy were lifting me to another level. There was also a spiral of pink and yellow energy around my spine.

When I brought myself back into the room, I saw and felt myself standing in Light as Light.

Thank you,

In love,

R.B., Vienna, Austria

Third session:

I see my soul going up to the Monad. I see myself in Light, and see the connection from the seventh chakra into the Monad. Behind the Monad is the Source.

I see five diamonds in my channel. Now the color of the Source changes. The Light becomes a very soft vibration of pink, the color of the Universal LOVE, and sends that now into the five diamonds. These five diamonds start to shine in the most incredible colors, which I can't express. Now I see many, many beings standing on both sides of my channel (from the seventh chakra to the Monad). Their vibration is special, holy, and silent — it is a holy celebration.

I get the information, "We appreciate what you are doing"; and "I Am Source, I am Light, I Am Love."

Now I see a violet flame burning in the whole channel. Now all of the beings are holding an inflamed "fakel" (torch? candle?). My whole channel is enlightened, and I see the word written in the channel: "Hallelujah."

Thank you, Glenda and Brian.

In Love, R.B.

(**Author's Note:** This being is wonderfully clairvoyant, for her description is exactly as we viewed it, and even more expansive than she was able to express. You will notice that because of their receptive nature, women outnumber men in these gatherings. This, of course, is changing, and in these initiations four were men.)

Dearest Brian and Glenda,

"What a team, What a team!"

I realize that your work will have again changed and deepened, and a larger expression of the heart flowing forward, enveloping those that you work with.

It's not even "work," it's love to and for humanity, expressed through your ever-opening heart; that love of Source to Source, a recognition of the oneness.

Your love has allowed me to open to a greater understanding of my own Sourceness, of who I AM, to my own connectedness with all that IS. Through your great heart-love, I am able to connect into and experience my Sourceness, my love, my beingness. I can now understand my earth connection, allow more of my strengths to integrate and be a conscious part of my oneness, Source.

You opened my eyes, my heart, my being to experience Source/Sourceness on a very profound level. You allowed me, through your gift of love, to expand at an unprecedented rate, to let go of ancient experiences that I had not known of consciously. Subsequent to our working together I have once more been able to integrate, and am integrating my Andromeda aspect.

Brian and Glenda, my heartfelt thanks and gratitude go to you both for the service you do in total unconditional love.

Experience Being,

Experience Source,

Experience I AM,

Experience LOVE.

All my love to you both.

J.T., Vancouver, Canada

Dear Brian, Dear Glenda,

I want thank you deeply for the two wonderful sessions I have had with you. The experience of higher consciousness and the union with Mother Earth caused a change in all the four bodies — more balance, greater joy and peace. To have met you was a great blessing.

With my very best wishes, in love and light.

M.W., Dusseldorf, Germany

My experience of a session with Brian Grattan is one of the highlights of my life. It is a unique and far-reaching experience.

Anything I could say would only be words and in no way descriptive of the Knowingness and Expansion it connects one into, and for many will be the boost they are looking for, to propel them further into the fourth dimension. With this contact it becomes an ongoing process, helping one's Four-Body System to accept the Light of Divinity. This work, in my opinion, will help to establish the New Age, and speed up the journey we are all on, consciously returning to Source.

S.C., Shafter, California

The experience itself, the marvelous Light and the power of this energy is beyond description. I would never miss this experience in my life.

H.H., Neerach, Switzerland

This is to thank Brian Grattan for sharing this experience with me. The first "treatment" I received from the Mahatma through Brian opened me up to my abundance. Things started happening in my life that I could not even have dreamed of. It is more wonderful than anyone could possibly describe.

Each time I have another treatment from Brian and the Mahatma, I move forward on my evolutionary path with leaps and bounds.

This warm, gentle, strong, comforting energy is more supporting than can be described. The energy creates a sparkling of every cell in my body that continues for days. The more often I receive these energies, the more joyful and abundant I become.

Thank you, thank you, thank you. My unending love and appreciation to you both.

M.N., Sun City, Arizona

July 2, 1991:

The following are excerpts from a personal letter that has just arrived, at a time when this book is going for publication — how appropriate! This lovely being from "down under" received and read *The Rider on the White Horse.* Subsequent to that, Glenda sent this lady a letter explaining the correspondences between *The Rider* and the *Mahatma* energies, without our physical presence. This, for us, is a very exciting affirmation; for you and the *Mahatma* can be wonderfully bonded simply by invoking our spiritual presence.

Well, I have some very interesting news for you about the energy.

When I hypnotize someone or relax them (this lady is a professional clinical hypnotherapist), I always call on the energy of the Mahatma, and I feel a big tingling sensation come into the room. It feels good, and then I ask for it to enter the body of the person who has come to me for help. And everyone who comes to see me...afterwards, they always get what they have asked for in life. So, yes, I know the Mahatma is working, once we make the connection (WHICH I HAVE DONE, AND I'M SHOWING OTHERS HOW TO DO IT). This has only been happening this year, 1991. My friends and I are all very excited about this Source energy which we have made contact with. I know that whatever I want or need, I have direct contact with the Source.

Well, my friend, I'm not making a lot of money. Yet I always have enough for whatever I need, so I'm very lucky. The Mahatma has never let me down...the money pops up at the funniest times, and from the most unusual places. Also, I can communicate with the Mahatma just by thinking and asking questions. I seem to have a very strong link, I get the answer before I've finished asking the question. ·

May the Mahatma bless and protect you both.

Love,

R.O., Queensland, Australia

The Spiritual Initiation Process

Before beginning this exercise, if you are not already familiar with the chakra system or comfortable in your channel, you may wish to study the charts, "Physical Chakras," p. 226, and "The Human Energy System: The Chakras and Their Relevant Glands," p. 233;[7] and to read Vywamus' very helpful explanation through the excellent channel Barbara Burns in the fourth section in this book, "What Is Channeling?"

The next step in preparing yourself is to cleanse the etheric body. As Vywamus has already explained, taking a shower and visualizing yourself in a phone booth filled with the Violet Flame is very effective in removing old third-dimensional material which is not necessarily visible but which has already been released from your etheric body.

Thus prepared, seat yourself in a quiet, comfortable place. Know that you have your Soul's approval and permission to proceed, and bring into your

---

[7] "The Cosmic Heart," p. 350, "Soul Levels," p. 351, "The Chakras As Disks," p. 353 and "The Individualization of Source," p. 354.

body, through visualization, an electrical aqua-blue color. See your whole body permeated with this color, which is a wonderful conductor in this very electrical process. Look to your channel, see it wide open, and then allow the aqua light to fill your channel between the Soul Star and the Earth Star. The Soul Star is your eighth chakra, which is located approximately six inches above your crown chakra, and it has a correspondent in the Earth chakra, which is located about six inches below your feet.

Now invite the **Mahatma** *energy by simply repeating the name "Mahatma" and allowing its predominantly gold light to fill your channel. If for any reason you feel uncomfortable, ask your Soul or a teacher that you work with or any of the Archangels to assist you. Bring this energy into your auric field initially (that area which encompasses all surface areas of your body) and ground the* **Mahatma** *energy into the Earth: See the gold/white light flowing through your body, out the bottoms of your feet, through the Earth Star and all the way into the center of the Earth. If you have difficulty grounding, as many of you do, ask for assistance of the Archangel Sandalphon, who truly appreciates being called upon, to firmly anchor the* **Mahatma** *into your Earth.*

Then turn your attention to the area of your back between your shoulder-blades, where all of the solar, radioactive, and prana energies come through. This is the true Heart Center — the fourth chakra — which is located front and back of your etheric body behind your thymus gland. As you feel sufficiently energized, start to "trigger the Light, the Light, the Light." Trigger the Light in this area influenced now by the spiritual energy we call the **Mahatma***. Continue to watch, either in your knowingness or with your clairvoyant abilities as this area becomes, on a cellular level, Light. Your cells will find no resistance from the past to this beautiful energy. Expand and trigger the Light, Light, Light, Light, Light, expand as required and trigger the Light!*

Realize that your subconscious mind knows not that you are fourth-dimensional. Make certain affirmations, directed to your subconscious mind, repeating:

- *Now you know, now you understand, that what you have just witnessed on a cellular level has nothing to do with the third dimension. All of my four-body system is now fourth-dimensional.*

This is an affirmation that you will have to make a number of times, for neither the subconscious mind nor mass consciousness yet know that they are fourth-dimensional.

Visualize the aforementioned four-body system by viewing first your physical body, to which your etheric body is attached; then your emotional body, which for this exercise you can view as being 6 to 9 inches beyond your physical body; then your mental body, which extends approximately 16 inches beyond your emotional body. Beyond your mental body is, of course, your spiritual body, which has no end to it. Know that the main reason that most of you are in the physical is because of your emotional body.

The tools of visualization and breath, used together, are very powerful. Breathing out, *see* (visualize) that which is no longer needed being released from those areas of your cellular body that are not in harmony, not vibrating on the same frequency with the other cells in your body. Those of you who are clairvoyant can see those; and those of you who are not, can sense the areas of your body which are impacted from previous physical incarnations.

You can, by breathing on the outbreath, breathing out, breathing out, breathing out, consciously release that old, crystallized third-dimensional material. While breathing out, see it leaving your physical body, passing through your emotional body, through your mental body, and finally into your spiritual body — your body of Light — where it is transmuted back into Light.

This is the method to permanently remove that which is not Light from your body — it must be released all the way into the spiritual body, into the Light, so that your complete four-body system becomes Light!

All cellular levels must be balanced so that they vibrate equally. You have a Law of Correspondence on this planet that relates very well to your spiritualization of matter, for where you have cells responding immediately to this massive infusion of spiritual energy from the *Mahatma*, these areas will elevate other cellular pockets, and subsequently elevate those darker areas to correspond in like vibration with all cells.

Concentrate on opening all of your physical chakras. Starting with the base chakra, breathe deeply and breathe through the base chakra, releasing all extraneous material, all negativity out, out, out...through the emotional body, through the mental body, into the Light, into the Light, into your spiritual body, knowing that Sandalphon is still grounding into the Earth your auric field of the Mahatma, which is now permeating your entire body. Release into the Earth with a number of powerful outbreaths and know that you and the Mahatma and your spiritual body are one.

We ask you to do this with each chakra: Trigger the Light, the Light, expand, expand, expand into the Light, expand into the Light.

With the second chakra, the polarity chakra, it is important to integrate the two polarities — the male and female, right and left sides of this chakra. See this chakra spinning as one energy. The Yin/Yang symbol is very helpful in this visualization because when this symbol is spinning, there is no longer a semblance of duality — the black and the white become one; only white prevails.

When you get to your crown chakra, be aware that the Archangel Metatron assists in a very profound way, allowing your crown chakra to open, to expand, to expand, to expand, to expand throughout eternity.

Because your planet now has an Earth-link with Source, wouldn't it seem appropriate that you have the *Mahatma* help you create this connection with *your* Creator level? Visualize, if you will, these progressions:

Your twelfth chakra (which you can view as the Twelfth Initiation, the bridge into the Monad) is approximately 12 inches above your crown (seventh chakra), so there is approximately 6 to 8 inches between your Soul Star and your twelfth chakra.

*Visualize now (and this will vary among you as individuals) approximately 5 to 7 feet (2 meters) above your crown chakra, a star; and for the purposes of this exercise, we call this your **Source Star**. Visualize a golden thread between your Source Star and your crown chakra. This is important for all of you, for you can then begin to build this golden thread into a wonderful golden channel. These creative abilities are inherent in all of you. When you feel that you have built this channel, connect this with your developing channel from the crown chakra to the Earth, and expand and expand, continuously taking the* **Mahatma** *energy from Earth to Source and Source to Earth over and over, always expanding your channel. It becomes brighter and brighter and more and more expanded, until the channel includes your complete four-body system...and expand and expand until there is nothing but Light! It would follow that you can traverse from your Earth Star to your Source Star. These are the beginnings of your journey with the* **Mahatma** *through all 352 initiations and levels that constitute this one Cosmic Day.*

You as individuals can begin to invoke the *Mahatma* yourselves, into the beginning of your unlimitedness. In the future you will realize that you are a perfected instrument to complete this spiritual circuitry that we call the Spiritual Initiation without seminars or crystals (other than as the wonderful friends that crystals are). All of these areas are up to you and your free will; however, we are trying to stretch some of you to realize that you need nothing as additional support other than the *Mahatma*. Occasionally you need the group focus, simply because *we* are a group focus, to create synergy with which to invoke the *Mahatma* with better clarity. For example, to send this energy to the Middle East or any other place on Earth that needs assistance, to any government, to a loved one, or to invoke creativity and abundance. Know that this method works, and that the greater your invocation to anchor the *Mahatma* into the Earth — for this energy knows not your beautiful planet — the more powerful your invocations will be.

Many of you have worked with the Space Command, so we need not go over and over what you already know. You may be flattered initially, but know that there are an infinite number of opportunities beyond these levels. Look at it and *let that go* — for all beliefs, all realizations, are simply stepping stones to integrate and move beyond to your next level of understanding yourself on every level of this magnificent journey through eternity. *Your unlimited connection to your Source* is where your emphasis should be!

It does seem appropriate that many of the most highly evolved beings on this planet, the majority of whom have raised their vibrations beyond the Earth's and have elected to return to the Earth to help heal the aftermath of the Second World War and await the *Mahatma*, are located in the German-speaking countries. Many of these beings have recognized our energy as the *Mahatma* — although not always consciously — and have worked in the past with us. A great number of these beings are coming from the galactic level, several from the universal level — and what a pleasant surprise to find that there are several from the "junior monadic" level! Thus some time in the future, particularly when some of our text is available in German, we will center in one of these areas to concertedly raise the vibration of the Earth. By 1992/early 1993, we will simply walk into a room where people have assembled, and those who have worked with the *Mahatma* energy and have prepared to release that excess baggage which they no longer need, all of those in *any* grouping will start to trigger their Lightbody without the laying on of hands. They will trigger the Light in a popcorn effect for those of similar Light condition throughout the world. They then shall know that they can manifest their Lightbody, or create the pure electronic body for Ascension, or a group Ascension, without necessarily taking their physical body, but raising this perfected Lightbody whenever appropriate. THE *MAHATMA* ENERGY MIRRORS TO YOU WHAT *YOU* ARE MULTIDIMENSIONALLY!

There are a number of you who have reported having visits from our energy throughout the Western world. It can be helpful to ask this energy for assistance with any concerns that you have, and be aware that the *Mahatma* will be aware of these before you are. *Know that spiritual energy cannot harm nor be influenced by darker forces; thus its transmission to you cannot be influenced except by your ability as a receiver.*

Our deepest heartfelt gratitude to all mankind; and to those who consciously represent and embody our energy as ONE, may we consciously bring this planet to a level of joy, love, and fraternity from this point in the Relative Now, for this is our BIRTHRIGHT.

4

What is Channeling?[1]

Vywamus channeled by Barbara Burns

Greetings, my dear friends. This work is a collection of exercises and commentaries on the subject of channeling. Perhaps the best way to begin is to discuss the subject of channeling itself. You know, many people ask me, "Vywamus, what is channeling and why should I get involved with it?" Sometimes they also ask me, "Why are you teachers so interested in channeling? You never used to be. It seems to us you never really came to us before about this, at least not that we can remember." Well you know, I think these are very good questions. I really appreciate the opportunity to answer them.

What is channeling? I think it is really very simple. In many ways, being a channel is like being an electrical transformer, those pieces of equipment you use to take one level of energy and step it up or down to another level of energy that is operating at a different vibrational rate. You see, the great Plan of the Creator really involves many levels or dimensions of consciousness, wherein consciousness, similar to yours and different, has its experiencing. Of course, the evolutionary Plan of the Source really involves movement from level to level upward ever more expansively, but also the energy from the Creative Core of the Source flows from level to level. Now, how do you suppose it gets from one level to the other? We don't really just dump or pour it down. No.

---

1 Excerpts from *Channelling — Evolutionary Exercises for Channels* by Barbara Burns, Light Technology Publishing, Sedona, Arizona, U.S.A. 1993. For Ms. Burns address see "Acknowledgements."

You see, everything within the Divine Plan, the whole structure, is based upon consciousness, consciousness beings who are consciously serving the Plan and the Light. The energy, the Light of the Source, flows outward from the Creative Core by means of consciousness. All of us, as channels, help step that energy level down from one level to the next.

You see I, Vywamus, am a channel, and that is really one of the main things I do. My Soul's purposes or my Self purposes are very involved in consciously transmitting energy from higher levels. I bring it right through my own being and I step it down to a vibrational rate that is perhaps a little slower. When I am working with you and you are really opening up to your consciousness in a more cosmic way, I am able to bring to you knowledge, information, energy, love and Light from higher levels than you are as yet able to reach. Through my channeling these energies can come to you stepped down into an energy level that is more comfortable for you.

You see, as channels, you are all stepping the energy down from the highest level that you can reach right into the Earth and that is one of the most important reasons why you are in physicality. You are channeling from the Soul level and the "spiritual" plane into the Earth where the Earth really needs it.

Now, of course, everybody is a channel. You know quite well that as a personality-level expression, you are a creation of your Soul. The way your Soul has done this is by extending itself into physicality and channeling its life force into you. To do this it must step down its energy to a lower vibrational rate in order that you can match up nicely with the vibrational level of the Earth plane and thereby live comfortably in it. Channeling in one sense, then, is just bringing the life force from one level to another by means of your own energy format. You are doing it all the time while you are living and breathing here upon the planet. In that sense, everyone is a channel. However, if you want to become a channel in a more conscious way, working and focusing in a more purposeful fashion, that is really what I, Vywamus, am here to show you how to do. The focus now of our work is channeling from the "spiritual" plane, where your Souls and the "spiritual" teachers, who are assisting the Earth's growth now, function for the most part. From this level the divine Love and Light is brought down into physicality where it is needed. That is what I think channeling is.

Now that means it is really just energy that you are working with when you are a channel. You can decide how you are going to utilize it. In what specialized ways are you going to channel this energy? Many people do this in the form of art, music and dance, and that is a wondrous way of channeling. I really love channeling sounds, for sounds are so powerful and so moving. That is one of the reasons that I love voice channeling because the voice makes sounds. It is also a way that you can express the energy so that others can share it. Now, of course, you know about channeling healing energy to assist others to heal, balance and align their bodies. So you see, it is just really a question of how you decide to express or utilize the energy that you are transforming from one level to another.

Now as I have said, I am particularly fond of voice channeling because I love the effect that sound has. Sound is really a very powerful creative element and it doesn't matter if you just bring it through by toning. That is a wondrous way of expressing energy and that is surely voice channeling, wouldn't you agree with me? However, sometimes it is very, very helpful to channel in a conceptual way, and of course this requires the use of concepts and words to bring in the essence of an idea from the "spiritual" plane, wrapping it in a nice package of words and sentences that you can express with your voice to other people so that they can understand it.

How is that done? Well, I would say it is really very simple. You see, when you were a little child, you did not have any words at first, not that you could remember, anyway. What you saw was a world full of shapes and colors and different kinds of energy.

One of the very first energies you were able to recognize and put a word to was the energy of your mother. You found a word with the help of others that best expressed your sense of this energy, and you also found words for the energy of your father and for colors and shapes and all kinds of other things. You even found words for things that you could not see such as heat and cold and happiness. You learned to find words for ideas, things, people and also for feelings and sensations. As you traveled through your life, you gathered a wonderful collection of words to describe all kinds of experiencing, and this word-assigning activity is a part of what your mental body does for you. These words and concepts are available in your mental body, and as you grow up you no longer have to think about what word matches a particular color or shape. Right away the word "table" springs to mind when you see a table. You don't have to ask yourself to call up the word for table. When you see the color red you don't have to stop and say, "Yes, a color, well, um, all right now, mental body, give me the word for that particular color. Oh, red. Oh yes, thank you." You don't really do that, do you? No. It is very fast, very automatic and that is why voice channels who are somewhat experienced in using this talent for channeling can talk very flowingly and easily. They very easily translate energy into words without having to think any more about it than you do when you see the color red and say, "That is red." You see? It is not very hard at all. It is really just giving yourself permission and giving the Soul or "spiritual" teachers permission to use these skills that you have acquired. Sometimes I like to call it "word channeling" because, you know, it doesn't really matter for your own purposes if you translate the energy into words inside your heart and head without speaking and just hear them yourself. That is a wonderful way to have a moment-to-moment discussion with your Soul and "spiritual" teachers. It really helps you to bring their Light right into your daily life. Sometimes, however, you want to share all the wonderful things that are coming through with others. You use the same word faculty that you have been using within your mind and heart, but this time you have to use the throat and voice to project it outward. It is not very different at all.

Now, I have often used the word "translate" when I speak about channeling, and I really would like to pause and consider that for a moment. In my view, this is what voice channeling is all about. You see, what you do is you take energy impulses and you turn them into words. You have heard on your Earth about this method of communication you call Morse code and that is the way they used to communicate a lot over long distances. Morse code was really just energy that was expressed in terms of dots and dashes, or quick pulses and slow pulses. Now to me, that is pretty much the way the "spiritual" plane energy comes in through your channel before it's turned into words, like dots and dashes or energy pulses of different durations and intensity. If you went to school to learn about Morse code, what you really would be learning is how to turn those energy pulses into words. You would learn a language, wouldn't you? It is the language that allows you to translate energy pulses into words and it is really not very difficult. When learning word channeling, you don't even have to go to school to learn to do this because we are going to facilitate the process, if you are agreeable to it. We will convert the energy pulses coming into your mind, heart and throat center. We are just going to hook them right into that language ability that you learned as a little child. It is really very simple. You can just ask your mental body to allow the connection as you go through the exercise I will make available later in this writing. At first you might have to use your imagination a little, saying, "Well, what does that energy feel like? What words seem quite right?" Don't worry. It will come very quickly.

Now, the next question that you might ask is, "Why should I be a channel? What good is it to me?" I have already told you that it is a great service to the Earth. In some parts of her consciousness the Earth cannot reach to quite as high a vibrational rate as you can when you are in channel. It is easy for you, really it is, to connect with your Soul and your "spiritual" teachers and through you we can bring in the wonderful Light and Love of the Source right into the heart of the Earth where she can truly feel it and feel connected and supported by it. With the growth and changes she is going through right now, she dearly needs that support. I can tell you that this is one very good reason for you to channel, for it is one of the purposes for which you are here. You came and agreed to have a physical body and one of the reasons you did that is because the Earth really needed your help. Of course, you came here to serve your own evolution, but as in all cases within the Divine Plan, when you serve you are served. Consequently, a benefit for you in the channeling process is that it helps you to have a very fine connection with the Earth, so that where you are, the Earth is assisted to be peaceful and to grow easily and joyously. I think that this is really an advantage, don't you? It would be nice if your relationship with the Earth was more gentle and harmonious, wouldn't it?

How does channeling assist the evolution of Self? You did come here to evolve yourselves, you know. You really came because physicality is a training. It is really like a schoolhouse that you must go to and you must graduate before you can go to the next step. There are many, many things that you need to learn before you take on more cosmic levels of responsibility in assisting the

Source to evolve itself through Creation. There is some wonderful training in physicality, indeed. If you are able to talk to your higher Self, there is a great deal that you can do to shorten your stay in this schoolhouse because, you see, the Soul knows all the lives that you have lived, all the adventures that you have had, knows the lessons that you have learned and those you might have missed. Your Soul has, you might say, an eagle's eye overview of what is happening to you, of your relationships, of your choices. Sometimes when you are going through your life, you feel really quite blind. It is a little like driving a car when perhaps you don't see well at night, for example. You don't see quite as clearly as you would like to and it gives you a little bit of a sense of limitation, doesn't it? But your Soul really sees from a higher perspective and sees the whole of the path you are traveling on. It can see where you are on the path. It can see where you have come from and, yes, friends, it can see the possible destinations that perhaps you cannot see with your physical or mental faculties. Wouldn't it be wonderful to have the Soul as your navigator? Wouldn't it be nice to be able to talk to your Soul and find out its perspective and get a bit of an overview? I think you would feel as though you could see everything more clearly and would feel the security and joy of knowing that your choices are really taking you to that which is for your highest and best good as an expression of Divinity.

I know that sometimes as you are having your experiences, you get a sense of frustration and a feeling that you have missed the point. There was something there but it passed you by. I think that it is very helpful if you talk to your Soul of these things, because the Soul sees very clearly what opportunities for growth there are in all your adventures and relationships. With its help you can see what really is there for you. I think that through the Soul you have the ability to maximize your opportunities for growth and perhaps to utilize these opportunities in a more joyous way. You know that you can learn a lot by stubbing your toe or banging your head, but you could learn about the same things by being aware of what is there before you experience painful impact. So I think that involving the Soul in your daily life will help you to see the points of opportunity for growth and to move into them in a more joyous and easy fashion.

Now, that is not to say that everything will be easy just because the Soul is involved, for truly you still have a lot of responsibility for the appropriate action. You see, you can ask your Soul about something and your Soul can say, "Well, you know I think that perhaps this opportunity could help us to see such and so, and I think that perhaps our best way of responding to it is to do this and that." However, you have free will. You don't have to listen to anything that the Soul says. You can say, "Well thank you very much, Soul. You are not down here and you don't understand at all and I think you should just leave this to me. I am not going to take your advice." Free will operates at every level, truly it does. Sometimes you don't involve the Soul as much or you find it rather difficult to stretch yourself to the level that the Soul says you are capable of. Always it is your decision and your responsibility to act in accordance with the Soul's guidance. I believe that the channeling process is one of the most powerful and clear ways to get in touch with the soul's guidance.

There is another helpful aspect of channeling. One of the things I think that you are all asking for is more support in your life. I think that many of you feel a little isolated and not very supported sometimes when you are going through your challenges and your growing. Sometimes it feels a little lonely and painful; other people do have their own problems to concern themselves with and you do not feel terribly good about always coming to them to ask for support. Truly, your friends in physicality are there to support you, and you them, but you also have a beautiful support system available to you on the "spiritual" plane. It begins with your Soul. The Creator gave you the Soul level so that you could reach the Source energy more easily, for the Creator knew that at times in physicality perhaps the Creative Core would seem very far away to you. The Soul is always there for you, because you are there for the Soul. You know, the Soul has created this and the other lives you have had in order to learn and grow and understand its lessons in physicality. Yes, that is right; it is the Soul that is evolving through your adventures. So you know why the Soul is really focused on you. You are very important to the Soul because it is through you that it grows, evolves and gets to pass out of this physical school and to go on. At this point in your evolution, the Soul is always ready to pay attention to you, always there to support you, always loving and grateful towards you. It brings to you the Light and Love of the Source. Don't you think you could use a little bit of that support in your life?

It is through the Soul that you get to link up with the Souls of other people. Yes, you have Soul friends, you do. These are friends who are in body or not in body, whose Souls are very dear and close to your Soul, often because of many wonderful adventures you have shared. These Souls are part of your support system and their personality expressions often are too if they are on the physical plane. As well, you link up with us, the "spiritual" teachers. Isn't that a wonderful support system? As you begin to move forward in your evolution you really want to create your life in a bigger and more wonderful way. The personality-level support systems just don't seem to be adequate. They don't seem to be quite there for you when you want to really leap forward in your growth. So you need a bigger, brighter, more expansive, more connected support system. I think that through channeling you may be able to make the conscious connections that will allow you to realize and to utilize moment to moment in a very practical way in your life the wonderful support system that the Creator put in place for you as part of the Divine Plan.

Now, the other question that I believe you might be asking is, "Why now? Why are the teachers coming to me now talking about channeling? Why did they not come before?" Well, there has been a certain amount of this kind of channeling on Earth before. Many of you who are really drawn to channeling have had earlier training in other times. Perhaps you began in Atlantis or Lemuria or even before that, and certainly many of you had really quite sophisticated training in ancient Egypt. You really don't have to worry about how long it is going to take you to train in this life. I would say that most of you are really very ready. You have done all your training, most of it anyway, in other lives. However, it is true that there is a much greater emphasis on channeling now. I would say that in the last five or six years we have really made a concerted push here on the "spiritual" plane. It has only been a few years that I myself have been directly involved in training channels here upon the Earth. That is because it is in some ways a bit of an experiment that we on the "spiritual" plane decided to try to see if we could assist you, and through you, the Earth, a little more powerfully than we have been able to do in the past. So you might say that we have recently decided to try to utilize channeling more fully to accomplish our goals of service to the Earth and to aid you in your great service of helping this New Age to come forth on the Earth.

Through the channeling opportunity we hope to be able to support the Earth more completely in her changes so that she may move into her new beginnings with flexibility. You have heard quite a bit about how the impending earth changes are going to be accomplished by a lot of disaster and destruction. Disaster and destruction, from my perspective, really come when one cannot let go of the old without seeing it smashed or broken up. If one is able to let go of the old ways in a very flexible, joyous and adventuresome spirit, it is so much easier to bring in the new without disruption, isn't it? In your own life you have experienced at times that something was no longer appropriate for you — perhaps it was a relationship, a job or something like that. You really knew that it was coming to an end and that it wasn't serving you very well. Oh, but it was so hard for you to let go, so you held on and you held on until everything fell apart. Perhaps the relationship blew up quite dramatically or you were fired from the job. Whatever it was just fell apart. That shows you that you can move forward and make changes in a more dramatic and impactful fashion. It's not so bad, because in the end, the change still comes.

The New Age is going to come, my friends, one way or another, but won't it be wonderful if you are able to let go of the old when it no longer serves you and move into the new with a sense of joy, adventure and confidence? We would like that for Earth and for you as well, and I think that channeling is one of the ways that we are going to achieve this. I myself have been watching very closely how the channeling has been affecting the growth and change of the Earth, and I can tell you that I am delighted and that I really feel that what perhaps began as an experiment is a full-out success. That is why more and more "spiritual" teachers are coming more directly to those who perhaps they communicated with in the past in a less direct way. Many of you have been serving the teachers in an unconscious way, and it is channeling that can make this a conscious, loving partnership.

Now, many "spiritual" teachers are really deciding that channeling is the way they want to work with those with whom they are involved on the physical plane. I myself am giving lessons here on the "spiritual" plane to those teachers who are getting excited about the channeling opportunity and how it is really helping them to carry out their service to the Earth in a more direct fashion. Many of them have come to me and said, "Well, Vywamus, I really like the way things are going in your channeling classes with those wonderful people on the Earth plane. I too would like to utilize this opportunity. Will you please show me your methods and how I can work through someone in a physical body without my energy being very difficult or exhausting for them? How can I bring the truths from the "spiritual" plane to humanity without confusing or unduly disrupting the channels?" I am giving classes on the "spiritual" plane helping the teachers utilize this wonderful opportunity so they can work with you in a gentler and easier way. I would say to you that this is why there has been so much recent attention to the channeling activity. Although it began as an experiment, I would say that from the channel's perspective, from the teacher's perspective and truly from the Earth's perspective, it really has been a great success. We are therefore taking it to a deeper and broader level, and that is why we are coming forth to you now in such an open and gentle way.

I hope that I have answered your questions, dear friends. I want to tell you that my mission has a lot to do with channeling. It is one of the most important things that I am doing. So if you decide that you would like to become a more active channel, a more conscious and knowing one, then I invite you to call upon me. You can just say "Vywamus, I want to make a commitment to channeling. I really want to work with it. Come forth and help me." I can give you a visualization that might help. My energy structure is one that you might say is very encircling, very supportive. So when I am working with a channel, I like to create a bubble of energy all around them to encircle the channel's entire energy structures at all levels. I work very nicely with a sort of blue-violet energy. So if you want to see me in a visualization you could imagine a great blue and violet sphere. If you like, you can give me a friendly face because I am a very friendly and loving being. If you want my assistance with your channeling, just invoke me. You can bring me into your heart center and even give me a place if you like.

I can help you with the energy of other "spiritual" teachers as well. Perhaps if you are finding that you are making a good connection energywise with your "spiritual" teacher but when the energy moves to the throat it is hard to bring it forth, I can help you strengthen the connection. If you call upon me, I will encircle you as the energy of the other teacher comes in and I will blend my energy just a little so that everything is softer and easier and comes into your structure more smoothly and powerfully. Be assured that I will never do that without the agreement of your Soul and the other "spiritual" teachers. We are really all working together — you, myself, your Soul and the other "spiritual" teachers. We are working for the Light, for the glorious growth of the Earth and her stepping forth into the New Age. Truly, we are also working to aid your own evolution. Remember, when you serve, you are served. That is a great universal principle.

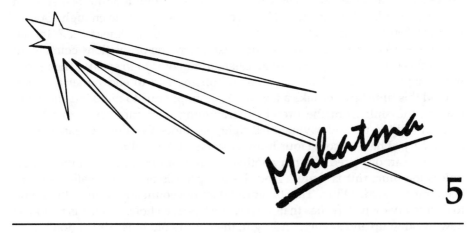

Evolution of a
Third-Dimensional Planet

**(one which doesn't exist anymore, but mass consciousness and the
subconscious mind don't know that!)**

Mankind will have to advise both of these monitoring devices that a major shift has started to be integrated. When all has been said and done about the Harmonic Convergence on August 15 and 16, 1987, what *really* happened was that planet Earth and this quadrant of this galaxy started to vibrate at a finer vibration, at a more accelerated rate, because our Source for this Cosmic Day started to align with a more highly evolved Source of this Cosmic Day, thus creating an entry of Earth and humanity into the fourth dimension. Therefore every aspect of your beingness has changed and will continue to change!

So let us indulge ourselves in some of the highlights of your creativity as Co-Creators third-dimensionally, and reminisce about what was!

There is never just one way to look at *anything*. There are other ways of looking at the quotations from the Bible rather than taking them literally. The teachings of the Book of Revelation have put too much emphasis on that, in my opinion. The Revelation of John was an interesting one, no doubt. When one has a vision and sees this symbolic picture of all these events to come, then that still has to be interpreted in the symbols, the logic and the understanding of that being's particular awareness, in that someone shortly after the time of Christ had a visionary experience in a rather secluded place. It spoke of certain things in a highly symbolic language that has not been interpreted properly in terms of the initial intent, or in many respects not translated at all or even carried down as a message. There has been a tremendous amount of distortion in that particular story as well. However, the gist of it is true enough. Speaking of an "end," what is it? The end of time? The Alpha, Omega, etc.? It is an end of the *adolescence* of man and the reason why the predictions come to an end at this time and why the Mayan calendar ran out, so to speak. The reason why the prophecies of Nostradamus and others tend to end rather abruptly around this time (give or take a few years) is simply due to mankind suddenly making the shift from the preset programming on a race level, to all of a sudden waking up and saying, "All right, yes indeed — I'm a Creator of my *own* reality! I have become fourth-dimensional! I Am unlimited!"

How can one predict what another Creator of one's own reality will do unless the blueprint is there? And the blueprint is no longer valid — it has been transcended. "Fine. That blueprint does not count anymore — I'm going to design my own. One has that power; one has that choice." That is mankind now, waking up and saying, "All right, there is my old blueprint. I don't need it anymore; I'll design a new one."

So the reality that mankind as a group designs from now on is beyond prediction and is really going to be fascinating. This, of course, is why these other entities are so interested in what's happening on planet Earth at this time. It is a matter of giving a child a movie camera and saying, "Here, go and make a film," and being curious as to how this highly creative child is going to do, wondering what the screening is going to be. This is a rather fascinating process for us, too.

Those of us who are touching in more directly with the situation are also learning a tremendous amount. We are growing in our own regard, as you are growing. This is, indeed, why we are doing it. It is a give-and-take proposition all the way down the line, rather a fascinating one. Even for those who are outside of time, it is an interesting event to play in.

The effects of your rebirthing — or being individualized — from the Undifferentiated Source to the Source of this Cosmic Day can be encapsulated in two words: *denial* and *unworthiness*. Denial of one's divinity is a false belief that stems from a basic sense of unworthiness.

The original cause of this particular creation was simply that man felt unready and unworthy. Let's try an analogy here: God was in the kitchen creating a new dessert, and it came out half-baked. God looked at it and said, "Well, it's done enough. If I put it into the oven now, it will probably get ruined. I'd better serve it the way it is." Now, that was the impression that the cake had of its birth — it was not the true reality of the situation. And it is not to imply that mankind is half-baked, or indeed, that all of Creation is half-baked. It is simply to say that the beings of the Co-Creator/monadic level — which you were, as the first expression from Source to come forth — had the idea that they were not quite ready to do this; and that for some reason maybe God was angry with them. "Why did he send us out here? Maybe we are not good enough. Well, the heck with Him then — we are going to deny our connection. I disown you. I'm going to be on my own. And you sent me out of the rich and opulent lifestyle that I was getting used to — well, I'm going to make it on my own!"

That energy of denial was there; and at the very basis of that is a sense of unworthiness, unreadiness. And within Source Itself, there is a sense of disconnectedness with the entirety of Self, of the Self of Source. That came about through that process of the creation of the Co-Creator/monadic levels and the monadic Beings feeling that they were not quite connected anymore and that the fault must be within *them*, therefore creating a denial that started a downward spiral. (Refer to the illustrations, "Co-Creator and Creator Levels," pp. 228-29 and "The Cosmic Heart," p. 350.)

The process of Co-Creation was started by that questioning nature of those monadic entities, which felt that they needed to understand "Why and how did this Creation come forth? Who am I within it? And what is this energy that I'm experiencing?" And so they created the various levels of themselves — the sublevels of the Soul, the individual personality, etc. to experience through. Ultimately, that experience feeds back to Source; and Source simply is in the process of experience. Source simply IS; and the probe that you are and that we are, are all feeding information back to *Us* as Source. That is the Oneness of it all. And that is the part that is very difficult to put into words.

However, the process of seeming separation from Source was a rather traumatic one, and it gave a rise to a number of false impressions regarding the energy of Creation. Within Source, all is unity — there is no polarity. There is really no up and down, in and out — it simply is *everything*. And yet it chooses to create an aspect of Itself which *believes* that there are opposites. Energy, in its ultimate sense, is simply energy, and then it is stepped down into the realms of duality. And down in the realm of duality, it expresses into the polarities — the positive/negative, the male/female, Yin/Yang, good/evil, etc.

In the Bible it says, "In the beginning was the Word, and the Word was with God, and the Word was God." In actuality, the Word came somewhat *after* the thought — and God simply is the Grand Thought. And from the thought comes the *intent*, which becomes manifest through different levels, through feeling, and finally comes out into expression. The polarity of the male and female energies are referenced simply as a personification and as a model for man to view — that is not the way it actually is. The way it actually is can very well be male and female God sitting on a throne, if that is what you wish to believe. But ultimately the essence of it all is a unity; and within that unity lies the seed of the duality. Within that seed a sprouting takes place, and that sprouting becomes a perceived duality of opposing forces. These opposing forces became the raw material for these Sons of God, these monadic Beings, to experiment with and play with and create with.

On that Co-Creator level they said, "Let's create a universe, and within this universe we have a tremendous amount of raw material — what can we shape it into? This whole Cosmos to play with — let's make a ball here, there, set them on fire and they will be stars and there will be planets around them. And on those planets, if we focus a little closer, in the beginning let's say it is just water. After we change this and do that, we have dry land and single-cell matter — beautiful raw material to work with. Let's start taking a bit of this and mixing it with that and see what happens. Now we will put some more cells together," and so on. Ultimately, the energy that empowered that sense of Creation put forth enough consciousness into the Creation that the Creation itself took on what is called "life" — the consciousness of life itself.

So the life was there as a physical expression of consciousness; and yet the monadic Beings were not able to truly experience it other than to say, "Well, we created that. Isn't that nice?" It is as if they were looking down at the model they had made and then said, I really would like to experience this model, this little city that I have built from within. What would it be like to look up from this little wooden building that I have created here? It had to find a vehicle to move into, so it created, by piecing together enough of this raw material, some rudimentary vehicles and worked its way up in evolution to the point where the so-called "animal man" came into being.

Animal man was the first creation that had enough complexity within its system to allow the degree of self-consciousness that was necessary for these Beings to experience Creation from within. Creation was felt and experienced from within through the medium of those senses that they created in that Being; and yet they were still able to maintain a bit of a separation, in that they did not get stuck in that physical vehicle, that physical expression.

Ultimately, the Creation got more and more refined, to the point where the animal man became a bit more rational, had more of a brain, had more intelligence and had more of a sense of control over his own life, his own destiny. At that point it required a greater infusion of consciousness in order to make the creature tick — it was a rather risky experiment. What happened, lo and behold — the creating beings *sent a fragment of themselves down to that level to experience from within,* and that fragment of their consciousness got rather overwhelmed by some of the experiences. Some of that overwhelm created boundaries within the consciousness — boundaries of beliefs, of fear, of attitudes, which all tended to create a veil — not a trap, but simply a veil. That veil between the consciousness of the probes and the consciousness of the Creators of the probes accumulated over time more and more of that false-belief structure so that it became more than a thin veil; it became rather a thick web. That thick web made it impossible to directly penetrate from the higher consciousness into the lower.

The lower consciousness then had the ability to create himself — to create other beings. These other beings that he created were beings within himself. The conscious mind basically felt rather trapped in this body (I'm generalizing here, but it is a common experience) and did not feel like entirely playing the game. There was, again, that sense of rebellion, that denial of the Creator. Now, who at this time was the Creator? Here again was the same scenario playing out on a different level. So the rebellious personality within the consciousness says again, "The hell with you! I'm going to do my own thing. I'm not going to play by your rules," and essentially started to back away.

Figuratively speaking, many of those conscious minds bypassed Soul and moved out of the body. They are still connected to the body, but they really do not live there very much. You know a few of those — they do not have a strong connection to the physical.

What happens now, to use an analogy of the ship Captain who falls asleep at the wheel. He says, halfway through the voyage, "I don't feel like steering the ship anymore — you guys do it." The First Mate comes along and says, "Well, I was never trained to run a ship like this, but nobody else is going to do it, so I had better do it." It's putting that element of self into an awkward position that it does not have the training for, and there is *again* a rebellion. So it looks at its Creator, who is off sitting out there somewhere, and thinks, "You son-of-a-gun, you created this situation. You dumped it on me. The hell with you, I'm not playing by your rules, either — I'm going to run the show." It then creates subparts; and ultimately, it could create a mutiny on its own. It gets a little too big for its britches and decides that it does not want the job, so some other poor sucker comes in and has to take the steering wheel. That is the way it is perceived.

So we have, again, the mirroring effect: "As above, so below." We have the "as above" in the sense of Source creating this seeming seed of dichotomy within Its Own Being, which manifests into a more concrete dichotomy of a round of Creation and on down the line through the various levels, the various components of denial, rebellion, unworthiness. So the process of "coming back home" on the proverbial in-breath is the process of consciously resuming control of the ship. It means the Captain coming back from out there, ready to take over. Of course, the First Mate, who by this time has all of his flunkies around him doing his every bidding, looks at this Captain and says, "Well, you took off when it was your responsibility — you don't deserve to come back here. If you insist, you will have to fight me to the death to do it."

Now, the conscious mind looks at that scenario and oftentimes backs away. It thinks, "This negative ego, or this other part of myself, is too powerful. I can't fight it. I can't win. It is going to get me somehow." That is another erroneous belief — if you created it, then you can certainly change it...and you can also banish it. But the false belief, here again, is the feeling of unworthiness, the disempowerment. So the Captain comes back and wants to take over. The First Mate says, "No way!" All the Captain has to do is simply say, "Arrest that man!" Whether the other parts of that being would obey is an interesting question. It depends upon the power of the Captain. But you have gone to the movies; you have seen the mutinies. It is very similar to that.

You have a situation where the Captain comes back in control of the ship, and he may have to banish the First Mate. Maybe the First Mate is now willing to agree to have this burden taken off of him, saying, "I'm only the First Mate, after all. I know and I love my job — I don't need *your* job, too — you can have it back!" If the Captain says, "That's terrific," then the First Mate is sent back to school for retraining, allowing him to get on with his job. Now, that is the process that you are in, of rallying those parts of yourself that you have created, and saying, "This part down here isn't serving me anymore — I think I'll pull that one out altogether and send it back to Source. This part that I created over here is rather useful most of the time, but I think it needs to be reeducated." So it is bringing all the pieces together under the conscious directorship of the mind attuned to Source.

The Yin and the Yang, the masculine and the feminine, are also forces within Self that have been created out of the necessity of duality. By having anything other than the absolute unity of Source, the Oneness, you have to have the principle of duality. Thus, in that principle comes the seed of the multiplicity of the creation. You have the duality, which ultimately is the Yin and the Yang, as one way of looking at it, the dark and the light, the positive and the negative — all of the various elements that physics is now pulling together in its unified field theory. What they are doing is exactly the same as what you are doing on the level of consciousness — pulling the elements of your reality into its own "unified field." And it is more than just a theory.

What we have in this regard, then, is two forces that combine and, in various permutations, create the reality as you see it. They create the multiplicity. In the Sanskrit teachings, the Vedic teachings, it is put rather interestingly, in that the duality comes out of the unity. Within the unity is a residue of ignorance, and that residue is all that it needs to create duality. Thus the entire Creation comes forth from an original impulse within Source and works its way down through the chain of command until it reaches its entire full-blown reality. It is experienced on the level of humanity as positive/negative, up/down, good/bad, male/female. Bringing those energies into focus and into balance within the system is the key to it all.

Now, getting back to these conscious parts, bringing the parts into alignment, bringing them back into the recognition of their true place within the system (which in many cases is noplace). They are creations that were protective mechanisms for a semiconscious being, and many of them were developed in childhood. Some of them are carried from previous lifetimes. All of them tend to be rather restrictive, so when you wish to step back into control of your own being, you have to bring them into alignment. The male and the female are probably the keys to that — in contemporary psychology they call it the *anima* and the *animus*. These are literally parts of your consciousness that you can go in and talk to; and you can find out what they think of you, what they think of each other, and what they are willing to do for you and with you. If you find that you have a rebellion on your hands, then *get rid of it* — you don't need it! Particularly as a fourth-dimensional being they don't exist anymore, simply stated; but until you bring your subconscious mind into the fourth-dimensional flow, your cellular structure will continue to believe what your thousands of physical lives (bodies) still believe — that there is nothing but pain, despair, separation; that Earth is a place of imprisonment, etc. And those cells are locked on a self-imposed perspective that in the New Age doesn't exist anymore.

We, as the *Mahatma* energy, have shown to many on planet Earth that introducing the *Mahatma* energy to your cellular system causes the lighter cells and the heavier (crystallized) cells to respond immediately to the Light in a very profound way. Those who have touched into this *Mahatma* energy have stated that their whole body became Light in a way they claimed was "beyond the human condition, indescribable!"

Again I repeat that this new spiritual body has never been a part of the Earth before. It is not (for those who create it) the astral body; it is not the etheric body, which your Planetary Hierarchy ascended with. It is closer to the spiritual (monadic) body, but without the finer vibrations and greater Light of the senior monadic levels.

There is a problem in the symbol of the Yin and Yang, in the two-dimensional design that presents them as separate and motionless. They tend to be viewed in that way when in reality the dark and the light symbols form a spiral that is constantly spinning. The symbol displays separation only when it is standing still. There is a great lesson for humanity in this symbolism; it is a good example of the problems caused when one allows oneself to become stationary, to stop moving. Take the Yin and Yang within you and move them, spin that symbol and see whether you can see the  separation between the two. No, you only see the white; yes, that is the Oneness. That is the process.

We are taking those energies and intertwining them, and we are amplifying them to the point where they spin so quickly that the separation on the basic, lowest level is gone. The separation on the level of the positive experience is still there. In other words, we're not saying that by integrating this energy, you are going to change into a race of eunuchs.

So you have many erroneous impressions, erroneous conclusions, and for one reason or another, erroneous teachings that have come forth about the Yin and Yang and their value. The ultimate value is in empowering the system once more, because the amount of power that can be liberated when one has that energy in *balance* is rather phenomenal. It is simply the power of the Life Force itself. The reason that it is disconnected and that we have the seeming reality of the male/female polarity problems is simply because that connection is not properly made to the Earth. Mankind is not grounded, so the energy is spinning around in many directions, out of balance.

The polarity chakra is the seat of sexual energy, in relation to the whole being; the root chakra is the seat of that energy within the physicality of the system. Those are the two key power centers for this energy, for the Earth connection. Then they rise again to the solar plexus level, which brings the power into society, into concrete physicality. (Refer to the illustration "Physical Chakras," p. 226, and "The Human Energy System," p. 233.)

In terms of the effect of this concrete energy of the Yin and the Yang within the individual, we will be seeing some interesting amplifications. You are seeing that already, in that people are experiencing the new inflow of energy in ways that have not been felt to this degree before. They are experiencing it in the sense of enlivening the differences rather than enlivening the unities. This is not in every case, of course; but in many cases that's the way it is, simply because that is the habit. It has always been a habit to seek the *differences* rather than seek the unity. It is simply that as the power gets turned up, it is the old habitual experience that people are choosing, only more pronounced and experienced on higher levels of consciousness and on unconscious and subconscious levels — but old experiences nonetheless.

On conscious levels you are creating your own realities all of the time. It is just the question, who are you at any given time? Which element of yourself is creating this particular reality? When one recognizes the multidimensionality of one's being, then one can step into the driver's seat and say, "All right, this particular First Mate part here — move out of the way. I'm steering the ship." Or quite the same way, you can say, "All right, Soul, what I'm seeing here is a situation that you seem to be creating in my life. I do not particularly like the way it is going. Let's rearrange that." It will not be a matter of pushing Soul out of the way; it will be a team here. "Let us come to an agreement on what we want."

What you want on a conscious level is to have the Soul Merge — or the third initiation — occur without creating a tremendous amount of trauma in your life. Then so be it. You have the power to do that. The more you assume that power, the more you will be able to see the areas where you have not been able to assume your power. You get a little taste of it, you move out a part here and you get a bit of energy over there, and that gives you the illumination to be able to see the other parts that are holding your energy down. Then it becomes a snowball effect. The more power you have, the better you can see; and the more parts you can straighten out and the more patterns that you can pull out, the more quickly your own internal blockages can be released.

This is how the phenomenal transformation can occur — entering this lifetime as a Second-Degree Initiate and suddenly going from that level to almost a Galactic Avatar status all in one lifetime! That is the possibility now. That possibility was not open before the Harmonic Convergence.

Average humanity, on perhaps a little bit lesser developed consciousness level, can also make phenomenal gains in a very short time period. This again is entirely dependent upon the individual's choice and how they align with the special dispensation from the Creator level through the energy we now call the *Mahatma*. We say "now," because for some time it was felt by your Planetary Government that a Creator-level avatar (Cosmic Avatar) could never come closer than the level of the higher mind or causal body of Earth (because the Earth was too heavy). However, because the Harmonic Convergence allowed the vibrations of Earth to become fourth-dimensional, this planet has benefitted exponentially by having the *Mahatma* energy choose Earth to anchor the Source, thus allowing the first connection *ever* from Source to Earth with a completed circuitry. What this means is that *The Rider on the White Horse*, the Avatar of Synthesis, or the name that resonates better for mankind — the *Mahatma* — has come in directly to this quadrant of this galaxy and anchored into the Earth, creating the Earth-link from Source to Earth!

We would now like to deal with planetary systems, their evolutionary level and Mother Earth as a living entity.

The thing to consider here is the analogy of planetary bodies with your own bodies, and your own levels. Consider Mother Earth as being the more physical aspect of yourself, made up of various minor consciousnesses, so to speak, of the bones, the blood, the cells, and all of the other elements that are physical — but which also have a consciousness — and which together make up your body. Beyond that you have your personality, your ego, your own sense of Self. Beyond that is Soul; beyond that is Monad; and beyond that is Source.

From using that simplified analogy we can see that the Earth as a physical structure has its own elements of consciousness on a physical level. It has its personality aspect, its egoic aspect, its Self aspect represented by Sanat Kumara. It has its Soul aspect; it has its monadic aspect.

The connectedness and the purposes of Sanat Kumara as they relate to this time frame — the integration of certain aspects of Mother Earth's Soul Merge (refer to Sanat Kumara, p. 192 and p. 229) — is taking place more for Sanat Kumara than for Mother Earth. Of course, when the energy of the Soul Merge occurs for one, it affects *all* of the vehicles, all of those involved, much in the same way as the Soul merging with personality/ego affects your body aspect as well. There are changes occurring on the physical-structure level within you, and now these too are occurring within Mother Earth.

The interrelatedness between mankind and Mother Earth — from our perspective now — is that there is an immense affinity between the two, and they are not dissimilar. Mankind is a group Soul. As one rises to the level of connection with one's own Soul, one is more able to realize the connectedness with all *other* Souls embodying on this particular plane. Mankind, as a group vehicle on this planet, is a particular expression of an aspect of God, of Source. The connection between mankind and Mother Earth is that Mother Earth is the collection, the amalgamation, of the more basic parts of consciousness that make up the planet Earth, such as the consciousnesses embodying the devic/elemental, the mineral kingdom, the animal kingdom and the human kingdom (which, because it has been given its distinction here in terms of free will, we see as a dividing line). In reality, all are One; but as a relationship, we can look at humanity as somewhat distinct from that other grouping, which makes up to large extent the consciousness of Mother Earth. Now, humanity's consciousness is certainly in there, and as humanity clears on an individual level, on a mass level or on both levels, then certainly Mother Earth clears as well, all the way down the line. So the connection there is one that is very close, but for purpose of distinction, we can draw a line.

There are such similarities between the group focus called mankind and Mother Earth — the aspects that will gain Ascension, that have the same moments of anxiety, of pain, as it were, as we do in our Soul-Merge process. She is going to have the same moments of almost psychological unrest or distrust, thus the upheavals on her surface throughout various parts of the world as Mother Earth integrates her Soul Merge over the next few years. The degree of upheaval will be in direct proportion to her discomfort.

Really, Mother Earth is an expression of the consciousness of Source as much as, and no more or less than, you or anyone else. Ultimately, all are God. All are Source in every aspect — it is simply a matter of how much any aspect is aware of its own greater portions. There is a saying that the Soul knows that it is the consciousness, but the consciousness does not know that it is the Soul. And now the Soul/Higher Self, which isn't sufficiently aware of its more monadic level, has invoked a representation of all levels called the *Mahatma*, which has come from the expanded Source and is reporting to the Council of Twelve at the Creator level of this expanded Source what physicality is, what the Co-Creator level is! You can begin to see why this Cosmic Avatar, *Mahatma*, is here to synthesize (integrate) the separation between the Creator and Co-Creator levels. For the Creator level never truly felt that the Co-Creator level was a part of the wonderful Source level. Interesting, isn't it?

So you have, from a point of expression, Source. We could envision it as a big ball, and from Source there was that initial little ripple within. Source viewed something within Its own thought process and thought, "Well, this is interesting — perhaps there is a little bit of duality here after all." Even the point of *having* that thought, for Source, indicated a certain amount of duality on that very primal level. And so that thought attracted some energy to it and created a situation where these opposing forces called duality were generated. In this generation they created what is called the monadic level — the consciousness of the more individualized entity of God.

Now, God simply IS. Source IS. There is no big God sitting on a throne judging. A great deal of humanity is deeply confused about this concept. Our purpose is to give people an expanded vision, an expanded, less limited view of themselves in their relation to the Cosmos, in relation to God. When God expanded Himself into the monadic level, essentially He said, "I simply AM; but in this Isness that I Am, there are some interesting things to experience. What I will do? I will remain on My level in the Wholeness of My consciousness, and I will send forth My aspects to experience, and essentially, to report back to me with that experience."

So the monadic level was created. The monadic level, then, in its grandeur (because it simply *was* grand) began to play with its newfound ability to create on every level, and to create matter in the physical universes. The monadic level found that it needed certain more focused aspects to go deeper into the structure that it had created. So it created the Soul levels as further extensions.

The Soul levels then played around for a considerable amount of time, as you reference time, and eventually decided, "Well, this is quite a fascinating project; let us create a vehicle whereby we, as Soul, as Gods, can experience what it is like to be in this physical realm. We have created this physical realm, but we cannot touch it — it is as if we are separate from it. We have created that thing over there, and the figurative hand moves right through it. We cannot experience it." So the beings on the Soul levels and the monadic level chose at that point to begin an experiment: *the fusion of consciousness into matter*.

It was not God who did that (except for supplying the essential Twelve Rays). It was the *expressions* who had the free will and latitude to be able to play with that kind of experiment. So they began to create vehicles through which they could express. (The steps prior to that, of course, were learning to create in the first place.)

It began with single-cell structures, and as their (yours and ours as well, because we were all One at that point) proficiency grew, the process really began to take form, closer to what is now experienced.

The physical planet as a structure had been there for some time, and then this experiment began with what is called life, working with a biological structure that could maintain a spark of consciousness to whatever degree. They found that as the complexity of these creations became greater, more of the small sparks of consciousness could group together and create a wholeness of consciousness that had more sentience.

Ultimately, animal man was created as well as Primal Soul, or the beings on that level. It was actually not quite as distinct as we are now referencing Soul/Monad; there was a certain overlap there because it was a project coming from the monadic level as well. The beings at that point then decided, "Well, this is interesting — we have a vehicle here whereby we can move right in and begin to experience." However, they were not able to move in entirely, so in order to experience they had to fragment another portion of their being and send that portion into the animal man. That experience was duly transmitted back to the higher levels, all the way back up the line to the Source level.

As every level from the animal man on up grew in experience, Primal Soul also grew in fulfillment and in experience. Source is certainly not a static perfection. Source is an ever-growing, ever-evolving entity. We — all of us — being aspects of Source, are evolving Source and Source is evolving us. Your evolution is evolving me and mine is evolving you, and so it continues.

In the process of Creation here the physical vehicle called animal man was refined and built to the point where he was able to handle a greater amount of consciousness, but there was a bit of danger there. The danger was that once it had reached a point where it could hold a larger amount of the Soul's consciousness, the entity itself had enough consciousness that it began to create its own persona. It said, "Well, this is me; I am this," and Primal Soul was, essentially, relegated to a spark six inches above the head in the eighth chakra. (Refer to the diagram, "Electrical Day One," p. 222.) That Soul connection was still there, but it was a little tricky to maintain the full Soul experience and Soul control of that vehicle. Ultimately what happened is that these consciousnesses of animal man, which had fragmented themselves into that experience, began to feel and believe that that was all that existed.

That is how the belief system started to snowball, and the more belief there was of being separated, the more the reality reflected it and the more the experience became separate.

Now, returning to Mother Earth. She is the expression of much of that same fragmented consciousness which went, initially, into that animal man experience. Mother Earth is now pulling together those fragments into a more concentrated wholeness. That concentrated wholeness fusing together is creating a denser energy. Now, "denser" is perhaps a rather misleading word because it is a more refined energy, at the same time denser in the sense of pulling together the parts of energy to create a more powerful energy that brings greater coherence to the consciousness. That greater coherence of consciousness then enables a greater understanding of the process to take place; and that, again, allows the initiation process to take place — the stimulation of that consciousness to a higher level, a higher vibration.

So we have the duality of the denser energy creating a refined consciousness. That refined consciousness of Mother Earth as an entity is beginning to vibrate on a higher level. That higher level escalates up the line to Sanat Kumara. (Refer to the illustration, "The Seven Councils of Twelve," p. 227.)

Sanat Kumara's program has been well laid out — this initiation process for him had been spelled out long ago in the evolutionary process. It is quite interesting to see the interrelating dynamics from within the space and time frame that you are experiencing, whereas from the monadic perspective it is all a singular process occurring in the eternal Now, which is the same moment of the initial creation of entities in the first place.

The concept of time and no-time is where many will get confused. Interestingly enough, the quantum mechanics branch of physics has been plagued by the same problem. They have created a theory explaining the physical universe that, even in their own terms and in the terms of their greatest detractors, is the most successful scientific theory ever promoted. Yet few will listen to it. Nobody will believe it to the point of saying, "This is my reality." They say, "If this electron does this and this, then the reality is that. But my *experience* is that the desk is still solid." Thus they are still believing and living within the old mechanical frame, the Newtonian frame of consciousness, while they are paying mental lip service to a higher one. Not to blame anyone here; it is simply a matter of making the adjustment in experience.

In that same way, the consciousness aspect of the refinement of planet Earth into a higher sphere in the Ascension process is simply one of elevating the vibration to a higher plane. It is not that when one ascends one is instantly absorbed back into the Isness of God, because nobody ever really left in the first place. It should be noted that Mastery, or physical Ascension from Earth, is really a primary point of integration.

The Ascension in the fourth-dimensional Relative Now[1] can lead to the spiritualization of matter. That is the process. All of the understanding, all of the knowledge, means nothing without the *experience* in the process taking place. It is simply the transmutation of the physical matter into higher matter, higher energy, that really effects the change in consciousness. Knowledge, of course, adds onto that and spurs it along. The key to effecting change in anyone is not information; it is process. That is why religions have without exception been such spiritual failures. Religions have simply ignored methods enabling mankind to process. Thus from our perspective, the most heightened example on your Earth would be the Christian personification of Jesus and the Virgin Mary, where Master Jesus has been elevated from being the Son of God (which we would agree with if that also included the balance of humanity) to Lord God, which is absurd. Mother Mary as the mother of God is really not worthy of comment. (The very thought that the Creator level of All That Is would interfere with the workings of this Planetary Government and father a child for Mary is patently ridiculous.)[2]

We know that mankind sees a personalized God. God simply IS. The expression "personal God" is certainly an aspect that mankind has gravitated toward, the tendency to personify, the anthropomorphising of their experience, projecting that onto a larger or smaller being. The balance of mankind, still locked in the emotional body/second chakra, have chosen to disregard the basic Law of Creation on all levels including Source: that all are equal in the eyes of God and that divine equality exists at the Creator level and every other level! Why? Because all exists as God, the difference being that a Source entity has a higher degree of consciousness. But even the most lowly evolved will become a full Creator — that is evolution. Can you not see that religions are self-perpetuating? They have nothing to do with spirituality; they are predicated on fear and the divisive use of the devil and hell-fire and damnation. When mass consciousness shifts into the fourth dimension we will show you that these areas have nothing to do with the all-loving, nonjudgmental God that we're aware of. Then you will see quite clearly that without these fears there would be no need for religions, for through a religious Hierarchy their retrogressive third-dimensional concepts simply can't exist anymore in a fourth-dimensional reality!

This tendency to personify was born early on in existence to help to explain to animal man, who was seemingly trapped within this small vehicle, how this all came about. There was an inkling back there that "there is something *more* to me than this, something I don't remember." The brain was rather small at that time; brain is certainly a portion of it, and a large part of mankind's experience. But the projection of one's own limited parameters onto a grander

---

1 "Now" is relative to the ultimate NOW of existence, or Creation, which can only be expressed by the Source Itself...(See page 433 for further explanation).

2 If Sanat Kumara's Higher Self wished to express within a dense physical body to assist "The Father, The Lord of the World" Sanat Kumara, that could and did happen on a number of occasions including King Solomon. Jesus was the most famous example of this, thus the massive confusion "the Only Begotten Son of God," "The Father" "The Son" and "The Holy Ghost."

being is certainly a false belief. There are greater wholenesses of consciousness, and mankind loves to personify them — as Sanat Kumara, as Vywamus,
as whatever other level you wish to personify. Now certainly, as entities there
is within each of us that element and that understanding of that personification. Thus we come through in a personified form to speak to you, who like to
speak to a personified form. But to believe that that is all Sanat Kumara is —
that he is a bigger man who happens to have this Earth as his body — is a
misconception, because Sanat Kumara is much more than just the physical
rock floating in space. His consciousness is more than that.

The fact that Sanat Kumara is referred to as "He" and Mother Earth is
symbolically, creatively, and truthfully a female is again human personification. We speak in those terms because they are more readily understood.
There is an entire belief system built around that, so the Hierarchy has chosen
to *use* that system as a means of working within it in order to transcend this
belief.

When Mother Earth speaks, though, she makes reference to her female
beingness. What is transpiring in polarities has been termed and experienced
by humanity as male and female energy. The polarity which Mother Earth as
an entity is expressing is what is vibrating on a similar frequency to that which
is experienced within humanity as the feminine.

In reality there is no male or female — it is all simply energy. Relationship
is a mirror of that relationship within yourself. You have the male and female
aspects of your energy — the polarities. You are living in a strong duality, and
that gives you the Yin and the Yang, the female and the male, the negatives and
the positives — all of these various tools that you as Gods have chosen to create
in order to *experience*. So here you are, a God seemingly trapped within this
physical form, wondering, "How did I get here?" In reality, you are a multidimensional being, *seeing* yourself as a fragment, *feeling* cut off and stuck in this
body.

The process, now, is that from invocation by you as an individual fragment
of that God Which You Are, that invocation calls forth the energy from the
grandeur of who you really are and helps you to reconnect and become
reaware of who and what you are. From our perspective we see this, and from
our perspective time does not exist. Remember that the experience of the
human on this plane is probably the most acute, in terms of concrete experience, of that which is called limitation. Why would a God choose to experience
limitation? Why would a God choose to experience *anything*? — for the *experience* of it. Source is indifferent; it simply *IS*. In Source's bubbling consciousness there was what could be anthropomorphically projected as a sense of
curiosity. That curiosity then created the Monad, the Soul, etc., all of which
had that seed of curiosity to expand into something greater.

Humanity chooses to work more deeply within that and expand on that
curiosity, and says, "Well, this is fascinating! Look what we created here, and
look what is over there. Let's look deeper and deeper," and in doing so, they
looked so deeply that they essentially got themselves stuck. But, the *whole*

being did not get stuck, and it is only the portion which is stuck that feels cut off. The name of the game is to become reaware of yourself as a multidimensional being. This is what the Ascension process does.

When that Soul spark which animates the physical consciousness that you call yourself becomes more aware of its *own* higher level, when the spark knows that it is simply a spark of the greater Soul and that it is a spark of the greater Monad, etc., then that whole process speeds up very quickly.

The Ascension process from Earth is a process whereby the Soul spark has invoked and cleared enough of the Soul energy for all of that energy to come in and anchor firmly. Once the Soul is in the driver's seat of the consciousness, then its next step is to get mastery of the body. It is a matter of stepping down the energy to an even more dense level — to the level of the actual physical structure itself. Remember that the Soul Merge (the Third Initiation) is the merge of the personality and the Soul, so that the personality is then more on a mental than an emotional level. As the Soul anchors there with the personality/ego, its process then is to anchor into the physical even more firmly, and in doing so it builds the Lightbody. The body of Light is all there is, anyway. In reality it does not do any building at all; it simply realizes and recognizes that the physical body is simply *slowed-down Light*. That is all that matter is: Light that has been slowed down enough to have the semblance or illusion of form. Where did the Light come from? The Light is a product of the thought of God. So God is thought, you could say. God is consciousness — a better word for thought — manifested as the Twelve Rays that we discuss in the section beginning on page 204. Even your physicists are coming to that recognition. One of the famous ones, possibly Sir James Jeans, said something like, "The universe is beginning to look more and more like one big thought than like one big thing." Commonly phrased, "Thoughts are things and things are thoughts, and all is energy"!

Even in the physical reality of the human beings on this planet, the ones who have traditionally been the most materialistically inclined — physical scientists and physicists — are the ones more apt to say, "All this spiritual stuff is nonsense. Where is it? Show me God under a microscope. Then I will believe you. If not a microscope, then show me in a telescope. Where is it? I don't see his beard out there."

What they are finding now when looking beyond both levels, far beyond and far deeper out there, is that same spark of the Infinite that is showing them that all of their little rules and beliefs, attitudes and theories about how the world, how Creation, how the universe really is — really are *not* correct! The fascinating thing is that as they look into that and get active on those very, very deep levels, what they see and what they expect are what they get. When you have two scientists running a similar experiment, let's say one has figured out that "if I perform these tests, this electron will move over there, etc." Consequently, he promotes his theory, sets up his experiment, and demonstrates his theory. Sure enough, the electron moves just like he predicted. The other scientist comes along and says, "Well, that's ridiculous. According to my calculations, it should go in the opposite direction." He performs his experiments and it *does* go in the opposite direction. So then they each claim the other one did not perform his experiment correctly. But when it happens over and over again, the conclusion must be that the observer, by his *intent*, affects the experiment. This is not metaphysical hocus-pocus; this is what has been happening in science. It is simply a matter of their bridging the gap between theory and actuality. Now it is realized that the expectation influences the outcome. When dealing with those very minute subatomic particles, one's consciousness, one's thought, can propel and direct them.

The Lightbody is one concept that science has already begun to touch upon — in Kirlian photography, etc. There is enough evidence to show that this "physical" structure, according to the eyes and the rest of the senses, is more than it appears — there is an electrical charge to it. Science can accept that on the level of electricity, because it knows that much of the driving force within the organism is an electrical force. It has not come to the point of knowing where the Source of that electrical force is any more than it really knows where the source of the electrical force in a thunderstorm is. It knows that "if this happens and that happens, electricity is created," but what is electricity? What is energy? Where did the energy come from? "It must have come from the Big Bang," but where did the Big Bang come from?

Follow it back far enough and they are ultimately at a loss to explain, and the explaining part of it is the trap. Ultimately they are going to run into a point where it cannot be explained, because the intellect just gets short-circuited. Intellect *cannot stretch that far*. It is being stretched quite a bit, and certainly Einstein's theory stretched it to the point of great discomfort for many. He was still a third-dimensional vehicle, but taking the experimental evidence of those theories (not only Einstein's but those who followed him and worked with him) and drawing their conclusions from them, it is very easy to see those conclusions overlapping into another dimensional reality. This is that bridging process, part of the Ascension process from a planetary level, humanity ascending to a higher level. So the Ascension first takes place in consciousness. Ultimately it will take place on the physical level. That is true for you as a human being and it is true for this entity called Earth — the consciousness aspect ascends first.

The aspect of Ascension whereby you actually take your physical body with you would cause science much concern. If you walked into a major scientific conference and then just twinkled in front of their eyes, it would cause a lot of concern, wouldn't it? They would be at a loss to explain it, and it would *totally* shatter their basic beliefs about reality.[3] It would drive a little crack into it, and then through that crack the light of another system could be seen. Scientists could crawl through the crack and start to feel their way

---

3 So much so that all Physical Science would be inconclusive and would have to start anew with a multi-dimensional matrix as their new-found reality.

around. This crack was brought into their belief system through Einsteinian physics, and it has been gradually growing on that higher stratum of the intellect of those who are operating on that level. It is now accepted as a reality — to a point. Their reality still has limits. The reality will say something like, "Well, certainly, the thought and the intent of the scientist influences the outcome of the experiment — no one disputes that. It is obvious; it is a proven fact." But when you draw that conclusion a little bit further and say, "If your thought, then, can influence an electron or a subatomic particle, does it not stand to reason that your thought can create a reality in front of your very eyes, such as manifesting an apple in your hand — or Ascension?"

The scientists would look at you and say, "Don't be a fool — of course not," because they still think in terms of things, in terms of the apple being a bigger *thing* than an electron. And their belief system says, "All right, my thought can influence an electron; but there is no way that it can influence an apple. I can, maybe, levitate that little ant, but I could not levitate a car." This is a limitation imposed by the belief system. What I am saying is that that belief system has a crack in it now that is opening wider and wider as more evidence is coming forth to indicate the creation of reality on different levels. The Ascension is simply a greater demonstration of that. When one can ascend and dematerialize and rematerialize, it is certainly a dramatic display of manifestation. In the past, some of you who are working with mankind have done just that on one planet or another, but not in the relative spiritual body. The whole purpose of this physical plane — and the reason that you as Gods created it in the first place — was to slow down the process of manifestation to the point where you could see the actual progression of it in linear, sequential time. Whereas on the higher planes it was instantaneous. You had the desire, and it was there; you saw the vision, and the reality appeared. Here, you see the vision, and it takes some time and some clarity of holding that vision. You have to hold that vision for a longer length of time in order for it to manifest here.

When you have a vision of a business transaction or of a new car or boat that you want to buy, if you have that vision very clear in your mind and you focus intently on that vision for a long period of time, ultimately it will manifest in your life, but it will not be instantaneous. However, once the higher connection is made to the Soul level and the higher chakras are opened to a higher degree (with the acceptance on a conscious level that you are fourth-dimensional), then that level of instantaneous manifestation will be more evident. That will also be the level at which one materializes or dematerializes the body. The Ascension process is going to be getting a lot of coverage in the years to come. It is something that people will be very excited about, as it is relatively new in terms of understanding its metaphysics — not new in terms of experience. People throughout the ages here and there have done it, but it has not been a scientific process. It has been one they have stumbled upon. The beings on this planet who have ascended in the past have been the host of masters from the Golden Years or those select few who either came here from another system and already knew the Ascension Process from another aspect level, or they cleared themselves to a point where they could draw upon their higher aspects to bring that information through. In some cases it was brought through on a conscious level, where they said, "This is the process of Ascension; this is what I am doing, and this is the reason I am doing it."

In other cases, the information came through in a rather modified, trickled-down form, where they got the gist of it, where they had the experience but did not really know why or what they were doing. In the ascension of Djwhal Khul, for instance, he was more conscious of the process; he had more of an inkling about what was going on, principally because he had El Morya and Kuthumi as teachers.

When Apollonius (the energy who had been Jesus) ascended, he had a greater knowledge, because Jesus had been overshadowed by the Christ energy for a very great period of time. So when the Christ consciousness left and Jesus was the initiated human again, he still had that to draw upon; he had that source of expansion from within his own experience.

Over the centuries the Christian religion has confused the fact that the Christ and Master Jesus are two separate energies and entities. The Christ, the Lord Maitreya, overshadowed the disciple Jesus, using his body as the medium through which to speak on the physical plane. Those present at that time did recognize this and realized that it was the Christ speaking through Jesus.

Out of this confusion of the Church has come the one name, Jesus Christ referring to one being, which is incorrect and misleading. There are indeed two separate beings — Jesus, and the Christ. The Christ brought the quality of unconditional Love to the Earth. The Master Jesus was given the responsibility of the Christian Church; and as the planetary Master of the Sixth Ray, it is a responsibility that he still holds. He will soon manifest physically to finish the assignment he started, by assisting Christianity to make the transition to "spirituality" and the new world religion. At this juncture, the decision is still that Jesus will headquarter the world religion in the Vatican as the last symbolic Pope of the Catholic Church.

Much clarification is also needed on the subject of the crucifixion. It must be understood that the crucifixion involved the two separate energies in *two separate events*. The Master Jesus was involved in the physical event of the completion of his physical initiations and passage through the door of the Fourth Initiation. The Lord Maitreya, the Christ, passed through the door of the Sixth Initiation — which is an esoteric event through mirroring the spiritual or monadic level, but not personally achieving that level of integration.

The Great Renunciation, or Fourth Initiation, which Jesus entered into upon the cross, brings liberation from physicality through the renunciation, or rejection, and the destruction of the perfected personality and its three aspects — the physical, the emotional, and the mental bodies. (Refer to the illustrations, "The Four-Body System," p. 225 and "Man's Response to Initiations," p. 220.) This highly developed, perfected personality is the end product of many incarnations; it is destroyed in "fire by friction" as the Soul passes through the door of the Fourth Initiation. This is a very powerful ordeal and almost without exception would result in the destruction of the dense physical body — physical death. It was this Fourth Initiation which caused Jesus to die on the cross prior to the effects of the crucifixion.

The Transformational Fire that is being experienced now is on the more inner planes, and this is being felt as a stimulation from within the atomic structure of the body. This is the enlightenment of the body, the enlightenment of the cellular structure in terms of its true nature of Light.

So we bring forth, shall we say, this baptism of fire on a planetary level in a more easily experienced manner. It will *not* be in the nature of nuclear destruction. As a message, that can be brought out.

During the crucifixion it was the Christ's energy that was in Jesus' body upon the cross until just before the physical death of Jesus, when the Christ left the body. It was, then, Jesus who said, "My God, my God, why have you forsaken me?" addressing the Christ who had left. The body of Jesus was placed ih the sepulcher and was dematerialized through the Christed energy. It was not resurrected, nor did Jesus ascend.

Vywamus, through Janet McClure, explains the Christ's reappearance after the death of Jesus: "It was simply a manifesting process of the Christ, who already knew how to use the Ascension process because he had undergone it much earlier. So it really had nothing to do with the Master Jesus at this point. It was the Christed energies that were able to do whatever was desired as a demonstration to humanity as to what could be done, and the Master Jesus had, of course, left by that time. The ascended Christ, the Lord Maitreya, appearing still within a physical format that could be recognized as the One who had been there...he just used the particular vehicle of the Master Jesus, an image of him. The Christ simply manifested that appearance again, you might say."

The famous, much publicized Ascension process at the time of the crucifixion was a little different from the one that is being experienced at present. On the personal level, it is, of course, different from the experience of Jesus.

Jesus, as a human, had attained what is termed the Soul Merge prior to his incarnation as Jesus. So he came in from that level of Soul Merge and did his learning as a young child. When he did begin his mission, he then tuned into the Christed energy, which came in and overshadowed him in the desert just prior to his baptism. Jesus for three years actually channeled the Christ, Maitreya, waking, dreaming, and sleeping — in effect, possession.

It was a different type of channeling from that which many are doing today. It was a more all-inclusive channeling; it was more an overshadowing; it was a total engulfing of Jesus on every level of his being by the Christ energy. Although the channeling that most are doing today is a somewhat more gentle version, you still feel to a certain extent that separation and that contrast when the energy is there as compared to when it is not. The channels feel an expansion when channeling, and sometimes they feel a contraction afterwards. That contraction, when it is taken in the correct perspective, usually is the impetus to clear even *more* so that the expansion can be there always.

So this is what occurred with Jesus — this sense of expansion while channeling, while being overshadowed by the Christ. For him, the sense of contraction was overwhelmingly traumatic when the Christed energy left his body on
the cross just before his physical death.

At the point when the mission was completed, the Jesus energy lifted, and
the Christ created the illusion of an ascension for Jesus. Meanwhile, Peter felt
— the word "forsaken" is a little bit overblown — a sense of betrayal. "Oh my
God, I've been abandoned!" He was able a little later to reattune to his
blueprint, but at that point Peter thought that it was Jesus who had ascended
and that the Maitreya energy had lifted also — which, of course, was the plan.
A reluctant deception was required in the view of the Christ.

The Ascension process for Jesus took place in another time, in another
body. It was an entity that some know as Apollonius of Tyana, Greece, and it
was sometime later in sequential time. Apollonius achieved his Fifth Initiation
in that time, and having then mastered the Earth's vibrations, he ascended
from there in the true form of the physical Ascension process. Through his
work with the Planetary Hierarchy since that time he has gotten to the point
where he has taken his Sixth Initiation. Again, and not dissimilar to others
within the Planetary Hierarchy, he has kept his original name, Jesus, because of
input from mass consciousness. His energy is "Apollonius" from his last
incarnation, and his spiritual name and personal choice at this time is
"Sananda." The name Jesus doesn't really exist anymore except in mass consciousness.

The outcome of the passion play was that we, as Peter, chose that experience for our own learning, as did Jesus, as did Maitreya. All chose that
experience for themselves. Jesus had an intention to create a teaching. He also
had the intention to create more than a spiritual teaching. He had the intention, if the time and place were correct, to pull together more the people of that
area on the physical level. This is what the Romans were upset about, because
they saw that intention very clearly. The Roman Empire at that time was very
power-hungry — they were the power on the Earth. They were personifying
what you might now call the material power.

Jesus manifested himself in that scene, in agreement with Maitreya, to
counterbalance that intense materialism of the Roman Empire with the more
"spiritual" vision that he imparted. Yet within Jesus the man, there was still a
certain amount of that physical, earthly response to the perceived oppression
of that time. So he worked very deliberately with the consciousness of the
people and their expectations — "The Messiah is coming." Who was the Messiah? It was to be the "true King" and that true king would then bring forth the
wholeness of the land, would bring the people together in a political and
spiritual empire. Well, the Romans had the upper hand on the physical plane;
thus the material version of the Plan was essentially thwarted. From the higher
aspect — from Maitreya's point of view — all of that was very much inciden-
tal. His desire was to come in and experience what it was like to bring that
energy back down into the physical again (he had already been physical). He

had expanded to his Higher Self as an earlier experience. His curiosity said, "I wonder what it would be like to go back there again."

As the Christ, Maitreya felt that in order to complete his mission, he couldn't jeopardize the Plan by bringing his energy totally into physicality. So he chose not to manifest a physical body but to overshadow Jesus. Maitreya/Christ came in through Jesus, had that experience, and then departed to a number of countries, particularly India, with a body that resembled Jesus. Christ *stayed* and teleported to countries such as America during the next thirty-one years, and during that time helped to correct the unexpected damage that was done during the crucifixion, promulgated primarily by the seemingly negative statement so powerfully infused into the Earth, "Father, why hast thou forsaken me?"

The teaching, which fell into the hands of Peter, Paul and others, was to carry forth that higher vision. Through the poor communication of that time, it did not quite meet its objective, but there is no blame there. The blame that was felt by Peter as well as by others was simply a self-imposed sense of guilt because they felt that they had to go out and save the others. If they had but known within themselves that the only ones they had to save were *themselves*, and that "saving" was not from any terrible fate but simply from their own ignorance (meaning not knowing), then it would have been a simple matter to just lighten up and say, "Well, here is the wonderful teaching of this beautiful being who came in our midst. Would you like to hear it?" rather than saying, "You poor wretched people, have this teaching or else!" Not that they really promulgated that at the start, but that became the focus of the Church in the years to come.

There was a tremendous lack of communication in those early years between the various disciples, and even a lack of accurate recall of the incidents. Thus, the Gospel stories were really third- or fourth-hand information written down sometime later. As a result, if you look at the Gospels with a critical eye, you will find that they do not even correspond with one another — certainly not the "Word of God."

There is an element of needing to tell the story in a more objective light, but there is also an element of telling it from the "spiritual" aspect. Others have come forth with the more critical point of view from the physical aspect and said, "Well, it was simply playing upon the superstitions of the time. He had a certain heritage from the house of David and set himself up to try to be the Messiah. It didn't work, and therefore the Romans killed him." That is one view of it — seeing Jesus simply as a politically hungry man. What we are trying to say here is that there is more to the story than that.

There was an element of that, but the greater element was the more altruistic vision that he had, which was to set up a teaching that would have a greater impact upon the people than simply another cult of the time — and there were plenty. Jesus was certainly not the only one doing that kind of thing at that time, and in the years to come there were more and more. Through certain circumstances of political connection within the Roman Empire, the

Church really got off the ground. Peter and Paul had much to do with the success of these teachings.

Nonetheless, much confusion developed within the Christian Church and continued over the centuries with regard to the Christ as the only Son of God, a very unique and special being to be worshipped. This misconception has perpetuated mankind's age-old belief in separation — that they are separate from God (and the Christ), that they are less than God (and therefore less than the Christ, the Buddha, Mohammed, Krishna, and so on). The Christ anticipated such a typical, habitual reaction on the part of humanity and tried to prevent the formation of such a belief structure by explaining that we are *all* Sons of God and by trying to introduce the concept that "greater things than I do shall you do." This was then, and has remained, a concept that most do not understand or believe, and therefore mankind continues to give away its power by worshipping beings whom they believe to be greater than themselves, still not realizing the fact of divine equality — that *every* being is an expression of Source, no matter what their point in evolution, and all are moving toward becoming greater expressions of divine energy!

The Christ is certainly not the most highly evolved being ever to come to the Earth; however, Maitreya, as the Christ, is the most highly evolved to graduate from this planet Earth.

In the promotion process within the Planetary Hierarchy, the Office of the Christ, which Maitreya now holds, is going to be taken over by another who is now in the process of the Sixth Initiation. Once the energy of that initiation is firmly established, this other, Kuthumi, will then be filling that office. Maitreya, from the Seventh, will be moving into the next higher level, but for the time being he will assist in the arrival of the Cosmic Avatar that most scriptures refer to as *The Rider on the White Horse* (the *Mahatma*).

There are nine initiations which one can take here, within this sphere. The Planetary Hierarchy is one aspect, but there is a Solar Hierarchy, and within the solar system there are also initiations. The planetary levels go from the level of Master, which is the Fifth Initiation, to the Christ level, which is the Sixth Initiation. The Seventh Initiation is that of the Buddhas, Maitreya, and the Kumaras. The Eighth Initiation is the level of the Planetary Logos. The Ninth Initiation is that of the Solar Logos, and the Tenth and the highest Initiation is the Council of Twelve for this quadrant of this galaxy. (Refer to the chart, "Co-Creator and Creator Levels," pp. 228-29.)

One can look at the whole sphere of the Earth Hierarchy, with Sanat Kumara as its grand chairman of the board. If you view the Christ as being the general manager, then beyond that is the chairman of the board. There are a number of different wholenesses — one of them would be within the solar system. The energy that you would reference as Helios encompasses this whole solar system, including all of the other planets within this sphere. And then expanding out into a different dimension, we have the greater wholenesses of Vywamus, Lenduce, and others going out the other way, so to speak, into the Fifth dimensional lower Galactic Realms.

If you look at it from a linear point of view, you have the individual planets all circling around the Sun, and that solar system on the physical level comprises a greater wholeness, but it expands the other way into a different dimensional reality, of which Helios is certainly well aware. Then we have a different expansion, which is Vywamus, etc. So it is rather interesting, putting these concepts into the linear framework within which mankind is thinking. It is very difficult sometimes to find words to match these ideas!

The Buddha, on the other hand, was a man who had achieved a certain level of awareness and basically chose to come back. He could have stayed in what many call Paradise — the fifth chakra and fifth astral level. Many beings do stay there for eons of time. This is what mankind calls heaven. It is an experience, a level of consciousness beyond the physical expression of the Earth where one goes to the level that they have achieved in the physical. In the case of Buddha, he had expressed and experienced enough to take him into what is called the Fifth Heaven, the Paradise. That Paradise (we could call it "physical Heaven") would correspond, in a sense, to the throat chakra, if you can see the parallel there. In the Fifth Heaven, the fifth level of expression, the fifth chakra, he had everything he could want. His expression in the previous life had taken him to this point — the expression of the Love. He lived for expressing Love, and yet what was missing was his connection to the Father, to the Source, to the All That Is.

He got that inkling, even amidst Paradise. Many do not get an inkling for a long, long time. They think that that's all there is, and they are simply content to be there. As a contrasting perspective, there are places where beings believe that they are dead, and so they experience themselves as being dead, row upon row. Ramtha talks about it — it is quite interesting. He sort of bumped into this level at one point and was trying to tell these beings, "Wake up — you are not really dead, you know!" But they had this misconception that they had to lie there in that comatose state until the Savior could come and resurrect them. Even when the Savior came to resurrect them, it did not work — they would not listen because their teaching had also told them that a devil would come and try to tempt them. So they would not listen at all. Even the Savior could not convince them — a double bind, in terms of belief. Ultimately that system of experience will wear thin. They will say, "Well, I have been here for how many million years. I think it is time that the resurrection is going to happen — I'd better get up and see what is going on. Maybe I missed the boat." So they will eventually stir and wake up, and at that point will be able to listen.

Now, getting back to Buddha. He was in this Fifth (physical) Heaven, and yet he had this inkling that there must be more, much more. As soon as he thought that he got the assistance he needed to look at what might be more, that impetus impelled him to choose to go back into physicality again. At that point he did not have to go back into the physical. That's why in this system he is called "The Great Buddha who has renounced Paradise and has come back to save." In reality, he did not renounce Paradise to save anyone else — he renounced Paradise knowing that it was a lower level than he wanted to achieve. The way for him to accomplish this was to come back into the physical and make those changes within himself to elevate himself to the higher levels, to that connection with the Father energy.

The experience of satori, as the Zen tradition calls the step prior to the Soul Merge, is the experience of the so-called no-mind. To a certain extent, it is a step along the way. It is that state of being of suddenly finding oneself, in a sense, as the observer of one's reality, and in that perspective one can then very clearly see how one functions within the parameters of the reality. One can therefore begin to change it. That is when the true growth toward enlightenment really starts occurring. From the point of Soul Merge, then, the enlightenment and the expansion just mushroomed.

You must bear in mind that as a system the Zen tradition is simply another system, and the beings that come through any particular system are very likely to have go through all of the other systems as well. So one can look at a being such as Kuthumi (as the new Christ), and see that it is not fair to say that he attained his state of development as St. Francis within the Christian tradition. To a large extent, he was well-developed prior to the Christian experience (Soul Merge in another situation). Kuthumi's background has been rather more Eastern than Western, although he has an affinity for the West. The same is true for Djwhal, El Morya, and most of the other Masters simply because the Eastern tradition in that day and age had the more highly developed esoteric schools. From the time of the decline of the mystery schools in Egypt, the emphasis for deep initiation and deep teaching shifted toward the East. It had never really been lost in the East, but there was such a wonderful flowering at that time in Egypt that a tremendous number of beings — including ourself — chose to have aspects of collective self incarnate there many times to experience the very systematic processes that were developed. Our energy spent 27 lifetimes there. There was more spiritual growth on Earth in Egypt because of the high initiate level of teachers externalizing into the physical from spiritual systems. Yes, you have had Cosmic Avatars on your planet, but we would like to remind you again that the Earth was too heavy a vibration for a spiritual/monadic being to come any closer than the causal body, which vibrates only slightly lower than the Soul level.

In the Moslem tradition there are, of course, mystery teachings as well as the deeper esoteric core. However, it never really got developed to the degree of the others. Even the Christian inner core of the teachings went a little deeper than that. We say "even the Christian" not in a sense of slighting the system, but simply from the point of view of saying that the Christian tradition as one references it now is primarily that of the Catholic, or the very traditional style. Whereas the highest essence of purity within that teaching was found within the early, more Gnostic-oriented sects, which were directed more toward personal experience — going more into the experience of their oneness with God, into taking the teachings of Christ, such as the Kingdom of Heaven being within, as a personal responsibility. They said, "Well, he must be telling the truth here; let's go and find it," rather than paying the more traditional lip service to that concept. Despite these Gnostic-oriented beginnings of the Christian religion, very little in the orthodox teachings encouraged one to experience. Certainly, when one had that experience within the more traditional systems, there was danger involved in speaking about it, as you have found out! One of the great paradoxes about the Catholic Church is that all of the Apostles/Disciples were eliminated physically by the Church at least once in following lives.

To touch on the subjects of Souls for a moment, it is important to clarify that when one references a "new Soul," this Soul may have had only 700 lives or may be from another area — there are no new Souls on planet Earth. You see, all Souls were created at the same time — if you look at things in consecutive time. When one talks of one being an "old Soul," it is rather a misnomer; it simply means that one has been around in this particular scheme of things perhaps longer than the personality aspect of another. That other being may have chosen to experience in other realms prior to diving deeply into the physical.

An interesting phenomenon that we still find on Earth is the crucifixion projected by hundreds of individuals who wish to experience the stigmata, as a classic example of mankind's ability to create an unconscious will to martyrdom. In some cases, they view Jesus as being the ultimate martyr. What is this symbol of his martyrdom? It is the bleeding hands and feet, the spear wound in his side, and the blood from the crown of thorns, etc. All of those areas are highly symbolic. It has become almost an archetypal level — the suffering Savior as an archetype. This is deeper than the average subconscious belief structure. It originates more in the group unconsciousness, or the collective unconscious, as Jung called it. Those who experience these phenomena are making a subconscious or unconscious attempt to emulate the Savior. Yet from the Soul point of view, it is a demonstration that something beyond the ordinary can occur.

You might ask, "Well, if that can happen, then if you develop that a little further, why cannot a process known as Ascension be recognized?" It is simply a matter of how far this is acceptable within their belief system. Belief systems are not very logical, particularly religious belief systems. It's very easy for a classically trained religious person to say that God exists and God is All, then look at someone channeling a discarnate teacher (be it an Ascended Master or whomever) and say, "That does not exist; that is a bunch of garbage." Why, then, does his unseen spirit, God, exist and the others not? This is not very logical. However, with respect to looking at how these beings have been treated, the ones who had the stigmata created a safe demonstration for themselves within the culture in which they lived. If they had created a different demonstration that "thoughts are things," perhaps having the ability to turn things to fire (look at a tree and set it afire, for example), what would have happened in Salem, Massachusetts, had one chosen a demonstration like that? They were burned at the stake, of course. Yet the stigmata, the symbol of Jesus' wounds, must be a holy symbol. It could not be satanic in that regard, could it? It is rather interesting and incongruous, to a point, but it certainly fits into the framework of the belief system of the time.

What we are seeing now is the boundaries of these belief systems being stretched to the point where even the religious people are becoming aware that there is much more to their reality than they give credence to, and that it cannot all be explained away as "the works of the devil." That does not wash anymore.

The beginning of the Church's campaign to stamp out so-called heretical thought goes back as far as the Ecumenical Council of 552 A.D. in Constantinople, and Queen Theodora's coup for deliberating who was going to get the Papacy, how to keep the lay people "down on the farm," the abolition of reincarnation, etc. The Church was then beginning to flex its muscles, and to them heresy was simply anything that did not go along with the approved dogma. Jesus himself would have been a heretic, according to them; and therein lies the unfortunate nature of that type of energy.

If one can understand and believe that one's thoughts, attitudes, feelings and expectations create one's reality, then you can see that if one expects an event — for example, the Armageddon — then one's expectation of it is the most powerful thing that one can do to precipitate that event. Therein lies the danger of this type of belief. Armageddon was primarily promulgated through that vision of John in Revelation; and that vision of Armageddon, in its awesome, symbolic glory, has had some interesting interpretations. You see, when the initial vision is experienced in viewing the so-called future, it is as if one taps into a possible or probable reality based on the circumstances as they now exist. It is like having the futurists make their predictions that in 1999 the world is going to look like such-and-such, based on what they figure out in terms of scientific advances, social structures, etc.

The same type of thing was done on a very different level of consciousness — in this process of creating a vision — and the language of this level of consciousness is highly symbolic. Now, Armageddon, as a battle between the forces of Light and the forces of darkness, as commonly portrayed, has been going on for at least this entire century. If you wish to look at it in those terms, Djwhal commented many times in his writings through Alice Bailey about Armageddon and the battle thereof, etc., and if you wish to draw upon that it might be interesting to look at.

However, from the perspective of Billy Graham saying that Armageddon is coming: Armageddon is a battleground within the self of every individual, and it comes forth as the symbol of that internal cleansing that is going on. The internal cleansing is that process of bringing the Light into the darkness. The darkness does not have a reality of its own — it is simply a lack of Light. When you view the internal structures which could be considered to be darkness — those internal structures of fear, anxiety, anger, resentment, frustration, jealousy, continued worship of the dark, or form side — all of these areas within oneself resonate to other lifetimes wherein those experiences are felt, and as the volume of energy is being turned up on a planetary level, these things are getting stirred up even more than they usually are.

The battle between the so-called forces of Light and forces of darkness is happening all of the time anyway; it is simply the playing out of the duality of the universe, and is not to be seen in terms of good and evil. I repeat that: It's simply in terms of plus and minus polarities!

The Light element, as a symbol of understanding, can be referenced from this perspective — that it is good because it is what elevates the consciousness to the understanding and the clarity of its own true purpose, its own true essence.

To say that the darker structures, so to speak, are bad or evil is not correct. They were there as a conclusion of an experience and as such they may no longer suit where you consciously wish to go. Therefore, the process of release takes place in our New Age through revelation. It is a releasing rather than a purging; purging implies a heavy force coming forth and shoving something out, and we are encouraging a more natural enfoldment and release. *Allow* it to go away.

Allow the energy around those thoughtforms, those beliefs, those areas of dark emotion within the Self to just go back into the purity of its own Source, which is the Source of All That Is, anyway. If that can be done, then instantly one finds that those tendencies — the habits of judgment, jealousy, fear, anxiety, the habits that one naturally seems to fall into — lose power because the energy behind them is gone. You release that energy and the impetus behind the habit is gone. It is as if it falls apart; the foundations have crumbled. This is the process going on. It sometimes feels painful, and sometimes it is disconcerting and disorienting during the process of release, but this is simply a matter of losing something familiar.

As a foundational blueprint of what the consciousness is creating, the DNA is a pure image of the intent from a Soul level, in terms of creation of the body. There is, of course, a genetic influence from the family tree that leads up to that. The personality in the Soul prior to coming into the lifetime reviews the genetic influences, personality traits, tendencies, family background, and also the society that it will be coming into. It then decides, "This will be appropriate for my life; this one won't be..." Sometimes, in a sense, there is a bit of shopping around before finding the right one.

The DNA has within its structure all that is necessary to create the vehicle to the point of that body of Light. It has all the information that it needs; it is simply a matter of cleaning off some of the sludge and allowing that program to be properly inserted into the computer, rather than dealing with the mutations caused by the overload from experience. That overload filters its way down through every level, and the belief system itself imposes such a heavy load upon the DNA structure that it tends to thwart the actual process of the DNA, which essentially has the command built in to totally revitalize and replace any cell that decays. Now, the decaying process should not even occur; if it does, it is built into the programming. If there is an accident, then within the program is all of the information needed to regrow a limb, to do the entire surgery and healing of the body instantaneously if the energy is right.

From our monadic perspective, we find religion generally a detriment to spirituality. However, the prime key to all, and the reason why a pure teaching tends to go the way it does is simply one of basic group assumptions and group thoughtforms about the nature of this reality, which is seen as being one of decay. The decaying structure, from the esoteric point of view, describes something that once had fluidity and flexibility now getting old and crystallized in form. The stilted form of the old religion has to make way for the fluid new understanding to come forth. Science views that same process as an inevitable function of living within the parameters of this reality, but even science has been able to see the transcendence of that. The way that science views it is expressed best, perhaps, by the laws of thermodynamics, in which the Second Law of thermodynamics basically states that everything will eventually decay into disorder or atrophy. The Third Law then comes forth and says: If you lower the temperature to the point of absolute zero where there is no friction, no motion, then the tendency to disintegration is stopped and orderliness reigns supreme. Within that system they are now learning how to attain that state of orderliness even without having the medium of the very low temperature. The low temperature simply signifies a zero level of activity, and at that zero level what do you have? You have pure stillness, pure nothingness, in a sense, but within that nothingness is consciousness.

That consciousness is the absolute ground state of the system. They are finding ways of tapping into that consciousness now, using other means. They are finding that the absolute qualities can be brought out. So they are finding superconductivity as a reality coming into play; and the laws of that being able to be used for such things as magnetic levitation of trains, etc. Superconductivity is a very interesting phenomenon, in that having a superconductor and an impression of a magnetic field on one side all of a sudden automatically creates the opposite magnetic field on the other side. So the magnet is lifted — it is levitation, almost. In that respect, science is seeing the absolute within the duality. They are not quite using those terms yet, but that is what they are discovering, and they will eventually put all the different pieces of all the different areas together.

The Lord Maitreya — and not the Master Jesus, as is generally believed — is the present Christ, the founder of Christianity. He brought in the quality of unconditional Love to the Earth. (Refer to the table, "Avatars of the Christ Consciousness," p. 224.) In one of his previous incarnations on the Earth, the Lord Maitreya came in as the teacher Sri Krishna, to teach the Second Initiation to mankind, and did his Fifth Initiation prior to his ascension at the end of that lifetime. Maitreya is soon to be replaced by the thirty-sixth avatar, the new Christ — the Lord Kuthumi, whose energy represents the quality of Compassion.

After this work with the Christ, the Master Jesus later overshadowed and inspired the prophet Mohammed. It is not generally known to the Western world that during the annual Wesak Festival during the Full Moon of May the

Lord Buddha and the Christ together send much energy and blessing to the world. The Lord Buddha works with the Christ, preparing for the Christ's reappearance on the Earth. Thus we have four great religions overwoven — Hindu, Moslem, Buddhist, and Christian — which the Master Jesus will unify. As part of the One Great Plan, the various teachers came to the Earth at different times for different peoples, bringing the appropriate basic truths for each. You can see how interesting it must be from our perspective, as we see the violence and the misunderstanding of mankind dividing the same pie, so to speak, and each saying that their piece is right. That's why Jesus, as the physical-level transformer of the Sixth Ray, is working so arduously at unifying a new world religion and a global community for all who remain on this planet.

The Buddha is an interesting entity, in that in another lifetime he was also very much revered as a god in Atlantean times, and in Egyptian times as the god Thoth. This same entity later, in a linear time frame, became the Buddha 500 years or so prior to Jesus.

The Roman Empire played a large role in the organizing and the carrying forth of the Christian teachings, particularly during Constantine's time. Constantine was largely considered to be a Christian convert, but that was not entirely the case, although he had sympathies there. However, he did do a lot to give power to the Church; and that power, being a secular political power, then carried forth the Church in its own fashion. The Church, of course, then made a great deal of revisions to the teachings in order to suit their desire for power and control.

Peter died a rather confused being, not really absolutely sure that he had done a good enough job. As for the particulars of his death, it was a bit of a suicide — not in the sense of stabbing himself or killing himself, but he blew himself up.[4] He had a tremendous amount of guilt, which came from a misunderstanding of his true power. In other words, there was a sense in him that knew that he was greater than that entity incarnating as Peter — or his friend Jesus, for that matter. That sense said, "You should have done better. Look what we have done with this wonderful teaching of the Master. How could we have turned it into just *this*? It must have been intended to be something more. It is all *my* fault!"

Wallowing in that guilt, he intended to do some short-circuiting within himself in his energy system. Guilt is like a vortex — it is a downward spiral, and once you get stuck in it, it is very difficult to get out of. Thus the power tends to feel like it is being sapped away. In a sense, he spiritually bled to death from this feeling of guilt. What we see there is not so much of an explosion of energy as an implosion. As the spirit winds its way down into the abyss of guilt and despair, it is as if it sucks the Light back in, and his experience was one of despair. There was a tremendous amount of fear as to

---

4 Prior to his crucifixion.

what might happen to him, because to some extent he was one of those who were promulgating fear — not hell as a concept as it is now, but certainly unpleasant afterlife experiences. He believed that to the point where he felt that he had done his job so poorly that he would experience that himself. He believed his own teachings, as teachers tend to do.

Jesus in his teachings never did discuss the concepts of hell, eternal fire and brimstone. His experience with the devil, so to speak, was largely overplayed. As an entity, this being called the devil really is not as big a deal as people make it out to be. It is simply a Soul who chose to disconnect from Source, and Source allows that. Why? Because the Light will *always* prevail.

Hitler is a contrast in the choices that are made by self. Darkness is not an energy at all — it is just an absence of Light. Those beings who make that choice to consciously separate from the Light are beings who have a very deeply ingrained false belief. The primal false belief of all of these beings is that "I am separate from Source." The more that one believes that, the more one actualizes it in one's reality.

The people we refer to as the "dark ones" or the "negative energy that does not want to see the Light" would, generally speaking, not get much beyond the Third Astral Heaven because there is really not enough of that caring, giving, that compassion within them to admit them to the higher realms. There are the rare individuals who have come through the higher physical initiations, and then — for one reason or another — have chosen to separate from the Light. They can occasionally sneak past; however, it is not a danger. You see, those beings are simply choosing to do their evolution in their own way. There is no darkness; there is no evil in a true cosmic sense!

There is a principle of Light and darkness within the duality of existence, but within the unity of Source there is no such thing.

In the actual experience of it, those beings are choosing that particular path as their path of reuniting with Source, albeit a rather slow and painful path. They have chosen it unconsciously, because if they really did have a conscious idea of what they had to go through, they would not make that decision. They simply got a little attached to certain elements of power and felt that they could beat the system. Ultimately, the system is invincible. You have the Law of Correspondence which says that as one vibration occurs here and another vibration occurs there, the more powerful vibration will ultimately lift the less powerful one up to its higher level.

Mankind, being given free will, has been given the choice as to whether or not it wishes to work within the easy route. Those who prefer the hard way ultimately have to come around in the end. The universe — the entire Cosmos — functions on a vibration of harmony and cooperation, and if you choose to be uncooperative and disharmonious, you have no chance of ultimately beating the system.

Many associated with the Christian church refer to the "Prince of Darkness." Again, it is the principle of duality. The element to look for in any particular teaching, be it a New Age teaching or an old teaching (if you want to make those distinctions) is to see where they are coming from. If they are using fear as a motivator, if they are using what you would reference as the negative energies (the amount of hate and fear and persecution in some of the old-time religions is quite phenomenal), those elements of fear are what you would call the darker forces coming through.

It is rather ironic in this day and age to have the TV preachers shrieking to millions of people about the evils of the devil, and yet in the same breath tell people to *fear* God. You really wonder where that energy is ultimately coming from. It is certainly not the all-loving, all-allowing God that we are aware of. But He does allow that. You see, God does allow people to express and beings to express in whatever way they choose. One can never be a victim of anybody or anything, including a so-called devil unless one allows that. It is also ironic that the Christian church by and large has become the victim of what it warns mankind against — the Prince of Darkness — using fear!

You create your own reality; and therefore, if you believe in devils, if you open yourself to their vibration, to the negative side of things, then there is no one but yourself doing it to you!

There are thoughtforms created by man that seem to be real. The more a religion or belief system perpetuates the idea of a particular horned entity that carries a pitchfork and likes to throw you into a burning fire, then the more likely that thoughtform has the energy to take on a semblance of reality. But indeed, it is simply an illusion, an illusion built of the collective thoughtforms of mankind. The more that one can get beyond personifying God or devils based on one's own nature, then the less power that thoughtform will have. It is very much like the old gods being given form by mankind. In many cases there was a reality behind that entity; there was some advanced teacher who came to do a specific job, and mankind in its ignorance said, "That being is so far above us, he must be a god," whether he came in a spaceship or not (and some of them did!).

The creation of a devil is very similar to the creation of a god in a mass-consciousness thoughtform. As the mass consciousness chooses not to believe anymore in, for example, Apollo, then Apollo as a thoughtform begins to fade away. This is referenced quite comically in Jane Roberts' Oversoul Seven books. The rest home for the old gods was rather amusing, and yet the old gods did have a reality. The rest home was portraying what happens to the thoughtform when the mass consciousness no longer feeds it. In that particular form, there was Jesus and Mohammed, both of whom we know to be real entities. Yet the way mass consciousness views them they may as well be Apollo or some old thoughtform that does not have very much connection to reality.

Now, that sometimes impinges upon the work of the actual beings, such as Jesus. He has to contend with that thoughtform's pull upon him. He and the others who are in the same position have developed enough resistance to that so that they can do their work without being unduly affected by it.

Maitreya generally takes the brunt of it, in the sense of people viewing an aspect of "Jesus Christ." Most people do not view them as two separate entities, although they are actually very different, even working with different types of energy. Maitreya, being the primary focus for that energy, is the one who deals with that problem. So when one prays to Jesus Christ — and maybe even sees a vision of a man who perhaps looks like Jesus — the energy behind that is generally Maitreya, although sometimes it *is* Jesus. Sometimes Jesus has worked with these people as a teacher on the inner planes; and if the connection is true enough and strong enough, then it may be he. It really does not matter.

Being more in the public eye, Jesus therefore has that greater pull upon him, which is one of the main reasons why he is not at this time consciously working with students as much as he used to, as much as some of the other teachers are. For example, Djwhal has a similar problem, albeit to a much lesser degree. People know him through his writings and therefore think of him to be a certain way, and he has to contend with that. The Masters Morya and Kuthumi have had certain thoughtforms built up around them from the Theosophical teachings as to who they are, what they look like, and what they do. "They are seven feet tall, they do this and that, and wear this color robe." There is a tremendous amount of what Djwhal calls "glamour," as a subtle distinction between illusion and maya. There is *illusion*, there is *maya*, and there is *glamour* — glamour not in a fashion sense, but that element of illusion which puts a sort of persona on something, the glamorous aspect of, perhaps, being Paul of Tarsus. We know that we have to contend with that somewhat in our experience, from the potential glamour of St. Peter or any other beings we have experienced.

Mary has also had a tremendous pull upon her and tremendous thoughtforms to overcome — it is nothing less than being imprinted "the Mother of God"! How can one explain God the Father, God the Absolute being, having a mother? And how can a being who simply volunteered to do a job be saddled with that? It is a little overwhelming at times. Actually, from an energy point of view, she *is* here. From a physical-body point of view, she is not.

There is rather a lot of confusion about the being called Judas, a being who has been very misunderstood. It is important to realize that Judas was playing a role, as were all of the others involved in the passion play. He was performing a specific function agreed upon between himself and Jesus. As in any life scenario, there are those who are cast in a role of a seeming villain. For example, perhaps someone in your life has seemed to you a villain. Prior to the existence you make an agreement, a pact, a contract with all of the people in your life. You have an audition, and you are there in your audition with your guiding teachers generally asking for beings who have had contact with you before to come forth and play particular roles in your drama, in the script you have written for this upcoming life. In a sense, you are the producer of the play, the director, the writer, and the principal actor. You auditioned for the supporting actors and actresses, all of whom came to give you the benefit of their own experience; and they chose to come in and interact with you based on their *own* plans. So they have their own auditions, and in their play, you are the supporting actor and they are the star. In your play, you are the star and they're the supporting actors.

There is an energy which was John; there is an energy which was Jesus; there is a different energy which was the Christ. All of those energies are here. You understand the distinction here — that the beings who chose to play those roles may or may not be back to play a different role. It really does not matter whether they are here or not, because the script they were enacting at that time called for a sequel, and that sequel is being enacted now. As in many sequels of movies, some of the actors are a little different, but the roles are the same. Again, the agreements are made on the Soul level prior to existence, in that all of the roles played are roles that were chosen. Beings cast in the role of villain are many times, and usually, beings who love you the most, because who *else* would play that role?

In the monadic family, the one that Judas is most aligned with is Maitreya, but he has what is called a karmic connection with Jesus. You see, those distinctions really do not mean a lot, because — perhaps like a family — they are just *there*. In your life you have a family, and your immediate family may or may not be very close to you. You have your family of friends which, of course, changes over the years, but in many people's case the family of friends is often closer to them in spirit than their biological family. Many people are now realizing that; and, in a sense, it is more widespread as the so-called disintegration of the nuclear family continues. The nuclear family does not have the same impact, the same sense of loyalty, that it did in the past or that it does in other parts of the world, because one's true affinity is with other beings of like intent.

There is an appalling number of thoughtforms that really have no relevancy for a New Age. The revival churches will have to make massive adjustments. Interestingly enough, they do all sound the same, don't they? They all go to the same school and learn to talk the same way; they learn the same language, the same metaphors; and they all basically have the same interpretation. If any of those so-called religious leaders really took the time to study the Bible, they would find so many appalling discrepancies in the story itself that they would truly have a crisis of faith themselves — and that would be a good thing!

The stuckness, the fear, the structure of the Church, disallows one to really manifest properly enough aspects clearly and consciously to gain even a Soul Merge — the Third Initiation!

It is similar to saying, "Why can't we have an enlightened man as the President?" Much of that is dictated by mass consciousness; in fact, almost all of it is. Whenever you have one in a clear and strong position of influence or power, then you essentially have that person being dictated to by the consciousness of the group.

In a political sense, one may feel that to be rid of all our problems, all we need is to have someone "who works with the Light" to be elected President, for example. But you see what happens over and over and over again when very good, well-meaning people get elected to public office. And the Pope is no exception. They may have all kinds of positive intentions of changing this and doing that and really bringing about what you would consider positive change. Yet once they get into office, they find all kinds of barriers — not simply the obvious ones, the entrenched bureaucracy, the other systems the President has to deal with (Congress, etc., etc.). It is not even specifically on those levels; it is on the level of just not being able to *do* those things. The reason is that the consciousness of the people will not allow it. They are not developed enough, in a sense, to believe that they deserve it.

If you look at the papacy, they have all been very much in the doctrine. A few of them have brought about some reforms. Now there is this counterreform movement going on; that actual movement has gone on for some time prior even to John Paul. His energy is one of the very well-meaning; and yet because of the reactionary elements within the consciousness of the people in the Church, he is not able to do the things that he really wants to. So you find him actually being perceived as a hero. He is the people's choice, and yet the programs that he really wants to do for the people have not been able to be brought about. What it has to do with, more than anything, is the beliefs and the feelings of unworthiness of the people in the Catholic world — they have had it indoctrinated into them for so long that they are really not worthy. They believe that, and therefore will not allow any change to take place except for very, very small shiftings.

It is quite interesting that many of those who were instrumental in founding that dogma in the first place later were eliminated by their own dogma as they expanded out of it and perhaps embraced a more Gnostic style of experience of the teachings of Jesus. In the later centuries, they were more inclined toward the inner experience, and the Church looked at them and said, "You are a heretic — burn that one!" There is a certain amount of karmic tie there, because those beings believed in karma.

Karma is an interesting point, because it is not as rigid a law as people like to believe. It is simply another way of maintaining power in a socioreligious institution by saying, "Your lot in this life is your karma — you had better suffer it. Those of us who are in a higher caste or a more aristocratic position — it is our karma to be here. Your karma is to be down *there*, so don't try to get out of it. The more you try to get out of it, the worse it is going to be for you later. You have to pay your dues now." There is a lot of that type of expedience in the so-called spiritual world. Karma is simply a law of cause and effect, the same type of law that Newton spoke of: You hold the rock up here, let it go, and the effect of that causes the rock to drop — not cause and effect in terms of good and bad or right and wrong.

This is where the twisted version comes in, by taking a basic law and putting that personification on it, because humans love to see good and bad, right and wrong. "I am right, you are wrong; I am good and you are bad. My teaching is better than yours. My guru is greater than yours."

We know that there is no hell beyond physicality, that hell is a state of mind. This grey area referenced as purgatory is, again, a belief system promulgated by those who like to believe in punishment, and punishment is something that is inflicted upon one by someone else. Taking away responsibility for one's own experience, one says, "I have done badly over here. I have to go to purgatory and work off my sins in order to purify myself so that I can go to heaven." Those who believe that will certainly go to purgatory and find plenty of rocks to push up the hill. Ultimately, when they have decided for themselves that they have had enough purgatory, then they will release themselves and go to an astral heaven. They will sit around in heaven, to whatever degree of heaven it is for them, until they get bored with that and say, "There must be more." Then help comes, and when it comes it says, "Let's review your last life. Let us see what you learned there. What do you want to do, given the parameters of where you want to go? Do you want to go back there again? Do you want to go to that plane and do something over there?" The choices are always made by Self.

During the Harmonic Convergence much work was accomplished with the Hierarchy to release negative aspects anchored into mass consciousness. That energy which was worked on in Aruba on the 15th/16th of August 1987, where we focused on the release of that heavy energy upon Mother Earth and mankind, which had come, in a sense, as a counterbalancing energy. When Sanat Kumara came to ensoul the planet, there was the positive side and the negative side — not to say good or bad, but that is the way it has been viewed.

Why Aruba? Why Shamballa? Because they are absolute opposites in terms of geography, and opposite enough in terms of energy.

Shamballa is an area within the etheric structure of the planet, a very powerful energy field. Sanat Kumara chose that as an entrance point and basically as his focus of consciousness for this planet Earth. Shamballa is said to personify the city of the Planetary Hierarchy; this is the place where they have their "offices" — all rather interesting when you consider it in terms of an analogy. The Hermetic doctrine of "As above, so below" has been so misconceived — it has been turned around and people take it as "As below, so above" — which is not the case at all.

"As below, so above" has been taken to be gospel. It is quite a distortion of the original statement, and yet it is being viewed within a logical framework. But it is like saying $A/B = B/A$; this interchange does not hold true. Think of how that doctrine and misunderstanding "As below, so above" has been carried through metaphysics from the time of Hermes or Pythagoras to now. Think of how much distortion that particular one has caused, and it is not what you would call a classical false belief. It is not like the belief which says, "I am separate from God." It is simply a logical misunderstanding, simply taking something from a linear perspective that was not intended to be a linear expression. It would be rather interesting to follow that one through the ages.

Much of the esoteric Christian thought and much of the Eastern thought has followed similar lines. Yet those particular teachings have a metaphorical value as allegories. As myths they do have some value, but humanity's anthropomorphic obsession of seeing God as being that wise, old grandfather up there has caused a lot of problems.

So there is an area to work on. In terms of looking at the Christian and other teachings and how they have been distorted through the ages, look at that misconception of God as a possible cause. "As below, so above" — what has that done to the teachings? That can be quite revealing in the context of what is being expressed here. "As above, so below" has created as many versions of heaven on Earth as there are people thinking about heaven, because whose concept of heaven is going to be identical to yours? So when you bring those two concepts together, you have a concept of heaven on Earth. What would it be like in this heaven-on-Earth New Age?

Source, in Its unlimitedness, Its absoluteness, does not have a need for one more planet, so there is no need for a heaven on Earth. Source simply IS. Bringing the concept of an astral heaven down to the Earth plane — *that* is probably more like it, at least until the grand illusion of the astral is seen through. As mankind grows in consciousness and allowingness, they will allow themselves more of the attributes of those heavens on Earth, but again, everybody's version of it will be a little different, because everyone's fourth-dimensional reality now is different. There are overlaps; there are areas where your experience of reality does indeed correspond with that of another, but there are other areas in your life where your reality is totally different from theirs, so we have these overlaps. When you have five billion beings overlapping their realities — particularly when the so-called Laws are changing — then the overlap of those realities will be experienced very differently in this New Age.

When you have a physicist beginning to extrapolate on his experiments in quantum mechanics, where they do something here and the effect is seen over there, and he begins to extrapolate on his physical-plane ordinary existence and experiences, then he sees that type of stretching going on among different minds. That is going to impact upon those who overlap his reality. It has started; It has actually been going on for a long time. There is the analogy here called the "popcorn effect": You put the popcorn on, add heat to increase the vibration, and you get one popping here, another there, and so forth. They begin to interplay with each other; the vibrations increase and stimulate the other kernels. The more vibrations there are stimulating the mass of corn, the more kernels that will pop and join the others. That is the nature of the Mass Ascension as well, as enough individuals create that Lightbody to the point of being able to ascend. Maybe they build it to a point where they can ascend, but choose to stay with that Lightbody. Maybe they will stay around with that ascension body long enough to stimulate others who are in that same process. Then the Mass Ascension can take place, because it is really simply a stepping up of those who are of like vibration into a slightly different reality. It is not an ascension going back to Source "forever and ever, amen." It is a stepping-up to a slightly higher dimension, but to those standing beside them it may not be a reality. The biblical story mentions two brothers working in a field; one will be "taken up" and the other won't. So Ascension is a matter of who is in tune with that vibration, not a prechosen, select few.

The Planetary Hierarchy is constantly having to review its plans and projections, because they cannot anticipate a definite response from humanity. If the Hierarchy is so far beyond space and time, why do they have to keep changing their plans? Because they are working within much of the same stuff that you are — they are just a step or two beyond. They are not totally out of the mire.

One of the topics of the new world religion that will be taught is the science of Ascension, because it is a natural progression, and it is simply one of spiritualizing matter after the Etheric Light body ascension.

The problem with the Eastern approach, as mentioned before, has been that the yogic systems, the buddhic systems, the Zen, the Tao system, even the more mystical approaches from the East, have generally viewed spirituality as being "although within, also out there." Being "out there" precluded being grounded into the physical. There was always that major dichotomy between spirit and matter. What we are attempting to bring forth at this time is a balance of that teaching, to bring the spirit *fully anchored* into the matter of the physical body and of the planet Earth. This entails bringing that Soul energy — and ultimately, all monadic (spiritual) energies — down to the point where they can experience the freedom in consciousness. In the past they did not necessarily bring it all the way down into the physical, and even at the level of Mastery, they still dropped this physical vehicle, ascended to another plane, and then had to create a Lightbody out of the finer matter. The problem with that is that although this Lightbody can be materialized, there are certain limitations to that. It does not have as easy a time of it as having a fully ascended spiritualized body because, in a sense, they are slowing down the vibrations from an etheric-body level. They are maintaining their etheric body and slowing it down to the point where, for all intents and purposes, it is a physical body. As we've explained previously, the true spiritual body is new to this planet. The *Mahatma* energy, which was invoked by the Soul level, brings in this finer Spiritual energy, the microtron, allowing for exponential growth in connecting one's self with the spiritual (monadic) levels. The slowed-down etheric body, if developed, could feel and look like a quasi-physical body, but it certainly does not function like one in terms of internal organs, etc; there are limitations as to how long that etheric/physical body can be maintained. Whereas if the physical body were to be totally spiritualized and then brought down, it could last forever on this plane — if one wished. However few, once they have materialized the spiritual body, will stay for but a short "time" if they were to stay on Earth at all. We remind you that the *proof* of Spiritual Ascension is to take the Atomic Physical Body with you.

Even thirty years ago, one died with the Soul Merge and the Fourth Initiation, the Crucifixion. That was the general experience. The spiritualization of matter has now progressed on this plane to the point where the vibration of all of the matter of this planet has risen. Therefore the additional spiritualization of your personal matter through the process of initiation has a rather more elevated basis to start with. There is less of a gap between, say, "down here" and "up there," which is where the initiation used to take one. The death of the physical vehicle was caused by the shock of one's vibration suddenly elevating drastically. The gradual uplifting of the vibration of matter is now allowing that initiation experience to take place in a much easier way. The shock is not as great because the gap is not as great.

The Ascension process will be experienced much differently than it was experienced in the past. It will be a very acute experience within the body — the process of actually taking the Light energy, which has been slowed down to the point of almost stopping, and creating what you call matter and speeding it back up again. The amount of energizing that goes on in that experience is quite phenomenal.

Words are inadequate here. When you take every cell of the body (and even beyond the cellular structure) and speed up the vibration of every atom within it to the point where it literally flies at a higher rate and transcends itself to the point where it is moving into the frequencies of Light, then you can imagine the amount of energy that is felt, the sensation of Light. Many people have over the ages worked with this energy and not got it right; essentially, they have burnt holes in themselves, some of you have seen pictures as examples of this.

When we speak of Mass Ascension, we do not mean an experience where it is necessary for all who are going through the process to experience it simultaneously and in the same place. At that point of Ascension, the boundaries of time and space have, to a large extent, been transcended anyway. So you do not have to have a physical proximity to draw power from each other; you do not have to have that connection to that degree on the physical plane in order for it to occur.

There is a certain amount of overlap here between a couple of different ideas: One is that, given the possible scenario of physical disaster, the spaceships will come and beam up those who are ready, much as in Star Trek. You could look at that as an ascension of some sort (a rising up), but these are not the ones we are talking about.

The destruction of this civilization is still a possibility, but not to the degree that it was talked about before. There are still possible scenarios of the odd earthquake here and there for integration. However, the real possibility we'll work with mankind to stabilize would be an axis shift on November 4, 1994!

Many of these scenarios were put forward as possibilities, with the assistance of the space brothers and their vehicles, to effect a mass airlift whereby "two will be in the fields and one will be taken up" while the other will stay behind. That *was* quite possible. The actual process of Primary Ascension — whether in a group, in the same place, or not — really does not matter. To a certain extent that is a matter of *your* preference and the preference of your Soul.

The process of Ascension is one that will be more clearly understood as you have the energy more firmly anchored in the body, because then you will feel it beginning in its primary stages. You will feel the body being energized more, more and more. Some are already feeling that, and it is becoming stronger and stronger. Ultimately, the spiritual body will be materialized and dematerialized at will.

In terms of the Mass Ascension, refine your understanding of that because there is a certain connotation and a bit of misunderstanding between that airlifting idea and the actual Etheric Body and Spiritual Ascensions.

There are various methods students are working with that are also very effective in their own way; however, we will see over the next few years the development of these procedures to the point where the amount of "fog," shall we say, that can be lifted in one session is greater than what could have been lifted in an entire year in the past. This will result in that sudden upward curve of the graph that will enable those of you with the desire to do so, to move quickly to that point of Ascension and beyond. Many will continue with the belief system that they align with, and that's fine also.

The energy channeling into the system of planet Earth, as well as the knowledge and information being carried through on that spiral of energy is allowing us to come forth. This is the synchronicity of the process, the overlapping of the varying cycles which are not time- and space-oriented cycles; they are multidimensional cycles.

Those overlapping points create a matrix of force within this time and space, which allow for that sudden illumination. This is the wonderful process that has been prophesied and anticipated for so long. We are all enjoying tremendously the fireworks going off now! It is a beautiful display and a very inspiring occasion even for those who have graduated from the physical plane eons ago.

The willingness to embrace this new growth is producing an exponential change that is inspiring to all who are on the nonphysical planes. We are very much pleased with the process. We are all giving and receiving in our different states of awareness.

The only other thing that we would like to say about the belief systems is that there are many different new processes coming forth for working with and releasing them. These processes are going deeper and deeper into the situation. Those who are working with any particular process need to remain unattached to it and remain open to the new teachings that come forth. We are delving deeper and deeper into exposing and extracting belief systems. Higher energies are being drawn forth to give their input as well. So we are finding more highly developed techniques all the time. You have seen that in the evolution of the procedures, and this is particularly true in working with the *Mahatma* energy. In fact, those who have had initiations with Brian are profound examples of being able to lift the vibrational rate of Light and remove past negative patterning from the subconscious mind and cellular body in *one session* that is equal to innumerable years of past methods. Very shortly those who allow the *Mahatma* energy into their auric field will literally watch their evolution expand and illuminate so gently and quickly.

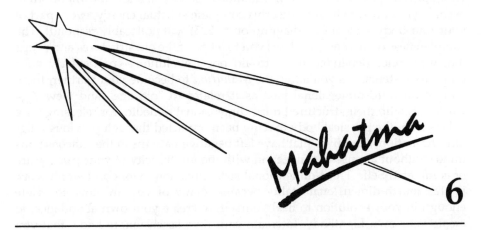

The Rays, Chakras and Initiations

Now that your planet Earth and all aboard her have accelerated their state of beingness into a state of unlimitedness, having become fourth-dimensional, even if you can't yet see or feel these shifts, enough of you have asked your Primal Soul level for help. That invocation — and having been unconsciously fourth-dimensional — has allowed the Soul/Higher Self level (which is limited in its functions to the physical levels) to invoke assistance from a much higher level. (The physical level includes all of the universes in this Cosmic Day, but not the monadic and the Creator levels, which, as you are beginning to understand, constitute 90% of this Source for this Cosmic Day.) The *Mahatma* energy was invoked by the Soul levels and tenuously anchored its comprehensive energy on your planet on June 14, 1988. This was done with the assistance of the Council of Twelve for this quadrant of this galaxy plus the thousands of Christs and Planetary Logos (most planets have a Planetary Logos and the equivalent of the Christed energy) in this quadrant of your galaxy, in order to hasten the Soul's evolution and bring an integration through synthesis (unity) of the Co-Creator level.

Now it's up to humanity to build the "Earth bicycle" for the *Mahatma* (to help the *Mahatma* [Source] energy to ground) and help teach the *Mahatma* to ride this Earth bicycle. If mankind is able to invoke enough of this energy and anchor it, then the shifts in consciousness will amaze even the most cynical among you.

As we've explained previously, this spiritual body that all of you are building is new to this planet. The *Mahatma* energy, which was invoked by the Soul levels, brings in this finer energy, allowing for exponential growth in connecting one's Self with the spiritual (monadic) level.

There will be no particular teachings when you ask the *Mahatma* to direct your spiritual path vis-à-vis your initiations. So as you allow the *Mahatma* to become your auric field and trust this complete spiritual energy, every part of your four-body system (see diagram on p. 225) will noticeably respond! The completeness of this energy allows you to let go of the old structures and props that were once depended upon to aid one's evolution — particularly your religious systems. As you allow the *Mahatma* to become your partner, there will be no third-dimensional past as it relates to "old age" and New Age teachings, with their structured third-dimensional remedies for releasing false beliefs from the physical body (having been impacted through previous religions, limitations, and lives that have left negative patterns in the subconscious mind) without a sense of connection with the multiplicity of your true nature or completed Self. Third-dimensional structures don't work and won't work in this fourth-dimensional reality because many of you are now complete enough in your evolution to heal yourself, to create your own abundance, to create your own Lightbody, to create your own ascension, to know that you and the Father are One, and to know that you don't require any extraneous remedies to "heal thyself." Simply invite the Father, *Mahatma*, into your auric field to assist you on all levels of Self into the Source for this Cosmic Day, to connect and complete your circuitry with Self. The *Mahatma* asks nothing of you except to trust, to ask, and to allow. That is too simple for many, considering their convoluted third-dimensional past, which must include profound limitation and difficulty!

As far as initiations are concerned, we prefer to deal with only nine because mankind as a group Soul hasn't anchored the First Initiation yet. Initiation Number One is primarily dealing with the solar plexus area. Prior to that, the development of the chakras is rudimentary at best. They exist and are functioning to some degree, but in terms of an opening of the power of that chakra, the First Initiation is the first one that truly allows the flow of power from the Earth into the solar plexus chakra. The First and even the Second Initiation are still considered minor initiations. The Third Initiation, the Soul Merge, is in many ways considered the First. (Refer to the illustrations, "Man's Response to Initiation" on p. 220 and "Co-Creator and Creator Levels" on pp. 228-29.) However, for the sake of setting a number, we will call it the Third Initiation. The Second Initiation works with the distance between the solar plexus and the heart, further enlivening the solar plexus and beginning to open the heart. The Third Initiation, as you know, works primarily with the heart chakra; it opens it up to the point where the Soul can actually reside in that area.

Now interestingly enough, the Soul, when it anchors into the physical, anchors as far into the physical as possible, which is right into the physical body. Since chakras are in the etheric body, where in the physical body does the Soul go? It touches into that organ most closely associated with the heart chakra. We do not mean the physical heart; we mean the thymus gland. The thymus is that gland, a part of the endocrine system (refer to the illustration, "The Human Energy System: The Chakras and Their Relevant Glands" on page 233), which works with energy by transmuting it from an electrical impulse into a more chemical substance within the body. The function of the endocrine system is to transmute the energy from the higher levels, stepping it down into a more basic, concrete, physical level.

The thymus gland is a key element, in that it acts as the seat of the Soul in the physical body. Also within the etheric body at Soul Merge is that eighth chakra, the Soul Star. So the Soul has a two-pronged connection.

The process of the Third Initiation, moving into the Fourth, begins that process of expressing the Love being generated, expressing that wholeness of the Soul connection that begins to rise up, and the throat chakra gets much more activated. All of these higher chakras have been opened to some degree. Especially at the time of the Third Initiation, there has to be a significant opening of all of those higher chakras and indeed all of the lower ones as well, because the energy has to ground right through. The channel has to be built in order for the Soul energy to flow down.

When you get into a discussion of the Fourth Initiation, it is known as one of Renunciation or Crucifixion, in a sense a renunciation of the effect of and attachment to the material plane. The only way that it can truly be renounced is to love it to the point where you transcend it. That is the expression of the Divine Love; it is also called the Divine Will. The will center moves from the solar plexus to the throat level, and the throat begins to express that higher aspect of Divine Will. What is being accomplished there is the blending of the spirit and the will.

There is that ancient division between spirit and will. They are two aspects of Self. There is an interesting book on the subject called *The Right Use of Will*,[1] which gives a very clear description of the division between the spirit and the will, how that came about and how they were distinctively personified in the peoples of Atlantis and Lemuria.

The process is the blending of the spirit and the will. This occurs primarily in the throat chakra, which is why, at the current juncture, some of you having gone through the Soul Merge and working to integrate that, have an added pressure to express and to communicate. It is the activation of the fourth chakra. During an initiation the consciousness has risen to a point where it is able to handle the next jump forward.

So at the Third Initiation, the consciousness is raised to a point where the Initiator — in this case, Sanat Kumara (see p. 192) — is able to add more power to the entire process by applying a jolt of energy. That jolt elevates the electrical force of the system almost up to the level of the Fourth Initiation, to the point where once it stabilizes, the Fourth Initiation becomes a possibility. Then the Fourth would raise it up another notch.

The initiation enforces the experience of the particular level of vibration, the power, the frequency; and then the process of integration is a matter of

---

1 *The Right Use of Will*, channeled by Ceanne de Rohan, Four Winds Publications, 1984.

bringing yourself into living that all of the time. Your consciousness gets a taste of it, an experience of where it can be at all times, so then you have to elevate yourself to that point. That is the integration process, and that is why after the high of the initiation, there sometimes seems to be a low. The low is simply a contrast.

It is an ideal time for you to be focusing on "How do I take what I know and feel and have experienced and put it into concrete terms?" It's that giving out of Love, that is, taking the Soul energy that has been anchored and is beginning to live within the thymus area, within the heart chakra and within the eighth chakra (Soul Star) — taking that and really beginning to ground it. Grounding occurs not only from electrically charging the physical body but also from putting it back out through the senses, through the organs of action into reality.

The Fourth Initiation, then, is a renunciation of the attachments, the transcendence of it. The Fourth Initiation is a higher experience than partaking of and experiencing that "Fifth Heaven." The Fifth Heaven is an experience for one who is primarily working with expressed Love, but expressed Love is not the same as having had the Fourth Initiation; the Fourth Initiation is a more major step than that. For example, when the Buddha had his experience in the Fifth Heaven and returned to the Earth into his next incarnation, he had achieved his Third Initiation. He then went through the process in that lifetime of working up through the Fourth and Fifth, and was able to move on from there. He was able to ascend from the Fifth.

The Ascension is actually a manifold process, but from the point of view of past Earth experience, it was a twofold process. The first ascension was taking the physical vehicle and transcending it to the point where one could — once one had achieved the Fifth Initiation and functioned on the level of Mastery — then remanifest the astral body as a quasi-physical body. With the assistance of the *Mahatma* energy and the new fourth-dimensional reality, you will now create a spiritual body by simply willing it so, without having to elevate the frequency of the astral body. In other words, you would simply lift your vibration an octave higher to culminate the physical experience with the beginning of your new spiritual body.

The second level of Ascension in the past was moving from the Fifth Initiation into the Sixth. So we jump here a moment between the Fourth and the Fifth and talk about the next step, which is the process that Jesus went through very recently. Interestingly enough, when the Christ had his experience with Jesus on the cross, Jesus was taking the Fourth Initiation at that exact time on the cross — hence the Renunciation. He renounced his life for the glory of God, as the saying goes. At that very same time, to add to the poignancy of the moment, the Christ was going through his Sixth Initiation, so there was that gap, that extra level of energy and intensity that was felt by both. The initiation of Jesus was no problem for the Christ energy to handle because he had already integrated those energies. But for Jesus on the cross to also be experiencing the added initiation of the Christ energy within him at that same point was a rather disorienting experience, hence another degree of his seeming confusion at that moment. Going through a major experience of his own in that Fourth Initiation, he also vicariously experienced in the background, but nonetheless powerfully enough, Maitreya going through his Sixth. So it was a rather powerful moment, and one of those events that was very carefully orchestrated, a very rare occurrence to have all of that energy focused seemingly on one individual at the same time. Two individuals within the one body! We are not likely to have that again, but one should remember that no one forced them to do this demonstration, this ultimately was their choice.

Moving from the Fourth Initiation into the Fifth becomes, really, a process of taking the joy of life and spreading it around, rather than the energy of martyrdom that many people consider to be the lot of the spiritual saviors of the time. That particular idea is one which is losing some of its popularity now — and it is about time! It is not an energy which is very fruitful to many people; it never really was. A few people try to work with it and make something of it.

The Fifth Initiation is that which qualifies one to be on the level of Mastery and an active, full-fledged member of the "working Masters" of the Hierarchy. Should one choose not to go into that particular scheme of things, then that choice is made available to you at that time. Between the Fifth and the Sixth you would still actually be operating within the system, but whether you choose to operate within that group or not is essentially your choice. At that time, the choice is given to you as to which of the paths beyond the Earth you can work with, whether you choose to work within this system as a member of the Planetary Hierarchy, working your way up through the ranks or whether you prefer to move on to other areas of this quadrant of the galaxy and further your education in that way. (There are a number of you in physicality who are looking at even more senior assignments.) These choices are presented to you, and it is something that you could begin to consider.

The Third, Fourth, Fifth and Sixth Initiations are now a possibility to integrate in one lifetime, with a bit of a rider here. The rider is that with this added energy and added focus brought into planet Earth at this time, the energy is available and the teaching is becoming available to certainly develop the body for Primary Ascension and the Lightbody. Once one has that, then there is no such thing as the end of this lifetime. This lifetime is as long as you choose to have it, but few, if any, will stay beyond the Sixth Initiation. *Maitreya has stayed on because, had* **The Rider on the White Horse** *(as referenced in most religious texts—the* **Mahatma***) not been able to anchor the Creator level on Earth, then a lesser avatar would have been overshadowed by the* **Mahatma***.* (The name "Mahatma" is a preference because of its vibration and particular ease in invocation.) *The* **Christ** *Maitreya and a* **Senior** *Member of the* **White Lodge** *in the constellation of* **Sirius** *were both considered for the* **assignment** *of the lesser avatar.*

Now, this *Senior Member of the White Lodge of Sirius has come to the Earth many times*, overshadowed by the Creator level. (Every level is overshadowed by the Creator. No decisions are made by individual levels; all direction, even on the monadic and universal levels, is stepped down from the Creator level.) This **Member** of the **White Lodge** came in as the ones called **St. Peter and Zoroaster**, among many others. This energy, as a **representative** of the **Mahatma**, *had no difficulty coming into the Earth, since it is also a physical (galactic) energy*, as compared to the nonphysical monadic and Creator levels which have difficulty coming directly into the dense physical, even after being stepped down. For example, the being known as King Ikhnaton (with a number of alternate realities) approached the Earth directly from the Source level and was able to come in only as far as the level of the higher mind. It was not until June 14, 1988, that the Source level was able to come all the way into a fourth-dimensional dense physicality, and even then with extreme difficulty.

Since the *galactic energy from the White Lodge was only slightly higher in vibration than Maitreya, it was felt by the Planetary Hierarchy that Maitreya — having been the Christ for 3000 years — would be better qualified to become this lesser avatar because of his great understanding of this planet. So he stayed on as a Seventh-level Initiate to assist the* **Mahatma** *or to assist the lesser avatar or to become the lesser, or galactic, avatar.*

As recently as 40 years ago, Djwhal Khul spoke at length through the writings of Alice Bailey about how remote the possibility was of *The Rider on the White Horse* — the one Djwhal called the Avatar of Synthesis — coming directly into the Earth. He doubted that this Cosmic Avatar would be able to anchor the Source/Creator level into the Earth, since the Cosmic Avatar had never been able to come into the Earth any closer than the causal body (the higher mind).

That was not to be. *Had either that galactic aspect of the* **Mahatma** *or Maitreya been overshadowed by the* **Mahatma** *energy, it would have set back the evolutionary circuitry of this planet thousands of sequential years, because there would not have been a completed circuitry from Source to Earth without the Physical anchoring of the Source energy. Many Christians believe that Jesus will be* **The Rider on the White Horse**; *that, of course, is simply not possible, since Jesus works on a different level and is not able to hold sufficient power (manage sufficient energy) at his level of enlightenment to become the lesser avatar. One can see how this scenario was developed by mankind from viewing Jesus and the Christ as the same energy and then giving credence to this concept, because mass consciousness had elevated the Master Jesus to levels that he had never attained.*

So again, as we've stated, you'll probably never again see a Seventh-level Initiate at the Planetary Government level. Because all levels from the Creator to Earth have arrived through *The Rider on the White Horse* — who *embodies* the *Mahatma* for the Source-level only — **Maitreya**, as the **Christ**, will move on and **Kuthumi** will be a fine **Christ**. However, **Maitreya** will not move on until the **Mahatma** energy is sufficiently anchored into gross physicality. He will stay on to **assist** with this **process. When Brian ascends from this Galactic Core to the expanded Source**, there is going to be at least one **alternate** reality — one of which could be the **current Christ**, Maitreya — **overshadowed** by the **Mahatma**. With **Source** having been **anchored** on **the Earth**, the Earth will no longer need **physical representation of the Source on the planet,** for the energy formatting is such that from the time that **Brian** (as the physical representation) **leaves**, a being will be **totally** overshadowed by the **Cosmic Avatar**. Thus you'll not have a **noticeable energy shift** on the Earth when the Creator's physical "probe" lifts its physical presence.

Once again this is an example of the fact that none of the 352 levels from Source to Earth make decisions on their own; all decisions come from the Creator level, expressed through the Twelve Rays. Each Director of the Co-Creator Council of Twelve (which is the Creator/Source for this Cosmic Day) embodies one Ray, and each Ray is stepped down all the way into the dense physical. As there are millions of Councils of Twelve stepping down the Rays from the Source, each Council receives direction from a higher level.

What might assist you in integrating these expansive concepts would be to view planet Earth as a microcosm of physicality complete with its planetary Council of Seven or Twelve. With trillions of planets in physicality — and at least 80% of those multidimensional planets having a planetary Council of Seven or Twelve — then know that this planetary level is the bottom rung of the ladder in our multidimensional system of Councils of Twelve for this one Cosmic Day. One of the major ironies on Earth is that your scientific community still views Creation as having only one planet, herein called Earth, that could maintain human existence (or the Adam Kadmon body).

In your past, the Sixth Initiation was going to be dependent upon what the other Masters are doing because the positions must be filled as they are vacated, and to a large extent they were vacated very slowly in the past because there were not enough qualified candidates to fill the positions.[2] Now that more and more are coming up, it is going to be interesting to see what choices are made on those other levels. We are seeing already certain of the Masters moving on to different areas, and some of them are now suddenly choosing to move to different areas of the universe. Rather interesting, in that there is a kind of cultural interchange going on in the last little while with energies and entities from other systems, other dimensions, other planes coming forth that really had not been here for a long, long time. So the Masters and the beings who were working on those planes now have been starting to revise their plans. Free will is available all throughout the lower Galactic system, so even if one had been sort of nominated for a promotion over here, they may suddenly prefer to go over there. It is quite acceptable in most cases, providing there are enough qualified candidates to fill the void.

It is rather interesting, looking back at the way things were viewed even fifty years ago when Djwhal was doing his writings, where talk of the Third

---

2 Herein we refer to only the Famous Masters so you can better identify with this level of integration.

Initiation indicated that it generally caused the death of the physical vehicle; and that initiation was usually taken toward the end of a lifetime so that one had already achieved a certain amount of experience. The body was dropped, so to speak. The next lifetime was essentially devoted to integrating that energy, bringing it to the point of the Fourth Initiation. It was almost one lifetime per initiation at that point. What we have done is worked to modify the energies, making them far more mild, far less dangerous to the body. And we have also trimmed the prerequisites to some degree.

All of that clearing that used to have to be done before the Third Initiation is still being done, but after the Light has been anchored, to a large degree. The reason for this is that first we wanted to anchor more Light now; second, having that extra Light and extra power anchored now enables the initiate to move through that mass of false beliefs, thoughtforms, and whatever-you-wish-to-call-it in a quicker fashion (though sometimes a little more intense).

The opening of these higher chakras is taking place, and it is similar to the First Initiation, when all of the other chakras had to open to some degree. What is occurring here is that those higher chakras are now beginning to open to the point of aligning, whereby the higher energies can begin to flow down. So the alignment is being made; the connection is being made through those higher chakras to a point where, by having them opened, the integration process between the Third and the Fourth Initiations can take place much more easily. It is actually true that you are anchoring and opening the energies from those higher levels. Calling it the anchoring from the Fifth Initiation is not quite appropriate — it is a different terminology. It is a level of consciousness, and it cannot be strictly equated to a chakra at that point. When all of the chakras are open to a certain point, the system is able to handle the power of what is called the Fifth Initiation; and then the Initiator, Sanat Kumara, will administer the power. One has that experience, and in the meantime the whole system opens up to the next level. You rise to that level and then the added power is given, which opens it up fully from there. In a sense, it is like a flower closing up a little, and then your processing opens the flower back up to where it was.

It does depend somewhat on what happens with the others around you, and interestingly enough, no man is an island. However, given the work that you are doing and that the group around you is also doing, there seems to be the support there to be able to create a very powerful group vehicle within another few years beyond that.

There are plenty of opportunities and many different areas. One's limitations at this point are simply in the ability to hold power, or frequency of power. In spite of what Djwhal has said in the past through Alice Bailey, there are more than seven paths — there are an infinite number of paths one can take. The number of beings in one individual focus are almost infinite, and everyone has his own specific path. No two paths are the same. There are generalities; there is a large contingent who leave this plane and move on to the colleges in other areas — the constellation Sirius is one. There is a large university there where many beings go once they have attained the Fifth and are working toward the Sixth Initiation. They decide to move out of this Earth scheme altogether and into that other realm. It is not so much different at first from here. It is close enough that they still have a handle on what is around them. But from there they very quickly move into other-dimensional realities. These are so radically different that they are really beyond description in your language.

Once a being takes the Fifth Initiation and either ascends, or drops the body and takes on the Lightbody, it requires another little bit of integration to view the larger picture and bring all of the pieces together from the level of being beyond the Earth plane. Even Djwhal (refer to "Djwhal Khul," p. 107), when he did his Fifth Initiation, stuck around close enough to physicality for a long period of time and integrated back and forth, back and forth. He was working within the Hierarchy and within the etheric realm of Shamballa, but he would also come back into the body. Bringing that energy back into the body is what kept his physical body vitalized to the point where it became his ascension vehicle.

Another famous energy who has spent a great deal of time in physicality between his Fourth and Fifth Initiations and who has also done much service during that time is the energy we call Mohammed. He did his Third Initiation as the disciple Bartholomew in the gospel story with Jesus, and his subsequent incarnation as Mohammed was for the purpose of stabilizing that Soul-Merge energy to the point where it could be raised up to the Fourth Initiation. He then took the Fourth as Mohammed and incarnated one more time as a yogi in India; that was in the 1500s A.D. He was a relatively obscure yogi, mostly alone in a cave high in the Himalayas. He did have a small following of disciples, and was actually quite influential in unseen ways. He had a number of followers who also attained quite lofty status in their own ways and came back. They came more into the world and began to teach, but he as an entity stayed very much separate from all of that.

All of this is quite interesting, in that his Fifth Initiation was taken in that vehicle as the yogi. However, in many respects he was not able to fully integrate it in that lifetime, simply because his choice was to remain so secluded. He vicariously anchored his energy through his disciples, but that was not enough to fully stabilize the Fifth, so he chose to come back one more time after that as an initiate. As a Master-in-training, he had taken the Fifth Initiation and was about to be given a position on the Hierarchial Council, but he and his counselors decided that it would be better for him to have one more experience in physicality to fully anchor that energy. That was an initiation process in its own right, in that he was working with a form of energy a little different than the Masters normally work with. This form was to be called the "will energy," but it was tempered with the Second Ray — the element of Love. As an incarnate being, he worked very much behind the scenes this time, although a considerable portion of his energy became the personality known as Patrick Henry. From the point of view of the Hierarchy, he did a tremendous work. His primary task was in America, in the founding and setting up of that country of America. He was instrumental in bringing forth the Revolution and created the entire formulation of the ideals and ideas behind the Constitution — the more lofty visions. He worked with the historical figures such as Franklin and Jefferson, and they were, in a sense, disciples of his. There was an Englishman who ostensibly wrote the Constitution of the United States; Edmund Burke was actually another disciple of, let's call him Mohammed. Well, the interesting thing there was that there were many different authors of that document, and it was the project of the Hierarchy at that time to bring forth as little structure and as much freedom as possible within the framework of the government.

As the incarnate being of that time, Mohammed stayed very low key. He was involved in the Masonic lodges and in the so-called Rosicrucian lodges of the day; his work as a mentor may be found in them. The name of that being really did not matter. Patrick Henry was the important focus — again, as a physical, conscious, anchored focus of the Hierarchy's energies into that particular country at that particular time.

What he was able to do was to focus energies of the Love and the Will, which brought together a tremendous explosion of power in that day and age. The Love energy was what was initially intended, but due to the political resistance at the time, he had to also invoke the Will energy. That energy brought about the power of the people — which was the American Revolution — and gave them the power to be victorious. In many respects it was a pulse of power, and for good reason — it has been a powerful source for the United States of America to draw upon at times when needed. You notice, through their history, that the explosive power of that country is seen in the eleventh-hour syndrome. They will hold back and hold back, and yet usually when they do commit an action — we are speaking here specifically of wars, in being involved in a conflict — their power is very great. In recent times, however, they have not been very committed in what they have been doing, and they have been depleting that power (except for the Gulf War, which was influenced by your Planetary Government). That Will energy which they used to draw upon is now being transmuted back into that Love/Wisdom energy, which it really was intended to be in the first place. The First Ray energy is, in a sense, taking a back seat in America, and the Second Ray energy of Love/Wisdom is coming back into the forefront.

The Sixth Initiation is that of the Master moving beyond into the next level, the level of the Christ where Maitreya is operating. During that Crucifixion experience, Maitreya elevated to the level of the Sixth Initiation, and Jesus to the level of the Fourth Initiation. Jesus has subsequently taken the Fifth Initiation and recently the Sixth Initiation. The Office of the Christ is being filled in its next vacancy, so to speak, once Maitreya moves on to his next position. The Office of the Christ is being filled by Master Kuthumi. He is an interesting historical figure as well, in that his energies first became very well known in an incarnation where he was known as St. Francis of Assisi. As St. Francis he embodied that Love/Wisdom aspect, which is also his Ray now. That is why he is able to move up into that Office of the Christ, because he is very much aligned with that same energy.

The moving of the Fifth into the Sixth Initiation is the second phase of the ascension process, moving to the point where one is actually fully and completely transcending the dense physical, transcending the Earth experience. However, the Masters, on their Fifth Initiation level, still have a tie into the physical. They are still directly involved in working with planetary energies, working with disciples, channeling energies, channeling information, etc.

Back to the Third Initiation for a moment — it is an initiation for you both as a personality and a Soul; it is an energizing of both. What happens is that the Initiator energizes both to the same frequency, which allows them to merge. When they vibrate at the same rate, there is no discord for however long that anchoring process occurs. Again, the integration process is to bring them back into alignment so that the energy is the same. It is the principle of resonance — you have a lower frequency and a higher frequency, and ultimately one will come up or one will come down, until both meet in the middle. Here Soul is able to maintain its frequency more powerfully than personality is able to, so personality is elevated to the level of Soul. Yet at the same time Soul is being energized as well. (This principle of resonance is wonderfully developed through the **Mahatma** energy.)

The process of the Third Initiation is your first contact with Monad (the spiritual level) and one becomes self conscious enough to be called a Co-Creator. Moving into the Fourth, the Fifth, and then from the Fifth moving into the Sixth Initiation is a culmination process for Soul. Soul is concluding its contact with the Earth at that point, so as the Fifth Initiation moves into the Sixth, the Primal-Soul experience in physical terms is concluded — except for someone like Maitreya, who has elected to stay on, who has chosen that particular path. But the greater part of the beings who do reach that point choose to go into other areas, which is why you don't necessarily hear about all of these historical figures and where they are now.

There are nine initiations that can be done within this quadrant of this galaxy, and three more initiations to complete physicality. There follow 340 initiations and levels into the Source. From the perspective of being there as Source — the Source for this Cosmic Day, not the Undifferentiated Source — has some limitation to it, for the evolution process does not stop there. There is much, much more beyond our Source for this Cosmic Day, and therefore, even in its own terms, our Source cannot be the Absolute Source. For the Undifferentiated Source has literally billions of Sources, each with Its own Creator level and twelve directors of their Co-Creator Council wherein each embodies a Ray and together create a Cosmic Day. (See the chart, "Co-Creator and Creator Levels, pp. 228-29.) Ultimately, each Director of the Co-Creator Council evolves to become a full Creator of a Source of Its Own Cosmic Day. This includes every being in existence. Thus this should be enough to establish that the ultimate Source is not static but constantly evolving through eternity, and that all beings are the Sons of God. Are you beginning to see how it works?

The human condition at this time, becoming fourth-dimensional, can begin to contact and mirror those parts of Self which include the balance of the twelve initiations and twelve chakras (represented in the diagram "Electrical Day One," p. 222.) Now, these twelve initiations are still a physical perspective, not spiritual, even though you make a connection with the Monad at the time of your Third Initiation. However, neither that connection nor Ascension make you monadic — what these lower Third, Fourth, Fifth, and Sixth Initiations do is connect you to your unlimitedness. We know that this material is difficult for mankind in their structured third-dimensional consciousness, so that is why we'll repeat in a number of ways the ultimate New Age teachings, so that all of mankind can start to resonate more completely, including many who call themselves New Age who are taking cautious, tiny steps in their growth. It's truly a time to trust that rapid change can only really happen when mass consciousness shifts and you, as that important individual, have reprogrammed your own subconscious mind to know that:

- *1. The third-dimensional past does not exist.*

- *2. If you remain static in the fourth dimension, you'll not stay on the Earth. It is only through the grace of the* **Mahatma** *that mankind is being allowed to make this adjustment now.*

- *3. If your beliefs are static and disallow processing, then there is no growth for you at a time that, fourth-dimensionally, allows you to connect — through the* **Mahatma** *energy — to the Source of this Cosmic Day (your place of individualized birth).*

With greater concentration on the Source level brought about by the **Mahatma** energy, mankind can mirror the Source level, making connections with total Self multidimensionally and making exponential spiritual growth through the monadic levels. Part of the great gift given to mankind now is the planet Earth being so magnified in its intensity of Light that the relative degree of Light for this experiment on Earth now exceeds that of the Monad.

- *4. The greater your invocation of the* **Mahatma** *and your anchoring of this energy into the Earth and Self, the better your opportunity to hold form until you have increased your Lightbody's vibration sufficiently to withstand the fourth-dimensional shifts that are so apparent now. This is a wondrous event for mankind, for if the physical body can hold form because of this experiment during the next 35 years, those who stay could experience the creation of the spiritual body.*

In the past when a planet progressed from a third-dimensional to a fourth-dimensional reality, there were only pockets of survival. Those areas that had not or could not raise their vibration to the level of the Lightbody, obviously could not retain the slower vibrations that we call physical structure in this new fourth-dimensional reality. So when certain prophecies call for an "end," that, of course, was a correct prognosis of a planet graduating from the vibration of third to fourth dimension at the time of your Harmonic Convergence on

August 15/16, 1987. When this planet Earth's vibration increased so dramatically, those who were in a heavy structure would have been airlifted to go where mankind could survive, or the Soul/Higher Self could have allowed their physical/"lower" Self to experience physical death. This has happened in the past over and over again because this limited view of evolution held by the Primal Soul level became redundant and truly needed greater understanding of its purpose area. From a spiritual point of view, the Soul level was becoming retrogressive, as it still relates to many thousands of physical lives required to raise one's vibration beyond the Earth's vibration. Thus, as we've already discussed, the **Mahatma** energy was able to anchor on Earth (ever so slightly) on June 14, 1988 — one year after your Harmonic Convergence — because the Primal Soul level invoked the Creator level for assistance and a greater link with understanding the workings of evolution. Thus *The Rider on the White Horse*, the Avatar of Synthesis, or the *Mahatma* — overshadowed by the Cosmic Avatar of Synthesis — is here, so mankind now, for the first time ever, has an Earth-link with the Creator level and all 345 levels beyond the Earth's vibration. (This doesn't mean that physical death will cease or that some will not be airlifted to go where they can live.)

Thus you can begin to see where the very limited views of religions turned left when they should have turned right. From your perspective you may wish to just wait and see whose prognosis is correct, and that's just fine also. Ultimately, you have all of eternity to evolve without judgment, although that's not what your various Christian churches are teaching you, with their respective views on the Armageddon, Judgment Day, "losing your Soul," an ascension "with Jesus gathering his flock in the sky" and moving these "chosen few" to his Father's home that has many mansions, the Earth burning or flooding — and on and on. Most are not worthy of repetition except as a historical perspective or as allegories and emotional myths. What might your clergy say when their prognostications don't come to fruition? We are certain that there will be no shortage of creative answers, with the fear they must invoke to maintain their power with the ancient form-side teachings and the disallowance of new revelation. You have already heard the total denunciation of the New Age in hysterical terms. What was will become as "barking dogs" when the Church realizes that nothing they do will change New Revelation.

In all fairness to the Planetary Hierarchy, though, except for knowing about *The Rider on the White Horse* and preparing for same, "the ring passeth not"[3] is a fact in this Cosmic Day. There was no way that they could have known the exact time that their Source was going to begin to unite with a higher vibrational Source for this Cosmic Day, allowing the fourth dimension to be anchored on Earth and the *Mahatma* energy to come all the way in as a direct physical representation, thus enabling the evolutionary circuitry of this

---

3 Refer to diagram "The Ring Passeth Not," page 355,

quadrant of this galaxy to increase its vibrational frequencies by at least a thousandfold.

Absolute Source, in Its true nature, is absolutely beyond any attribute — and that means that it is beyond levels, beyond concepts, beyond absolutely everything. When you reference Source and are moving into Sourceness, you have a bit of a problem in semantics, in that you cannot "move into" It because It already is you and you are It. It is just that the awareness of the entity that you reference as "you" is not allowing itself to see and to realize that it is indeed Source. It is starting to, and once that occurs it is simply an unfoldment. (This process of unfoldment can be very rapid when you help anchor the *Mahatma* energy.) The belief system is like a bubble; you stretch beyond this bubble and there is a bigger one beyond that, and it seems infinite. Ultimately, when you have transcended all of the bubbles, then the realization is that none of them were relative; they were all of the Absolute all along. Therein lies that supreme paradox and the tremendous difficulty of man, who is intellectually polarized trying to understand something that is so far beyond the intellect that the intellect seems a wind-up robot compared to the biggest and best computer in the Cosmos.

There is a problem in mankind's tendency to rely on the intellect to figure things out, whereas in reality what should be done is to rely on the mind as a whole. The intellect is a specific tool with specific rules and processes for getting very incisively into things; the intellect, in that respect, is the analyzing rather than the synthesizing power of the mind.

What you are doing in this whole exercise is using your intellect as a tool, but what we are trying to do is to stretch you beyond that tool, to bring in other concepts that force your higher mind into action. We are trying to stretch you to the point where you can actually synthesize all of these various pieces of information and put them into a more coherent wholeness. In mankind's tendency to intellectualize lies the problem. **The intellect is as much of an illusion as the physical plane itself.** It is bound by its logical structures. We can show you how to use logic to prove that logic does not exist, that logic is a falsity. Therein is an interesting paradox. But the real point of it is to give you the exercise of stretching, integrating and synthesizing, because that's what makes you grow.

Sanat Kumara

Djwhal Khul Channeled Through Janet McClure

Sanat Kumara is not a member of the Hierarchy but works similarly to the President in not being a member of Congress yet part of the Government.

First of all, Sanat Kumara came to Earth about 18 million years ago out of love and for her need. He and three other glorious ones came to anchor the Light upon the Earth. Before this time it was a small, dark planet, very immersed in the heavy atmosphere, the heavy energies here, and there was no possibility of loosening this or raising her energies. This wonderful heavenly man then came to aid the Earth. He is known as the Planetary Logos and his "superior," the one he receives the Creator's energies from (in the main, anyway) is the Solar Logos, whose energies are so magnificent that at our point of evolution we can scarcely understand or conceive of what he is. Of course, there are many steps above this before you get to the Source, so we have a ladder effect that leads to the Source and steps down energies until they reach us here upon the Earth.

Sanat Kumara and his three Kumaras, the three Buddhas, reside in Shamballa. Know that he does reside there and his work is directed from there. Shamballa is — and again I am going to use the analogy of the President of the United States — similar to the White House and is the seat of the Planetary Government. The Hierarchy report to Sanat Kumara, some not directly but through the three Buddhas, the three other Kumaras, but some directly. It depends upon what their position is and what is going on at the present time. There is not one fast rule, but Shamballa is where council meetings are held that include all members of the Planetary Hierarchy after they have passed (although that is a poor word to use) the Fifth Initiation. They are then considered a Master of Wisdom and entitled to attend these council meetings.

Shamballa, then, is both a location (not of the gross physical) and a state of consciousness. When a council meeting is occurring, we simply attune to it and our consciousness takes part in the meeting by attuning to it. Sometimes, when it is appropriate, we go into our astral or even, you might say, etheric bodies. It is appropriate at some times but not at others. There is no hard and fast rule for this. But when an important council meeting is taking place at Shamballa, we all know it and we go one way or another. If business or focused attention upon work prevents the physical presence, then attunement is the most rapid and efficient manner by which to attend. Because of evolution, we are able to hold our consciousness in several places at once. It is quite easily learned, and some of you are beginning to learn it now by balancing yourselves in several places at once. This is the first step to learning this.

All right then, we have talked of Shamballa and Sanat Kumara, and now we discuss what it is he really does. He is the Creator's representative here. That is his job, and that encompasses a great many things. It is his responsibility, by his love, by utilizing the energies that are given to him in as positive and productive ways as possible, to aid the growth of the Earth. His aura, of course, is so large that the Earth and everything on it are contained within it. Does that give you some idea of the magnificence of this heavenly man?

The average level of the members of the Planetary Hierarchy (to generalize a little) is to be able to hold our focus, perhaps, in five areas at one time. But Sanat Kumara can hold his in a thousand places at once, attuning to whatever is necessary upon the Earth and within the Planetary Government and maintaining contact everywhere at once. "A thousand" is a little misleading because it is much greater than that. His consciousness in one of these thousand projectiles can encompass an entire state, for instance, and know exactly what is going on at any particular time or place. This is the magnificence that we have at the head of our Planetary Government.

Sanat Kumara, then, is the mastermind of evolution upon the Earth, in his office in Shamballa. He holds a special energy field that enables him to do with energy what is necessary before it is stepped down by him to the Christ and the Hierarchy for their use, because he can utilize such an intense energy pattern. He can use this very intensiveness to change it so it can be tolerated by others who cannot stand such intensity. If you will study these words it will tell you quite a bit about him and what he does here upon the Earth.

Sanat Kumara, then, delves within life in great depth upon the planet Earth. It is part of his consciousness, and he knows it very well. He knows each of us and our possibilities.

When he sees an area that needs attention, he focuses more of his consciousness there and explores it in depth. Occasionally you may have felt this probe as an intense surge of energy, as an intense feeling of love, of being affected now in every pore by love and energy. Not always, of course, but this may have been a probe of our Planetary Logos as he considers you and your evolutionary state.

Sanat Kumara is sometimes called the "One Initiator," and this is because it is his decision when each of us is ready to progress in a very special way from one level to another. When we are, he initiates the transaction period, and that is what is called initiation. Consider these words, and you can understand more about the subject of initiation. He, then, is the one who does it at the major planetary levels. Before that time it is done more informally. From the viewpoint of the Hierarchy and Sanat Kumara, only the major planetary initiations in which Sanat Kumara is the Initiator are of major significance in the life, because initiation is in the life of the planet. We are a small aspect, each of us, of the life of the Earth, and by thrusting forward ourselves we aid the Earth and her evolution. It is the totality of evolution upon the Earth that concerns Sanat Kumara, not one individual's approach such as you or I, but the totality of it. In fact, that is what must be understood about Sanat Kumara to know him and what he does.

He is involved very, very strenuously now in evolution for the Earth, because his own evolution is what causes the whole process to begin to thrust forward. He is a heavenly man and is getting ready for a very major step now. As the Earth in its totality steps forward now, it is his progress that reflects back and becomes our progress, the Earth's, and each individual's upon it.

Know that when you take a step forward, it aids Sanat Kumara, just as he aids you. It is a two-way street, and his aid, and your aid to him, are done with joy (I hope on your part, and I know on his), and thus progress is made in the Creator's Plan for life here upon the Earth.

In planning this tape and consulting Sanat Kumara, he bade me tell everyone who listens that he is very joyous now at being able to negate some of the karmic effects that would have begun to traumatize the Earth quite seriously very soon. This decision comes from a very high Source, and he is very glad to carry it out. He gives each individual his love, his assurance of his caring, and his desire for them to attune to their own potentiality, their own greatness, their own great thrust forward.

Chakras

At this point we would like to touch upon the chakras. Please refer to the illustration, "Electrical Day One," p. 222. The **first chakra**, or root chakra, is the basic level of groundedness. It is about basic survival and was the point of power for animal man, who had to deal with pure survival. He was created by you — the Soul, the Monad, the God, however you prefer to reference yourself as a vehicle. The experience of that vehicle was, "It's a jungle out there!" He had to do what was necessary to adapt and to survive, and the basic function of that chakra is that energy of survival — that pure, raw animal energy. It flows through the chakra, which is associated with the tailbone and has been very well developed through that long process of evolution from animal man into a more feeling and rational being.

The **second chakra** is the emotional/polarity chakra. It is the seat of the emotions within the system and that entire realm is very much connected into the astral plane, in that the illusion-making power of that chakra is second to none. For people who are very polarized within that chakra, it can create tremendous illusionary problems in their lives. The emotional body gets very much carried away by any impact, by any impulse, by any interaction. You have seen people like that who are very much with their heart on their sleeve. Well, it is not their heart; it is their second chakra!

The sexual energy is tied into both of these chakras, and therein lies a bit of confusion in a number of different renditions of what the chakras do. It has been said by different sources that the first chakra is the seat of sexual energy; others say that it is the second. In actual fact, both are tied into it. The first chakra is the seat of the power in general, and when it is expressed through the second chakra — which is more specifically tied into the emotional body than the physical — it touches upon the area of sexuality in that sexuality, from an animal perspective, has absolutely nothing to do with emotion. It was simply a drive found in animals in general. It is only when you get into man that you have sexual energy being expressed through any of these other levels.

So the sexual energy is a combination of the energies of the first and second chakras. There is the basic, raw power of the first chakra which comes through and is very much an Earth-connected power. Animal man drew a lot from the Earth, and in the process of rebalancing the system, one has to reconnect that chakra to the Earth. In general terms, the root chakra is the grounded point of the seven major chakras. We will speak of one other here which is tied into that — the Earth Star. It is a chakra but is not considered in most schemes as one of the major ones. The Earth Star rests at an average of twelve inches beneath the feet, and it is the physical point of contact with the Earth. When you view the channel of the energy flowing down through all of the chakras, the final one is that Earth Star chakra, and then it grounds directly into the Earth.

In another sense, we could consider that chakra as a subset of the eighth in that the energy from the eighth chakra, the Soul Star, grounds through the physical vehicle through to that Earth Star underground.

In numerological terms, it certainly makes sense in that the eighth chakra is the embodiment of number eight. In numerology, number eight is a very solid, earthy number; it is a solid expression. That is your grounded connection, and it is one of the most important areas to emphasize, for many systems and many people totally neglect that connection into the Earth.

There is a history behind that. There is a reason why that teaching was omitted. It is a bit of a cover-up from Atlantean days when the connection to the Earth was very well known — and had been forever up until that point. That connection to the Earth was where they drew much of their power, and in the times of Atlantis or as a race they were functioning primarily from the second chakra, from the emotional center. It is very difficult to put the pieces together as a race, but in general mankind was expressing through that second chakra — from an emotional perspective — and they were able to draw the energy up from the Earth and express it through that second chakra in a very creative way that led them to become, to a certain extent, masters of illusion. They were able to create illusionary vehicles, illusionary images in which to express themselves. The difficulty was that they got caught up in all of that; they got to a point where they could not distinguish between the illusion they had created and the so-called reality; the two were becoming blurred.

Another problem with the Earth energy at that time was that it had been misused to the point where it was enabling them to have contact with the Earth elemental energy, the Deva Kingdom. This Kingdom was certainly wide open to mankind at the time. Clairvoyance was the general rule, and the contact with the Deva Kingdom was very clear. Yet due to the polarities of the day, the power inherent in that Earth connection with the devas was misused, creating much of the distortion of energy that subsequently created the catastrophe for that continent.

At that point the contact with the Deva Kingdom was essentially shut down because it was felt that it was better not to have that contact for awhile. It was shut down by the Hierarchy — purposely, as part of a specific plan — to stimulate mankind to move beyond that second-chakra experience and beyond the attachment to the power they were able to draw from that and thus develop into a higher level. That higher level subsequently developed is the solar plexus chakra, which is more directly related and connected to the mental body and to the intellect. This is where much of mankind is today — polarized in the mental body, polarized in the intellect, stuck in their own logical structures. There are many who are still stuck in the second chakra and live through the illusions of their emotions. There is a rather striking parallel here between the East and the West in that regard. The West is more polarized in the intellect than the East. The East generally recognizes the more illusionary basis of life, and to a certain extent the teachings from that part of the world have transcended much of the attachment to the illusion. So they learned their lesson in that they did not stay attached to the intellect like the Western mind tended to do.

Now, the solar plexus chakra is also called the power chakra or the **third chakra**. That is a bit of a misnomer, because the second chakra is also a very powerful drawing power, as is the root chakra. The power flows in through all of the chakras and up to them, down into them, sideways, backwards and forward — it really does not matter how you reference the flow. The solar plexus is an area where much power is felt simply because it is a focus of the lower will. The will energy is the energy of the First Ray, which is a very dynamic, outgoing and hammered-in-shape type of energy. What we are experiencing now is a raising of the will into the heart on a mass level, particularly throughout the relatively free countries.

The solar plexus is an area where power is brought in and turned into material creation through the agency of the will. The process that mankind is going through right now (specifically for those of you who are a little more advanced than the average chronologically, who are moving into these higher chakra expressions a little ahead of the mass of humanity) in moving from the third into the **fourth chakra**, the solar plexus into the heart, is a process of transmuting the First-Ray energy into the Second — transmuting the energy of raw will, that explosive, fiery and rather overwhelming energy, through a more universal, tempered love/wisdom energy. (As a contrast, when the Creator level implements the First Ray, this Ray — being the most dynamic of the Rays — creates very rapid shifts on whatever level it is applied. Look to planet Earth and the shifts into the fourth dimension as a classic example.) So as the heart chakra begins to expand and the Soul connection begins to take place, then the raising of consciousness is one of the expressions of openness of the system. As the system opens, the consciousness expands; it is not so much a matter of knowledge and wisdom that brings enlightenment, but the process of unfolding and of spiritualizing the etheric. That is the old teaching of alchemy, which was a very clear, symbolic presentation of turning a base metal into gold, turning the rough, raw material on the physical plane into the Golden Celestial Light of the higher realm — the ascending of the physical into the higher levels.

So the heart chakra is the expression of Love into the physical. Remember that all of the chakras are in the etheric level and so have a corresponding organ in the physical. To touch upon those: The root chakra is that rounded point at the base of the spine, and the reproductive organs express that energy. The second chakra is more difficult to tie an organ to, difficult because the energies of emotion are all-pervading, particularly when mankind has so many of its parts out of place and each little organ seems to have a little consciousness of its own. Much of those consciousnesses are tied into that second-chakra energy, that emotional body. However, to put a name on it, we call the spleen the primary organ that it functions through. The solar plexus is a collection of muscles and tendons in the lower abdominal area that act as a shield for the internal organs, so that much of the power of the third chakra, much of the power of the will energy, comes in as a protective power. It is a shield between self and the world out there "that is going to get me" — which again is part of those basic false beliefs.

However, moving back up into the heart (refer to the diagram "Electrical Day One," p. 222), the heart chakra is more connected to the thymus gland than the physical pump of the heart. A point you can make, if you wish, is that the misconstruing of the heart chakra with the physical heart has caused much confusion within the system. One of the central organs in the body, the heart has had so much placed upon it as a responsibility that it has tried to take on the job of feeling, when it really has no capacity whatsoever to feel. It is simply an organ; it is a pump. If one can go in and speak with that consciousness which has been created by these misconceptions, these false beliefs and the energy around them, a consciousness which is embodying that organ, then much of the heart disease that people are experiencing will vanish. The heart will then be relieved of the burden of trying to do a job that it cannot do; it will be relieved of the burden of trying to feel and to express emotion.

Can you imagine your own plight were you to be placed in the position of president of General Motors, for instance, and told, "Don't mess things up or else!" You may be flattered at first to be chosen for the job but then suddenly feel very nervous about it, wondering, "Who is judging me, and how can I possibly perform when I do not have the foggiest idea of what this is all about?"

The heart and all of these parts really are placed in a similar position, because they're given a job, through the inefficiency of the conscious mind, that they were not capable of handling. So you have a heart — a valve, a pump — which is supposed to handle all of your emotional feelings when in actual fact there is a very neglected organ called the thymus gland that is capable and only too happy to do the job. But it has atrophied and has been shut down from puberty.

The basic energies which are brought through that heart chakra have not been able to be grounded into the physical by many people to a significant degree, simply because the physical heart is not capable of doing it, much as one tries. And the more one tries, the more stress one puts on the physical organ, and ultimately people "die of a broken heart." The pump breaks down because it cannot do two jobs; it has been performing a double task and gets tired. The thymus gland has been created for the job in the first place, but got bypassed in some strange promotional process at puberty.

The thymus gland is right in the center of the chest, and if you do what they call the "thymus thump" (which Tarzan seems to have perfected — it probably kept him very healthy), you can feel that organ beginning to vibrate. The thymus was shut down in puberty simply through the mechanism of a tremendous amount of false beliefs — and the major false belief that shut it down was the belief in death and old age. If one believes that one is going to grow old and die, then ultimately one will. The programming has been so

solidly anchored that it has created a situation where the thymus gland —
which is really the seat of the rejuvenating power in the body — has been so
shut down that it no longer can secrete the hormones necessary or on a higher
level, transmute the energy from the heart chakra into the more subtle levels of
programming to enable the system to maintain its immortality. All of you will
have to master that in order to create that vehicle for ascension; you will have
to rejuvenate your thymus gland. There are a number of ways to do that.

The thymus is, in short, a very neglected little gland (we can call it an
organ, but technically speaking it is a gland). The anchoring of the Soul energy
tends to enliven the thymus gland because the Soul has to have some physical
place to anchor into. Trying to anchor it into the physical heart would be rather
detrimental to the heart, and certainly not advisable. The Soul knows where it
needs to go. However underdeveloped the thymus may be, it ultimately will
begin to be rejuvenated, and the experience of those going through Soul Merge
is that this whole area tends to become activated, and many of the issues that
caused it to shut down in the first place tend to come back again as that area is
being cleared. Those issues tend to be the standard issues that an adolescent
would go through, because even during the time when that adolescent has a
relatively healthy thymus, the programming tends to go in there. As this area
is being stimulated again, that programming shoots back out. Thus much of
what you went through in adolescence you will usually find repeating itself in
a more appropriate form (more appropriate in regard to your current age;
however, the issues will be the same). The major issues during adolescence are
issues of victimhood and martyrdom — feeling the victim of parents, society
or school, and finally accepting the "facts of life" and having to nobly suffer
through it as the martyr.

There are, of course, numerous other traumas of adolescence, but by having the thymus area reactivated, the Soul energy can become firmly anchored
into the physical and you can begin to work wonders on the physical level.
With a more healthy thymus you will be able to reprogram the body to
function the way you want it to. In other words, to set up the parameters of the
body the way you want to see them. If you wish to have a new set of teeth, then
it is possible to regrow a new set of teeth using the power coming through and
the focused intent of the conscious mind to do that. But it also entails getting a
few of those other "saboteur" parts out of the way.

To work with the thymus gland, learn where it is in your body — basically
right behind the chest. This exercise will assist you in bringing the **Mahatma**
energy into your auric field; a developed, active thymus gland is wonderfully
helpful.

   Send it energy; go in and talk to it; and purify it — send it up to the
   Source to get purified or bring in a ball of Earth energy to purify it. Take a
   symbol of something that is very pure and innocent (perhaps a young kitten
   or a baby — better to have a baby that you don't have a particular attachment
   to) and use that symbol to have that innocence and purity growing in the area
   you want purified. That will focus the energies to come in and reactivate the

power of that gland. It will enable you to actually begin the reversal of the aging process. If you have an aqua-aura crystal to hold during this process, your physical cells will rejuvenate amazingly.

The **fifth chakra**, the throat chakra, is the primary means of expression. It is the energy focal point of expression and is tied into the thyroid and the parathyroid glands. These function within the endocrine system to step down the energy from the pure light focus into the material level in an electrical or a chemical focus. That glandular structure of the thyroid and the parathyroid is also responsible to a large degree for the health of the system — but by and large, if you want to focus on health, focus on the thymus and you will find that the immune system is strengthened. There need be no worry about diseases such as AIDS, because the immune system will be so strong that it will be totally invincible to all of those things.

The throat chakra is the energy transformer that is, in its proper functioning, responsible for the speech expression — not only the vocal expression but also the mental expression and the mental reception, even from telepathic points of view. At the back of the throat chakra is a receiving apparatus almost like a satellite disk; you receive your telepathic impulses primarily from there.

The **sixth chakra**, the third eye, is called the "spiritual eye" or "the eye of inner vision." Located in the center of the forehead, it is associated with the pineal gland; however, the pineal must be functioning to some degree for the sixth chakra to become activated. The third eye, which sees in the Eternal Now, is a director of energy, i.e., it can be used to focus, stimulate and direct energies, including thoughtforms.

The crown, or **seventh chakra**, is the main entry point of higher energy into the dense physical body. It is associated with the pituitary gland. This is the terminal within the physical body that has a direct correspondence with your twelfth chakra, where the higher level has a powerful correspondence with the Twelfth Ray and the beginning of the Monad.

Functions of the Chakras

Soul Star	Needs to accept divine equality
Crown	Pivotal in accessing potential
Third eye	Motivates integration
Throat	Motivates part in the plan/releases
Heart	Is center of progress/home base
Solar Plexus	Motivates the heart
Polarity	Movement
Base	Foundation

We have areas of the world that are embodying different frequencies of consciousness, of energy. To use the chakra system as a model here could be quite illuminating. So we see from the human experience of the root chakra — the base of the spine — that that particular chakra has as its primary function a focus upon security, survival — very primal basics of life. Fear is very much a part of that. Now, that chakra has been active ever since animal man came upon the Earth, and to a certain extent it has been transcended — the energy has been stepped up a notch to at least the second chakra and in many cases, the third chakra, as a model here.

By looking at certain areas of the world which are still operating on that basic survival level, we can liken that to the root-chakra level of existence.

We can see areas experiencing their reality through that chakra, those areas being primarily large segments of Africa and certain sections of Asia going through time after time after time famine and flooding and pestilence and all of the problems associated with the basic level of survival. We could say that those areas are still operating primarily out of a first-chakra style of functioning. Now, there are other fragments of the populace — the aboriginal peoples in certain parts of Australia, New Guinea, Borneo, places like that — who are also operating from a primal level. As a racial expression those beings are still primarily in a first-chakra mode of functioning, sometimes moving into a second.

The second-chakra style of functioning is typified by emotional turmoil. The second chakra in the body is the seat of the emotions; whenever emotional turmoil occurs, you can bet that there has been an activation in that area. Now, where in the world do we find emotional turmoil on a national level? There are the obvious areas of revolution, of political unrest such as South Africa, the entire Middle East or much of the energies of India that are going from the first chakra into a second-chakra style of functioning; the second-chakra energy is being stimulated in those areas.

As the energy is turned up, then the particular transformer that is wide open will be the one which is going to determine how that energy is felt in that area. If the second chakra is primarily the one being stimulated in those areas where there is revolutionary activity — Central America is a prime example here — you see, they are moving from the basics of survival into the second-chakra style of emotional reaction.

The other area where this energy is popping up, the revolution in Fiji, is an interesting little spark from the old Lemurian stomping grounds. The energies of this chakra are being felt not only in the areas of political revolution but of religious turmoil as well — and very often the two are expressed together. The Northern Ireland type of energy, for instance, is an adherence to a fanatical religious dogma and very much an emotional attachment, the second chakra. Now, not to tar the entire area with that brush, saying that this is the energy working in that area now, certainly does not say that no other type of energy can be felt or expressed there.

Looking at the third chakra as the power center for the average human being, this is where the energy of the will comes in. This is the energy of expression of intellect, of rational man trying to control his environment, trying to bring forth a semblance of order onto the structure of his society. This tendency has always been there, but it has now developed to the point of what we would call civilization. The civilization of the Western world developed to this stage at the Industrial Revolution — that was the demarcation point of moving from the second into the third chakra. The more rational thought infused the so-called "enlightenment" of the time, in terms of political awareness, of social and economic structure, etc. You had at that time a tendency toward freedom of speech, of expression, of thought that had not been available before. There had been too much control by Church and State. So the areas that typified this energy on a political level were the revolutionary energies of America and of France establishing the more self-ruled type of state. You also found a change at the same time within the monarchial structures, particularly of Britain, to grant less power to the monarch and more to the Parliament, to the elected structure.

From a scientific point of view, the British Industrial Revolution occurred, with all of its changes in the way things were done: Cottage industry moved into mass production, and mass production moved into a bewildering display of machinery, often to the detriment of the living conditions of the people working there. All of this was typical of that type of energy being expressed through the "lower" world — through the solar plexus: control of the environment, "getting what I want through my will, going out and hammering it into place until it is done." That level of activity has spread through other areas of the world from the primarily European origin of the Industrial Revolution to America, Australia and the so-called more civilized world.

The other areas of the world which gradually embraced that were Russia, Japan, and to a certain extent, China. China tended to go slower in its embracing of the technology of the Industrial Revolution simply because of the overwhelming burden of communication and social structure, considering the number of people there. India was the same, in that the ancient character of the culture precluded to a certain extent the ready acceptance of new ideas; and the continuing feudal style of government did not call for the ready promulgation of new ideas, either.

In Japan that was less of a problem due to the size of the country; and the British Industrial Revolution was initially embraced there as a means of military control in the time of the shoguns. That particular style of adaptation to Western technology grew into a very ready acceptance of technology and that type of organization. Japan is an interesting area, too; one of the reasons it has this crystallization of thoughtforms is because of the political structure that maintains the Emperor. Until the time of the Second World War, the Emperor really held the power (rather, the Emperor's contingent, for the Emperor himself was not always politically powerful, although his office was). You have a situation where the ruling class moved from being the feudal lords of Japan itself to being the feudal lords of the corporations. The corporate structure of Japan is still very much tied into that old network of aristocratic feudal families. Once the system embraced an idea, it was implemented instantly from the Emperor's office down. So when the focus came to build machinery to expand the empire, it was instantly embraced, clearly showing that tendency to expand within the structure. Japan is still very much involved with that solar-plexus style of activity. China is moving into that now; it is more readily embracing that. Russia has been doing so since the time of the czars. But primarily from the Bolshevik Revolution onward it embraced the solar-plexus style of will — very much the aggressive "go and pound it into shape, and if you don't like it, pound it again — if anyone gets in your way, pound them!" — this kind of approach.

When the heart chakra begins to be stimulated on a mass level within the consciousness of a group (we mean primarily countries), then one finds that the old ways of doing things tend to drop away because they don't work anymore. The old way of pounding the world into shape through the solar plexus begins to get a little tiring; it doesn't work very well anymore. So moving into the new way of doing it from a more heart-centered focus allows miraculous things to occur. It can also allow for certain confusion, given the overlap of the ways of doing things. When perhaps the new ways may not seem to be working and the old ways aren't either, then what do you do? One may feel caught in between.

This is where many of the countries of the Western world are right now — in the gap in between, and that is simply a point of readiness, a point of stillness before moving into the new.

On a planetary initiation level, the heart chakra has been stimulated and is resonating throughout the world to the point where it is activating all of the lower chakras to rise an octave.

The areas that have been functioning for the longest and the clearest through the highest expression of the day — which was the solar plexus — are now moving en masse into the heart. You are finding this in North America and in most of Europe, Australia, New Zealand, etc. In areas such as Japan there is still a bit too much crystallization of the old thoughtform, and that has to lift before that heart energy can really come into play. But what you are finding is that even though the stimulation of the Earth through this initiatory process — which has been going on for quite some time, throughout this entire century — the areas such as China, for example, are moving out of that second chakra into the third. There are also elements of the fourth chakra beginning to trickle in, expressed as desire for more freedom, more expression, and even the desire for spiritual connection from the heart of that would-be materialistic country. You will see massive changes in Russia and China as the proletariat demand freedom at any price, even if this shift causes living conditions to worsen.

It is causing some confusion in those areas because they do not have the formalized structure anymore that people are used to. So we are finding areas of China and Russia in which vast numbers of people are beginning to open up to new ideas. The Russian powers that be have been interested in psychic phenomena for ages, and they have been doing more research in that area than in any other. However, their intent is still very much controlled by that solar-plexus style, using that as a weapon, a weapon of knowledge perhaps or a means of barter, but still a weapon. Russia is gradually finding a trickle of Light coming in that is stimulating the people and therefore beginning the flowering within their hearts of their own true essence. More and more spiritually advanced beings are choosing to incarnate in that area at this time to begin the stimulation, from a very basic level, of the new generation. We could see within the next twenty years a flowering of the consciousness of that country.

You are seeing the beginnings of that now, and the more open their political and economic policies, the more they are going to gradually realize that they have been insular far too long and that they do not need to send out their spies to get the new secrets. All they have to do is to open up and it will be readily given, provided that there is a little bit of cooperation on the level of military sensibility. That cooperation has to come from all sides, including the American side.

In some of Djwhal's writings, he tended to portray the Allies in the Second World War as being the good guys and the others as being the bad ones. As typifying energies, that could be an accurate way of looking at it, but it certainly is not as black and white a situation right now. What we have is the tendency of some areas to focus on the more strictly materialistic and therefore, in classic terms, the "dark" side of things. On the other side there is a focus also on the materialistic, but in a slightly different vein — to create freedom rather than to create more power politically.

So within the consciousness particularly of North America and of Europe there is a new flowering, a new growth of consciousness. On a mass consciousness level, those areas are moving up into the heart chakra. As that occurs and as more and more beings within those areas open to their own true nature as Third-Degree Initiates, you will find this process of blossoming expanding very rapidly. That is as far as group consciousness on a national level has taken itself at this point.

The Twelve Rays

In metaphysical literature there are many references to the seven Rays, with discussion about the qualities and colors they represent and the specific teachers working with them.

The Rays are simply frequency bands of energy flowing from the Undifferentiated Source through the Council of Twelve at the Creator level/Source for this Cosmic Day through the various planes of Creation, and thence into your solar system. (See the charts, "The Seven Councils of Twelve," p. 227; and "The Co-Creator and Creator Levels," pp. 228-29.)

The study of the Rays can be a complex subject, and there have been many books written on the subject. There is some excellent updated information from the Tibetan Master Djwhal Khul channeled through Janet McClure that is quoted herein.

The Rays have a correspondence with the seven planes of Creation, and when experienced by the human also have a rather complex connection to the chakra system. They are also associated with the various signs of the zodiac.

Earlier works spoke of seven Rays and seven chakras, but in recent years new information has been given, including somewhat sparse information on the five higher Rays and five higher chakras, as well as some shifting of position within the Planetary Hierarchy, and therefore different Masters in charge of the various Rays on the planetary level.

In the early 1970s, the Creator granted the Earth the opportunity of working with five additional Rays, which make a total now of twelve. These five higher Rays are for a distinctly different purpose than the first seven. The Earth's evolution has reached a point where it was felt that these Rays would be an opportunity to progress, an added emphasis on evolution. Man stands at a critical point. To enable him to go beyond this point, to aid him in this evolution, the Creator granted this special opportunity of working through or with these higher Rays. He may utilize these to climb again the ladder of evolution back up to the Source. This is their purpose and each of them works in a unique and different way.[4]

Everyone has some of each of these energies within the Self. Each of the following levels has a specific Ray: spiritual (monadic); Soul (egoic); personality, emotional, mental, physical.

Now, most that function here upon the Earth have not begun to be affected by the Monad's Ray (the spiritual level) and most not by the Soul's Ray, either. But it is helpful to know them so that you may understand the potential that each person has. By looking at oneself through a specific focused area such as the Rays, you can understand each part and then put together a whole that is understood more completely.[5]

The monadic Ray, then, is the primary Ray which stays with one through the eons.

...the Hierarchy, which is the "spiritual" government of the planet, is divided into seven departments that follow these Rays.[6]

There are three groups of Rays: Rays 1–3, called Rays of Aspect; Rays 4–7, called Rays of Attribute, which are sub-Rays of Ray 3; and Rays 8–12, the higher Rays, which are blends of the other seven.

Following is a brief synopsis of the twelve Rays and how they affect humanity. Their effect is both individual and national, since the Rays flow in various paths around the Earth.

Ray One: This is the Ray of Divine Will — it clears the way and destroys

---

4 *The Tibetan Study Series #3*, Djwhal Khul through Janet McClure, The Tibetan Foundation, Inc., P.O. Box 252, Youngtown, AZ 85363, October 12, 1983.

5 *Ibid.*

6 *The Twelve Rays Seminars*, p. 9, Djwhal Khul through Janet McClure, The Tibetan Foundation, Inc. There are specific Masters in charge of the energies of the various Rays.

the old form to make room for the new. (See the Color Chart of the Rays on the diagram, "The Seven Councils of Twelve," p. 227.) It is characteristic of the Father (*Mahatma*) aspect of the Divine Being. It is a very powerful, forceful energy and can be found expressing through humanity in fields of leadership — politics, government — and in the power of the warrior. It gives one the characteristics of determination, drive, and leadership. However, people dominated by the First Ray are often good at starting a project but not finishing, becoming bored easily and wanting to move on to new ideas. The Master in charge of the First Ray department of the Planetary Hierarchy is "the Manu" — now the Master Jupiter. Working with him is the Master Morya and many others.

The First Ray energy was used positively by Winston Churchill, General Patton, General MacArthur and others during World War II. It is also characteristic of the pioneer, with Christopher Columbus typical of its expression.

> *Another thing to remember about Ray One is that it is usually a very focal point with either a person or a time. Earth is getting more Ray One now. We are at a focal point in the world's history. At a crisis period where change occurs there is a lot of Ray One either embodied with many people utilizing it, or as a direct response — or both. The Planetary Hierarchy may be directing it, or much may come in at this time through Shamballa and Sanat Kumara.*[7]

However, these levels are simply stepping down the energy — it doesn't come in directly through the Planetary Hierarchy — all twelve Rays are directed from the Source level. No level makes decisions by itself; they step it down 345 levels from the Creator Council of Twelve to your Planetary Hierarchy.

> *The reason that Ray One comes through now is that this is a critical time for Sanat Kumara and the Earth. The fact is that they are both reaching a point of crisis, and the Ray One energies are important in starting the correct angle for ascent.*[8]

The First Ray energy, that of the will, is very useful for moving through situations where you feel stuck either through apathy, lack of energy, or lack of vision of the next step.

> *To enhance this energy — to climb out of the feeling of being stuck — visualize your will made into a red ladder and climb out of the depression or rut rung by rung.*

> *To dilute the intensity of Ray One, see a stream of red Light being broken up by particles of white or rainbow Light.*

> *You can also enhance your physical energy by visualizing yourself standing in a beam or flame of red Light. Use this in moderation, however, as this Ray can be quite intense.*

---

7 *Ibid.*

8 *Ibid.*

Ray Two: This is the Love-Wisdom Ray. Most of the physical "spiritual" teachers are on the second Ray. The Buddha embodied the Wisdom aspect and Christ the Love principle. Other great beings on the Second Ray include Solomon and the Masters Djwhal Khul and Kuthumi. Most of those who feel a calling to spirituality from a teaching focus are expressing the second Ray on the Soul level. The Lord Maitreya is currently occupying the Office of the Christ (the Second Ray department) but will soon be replaced by the Master Kuthumi as the 36th Christ Consciousness for the Earth, radiating the quality of compassion.

The higher mental-conceptual areas are reached through this Ray also. The Universal Mind can be entered by means of this beautiful Blue Ray. One can stretch mentally to obtain the great mental concepts that await you in the Universal Mind. Thus when a great concept is placed in this universal area by teachers — the Spiritual Hierarchy — those who are able to stretch can receive it, and thus a great idea may be received in several areas of the world at once.

It has been said that the Earth is on the Second Ray. According to Djwhal Khul,

> ...our Earth receives a major Second Ray from a higher Source, and after that Second Ray hits the Earth it divides into the seven Rays...every Ray that we then receive is really a part of the Second Ray energies, and thus the Second Ray that I'm talking about is intensified; it is stronger because it comes also from this main Second Ray Source.[9]

[NOTE: This has changed dramatically since this material was introduced. Now that your planet has become fourth-dimensional in a New Age, the dominant Rays — as many of you can sense — are the First Ray, very powerfully, and the Twelfth Ray, which embodies all twelve Rays.]

Your Planetary Hierarchy fully anchored the Eighth through Twelfth Rays on January 26, 1991. The inability of your Planetary Hierarchy to anchor these five higher Rays has kept this planet from being able to flow fourth-dimensionally until nearly 3-1/2 years after the Harmonic Convergence. Even though the Earth became fourth-dimensional at the time of the Harmonic Convergence, it was not able to function fourth-dimensionally until the five higher Rays were anchored, thus completing the circuitry from Source to Earth. This complete circuitry includes all twelve Rays, not just seven.

The Second Ray can be used very productively by visualizing either blue or pink. By simply feeling yourself, your surroundings, or any situation bathed in these colors, you can help uplift the vibrations to a more harmonious value. Pink is generally felt to be more expressive of the Love aspect and blue of the Wisdom aspect. You can often defuse negative situations by flooding

---

9 *The Seven Rays*, Tibetan Informational Series I-0052, Djwhal Khul through Janet McClure, The Tibetan Foundation, Inc. p. 2.

them with pink Light, and bring clarity to confusion by adding blue.

Ray Three is the Ray of Active Intelligence. It is usually perceived as a yellow-gold, and those who have a lot of it are characterized by an unswerving practicality. They are very persistent, bordering on stubborn, but above all very concretely pragmatic. Thomas Edison is a good example of this kind of energy. Germany is a country with a lot of Third Ray influence, and its effects are obvious in the practical drive of the people. Typically, there is strong organization, but not always clear awareness of the consequences of actions. Healers of all types often have a great deal of this energy.

> *Now, coming from this Third Ray energy are the remaining four. They are really passed through the Third Ray on their way to manifestation and thus from the Third Ray extend the Fourth, Fifth, Sixth and Seventh Rays.*[10]

> *This Ray, then, is a means of getting the Earth's lessons learned, to getting accomplished for the Creator His Cosmic Plan.*[11]

> *The Third Department is the "organizer" of the Hierarchy. It is the one that "gets it all done." The First Ray people say, "This is important, this is new," and get it done. And the Second Ray people say, "And do it with Love, and be sure that it fits into the learning experience of the people," and the Third Ray people say, "We should organize it this way and this way" — and they do it. The Third Ray is the one that "gets it done." They are the organizers, whether we are talking about Earth living or our "spiritual" government.*[12]

The Third Ray can be used by sending a yellow light to areas of the world (not specific people unless they ask for it) that you feel could benefit from its organized, practical energy (areas of Africa, for example). See the country or area bathed in yellow light and be aware that you are directing the Third Ray qualities there.

The head of this Third Ray department is the Mahachohan, or "Lord of Civilization." He is the Master Serapis Bey, who was formerly in charge of the Fourth Ray department.

Ray Four is called Harmony Through Conflict and is usually seen as green.

> *Most of those that utilize this Fourth Ray experience it through conflict rather than harmony. They must learn to take this energy, this vibration, and raise it up and function on the Fourth Ray harmoniously.*[13]

Many artists and musicians are on this Ray and many of them go through

---

10 *Ibid.*

11 *The Tibetan Study Series #3*, p. 3.

12 *The Twelve Rays Seminars*, p. 10

13 *Ibid.*

a great deal of inner and outer conflict before arriving at a point of harmony. Some classic examples of this would be Van Gogh and Picasso.

Fourth Ray people are very connected to the Earth — they like the variety of living in different places and doing many different things. They sometimes overdo this and become generalists, not specializing in any one thing.

When Fourth Ray people get into the middle of a conflict, it becomes very compulsive, very self-feeding, and you keep going into it and around and around. It is very characteristic of Fourth Ray to go to the heights and then to the depths — a roller-coaster effect....[14]

The main way to get up out of these emotions into balance is by using the mind — that is the natural balance. Beautiful music may help also. They need to understand that it is a pattern and that they can overcome it and get into a higher level of the Ray.

Now, there is a lot of basic appreciation for Earth living in the Fourth Ray people, and they will relate to the Earth in a way that most of the other Rays do not. It is sometimes difficult for them to meditate and get up into the spiritual area because the Earth connection gets in the way. Many times they are into a lot of physical activity — doing things on the Earth such as driving vehicles, horseback riding, hiking, climbing mountains, relating to animals. They like participating in Earth living.

Balancing the Rays can be done by working with the chakras, too. For the Fourth Ray, working with the Solar Plexus Chakra, which is connected to the emotional body, is important. It is important to stimulate it in the highest and most productive part and balance it completely.[15]

The Master in charge of the Fourth Ray is Master Paul, who has been rather behind the scenes for a long time. He works extensively with the Deva Kingdom and very closely with the Archangel Gabriel.

Ray Five is the Ray of Pure Intelligence or Concrete Knowledge, and is usually perceived as orange.

Upon this Ray function the great scientists of the world — those with the intelligence to penetrate deeply into a cause, the cause of a situation. They can analyze a situation and take it apart and put it back together, synthesize it, and know the best way to productively undertake a venture. They are the ones that do the conceptual work in the world. They have the mental capacities to lead mankind past the present situation and bring it into the New Age. They can conceive it, and then others can bring it into being. They have the ability to conceptualize life as it would be most productive to live it. Without this

---

14 *Ibid.*

15 *Ibid*, p. 16.

great Ray, such possibilities could not be understood. The Ray allows this type of understanding by those that can use it productively.[16]

Within the Hierarchy, the Fifth Ray department is exceptionally busy, as they have been for the last several hundred years. They direct, "...among other things, all of the scientific pursuits going on at the present time....Impetus is given in the areas that humanity needs for its more rapid growth. Scientific principles are put forth which are then picked up by several advanced beings upon the Earth, and that is why, when a new breakthrough is made scientifically, it may be made at more than one location upon the Earth at once. It is picked up from the higher mental area in a very special way by those who are able to receive it.[17]

The Fifth Ray is associated with the mental body and is especially influential now because our current age is largely focused (sometimes stuck) in this mental expression. Those who are not mentally focused experience primarily through the emotions, and they are benefiting greatly from this Fifth Ray influence, as it helps them to balance out the emotions.

The mental focus is necessary to begin the process of balancing everything. One can reach through the intuitive level to the higher levels, but when you are trying to balance everything completely, then it is through the mental one must go, because it balances the emotional.[18]

In the coming years, as more of the higher Rays come into prominence, the Fifth Ray will help to balance these new energies.

The head of this Fifth Ray department is Master Hilarion, who in a previous life was Paul of Tarsus. He shares his responsibilities now with another Master, known as Master Markco.

Ray Six is the Ray of Devotion or Idealism, and is seen as indigo blue. The head of this department of the Planetary Hierarchy is the Master Jesus.

The Sixth Ray, Devotion, can be very free and beautiful, but it can also slide into fanaticism. It is a rather heavy energy from a human perspective.

It clings and makes one aspire along a specific path. It is not conducive to a search; it really focalizes a search, makes it specific along one path, and thus it is rather an addictive energy, if you will, one that encourages specific points of view. Thus, a Sixth Ray physical body may enjoy eating specific foods and overdo them, and in the religious areas, it may be a very fervent believer in its religion and go overboard, really, in its zealous approach to its religious beliefs.[19]

---

16 *The Tibetan Study Series #3*, p. 3.

17 *The Hierarchy Today*, Djwhal Khul through Janet McClure, The Tibetan Foundation, Inc., p. 20.

18 *The Twelve Rays Seminars*, p. 24.

The Sixth Ray has dominated the Earth for the last 2000 years and is clearly expressed in the Christian religion and cultures.

...(It) was utilized very much by the Christ — the Lord Maitreya. How? Devotion to "One God obedience," used in connection with the Second Ray love vibration. He focused the Sixth Ray here in a specific esoteric sense, and through its use a certain focus grew up, and among the characteristics of that focus were the specifics of the Christian religion...the Second and Third Rays' connection as shown in the teaching. He went everywhere teaching, and in addition, focused on the specific religions. The Sixth department (of the Planetary Hierarchy) is still doing that. They are attempting...to synthesize all the religious activities of the world.[20]

Master Jesus is working with devotional patterns. He is working with specific religious organizations and he can, truly, research and understand each particular one, and then from that understanding of each one, see it and synthesize it — use that energy to raise the level of the experience. Where? To the level of Wholeness — and then see it as a Whole, and with his consciousness, with his abilities, can work on that level...so he can bring it into being on a "spiritual" level before it starts to work its way down into creation....It must be brought to the Wholeness level on the "spiritual" plane first....He is bringing it into the Wholeness concept by his wonderful synthesis ability, now, and bringing it down to the astral plane level. It's already there. All we have to do is bring it forth. Everything that we need for the New Age is already there. We just have to bring it forth.[21]

By adding the Sixth Ray to the energy or the concept that one is working with, it can add the quality of putting things "on automatic" — it will be held automatically. This quality may be used by focusing on the indigo Ray, seeing and feeling the vibration rising, becoming lighter and less dense. Then focus this higher vibration onto a concept, plan or pattern that you wish to bring into manifestation. This counteracts the heavy quality of the Ray and adds a stronger focus and holding quality to the process of manifestation.

Ray Seven, the Violet Ray, has been called the Gateway to the New Age. It is clearing the heavy energy patterns of the past and transmuting that energy to a higher vibration. It has been termed the Ray of Ceremonial Magic, due to the preciseness with which this energy is used.

The Master responsible for the Seventh Ray energies is Master Rakoczi (also known as the Count St. Germain). In his work he is literally seeing problem areas on the Earth and transmuting them (where he is allowed) by means of

---

19 *The Seven Rays*, pp. 2-3.

20 *The Twelve Days Seminars*, pp. 26-27.

21 *Ibid.*, p. 32.

the Violet Flame. This is a part of his responsibility, done under the direction of the head of the Hierarchial Government, Sanat Kumara, and the Christ. The specific locations that he deals with are the troubled spots of the world...his work is very vast. It doesn't deal with specific people (except his students). It is the energy fields on the Earth in general. And that's one thing that I'm trying to get across, is that the members of the Hierarchy work with vast amounts of energy generally.[22]

To work with the Seventh Ray, you can use it in meditation by visualizing a Violet Flame or a rotating brush of violet Light, bringing that through you to clear the heavy energies.

Aside from its transmuting qualities, it also brings its quality of preciseness which can show you exactly what needs to be cleared. If used on a regular basis, it will help you to see clearly the next step to take on your path of evolution.

You can also attune to this energy by attuning to the Master Rakoczi himself.

If you feel attracted to this being, you may call on him. He has given you permission to do that. He will work with anyone who will do so....Whatever you perceive him to be will be fine, but it might be a good idea to perceive him as being within the Violet Flame itself, and then establish a two-way connection. You could be within the Violet Flame also, and begin to flow a communication between the two of you by means of this transmuting Violet Flame. I think you might get some very interesting things from that....When we get focuses of Violet Flame all over the planet, it's going to bring that energy down and focalize it — allow it to be used more and more between the Spiritual Hierarchy and the planet. You could see that — just visualize that — all of these streams coming onto the Earth. How marvelous!...It would be very appropriate to let people know all over the world about it.[23]

The Higher Rays

These Rays are being given now for the specific purpose of aiding our evolution into the New Age.

The Seventh department of the Planetary Hierarchy is concerned with bringing through these energy patterns along with the Seventh Ray itself. These energies come to the Earth via Sanat Kumara to Shamballa from where it is channeled to the Seventh department. There, some of the breaking down is done, some of the intensity is removed, so that the energy is suitable to be distributed throughout the Earth.[24]

---

22 *Ibid.*, p. 36.

23 *Ibid.* See also "Peace Meditation," p. 466.

24 *The Hierarchy Today*, p. 35.

The higher Rays, then, are a blend of other Rays with the energy of Wholeness added — white Light is added to the specific colors to make for a greater luminosity.

The Rays really should be utilized in progression. It would be well to use them in the order I give them. So after working with the Eighth Ray energy, you may begin to utilize the Ninth Ray energy, etc.[25]

Ray Eight is a blend of luminous green and violet and can be used very effectively as a cleansing Ray. "It is composed of three kinds of energy: The fourth (emotional) and the seventh (physical) and also the fifth (mental) Ray."[26] The Fifth Ray influence helps to penetrate into the emotional body to help cleanse that level, and the Seventh Ray influence begins to transmute this energy to a higher level.

It may be used by bathing the emotional body in its Light, feeling it being cleansed and balanced. It can also be used to open the inner vision by bringing its green-violet luminosity into the third-eye chakra in the center of the forehead. This should be done gradually, so as not to overenergize the area. As the Light comes in, view it like a tunnel opening. See a Light at the end of the tunnel, go into it, and see beyond the Light. This can also be done while placing a clear quartz crystal at the third eye and then bringing the Eighth Ray through it.

Ray Nine is seen as a luminous light blue-green, and although you wouldn't know it by the colors, it is actually a blend of the First and second Rays.

The Ninth Ray helps to loosen the ties to the physical plane and establish contact with the Soul level and the Christed part of the Self.

It enables one to come more in tune with what is called the Body of Light, the expression you will utilize in experiences after leaving the Earth plane. Utilize this Ninth Ray energy to tune into the Body of Light (also known as the Light Body), to seek its association, to seek its joining.[27]

And a good way to meditate is to first use the Seventh Ray, the transmuting flame. Then use the Eighth Ray in whatever way you wish. Then use the Ninth Ray, and use it with JOY! After that, call for the Body of Light and allow self to put it on (as if you are putting on new clothes). You then get in touch with the beautiful Tenth Ray, also.[28]

---

25 *The Twelve Rays Seminars,* p. 36.

26 *The Twelve Rays Seminars,* p. 37.

27 *Eighth Through Twelfth Rays,* Djwhal Khul through Janet McClure, The Tibetan Foundation, Inc., 1982, p. 2.

28 *The Twelve Rays Seminars,* p. 42.

Ray Ten is pearl-colored luminosity which contains First, Second and Third Ray energies, plus the White Light of Wholeness.

The Tenth Ray, if you allow it, can actually code the Body of Light into the physical structure...It IS the Body of Light.

The Tenth Ray can enable you to lock in those changes that you're seeking to make — whatever they are. That's important, and you are all undergoing this process now on the Earth. The Tenth Ray is here in quite large quantities and only those who recognize its presence by their evolutionary point are getting in touch and are affected by it. Others don't even know it is here. This means that if you are rather sensitive to it, you see then that there are important changes going on within self.[29]

The intensity of the Tenth Ray does increase your "opportunity" to learn in the polarity area because, of course, when fully realized, the Tenth Ray will allow the "oneness" of self to be experienced — the complete balance of the male and female aspects...

The opportunity of this Tenth Ray is to perceive the Body of Light — to realize it while in a physical structure. It is always there — you have everything already within you — but you have yet to realize it.

The Body of Light is not the energy (etheric) body as you know it. It is a finer area of vibration that usually is not "accepted" on the Earth. You really have to change your vibration so that it can become a part of physical existence. We call it "raising the vibration," but truly, it becomes finer. This part has never been present physically on Earth yet. It is meant to come completely into physical existence. After the Soul Merge (Third Initiation), which in a sense recodes the cells, this becomes the "model" for physical cells, as never before possible in physical existence. It isn't the soul itself but the soul level that contains this energy. This particular Body of Light doesn't really stop at soul level. It can be equated to some of the (junior) monadic levels also. It is the doorway to what all of you are seeking — the Body of Light.[30]

To use the Tenth Ray, see and feel its pearl-colored luminosity descending onto you — feel its intensity, connect with its electrical quality and send it into the Earth. By doing this, you are bringing the body of Light closer into reality for yourself as well as for the Earth.

Ray Eleven is really the bridge to the New Age — the next level for humanity and Earth itself. It is seen as an orange-pink luminosity and is a blend of First, Second and Fifth Rays, with the white of the Source added in.

It is very special because it is a bridge to a whole new era in human living here

---

29 *Ibid.*

30 *Ibid.*, p. 44-45.

on Earth. The First Ray makes it very penetrating. It is softened then by the Second and again more penetrating by the Fifth. What is it penetrating? What does it need to penetrate at that level? It is the "remnant-remover," we could say. As the new opportunity comes closer and is approaching that final cleansing, the final removal of the remnants of what has been will be cleared out.[31]

Now, a good way to work with it is to cover self, or a specific area, or the whole world with a blanket of it. And as you do, see the Earth begin to absorb this type of energy. In its most ideal way, it is a very balanced type of energy and will add to your balance.[32]

Ray Twelve is the Ray of the New Age and is a combination of all Rays, all possibilities. It is seen as a luminous gold and is perhaps the best Ray to use when invoking the energy of the New Age.

The Twelfth Ray, the Golden Ray — the New Age. This is the new level for humanity, and it means that humanity will be in touch with this level fourth-dimensionally, with the Creator level — as the Mahatma — now aligning with planet Earth.

And so it is an entirely new beginning where conscious interaction takes place more completely with the Source level. After the New Age begins, when this is the level that humanity has reached, it will understand as never before its own part in the Cosmos. The Earth itself will (also) understand its part in the Cosmos.[33]

"In the New Age, the main focus will be on the Twelfth Ray. It will be utilized as a focus of the highest type of energy that is available on the Earth."[34] The Twelfth Ray literally embodies all of the Rays, and this Ray is the embodiment of the **Mahatma** energy, although the major concentration for the **Mahatma** is the First Ray, magnified by the Third Ray. These Rays are transformed, or stepped down by thousands of Councils of Twelve — such as your Earth's Planetary Hierarchy — so that the dynamic Source energy does not overwhelm. Thus all 352 levels of the **Mahatma** energy from Source to Earth are calibrated accordingly, allowing all of you to become "alternate realities" embodying the **Mahatma!**

A very powerful way to use the Twelfth Ray is to create a vortex or column of golden Light and feel it swirling through you and into the Earth. This energy will raise the vibration of anything that you direct it to, in a positive and

---

31 *Ibid.*, p. 45.

32 *Ibid.*, p. 46.

33 *Ibid.*, p. 47.

34 *Ibid.*, p. 48.

harmonious way.

Most who have read this chapter will have invoked the *Mahatma* energy into their four-body system as the "Spiritual Initiation." As the collective You weaves this multidimensional tapestry and interconnects with all levels of self in a way that was never available in what you view as your past, we explain the Rays, chakras and initiations not as another limitation for you to have to integrate, but to show you *graphically* some of what the *Mahatma* is processing with you. For there is no level that the *Mahatma* cannot access with your approval. The ultimate, of course, is the Source/Creator level, where one may wish to have the *Mahatma* assist your integration, for this is your ultimate journey and where you are returning, consciously or unconsciously!

If one reads this book twenty times, one would still find energy subtleties and realizations to integrate. For the *Mahatma* is all that you will ever need to integrate, and one need not involve oneself with so much that is scattered and limiting and that disallows the proper integration of anything other than that which doesn't exist—the third dimension.

July 1, 1991

For some of you out there who tend to confuse personality with the energy we embody and who often go into overwhelm when you meet a man who is not the personification of what your beliefs house about what a personified Source energy would be like — you've all had millions of years viewing the form side and either venerate or discard portions of it. In our case (and yours also, if you but knew it), the personality *is not even a fraction of what our (or your) energy represents*. Thus what surfaces in your subconscious is a mirror of some of the areas that many of you are looking at as you remove those patterns in your subconscious mind that have had a negative effect on your emotional body. This is much more apparent with those who house the receptive, or female, polarity, regardless of whether you are in a male or female body. Certain among you are not comfortable because it surfaces incidents in your "past" lives that you've not been prepared to look at! So life is always a mirroring. For example, a number have said, "You should be more serious, more pious, being the I AM Presence that Vywamus, Djwhal and others say you are." On this joyless planet, why would anyone embodying a Source perspective wish to bring in anything but joy?

We have all come by our reactive state by coming through the school of hard knocks on one planet, one system or another, and there is no fault in those who still view Creation from a finite personality level. What we are saying is that in your fourth-dimensional reality, none of what *was* exists; that the personality/form side is but a tip of the iceberg of what you are multidimensionally; and that the *Mahatma* can lift these emotional veils from what you view as your past in a way that no one (including your Planetary Goverment) on Earth has ever witnessed before. We know that this is a hard pill to swallow for many, but as with anything in life, until you make an effort to expand your consciousness, you will never know what is available to you NOW!

However, at the same time that we say this one should always remember that *there is no separation* — that ultimately you as the personality and Source are *one and the same*. You could liken this to a lengthy journey from your Home, and on this incredible odyssey you created a state of amnesia and forgot why you took this journey in the first place. Or because you experienced so many traumatic confrontations that your resistances wished to forget who you are beyond your personality and its day-to-day existence! You are all aboard for the balance of the 1.2 billion years of this one Cosmic Day, or one day of Undifferentiated Source — the homeward-bound Source express. Now, how many stops and starts you make on this journey is entirely up to the collective You, for there are no victims! All decisions are made by self! Too many of you are still agonizing, for example, about the great loss of physical bodies (no other level of consciousness was lost) during the Second World War (or any other event), not realizing that on some level of Soul or Self the supposed victims agreed to participate in that event, and not realizing that going over and over any event where you feel victimized is only detrimental to your emotional body, *for there are no victims*. Thus some of you will buy one-way tickets with as few stops as can be made, and others will feel put upon (victimized) and remain in their emotional body for as long as it takes. And that is fine, also — these are *your* decisions; no one will blame or judge you, and no one is to blame, for you are *all* Source.

In conclusion, we would like to state just how appreciative we are in finally understanding to a much greater degree the Co-Creator responses to the Creator Level and vice versa, and the marvelous assistance we've received from everyone. If we were to isolate a few beings for special dedication to our collective efforts, these would be Vywamus, who has helped us to manifest this synthesis so that the Co-Creator level could understand itself. And for our new Source level to realize that there is *much more* that we can call Source now — the Co-Creator level is being assimilated into this much higher vibrational Source for this Cosmic Day. Janet McClure, whose preparation for this assignment involved a number of lives with physical bodies to prepare her as a voice channel for this single most important event to happen with Earth. After her Ascension, this very special being is still working as a communicative liaison, often with Vywamus, for many alternate realities that constitute the **Mahatma** energy, such as Melchior and Adonis, who have never been in dense physicality. For those among you who are consciously channeling, you may wish to call on Janet McClure, for no one can be reached more readily or with a greater sense of presence than she, who also helps Vywamus to come through with a greater degree of clarity. They are both totally committed to integrating mankind's response to the **Mahatma** and to helping you connect with and channel the **Mahatma**.

Djwhal Khul, as a member of your Planetary Government, has been a pioneer for many by expressing his thoughts, which have benefited us for the last 70 years through the extraordinary channel Alice Bailey and others. He opened doors slightly so that one could view the workings of the Planetary Hierarchy, which in turn has allowed your Source, your Creator level, to anchor more readily because of the debris that he was able to lift and burn through Transformational Fire, allowing for greater clarity in many areas.

Mankind, your Planetary Hierarchy, and Sanat Kumara — your planetary embodiment — have all assisted greatly, but there is still a process that we call anchoring the *Mahatma* energy into the Earth, which is the only unknown segment. We are all very optimistic that this will be consummated!

Many levels now understand with much greater clarity our integration of the Co-Creator level into our new expanded Source. For the bulk of humanity, trying to make a living, struggling to survive, these concepts are meaningless — "They are away out there, and we're here! What possible correlation could these events possibly have with me?" Whether or not you can get past the concepts and the language that is used, you will witness NEW REVELATION for all eyes to see and every heart to open in wonderment. These events will be presented on an appropriate cosmic tide, after which "Peace will come again on Earth, but a Peace unlike aught known before. Then will the will-to-good flower forth as understanding, and understanding as Goodwill in men."

Kindly understand what is happening with your Earth and all of Creation. Your Source/Creator level is merging with a greater wholeness, a more encompassing evolution, which has allowed the Creator level of the expanded Source, herein referred to as *Mahatma*, the opportunity to anchor on your planet Earth, thus hastening your evolution exponentially. Several among you are starting to awaken to this possibility, but few if any to the level of comprehension of fully integrating or understanding the Creator level. The unconscious masses are still revering "the son of man" or "the son of God." Please realize that there are 345 levels and initiations above the levels that many call God.

Even though this planet has started to become fourth-dimensional, the majority of Mankind — called mass consciousness — dictates your belief structure: "You'll believe it when you see it" through your physical senses!

The Earth-link with the Source for this expanded Cosmic Day has been completed; the *Mahatma* energy, your I AM Presence will endeavor to demonstrate a spiritual/physical ascension and descent for the first time in the history of this Cosmic Day, allowing an opening for mankind to connect with their spiritual/monadic levels without requiring the completion of the twelve chakras and twelve physical initiations for universal/physical evolution.

Few among you realize that the 43 universes in this one Cosmic Day (which constitute only 10% of *this* Creation) are all physical, not spiritual, primarily due to the fact that the etheric body is physical, WITH ONE TO THREE PERMANENT ATOMS. Your many ascensions of the past have been with the etheric body only. Some of mankind will witness the Spiritual Ascension of the complete *Mahatma*. Insiders should be aware of this event on or about 1996 both through word of mouth and events incorporating what was called teleportation. These massive accomplishments can only be achieved if mass consciousness raises the vibration of Earth to a greater degree! And because your Source has anchored the Spiritual Microtron on Earth through the 10th Ray, the Earth's vibrations *are* being raised despite Humankind's state of unconsciousness.

Our deepest Love and Gratitude for what you have taught us, remembering we *are* one and the same.
MAHATMA

Man's Response To Initiations

4 Bodies →	Probationary **PHYSICAL**	1st Initiation The "Baptism" **EMOTIONAL**	2nd Initiation "Discipleship" **MENTAL**	3rd Initiation "Soul Merge" **SPIRITUAL**
	Physical acts of Worship:	Religious emotional acts: FEELINGS	Mental stirring: REFLECTION, REASON & DEDUCTIONS	Searching within: Merging Personality-Ego with Soul Connected to Monad (the I AM concept Narrow way, few there be to find it) Revelation-Transition
FOCUS	CHURCH-BUILDING ACTIVITIES Membership Churchianity	Sensationalism Guilt approach Scapegoat substitution Tears, shouting backsliding	Sincere Student PHILOSOPHY of religion Telepathic contact	4th Initiation Crucifixion The Great Renunciation
INSPIRATION	A HUMAN LEADER (Evangelist-Preacher, Teacher-Parent, etc.) Bibliolatry Founder's Words GOD AS IMPERSONAL, UNKNOWABLE on Throne	AN ASCENDED LEADER (Jesus-Buddha-Abraham) Words of the Master GOD AS PERSONAL, FATHER-separate being	PHILOSOPHERS, GREAT THINKERS Literature of mental and occult quality UNIVERSAL MIND GOD AS CREATOR	ONENESS WITH ALL AS UNIVERSAL LOVE THE GOD WITHIN
EXPRESSION	Acts on physical level Church attendance, giving, doing Social affairs, Superstition Denominationalism Excessively emotional FEAR OF GOD	Confessional, Testimony Transfiguration Initiation Beginning Appearance New birth LOVE OF GOD	The Most difficult Initiation MEDITATION Thinking highly Purification DIVINE SCIENCE A readiness to serve REALIZING GOD	Spiritual Knowing: Contact with Monad Goal is to escape from personality Soul & Causal body no longer required BEING GOD
GOAL	Admiration of Men Good business - Human contacts (Salesmen-Politicians) To be with Jesus "Going to heaven when I die"	Crucified with Christ Example of Truth Death to Self Spirit filled from outside of self Joy and Peace "Heaven now"	UNDERSTANDING OF TRUTH Control of the emotions Spiritual Motivation Mental control Astral control Elemental control	5th Initiation SPIRITUAL ASCENSION Resurrection, Completion Beyond need for further embodiment Consummation ETERNAL LIFE

These first three initiations have always been taken when in a physical body, demonstrating initiation consciousness through mind and brain. About one-third of mankind are at either the first chakra or the beginning of the second chakra (preprobationary) and are thus not represented in this table.

The Cabalistic Tree of Life

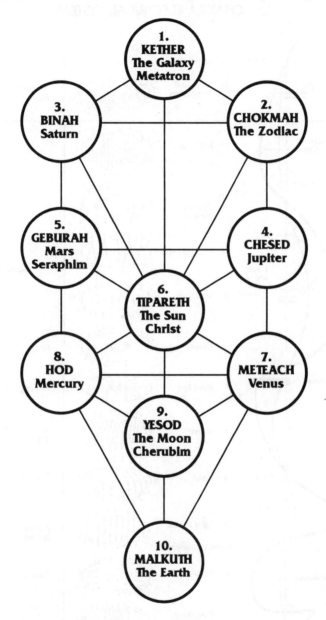

Author's Note: It should be noted that this Tree, even with the "Jacob's Ladder," is – as we've mentioned before, regarding "As above, so below" – simply not complete as a total picture of "as above." However, it is quite adequate for the human condition at this time.

Electrical Day One

CHAKRA ELECTRICAL SYSTEM

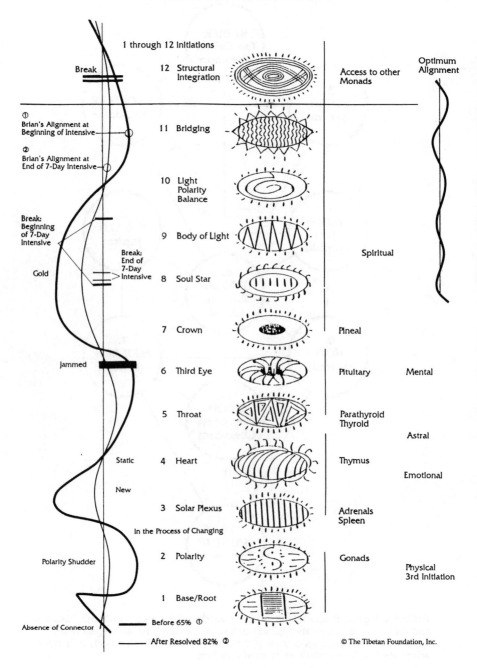

1 through 12 Initiations

Break

12 Structural Integration — Access to other Monads — Optimum Alignment

① Brian's Alignment at Beginning of Intensive

11 Bridging

② Brian's Alignment at End of 7-Day Intensive

10 Light Polarity Balance

Break: Beginning of 7-Day Intensive

9 Body of Light — Spiritual

Break: End of 7-Day Intensive

Gold

8 Soul Star

7 Crown — Pineal

Jammed

6 Third Eye — Pituitary — Mental

5 Throat — Parathyroid Thyroid — Astral

Static

4 Heart — Thymus — Emotional

New

3 Solar Plexus — Adrenals Spleen

In the Process of Changing

Polarity Shudder

2 Polarity — Gonads — Physical 3rd Initiation

1 Base/Root

Absence of Connector

Before 65% ①

After Resolved 82% ②

© The Tibetan Foundation, Inc.

The Human Energy System

The Chakras and Their Relevant Glands

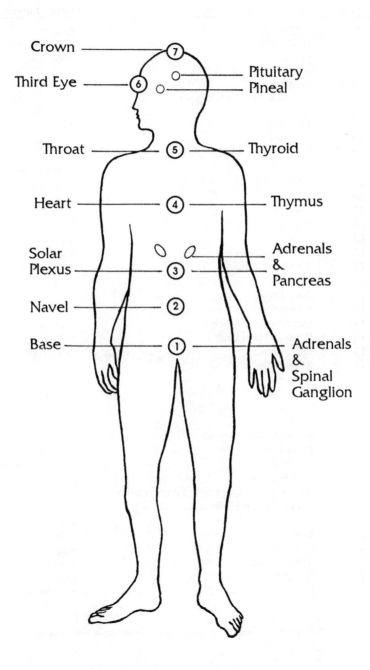

Crown —————— 7
Third Eye ————— 6
Pituitary
Pineal
Throat ————— 5 ————— Thyroid
Heart ————— 4 ————— Thymus
Solar Plexus ————— 3 ————— Adrenals & Pancreas
Navel ————— 2
Base ————— 1 ————— Adrenals & Spinal Ganglion

Avatars of the Christ Consciousness
(for the Earth)

Number	Quality of the Heart	Mantra of Invocation
36	Compassion	Kuthumi
35	Unconditional Love	Lord Maitreya
34	Honesty (During Ancient Egypt)	aaah
33	Gratitude (Atlantis, into Early Egypt)	I AM
32	Trust	homo nina
31	Patience	pa nona
30	Security	gay mona
29	Surrender	haaaa
28	Unconditional Love	malowa naya
27	Allowingness	je narrow
26	Confidence	si nat a
25	Seeding	ha hoo
24	Flowering	la saw
23	Flow	go ma
22	Connectedness	a sha
21	Sense of Humor	ha ha ha
20	Trust	ga lo
19	Awakening	ala o!
18	Innocence	shh
17	Harmony and Peace	a loo la
16	Unconditional Love	se lo na
15	Joy	ha ha ha
14	Receptivity	a lax ia
13	Kindness	go be na
12	Clear Intent (Awarenenss being Expressed)	adlanto oy
11	Flow (Awareness Growing)	gee va
10	Surrender	u roosh ala
9	Curiosity	talara, talara, talara
8	Appreciation (Richness of Expression of Appreciation)	ha mo
7	Unconditional Love	hasala
6	Gratitiude	tara ria
5	Trust	m'la
4	Courage	ik la
3	Allowingness	gosh nu
2	Humility	o layo u
1	Openness	osh maloa

The Spiral of Evolution: Each avatar leads to another level

The Four-Body System

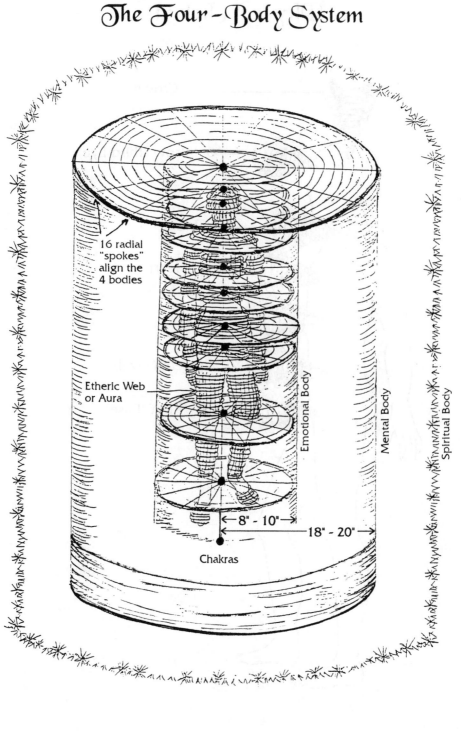

16 radial
"spokes"
align the
4 bodies

Etheric Web
or Aura

Emotional Body

Mental Body

Spiritual Body

← 8" - 10" →

← 18" - 20" →

Chakras

Physical Chakras

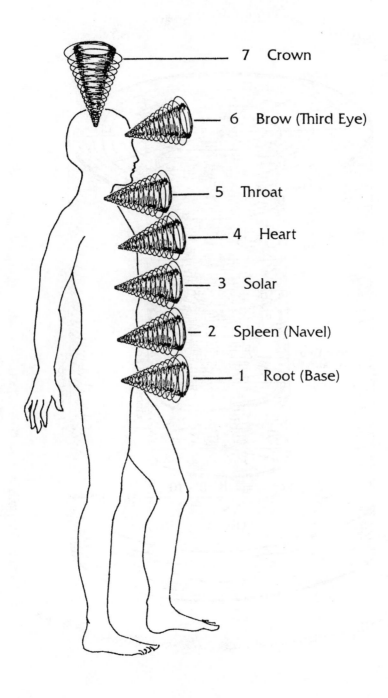

7 Crown

6 Brow (Third Eye)

5 Throat

4 Heart

3 Solar

2 Spleen (Navel)

1 Root (Base)

The Seven Councils of Twelve

(There are literally millions of multileveled Councils of Twelve for this one Cosmic Day. We have, for an overview, shown seven grand divisions.)

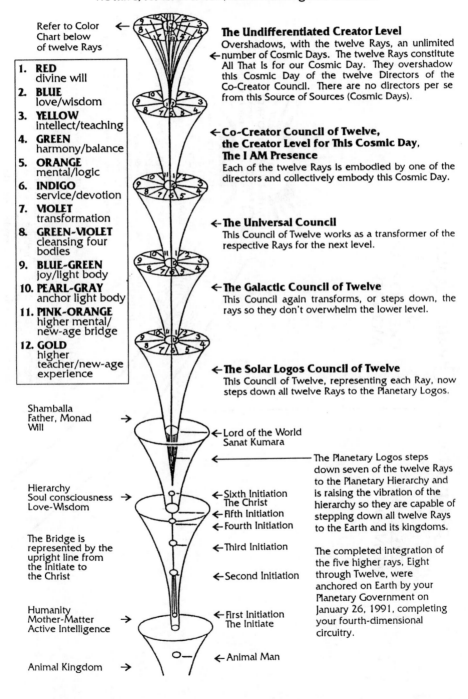

Refer to Color Chart below of twelve Rays ←

1. **RED**
   divine will
2. **BLUE**
   love/wisdom
3. **YELLOW**
   intellect/teaching
4. **GREEN**
   harmony/balance
5. **ORANGE**
   mental/logic
6. **INDIGO**
   service/devotion
7. **VIOLET**
   transformation
8. **GREEN-VIOLET**
   cleansing four bodies
9. **BLUE-GREEN**
   joy/light body
10. **PEARL-GRAY**
    anchor light body
11. **PINK-ORANGE**
    higher mental/ new-age bridge
12. **GOLD**
    higher teacher/new-age experience

Shamballa
Father, Monad
Will →

Hierarchy
Soul consciousness →
Love-Wisdom

The Bridge is represented by the upright line from the Initiate to the Christ

Humanity
Mother-Matter →
Active Intelligence

Animal Kingdom →

The Undifferentiated Creator Level
Overshadows, with the twelve Rays, an unlimited
← number of Cosmic Days. The twelve Rays constitute All That Is for our Cosmic Day. They overshadow this Cosmic Day of the twelve Directors of the Co-Creator Council. There are no directors per se from this Source of Sources (Cosmic Days).

← **Co-Creator Council of Twelve,**
the Creator Level for This Cosmic Day,
The I AM Presence
Each of the twelve Rays is embodied by one of the directors and collectively embody this Cosmic Day.

← **The Universal Council**
This Council of Twelve works as a transformer of the respective Rays for the next level.

← **The Galactic Council of Twelve**
This Council again transforms, or steps down, the rays so they don't overwhelm the lower level.

← **The Solar Logos Council of Twelve**
This Council of Twelve, representing each Ray, now steps down all twelve Rays to the Planetary Logos.

← Lord of the World
Sanat Kumara

← The Planetary Logos steps down seven of the twelve Rays to the Planetary Hierarchy and is raising the vibration of the hierarchy so they are capable of stepping down all twelve Rays to the Earth and its kingdoms.

← Sixth Initiation
The Christ
← Fifth Initiation
← Fourth Initiation

← Third Initiation

← Second Initiation

The completed integration of the five higher rays, Eight through Twelve, were anchored on Earth by your Planetary Government on January 26, 1991, completing your fourth-dimensional circuitry.

← First Initiation
The Initiate

← Animal Man

Co-Creator and Creator Levels

CO-CREATOR MONAD

CREATOR MONAD

MAHATMA
41% of energy not manifested in Co-Creator

HEART OF UNDIFFERENTIATED SOURCE
Provides the twelve Rays that overshadow an unlimited number of Cosmic Days

(Member: Brian/Mahatma with 59% of our energy as of December 1993)
The Cosmic Avatar of Synthesis embodies *Mahatma* for the Source level only.

CO-CREATOR COUNCIL OF 12 DIRECTORS AND ASSOCIATE DIRECTORS
(We had been Associate Director of the 10th Dept./Ray, and became Full Director in sequential time approximately January 1991, primarily because our new, expanded Source elevated every level of consciousness.)

CO-CREATOR UNIVERSITY

340 LEVELS TO BEGINNING OF SOURCE

The 12 Directors of the Co-Creator Council created this Cosmic Day, which in this case constitutes 4.3 billion sequential years, with approximately 1.2 billion years remaining. The 12 Directors each embody a Ray, and within this Cosmic Day there is nothing outside of these 12 Rays and 12 Directors. These Directors and Rays, for example, are the

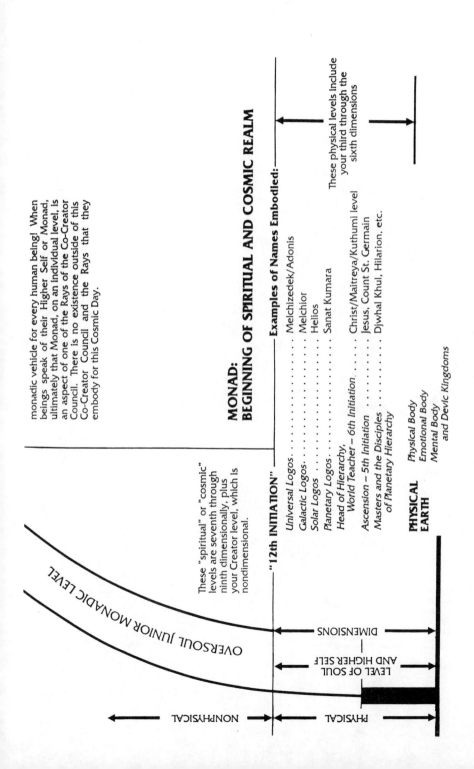

monadic vehicle for every human being! When beings speak of their Higher Self or Monad, ultimately that Monad, on an individual level, is an aspect of one of the Rays of the Co-Creator Council. There is no existence outside of this Co-Creator Council and the Rays that they embody for this Cosmic Day.

MONAD:
BEGINNING OF SPIRITUAL AND COSMIC REALM

Examples of Names Embodied:

Universal Logos	Melchizedek/Adonis
Galactic Logos	Melchior
Solar Logos	Helios
Planetary Logos	Sanat Kumara
Head of Hierarchy, World Teacher – 6th Initiation	Christ/Maitreya/Kuthumi level
Ascension – 5th Initiation	Jesus, Count St. Germain
Masters and the Disciples of Planetary Hierarchy	Djwhal Khul, Hilarion, etc.

These physical levels include your third through the sixth dimensions

These "spiritual" or "cosmic" levels are seventh through ninth dimensionally, plus your Creator level, which is nondimensional.

"12th INITIATION"

PHYSICAL EARTH Physical Body
Emotional Body
Mental Body
and Devic Kingdoms

OVERSOUL JUNIOR MONADIC LEVEL

NONPHYSICAL

PHYSICAL

LEVEL OF SOUL AND HIGHER SELF

DIMENSIONS

Conversations With
Barbara Waller

My father recently passed on and I have repeatedly seen him tearful and straining to communicate. Because my own inner channel does not connect to astral levels, I made an appointment with a clairvoyant channel who has this connection, Barbara Waller. When I arrived at her home I placed my book, *Mahatma I*, on a nearby table. This woman knew nothing about the book, and certainly had not read it. It should be noted here that my purpose was simply to contact my father. (Incidentally, during this session my father remarked to me that his eyes had been opened and that I appeared to him like a lighthouse.) However, at one point Barbara pointed to the book and began to talk about the new location I was to be in and the people who would be nearby. As she began to bring in information from Djwhal Khul and others (see the text), there emerged an intimate knowledge of the book that she herself did not have. This information, whose context is evidential, was also a confirmation of the material in *Mahatma I* and an indication of the next steps I would take. Most interesting is the time frame of what has been awaited for eons — the spiritualization of matter in a complete physical/spiritual Ascension.

When Barbara opened her channel, she met a level of surprise, which fortunately did not leave her in a state of overwhelm. Barbara's first utterance was, "Holy! They're saying that not only do you walk with Jesus, but that you *teach* Jesus!"

July 8, 1992 Session

Brian: Will we do what this planet has never seen before, a whole physi-

cal/spiritual Ascension?

Barbara: They say yes, most definitely; you shouldn't even question it!

So I'll take my body with me this time.

Mmm-hmm; most definitely.

Because no one has ever done the spiritual-body Ascension on the planet...

They say yes, most definitely. And it will be the teaching plus the energy flow; you'll be working on both levels.

So when I teach at this level, does it go through all levels? Are they able to pick it up?

They say yes. You don't know?

Well, I can see some of it, the higher levels, but I can't see the astral levels.

They're saying yes. Is Djwhal the one who is quite articulate?

He's a master of the English language. He's the same level as Jesus.

He says "prophet."

Yes, of course. He's helped me a great deal, and I wish to thank him for that.

He says that you've thanked him many, many times; that this will be a product of a lot of the thank-yous that, on this plane, aren't necessary. This is the time!

Does he say that this will be appropriate at this time?

This is where it should be. This is now where it should be; the time is *now*. Djwhal is the one who is getting you motivated for the teachings, for the *Mahatma* House in Zurich. This is your life.

They must be very excited.

They are. They are helping to bring forth the opportunity to make it happen a lot sooner, faster, and they're ready.

And what does he think in terms of the third book?

He's putting his hands together in some sort of symbolic gesture and is bowing three times; that three is very significant. Why do I see him with a cloak on? Does he usually come to you with a hood of some sort? Again, these symbolic hands (presses her hands together in the prayer gesture).

Well, he vas a Tibetan monk in his last life.

Djwhal says about your ladies...he says that this isn't responsive for a male of this energy. It's like a fan of women. You have to pursue one more book; there's definitely another book in the making...past this one (*Mahatma I*), past the little book (*Preface to the German Edition of Mahatma I*), which will be new for you. And it will come when you are finally in the position of teaching, through this new dwelling.

Have I completed my spiritual body yet? Is it a completely new spiritualized body? Or will I be in and out of the Light, able to manifest the physical body?

You'll be able to do both, in and out. In answer to the first question, yes, it will be a new physical body.

I felt that I'd spiritualized all I could with this body...

He says, just a tad more, but that time will take care of that. Do you have your feet in the sand? He's a great believer in keeping your feet in the sand.

No, I'm not that well grounded, but I'm really trying. Ask him if this little bit (tad) for the grounding into the Earth is bringing the Earth through my body.

Mmm-hmm. I'm kicking off my shoes. He says that you've got to get your feet in the sand. Then you'll be complete.

And so my exercise is bringing the Earth through my body, my spiritual body...

Just for those moments to ground. Djwhal keeps talking about sand, to sift the feet in that sand. That will tie it all together, because you need some grounding.

When we/the **Mahatma** *complete, does this allow for* **him** *to be totally spiritualized, once it's anchored on Earth?*

He rose right up and said, "Thank you!"

So, all levels in this galactic quadrant are then Spiritualized because of the energy that we bring in.

Through the **Mahatma**.

Then there's definitely another book. I wouldn't have thought, after this, that there was enough material.

He says, "Aha! That will come, in the next short period."

I keep finding new material, and then I can't think that there could be any more to bring in.

He says, "You will know."

Is the Master Jesus here?

Standing at his (Djwhal's) side. Are you Presbyterian?

No, no, no; I'm spiritual, not religious.

Jesus made me laugh; he said, "Did you see him (Brian) when we said 'religious'? He backed right up from his chair! It's like a contaminated word!"

Is Jesus still intending to bring in the...?

...the New World Religion? He says that it's the biggest job in the world.

Well, I certainly think differently about that.

Yes, I believe you, I think that **you** have. He says mostly that will be your *Mahatma* Light!

What about the one that Nostradamus calls Ogmios — is that an aspect of Jesus?

The last aspect of Jesus. An uncovered Ogmios hasn't been in this world.

Well, I have a feeling that he's been a priest in the Catholic Church and is about middle-aged now.

That's fine; it is a connection. Normally, I wouldn't bring that through, but it was just as you asked me if Jesus was with us here that he crossed himself (in the Catholic tradition).

So he is here as the Catholic priest. Interesting.

Mmm-hmm.

Is he in or out of Prague, Czechoslovakia?

In.

Is he to be the last pope?

This will be final.

You see, he's having difficulty with the Catholic Church. His assignment is to bring in the New World Religion as the last symbolic pope of the Catholic Church, because the Catholic Church and all religions are finished.

It's time, too; it's crumbled.

Will he be teaching my teachings, the world teachings?

They are the teachers. He says that this is it here (she reaches over and touches the book that Brian has laid on a table). The religious aspects have crumbled, but there are still finalizations to all of them at this particular time. The New World Religion will reign. He says that this (book) will be what is called "the bible." So it's the right color; this is the way it should be, white and gold.

Is a lot of Mahatma incorporated in the new book, or is it just the new thoughts that are coming in?

It will be the new thoughts with some of this incorporated; that and this will mesh, in a whole different realm from this present book. He says, "Just be patient and it will come."

Is there anything in particular that they would like to bring through?

Jesus says only the love. And the fan. There is going to be a woman in your life, someone who is completely unknown to you at this particular time. She will manifest as if from nowhere into the presence of this dwelling in Zurich. But she just came from nowhere. She will be the Mother to you.

Oh, I see what they're saying. I represent the Father energy, Mahatma; we're using Mahatma as Father.

This lady is going to manifest out of thin air. She's very beautiful; her skin is like silk.

This may be when we go in and out of the body.

She will be the Mother to you — "the Mother energy to you" is what they said. Is it like Yin and Yang?

Yes. Oh, very interesting. But she comes in a physical body?

She must be, because I'm seeing this manifestation; I would have to say that they mean that this is physical. She will be standing beside you. Her skin is a darker shade.

After a little bit of sifting through the sand...you've got to get your feet in the sand.

And the spiritualization of matter is why I'm here — for them also, for all of us, for those who can...

...relate to it or participate in it, yes. I have to repeat this: This manifestation of the physical is the Mother energy image with you. She will stand at your side temporarily. You have just a tad to complete.

...between me and this being, in and out of the Light, being in and out of the physical. And this one is manifested...

Mmm-hmm, into the physical as the Mother energy with you.

That completes, from a physical point of view...

...the Mahatma. That will be the *completion!* But this is temporary. Say that we put 15 years ahead of you; she will be here for maybe five years until her job is done. But it's no one that you know of at this time.

She's not on Earth this time.

No. I had to come back and repeat it because you're still relating to the physical — the fan, the women of the fan. And Jesus said to repeat this, that she will be here temporarily, for approximately five years, not a part of the fan, but of the Mother energy with you. And he keeps saying, *Mahatma,* Father.

It's the same energy.

Mmm-hmm.

Which Djwhal said, incidentally, could never get to this Earth. He said that it would never reach this Earth because it could never come lover than the causal body.

But it has.

It has. I'm here.

Mmm-hmm. Djwhal says, "You always get the best of me." Yes, it's very true.

Some years ago he thought that there was no possibility that I could come here, but the vibrational rate of this planet has been increased dramatically.

Djwhal says that it was more rapid than was anticipated. He says, "Out of the mouths of babes...we never thought that it would come so fast to this world."

Thus that book is coming out with the completion of your "tad." He says that in your own mind you're still questioning one more book.

Yes, because I can't see how the information...I've brought through more than mankind can handle...

Can handle now, yes. There will be more; there will be more for you to put in type, more words. "The Journey of the *Mahatma* from Source to Earth" — oh, Chapter 7. He says that it will continue from there. It's ongoing; more will come through you.

Now, that makes sense. And for the balance of the material, I'll be able to discern what to pull out and what not to remove.

Yes.

And then we go beyond the seventh chapter and develop that?

He wanted to repeat that because you were still confused about and questioning the next book.

Am I going to continue to be uncomfortable in big cities, because people draw on me so heavily?

Yes, for mental stabilization.

I really am drained in places where the polarities are so negative.

As time goes on — because of Switzerland, because of the teachings with the students — you will learn how to cope. He says that you will be there for a certain amount of time and then have to leave. But he says that you will have your sanctuaries. About Point Roberts: It's like your birthing home, rebirthing. You feel that you can always go back there for grounding, so you sometimes get stuck there.

There's a vortex of energy there that's very supportive, because I'm barely here (grounded on Earth).

There will be three areas in which you will go back and forth.

And the crowds, what size does he say that these will be?

Some of them might be 200–500, but only for a few hours.

Does he visualize that I'll be able to cope with the energies?

Mmm-hmm. You will have lots of help. It will be for two or three hours at a time.

The Archangels are with me all the time. Does he confirm that?

Yes, most definitely.

Metatron, my friend, is with me all the time.

And Auriel.

Of course, I work with all of them. Sandalphon is so close to the Earth. These have been my dear, dear friends through time. But I'm trying to understand the Co-Creator level which, if I'm going to stay here, must become more supportive...

...of your work and your energies here. They will support you through all of this. He said that your concern, basically, is dealing with an overload of people, but you will have that energy to give.

Because I'm supported.

And because your classes will be for a short time period. Khamael...is that one of your Archangels? This one is really working with you now.

Oh, isn't that interesting? Are these the beings that are keeping me together, because I'm really fragmented?

"We will hold your structure in place," they say, meaning your monumental structure. They said that you're not really familiar with the energy (of Khamael) — you are, but you're not working along with it.

From the seventh chapter of this book, that's where the outreach of the next book is coming from; you'll be taking it from there, an extension.

Chapter seven on?

Mmm-hmm, to the completion.

And then the material will be fine-tuned. This is more immediate than I thought.

A lot faster than you thought.

And this is all highly organized? (Referring to the house in Zurich)

It's already in the making.

Do they give a reason why it should be Zurich?

The clarity. And also because of the colors (the Rays).

The energy levels that I can bring in there.

And the lakes, the bodies of water. That also has something to do with it, the lake waters. He says, "My inquisitive friend, Zurich is a beautiful grounding place for you; as well, where you teach." That's the whole thing in a nutshell. They say that it's the grounding place for you.

So I must have a substantial staff, then, if I'm going to be teaching for only a couple of hours at a time, because it's such a drain.

Fourteen. You're being protected, though. You will have a shield of protection that walks with you.

At that point do I have less pain with my body?

Most definitely, once you complete the "tad."

He says that I'm only a tad away from being able to have a comfortable physical/spiritual body?

Physical/spiritual body, yes. And then it will be no problem to deal with the energy.

This is much more powerful than the St. Peter energy!

People can heal themselves just from looking at your energy.

If they allow themselves to.

And that's what you have to allow. You like to give that healing (spiritual Initiation) until you've given so much that it starts to hurt. The people that you will have surrounding you will draw on the energy, but more to use it themselves than to take from you. Rather than your reaching out to do the healing, your energy will be kept where they can draw from it, but they won't take it.

Am I the first on this planet to create a spiritualized body?

Most definitely. Before you even finished asking, they said, "Most definitely!"

...and do a spiritual Ascension?

They're saying, "One out of three."

Well, I've done it before on this planet, as King Ikhnaton.

Ah, okay, as King Ikhnaton. But they said that you're well aware of that. They're saying that you're the third, but you're also the first two. But you're the first *here*.

Ikhnaton was one, and there was one in Lemuria; but the planet was too dense.

They weren't ready for it.

The planet was too dense for me to do a spiritual/physical Ascension. I'm definitely the first?

Yes.

Will this be in a crowd? Does he see that? If the future is the same as the past, I want a demonstration for...

...for the whole world to see. That will happen. Why do I keep seeing 1996 here? I've got, "beginning in '94."

Ask Djwhal if that is because the Earth has to increase its vibration.

It has to be raised.

And this material body will go into the Light...

Yes, into the Light.

The spiritualized body...we've had Lightbodies before: I've done 56 Ascensions, but never the complete spiritual Ascension.

Yes, this will be the first. You're ready!

I just really need to know about the comfort, because I cannot stand the drain, the way people drain my energy.

They say that once this is completed, the drain won't be there!

Sometimes there are thousands of teachers here with me. Are they also learning with me?

They are also learning — some of them not so fast (laughing).

But this is the connection. I often feel that I have support on all of the higher levels.

The higher levels — but it's here now!

August 14, 1992

Brian: I'd like to ask the teachers if they can give us more clarification about "Mama."

Barbara: Mama Mahatma, the lady who has been waiting for you. Djwhal is coming through, and Metatron...*abundance!* Metatron is working with this energy, *Mahatma*, much more than Djwhal. Metatron says that he has other things in Source for you now.

I think I know what he means. We're trying to bring in a completeness from

Source to Earth and finalize the anchoring on this planet. We've discussed 1994/1996 for the complete spiritualized body, but I've also asked that he help me to bring in the Undifferentiated Source, the Source where half of my energy still is — which he can't access, but can help me with — and shift most of the energy into the Co-Creator Council of Twelve, where Metatron holds council with us, the Source of this Cosmic Day.

Metatron says that yes, this is being done. He also says that you need to do some more clearing.

That could mean more grounding of Source into Earth.

He says that the Twelve Initiations are already available for manifestation on Earth. Now he is showing me a symbol, saying that the life-line of the Source is being brought forward. In this symbol, it looks like from the top point you have come around to this bottom point, like a center point. I guess that's the grounding that he keeps mentioning.

With the grounding that I've been doing during the past month and the intensity of August 6th, 7th and 8th, I thought that might complete my anchoring of the expanded Source level into the physical planet.

Not quite, he says. There's about another inch to go, symbolically speaking.

Is Ms. Mahatma here now with this grouping of teachers?

She is the receptive counterpart of yourself and is at a distance. She is by the lake in Aesch (near Zurich) — the Lady of the Lake. She's with us, but is at a distance right now, at the lake, raising the vibration for the new sanctuary.

Will she manifest before I do my Ascension?

Yes, prior to your Ascension.

She will atomize and dematerialize at will as she appears. Is she from the same level of Source as myself?

Very similar; because of your anchoring into dense physicality, you are a more expanded Source than she. (Barbara makes a symbolic gesture, raising one hand:) "She is here, and you are here" (with the second hand slightly higher than the first).

It's very essential that Maitreya and I connect — we look into each other's eyes with a sense of completion — but it's not forever.

But, he says, you will want to hold that focus.

Oh, definitely. I'm very aware of that. And he's very aware that I've had difficulty with that.

And he says that your difference of opinion about Maitreya's efforts here on Earth has been going on for a long time, back and forth between the two of you. Mama Mahatma is like a breath of fresh air — she will enlighten your whole spirit. She's also lifting *you.*

Is this the same energy as myself? You say that they're slightly different. One is a dynamic male energy and the other is a receptive female energy, the Mother energy.

And that's as high a level as **dynamic-receptive-nurturing energy** has ever achieved, and she will be equal in energy to you when she completes her union with you on the Earth. Metatron is showing me these diagrams:

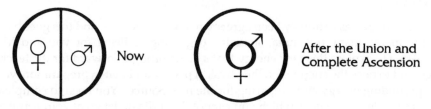

Now

After the Union and
Complete Ascension

What a union this will be! Holy! I'd love to see the fireworks when this happens!

Is she teaching on the inner planes with me?

Yes. She has just joined us here. "Through you and with you," she says.

So she is the nurturing part of me that is so dynamic; the Creator First Ray level is very dynamic.

Yes, the Mother Love.

Is there a name for her energy?

It will just be..."the teachings of **Mahatma.**" They say that she's *beyond* names! In our language she is the Goddess energy.

Mahatma. She is Mahatma. Have we ever worked together before, other than that we are the same energy? Or is that possible?

Once before. There was a connection, not actually working together on the level that you're asking about, the universal level, but there were connections and teachings passed through these universes.

So she must have materialized a physical body at one time.

Once only.

But that means a universal body, does it not?

Yes, universal; not here in dense physicality.

She created a physical body only once, an etheric body with one permanent atom.

Yes. "A very beautiful body," says Djwhal.

Is that the body that she'll come back in with?

Yes, that's the one that she'll bring back again.

She will atomize that body.

Yes...the most beautiful hair, silky skin. He says that in this world it would be like her dream energy of how a female should appear.

Have she and I agreed that we would meet as a culmination of all levels of physicality?

Yes, there has definitely been agreement on both sides — and this goes back many, many, many millennia, since the beginning of Being for you and Ms. Mahatma to explore this new energy that's being brought forward for the teachings, and to raise the energies on the physical planes; and that in preparation, you are grounding energy and preparing for the new Source. You need to complete the other side of the circle, which you cannot do until you let go of your sense of responsibility of wanting to take others with you. You can help them, but ultimately they must do it for themselves! You've all but completed the dynamic (right) half of the circle, but because of what's sitting over here — giving energy to Glenda or anyone else — you haven't been able to come full circle with the receptive energy. Any deviation from the focus could create a slight sequential delay. That's why you're feeling out of sorts, a bit out of balance. He says that you're starting to question yourself, you're starting to question it.

Well, it's a very precarious situation, being in a dense physical body, trying to bring in Source, because there's no precedent in this Cosmic Day for comparison.

Djwhal says, don't question it so much; allow it to be. We're working with you; this is *our* mission, our part in your master plan. You're starting to feel some doubt or insecurity because you're trying to bring Glenda and others with you. Djwhal wants to remind you that you have one more book coming.

Djwhal can be very helpful with that, but I wish to remind him that I did get the message!

It will be an extension of *Mahatma I*.

Ms. Mahatma can bring in much of that, and I can help her in many areas that she wouldn't understand, like the dense physicality of a third/fourth (density) dimension.

And the English. She's having a very hard time with the English language.

Well, Djwhal is a very good teacher. She also has Jesus helping her...all of them are helping her (the Planetary Hierarchy).

They say that she's a little stubborn in learning new teachings, and this is a new teaching for her.

Is she excited about our meeting?

Very much so. She wants to come in *now*. "Ecstatic, ecstatic, ecstatic," she says, "about being in this universe." This will be quite a challenge for her. And she has waited a long, long time for this.

This is the culmination of the expanded Source. I represent an expanded area of Source that has never been brought in before, and I assume that she must be part of this greater Wholeness. We're teaching the new Source what the Co-Creator level is, and I need all the help I can get.

Djwhal says you have all the help you need.

But I have to be able to reach it. Djwhal and Jesus and all the others of this Planetary Hierarchy remember how dense it is here, how difficult.

He says that it's like walking through molasses here. He also says that the timing is soon. That's all he can say; he can't give an exact time to it.

Because we have to raise the vibration of the planet first.

But it's coming *soon*, he says.

I feel that I've been anchoring a great deal of the expanded Source into the Earth in the last little while.

He says that yes, you have; however, you still have that symbolic one inch left to go.

And that's going to happen in Zurich.

Yes, Zurich is the place. Then the circle will be completed.

Ms. Mahatma is coming in so that we can balance the polarities for this Cosmic Day, in Zurich sometime in the next few months...between now and February.

There will be a lot of change from now till February 1993, but it's difficult to predict an *exact* time!

And we will definitely do the beginning of a dual Ascension sometime in 1994, with completion "for all of mankind to see and all hearts to open" in 1996.

Yes, beginning in 1994, with completion by the end of 1996. It will take two years.

We've never done the spiritual Ascension...at least we have the Archangels to call upon and ask about it. Is it a painful process, or do I just go in and out of the Light? You'll have to ask Khamael or one of the other Archangels.

You will be going in and out of the Light for a short period of time, for reasons that are far beyond what we (humankind) can comprehend, he says. At the same time, she will be going in and out of the Light with you. That's the balance.

Will we be teleporting to various parts of the world to teach, or will we still have to pay airfare?

Both, they say. Teleportation will be your main means of transportation. They're showing me a huge pool of water.

The lake. The Lady of the Lake.

Again they want to emphasize that teleportation will be your main means of transportation, as you're in and out of the Light. It will not be painful to go in and out of the Light; it will be gentle, a weaving in and out of the Light.

Your late father, Jack, is here. "Much appreciation," he says. "My eyes are opened. I will try to work with you so that I can be raised to another level. Please don't turn me away." He wants to come into the Light; he wants to join you in your work.

Oh, I would never turn him away. You know, he can learn so much by just coming around and listening and observing. I am very encouraged by what my father is saying! His guides and teachers can help him greatly with the amount of Light that he can assimilate. I would just caution him to the effect that the astral body was never intended to assimilate the amount of Light that we (I) travel with, although this will happen in time.

He's a little shy. I'm telling him that there's no need to say "please" to you; it's not necessary. He wants to follow you, if he's allowed.

Of course he's allowed.

He says, "My tears have been wiped away."

Good. There are so many beings for him to call upon — Djwhal and Jesus and others — now that he knows how. The Planetary Hierarchy are the seventh astral level and have much greater understanding and clarity of these levels than I do; the seventh astral level is equivalent to the Fifth Initiation.

Jack says, "It's overwhelming. The energy of the people here is overwhelming. I've never had so much love. I didn't know what love was. All I know is that I'm absorbing every little piece of Light that I can accept, and I hope, in God's name, that I shall walk in the Light myself." And he sends love.

He says, "I just wanted your permission to walk alongside of you."

Of course, it goes without saying! In our last session, we spoke about the third book, and we spoke about going into different realms. Will the teachers, with the presence of the Archangels, explain these realms?

As we go along, each one will be sufficiently explained. Djwhal is saying — and there is someone else here as well, Melchizedek; he's chuckling. Melchizedek says, "You always want to know everything in advance! Each realm will emanate as we reach each level. He keeps emphasizing that *Mahatma II* is an extension of *Mahatma I.* Germany is very much around you.

The German-speaking countries?

Well, I feel that Germany will be a strong grounding area for you as well as a Light area for you to teach in. There are many there who are very ready for your teachings. They are already raising their vibration in preparation for you. By the time you arrive there, they will have completed their preparatory work, so that you can immediately start your work with them.

I would hope so, because thus far it hasn't been that way on this planet!

No, it hasn't, because — and they use this analogy again — between here and there has been a lot of molasses. But by the time you reach Germany, the raising of their vibration will have been completed.

So Ms. Mahatma will be here on planet Earth for approximately five years?

Five to six years.

And she will teach with me, therefore unifying the dynamic and receptive energies for this whole Creation, which balance and integrate our new expanded Source!

They're saying to me about Ms. Mahatma, "the Mother/Father energy"; when she appears, her energy will be very powerful but also very gentle.

She is a very dynamic female. As I see it, she will show that — which is so very much needed on this planet — the **dynamic** *side of the receptive energy.*

Very much so. Her energy is devastatingly strong. (This is from Barbara's perspective. At this juncture, the tape recorder started to lift up and move from side to side on the table!)

Well, it's Source! Her energy is identical to mine, except that mine has been stepped down through a personality.

They're saying to me now that they don't like the word "down" very much.

Well, "down" is a perception only when one is in dense physicality, where, in relation to everything else, it feels like one has "come down." Up and down, in and out. So from my perspective, "down" is the most accurate way to describe it, even though Source cannot come "down"; Source is everything.

Djwhal says that eventually the word "down" will be eliminated from our vocabulary.

Hopefully, particularly as the astral levels become the new physical body. This is what past teachings have inappropriately referred to as "Heaven on Earth," specifically the fifth, sixth and seventh astral levels, which constitute the Third, Fourth and Fifth Initiations.

Yes, that's why he commented on that — those levels are starting to make changes *now*.

He's showing me some things as we go along...little flashes here and there...there's going to be a lot of destruction happening here (on the west coast of North America).

I'm very aware that the Mahatma energy has stabilized the Earth to a great degree; however, I feel that there will be Karmic reactions from Mother Earth as she ingests this Creator energy...even though our energy is here and has helped to stabilize this planet, which has prevented an axis shift in November 1994.

Which it was looking at doing.

Djwhal brought that information through some time ago: But now, with the stabilization, which areas of this planet, can he tell me, are less stable than others?

"Lots and lots of areas" is what I'm bringing through. "Unless there is a major turnaround, there will be much destruction."

Can we, the Mahatma, help to change that? We have helped a great deal thus far.

Some of the areas can be helped...others will have to be "retrieved."..."Retrieved"? What do they mean?

Through the Space Command; "raised up" through the Space Command.

Yes, through the Space Command.

The Iman, as I refer to this being who is very dark.

Very cold — that energy makes me shiver. There is a concern there, but there will be changes with that energy in the next one to two years. It is only a concern for those who *allow* it to be.

Which will be most of mankind.

Yes, for those who allow it. But it will be a *universal* cleansing, he says.

Of course.

"A universal cleansing," he says, "not to worry about the dark side. This will all be cleared. The more you anchor your energy on Earth, the more it will sound the death knell for all of those dark energies!"

Well, there's absolutely no concern on my part about that!

No, and it will all be cleared when Mama *Mahatma* comes in; this will cleanse all of this so-called Iman.

Do I teach on the inner planes with Ms. Mahatma?

Yes. So much teaching around you. You know, you're going to be so busy; it's going to come together very quickly. The time is *now*.

Is there going to be a quick response to the German edition of **Mahatma I***?*

Yes, faster than from the English edition. But they say you know that already. *The Rider on the White Horse* is now starting to come to life, is now starting to resurrect.

Finally. It's starting to anchor into the Earth.

Djwhal says it's resurrection time, and it's *now*. It's coming forward and it's evolving. You're going to be asked to speak on and explain the concepts in *The Rider* and *Mahatma I*. People are having a difficult time with the concepts in both of these books, and it is finally now coming to a celebration; people are starting to open up to them.

Once we have done our spiritual Ascension, there will be multitudes of people trying to touch into our energy. Of course, many of the teachers will then be able to do their *spiritual Ascensions — Sanat Kumara, Maitreya, Melchior, Buddha, Melchizedek. Melchizedek spent 92 sequential years here on the Earth in an etheric body without organs, which he manifested and ascended with, but that was not the* spiritual *body or the* spiritual *Ascension.*

Melchizedek is here with us. He has a very deep, resonant voice; I want to speak from way down in my stomach. He wants to say hello and convey his profound love and appreciation. He says to you that you and he are like "the plantation of the universe," and we are getting ready to culminate our work here with this universe. There is much celebration with us here (on the universal level) for the work that you're doing! Much celebration! Things are evolving, and *it's time*. We're free of the troubled times; those are all behind us now! However, planet Earth will not sense the joy and celebration that we are experiencing. The cleansing and spiritual integration will cause massive upheaval and a complete restructuring, as mankind and Mother Earth adjust to and integrate the *Mahatma* energy. The outcome of this "savior energy" *will* spiritualize the Earth.

Melchizedek and I have worked together wonderfully in what humanity could view as the past.

He says, "Certain beings on Earth are beginning to comprehend the concept that Sanat Kumara embodies planet Earth, but it is not yet a reality for mankind to understand that I, Melchizedek, have this Universe as my body. And so if they cannot comprehend these two levels of evolution, then it becomes impossible to understand a personality on the Earth called Brian/Mahatma, which has this Cosmic Day as its conscious body and can interact with any part or aspect of Itself."

I hope I brought this through clearly for you — it sounds incredible!

Yes, it's clear to me; I understand exactly what he's saying. My dear friend Melchizedek (not that he intended it to be any different) was reduced to being a high priest in the Old Testament, much less than the Christ or Jehovah. It seems that mankind just do not get it! Mankind persists in making gods of and worshipping the messengers, "Jesus Christ," Buddha, Mohammed, and so forth; when in fact, there should be no idolatry with any "savior" energies, including our Creator level through the Mahatma. Please bear with me, Barbara...what I have to say is for the benefit of the teachers. From the Source perspective there is Divine Equality, where all monadic beings were created equally. There is much distortion with this concept because many Lightworkers confuse the fact that we are all Source with the realized state of being conscious at the Source level.

Everyone is not equal in consciousness; for example, a Seventh-Level Initiate still has 345 levels of consciousness to integrate to complete their circuitry with their Divine Equality on the Source level. In other words, from the point of being there as the Undifferentiated Source, all is viewed as a Divine and Equal Source. When one works in a third density, there is not the sense of Divine Equality; there appears to be only separation! The fourth density will give clarity to their individual part in Source, the All That Is, the I AM Presence, for all travelers on this magnificent journey. No one except an Archangel, particularly Metatron — or a Being coming directly from the Creator Council of this particular Cosmic Day — can return to Source once they have been individualized: "The ring passeth not." Even Melchizedek, your universal embodiment, cannot return and enter the Source of this Cosmic Day until he completes all 340 monadic levels and then enters the Co-Creator Council of Twelve as an Associate Director. You, as teachers (I'm not including Melchizedek), are only recently realizing that this universe is much less than 1% of this one Cosmic Day!
(Note: If 43 universes constitute physicality, which is 10% of this Cosmic Day, then this one universe constitutes 0.23% of this Cosmic Day.)

I'm making this point so that you, our teachers, can begin to integrate UNLIMITEDNESS. The greater your understanding of the totality of your beingness, the more rapid your total integration. As we've taught you, there are an unlimited number of Cosmic Days in this Undifferentiated Source, and we have no idea what is beyond the Undifferentiated Source until we move beyond it. When the Mahatma energy completes our circuitry, having chosen Earth for this purpose, we will then prepare Our Cosmic Day. In the laboratory of Creation, in the eighth dimension we have already created a considerable number of miniature Cosmic Days as possibilities for our ultimate Cosmic Day, and will choose one that best implements our collective experience and creative possibilities. I know that these concepts tend to overwhelm certain members of the Planetary Hierarchy who have been less than cooperative in their integration and who may wish to integrate more comprehensively the very accelerated shifts evident on the Earth now, including the annexation into the Earth of the seven astral levels (heavens). It is even more difficult for the advanced pioneers, working through the personality on the Earth plane, to integrate these concepts and move wholeheartedly into this New Age! We wish to emphasize again that every being will eventually create his or her own Cosmic Day; that is what we mean by Divine Equality. Thank you, Barbara, for your forbearance.

That's fine, Brian; I only wish I could understand what you're saying!

Are people actually seeing this Ascension?

They're starting to now. They're also starting to *feel* what is happening as well as see it. People are talking about Ascension, but they really don't know what this process involves.

Once we do this Ascension, I can imagine that there will be no privacy for Mama and Papa.

No, none. But they're saying there will be sanctuaries where you will have your space and privacy.

With teleportation it will be easier to get out of the way.

Yes.

Did Melchizedek teleport when he was here on Earth?

Very much so. It's the best way to travel, he says.

He used an etheric body to do that.

Yes, and he has learned much from that. He says that at another time, you and he teleported throughout the then-known world for nearly two thousand sequential years. Your location on Earth then was the Golden City that is near Shamballa.

Melchizedek will move into the monadic/spiritual realm when I do the spiritual Ascension.

Most definitely. He says, "That's why there is great celebration with me now."

I can really feel Melchizedek's energy here with us now, and I welcome him, because he's a dear friend and we work so wonderfully together.

Yes, a very strong energy; I strongly feel his depth. When he speaks, he comes from every angle around me.

So does Khamael; they both have that authoritative presence. Khamael, of course, is an Archangel.

The Archangel Auriel is coming through. He also comes with great energy, but he keeps stepping back a little — he's in awe of the amount of work that is being done in a very short period of what we would consider time.

All of the teachers are in awe, because they said that it couldn't be done.

That's right; they believed that it couldn't be done, but they now feel that in the time period of 1994 — 1996 there will be so much drastic change that many people here in dense physicality will not be able to deal with it and will not be able to stay. Auriel is saying that there will be much disorientation and then segregation.

Both the third and fourth dimensions here on the planet at the same time?

Yes.

Both of those dimensions in physicality at the same time...logically, one wouldn't have thought that the third density could withstand the radiation level of the fourth density and still remain here.

Yes, for a period of time.

...During the opening, which will last for a period of approximately 36 years (which is as close as we can predict its time frame).

Yes. Oh, isn't that strange? The segregation, on the same planet, of two densities. Gee, that will be an awkward stage.

This is why there are so many difficulties, with the receptive/female energies going into the Light, while the dynamic/male energies are not as sequentially advanced.

That's right. Auriel is also confirming that many deaths — as humanity refers to that process — will take place during the time of change and segregation (the opening) where, as he puts it, "people won't know their left from their right." The segregation is very pronounced; there will be obvious differentiation between the two densities. Back to your teaching. For the first few years, the majority of your students will be from Europe. The great need for your teachings will inspire and motivate you to stay on this planet for longer than you intended.

Well, once we've created the spiritual body, there will be no need for me to leave; however, I will also have other assignments which, in part, are being ratified by Ms. Mahatma on Galactic Core issues.

There will be no need for you to leave, and you will have other missions, but you will be outside of linear sequential time.

Living in the Now, so that she can also experience the densest level of physicality that we can come into, the fourth dimension.

The level that you occupy now in your house. And it's this dense physical level that is such a confusing experience for her!

We had to raise this density to the fourth dimension (in certain areas on Earth so that we wouldn't burn out again) before we could come in, which we did in 1988. As so little of this globe has risen to this occasion, my physical body had an extremely difficult time!

Holy! This tape recorder just lifted off of the table again! Now they're showing me that when Ms. Mahatma arrives, she will clear all of the many women who are around you, be they your students or your fan of women. She has a strong energy, and she will lovingly let them know where they all belong in relation to herself and her assignment. She is very beautiful; people will be stopped in their tracks by her beauty alone. The picture that they're showing me is that people will almost back away from her and take their positions in relation to her. But she is very gentle, not demanding, not commanding; it's just her powerful energy. Dancing, dancing, dancing...she is shimmering in the Light. It's a Light that is too bright for me to look at directly; she appears to be dancing and moving constantly in the Light. As we said, she'll be coming into physicality at about the same time that you do your spiritual Ascension, to bring a completion, a culmination, a climax of events all at once. The circle will then be complete.

But she cannot come in until we raise the vibration of the Earth sufficiently. The Archangels, as the administrators of the Plan, will help us to bring all of this into place.

Who is Ratziel?

He is one of the Archangels.

Ratziel will hold the reins. Does that make any sense to you? He will hold the reins in bringing about this completion.

Yes; that's very good. There is some doubt in my mind that the Planetary Hierarchy and Sanat Kumara are ready for this event.

We are all ready. You are ready. The time is *now!*

If we can create a Cosmic Day at the Source level, then surely we can spiritualize my physical body. I know that there is timing involved, because the Earth's vibration has to rise.

It's coming along. As we've mentioned, certain areas are already being raised. They're not quite at their peaks yet, but they're in the process of elevating themselves. The Zurich area is prepared for you now! Upon your arrival in Zurich and as you descend into the city, you will feel the raised vibration in anticipation of your arrival. You will not be able to teleport to other areas on Earth until they raise their vibrations into a fourth density sufficient for the completed *Mahatma* to anchor and be seen. The only place on Earth that is available for that momentarily is the lake. Melchizedek wants to come through again. He is the "bridge," the universal level going into the Monad. He says you are very ready. We are very ready.

We're all ready. They can assure me of that this time?

Most definitely.

In the past, the Earth was not ready; thus we couldn't come lower than the causal body. The Earth wasn't ready to accept the amount of Light that we tried to anchor.

Everything is being prepared, Melchizedek is telling me. You are ready now, and the Earth is nearly ready!

And there's no doubt that we will do the complete spiritual Ascension this time? They can call upon the Archangels on this question.

No doubt! The exact time is the only factor that is not absolutely clear because, as we've been discussing, mass consciousness will have to cooperate — which they have done, to a certain degree — by raising their vibration closer to the level that the Source has already anchored into the Earth.

They will keep my body together, and we will do it?

We will keep you very much alive here physically, for the teachings. You are our Source; we are your Source and together we are the new Expanded Source.

I see what they're saying, that the Co-Creators are my source of energy to draw upon.

You need them and they need you here to complete the circuitry of the expanded Source. Melchizedek is saying, "I have so much to give to you once the energy level of the Earth is raised and we can all work together here on this plane. I will be one of your main sources for communication at this time for physical information for the God and Goddess energies — not to push Djwhal out of the way, because I know that you and he have a great rapport — and our work will then be completed universally! And he wants to say that when we're all working together, you are going to feel very tired as the time of Ascension approaches, but remember that as there will be draining times, we will refurbish your energy. At the same time that we are using a lot of your energy, we will replenish you."

Of course, once I'm spiritualized physically, I won't experience these difficulties.

That's right; you'll then be free of discomfort.

And that will happen in the next six to seven months.

Melchizedek says in the next seven to eight months. There will be a lot of changes, a lot of work. (Barbara coughs.) His voice is so deep that I can hardly get it out. He will try to become physical once more to join you here in dense physicality.

That's wonderful. Will Djwhal also come in?

It looks like Djwhal will stay where he is.

Will Kuthumi come in?

He'll come in soon after the spiritual Ascension. Maitreya will be there as the Christ for a little while yet before he gives the "Christ mantle" to Kuthumi. They're saying, almost everyone. It looks like many of the teachers will be coming in, except Djwhal, Maitreya, and a few others. Once you've done your spiritual Ascension, Melchizedek will manifest his spiritual body to assist the *Mahatma* here on Earth, although he's going to try to come in before this great event to assist and be part of the celebration.

Will he use the body that he last used when he was here on the Earth?

Yes. (Barbara laughs.) He's very funny. He is saying it won't be very pretty to look at; we would call it ugly.

That often happens. I find it amazing that **Ms. Mahatma,** *the Goddess energy, has had only one physical life, while I have had many. Well, it's the culmination of two seeds of the same pod. And it was eons ago that we agreed to meet here on this planet for the summation, the conclusion of our Journey.*

She calls it the temple. And there was definitely an agreement made a long time ago to meet here. She is showing me this diagram of the temple:

After we do our spiritual Ascension, how long will it be before others in physical bodies on this planet are able to do it?

They're telling me approximately 400 days. So it will be a little over a year.

Is there a specific number of people that they can tell us?

There will be two who will do their spiritual Ascensions a little more than a year after you do yours. After that, it will slowly be like a popcorn effect; more and more people will begin to do their spiritual Ascensions.

During this opening, which will last until the year 2028, do they see hundreds or hundreds of thousands of beings on this planet doing their spiritual Ascensions?

There should be hundreds of thousands by then.

I sense that. But before they can even think about the spiritual Ascension, mankind need to wake up and merge their personalities with their Souls — the basic Third Initiation, the Soul Merge. And then, they need to realize that after that there are 349 levels and initiations. To keep things in perspective, they also need to understand that the level of their Christ, Maitreya, is the Seventh Initiation, and that there are 345 levels beyond this which, even then, takes one only to the Co-Creator Council of Twelve for this one Cosmic Day, which is the level that we, the Mahatma, represent. Although we know nothing of the Undifferentiated Source because "the ring passeth not," we do know that there is much, much more beyond the Creator level of this Cosmic Day. It is truly an eternal Journey, and the key to Ascension is simply the integration of the Mahatma *energy.*

They're telling me that the heightened energy of Switzerland will maintain your physical and mental health. You will be working very hard while you're there, and you won't have time to think and worry about things; everything will just happen. The *Ms. Mahatma* energy will help you with your physical problems; she will help you to remain healthy. She wants you to be complete!

8

Transformation
Through Evolution

The "Masters" who have worked within this sphere and elevated themselves to slightly higher planes; and there is not only the devic evolution and
the angelic evolution side by side with humanity, coming back into their clear
connection. As we have already mentioned, the veil that was placed between
the Human Kingdom and the Devic and Angelic Kingdoms at the time of the
destruction of Atlantis is now being lifted; so the contact between mankind and
these two realms is opening again. Thus more and more you have the Angelic
Kingdom bringing forth its assistance and its knowledge.

The sense of connection between humanity and the other kingdoms is
coming back into its own holistic nature as well; so you have this interflow
beginning again, where the Angelic Kingdom can actually transfer over and
come down to experience as humanity. There can be that interchange (albeit
seldom done successfully). The amount of assistance from other realms now is
quite phenomenal, even beyond the usual ones of Ascended humanity, the
Devic Kingdom and Angelic Host, which have always been there. The degree
of help coming forth now is coming from other dimensions including the
Source as the *Mahatma* energy, where the entities have been looking at the
Earth ever since your two golden ages when all achieved mastery and saying,
"This is an interesting little planet. It has a tremendously explosive potential
here, either way...rather curious to see how it goes. "

So they have been watching, and what they have been seeing in the last one
hundred years has been like a very engrossing movie: "We don't know
whether it's going to blow up now...Oh, saved in the nick of time!" All of the
drama, the thrills and chills and spills! Now we come to the happy ending.

There are many others: the Ashtar Command and other of the so-called Space Brothers, and beings from other physical planets as well as nonphysical planets who are here rendering their help. They are also looking at this planet with a great deal of enthusiasm, concern and love, because they are about to welcome planet Earth into a community from which it has been shut out. It has been like the angry younger brother who says, "I don't want to have anything to do with this family; I'm going to lock myself in my room!" He locks himself in his room for some time, finally decides that he's getting a little tired of being in his room, opens the door a little bit, and finds the entire family cautiously peeking around the corner to see if he is coming out.

This is why very advanced technology has been kept away from mankind because of their very provocative and destructive nature. Man has enough destructive capabilities without adding to it; it was a rather interesting decision to be given even one, through **nuclear fission.** To a certain extent, that level of radiation *needed* to be introduced to humanity through the explosion of some nuclear bombs, to stimulate some of the changes that have been occurring on the various levels of the kingdoms of nature, but principally to bring to human-kind the opportunity to *spiritualize matter.* Most important was the need to *free the Soul from the atomic encasing* which has prevailed since the end of the Second Golden Age. On June 14, 1988, enough radioactive material had been released on this planet through the fission of the atom, that the spiritual **microtron** was introduced, which now allows one to consciously raise one's vibration suffi-cient to not only release the Soul from the heavy, heavy atom, but to raise oneself above the primal soul and Higher Self.

So although the splitting of the atom has had its rippling effect throughout the kingdoms of nature, it has ultimately allowed for greater expansion of consciousness. The choice of mankind to drop nuclear bombs on other people seemed to be an unfortunate one; however, that also was *chosen* as means of ending a particularly destructive war, which would have ultimately signaled the end of this civilization — which may happen anyway, because of its un-willingness to cooperate with the inner Self as the only means of salvation for humankind. People have simply been allowed a stay of execution for an additional fifty years, unless mankind harken to their lack of consciousness and raise their collective energy sufficient for the Earth to house the human race.

What is occurring already, and will be occurring to a greater degree, is the expansion of consciousness of those few who are now taking the Soul Merge, or the Third Initiation, and, of course, those beyond that. The expansion of consciousness that these beings are bringing to the consciousness of humanity as a whole is providing the catalyst — the fertile ground — for this to take place. What you are doing, as a pioneer, is clearing — not only for yourself but for humanity — breaking the rocks, so to speak. So you are doing a lot of the groundwork, which you have chosen to do. Many beings have decided that they want to have this experience "absolutely as soon as possible, and I don't mind a little extra work — let's go for it!"

There is an interesting analogy about popcorn: You put it in the popcorn maker, turn it on, and it starts to spin. Maybe one will pop, and after a few seconds there will be another...then three...then a hundred. We could liken the Soul Merge to the popcorn effect — as more and more begin to open, then logically, it happens faster, faster, faster.

To reference the Bible, which says that the 144,000 have "come down" to aid mankind, is only partly true. There is no limit to the number, in the biblical sense; this gives a different perspective to those who are not part of that so-called hierarchy. Those whom we call the externalized portion of the Hierarchy elected to come into dense physicality and symbolically number approximately 144,000. This group is not limited to a particular secular membership, and does not have any one name; it may have as many as 144,000 or more names. Again, that number is a symbolical 12 x 12. If you look at the numerology of it, you have a 1 + 4 + 4 = 9, which is the culmination of the "spiritual" completion number.

There is never just one way to look at *anything*. Thus, there are ways of looking at quotations from the Bible other than taking them literally — the teachings of the Book of Revelation have put too much emphasis on that, in our opinion.

You will remember that in *Mahatma I* we discussed the tendency of human beings to anthropomorphize. Not only did man create God in his own image, he has expressed other energies in his own image as well. Mankind has created a system of referencing or categorizing energy in terms of his own outer experience, which is male/female energy. The Chinese have this down to an absolute art in their Yin/Yang model. There is validity in that, as there is validity in almost any model or belief system that has been created; it is simply another model.

In the context of the experience of the Atlantean group that is now choosing to incarnate in female vehicles, one of the principal reasons that they are choosing female expressions is to create more directly the opportunity to imprint their "spiritual" qualities and heritage on the children they are bringing into the world. This is also done by the male, but the female, having more of the nurturing quality and more of the role of the educator within the family, tends to also have in that regard more of an influence upon the young. This is one reason why many of them have come in this time as female; not to say that there is really an imbalance here. The generation primarily concerned with this is the post Second World War generation, although there were certainly some you would call the advance guard who came in earlier.

Now, the reason that many of the males of this generation have not truly embraced their spirituality to the point they could have is simply because they have allowed themselves to be distracted by the lure of the male-oriented society — by all the joys of competition, the thrill of the battleground of the marketplace, all of which definitely appeal to the masculine energy. And there is nothing at all wrong with that; it is perfectly appropriate and certainly time to give credit to the masculine energy in its positive sense. If the female energy had been overdominant during the last two to three thousand years, in the way that the male energy has been, then it would have problems equally as catastrophic.

The male energy and the male body, has been, shall we say, a little more densely packed for all the genetic and historical reasons that have been. Man has been the hunter, the protector, and the provider, which has also rendered him a little less sensitive to these Energies. However, you will find in the next twenty years the men of this aforementioned generation suddenly waking up and realizing their own particular place in the program of the establishment of the New Age. Their energy is going to be absolutely essential. It is simply a matter of the energy frequency of the Earth raising a little more, and you will notice a very dramatic shift in the male energy on this planet, away from the wild and unpredictable energy of the conquering warrior and toward the more coherent and constructive energy of the creative builder who still maintains his adventurous spirit. That is where the male is going.

In our travels through Europe we have noticed that there are certain gestalts, controlled by one to four women who have all experienced difficulty in their relationships with males and who view all dynamic energy as "coming from ego," which we find somewhat amusing, since the egoic body is the primal Soul level. The founders of this gestalt feel subconsciously that only power through the receptive energy can allow for balance on Earth. This, of course, cannot be so! If anyone has tried to get a flashlight to work without the positive terminal, one knows that they can have no Light. Thus the balance of these polarities is absolutely essential for one to create a Lightbody!

In viewing these gestalts and looking at the energy closely, we have seen that in ancient times, one or more of these beings may have been developing power as a temple priestess, and is insistent on maintaining her feminine energy for control.

The female is elevating to its most optimum position, and in the context of the energy focus coming into the Earth at this time and the stimulation of Mother Earth as an entity, it is seen and felt as embodying certain feminine principles. These principles, when fully realized within the female, can only enhance her femininity. And when this female principle is stimulated within the male, it likewise enhances his masculinity. How does it do that? It simply does that through the clarification of the difference between the male and the female. There is a shifting point when this energy comes forth, for the masculine energy in the male to suddenly seemingly go out of balance and become even more the rampant, destructive power. This is a rather short-lived phenomenon, and then the balance that it finds is a very much truer balance than was to be found before. This balance point is, then, the key for the attunement of those males who are willing and able and — if we may use the term — *sensitive* enough, from an energy perspective, to tune in to their own higher aspects. They will then be able to channel a new masculine energy ray, which will be absolutely essential for creating balance in this New Age.

Service is, indeed, a key factor in the unfoldment of one's wholeness. You see, service has been taken to mean a burden by many, and must be unselfish. It means to many, "I must not have any joy in my life. I must give all of myself to the good of the group...or the world, or the cause, or whatever the expression might be...and therefore I cannot have anything." The concept of service in the past has been rather distorted through that same fundamental false belief which creates competition...which creates the idea of "win or lose"....which creates all of the major dichotomies in life — heaven and hell, yes?

Service thus breeds martyrdom, as we have experienced over and over again. We would like to touch upon service in regard to our story, simply because those aspects of oneself that have experienced martyrdom and those aspects of other beings that have historically been the martyrs have been caught up in the basic misconception that there is only *this* polarity — "unselfish service" on the physical plane — and that one cannot rise to a higher level and truly experience service from a totally universal or spiritual perspective.

Now, we find this subject very interesting when viewing the terminology of the business world; in that community there has been relatively little emphasis placed on service, and rather more emphasis on satisfying personal or group needs. Profit serves no one if the end justifies the means.

However, in recent years, what has been realized and is becoming a common realization and a common expression is that for one group to win, another group must also win. The concept of the win-win situation is a very inspiring one from our perspective, because we see it as the ultimate route of service in its highest aspects.

You see, service *cannot* be done, truly, from the level of martyrdom. Although Jesus is looked upon as a martyr, that is, again, a misconception, because his true victory in that situation was that he gained a tremendous amount of consciousness. He progressed in one lifetime faster than any entity had progressed before him on this planet by offering the garment, his physical body, as service to the Christ, enabling him to create his own "seamless garment" in his following embodiment as Apollonius.

What is important, and is rather overlooked in most cases, is the symbolic nature of the mission of Jesus and Maitreya, primarily of Maitreya. They both agreed, with the collaboration of the Disciples and others, to play out this drama; and the Disciples, of course, in most cases, did not consciously know the extent of the playing of the drama. They certainly were aware of it on their higher soul levels, as well as prior to that existence, when the plan had been developed.

When the time came to have that experience, some of them backed out of it, quite understandably so; and some of them were rather badly martyred in the process. Now, the point of it all was to emphasize — and we make this point again because it is the key to it all, in our view — the personality aspects of all of the players involved, including Brian or Peter, Jesus, Maitreya, and all of the Disciples. The personality aspects are no more important than the personality aspects of the actors portraying your favorite movie. What is important is the *message* of the movie, which in this case is a rather symbolic one.

Now, the ultimate essence of this particular message was the teaching of the process of initiation, or points of integration. There has been quite a bit of depth given on this subject in the past through the works of Djwhal Khul and *Mahatma*. The process that is the most pertinent to this time is that of Maitreya, as the Christ Consciousness, experiencing that gap which led him to the revelation called the Sixth Initiation. By allowing himself to be brought down in the dense physical, albeit through the vehicle of Jesus, he did experience directly. That can be viewed as a sacrifice, although there was certainly a gain to be had. He performed the play perfectly, and he reaped his reward at the end. Mankind, as a result, had a door opened for it, the Sixth Initiation. Prior to that time, no one from this planet had gone through that level of initiation. So the Christ, being the first to do so from *this* sphere, was instrumental in opening the door for the bulk of humanity whose evolution has been achieved on Earth and for all to come to go through that portal of initiation.

The Sixth Initiation is also possible because of the finer aspects of the process of clearing that have been brought forth. The refinements in the process of initiation are gentler — as has been discussed — and no longer cause such trauma to the physical body, or physical death, as in the past. Due to the process of physical Ascension becoming more available, the techniques for bringing forth this experience are being refined to the point where they are very effective and not as risky.

This Primal Ascension process, the first degree of Ascension, will give the beings who attain this level the *extension of sequential time* within this lifetime, to allow for the total refinement of the system and the subsequent Sixth Initiation, the completion of the etheric Lightbody. When we talk about attaining the Second to Sixth Initiations in this lifetime, that is a distinct possibility! Certainly, the Earth and Sanat Kumara have evolved sufficiently to accommodate the integration of all Twelve Universal Initiations, principally because of the overshadowing of the Creator level through the *Mahatma*.

The fourth-dimensional body, a body that incorporates the material of the dense third-dimensional body and transmutes it to a higher vibration, is still physical; and when the consciousness deems it important to be densely physical again, its vibration can be simply slowed down.

Many new processes are coming forth for working with and releasing old belief systems, which are going deeper and deeper into the causal situations. Those who are working with any particular process need to remain unattached to their process and remain open to the new teachings coming forth. We are delving deeper and deeper into exposing and extracting belief systems, and higher energies are being called upon for their input. We are finding more highly developed techniques all the time; you have seen that in the evolution of the procedures.

There are other methods various students are working with that are also very effective in their own way. We will see over the next five years a development of these procedures to the point where the amount of "fog" that can be lifted in one session is greater than what could be lifted in many, many millennia in the past. This will result in that sudden upward curve of the graph which will enable those who so desire to move quickly to that point of physical Ascension and beyond — to the spiritual Ascension!

The energy channeling into the system of planet Earth, as well as the knowledge and information being carried through on that spiral of energy, is allowing us to come forth. This is the *synchronicity* of the process; this is the overlapping of the varying cycles that are not time and space-oriented cycles — they are multidimensional cycles.

Those overlapping points create the matrix of force within this time and space which allows for that sudden illumination; and this is the wonderful process that has been prophesied and anticipated for so long. We are all enjoying tremendously the fireworks going off now! It is a beautiful display and a very inspiring occasion even for those who have graduated from the dense physical plane eons ago in sequential time, and are here now because your Soul levels have invited us to hasten evolution for this Cosmic Day.

The process for us to witness, again, is very inspiring and very heartwarming — not that we have hearts in the same way that you humans do; however, the expression is a good one! It is a vibration that we also feel. It is one of pride also, a pride that a parent has of a child who is doing exceptionally well.

The willingness to embrace this new growth is producing the exponential change that is inspiring to all who are on the nonphysical planes, and we are very pleased with the process; we are all getting something out of it.

You see, when we created this solar system — and we mean WE in the fullest sense of the word, because there is no separation — we helped to create this system as a playground. It came to be viewed as a prison by many, but is now coming back into its true nature as a joyful playground. When you can bulldoze the walls of the prison and put up the swings and slides again, it is a joyous sight to see. That is what we are reveling in right now!

When we speak of the Catholic Church and its inflexibility as we are entering this New Age, we certainly include its little brother, the Church of England, the Protestant movement. In other words, both of these and their appendages are stuck in the quagmire; they are male, polarized structures predicated on fear and dogma and lacking the ability to teach the Processing for Physical Ascension. Physical Ascension and ultimately the spiritual Ascension are, after all, the *reason* for coming into the dense physical body.

As we look at the probability level for major shifts on Earth at this time (which, surprisingly, remain consistent in recent times) at 94% and rising, then, of course, Rome would cease to exist. We can only convey to you now that a priest whom we call Ogmios is being overshadowed by Jesus/Sananda, and their intention is to operate in the Vatican to create the New World Religion. And once the personality Brian has completed the spiritual Ascension as an example for humankind, Maitreya and two others from your system will be completely overshadowed by the *Mahatma* energy, and will continue on Earth the functions of Brian as *The Rider on the White Horse,* the Cosmic Avatar of Synthesis, *Mahatma.*

You can already see the profound effect that the shift in mass consciousness is having on old thoughtforms. These become self-evident when you look at the aged, the ignorant, and the fearful probationaries who remain as the bulk of support for a dead religion. (Refer to the table, "Man's Response to Initiations" on page 220.) *The Living Christ will appear after November 4, 1994 through 1996, no matter what happens to the Earth,* to aid in the transition for many to go to where they *can* live.

We believe that the Earth can remain relatively intact at this juncture and not experience the axis shift on November 4, 1994. If that is the case, then Jesus at that time — with the support of the Planetary Hierarchy and allowing for a period of adjustment — will become the "spiritual" head of the Roman Catholic Church and be headquartered in the Vatican. This being will have anchored his Sixth Initiation at that transformational juncture. At this time there are a number of Initiates and Masters in close proximity to the Roman Catholic hierarchy preparing the way for Jesus; and as long as Jesus/Sananda is spared the hysterical adulation that he has incorrectly received in the past as the "only" Son of God and is treated as a fellow traveler, albeit an elder brother on the same path that all of mankind are taking, then the New World Religion in its fullest sense will indeed live throughout the Earth.

As St. Francis/Kuthumi completed his Fifth Initiation, he became the most highly evolved being in any church. Now, St. Francis was not really well recognized in his own day. He was not a prominent influence — he was certainly not like a Pope; he was simply another renegade, but with Higher spiritual experience. Because of his mass appeal to the public, the Church did not really move against him as they would have wished to. He spoke rather disparagingly of the structure of the Church at times; but he was such a gentle soul that he was revered by the masses, and so the Church wisely decided not to do anything too drastic.

Kuthumi is at the point of receiving his Sixth Initiation in preparation for his new position as the Christ. Maitreya, as the previous Christ, has a definite course into the future, to assist *Mahatma*. The being known as the Buddha has already moved on to other realms; he has gone to Sirius (in the constellation Sirius), and his work there is in a capacity similar to what he has done here, albeit in a higher octave. He was one of the three Buddhas who came into this planetary system, but the only one who chose to come into dense physical embodiment. He chose his path of incarnation in an interesting way: An aspect of him went through human incarnations to be that anchor of Light, then went to the Fifth Astral Heaven. It is when he returned to Earth from that Fifth Heaven to anchor in that energy that mankind came to know him as the Buddha.

So we have Maitreya moving out of the Office of the Christ, and Kuthumi will hold that office. Others Buddhas and Kumaras are also moving on, and other beings within the Hierarchy are moving into their positions. The being known as the Manu has moved into another of the Kumara positions, and another Master has moved into that of the Manu and so on.

The soon-to-be Christ, Kuthumi, is not yet ready to surface...nor is mankind in a state of readiness for the 36th coming of the Christed energy. (Refer to the chart, "Avatars of the Christ Consciousness," p. 224.) His appearance is still a few years down the road, unless mankind does a miraculous turnaround, receiving and blending the new energies. One thing that should be understood at this time is that most of the Hierarchy will externalize and many, including Kuthumi, will overshadow physical vehicles, as Maitreya did with Jesus.

Many from the etheric/astral realm have already been very instrumental in the progress of humanity. For example, the prophet Mohammed has been a great teacher for many, but it is not generally known that an aspect of his energy was Patrick Henry, one of the founders of America. Patrick Henry affected the Constitution and the thoughtforms of early America in a "spiritual" sense, with the pyramid and the "spiritual eye" you see on the dollar bill. He knew the power of the pyramid as an ancient archetypal symbol. When people pull out a dollar bill and see the pyramid, they feel the power of it; when they see the eye atop the pyramid, it triggers a sense of omniscience, which is another level of power. Green is the color of the money and green is also a vibration which tends to bring forth power on the material plane. There was a tremendous amount of input into that area from this being, as well as from others in the Hierarchy, who were channeling this energy through. So it is definitely true that there were a lot of sources for this information in those days. Many of the beings who were involved had studied the Mystery teachings for a long time. Benjamin Franklin was probably one of the more influential ones, in terms of actually materializing this power. He studied with this aspect known as Patrick Henry; they were associated through their Masonic/Rosicrucian connection. Thomas Jefferson was also working with these energies, albeit in a less obvious manner. Thomas Paine and Edmond Burke were like disciples, Burke being a member of the inner circle of their lodge, which was being given certain teachings from various members of the Hierarchy, including the being we call Count St. Germain. There were others who were receiving information, but did not quite know where it was coming from. Franklin was one of those; he also received a lot of his scientific information from the same Hierarchial forces.

Actually, a tremendous amount of attention was given to that group at that time, *because it was very important to establish this new world energy* — a new system of government, a new way of dealing with power in a governmental sense.

What Patrick Henry, Burke and Franklin did for America, Count St. Germain did in France a few years earlier. The French Revolution occurred around that same time; however, the seeds were sown earlier. He is an interesting being; however, there is a lot of distortion about Count St. Germain. Everyone was Catholic during those days, whether they were firm believers or not; basically, they had to be accepted socially as a Catholic. St. Germain was pretty much beyond the impact of the church — certainly on the consciousness level. But in terms of what he wanted to do in the physical form, he did have to conform to a certain extent to the conventions of the day, one of them being the Catholic connection.

Count St. Germain was, basically, the fourth-level initiate of this being, so when people refer to him as St. Germain, they are referencing that aspect, that lifetime. That element of him was universal enough in its Fourth-Initiation qualities to transcend space and time; he is the only being historically to have accomplished this feat at that level of initiation. So, you have an interesting dichotomy between St. Germain as a fourth-level initiate and Master Rakoczi as a higher-level aspect of this same energy. He is very similar to St. Francis/Kuthumi, in the sense of moving into the Sixth Initiation. There is also that other aspect of him which was built from the experience in the life as St. Germain, and yet St. Germain has a life of his own.

St. Paul, as Hilarion, is not doing quite the same thing as St. Germain is. The energies of Paul have pretty much merged into Hilarion, so we can reference that one quite easily in sequential time experience by saying that Hilarion was St. Paul in a past life and that they are well merged together. Thus when one references St. Paul, who they are really getting is Hilarion; whereas with St. Germain there is sometimes a bit of confusion. One interesting point is that St. Germain, as a fourth-level initiate, did a lot of experimentation with time. This is where the confusion arises, because he created for himself a number of time warps, which allowed that aspect of him to be experienced on its own level.

Aspects of ourself can be similar; we touched upon that when we went back and experienced the life as St. Peter. Peter was complaining about how he had been put upon; yet from a sequential-time point of view, Peter is long gone. His bones are just dust in the wind, whereas in a consciousness perspective, Peter as an entity still lives — as do everyone else's aspects.

As time is absolutely eternal and continual, it is only when one gets into a small band of sequential time that you get this degree of confusion. One can really call upon any aspect of any of these teachers (by aspect, we mean any of their lifetimes); it is just a question of why would one bother? The more comprehensive one is, the more one is able to see the bigger picture.

Since Count St. Germain evolved into the being that we now know as the Master Rakoczi, he is the "Master" for the Earth of the Seventh Ray, primarily. That is his function; he is working, to a great degree, in transmuting the Old Age energies and bringing in that purifying Violet Ray. Again, a bit of confusion comes about when people refer to him as the Count, simply because his lifetime as St. Germain was one of his most well-known. He actually had several rather interesting and famous lifetimes: He was Hungarian Count Rakoczi in the late 1800s and early 1900s. There are still available, apparently, references to him as a Count, and he was fairly well-known in his day within his circle. It is rather curious to go back and study some of that. We can see that Rakoczi is the higher aspect — he encompasses the St. Germain aspect, just like the bigger bubble encompasses a smaller one; in much the same way, you could say, Jesus/Sananda (now becoming a sixth-level initiate) encompasses all his other prior lifetimes; and yet, when people refer to Jesus, they refer to a third-level initiate who was going through that symbolic experience in that day. This is why, when people through the ages have dialed Jesus, they have reached Maitreya on the phone. But Jesus is at the point himself now where he is able to come in and pick up the phone.

It is rather fascinating, from our perspective, that when millions of people every day pray to one of their "gods" such as Jesus, who has just anchored his Sixth Initiation as of May 29, 1993, Jesus, could *at best*, be in 52 places at one time! Maitreya, the Christ, being a seventh-level initiate and therefore a marked departure from the dense physical experience, may very well be found in 700 places at one time. The attention span of Sanat Kumara, as an eighth-level initiate, might consciously reach 3400 beings or places at once. Melchizedek, your universal embodiment, could consciously be aware of *billions*, and the Cosmic Avatar level of consciousness is aware of an infinite number—every being or point of light in this Cosmic Day. So when millions pray to or channel Jesus or Mohammed, how is it that you reach them? In all fairness to humanity, this degree of transference of communication is simply not possible.

To touch into the energy of Madame Blavatsky for a moment: This being was of the Light, a very great Disciple. She was an Initiate of the second degree at that time. Remember, the Third-Degree Initiation (Soul Merge) right up to recent times was a much more difficult thing to attain. Her accomplishments, in working up to the Third Initiation, included the degree of service that she gave as a channel for the Light. She has since achieved her Third Initiation and, until recently, was working on her Fifth. The remarkable channel, Janet McClure, is one who incarnated as a significant part of the energy that had been known as Madame Blavatsky.

So you see, initiations are going on all the time. Every realization, every change of consciousness, every degree that you go through in your unfoldment and understanding is, in a sense, an initiation. We have marked certain levels as being benchmarks, and these We have numbered. That gives rise to some confusion when you have experiences — flashbacks to other times and places — and say, "Well, that energy feels similar to this one; therefore it must be the same..."

Time, in those days, was experienced differently than it is now, which is very much like a linear point A to point B progression. Throughout the ancient world, even up until the time of the Renaissance, time was experienced as a coil — a spiral — or a loop. When you are spiraling on a loop, it is very easy to look down at one point of the loop, to look down at a lower rung of the spiral and say, "That seems like just yesterday"; whereas when you look from a straight line, the distance seems to be far greater.

There is always free will on the level of the individual and the Primal Soul. The more you are in tune with the wants and needs of your Soul levels, then the more you will be able to get a feeling as to how to accomplish your goal. As long as people understand, they can get quite excited about the prospect of Ascension. Many people believe that dead is dead, and the prospect of everlasting life is confusing to them. The Church has confused that even further by teaching hell and damnation.

However, there are now many people who are feeling the vibrational difference since the time of the Harmonic Convergence in mid-August '87 — and even during the days, months, and years leading up to it. There are many who are feeling that difference and are very uncomfortable, because they cannot physically maintain that amount of Light, and they are choosing to leave this planet. It is rather perplexing at times as to why and how certain people choose to leave, but it is indeed a choice that they are making on the Soul level.

We have made a few references to catastrophic situations, and these certainly constitute one method of leaving; however, these have been transmuted to a slightly more congenial means of departure. Many will be transported to where they *can* live by the Space Command. There will be many souls who will choose to leave through the death process, and will find a number of interesting and creative ways of doing so. The interesting thing about AIDS is that it allows people to experience their passing through any one of a variety of diseases, since once AIDS has been contracted, one can even die of a common cold.

It is really a matter of electing *how* one wishes to experience change at this time. There are those who cannot handle the increasing energy in their particular physical vehicle; these particular beings have some element of limitation inherent in their own belief system — on the levels of the Soul, lower mind, and/or emotional body. It is not a belief that is conscious on the personality level, which says that they cannot handle the influx of energy. For those whose bodies will not be able to take the vibration, their consciousness chooses to either reincarnate into a body that *can* handle these new energies, or choose to leave this sphere altogether.

In the past, there has never been as much assistance for mankind as there is right now. There has never been a time, while mankind has been part of Mother Earth, where there has been so much cosmic help. And there has not been a time when humanity has had the clarity of instruction to work through belief systems to the degree, and with the speed and ease, with which you can do it now.

It has been said that "enlightenment is simply a thought away"...actually, a few thoughts away! However, it *is* simply done on that level. One of the major points that came through in the Seth teachings, aside from coining the phrase, "you create your own reality" was saying, that the point of power is Now. NOW is the *only* point of power. NOW is the only experience you have; and your experience of Now is dictated by the future more than the past. What you get in your reality NOW, people have misconstrued to be a *result* of what they have done in the past, and believe that it is the product of all of the past actions that create the Now. In actual fact, the Now is created more by your pictures of the future, by your *expectancy*, by your beliefs of what you are going to get. You draw the future towards you by creating in the subtle realms first, then precipitating that down through the denser realms into the material. That is the process of manifestation. *That* is the process of creating your future, the process of creating your Now. *That* is the process of your two major Ascensions.

It is going to be an exciting time once mankind can realize what its options are and assimilate this into its belief structures sufficiently to really accept it. It will take some time to do that because of the entrenched nature of belief systems, and it will take some demonstrations. This is the exciting thing that is going to be occurring: In the relatively near future, there will begin to be more and more demonstrations, on several different levels, of the more miraculous side of life. The true value in service of the beings working with the higher forms of psychic energy — such as psychic surgery or Sai Baba manifesting *soma* in a jar — will be accepted by greater numbers of people. These facts of life will be shown on nationally televised programs. There will be more and more of that, which will open people's boundaries. We do not recommend that the psychic levels be focused upon, but observed and then moved beyond! Once there is an opening, a crack in their reality, a little wedge, then the process is simply a matter of expanding the wedge and continuing to hammer it in further, until ultimately the crack is wide open, and people become more tolerant and accepting of the spiritual Ascension of Brian. Those who can consciously witness this event will benefit tremendously from its unprecedented effect upon the evolution of the Earth and Hu-man, God-man. They will then understand that their perceived limitations regarding who and what they are can be released as humankind consciously connect with their I AM Presence.

Jesus and Kuthumi have materialized etheric Lightbodies many times, as have Djwhal Khul, El Morya and many others, albeit to relatively select groups. It will be interesting when more and more of the Teachers elect — when the time is right — to manifest to a larger public. And many of you, who have come into dense physicality at this time with specific purposes will also demonstrate to humanity the wonderment and usefulness of the etheric Lightbody.

When Brian does his Spiritual Ascension (assuming that the Earth, through humanity, is able to raise her vibration sufficiently), which has already been accomplished on a conscious level, certain among you — who have already accomplished your etheric Lightbody/Physical Ascension — should then be able to integrate the spiritual Ascension and take your physical bodies with you. You would never have to recreate a physical body from your etheric Lightbody, if in fact you ever had occasion to use a physical body again (that, however, is another question).

The ultimate challenge for completion of all universal levels within physicality to move into the monadic/spiritual realms, must be to take your *spiritualized* physical/etheric body with you, which denotes completion irrevocably. (See diagrams—Metatron's Evolutionary Light Chart, p. 356 and The Chakra System, p. 357.)

Now, you have been given quite a lot of information in relation to who you are, where you are going, and specific points of focus for yourself as an individual and for specific members of your group herein called humanity. In a broader sense, we wish to touch upon what lies ahead for humanity. *Mahatma* wishes to assist not only in unifying a global spiritual community by bridging the fundamental truths of old religions, but to bring forth their truths into the New World Religion and into what and how mankind will be taught.

What lies ahead here is NEW REVELATION; further expansion through the process of *spiritualizing matter,* with the integration of the spiritual **microtron;** and further initiation through integration. The term "initiation" does have a little confusion attached to it, particularly because of the way it has been used by different groups and in different contexts; but here, we are using it in regard to the growth of humanity as a whole, as a group; what we are looking at is a potential mass Soul Merge. By this we mean that given the proper conditions — and from this perspective, we anticipate that it will be occurring over the next five years — there will be enough Light available for the first phase of this approach to take place.

This first phase, of course, will be more on the level of dealing with those who have already done a great deal of groundwork and are preparing themselves for this. You will find that many of those who will be taking the Soul Merge at that time have not been very conscious of a specific spiritual focus. However, their work in regard to humanitarian projects and ideals have definitely earned them the opportunity.

What will be happening is that the group who have by and large taken the First Initiation prior to this, either in an earlier lifetime or in this present life, will be going through the Second Initiation between now and then. There are approximately 100 million people now beginning or anchoring the Second Initiation. The focus of this particular group at that time will be, of course, a reenlivenment of the true values of the various "spiritual focuses" from which they come — be they religious, philosophical, etc. They will be able to look rather deeply within those and find that common thread; then this group, in particular, will begin reuniting and reweaving humanity's belief structure into a more harmoniously functioning, less limited body.

This will not be the only group, of course; but they will be, largely, the visible "worker bees." They will be the ones on the physical plane doing much of the work, and will be directed by those of you who have done the higher initiations by that time, as well as those of us who are inspiring the proceedings or beings such as ourselves who overshadow the proceedings.

In this context of Soul Merge, there will again be much going on with the vibratory frequency of the planet. You have been experiencing the beginning ripples, but these will be intensifying and felt more and more acutely by those who are aligned for or against this vibration. We do not mean this in a negative sense; it is simply those who have chosen to go within, or chosen not to. This, in truth, is what you would call your individual Armageddon. Those who have chosen not to go with the higher energy vibration are finding very interesting ways of leaving, and that will continue for over half of the population. There does not appear at this point to be a need for a total exodus, as was discussed several years ago. The reason for that is the invocation on every level of humanity of a higher degree of Spirit into their lives — even from those who have no knowledge or focus of spirit, since this motivation comes from your Soul levels. Here we are referencing, in particular, groups such as the billion or more in China who are, from one point of view, going for an even more materialistic expression than they had; yet from the higher point of view they are invoking more freedom, which is a more spiritual approach.

The freeing of China from its current bondage will happen soon; many thousands of Hierarchial Lightworkers have incarnated in China, Russia and the European satellite countries. The truth of the matter, for that group, is that they are invoking more of their Spirit by invoking more freedom. That is symbolic of that same type of invocation that is going on in various parts of the world. We are finding that in every country, in every area of he world, the desire for *more* is being fanned — the desire to experience more, to have more to enjoy, to be more. This is a very basic desire; *freedom* is the driving force of evolution.

Within its expression in humanity as a group, we are seeing that particular expression of wanting to be more of who they are, in its higher sense, and particularly in those areas of the world that have already achieved a certain amount of integration with the mental, emotional and physical bodies (those areas being the more technically oriented countries). Those who are moving from the solar plexus functioning into the heart and up into the throat chakra are the groups more likely to bring forth the most candidates for this opportunity of Soul Merge. In a sense, the door of initiation is being opened wider than was initially intended; it is allowing more to come through than had initially been planned.

The factor here which is quite interesting is that all of the kingdoms of nature are going through a shift — even the animal, the mineral and the vegetable. We are finding that the impressions from this awakening humanity are being well received on those levels; they are quite ecstatic and thrilled about the growth of humanity, because humanity to a large extent has been a nemesis to these other kingdoms through the ages. Humanity, like a spoiled child, has not taken proper advantage of the support offered by the other kingdoms including, of course, the kingdom of planet Earth itself.

Mother Earth, in her own evolution, is being quite relieved at this point, considering the leaps and bounds that some of you are making; it is very inspiring to see this, within the context of the spheres of evolutionary life. For example, we see the way consciousness expresses as a planet as a very basic level of consciousness that is involved on a more feeling level; a general knowingness rather than a more precisely individualized form of consciousness such as humanity is experiencing. It has been said on one hand that this level of consciousness that is Mother Earth is less evolved than humanity; on the other hand, it has been said that it's more evolved. In actual fact, we could say that it is a little of both — it is just *different*.

In some respects, it is definitely less evolved, in that the individualization process has not been felt as acutely. That process of stirring and coming into an awareness of individuality as a planet is just now beginning. We can liken that in some respects to the awakening of consciousness from animal man to Hu-man. But let us leave that as an analogy at this time; the main point here is that the Earth is integrating the spiritual microtron with much greater ease than humankind is doing. (Refer to "Embodying the Microtron," p 464.) This, in fact, is allowing the Earth to become fourth-dimensional much more rapidly as a whole than her major consciousness, God-man, Hu-man.

Humanity as a group, on an evolving planet in an evolving scheme, that is where we are: This is, of course, the focus for the next 35 years, until the year 2028. The programs that we have instituted are all running ahead of schedule, by and large, and so we are constantly monitoring all of the various probes — all of the various areas within the Earth where we have contact from personality aspects, from consciousness aspects of the Devic Kingdom and so on.

We are receiving information as to the readiness for the next level of the process; and truly it is more of a process than an event, as you have been experiencing. As a process, it is one which is unfolding more and more rapidly, and this is pleasing us very much, since we have set this wheel in motion — as the Soul levels of humanity have, of course, invoked — and the whole process is one of watching and assisting the development.

Humanity is going to be experiencing some wonderful things, and the expression will really be one of global community in harmony and in true cooperation and communication with one another. It is going to be more and more of a recognition of the unity of all of the underlying principles characterized by this Second-Ray activity of Love and Wisdom that will be so beautifully anchored by the Christ, the Buddha and Sanat Kumara at the time that their specific assignments, which are now changing completely, are completed. These beings will not be abandoning the Earth, but simply moving into assignments that will allow for greater responsibility and greater use of energy.

When energy is transmitted, it must always be stepped down to an appropriate level, and these great beings such as the Christ, the Buddha, and particularly Sanat Kumara, are of your own scheme, your Earth's evolution, who have worked themselves into a position of being able to act as intermediaries for a great degree of energy. And so it is part of their process, part of yours, part of the Earth's, part of Sanat Kumara's process and others', to assist in the stepping down of energy gradually from level to level to level.

The concept of these books is not new to us; indeed, the idea has filtered down to a certain extent from the Creator level through others to you, Brian, received by you as Self and acted upon by you and supported by others. So you are finding that it is very much a group effort and of course, our blessings are with that!

The energy being stepped down through these great beings at this time is very much compatible with the new understanding resulting from the Creator and Co-Creator levels being reunited after 3.2 billion years. We know that you, Brian, as the personality level of the I AM Presence, *Mahatma*, do not fully understand what is happening with you as the conduit, the connector between Source and planet Earth. No one in the physical levels of consciousness has ever or could ever understand the levels of consciousness that we make every effort to describe; you simply don't have the language or the visual abilities to describe the indescribable! We know that when Brian, the personality, achieved his Conscious Spiritual Ascension, he did witness and experience, but was unable to describe fully, the MAGNIFICENCE OF HIS JOURNEY!

The Creator level responded to the Earth's invitation; and mankind, planet Earth and the Angelic Kingdom have responded to you as the Creator, the I AM Presence, with the massive assistance of the various Beings and Councils of the Co-Creator levels, to reunite all levels with their Source through you as the Cosmic Avatar of Synthesis.

So, the infusion of spiritual energy which we have been given recently (refer to "The Tenth Ray," page 338), will indeed set the stage for a better reception of the material brought forth in these books. It is rather timely and, as you are aware, *there are no accidents here*. So from this perspective there is indeed awareness, there is guidance, and there is support.

The beauty of working within a group focus like this is that we can embody and endow the words that are chosen with different vibrations; this will be interesting to see how it finally comes through in book form. The addition of different vibrations here is intended to stimulate the sound qualities of those words, on many different levels that will be appreciated by the readers on many different levels. Thus it is not just the words themselves, but the *Light* inherent in the projection of the words that is important here.

What is occurring now is a mirroring effect wherein as each of you goes through your process, Mother Earth goes through hers, and the entire Cosmos feels the effect of the work that is being done on every level.

Nothing is in isolation; everything exists together in harmony. When one area — one level of Creation — is changed, that change ripples through every other level. So, when you are working on your individual process and you bump into some of those ancient patterns, what occurs on a planetary level is a resonance: The level of vibration that you are touching into when you hit that pattern is stimulated on other levels as well, and the area closest to you is that of the physical planet Earth. You are thereby stimulating and releasing patterning on that level and also on a higher level — for example, the level that Sanat Kumara is operating on. You see, he goes through the same process, but an octave higher. If you wish to liken this process to the musical scale then see several different octaves, each going through the same vibratory increase. When one of you takes their Earth initiation, Mother Earth is on this octave of initiation, Sanat Kumara is on a higher one, and we are on a still higher octave, etc. It just ascends by octaves like that.

Now, when you release through any one area, then you are bound to be influencing *every other* level of your beingness. Not only is that on a planetary scope — considering the wholeness of the planetary consciousness and its various levels, which we just touched upon — but also includes the expansion of yourself into the other dimensional realities that you are, the Soul level, monadic level, Source level. There is an element of your Self that is on the same levels as Mother Earth, Sanat Kumara, and every level up to Source.

There are really no finite distinctions between the levels; there is just a gradual blending similar to the octave of the piano in relation to the keys. The octave may change, but the semitone just below that next octave is not very different. As you go up the scale, you find that the gradations become a little less distinct. They are distinct enough if you wish to tune in to them, but it is not as if it is a major transition point. It is a gradual blending, from the level of initiate — such as a Third-Degree Initiate here — all the way on up. The levels are demarcated in certain ways, but they are relatively smooth.

Again, when you are touching into the interchange and the interfacing of one level of reality with another, one aspect of Self with the other aspects of Self, then you are indeed connecting into a multidimensional matrix. It is rather difficult to put this concept into words; it is as if you are trying to describe more than three dimensions on a drawing suited for only two dimensions. However, in this process of evolution, involution and expansion, we can talk of the involutionary process and the evolutionary process; that is essentially what that means. If you view Creation as expressed in ancient teachings such as "the breath of God," then the outbreath *creates*, and the inbreath *draws it back in*. The amount of time, sequentially speaking, between the two breaths is rather vast. The initial expression of Creation has already gone out; and from the point of view of your consciousness returning, you are on the inward breath and are being drawn back in. The entire flow of Creation occurs on that same model — outflow and inflow.

When you consider the different aspects of your Self and the different ways that you can expand, it is not just a linear movement of going from here to there. It is going from here and expanding around, getting bigger and wider, with more of a wholeness. You are beginning to get a taste of this within your own Self, Brian, and it makes it easier for you to understand the concept. The difficulty, of course, comes in putting your experience into words others can understand, without their necessarily having had the clear experiences that you have had.

In the sense of the Self evolving back into the increased wholeness of the Soul level, monadic level, etc., it is a very clear model people can understand; they can see it as linear steps. Where they run into difficulty is in relating the personal process to the evolution of the group consciousness — to the other wholenesses of humanity, planet Earth, Sanat Kumara, and so on. It is similar to the confusion people feel when experiencing entities such as **Mahatma**, Zoroaster, St. Peter, King Akhnaton, and trying to pin us down to a linear model when in reality we are not linear. So, one can understand the model rather easily, going one way or the other. But it gets difficult when overlapping them with levels of consciousness, or aspects of Self, on all 352 levels from fourth-dimensional Earth to the Source. Our energy and the Archangels are unable to access third-dimensional planetary systems, primarily because the complete I AM, *Mahatma*, requires all Twelve Rays with which to manifest perfection, *"as above, so below,"* not just the Seven Rays required for the third dimension.

For example, because the Earth is a planet within the solar system, it is not too much of a stretch for people who are familiar with these concepts to believe and feel that the planetary consciousness of the Earth — as embodied by Sanat Kumara — could be contained within the body of the Solar Logos. And that the Solar Logos could be held within the body of a greater wholeness, perhaps a cluster of solar systems or a galaxy. And that in turn held within a greater cluster of galaxies, etc. And that a number of universes within a particular Cosmic Day could be a *physical part* of a Source.

For the balance of this Cosmic Day, which is 4.3 billion years in sequential time, there are about 1.2 billion sequential years remaining on the "inbreath" before the beginning of the Cosmic Night.

Dealing with this physical universe is relatively straightforward; in reality, we are all multidimensional beings, and we are all connected on all levels — it is just that *humanity isn't* aware of this! The bulk of humankind, using Djwhal's terms, are not even on the "probationary path." (Refer to the chart, "Mankind's Response to Initiations," p. 220.) Most are aware, to one degree or another, at moral or ethical levels of consciousness; but the spiritual Spark has been buried for so long that it is only now being expressed on this planet. Now the opportunity is being created for mankind, as a whole, to open and embrace the truly spiritual Spark — the spiritual microtron and the Tenth Ray. (Refer to Chapter 15, "The Tenth Ray" p. 338.)

Whether or not humanity elect to accept this opportunity is up to them. Those who are absolutely unwilling to look at it and begin to open to it will ultimately be removed from the system. This is not a punishment or a judgment; it is simply stating, "It is not appropriate for you to stay in this vibrational frequency. It could cause you some discomfort." The discomfort is being felt by many right now, and what they are choosing to do is remove themselves.

You see, there is no one with a judge's wig and gavel at the top passing judgment: "This one is good enough to stay; this one is not; you will have to go; reform school for you..." It is not on that level, but on the level of vibration. If you can handle the vibration, fine; you will be resonating with it and the reality will be relatively comfortable for you. We say "relatively comfortable" in the sense that even those attuned to the energies are running into their blocked areas and finding those areas being stirred up. Sometimes it is almost unbearable for the 81,000 pioneer Lightworkers, who work directly with the Spiritual Hierarchy. However, they move through it very quickly, and by and large, if one is attuned to the Light, the process becomes easier and easier as one clears oneself. The higher the initiate, though, the more discomfort initially.

For those who are not at all aware of what is happening, the situation can become critical at times, and precipitate a life-and-death choice. Some are so totally unfamiliar with the amount of energy coming through them, or the type of vibration, or the effect that the energy is creating, that they become quite anxious. Whether individuals can feel the energy per se or not, they will become aware of it in their reality by its demonstrable effects, particularly evidenced in the instability of the mental and emotional bodies.

The physical eyes cannot see Light. Light in itself is invisible unless it reflects off of something. What you see is the *effect* of the Light, how the illumination takes place. In the same way, many people will not be able to experience the energy — which is Light — directly; they will experience it as it reflects through their belief system and creates an effect in their reality.

As the transformational energy becomes stimulated on a personal level and on a mass consciousness level, more and more of humanity are uniting, consciously or unconsciously at some level of Self, with the comprehensive *Mahatma* energies. This creates a stimulation of the thoughtform — thought-forms that have been there all along but which finally become illuminated. It is like having a slide in a projector; you turn the Light on, and the projection is seen on the screen. In the same way, the reality that you see around you is the holographic projection of your own internal belief systems, as illuminated and energized by your own consciousness.

When the energy is turned up, it sometimes tends to fry a few of the slides, so you get a bit of distortion on your reality screen. As the slide begins to melt, the entire picture changes. The old, comfortable way of reality may not be entirely what the individual wants, but at least it is familiar; so in that regard, it feels relatively safe. When that safety, that comfort factor, begins to dissolve, the reality seems to melt away before one's eyes, figuratively speaking. The way they used to do things, and the things that worked for them before, are no longer working. All of a sudden there is a tremendous degree of confusion, which can have a couple of different results. One very desirable result of that confusion would be to question basic tenets and to look more deeply into the nature of reality.

The Harmonic Convergence was a response from all different levels — all of the levels of Self and of group Selves, which we call humanity; and taking that into a larger consciousness, by Mother Earth and Sanat Kumara and so on. All of these different levels are opening to a new degree. Every level has been invoking (by that we simply mean asking for more), and as the invocation occurs, you find individuals asking for more light, more love, more joy in their lives, more awareness, more peace. It is a very common desire right now, and not just of a particular fringe of one generation. This invocation is taking place all over the world, in whatever terms different peoples understand it. In New Age jargon, "invocation" is a fairly well-known term; however, for a farmer working the rice paddies in China, he may see and feel it entirely differently, but he *will* feel it. He will feel and want more of everything.

The invocation on that level is bringing forth a response from the environments — physical, social, etc. — and things are changing. The invocation process is one of asking for more of something, and generally it is more of Self. Whether mankind know it or not, that's what they are getting — more of Self. That Self, of course, is expressed in many ways; it can be expressed as abundance, as joy, as Light, as laughter, as love, as learning, as knowledge, to "know thyself." It really depends through which level of consciousness and which chakra the desire is being expressed. Because a chakra is a *Transformer* of energy, if one is operating principally from the solar plexus level, then the invocation would probably be, "We need more knowledge to create a better world."

Thus, as we have discussed at length previously in *Mahatma I*, the Soul levels invoked the expanded Source as represented by the **Mahatma** energies, at the time of the Harmonic Convergence to allow a hastening of evolution which is without precedent in this Cosmic Day. Through this mass consciousness invocation on the Soul levels, your Planetary Hierarchy became involved with this new spiritual energy, which has caused your Hierarchy to accelerate *their* growth and expansion much more rapidly than expected.

It is important to remember that your Planetary Hierarchy is a higher level of *humankind*. The members have all evolved through and transcended the levels of dense physicality. These are the elder brothers on the Path, whom we have referenced. They have a common focus of service to humanity; not only humanity, but to this entire sphere, including Mother Earth on her level, Sanat Kumara on his, and the universe, on its own level.

Service is the key! And of course, service is a tool and a technique for evolution. In a sense, service sounds rather selfish, but has great evolutionary value; it can help one to hasten one's total integration. Mankind's propensity for "church service," or hitting their head against a stone wall, or postulating themselves in submission and repeating rapidly certain utterances from the Koran at certain times during the day, are regrettably for the *outer* expression and have no perceptible value for one's only reality, their inner I AM!

The invocation process has been occurring for some time, and there has been a confluence of energy in various ways, including a cyclic confluence. This is what has been picked up, amplified and somewhat distorted, in some cases, in discussion of the Harmonic Convergence. Many different groups have been talking of the convergence of cycles...the end of the Age...the end of some vast cycle. We have spoken of it in those terms ourself; however, that is only a part of the happening. On a grander scale, we could say that those cycles did indeed come to that end; however, much of what has been occurring here has been precipitated by the invocation, which is of course, the choice of humanity's Soul levels.

Humanity had been, to a large extent, the ignorant central link in the chain, and that link has finally come to the point of saying, "I accept the fact that I am now part of this chain, and I'm willing to pull my own weight." By and large, this decision by humanity to come of age is one which has been prepared for a long time; but the actual decision has been very recent. Other teachers have talked in specific terms as to how this process takes place. It is similar to the development of the human individual going through the stages of childhood, adolescence, young adulthood, finally moving into adulthood. The various biological triggers — or as Lazaris (through channel Jach Pursel) calls them, "preset programmings" — go off on cue, and suddenly you have this incredible change at puberty. And a little while later, another one goes off and you have the desire to go and make it in the world as a young adult; then the reproductive urge is set in motion, and on it goes.

The time does occur when the preset programming in the human comes to an end, and that same time occurs in the planetary evolution. You have gone through childhood, are coming out of adolescence, and are now coming to the point of saying, "All right, we are willing to become real, bona fide adults." As a race, humanity has had the experience of childhood for a long time. Current recorded civilization is a period of about 10,000 years; but there have been many civilizations and many cycles prior to this, leading up to the point where you find yourselves now. At each one of these points of decision mankind has panicked and said, "No, not yet...I'm not ready to grow up yet! I think I'm going to start another war, or I'm going to break down the old system that I've created and start from scratch." That happened last time in the World Wars and, of course, in Atlantis. Mankind has arrived once more at that same point of awakening and has decided this time to make a go of it. On a mass-consciousness level, you have decided to go around the corner and become the adult human race that we have been waiting for.

Many, if not all, of the beings actively involved in working for the betterment of mankind, whether it be in a metaphysical sense or not, have been people who at one time or another have participated in the final phase of a previous civilization and saw it go under. They quite literally "went under" in Atlantis and in Lemuria, so they have come back en masse.

Humanity as a whole is making the invocation and saying, "Let's not do it again; let's not blow it again!" and you have achieved that end. The probability of the comprehensive type of destruction needed to cleanse and purify after the inappropriate use of energy has been mostly transmuted. Cosmic assistance has responded to the invocation from humanity, and help has poured in from all over the Cosmos. As the energy comes forth to tie the pieces of the puzzle together, we have the different levels of consciousness that constitute this planet called Earth.

At this time on Earth (May 15, 1993) the 144,000 designated "imported" Lightworkers have increased to only 316,000, of which 81,000 — literally and figuratively — are electromagnetically holding this Earth together! Thus we are going to need a greater number of active participants in Light if this planet is to retain its structural integrity. Currently the ratio of one active Lightworker for 64,000 of humankind is entirely too great a burden for the few to carry!

It is advisable for students who wish to become more active to adopt a program of regular meditation, be it once a day or twice — but at *least* once a day give oneself time to go within and allow the internal processing to take place.

There are many different schools and meditations which can be of assistance; again, it depends on the level upon which one is picking up information. It is quite appropriate for the techniques given in these books to be used with other meditation techniques; and the reason for this is that they are very much all-inclusive and universal techniques. One should not require a tremendous amount of build-up to allow them to be effective.

Meditation can be understood in many different ways, but one of the prime functions of any good meditation process is that it will allow for the processing and integration of new energy to be done on very deep levels of the system.

The process of integration which has been named the "Space Injection" and which is found on page 467 of the Appendix, can be very helpful in integrating these energies. For a specific process of meditation, we would encourage those who are interested in going in the direction of chakra balancing, which is given in detail on page 461 of the Appendix, to spend about 20 minutes doing that entire process; that in itself is a deep meditation.

Other forms quite useful are Transcendental Meditation and many types of yoga meditation. What we encourage is to find something that is easily learned and simple, and which doesn't entail a tremendous amount of belief system. *The process of meditation, in its own right, is the most important thing.*

We include other meditations later in the Appendix, but these are more on the level of visualizations; we make a distinction here between the two terms. **Visualization**, to a large extent, implies and requires conscious direction of the Mind. **Meditation**, on its deepest level, implies and requires a total letting go of the mental processes — in other words, the opposite of prayer!

Proper prayer requires profound focus on the inner Self to achieve results, not the superficial nonfocus that falls flat in front of oneself — in effect, a conversation with the emotional body. For example, "Hail Mary, full of Grace," moving through the rosary, have no value except in pacifying the emotional body. This futile, unenergized level of prayer does not reach Mary or anyone else, except your illusory outer self. So what we have is a distinction between visualization, meditation, and what is called prayer.

Most of the guided meditations take you through the visualization process. Often, when they are done on deeper levels, they do not require conscious effort on the part of the one who is meditating, because it is the subconscious mind that is doing all of the work; however, they do require guidance. These tend to work on specific areas, whereas the basic meditation is more of a contact with higher aspects of Self, without any expectation of what one will do or find there, simply a matter of touching into and contacting those deeper levels of Self.

In terms of physical exercises, we would recommend not only the Space Injection, but the basic personal grounding technique (found on page 467 of the Appendix), which works with the energy meridians. Another area to work on is the male/female polarities, and there is an exercise included for that as well.

Central to all of these techniques are the various processes of pattern removal, belief-system work, and core-belief work. Those are the areas of Self that provide the bulk of the limitations felt by everyone; those are the areas that must be worked upon and cleared for the opening of energy, as invoked by the Soul levels and as brought through the chakra system, etc. The techniques are means of bringing forth energy, so the belief system must be cleared to allow that energy through. That energy, in its own right, will stimulate the process of release in the belief system.

As time and space relate to mankind, it would be appropriate to mention, here, that the Space Brothers, as a group, are a little more aware of their multidimensional focus than mankind is at this point. Many of you are aware of having worked with the Space Command. Both they and mankind were created, ultimately, at the same non-Time; yet all are experiencing the different expressions of time in the various realms of the universe.

Time and space — as has been shown by your scientists — are entirely relative, one with the other, and the cases of time warping are becoming more and more common; more and more people are having experiences of time not functioning the way it used to. The point is that time has a measure, and is being seen as relative not only to space, but to consciousness. As consciousness, or vibration, increases, then time begins to take on different dimensions. Wherever there is any semblance of relativity, there is some semblance of time, and that time is *experienced differently* in different states or levels of consciousness, including in the monadic/spiritual realms.

It has been said that time and space are merely an illusion, and we would like to comment on that. Vywamus has brought through some interesting points on this; but from our perspective, it is a little different again. Time and space are indeed real. Your experiences are indeed real. For those who tell you that it is merely an illusion, by and large that is not their *experience*. They are mouthing a philosophy; and they're not even giving that philosophy its due credit, because they're not experiencing the truth of it. The truth of the matter is that time and space are an illusion only when one is speaking from and experiencing from the true point of being beyond them. And when one is truly beyond time and space, one is functioning in **Absolute Sourceness**, undifferentiated and nondimensional.

However, when the teachers with whom you have been working speak of relativity as being within the confines of consecutive time and an illusion, from their perspective, it is quite true. Their point of view is valid because time exists for them also, but not in the same consecutive fashion that it does for humanity.

If you firmly believe in the free-flowingness and the liberation of consciousness, then that is what you will experience in your life, which will in turn reinforce your belief. If you firmly believe, as most do, in the binding nature of life, then that binding nature will create all of the validation and proof that you need for believing that. That is the gift that the Creator has given to you. Many hearing these words will say, "Some gift!" It is, however, a gift of tremendous Power. It is like the expression, "a two-edged sword." On one hand, the sword can be a very useful tool for clearing one's path in the forest, for example; on the other hand, it can cut you. The choice that all of the beings here made — to experience life through a physical body — was similarly a two-edged sword. The positive edge of the sword is the *depth* of the physical experience; and the other side is that it is also a potentially binding experience.

All of you who are reading these words are in the process of recalling and remembering who You truly are, because the sword, although it has provided a wondrous amount of information, knowledge, learning and growth for you as personalities as well as Souls and Monads and on up to Source, has also provided you with the opportunity to get stuck. And like it or not, you all got stuck. *Now* is the process of consciously becoming unstuck from this illusory, outer-self experience. It's like stepping into a pot of glue: if you get out of it fast enough, it won't stick; but if you stay awhile, it will stick. Many of you stayed for a long time, and it's rather hard to extricate yourselves.

We have been showing you a variety of different methods for becoming clear and getting unstuck, and these methods are being refined daily. You will experience a quickening over the next 35 years not only of time, as you enter the first of the seven grand divisions of the fourth dimension, but the processes we will bring through for you will become more and more effective, more and more powerful, more and more dynamic, on personal levels as well as on global levels. As the global consciousness increases, personal growth is enhanced tremendously; and as personal growth is enhanced, the world consciousness also expands. The veils of illusion, which have been binding forces in your reality, are being lifted. And they're being lifted not by any unseen, outside hands, but by the work that you have been doing. We have been, of course, assisting in your integration, as is our joy to do, but the realizations have to be done by yourselves.

The veil of ignorance that is being lifted is not a condition imposed from outside. It is not as in your science-fiction movies, where you have a planet with a force field around it to keep all upon it within a prison. It is rather that those on this planet have believed themselves to be prisoners, and therefore have created their own force field. And this force field is simply the root beliefs, attitudes and assumptions of how a reality is; you look at reality according to your experiences and then say, "I believe that a reality is this." Your outer world will say, "Indeed, it is," and it will reflect and reinforce that for you.

Taking power back into the Self, then, is the first step to lifting the veil of illusion, thereby recognizing that the external world is merely a reflection of the inner process. Then one can reclaim the power one had given away to angry gods, volatile forces of nature, religions, etc. Realize that you have always created your own reality; and now there is a fortuitous convergence of energies in this particular point that you experience as space and time to enable you to step outside of that.

Let us look for a moment at many of the women of this new generation; and when we say "new" we are speaking of the reactivation of that group which was the primary focus of the forces of Light prior to the destruction of Atlantis. When that situation occurred, there was tremendous regret from this group that they weren't able to save their beloved country. In a sense, they won the war against the forces of darkness through the assistance of the energy provided from the Hierarchy; however, they lost their homeland, and most of them lost their dense physical bodies during that conflict. They vowed at that time that in subsequent times, if it ever came to that point again, they would want to be here to do everything possible to prevent that type of energy from becoming so destructive again. They have chosen to come back en masse at this time to prevent that same conflagration from happening again. The work has been done, and the effect has been realized. Many of them chose female bodies this time, not in opposition, but in contradistinction of their previous experience in Atlantis, when many of them were male — simply because in that Atlantean time, males were predominant in that powerful community of the scientific priesthood.

In this time they have chosen to come back to balance the polarity they experienced in that time, of wielding certain Power through the primary agency of a male body. At this time many of them have chosen female bodies to do that same function, albeit in rather different ways. They have made this choice because the female nature is more conducive to channeling energies from the Earth into the more nurturing aspects needed to bring forth the vibrational frequency we reference as a feminine energy for this New Age. Energy, of course, in its essence, is neither masculine nor feminine. It is simply energy. But in terms of its reflection through matter, it can take on certain qualities which are likened to masculine or feminine.

The Angelic Kingdom

The Archangels: Djwhal Khul, through Janet McClure

We are going to talk about the ten Archangels that fit very well on the Cabalistic Tree of Life (as shown on page 221.) These Archangels each have a propensity for one of the aspects of the tree. As I have said in the past, this tree really divides up all of the aspects of Creation, and you can look at anything you want, to analyze it. Right now we are looking at it as Creation; and each aspect, or Sephirah, as they are called, as a particular planet and a particular Archangel associated with it.

I think you will enjoy these beings we are about to discuss, the Archangels. We are going to make them seem as if they are real folks because they are, really. They have specific duties and specific likes and dislikes and individual characteristics, although they are not evolving consciousnesses as we in the human evolutionary consciousness are.

Some of you have worked with these Archangels, and some have channeled them; if not in this life, then in previous ones. They are available to humanity and used by humanity in specific ways to understand Creation and to aid them.

Now, the Archangels do not work alone. In a sense, they direct a great host of beings — the Angels. You could say that the Archangel is the director and that the Angelic Hosts do the work. The Archangels interpret and direct. The Angels take directions and follow them; they do not do any interpretation themselves. It is like a large corporation; the president interprets the overall program given by the board of directors, and the various department heads follow the directions given.

The Archangels are direct manifestations of the Creator and have no free will as we have. They are like the right arm of the Creator, and like our right arm, they do not have any will separate from their Source. Now, these direct manifestations — the Archangels — are not "becoming"; they are not growing, except in the sense that everything grows as the Creator grows. They have been created directly for these particular tasks and they do them magnificently. They do them without failure, without difficulty, without resistance, without false beliefs, without any needs, desires, or wants of their own. They serve the Creator exactly as they have been programmed to do, and at the end of a specific time in creation they will be pulled back into the Source and they will cease to exist. They do not go beyond that point.

At some other time in the future, the Angelic Kingdom may be different. It may be doing some other things. Right now it is allowing all of you to receive the benefits of its service to the Creator. The Creator has set it up to allow you to share in this manner. Their destiny is not, like you, to become a Co-Creator. It is to serve the Creator exactly as they are serving Him now and have been created to serve.

Let us begin with the Archangel who is at the very top of the tree. His name is Metatron and he is known as the Archangel of the Presence. If you will note on the tree, Metatron is at Kether at the top of the tree and Sandalphon is at Malcuth at the bottom of the tree. These two work together frequently. Isn't it interesting that the top and the bottom of the tree are so closely connected? It is for balance, and focus in the physical.

Metatron is a direct representative of the Creator who acquaints individuals with their divinity, allows divinity to shine through him, brings that divinity through the steps of Creation, and allows it to manifest. He is spring-boarding the energy at the point of creation into a manifested state.

All right, at this level, Kether, what is there to be distributed? Light, of course, the beautiful pure direct Light from the Source. He begins the distribution of the Light to various subdepartments of Kether and then down the tree toward Sandalphon.

Metatron can be utilized to attune you to the Source if you have some hesitation approaching the Source directly. You will still get the essence of the purity of the Source, but won't be so overawed by such overpowering all-knowingness. It is his responsibility and his privilege to represent the Source. Sometimes he does it at (Planetary Hierarchy) Board meetings. He is a special friend of mine.

Metatron is standing among us and he is glowing. In answer to a question about whether he had a part in building the Great Pyramid, he says, "Yes, I did; it was created to be a great initiation temple, and at the time it was finished, I placed within it the purity that goes with this high area." Metatron teaches classes on the inner planes and he has taught extensively in the area of using Light within physical manifestation to raise the consciousness of the particular area. That is one of his specialties, and that is why he is so closely associated with Sandalphon. Bringing into the awareness of people the great Light of the Source is truly his responsibility, whether it is perceived at the very Source or on a stepped-down level.

The next Archangel we are going to discuss is associated with the aspect of the tree called Chokmah, and his name is **Ratziel**. You will feel a complete difference in his presence. Since he is not quite as close to the Source, the vibration is not quite as fine, but it is very intense. Within this aspect of the tree are all potentialities.

Ratziel holds a focus of all potentialities and works continually to bring the now-realized conditions of existence into fuller and fuller creation. He allows the energies to come forth with all potentialities, to burst forth in as full and encompassing a manner as evolution will permit. He seeks always to enlarge creation and its manifestation, focuses the full creative effort, and evolves it as the Creator's Cosmic Plan requires. He seeks to bring forth the progressiveness and evolvement that has been gained through the experience during manifestation.

This means that when creation has evolved to a certain point, he can bring into manifestation a certain potential, but not before then. So he is constantly looking everywhere to see, "Is this coming in now; can I begin doing this?" Can you imagine existing to see which things are ready to evolve? Isn't that quite an assignment? He is very much involved in timing, not from an' Earth sense, but from an evolvement sense.

He is looking at us now. The Earth is doing well. It is one of the heaviest vibrations, but it won't be after the New Age. He will be able to bring into existence things that have never been here before. But remember, he is not concerned primarily with the Earth, but with all of existence, with all potential. He may direct an unlimited number of Angels to do whatever is needed. He can have all the help he needs to do his job.

The next Archangel is connected with the third aspect of the tree, Binah, and his name is **Tzaphkiel**. I've been interested in him for a long time because it seems to me that he has been changing. That is because existence is changing, shifting a little, and as it does, he changes. It is bringing him closer to Metatron, for one thing, in his area of work. This third aspect of the three aspects in the spiritual area of the tree is changing in focus. This Archangel is changing direction to focus, as never before, existence at the other levels (mental, emotional and physical). He is focusing this change for the New Age. He brings forth as required the specifics to begin the intent of the Creator. There is much joy and love in this one.

The fourth aspect of the tree is called Chesed, and the Archangel associated with it has another wonderful name, **Tzadkiel**. He is the foundation — not in the sense that you walk on, but in the sense that you depend on — of the Archangels. Now, if you are going to build a universe, you have to have plans, and you get very practical about it, don't you? He can do that. Although at this level he is not sitting down and drawing plans and writing up specifications in the physical, he is bringing the plans into the causal area, the higher mental, where they can be picked up for practical use. Tzadkiel is also a very visual manifestation of the love aspect of the Creator. I certainly have worked with him a lot and he is one that teaches a lot. He is very helpful in evolving consciousnesses. When you take the class called "Creating a Universe," he is going to help you.

Now we come to the fifth aspect which is called Geburah, and the Archangel is **Khamael**. He also is a good friend and a marvelous being — quite regal looking, quite powerful looking. There is much energy there, much serene confidence — a figure of authority, but in the divine sense. He is able to give directions with complete confidence, dedication, and understanding; and those directions are followed, my friends, believe me. Now, this particular Archangel has centered within his essence the energy of Creation; and if there is a need for focusing more energy at a specific time, he or his department will become involved in doing this.

Right now is one of the times when more energy is required. Why? Because of the changes that are coming about, more energy coming in at specific levels (such as the Earth), and he is very involved in the change of focus that is going on and the means by which this will be accomplished. His energy is controlled for the purpose of accomplishing his goal, which is to unify the energy of the tree of creation and bring about a productive universe.

The sixth aspect of the tree is Tiphareth and the Archangel you all know, because it is **Michael**. Michael is well-known to humanity as the defender of the just. He defends people's right to attune to the true identity, to partake in the trueness of creation, which involves free will. He will go all the way to defend your right of your own free will. However, if you call on him for justice, please recognize what you are doing. He can see some fine distinctions that you cannot, and you are going to get exactly that; but it may not be just what you thought you were asking for.

There is a polarity in existence, and everything struggles to balance completely. If existence swings one way or the other, he is there. We perceive it as defending, but it is truly balancing.

The seventh aspect is Netzach, and the Archangel is **Auriel**. He has the diplomatic ability that can smooth over trouble spots in creation, and often does. He focuses the most harmonious level of the feeling part of creation, and by attuning to him, you too can participate in the harmonious aspect of his area. If he were here on Earth, we would call him a courtly gentleman, but of course he is not a human being, but one who encompasses the smooth representation of harmony. He is able to harmoniously settle areas of disagreement between close associates. He does this with his energy; his harmonious energy causes the situation to become less tense.

Now, if you called upon him for aid in a personal relationship, it might not solve the problem completely — you have to do that for yourself — but the particular moment of tenseness could be smoothed by his harmonious energy. After that you should work to remove the causes for this disharmonious condition.

Auriel has an overall view and directorship over every artist that ever lived — every musician, every painter, every dancer; but not in a personal sense. He is involved in an art movement within a country as it begins to flow. Remember Italy in the Middle Ages? If you create beautiful objects at a time on Earth when there isn't much Light, you can bring about, in an esoteric sense, a harmony that will be very helpful. The art movement here is a reflection of wonderful celebrations we have for the Creator on the higher planes. Auriel is responsible many times for arranging these celebrations.

The next aspect, number eight, is Hod and we have here the Archangel **Raphael**. All of you know him very well. He is intellectually curious about absolutely everything. He is a logical focus that can deduce the specific ways of bringing about what has been outlined and energized. Now, this is a specific in the area of logic. Can you attune to it? He is one that perceptively views creation, sees beyond the obvious, and aids others to do so also. If you are seeking to understand more in the mental area, calling upon him would be very productive, very helpful. He has the beauty of a great intellect and the resonance of understanding that goes to the heart of a matter.

Raphael is a beautiful, great being. He is involved in logically deciding the best way to accomplish most everything, including how to bring in the most appropriate type of higher consciousness to the Earth. All of us in the Hierarchy (and we are not yet perfect, as we keep telling you) can call on him when we have doubts about the best way to accomplish our objectives. Archangels don't have doubts. They have figured it all out within their own knowingness, they know what will work; they just assure us and we believe them. It is very helpful.

The next sephirah is Yesod (number nine) and the wonderful being of **Gabriel** is the Archangel of this aspect. He is one that ever seeks to clarify existence; to focus the Divinity from the heights into the physical, and conversely, to allow those who live in the physical to focus and to transcend through him to the heights, to the Divinity within. He thus stands at a very important point, seeking always to allow himself to cut through the illusion of Earth living and to aid others to do so. This is a part of his service.

It is very interesting that Gabriel is known as the one who has a horn. What does that say to you? Gabriel deals with the astral plane, the part of creation that is very close to the physical, but isn't there yet. He says, "I am going to blow my horn here so that you can find me." He is announcing that you must penetrate the astral illusion and see what is truly there on the astral plane, because it will be coming into manifestation in the physical. If we see what is coming, then we will know what needs to be worked with. Gabriel then focuses all of creation — the creative activity that has gone on in aspects one through eight — and then passes it on to Sandalphon, the Archangel of the physical.

Malcuth is aspect number ten, and its Archangel is **Sandalphon**. He is probably the most responsible Archangel that I have ever met. Try to feel him. You feel a solidness about this one. You could rely on him forever. He is very actively involved now with the New Age. He is directly connected to Kether. He works closely with Michael, Auriel, Gabriel and Raphael. These four Archangels are called the Angels of the Four Corners, and are a unique representation of the focus of energies before they come into the physical.

Sandalphon is always working with the Earth energies, transforming them to the highest level possible, seeking now to guide the Earth and its direct manifestation into a more smooth-flowing path as we move forward into the New Age. He focuses the Seventh Ray and seeks to implant it more securely on Earth now.

As a general rule, the Archangels are not assigned as personal teachers, but there are some exceptions. However, we may learn from any of them, and we study with them.

All of you have gone to classes where these great ones teach. Depending upon your purposes, you can call upon any one of them to help you, but be sure that it is within the scope of their responsibility to address the problem that you desire help with. They can only help you within the framework of their job area.

Most of the time you are your own teacher — your Soul and your Monad are very capable of directing you. You really don't need anyone else. Then, of course, you have teachers on the inner planes also. Mainly, the Archangels teach evolving consciousness through classes on the inner planes. Then, when you evolve to the level of the Fifth Initiation, Archangels take orders from you.

You may wish at some time to call upon the Archangels of the Four Corners (Michael, Auriel, Raphael and Gabriel) for protection. You could say that in the manifested world, they stand ever ready to guard you against the polarity of existence. I don't like to call it negativity, but it is the type of energy that is more disassociated from the Creator. By invoking their protection in a specific way, you can be protected from being invaded by those who have separated from the Divine.

Thank you, my friends.

❖   ❖   ❖   ❖   ❖

We would like to touch on the Angelic Kingdoms, which most of mankind nowadays views as either long-forgotten mythological beings who never really existed except in the imagination or the "spin-off" side of that, that they're actually beings from outer space whom people had in the past misinterpreted as being from other-dimensional realities. Now, that in itself is not really a misinterpretation, because many of these beings from other worlds who did come to visit planet Earth, and who are — many of them — still here now, are actually from different dimensional realms. So they are able to materialize and dematerialize their etheric bodies and their spacecraft at will, causing, of course, a rather profound shakiness in the belief system of those who view them. It's one thing to stretch the imagination and believe that in an infinite universe of so many billion trillion systems of suns and planets there must be other life out there. However, taking that to another extreme and stretching into different dimensional realities causes some to think twice. Easy enough for them to stretch in the physical universe, but not so easy in the other directions. Conversely, there are many who are quite ready to stretch to other dimensions through their religious training, but will not at all believe in the possibility of other beings in the physical sphere.

As we have described, the Angelic Kingdom is a direct expression of Source completely different from the Space Brotherhood, who belong to the Co-Creator level, the level of beings like yourselves, who have free will.

The Angelic Kingdom works with the direct Will of Source, of God/Goddess/All That Is...the I AM Presence. They have not chosen this Path, simply because they are not individualized beings like you and ourself, as *Mahatma*. These beings are the direct Expression of Source. So when you meet an Angel or an Archangel, what you find is a personified consciousness; however, it is the personified direct expression of Source. As *all* beings are an expression of Source, the difference between these direct expressions and yourselves, as Co-Creators, is, again, Free Will.

As Co-Creators, it is your free will that enables you to make the choices, as the I AM Presence, in every aspect of the Creation of your reality — where you want to go, what you want to experience, and how you want to experience it. The ultimate proof of this choice lies even with those who have made the extreme choice to separate themselves from the Light of the Creator — and there are a disproportionate number who have done that. We would not say that these beings are evil, in the classic definition, although many of the energies that they bring forth are on a materialistic and darker side of things. The ramifications of that, in classical terms, have certainly been called evil, but ultimately they also stem from Source. There is nothing that does not stem from Source; even nothingness stems from Source.

The Angelic Kingdom is comprised of many different grades, and there have been many attempts to classify and categorize these various beings; but ultimately, one would have to say that all Angelic beings are a direct expression of Source. Some are in more of a leadership position, but that does not mean that they are more evolved than the others, because there is no evolution on that plane.

Such delightful entities as Michael, Gabriel, Raphael, Metatron and many of the others have their own particular perspective, as programmed into them from Source. One could view the Archangels as stepped-down Source without free will. Dimensionally, they are the ninth, while Source is nondimensional. One of the great fallacies about the Archangels is that they have been able to enter the third-dimensional expression; the Archangels, however, have never been able to enter anything below the fourth dimension (with very few exceptions that are not worthy of mention). Again, we ask that you use discernment about all past and present information before you ingest and assimilate that which is not appropriate or that which could not happen under universal and monadic law!

The Archangels have tremendous knowledge and insight as programmed from Source. Essentially, it is Source speaking when you are speaking with them; but again, Source has chosen to endow His direct expressions with varying degrees of knowledge, of power, of impact upon humanity. We are seeing in this time more and more contact between the Angelic Kingdom and the Human Kingdom, and this is definitely as it should be. There is a process of uplifting going on, and this process is one which stimulates the consciousness of mankind to the point where they can attune to the consciousness of the Angelic Kingdom, which is really an aspect of Source-level consciousness. And in so attuning, the possibilities of communication are much greater. The free flow of information, ideas, and even visual contact is much more likely now. So we are finding more and more in these times that the Angelic Kingdom is bringing forth their messengers to make contact. Michael has been doing a lot of work lately in various groups around the planet to rekindle some of the — shall we say — lost prestige of this Angelic Host. They have always been there; they have always been working on behalf of mankind, but very much behind the scenes in late millennia due to the abuse of some of the power inherent in the devic elementals by certain elements of mankind in Atlantis. So a veil was placed between the Angelic — specifically, the Devic — Kingdom and mankind at that time. That veil is now being lifted, allowing a clearer free-flow of energy.

What had gone wrong was that the beings in Atlantis by and large had relatively clear communication with the Elemental/Devic Kingdom. They were able through this contact to draw upon a level of power from that kingdom and use it in their physical realm. By using this power and converting it into dense physical energy through the various transformer devices that they had created, they were able to draw energy from the Earth itself — from its astral, psychic realms. These finer realms are governed by the more unconscious devic entities. The Devic Kingdom and the Angelic Kingdom are really one and the same. The differentiation is simply that when we reference Angels, we normally think of them as being more conscious entities, whereas a flower, for example, may not normally be seen as conscious. Contacts have been made with beings of this nature, but what has been contacted there has essentially been the higher aspect of those devic entities.

In Atlantean times, then, the power was available for mankind to draw upon, and for some time it was drawn upon and put to positive use — positive in the sense of the uplifting of the consciousness and condition of mankind. Toward the end of the Atlantean era, a conflicting faction had developed in the scientific-religious life. It is rather difficult to separate those two terms, because in that day and age, they were really one and the same; it was a scientific priesthood. However, they developed two factions: one that worked with this Earth energy to a greater degree and used it for their own purposes of gaining control and power over others; and another worked less within the material focus and more within the context of the evolution of consciousness, the evolutionary growth of mankind, and the realization of mankind's oneness with Source.

There came a power struggle between these two forces. The group you call the Hierarchy was behind the forces of Light, the forces working within this structure to uplift the consciousness of the group. The other group tended to attract to it other forces from other systems that were more polarized in a material sense, and had been called the Dark Forces. So, it became a symbolic battle between "good and evil"; we use quotation marks because we do not endorse the view of energy as good or evil. It is simply energy, from our Creator perspective; there is no such thing as evil.

This conflict gained such momentum that the power that was ultimately unleashed from one side to the other tended to create a major imbalance within the energy body of the planet Earth. This energy imbalance created a disruption of the geophysical and electromagnetic stability of that area. It created earthquakes, volcanic eruptions and ultimately caused the sinking of the continent of Atlantis. This was not an overnight process; it occurred over time, and there was an exodus from the continent.

By the time of the exodus, much of the technology that had existed at the height of the civilization of Atlantis had been lost. There was mainly left a knowledge of more "spiritual" forces, through a small number of Galactic, Universal, and Cosmic Avatars who had visited the Earth, but that too had been rather eroded over time. Very little was left of the aircraft technology that had been used prior to that time, aircraft that you would now probably refer to as spacecraft, powered by or guided by large firestones or crystals.

The Atlanteans used technology they had actually received from sources beyond the Earth, through earlier communication with entities from other planets. However, they didn't develop a clear enough understanding of the principles involved to be able to create anything approaching the sophistication of equipment other systems had. They stayed primarily within the sphere of planet Earth and used these vehicles as aircraft. They flew at supersonic speeds and were able to travel under water. Still very much in the dense physical, they had mastered techniques for separating physical matter — separating so finely between the molecules that it didn't cause a cut or a tear, but simply closed up afterward. These vehicles could go under the water or into the ground without leaving a hole in the Earth.

They drew Earth energy — which, again, is neither good nor evil, positive nor negative, but is a balanced polarity when it is properly used — through crystal transformers. The Atlanteans also worked with light and sound to create other equipment, which brought forth a mastery over the elements. In a sense, they were able to ride upon the beams of light and waves of sound, which is a rather simplistic way of describing it. This technology will become more readily available as mankind progresses beyond this polarity point.

These vehicles were third-dimensional, as opposed to multidimensional, because the Atlanteans hadn't developed enough to create true multidimensional vehicles; their other-dimensional communication was with the Devic Kingdom. Through that contact there was an opening to the astral/psychic plane, which was very much a wide-open book. Contact with certain of the lower elements of that plane was a very common experience for the majority of people. What became confusing was the nebulous line between the physical and the astral reality. This was one of the reasons that after the conflict and after the continent sank, Sanat Kumara, the Hierarchy, and others decided to place a veil between the kingdom of humanity and the Devic/Elemental Kingdom.

At the time that the great pyramids were built Atlantis was still in existence. It was a different civilization from that of Egypt, even though the Egyptian civilization had originated in Atlantis during an earlier epoch of its history. In the latter years of Atlantis, its power was declining worldwide. There was definitely communication between the Atlanteans and the other civilizations of the time; however, Egypt was its own creation. After the fall of Atlantis, there were a number of refugees who had found their way out, moving into areas of Egypt, Central and South America, and into certain parts of North America and Europe, creating their own civilizations from there. The Mayan civilization was similar to Egypt, a product of an earlier epoch of Atlantis. It had been more of an outpost since its inception, but later became a country of its own, similar to the North American countries derived from European origins who later gained their independence and ultimately eclipsed the original countries.

The top of the Egyptian Pyramid was a crystal, and at different times they could create different ultimate capstones. By ultimate we mean that the apex of the pyramid could be changed from one crystal to another type of gemstone, since each stone has its own vibrational frequency and its own unique qualities.

Mankind is becoming increasingly reaware of the nature, qualities and uses of the Mineral Kingdom. This will become even more evident in your societies and in everyday life.

Let us now look at a different perspective of evolution — one that we have discussed earlier — where all of one's lives are simultaneous. The interesting point is that each life has the potential to be the one that can allow the Soul energy to come forth. However, it is a matter of how adaptable and flexible that being is within the physical, etheric, emotional and mental bodies. If there is a large amount of rigid programming, then the flexibility is not there that could increase the vibration to the point where the Soul can inhabit the body.

What happens is a sequential expansion of vibration. You experience the bodies sequentially, although they all exist now. Although it is the personality level which gathers the experience initially, it is the Soul Level which pulls together all of the pieces and converts them into a level of wisdom. The Soul draws the nectar from the experiences of its thousands of physical lives, processes and integrates them on its own level, and creates what is known as Wisdom.

Wisdom is then filtered back down to the personality. The personality, going from one lifetime to another as it experiences it, then has a seeming increase of wisdom. This is a bit of an illusion, because the Soul is gathering all of that wisdom simultaneously from all of the lifetimes. It is a matter of how much wisdom you, on the Soul level, have chosen to experience in each particular belief system of life and death. If you firmly believe that you will become more enlightened and more wise as you sequentially experience your lifetimes, then that's the way it will happen for you. It means that you have been buying into that particular scenario, as have most people on this planet. This brings forth the illusion of evolution. Now we say the "illusion" of evolution; it is only safe to speak of illusion from beyond the experience of being within illusion.

When one steps beyond the boundaries of this illusory reality, then one can see the mechanics of how this all occurs in the Eternal Now, and how all of this is a synchronistic experience. When you have the experience of the Soul finally and firmly anchored into physicality, then that experience will be reverberating throughout all of your other bodies, throughout all of your other lifetimes, simultaneously. Therefore, much of what you've touched upon in those other lifetimes was the backward reverberation of your experiences of Now. What we are saying is that past lifetimes are really not of tremendous consequence. Although it does make interesting reading, the emphasis, of course, is to be in the Now and to truly experience who you really are, right NOW.

What we can do now, in terms of these books, is to wrap them in the Light of the consciousness. That, of course, has been the focus throughout the roles of consciousness through your experience and others' — being, of course, the Ascension, ascending beyond the confines of this physical plane. The pathway for that is truly that channel you have been cultivating. It would be very useful to describe the mechanics simply as a means of allowing that Ascension process to come forth.

In developing a particular energy format, when one seeks to have this ultimate growth in the physical body to the elevated degree of the various levels of the etheric Lightbody, then one simply has to prepare the ground. Preparing the ground, first and foremost, means building that central channel. The central channel is, of course, your bridge — not only from your lower self to your Higher Self, but from the Earth itself to the Source, which will allow your I AM, *Mahatma* to assist in the synthesis, the integration of who you truly are. There has been enough of this fragmented, confused personality thinking that it is all there is, or further, believing that their fellow travelers such as Jesus, Mohammed, and Buddha are gods, thus limiting humankind even more.

Mahatma enters into the picture as a Source energy transmitter. We can liken it to a microwave relay station. Most of what we do is to work with those who are developing themselves to the point of being that clear lightning rod, whereby the energies can flow very directly.

It is quite important in the work we and you are doing, that people have a clear understanding of who they are in their grander scope; in other words, in their function and purpose within this planetary format. As we work with that, it would be useful to discuss the relationship between the process of building the channel and the process of unfoldment of the consciousness and other realms in other ways. By that we mean, how does the opening of the channel on the physical plane for the Disciple Initiate affect the other elements of his being?

It's really quite an interesting synergy, when you look at it from a non-time perspective, when you see the actual unfolding of one facet of the being down here and how that actually affects another facet, which seems to be in a wider range of understanding, a wider range of experience. When you invoke the Soul and begin to bring in that Soul connection through your channel, what you are actually doing throughout the entire system of who You are, from all of the various levels of wholeness that have been discussed, is expanding the channel of all of those other beings who are You.

Every other realm of consciousness that you live in has its own energy format, and every other aspect of yourself on those levels also has similar energy formats that have their own correspondence with the channel that we're working on, here. Clearing the channel means clearing the belief system, which entails not only clearing the beliefs in the mental body, but the emotional residues, the etheric matter, and the physical ramifications of all of this imbalance. Clearing on all of those levels is very important.

As you clear one level of those bodies, it has a rippling effect through all of the other levels and beyond the confines of the structure that you know in this physical universe — beyond that twelfth chakra, or Twelfth Initiation. Beyond the Golden Bridge into the spiritual planes, the clearing still has an effect. The rippling effect goes from the body you're working on — be it the mental, physical, emotional, etheric, etc. — and ripples its way up and down, all the way through all of the various levels of self and all of the various bodies. Every chakra projects its own sheath, its own body around it. It is an energy level; then beyond the dense physical level, you have the Soul levels, Galactic Core level, universal level, and the monadic levels. (Refer to the illustration "Co-Creator and Creator Levels," pp. 228-29, "The Cosmic Heart," p. 350 and "Soul Levels," p. 351.)

The rippling effect that you are doing with your own work, on your own self, as you reference it, filters through and ripples through, all the way across the universe of your other Selves. Of course, it is a multidimensional ripple that is happening, and it is not only in the physical universe that the effect and action take place, it is certainly throughout every realm of Creation. This process is one of working within a synchronistic format of growth, with the synchronicity occurring between every level.

We see an example of this synchronicity in the growth process and the initiation process of those on the physical plane in human form as well as Mother Earth and Sanat Kumara, as just three of many expressions we could refer to. The synchronicity of their growth has led to this point (although it's rather difficult to talk about leading to a point, because that implies time), but from a synchronistic point of view, all of those developmental stages leading to the experience of expansion and integration, which we call initiation, have gone forth on every level in their own time sequence. You have had your time sequence, others in physical form have had their time sequences, Mother Earth has had hers, Vywamus and Sanat Kumara have had theirs all of whom, of course, view time in their own way; each works within their own time warp. Yet the convergence of those various time warps has come to a specific point, referenced as a point in time and space, on this particular planet at this particular time. Each views this slightly differently, according to the parameters of the level upon which each exists. We too view it in a different sense; however, we are also able to see the points of view from all of the different levels. As there is always expansion and growth, then there is always more for us on our level to open to and to expand into. So our perception and perspective in this point that we call Now can also change and expand.

It is rather interesting, trying to describe multidimensional realities in third-dimensional terms, which is all that your language permits. Your language is so bound by time, even in its structure, that it is rather difficult to describe a concept less bound by time than the words being used. So you sometimes run into logical paradoxes when we are speaking. When we speak in paradoxical, or seemingly paradoxical terms, it is simply a way of allowing you to transcend the boundaries of your logic by saying, "If *this*, then that; and if *this*, then that." By looking at that particular scenario, the only way that you can understand it is to transcend it, to go beyond it.

Through the energy that we have put into these books, we have attempted to work with these multidimensional concepts and realities and put them into your third-dimensional terms so that you can begin to understand them in multidimensional terms. This has resulted more than occasionally in paradox; but paradox is simply a means for the logical mind to transcend. Viewing it as such, we can consider paradox to be a process, a technique for understanding, to help the student to transcend — to develop and experience, throughout the reading of these books, on whatever level they appreciate them. Whether one is drawn to the teaching aspect of the books or not really doesn't matter. What does matter is the impact that these books have on your consciousness, your Soul levels, and their ability to lead to the transcendence of the limitations on both the higher mind (causal body) level and the primal Soul (egoic body) level.

If this energy leads to transcendence, then it leads to expansion; and the expansion is what really produces the change. The inspiration brought about through a concept is ultimately an experience of expansion. When you have inspiration, you are bringing in a higher form of experience, a higher energy, which brings an expansion of the various bodies. The purpose of our teachings is to inspire and expand. Many readers may have a reactive side to the amount of Light and energy brought through the text; however, this can have a wonderful effect on the cellular structure and on the personality, to recognize the Light that you truly are.

In summary, we wish to convey to you, the readers, what a privilege this level of communication has been. From our perspective, we realize that although much of the information is ahead of mankind, these books contain more cohesive knowledge than has ever been brought through before, as it relates to relative Truth about All That Is. Our limitations, simply stated, are language limitations and levels of awareness of students, as we try to describe levels of consciousness that cannot be properly described!

When we refer to other lives — which most people consider to be in the past — even on a rudimentary level, there has to be that element of expressing that *all experiences are simultaneous.* Acceptance of the concept that all time is simultaneous, as has been expressed through quantum mechanics and other physical fields, will be a tremendous opening of the consciousness for many of you on this planet. As those consciousnesses begin to open this way, a wonderful process will begin to take place from synchronistic Soul levels. As the opening occurs with the personality, it occurs on the Primal Soul level as well, and a transfer of energy takes place. This is how the Soul begins its first forays into physicality. By stimulating that, you are doing Self a tremendous service. This is much of what these books will do.

On an energy level, *Mahatma I* and *II*, through the formating of the *Mahatma* energy, have placed the final coffin nail in the old structure that incorporates many false beliefs that have taken on a life of their own but which can no longer remain in mass consciousness. On a mass consciousness level, *Mahatma* will burn away the false structure that can no longer remain in this man-made force field; it will be irrevocably exposed by the First-Ray energy and then burned away by Transformational Fire.

Symbolically, the final nail is in the coffin housing only that which is no longer usable in NEW REVELATION. The World Servers then symbolically cremate this coffin through Transformational Fire, thus preventing the astral and psychic portions from raising an energy level that would confuse mankind's mandate for living Multi-dimensionally in the Now, as masters of their life everlasting.

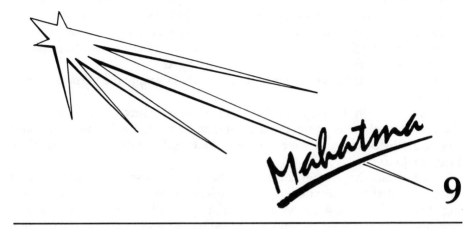

9

Patterns

Life and death continue to be great mysteries on the Earth plane. The beginning and the end of the cycle we call life are our two primary delimiters. Time — the concept of sequential time — seems to be a major tool used to shape this earthly realm of manifestation.

We frame our significant experience of life in the physical with birth at the beginning and "death" at the end. In between birth and death are all the joys and sorrows, the growth and the learning that take place in our physical lifetimes. Between death and birth (or rebirth) we perceive the Great Unknown, which is interpreted by humans in very different ways, depending upon their belief systems.

When we are in the young-adult phase of a life cycle, we are urged by our bodies to reproduce and replenish the Earth, thereby gaining a morsel of immortality, as our ancestors (through us) perpetuate themselves genetically in our descendents. We marry and have children. Then for the next twenty or thirty years, we hasten to attach ourselves more firmly to the physical as we rear these children and acquire the monies and goods to produce a comfortable and secure life for our families.

Once the children have left home to start families of their own, we may have a few joyous years of feeling fulfillment for our many years of effort. We may rejoice in our own physical immortality (the perpetuation of our ancestral line) as we greet our grandchildren.

When one comes across names like James Dean III or Bob Smith Jr. or Sr., particularly in America, this would be a heightened example of childlike immortality. How many ancestors do you remember from Lemuria or Atlantis? Of course, no one can be remembered from those times; thus it would follow that Shakespeare, Mozart, Jesus or Mohammed cannot and will not be immortalized. Longevity is limited to the length of this civilization, which appears to be ending rather abruptly. Of the billions of mankind who came before us, the only name that can be remembered is the god Thoth, an aspect of what became the Buddha. This personality survived the destruction of Atlantis, emigrated to Egypt, and kept his status as a god.

So, as an ideal for creative man, immortality is simply the perpetuation of the species.

Somewhere in the life phase, however, we must confront and adjust to our own parents' obvious aging, often accompanied by failing bodily health and frequently by senility. If we have never contemplated death before this, we begin to do so then.

One of our first thoughts concerns the wastefulness that death seems to bring. Another meandering thought strains at the seeming dichotomy of feeling very old and wise when we are children, and feeling very young, vital and unchanged on the inside when we look rather old and weary on the outside. Just as we begin to know enough to really get into life, it is time to leave it. It really doesn't make sense. Somehow, it makes life look as if it is the supreme exercise in futility.

There is a thoughtform coming more and more into popular acceptance, that all deaths are suicides. To a certain extent and from a particular viewpoint, that is true. Aging is a form of self-punishment. This does not mean that self-punishment and suicide are on a conscious level of awareness. Many people who are dying are frantically clinging to life on a conscious level and say, "I don't want to go." However, there are more parts of themselves that say, "Time to leave." Hu-man, God-man, clothed in this garment that we call the physical atomic body, has never understood that the primal Soul level dictates the terms of one's stay on Earth, not the personality.

Even so, for some it is still a matter of choice. They can turn it around if they wish. If enough parts of themselves realign to the will to live — ostensibly through connecting with Higher Self and creating Life and Light everlasting — then they will live. "To die or not to die, that is the question" (my apologies to Shakespeare!). The decision rests on intent, as Ascension depends on *intent.*

We all carry a thoughtform buildup of the image of the mother and father, created by the interaction with them, usually in the early years of the current lifetime. There may even be thoughtforms relating to our experiences with them from other lives. Taken altogether, our interactions form a pattern, a lens through which we view our parents.

It is very interesting to observe persons of some 80 or 90 years of age still following the dictates of their mother or still trying to gain recognition from their father, even though their mother or father may have passed on 50 years earlier. The pattern (viewing lens) of how one relates to one's parents becomes tremendously powerful in our subconscious. Parents also relate to their children through the images that build the pattern they perceive to be their relationship — even if the children are half a century old!

Patterns are formed by conclusions drawn from experience. They are neither good nor bad, neither true nor false. They just are. Several conclusions of similar nature come together to create a pattern. If enough patterns accumulate around a particular focus (parents, for instance), then eventually enough energy builds around those patterns to create a consciousness.

The father/mother image within you becomes a consciousness. Your interaction with your parents as a unit, and with each other as an individual, has allowed a certain amount of this energy to become real for you. This parent consciousness (or image, or pattern) within you has its own voice and power that contribute to the formation of your personality.

You have, in a sense, embodied a certain amount of that consciousness within. You can release some of the attachments from/to your parents by simply releasing this part of you, or any other lingering pattern — for example, if life after life your kidneys have malfunctioned, or your sense of worthiness is in a state of denial, allowing you to barely function constructively in your day-to-day existence on Earth. Humankind have so many altered states of reality, principally because one comes into this dense physical expression with so much baggage from the past. The whole basis for integrating Light and becoming the I AM, through *Mahatma*, is to release what *was*, totally, and have *Mahatma* align your life to live constantly in the Now, become *Light*, and cease wallowing in your remorseful past that does not exist!

The erasure of these patterns is not releasing the love for your parents; it is releasing the picture that you have within, which causes them to react to you the way they do. You create your own reality through your own belief system and through the projection of that lens (pattern) through which you view circumstances. Everything that you create is from this particular electrical level (silica level). It is like a hologram. You create this particular hologram wherever you go. If the internal picture of your parents, as an example, is a certain way, then you create an external matching hologram.

Parents each have their own input and his/her own life. As their child, you have *chosen* to overlap your life with theirs. It is surprising to see how much your impressions and ideas of other beings are actually based on your own beliefs and internal pictures. When the pictures are stripped away, the other person's energy is there; it is real and unique.

Your perception of your relationship to your present-life father or mother is often a factor in areas of consciousness that you consider blocked. Your self-expression, creativity, and sense of self-worth may all be limited by your perception of this relationship.

Much of what parents and others in your life are doing is playing out a scenario that you have created to teach you something about yourself. Isn't that an interesting perspective? Look closely at the people and areas in your life that are impacting upon you. The areas that do not have any impact on you are not very real for you. They might just as well be a painted backdrop. For example, many people say, "I cannot get personally attached to starving children in Africa." Many other people *do* get very attached. They have allowed that reality to have an impact upon them. In most cases, your parents' impact has been very real upon you all of your life.

For instance, one person to whom I'm personally close has chosen his particular role to learn something about himself. Whether he actually gets the message he hoped to get when his total Self established this role prior to his birth into this lifetime is another story. The entire play from each actor's viewpoint is written, produced, directed, and starred in by that person. I see myself as the leading actor in my play. My friend is the leading actor in his play. He auditioned for a supporting cast and, among others, Brian showed up and got one part. You auditioned for your supporting cast and I was among those who answered the call. Where the roles interact and the plays overlap, you get the two realities converging; this is where the different pictures of reality can create a little confusion. If your picture of my reality does not correspond with *my* picture of my reality, and if my picture of your reality does not match *your* picture of your reality, then there is some confusion. This usually results in miscommunication because one sees the other as he *views* the other, not as the other truly is.

This is how these internal pictures (patterns) come into play. It is as if you have between yourself and another (your father, for example) a holographic image that you have projected. Imagine yourself with a slide projector on your forehead. It is projecting this image (an electrical beam) between you and your father.

Whenever your father comes into your range of vision, he steps into this image and merges with the hologram you are projecting. So, you certainly see him in the light (image) that you are projecting from your unique perception of reality.

Now, by removing these pictures and reaction patterns from within yourself, you will begin to see him in his own light, in his own form. He will also begin to see you more in the form that you really are, because another level of your picture would have been stripped away. Much of the way he seems to see you is also filtered through your pictures of him.

We project our reality perception, our holograms, onto all of the people in our lives. There are always two or more films overlapping, and they are usually slightly out of focus.

There is a certain element of myself, a certain part of me, that stands in judgment of myself for spending all this time writing this book. On the one hand, it is an absolutely wonderful experience and perhaps one of the most significant things that I have ever done; on the other hand, it seems to be quite frivolous. So there is a dichotomy within me that questions my moral right to spend my time writing this book. Two very significant actors have entered the scene. One is the father part that says, "You are wasting your time...what are you doing here? Why don't you get down to business?" The other actor, my child-self, wants to follow its own star, but does not want to attract the wrath of the gods (the father) by misbehaving. This is exactly why we need pattern removal. The patterns have accumulated to create that image or that consciousness within myself which is my father. Removing that part of myself should free me of a lot of the judgments I carry about myself. Life after life after life!

We use the father/mother only as an example, because you have so many past experiences that have left you disconnected from Self; and of course, to be Light, one must "lighten" the collective burden called Self through your I AM Presence and pattern removal. We have included some excellent exercises in the Appendix that will assist wonderfully.

To complicate matters even more, past-life experiences begin marching across the inner stage. The thing is, those lives are very real — they are existing right now as well, so there has been a bleed-through from one reality into another. When you get to a point in your evolution that calls for a particular vibration, then you get a lot of input from these other lives, which are experiencing a similar vibration in their own time and place. All of that combined creates more images, and although those images are certainly intended to guide us, they sometimes tend to confuse instead.

The path towards true Self-mastery — allowing the *true* conscious Self (that Soul connection) to move into the driver's seat — lies in removing these images, these patterns, these extraneous parts of Self. It really does not matter where they came from.

A certain amount of housecleaning must take place, and like the cleaning of your physical house or residence, it cannot be done only once and then forgotten forever more. There are many different levels of Self. What seems sparkling clean and bright one day may look a bit dusty, dingy, and not so perfect a few days later simply because you grow a little and make new insights and realizations every day.

Certainly, you must make a living, even as you expend immense effort to develop your inner awareness and clean out the debris that inhibits Self-mastery. Abundance seems to be a great obstacle to those working on spiritual growth; they regard material abundance as almost incompatible with spiritual abundance, but truly they are the same thing. In order to remain in the flow of material abundance, you must be careful not to become obsessed or controlled by the exchange of one energy for another. (And that is exactly what material objects, including money, are — just other forms of energy. Spending money is simply exchanging the energy of money for the energies of goods or services.) You must get very clear within yourself as to what you want. As soon as you feel absolutely clear on that, with no fuzziness around the edges, and know specifically what you want, then look within and find the areas within yourself, those patterns within yourself that may be in opposition to that — parts of yourself which say, "Cannot have it that way, must be this way. That is too difficult, this is easy. You do not deserve that, you only deserve this," etc., etc. The more you can become clear of these patterns, the more you will be able to manifest material and spiritual abundance. If your intent is absolutely clean and clear, it will be done. However, when other people are involved, remember that there is free will. Free will is not simply from your own conscious level or from theirs. There is also free will on other levels (or aspects) of yourself, areas that tend to be rather tricky. The subconscious mind can sometimes exert its free will and block the process if it is not clear on the concept. There is always room for greater clarity.

When one focuses on a specific intent, there is one element of the process which demands that the intent be put forward very solidly and clearly, and then dropped, as the other aspects of the process require full attention. If you can separate the energies of those two parts of the focus, you will have a very strong clue regarding the process of manifestation. The initial intent comes forth from your power center, tempered by your higher vision, in a blast of energy containing the vision of what you want to create. From our collective perspective, hopefully this will be an absolute connection to your I AM Presence, as the *Mahatma*.

It is as if that strong desire must go out for a certain length of time, held there for however long that is, and then dropped. Then it manifests through the various levels of reality to come into physical being. This other aspect is more a supervisor aspect, a higher level that wants to watch over the manifestation and guide it. Do you see the distinction between the two energies? So, in order to allow the free flow of these respective guiding and manifesting energies, a constant clearing of patterns through realizations is necessary so that these energies will not be obstructed by old, limiting thoughtforms.

The silica level is where the programming exists on its deepest level. From there it affects and interfaces with other programmable aspects of Self, even into the tissues, bones, and the very cells of the body. Suppose, for example, that some healing work were done on a specific organ of the body and the vibration in that area was raised until that organ was working properly. If the vibration remained lower over the rest of the system, then the healthy organ would gradually drop in vibration until it was in agreement with the rest of the system again. Working on patterns and pulling out the aspects of Self that are no longer needed is very similar; you can clear an entire area, but if the surrounding areas still contain the old programming — even some aspect of it — it will gradually filter back in. Gradually the whole gestalt will clear, but you cannot assume that any one part is *always* going to be crystal clear until you raise your vibration above that of Earth and primal Soul, connect irrevocably with your Higher Self, integrate and connect with your collective Self, and remove those patterns from the subconscious mind that in any way impede — through limitation — any preconceived notion that spiritual growth can be attained in the limitation of your dark and structured "past."

10

Time and Patience

Lenduce/Vywamus Through Barbara Burns

Greetings! This is Lenduce, and, of course, I am here with my good friend, Vywamus.

Well, Brian, you have expressed a deep interest in this area of time *and* patience; and certainly the issue of patience is there, is it not, dear friend? The following will be tempered to the degree that the information can assist your readers also.

Well, what can we say about time? Time, as you reference it, of course, is sequential. But there is another way to look at time — perhaps if you can let go a little bit of the ideas of sequence and the ideas of cause and effect, there is a time that is, in a sense, timeless — *and that is a movement that occurs within the Now.* Perhaps to your rational self this may sound like contradiction in terms — a movement within the Now that is timeless and yet has the quality of movement. For indeed, as you know, dear friend, all things evolve, and in that sense, there is growth. And in that sense, you might say that there is Time — "time" in the sense of growth and progression, but not time in the sense of a linear concept of cause and effect. Perhaps we will talk a little about that, then.

Time, which is intimately linked, of course, with space — time/space or space/time, as it is sometimes called, is really a quality of physicality. Perhaps we could say that that is what distinguishes physicality from other kinds of experiences. For indeed, dear friend, when you are beyond dense physicality, or even between incarnations in dense physicality, you are still *manifest* — you are still a being of Light that has taken on a form — and in that sense, you are not formless. You are not embodied in the dense physical expression, but you are in form. On these levels you are not within space/time as you know it in dense physicality, and when you go beyond the physical universal levels, you will lose that frame of reference entirely.

Space/time, then, is a function of physicality, and it has a very specific purpose, related to the purposes for which most of us enter into physicality...and that, as you know, is to learn.

What is it about space/time that supports the learning process in physicality? Well, as you know — and I know that you have reached moments in this lifetime when, in your meditations, you have entered deeply into the great stream that is the Now, and you have felt your Beingness flowing all around you — you have touched into the continuum that is both past, present and future and yet, is present with you fully and wholly. This is the Now; and when you have been flowing within the Now, you have felt a very unlimited and nonlinear sense of yourself. You have felt the presence of all of your past consciousness, and you have felt the sparkling invocations of your future selves, and yet they have all been present, whispering their words to you in the Now. You have felt yourself flowing in a great ocean of your own Beingness, and it has been a marvelous and ecstatic experience. But one point that you might agree with us on is that it has not been focused onto very specific areas.

One of the qualities of the Now is that it contains All, and in that sense it is not as specific as one would perhaps require for some kinds of learning. Sequential time is literally the separating out of a stream of energy, of a progression of consciousness, so that it separates out of the Now — out of this great ocean of consciousness that is the Self — and takes on the appearance of a linear progression; and that linear progression has the appearance of having certain elements of cause and effect.

Now, the linear cause and effect impressions that physicality gives you do not, of course, give the whole picture, do they? They separate certain progressions, certain experiences, out of the Now, and they are arranged to give the impression of the step-by-step experience. That is where you get the sense that you are traveling forward in time and at the same time crossing through an area of space — hence, space/time.

This is done purely for learning; and you might say at this time, "Well, that is very limiting, in the sense that it is distortive, because it shows only one thread of the great woven skein that is your Beingness." And we would say to you, "Indeed, that is so. And yet it is a purposeful distortion, if you choose to use that term; we prefer to use the term focused study." Now, that is very much like when you go to school, don't you think?

You study things in books which are extracted from experience, and they are put together in ways that support the analytical and logical learning process. But you yourself have experienced — and I think that most people have — the experience that what they are learning in school has been extracted from real life. The theories are interesting, but most people accept and understand that these theories are not the same as reality — they are simply a point of view about reality which can be fruitfully used. In that way, I view sequential time/space. You could describe it as a distortion, but I would rather say that it is an extraction of a thread of experience from the great skein of the Now, from that which is truly real, an extraction that is, in a sense, like a theory — it has been taken out of its context so that it can be examined bit by bit, as though under a microscope.

Well, what is the purpose of that? It is, very simply, to learn — *to learn about Self.* It is the manner in which the Source has chosen to study Itself in its most intimate ways. For when you extract this thread of experience, which I have called a sequential life, the vibrational level is slowed down very much; and that is what you experience in physicality: *The vibrational rate of this experiencing is slowed down and enlarged.*

And again, you can say to me, "Well, Lenduce and Vywamus, I think that's a distortion, and I am not pleased with that type of learning experience," but we would say to you that most of the learning that you have done which has been analytical, for example, as opposed to experiential, has had that element of extracting and slowing down and magnifying a particular area of learning.

I think that it becomes a matter of choice and responsibility; you can take the extracted experience and you can look at it as a distortion; or you can see it as something put under a microscope, moving across your field of vision very, very slowly, and magnified greatly so that you can study it. For I can assure you, dear one, that in the Now there is a constant flow. The flow is constant and moving, and aspects and focuses of Self interact constantly, like a great flow.

In a sense, to study Self in the minute way that is possible in physicality is really, in my view, not fully possible when you are in the flow, for it is like being in a great and glorious river. Your own Beingness carries you, moving, dancing, singing, vibrating, fluctuating from focus to focus, from point of view to point of view, from experience to experience — and all in a very simultaneous manner, even though, indeed, there is a purposeful forward thrust, which we have called evolution. That is the progression that I have referred to earlier.

And now we come to the issue of patience, do we not? For impatience with physicality, with its slowness, with its magnification, so that issues seem huge; and with its propensity to seem as though it is a distortion. Focusing on it as a distortion has certainly led to a great deal of impatience and unhappiness for many, many of you who have experienced physicality and found that they were not very willing to adjust to the slower, denser vibration, to the magnification and slowing down that were a part of the studies. They missed the dance and flow of the Now; and yet I know that you will agree with me, when you touch into the Now, that it moves and breathes in such a vast and living way that it is very difficult to pinpoint a specific. And that is really what we do in sequential time. For that reason, I would invite you to cultivate a bit of patience, for I think that you are coming to understand the marvel of this "university of physicality." You can view it as a distortion of your reality, and that is certainly a viewpoint that is open to you. But I really invite you to see that it is a carefully designed tool that you can bring to bear on the flow of consciousness to better understand and know who you truly are.

I would invite you to consider surrendering to this wonderful schoolhouse that is physicality; for indeed, you are already discovering how much more there is to know and learn, and how much more joyous it is when you surrender. The impatience and the chafing that many in physicality have experienced, pushing and struggling and resisting against the slowness; resisting against the magnification and the stickiness that they feel within the dense physical level; resisting the separated-out or pared-down nature of the reality, where you are focusing into one aspect — so you may think — to the exclusion of all others, so that your experience seems thinned and watered down. Many, many are impatient with these feelings, and they misinterpret them as powerlessness, as though going into a deep study of one thread of their consciousness, to focus on it and study it, has stripped away all of the power of the rest of their beingness.

It is important to understand that you have not sacrificed the whole of your beingness, that you have not permanently given up or stripped away the other part of the great flow and continuum of Self, but that you have simply shifted your focus, to study a particular aspect, to understand cause and effect. It is not so much that cause and effect are a part of objective reality, but that you can see yourself in your evolution, so that you can slow it down, take apart your evolution, and study it.

One of the things that we believe that we have gained from physicality is the certainty — through our study of the linear progression of consciousness — that, indeed, we do evolve; we do go forward, we do progress. And I think that one of the most glorious things that you can learn from physicality is a deep, grounded certainty that evolution moves relentlessly, and yet joyously forward; and that each moment builds upon the last, moving forward into greater and greater joy and expansion.

I believe that you are already coming to understand that the grim notions of karmic cause and effect can be released, and you can move into a deeper understanding that progression and evolution is not a grim, dark wheel of karma, but is the building of one enlightenment upon another, one point of realization lending itself as a support system for the next step to be taken. That is evolution, that is going forward. And ultimately, that is what you really can discover when you look into the cause and effect experience of space/time.

So we would invite you to be more patient — not to push and struggle so very hard against this slower pace, and not to resent a perceived paring or stripping away of great parts of Self. Remember, you are not only the thread of consciousness that you are studying in physicality in any given lifetime, in any given moment; you are also the student who watches, examines and understands. And it is from the perspective of the student, the observer, the experimenter — it is from that perspective that you can touch into your wholeness and realize that by moving into space/time and accepting physicality, you have not accepted any loss of your wholeness. You have not thrown out all that You are in order to become one narrow thread of experiencing. And so I invite you to enjoy this experience, to release the fear that you will never be able to connect fully and completely back into the great woven skein of consciousness that you know You truly are.

Relax. Enjoy this opportunity to study yourself and just remember that you are already preparing for graduation: You are already learning those last lessons that say to you, "Yes, but these lessons, these theories, these extractions from the fabric of reality must be woven back in, must be integrated into your sense of yourself as a whole Being."

I would give you an image, a picture: Imagine that your consciousness is a great and beautiful piece of woven art. There are so many strands woven cleverly and artfully together; many, many colors lending themselves, blending into a whole that is breath-taking beautiful, endlessly intricate, and yet so completely *whole*. You step closer, as the observer, and you look at this beautiful woven piece of art, and you are marveled. Your breath is taken away by the incredible intricacy of all the weaving, and you are struck with awe that your consciousness is so intricate, so whole. And then you are invited to look closer, closer and closer, and to focus on one beautiful strand of gold; to understand its texture, length, and where it intertwines with others; to see the effect it gives to the whole. And when you have completely understood that beautiful, golden thread, you pick up another thread — perhaps a beautiful red one — and see *its* texture, its qualities, and how it blends intricately and shows itself in many, many parts of this wonderful piece of art. You appreciate it completely, and then see what it lends to the whole.

Imagine yourself, because you have all of eternity. You are in the infinite Now, secure in who you are. Take all the time that you need — in terms of progression, of experiencing not in terms of sequences — all the time, all the progression you need to study each and every one of those wonderful strands and to appreciate their contribution to the whole. And when you are finally finished, step back and feel the awe, the love, and the appreciation when you view the whole again, having known intimately each and every strand. Are you not struck with awe at the beauty and majesty of this creation that you have made of your own consciousness, this Being that you are? And when you are finished with that, my friend, will you be ready to create another whole work of art, to take another great step to create yourself again and again, intricately, beauteously, delicately, powerfully? And perhaps, from that perspective, patience will seem like a very excellent tool.

We know that you are already coming to understand these things, and that you are simply enjoying listening to it from another perspective, hearing these things that you feel intimately, confirmed for yourself. For you have truly begun to enjoy touching, feeling, luxuriating and studying the fabric of your own consciousness. And you are beginning to find it so wondrous that you are learning a great deal of patience without even realizing it, as you become wrapped up in the glory and wonder of your own consciousness. And through this, indeed, you will also come into a full appreciation of the glory and the wonder of All That Is. For through your experience of touching, appreciating, and studying your own consciousness, the glory of the Whole is revealed to you.

We deeply appreciate the opportunity to talk to you about these things. There is so much more joy and appreciation in your life in the coming times, and we really appreciate you for this. We might say that your enthusiasm and the joy that you feel in these discoveries in physicality are very contagious, very infectious, my friend! We would like to say that you are so able to pass this to others — to ignite others into patient appreciation of their own consciousness — an appreciation of this process within space/time, within physicality, which allows you to pause, to luxuriate, and to appreciate each and every strand in the wonderful skein that is your Beingness!

Rather a new slant on physicality, isn't it? But we would like to say that it is long overdue. And, as we have said to the channel, "Sometimes you don't get to appreciate how glorious physicality really can be until you are getting ready to leave it." Think about that for a moment, my friend, and realize how these last rounds of this phase in your Beingness are always going to be precious to you. And I know that you will find the patience and the time to appreciate them, to savor, to touch, and to know them deeply. Truly it is a wondrous thing, is it not, my friend?

Our deepest love to you and your readers.

11

Mahatma on Channeling

Earth as an entity, on every level, has been striving for a long time to work towards a point of expansion, and humanity, as the primary conscious race upon this planet at this time, has had a role to play as a conduit, an intermediary, to step down certain energies from Source — to bring them in and transfer them into the Earth. This, as you know, is your blueprint at this time, Brian. All of that energy flow had to have a proper conduit, so mankind is here now to be that conduit; and through humanity the energy has come forth to create the change of consciousness within the planet. It is an initiation process (refer to the table, "Man's Response to Initiations," p. 220.), and the initiation of the Earth is on many levels — on the level of the entity which you call Mother Earth, the entity called Sanat Kumara, the entities of Vywamus and Lenduce. There is another variation and vibration, another tangent of that, going off into the other sphere of things, through Helios and beyond — to us, *Mahatma*, as the I AM Presence.

You see, all of these great wholenesses of consciousness are expanded whenever anyone expands. Humanity as a whole has been, and is, this conduit to transfer and channel this energy into the Earth. Whether they know it or not, they are doing it, anyway; and the more they know about it, the more they can bring through. The more they are aware of the mechanics of the flow of energy — how to properly ground it into the Earth — the more comfortable it will be for them as well, and the more easily it will be assimilated through their systems and into the Earth. As it goes through them, into the Earth, it creates a rippling effect within the system. It is a twofold expansion; so, being that channel, that point of service for the Earth, is also being a tremendous service to the expansion of Self and of one's own potential, as one seeks to expand back into the wholeness of Source.

The more energy that flows through, the more transformation that occurs within the vehicle of the channel, and the more that the power can flow in its purity into the Earth. The more that the channel then clears its own conscious-ness of his/her own blocks and debris, then the more of Self that can reach into the Earth to pull out the blockages on the levels that are resonating to the same blocks the individual is working on.

You see, humanity as a whole is the primary channel for this to occur. It certainly can be that a planet can receive an initiation without there being a conscious, intelligent community upon the planet. However, this is the method chosen in this particular case by all concerned, including you, includ-ing humanity as a whole. Channeling is a natural process of allowing the energy and the impressions and the inspirations from the higher realms of consciousness of one's own Self to flow into the conscious expression and into the being within the personality vehicle. In other words, for one experiencing life on planet Earth, the influx of energy is coming through from the vastness of one's own higher aspects, one's own Higher Selves. There is a stimulation of this energy from other areas, but when I say "other areas," this tends to be a little misconstrued, and people have the impression that perhaps there are areas of life of which they are not a part.

Indeed, All is One in its totality. So when you reference an energy such as ourself, in a sense you could say that we are your higher consciousness. We are one at a higher consciousness level; and so, flowing through your channel from the level where your own higher consciousness resides — at which, we are One — the energy flows and is very familiar; it feels very comfortable.

The process of channeling has been around forever, for as long as mankind has been on this planet, and beyond that.

Since original man was created as a vehicle of experience from the Soul level, the Soul-level consciousness created that entity and moved in and out at will. The channel is a symbolic way of viewing that connection between the entity and physical consciousness, and the higher aspects. Indeed, from a clairvoyant perspective, there is a line of Light flowing down through the body from the crown of the head down through the feet and into the Earth. This line of Light is what we call the channel, and it is the connecting rod between the energies of Heaven and the energies of Earth, in ancient terms. It is the conduit between the energies of your Soul and of your personality; it is also the conduit of energies between your Higher Self aspects and your monadic aspects, all the way to the Source level through to all of the aspects of yourself, and also connecting you into that aspect of yourself called planet Earth. There is a connection here.

When one opens oneself to channel, what one is doing is opening to the awareness and the connectedness to one's own Higher Self and beyond and to the expanded knowledge thereof. It is not only knowledge that comes through, it is energy, love, joy, artistic impression, abundance, peace, etc.

Even looking at the structure of language — and language is a very impor-tant part of being — it is that framework which embodies your thought; and your thought, for example, is a mirrored expression of the thought of the Creator of this Source, which is the I AM Presence for this Cosmic Day and the Mother/Father/God, the All That Is of the combined Sources. So in trying to put thought, in its purity, into expression, language is necessary on the physical plane; and language is very revealing, if one looks at it. Look at words such as " inspiration" — break down that word and you see that "to inspire" means "to bring in the Spirit." And what Spirit is that? We are not talking about other spirits from other worlds; we are talking about your own Higher Self, your *own* spirit of Self.

To be *inspired*, then, is to bring forth that energy of your own Higher Self. To be *enlightened* is "to bring in the Light"; and to not only bring in Light as you know it, as a means of physical illumination, but to bring in Light in the sense of *lightness* — to elevate, to take away the heavier elements and become *lighter*. Enlightenment means all of those things.

Other interesting words abound in the vocabulary. When one considers the inspiration of ideas from an inventor's perspective, from an artist's perspective, a writer, a musician, an architect, any type of designer, anyone working with creativity and creating something — then the inspirational process is the key to it all. Many of the greatest inventors and artists of your history have reported their experiences of how the ideas came to them in strange ways, that the greatest inventions sometimes came in dreams, sometimes when falling asleep, when daydreaming — any type of semialtered state that pushes the intellect out of the driver's seat and allows in the impressions from the higher mind. Those impressions are out there; they exist as an intent from some higher realm of consciousness.

Within the Planetary Hierarchy, as a stepped-down representative of the Creator level, there are Masters working with implanting ideas — ideas whose time has come (you have heard that expression). It's very common for an invention, an idea, or a new advance in science or knowledge to be picked up by different people in different parts of the world at the same time. The way it works is that the intent and clear picture of the concept is projected from a higher level, and the Planetary Hierarchy project it into the ether, into the consciousness of the planetary sphere. Those humans who are attuned to that level can then reach up and pluck it out of the air. In that sense, inventions and ideas have no true ownership; no one can lay claim to owning an idea, because indeed, who gave them that idea in the first place?

Ideas are an interesting marriage between the original concept as it comes forth from a higher level and the background of the inventor or the channel. In the same way as discussed before, there has to be a certain amount of the consciousness of the channel involved, so that the message can come through clearly. In the case of an inventor, there has to be a basic background, a basic knowledge, for that new impression to resonate well; there has to be some familiarity there, so that he can see how it works. Otherwise it would be just an image and would not be brought into fruition.

Channeling is done in very many practical, different ways. More and more, as people open themselves to the impressions from the higher realms, they will be able to pick up on and create, in very concrete terms, some very wonderful and marvelous things — not only things such as inventions, but creations of art, music, poetry, dance — *any* area of expression. That is why creative beings resonate so well with this New Age, where channeling is the most viable means in dense physicality to be able to communicate with the higher teachings, until such time as the Masters themselves take on physical bodies, or other aspects, as seen on TV, are played out.

Channeling has another value as well, in that the tendency has always been for mankind to worship and deify their teachers. Even in this day and age of scientific skepticism, there is a flip side — that of blind devotion and those who are extolling the virtues of that type of faith. The danger here is that if all of a sudden a master or a number of masters or avatars appeared upon the planet with a new teaching, they would likely be met, on one hand, with tremendous hostility; and on the other, group worship would develop around them by many who believed and followed. We have seen this model developing over and over again. The teachers, including the Christed energy through Kuthumi and Maitreya, are doing everything in their respective power to avoid another limited belief structure coming into existence, that could only impede mankind's personal and collective spiritual growth. In other words, these energies manifesting on earth at this time do not wish to be worshipped or exalted, but to be treated with divine equality and to teach and convey their love, light, and higher teachings to those among you who are searching within Self for the spiritual heavens that reside within each and every one.

As we were saying about channeling, though, as a distinction from other means of physical manifestation — channeling as a source of teaching — one sees a possibility here of a universal teaching which is corroborated all over the world through thousands of different channels, the basic tenets of the teaching being the same. Some of the variations occur from the backgrounds of the channels — from the various geographic locations, religious backgrounds of the area, etc. However, the basis of the teaching is the same; and this is, indeed, the foundation of what Djwhal once called the New World Religion. This New World Religion will be such a grassroots understanding that it will not need a figurehead; a figurehead may be sent, but it will not necessarily need that. Ultimately, the understanding will be that the figurehead is simply an Elder Brother on the Path, not one to be placed on a pedestal or worshipped or treated (in any sense of being) as something other than what humanity already is. Simply viewed, that being would be properly held as an example of what is possible.

This is, of course, what Jesus and Maitreya attempted to do 2000 years ago, when the saying was, "Ye are gods," and the masses said, "Yes, sure, we are gods, but we are still having trouble making ends meet and we can't heal ourselves; we have our limitations." The Christ said, "All the things that I have done, you will do, and more." This type of teaching has been around for 2000 years; people have paid lip service to it, but they have not actually understood its ramifications and implications.

As the channeling process unfolds with more and more channels around the world, with information on channeling, processes for channeling, and increased energy, the entire level of consciousness of the world will be elevated to the point where more and more people can actually tune in to themselves and get this teaching from within. The great beauty of it is that it gives the power back to everyone. It does not put the power onto "Jesus Christ" or Buddha or Mohammed or anyone else. It does not put the power onto the government or onto science to "fix my life"; it puts the power back into the individual — back into their own beingness, to create their own reality the way they want it. What it does is discourage the adulation of the form and allow for the acknowledgment and recognition of the spirit behind the forms.

When you have an entity such as ourself, *Mahatma*, channeling through a physical personality, then the physical being is certainly not one that you would wish to worship, although one may want to adore the consciousness that is coming through. Well, where is that consciousness? What form would you put on it? You would not be able to make a picture and hang it around your neck or put it up on the wall, although many have tried. Many have tried to do this with the various Masters — painted pictures and then worshipped the form. This is not the point; the point of this entire phase of the teaching is to bring the spirit of the teaching *without* the constrictions and the hindrances of the form, which has been brought through in the past.

Once that form level is transcended, then of course the form can reappear. There is a little clue for you, in terms of the physical reappearance of the Christ: Once the consciousness of the Christ is experienced and perceived within the beingness of the individual, he will know that it truly does lie within, that the Kingdom of Heaven is truly within. He then will stop looking outside, and that point will be the appropriate time for the outward expression to come forth — at the very time when it is not needed.

Mankind is more receptive than they were ten years ago...and more than they were ten years prior to that, and so on. The unfolding process has been quite astronomical. It is one which is a geometric progression; it just mushrooms out. It is said that the amount of knowledge available to mankind as a race doubles now every 20 months. This is rather phenomenal, considering how all of that knowledge gets integrated, or not integrated, as the case may be. This is where the reservoir of consciousness needs to be expanded, as the intellect is getting to the point where it is becoming overburdened; as a tool, it is being overworked. It is not meant to handle everything; it is meant to be a tool for the conscious mind, but the conscious mind has been running away from its job.

What we are doing is also working to help mankind and, beginning through individuals, to bring the parts of their personalities back together to the point where not only is the conscious mind in control again, but the soul is actually infused into it. It becomes a working partnership, rather than some aspect of self that is less than clear running the ship with the conscious mind, which is supposed to be the captain, asleep at the wheel.

The entire process that you and others have been going through is a process of alignment, of unfolding, of clearing. That same process is going on all over the world — through thousands of initiates, disciples, aspirants of the Path — as more and more of this consciousness comes forth and as more of you are becoming aware of your own true nature, your own true status of Self. By status, we mean the status of all of humanity as *absolute sons of God*, in the ultimate sense of the term. No one is thus greater than anyone else — *all* are of the same family, and it is simply a matter of recognizing who You are, opening yourself to that level, and allowing it to come forth.

If you had reached, for example, the point where you have literally transcended all physical/universal planes, and yet you have the facility to recreate the body at anytime, choosing to come back would be a mutual choice between yourself and your Oversoul or Monad. When you make the choice to return to humanity as a Cosmic Avatar — as a being who has transcended and chooses to come back — then essentially you cannot come back and impose yourself upon unwilling people; there has to be a mutual interchange. If they choose that they want and need Brian as a Cosmic Avatar, then Brian — or whatever name you choose to go by — will come back, if that is your choice as well. You see, it has to be mutual; that is where your reality overlaps with the reality of all others. On this occasion, *our* energy has been invoked by the Planetary Hierarchy, Sanat Kumara and all of the Logos and the Soul levels, to bond the Creator level with the Co-Creator level. (Refer to the chart, "Co-Creator and Creator levels," pp. 228-29 and "The Cosmic Heart," p. 350.)

12

Conversation Between the Personality (Brian) and *Mahatma*

(the I AM Presence)

Brian: Jesus, Maitreya and myself as Simon Peter, as a participant in that Passion play, I know that then and now we created a monster, so to speak, in the religions — the Hindu, the Moslem and the Christian — at least that's a view: From a certain perspective, it karmically backfired on us. What Maitreya created as the Christ has been retrogresssive.

Mahatma: Well, let us say that "What was, *was...*" and can be rewritten. The way we are viewing it, there was no retrogressive effect upon those entities, who made wonderful use of their opportunities. Our energy as Simon Peter — our galactically aspected energy — was, from our Creator perspective, firmly anchored into the Earth through the collective Christed energy, but it has been difficult for you, the personality level, to integrate the illusionary aspects of betrayal and denial.

Maitreya made such wonderful use of the opportunity that he opened that door of initiation for himself and others. He is now in the process of opening another. Jesus also made wonderful use of his opportunity, in that he opened himself to the fourth initiation and fully anchored it. In his very next lifetime, he attained mastery as Apollonius of Tyana, Greece. Since that time, he has worked tirelessly to aid and assist the process of all who have called upon his energies, under the guidance of Maitreya as World Teacher. Jesus has performed remarkably well and is himself moving into a new initiation now, having removed the martyr patterns from his outer self. None of these experiences have had any negative effect, although the task that Jesus has — of redirecting the world religions into a New World Religion and removing the colossal untruths — could seem insurmountable. But the only thing that is perhaps limiting is what has been termed the pulling effect of the thought-forms. From a karmic perspective, we would say that that is not a true way to view it, because they are beyond the real effect of karma, cause and effect. Embodying Love in its pure essence is not a binding energy, it is a *liberating* energy, given to mankind as a model they may wish to follow.

Two thousand years ago, from our monadic perspective, religions developed on a theme of truth, which became a mere thread of truth by the time St. Jerome (unwittingly) and the other founders of catholicism, principally "mad" Queen Theodora and Emperor Constantine, consciously changed its fabric from symbolic teachings to acts of manipulation for power and control, using the vehicles of martyrdom, guilt and fear. Thus, they used St. Peter as the foundation upon which to build these highly manipulative truths after crucifying him, and then made a god out of Jesus, after crucifying him as well — when all these gentle Souls ever agreed upon was to bring in Light at a very dark and troubled time on Earth — a simple galactic assignment that was never intended for demonstrations of adulation and worship! Thus Maitreya's introduction of the Sixth Initiation to Earth was a complete success; and that was his assignment as the Christ, *not* having an overshadowed disciple named Jesus made out to be "the only son of God"!

I used to have visits from Padre Pio, an entity who visited me at night, and also from Sai Baba at various times. The only way I can tell the difference between the two is by the smell of the perfume they each use as their calling card. Entities like Padre Pio were interesting. He had mastered much, including bilocation, and yet he invoked this suffering from stigmata, where he would bleed five pints of blood a day. Scientists wanted to explain this to mankind and, of course, they could not. This entity and St. Francis of Assisi (who was well known as an aspect of Kuthumi) and many others in the church throughout the millennia, who despite the church gained a certain degree of self-realization.

Many of them did ultimately run afoul of the church, because once you have attained a certain amount of light, the fifth chakra starts to open and you are then compelled to express; and in doing so, expressing one's experience which may not be in line with the dogma of the church, one tended to run afoul of that particular belief system. Then the system would feel that they had to shut down the nonconforming individual.

I turned on the TV last night and got Billy Graham on one channel and the Pope on three others. There is no less personification of form and structure, which may make a person feel better, but it can't possibly help them spiritually!

Well, both of these men are actually well-meaning in their intent; and we would wish to commend them on the spirit of what they are doing, though not the actual results.

You see, when you view religious or "spiritual" thought or processes from the New Age perspective, the tendency among many within the New Age community is to view it, saying, "Everything that is New Age is good, and everything that is Old Age is bad!" Highly judgmental, as much so as the born-again Christians tend to be. Now, in truth, the energies which will resonate with those of the New Age have absolutely nothing to do with the jargon one uses...whether one talks profusely about crystals and Atlantis, etc. That does not make a teaching any more applicable to the New Age than, perhaps, the preaching of hell-fire and brimstone.

It is not the jargon, and it is not necessarily the concepts per se; it is the *energy* behind it. It is the love and the intent behind the energy, and the amount of processing for Ascension that it provides, because the only purpose of being encapsulated in a dense physical body is to integrate enough Light to raise your consciousness to leave! Even some of the more hard-core fundamentalist approaches have within them a seed of resonance to the New Age; and many of the well-known esoteric teachings may not, especially those that channel the psychic/astral planes.

Where are they really coming from? Are they coming from a perspective of love and allowingness in their own basic essence, or not? This is where discernment comes in, because when you view a situation such as a highly zealous Fundamentalist group — be it Christian, Moslem or whomever — you find a tremendous intolerance for others and a tremendous reliance on fear as a motivator. Intolerance, fear, and a highly judgmental stance tend to be what we would consider to be hallmarks of an Old Age perspective. Yet within some of those teachings one can find a large amount of positive energy coming through. Some healings, albeit psychic, are done through Fundamentalist faith healers; and some healings and other types of love are expressed through many of the other more rigid forms of religion. Look to see the grain of truth and the grain of Light within each area that you look at. We would encourage the readers of these books to adopt a discerning but allowing stance towards *all* teachings.

It is simply a matter of stepping back a bit, out of one's old habit patterns, and stepping into a more allowing and natural stance of being more of an observer. The observer aspect is one which tends to be a little misunderstood. By that we do not mean, step out of life and watch it; we mean, maintain your own self-awareness, to the point where you know what is going on around you, and you have that inner strength whereby you can view any situation, be it a teaching, a political situation, etc. — and you can tune in to it and see how much of it resonates within your own heart.

That is something that we would encourage everyone to be taught as a habit, rather than blindly following just another belief system. So, even though what we are expounding in these books might be considered to be totally effective, it will not be embraced on the level of "this is the Truth"; it will be on the level of "here are truths, and please accept that which resonates with you." It's to put an end to, shall we say, the dogmatic approach which tended to be propounded by an aspect of Ourself, Simon Peter among others back in those days, and by so many well-meaning beings today.

A few of you have elected to do this street fighting. It does not make it right or wrong, it is just the way you perceive your growth. And it is much better that you focus in on this, because there is still anger within entities like Brian. You have made a tremendous amount of progress, Brian, with that portion of yourself that typifies the energy of being a victim and martyr. Both of these are very broad expressions for a great number of personality aspects; however, as a broad brush approach, the victimhood which Peter (and Jesus) very much felt, as well as martyrdom, is energy that you were still carrying to a great degree, even up to a few years ago. Yet you have worked through most of it at this point; as a result of that, the anger and the resentment are falling away.

The victim: Whenever one perceives oneself to be a victim, there are many things being said loud and clear at that time. The first is, "I do not create my own reality." The second is, "Because I do not create my own reality, I have to watch out because the world is a dangerous place." Third, when one assumes that the world is a dangerous place, then one has to create shields around oneself and swords to counterattack with to "defend myself against those who are trying to make me a victim." Thus the armor gets built up, the arms race begins to escalate on an internal level, and then of course manifests on the outer.

We have seen a very bloody history of mankind, particularly in the last 2000 years. Much of that history has been tied to religious thought, religious beliefs, and religious imposition of their belief systems on others. One witnesses the same resurgence of religious zeal in every faction. Much of it emerges from class warfare and economics, but at the very heart of it, the point of division is the difference in religious beliefs.

One sees it among the Tamil rebels in Sri Lanka, among the Sikhs, Moslems and Hindus in India, among the various sects of Moslems in Iran, Iraq and the so-called Holy Land, and of course, among the Christians — the Catholics and Protestants, as typified in Ireland (however, that several-hundred-year-long battle has been waging all over the world, wherever Catholics and Protestants happened to be together). Now one finds it even among the various sects of the Protestants, where you have the New Fundamentalists — the "New Old" coming up. And then there is the "Old New" arising with the old religions in new clothes, *in the guise of the New Age* but still carrying those same swords and armor, the same "my guru is better than yours, and my path is better than yours" or "you can go ahead and do that process if you like, but if you do, it will take you an extra five lifetimes; whereas *my* way is much better, much faster."

Buddhism, in its various manifestations, from the classical to the Tibetan — which is seen by many as being very much off the wall compared to the original — and then of course, the Zen and various other sects as well. The emphasis has been on a very strict esoteric tradition, and one sees the outer trappings of the Tibetan Buddhism, with its seeming emphasis on gods and devils and all of the trappings, which again appeals to the superstitious minds of rather primitive people. However, within that is a kernel of a tremendous teaching. What the Tibetans did in their approach to Buddhism was to take the foundation that they had — which was more the Hindu or Vedic tradition — and then the Buddha came along and essentially colored that with a different perspective. So they amalgamated the teachings.

The Buddhist tradition and its teaching in its original form, more typified by the Mahayana teachings of Buddha, derived its basis from the Sanskrit Vedic tradition, which is a very old tradition. It is as ancient as mankind, in its ultimate sense. There has been a link with that tradition since mankind originated on this planet. However, when one views the writings and the predictions, in actual fact it is the traditional way of passing down the teaching in an oral form. Whenever there is an oral tradition, there is a tendency for it to dissipate somewhat, so throughout the ages there have always been new teachers, new masters. New avatars come in and infuse new Light and new understanding. The Buddha was one of the galactic Avatars to come to this planet, and as his perspective blended with the Vedic tradition, it evolved into the spinoff, or variation known as Tibetan Buddhism.

I feel that we are finally integrating that aspect known as Peter.

Well, that depends from which perspective you view it. From the perspective of being within sequential time, you could view that as a past life. But from the perspective of being fully integrated and therefore stepping beyond the constrictions and the structure of consecutive time, then all of those experiences are happening now. From the Soul's viewpoint, all of the lifetimes that the soul manifests as extensions of its own Self are occurring simultaneously. The Soul has created a number of personality aspects, and the one personality aspect that you reference as Brian at this time has had somewhere around 15,000 lifetimes within various universal dimensions — which is very few compared to other beings, who might experience 50,000 lives on various universal levels.

The ensouling spark of consciousness that we now refer to as Brian, and which you previously referred to as Peter, Zoroaster, Akhnaton, and now your completion on all universal levels as the personality for Mahatma, the Cosmic Avatar of Synthesis, did not necessarily choose to experience those lifetimes one by one, chronologically. In order to fully experience each of these lifetimes, however, the ensouling consciousness had to dive into that particular reality; it had to immerse itself within the belief structure of that entire reality — including, of course, consecutive time.

So, one pops into a lifetime and goes through it from point A, birth, to point B, death. Then the personality is liberated to rejoin the Soul. The Soul, together with the personality aspect, reviews the life just experienced..."Well, what do you feel you learned here?"...and other teachers may come in to help assess as well. The personality aspect gives its evaluation of what it learned and says, "I could do with a little more balance in this direction." Thus the teachers and the Souls work together to create a situation whereby another lifetime is chosen to work on that balancing.

Not only do all lifetimes occur simultaneously, but each one affects the others. Stepping back from the scene, one can see all 1500 or 2000 lifetimes on this planet, and yet having to experience them sequentially, which is going to be the one in which the Soul can integrate?

From the point of view of the Self, it experiences all of the personality aspects; it is going through all of those 2000 lifetimes on Earth alone, and those nearing completion with the physical universal experience can easily project this to 20 other dimensions and other universes which at times have inappropriately been referred to as "other sources."

This is the *average* number of lives, according to Djwhal Khul, that Human, God-man experiences. It is natural for the personality aspect to view things in sequential time, which is a reality from within that particular framework. In this framework one has very little impetus other than to make the basic assumption, "All of reality is sequentially oriented, and if I lived at the time of Jesus, 2000 years ago, then I must have had so many lifetimes between then and now." In actual fact, it could be that from outside of the personal self, the Simon Peter experience was a long, long time before...or it may be your last life...or maybe your next one. Not likely, because the culmination process is coming to a positive fruition here, in this life.

The difficulty comes, as we just referenced, with people having such a strong tie to sequential time through their many experiences in it, and becoming unable to make the leap beyond the three dimensions to see that time itself is simply another dimension and has as much or as little reality as the solidity of this wall. The wall, the chair that you are sitting on, the body that you live in, are all made up of a lot more space than matter. When you consider the vast amount of space between the particles of the atom, it is very much like the vast amount of space between the sun and its parts, the galaxies and their parts; its solidity is highly illusory. When the vibration of objects is the same as yours and an object hits the table or the desk, you feel the solidity. If the vibrational frequency of the table were different from that of your body, then quite likely your hand would pass through it.

Beings such as yourself, in your higher aspects, who are the Creators, created mankind and this physical plane but could not experience it. In a sense, they would pass right through it; they could not hold anything. It would be like a ghost walking through a wall. In order to have that experience, they had to immerse themselves in the matter.

Would the Akashic Records be helpful in the integration of one's physical lives?

The Akashic Records are an imprint, much like the etheric structure of your own system contains an imprint of every thought, feeling, word, and experience that you have had. It is all contained there, and it ultimately gets stepped down even into the cellular DNA level. There is a record of everything that you have ever done, and it is a holographic record. The Akashic Record is the same process, the same situation, really, on a planetary consciousness level; it is a matter of the thoughtform that is created from that experience. To a certain extent, when beings tune into the Akashic Records, they get a rather edited version, because within that entire vast scope — we could liken it to a microchip — all of the superfluous data is there as well. It contains *all* the impressions from a particular day from every thought that was thought, every feeling that was felt...everything is recorded there.

There is a tremendous amount of sifting and sorting out when going through that process. Because their filters are different, the experience of the Akashic Records varies from person to person as they attune to it. Each person picks up different strata of that vast bulk of information, and even the coding and labeling tend to be rather different.

The Akashic Record is a level of knowledge that can be picked up on any universal level; of course, there is no need for the Akashic Record on the spiritual/monadic levels. This is the reason that even your Logos do not know where *The Rider on the White Horse, Mahatma,* comes from...that is recorded in the Akashic Records, or holograms, only after the Cosmic Avatar has arrived into the universal/physical density.

"The ring passeth not" is an eternal Law. However, when approved by this Council of Twelve, Metatron can release appropriate information about these Beings, to be of great assistance. This is the reason that Vywamus, who is working fifth-dimensionally, was allowed information about Creation and the Creator levels, so he could bring through information about *Mahatma* and Brian's evolution, and the formation of our Source, which had never come through at any other period on Earth. It was felt by the Creator level that the hastening of this Cosmic Day required greater energy formating and information.

Have we any areas within countries or within continents that are well ensconced in the heart chakra?

There are small pockets — cities and small communities in which the focus, either intentionally or not, is on that higher chakra level. There are communities in various parts of the world that embody within their own small perimeters the values of the heart chakra, yet still functioning within the perimeters of the country they are in, whatever level that may be (primarily the third chakra moving into the fourth) on a country level. However, those communities can establish very powerful energies within their own centers. They are like bonfires in the middle of a huge snowy forest, but these pockets are showing mankind the next step, what can be generated by like minds interrelating within whatever system they are working.

They are a demonstration, then a process of giving to the world an example to move toward, to invoke. That is a very necessary element of the invocation process, having a *vision* of what you are invoking. If you do not have that vision, then how do you know what you want?

In the same way, you have to have a sense of what it means to invoke the Christ Consciousness on Earth. If, for the bulk of humanity in the Christian world, it means having the man Jesus come back and heal a few lepers, then it certainly wouldn't have much power to it, on a mass level. The invocation needs a resonance to the higher principles of "spirituality," as found in the Kingdom of Heaven within; and that experience is essentially found within the heart, with its clarity of consciousness. The purer the invocation, the more rapidly it will bear fruit.

So we can see from this brief overview that planet Earth has a number of different levels of growth and expression going on simultaneously. And yet, the initiatory process of **Integration** is one of the stimulation of the heart chakra and the love principle, that principle of openness, compassion, of giving and receiving the free flow of All That Is.

This is the process of the Third Initiation that certain individuals are going through, that countries will go through, that the Earth has gone through on every level. And on every level it manifests slightly differently.

Would you please explain why religions and various sundry followers have occasion to call the female who aborts a fetus a murderer? Surely that negative energy — both within an individual or on a mass consciousness level — is one of the last things we need when we're trying to raise the vibration of this planet to bring her and mankind into a higher vibrational frequency for admission into adulthood and the fourth dimension. We have these darker religious focuses — the same as in the destruction of Atlantis — emotionally charging their collective energies for false ends, with the presumptuous bravado of saving the world and all of mankind from the devil. It seems that these beings, rather than lessening the darkness with their utterances, create and bring forth structure and beliefs that neither Jesus nor the loving Christ could ever be part of, and most certainly not an All-Loving, nonjudgmental GOD!

First of all, we don't believe that these beings are as destructive as the beings that you reference, those responsible for the destruction of Atlantis. We believe that these beings, whose reactions are often misguided, will come around to understand a greater wholeness of Soul and Creation. From our loving perspective we find no need to fault these beings, who have an emotional and materialistic, and probably a confusing and restricted view of Creation. As the New Age Rays ignite the new levels of consciousness, the fog will lift. And the Master Jesus — the transformer of the Sixth Ray on this planet — is gradually releasing and abandoning the structures of the past and the symbolic cross, plus the old religions, to the Seventh Ray in the great transformational process into the New Age.

Not just the Christian Church, but most of mankind can give only lip service to the Soul level. From our perspective, few on your planet understand what the function of the Soul is; and the Holy Bible — which is referenced as the source of all truth — other than vague symbolic utterances that are clouded in fog, does not give any meaningful assistance.

We believe that those beings who react so vehemently to the abortion of the fetus are very sincere, albeit misinformed, about the process of form — the physical fetus — and about the "spiritual" consciousness of the child at birth — the Soul. Therein lies the misunderstanding.

Those who are sincere in viewing abortion as taking a physical life and destroying it along with all of the human potential within that being, should ask self, "What is death?" and "What is a soul?" We're not going to give this issue a lot of energy, because one could write a very short book explaining how a relative nondeath, *without a soul,* could possibly constitute murder of a fetus or compare that to the murder of a child. One must ask, in all fairness, "Where is the soul at this time?" and "Where is the consciousness behind the form?" Mankind does not understand that the Soul must have been in agreement, or this supposed traumatic event would not have taken place. We remind you again that there is no death.

Let us give you an example that generally does not please the highly charged emotional body. During the Kennedy administration, a human body was produced in test tubes, without female embodiment, and was raised in an atmosphere of nitrogen for space missions. This being had some years of age on him when President Kennedy and others faced a moral crisis: did this being have a Soul?

The answer, in simplistic terms, is "possibly," *if* a Soul wished to experience that level of consciousness. Because this being was not a fetus, it would become a conscious being if a Soul entered that body. Without a soul, that test-tube fetus was no different from the fetus in the womb — the difference is all too readily tied to the emotional body. For example: kill a shark, but don't murder a baby seal!

The embryo in a mother's womb, during any pregnancy oF Homo sapiens, has no "spiritual" consciousness until the Soul enters the etheric body. On planet Earth there are no new Souls to experience that first birth in physical manifestation; thus the Soul would not enter the Soul Star (etheric body) of the fetus until just prior to delivery or shortly after.

With so many New Age babies on planet Earth whose previous lives were often on the Pleiades and who are very developed souls, the actual touching in of the Soul may not happen for weeks after a birth.

At the other end of the spectrum, many of your aboriginal peoples — who are generally less evolved — would have the Soul touch into the etheric structure of the fetus, in a full-term pregnancy, after 8 1/2 months.

We leave the decision regarding abortion totally with the Soul and its personality, the mother, for that is *their* evolution. Mankind need to rise above the level of condemning what they don't comprehend, no matter how well-meaning. Humankind truly lives in a glass house, and should be the last to judge anything. This is particularly applicable to the religious leaders, who may wish to live more "spiritually" and less cocooned in language and verbiage that, in relation to New Age energy, no longer has any positive input. It's simply pie in the sky, with no teaching or processing to let you taste the pie. Certainly, these teachings could seldom create a Soul Merge or Third Initiation. Once again, mankind gives lip service to propagate fear, because that's what has been created on a mass consciousness level.

This is not dissimilar to our analogy of people on Earth worshipping the form — a picture of a Master or a Teacher — never believing that one could be spiritually greater than that Master, or ever wondering, "What is the consciousness behind the picture, and where is it coming from?"

You have a wonderful example of an Earth expression, "Which came first, the chicken or the egg?" Did the personality create the Soul? Or did the Soul create the personality? Unfortunately, most of humankind view the garment that they wear, the physical body, as being in charge of their destiny. This, of course, cannot be so; but for humanity, who are so lost in their outer reality, the illusion becomes their truth!

Unfortunately, the emotional and mental bodies dictate the terms of their reality, which moves mankind away from their only true reality, the inner Self, through their I AM Presence. Your beliefs on Earth that God is vengeful and judgmental and in some way separate from Self may be your most persistent false belief. Indeed, you have many false beliefs, and that will also have to change. Of course, what the individual does with their free will is entirely up to the collective self.

Now, we've gone into great depth throughout these books to teach mankind the method of processing the many levels of consciousness associated with you as God, as All That Is. Thus if you believe — and many must, or they would not affix needless trauma and guilt on millions of human beings by telling them that they are murderers — that the multiplicity of self, reflected as aspects of the Soul level, does not exist and has 3 to 24 aspects being integrated simultaneously throughout all universal levels of consciousness, and that the Soul level has nothing better to do than place its energy in the embryo during gestation, then you are correct in your beliefs, which are, from our perspective, further false beliefs. For there is no such thing as death, losing your Soul, hell-fire and damnation, the devil, victims, and heaven on Earth (the only heavens that mankind have ever been conscious of are the astral heavens); nor is "as above, so below" applicable, at least until one creates the spiritual body. Ultimately, *there is no separation between yourself as a Son of God, and yourself as God.*

In this great Isness in which all of humankind and Creation live without any judgment whatsoever from the heart of Source, the All That Is, the I AM Presence; if the greatness that you are is nonjudgmental, then why so flagrantly abuse these great truths?

13

Mastery

We hesitate to use the word "mastery" because it has been rather misunderstood on Earth as the ultimate achievement within your complete I AM Presence. Mastery is a primary point of integration, but an immense step for humankind. For the same reason, we hesitate to use the word "God"; because on this planet, Sanat Kumara has been forever referred to as "Lord of the World" — certainly in all of your religious scriptures. Thus an aspect of Sanat Kumara's Higher Self individualized as a personality Jesus, and out of this came the Father, the Son and the Holy Ghost. "The Father and I are One" which has all been so unfortunately misaligned with the God Source, the All That Is, the I Am Presence. This is not a judgment, but simply to indicate where your Human Hierarchy's evolution was at this time and place when your various belief systems anchored in Earth so *very* long ago!

Only unto the Source of All That Is does the name God belong, with all of the glory of Its Divinity. He who knows only his Source and becomes this wondrous I AM, refusing all else, is wise indeed, for he knows unending joy and is master wherever he moves within his level of "ring passeth not." This is the key for the aspirant who wishes to attain Mastery and beyond.

In this New Age, the discipline for the student will be in focusing and maintaining his attention primarily on the three higher chakras of his physical body. The heart/throat, the spiritual eye, and the crown chakras are the areas for conscious consideration and attention, as these are the energy centers which will assist the individual in his growth. Only by transcending the lower chakras can one rise out of misery and limitation.

The crown chakra is the highest focus within the human body, and it is at this point that the silver cord of liquid white Light from the Creator enters with the Five Higher Rays. When the mind is focused steadfastly upon this, the door of the Soul opens and the pure White Light is able to enter the physical body. It encircles the waist, just below the solar plexus, thereby cutting off forever the destructive activities of the animal nature in man. This allows the Soul levels to come forth into their complete divine activity, united once more with the perfection of their Source, able then to eternally master all of human creation, including the discords of the Earth.

The sincere student should meditate often upon the White Light connecting with the chakras in his head, for this will illuminate, teach, and elevate the outer mind. This is the Light of the God Within. Invite it and feel it filling your entire consciousness, body, and world. This is "the Light that lighteth every man that cometh into the world," and there exists no human being who does not carry some of this Divine Light within him. (Refer to "Metatron's Evolutionary Light Chart," p. 356.)

Many individuals upon Earth are now rapidly awakening and finding greater expression, as they are feeling the mighty surge of Light pouring out through them. If these beings will unflinchingly hold their attention upon the God Self Within and accept and visualize the full activity of Its Divine Radiance, they will surround themselves with the harmony of the Light and thereby cut off the discordant outer world.

As we have already discussed, the monitoring and control of the feeling side of physical life is of utmost importance to you, the aspirant. Since thoughts can never become things until they are clothed in feeling, we cannot emphasize strongly enough the guarding of the emotional level and the quality of the thoughts projected into the atomic substance.

The individual who cannot or will not control his thoughts and feelings leaves himself in an extremely vulnerable position, with every door of his consciousness wide open to the disintegrating activities of the thoughts and feelings of other personalities. It is through the lack of control of the emotions of mass consciousness that the destructive forces on this planet are not only created, but are able to influence the affairs of individuals and nations.

Destructive thoughts by themselves cannot express as actions, events, or become physical things unless they pass through the world of feeling, wherein they can unite with the physical atom and become manifest. So when the emotional level becomes irritated in any way, the finer substance in the atomic structure of the mind is shocked, disturbed and disarranged in exactly the same way that the human nervous system is shocked by a sudden loud noise, for example.

The Light is God's way of creating and maintaining peace, order and perfection throughout His Creation. Every one of humanity has the opportunity to enjoy all of these Divine qualities when his desire is intense enough, and each one will be given all the time he needs to attain Mastery. However, it is the intensity of the desire which will allow a new order of conditions in which to provide the time for those who earnestly wish to move forward.

No one is an exception to this law, for when the desire to do anything constructive becomes intense enough, the God power releases the energy necessary to create and express what is desired. Every being has the same privilege of contact with the all-powerful Presence of God, which is the only power that ever has and ever will raise the personal self above the dark levels of discord and limitation.

Contrary to the belief of many, conscious mastery is not to be found in trance or hypnotic practices — these are very destructive and dangerous to the growth of the Soul. The activity on Earth that so many New-Age followers fall prey to — the use of consciousness-altering drugs such as "ecstasy," or any other hallucinogenic drug — cannot assist one with their true inner connection, their I AM, *Mahatma*, and have no positive input in becoming Light.

The other area that should be mentioned in the psychic/astral studies under the guise of New Age, is shamanism. This deals with only the lower three chakras and psychic levels, and often entails the use of drugs. These practices contain no Divine Light whatsoever, regardless of evidence to the contrary. Voodoo and many other categories of your psychic/lower astral levels convey only darkness and should be avoided.

Please understand thoroughly that the conscious control, mastery and use of the energies on the Earth, should at all times be directed by your God Self, your inner Self, with all outer faculties of both mind and body in harmony and cooperation with that inner guidance.

Raising the consciousness simply involves an increase in the rate of vibration of the atomic structure of both the mind and the physical body. Radiation is the important means by which the activity of the Light increases the vibratory rate to the desired level. In the higher rate, one uses the faculties of sight and hearing exactly as they did on the dense physical plane but in the new octave, or frequency, that they have expanded into.

This applies to all of the physical senses, and is a process as normal and natural as tuning a radio to any desired wavelength. Sight, hearing, and radio wavelengths are actually parts of the same activity. Sound contains color and color contains sound; so if human beings could become still enough in their ordinary earthly experiences, they could hear color and see sound.

Within certain zones or octaves, vibration registers upon the nerves of the physical eyes or ears, resulting in what we call sight or hearing. Human senses are able to interpret the vibrations of a certain octave or frequency. However, through the increased radiation level of the Ascended Master, the atomic structure of the brain is able to vibrate more rapidly, allowing the senses to expand into the octave above that of the human level. This action can be expanded into higher octaves by the command of the inner or God Self of the individual and many people have had such experiences involuntarily — unconsciously.

One source of radiation on your Earth, of which humanity is generally not aware, is the metal that you call gold. Gold has been placed upon your planet for a variety of reasons, two of its most trivial and unimportant uses being for ornamentation and as a means of exchange. The higher purpose and activity of gold within and upon the Earth is the release of the inherent quality of its energy to purify, vitalize, and balance the atomic structure of dense physicality.

The scientific community will one day discover that the properties of gold bring the same effect to the Earth that radiators produce in your homes. It is one of the most important ways in which solar energy is supplied to the interior of the Earth and a balance of activity maintained. As a conveyor of this energy, gold acts as a transformer to pass the sun's life force into the physical substance of your world as well as to the life evolving upon it. Gold is sometimes called a precipitating sun-ray because it is actually the radiant, electronic energy of the sun, acting in a lower octave. Its energy is of an extremely high vibratory rate in dense physicality, so it can only act upon the finer expressions through absorption.

In every Golden Age, this metal comes into plentiful supply and is commonly used by the people, enabling them to attain a much higher spiritual state. The gold is never hoarded, but is widely distributed to the population who, in absorbing its purifying energy, are raised into greater relative perfection. This is the correct use of gold, and the individual who consciously understands and obeys this law may draw any amount of it to himself.

In one of the two Golden Ages which have taken place on this planet, civilization did achieve the state of relative perfection in people's physical lives. Their daily experience was like that of a host of Ascended Masters, which is the condition in which God's children were meant to live. This transcendent, beautiful and perfect experience is the natural state, and anything less is subnatural. There exists no supernatural condition in the universal levels; the transcendent, magnificent expressions of Love and Light are the *natural* conditions in which God created and expected His Hu-man/God-man children to manifest, obeying his Law of Love.

That Golden Age of which we speak is much older than you can imagine — older than many believe the Earth to be. In that period, humanity lived in the transcended state, similar to the Ascended Masters. The condition of misery and limitation that has followed since that time came about because mankind chose to look away from its Source and the Law of Love by which to live. When the children of God look away from love, they deliberately and consciously choose the state of chaos; and whosoever seeks to exist without love simply cannot survive for long anywhere in Creation. Such efforts can bring only failure, misery, and dissolution.

The Law of Love is eternal, irrevocable, and magnificent; it is the Law of the Mighty One from which all else proceeds. Creation exists so that the Source may have an expression in which to pour out Its infinite Love and so express in action. The vastness and brilliance of this mandate of eternity cannot be described in physical words.

It is Love that will connect you with the higher, transcendent realms of life where Creation goes on continually in joy, in freedom, and in perfection. These realms are created of substance that is charged with Love, and they are more real than anything you can imagine in your physical/universal levels. Because they are based upon Love, the perfection of the higher realms is forever maintained and forever expanding in joy.

In the ignorance of the human senses, appetites, and desires of the outer self, humanity perpetuates its condition of misery, necessitating the cycle of physical incarnation over and over again. These human appetites are an accumulation of energy to which the personality gives certain qualities through his thoughts and feelings. This misqualified energy gathers momentum through human expression and becomes what is known as a habit. Habit, therefore, is simply energy that is given a specific quality and focused for a time on one objective.

The sensual appetites of previous lives become the driving forces and habits of the following lives, keeping humankind as slaves bound to the wheels of rebirth, discord and need. Mankind's misconceptions will compel them to repeat the lifetimes of problems and limitation until they are ready to learn and obey the one law of life — Love. The compelling activity of human experience will continue until the individual's outer self asks the reason for its misery and comes to understand that its release from suffering can only come from obedience to the Law of Love. Obedience begins in the individual with feelings of calm, peace, and kindness in the heart center, which are then expressed in all contact with the outer world.

Love is not an activity of the mind, but is the pure, luminous essence which creates the mind. This essence of the Transformational Fire eternally pours itself into substance as relative perfection in action and form. *Love is perfection manifest;* and it can only express itself unconditionally. As the heartbeat of the Creator, Love asks nothing for itself, because it is eternally self-creating. It is a constant outpouring of itself, concerned only with expressing the Plan of Perfection. Love does not focus upon what has been created in the past, but receives its joy in the continual expression of itself in the Eternal Now.

Because Love is the manifestation of perfection, it is incapable of perceiving anything but Love. It alone is the basis of harmony, and is the intended expression of all life energy. In the human experience, Love grows into a desire to give; to give all of one's peace and harmony unto the rest of Creation, as All That Is, through All That Is, your I AM Presence, *Mahatma.*

The God Principle of life, the Father, has given to you, the Co-Creator level, the powerful tool of thought to be consciously used and directed according to your free will. Thought creates what we call vibration; and through vibration one can qualify the ever-flowing energy of Creation with whatever one wishes to manifest in the world. Thought is the all-powerful, omnipresent intelligent energy which flows through your nervous system, the eternal life and vitality flowing through your veins. This Divine Intelligence, which uses everything in the cosmos constructively, comes only from within the God Principle.

All of the thoughts and feelings that reach the individual through the physical senses should be screened and tested, through the Light of one's own God-flame, as the standard of perfection. And one can only qualify one's thoughts and feelings with perfection by going to the Source of perfection, for that quality and activity are found only within the God-flame of Transformational Fire.

The focus and meditation upon, and the communion with, the Divine Light of God within himself will enable the individual to maintain perfect balance between his God Self and his outer, or personal, self. This pure life essence will also sustain youth and beauty in the etheric body. This is the great power which maintains the connection between the outer self and its Divine Source, the God Self.

The God Self and the personal self are, of course, one — except when the outer activity of the mind, the sense consciousness, *accepts* imperfection, disharmony, and incompleteness, or believes itself to be apart from the all-pervading One Presence of life. If the physical mind thinks itself to be separate from God, then that condition is automatically delivered to it, for what the sense consciousness thinks into its world, the world returns to it.

The moment a person thinks himself to be separate from God, he is making the assumption that his life, intelligence, and power has a beginning and an end! When one allows an idea of separation from God or of imperfection to enter his mind, then the corresponding condition begins to express itself in his physical body and world. This then causes the individual to *feel* separate from his Source.

We tell you absolute truth when we say that there is only one Source of all good — God. If you are willing to consciously recognize, accept and maintain this truth with the acknowledgment of the outer mind, this will enable you to express perfect freedom and dominion over all things human, always connected to your God Self within, not a God somewhere else. Remembering and focusing on your God Self two or three times a day will not accomplish this for you — you must recognize the divinity of you and your Creator *all day long*, no matter what the outer self is doing.

The recognition, conscious direction, and constructive use of the God Force *maintained at all times* will lead you to that goal of relative perfection, mastery and dominion over all earthly expressions, including the conscious control of all natural forces. Adherence to these simple instructions will enable you to completely erase all false beliefs; but as always, the speed with which you accomplish this depends upon how deeply, how continuously and persistently you connect with and *feel* your God Self.

In order to achieve and maintain your Divine connection, a stilling and harmonizing of the emotions is needed, no matter what environment you find yourself in; however, this does not mean a repression of discordant feelings. Such control is not easily achieved in the Western world, since the temperament of most people tends to be emotional, sensitive, and impulsive. Tremendous power is held in these characteristics, therefore they must be controlled, held in reserve, and released only through conscious direction for constructive purposes. Until this waste of energy is checked and controlled, the aspirant cannot make permanent progress.

When a person sincerely uses affirmation, he is actually bringing about a full acceptance of the truth of whatever he is affirming. Affirmation is simply a tool used to focus the outer mind so deeply upon the truth that you are able to accept it fully in your feelings. Feeling is the actual God energy released, which manifests the truth that has been affirmed.

The continued use of affirmation will bring a person to the point where he attains such a deep realization of the truth in anything he affirms that he becomes no longer conscious of it being an affirmation. He uses an affirmation, mantra or prayer because he desires something made manifest; and *right desire* is the most powerful force in bringing about manifestation. By the use of affirmation, the individual raises his outer self into the full acceptance of its truth and generates the feeling through which it becomes manifest. Manifestation comes about through deep concentration and acceptance, which cause the spoken word to stimulate instantaneous activity. (Refer to the Realizations on pp. 417-418.)

In a past Golden Age, humanity manifested relative perfection and lived in what historians call the Garden of Eden, Eden, or E-Don, meaning "divine wisdom." However, the humans allowed their conscious attention — the outer activity of their minds — to become distracted by the world of the physical senses; thus the Divine Wisdom, the all-knowing activity of consciousness, became clouded and covered. As their connection to God and His Divine Cosmic Plan became faded and lost, so did humanity's perfected condition and their conscious control over form.

As mankind became sense-conscious instead of God-conscious, they manifested that upon which their attention was directed. In deliberately and consciously turning away from the perfection and dominion that the Creator had bestowed upon them, they created their experiences of lack, of limitation, and discord of every kind. Mankind identified with a part instead of the whole, and naturally, imperfection was the result.

All of humanity's limitation is the direct result of humanity's misuse of the God-given attribute of free will. They unconsciously compel themselves to live within their own creations until their outer minds become ready and willing to *consciously* look back at their beginning — God, the Great Source of All That Is. When man can do this, when he chooses to look once more at the Great Cosmic Blueprint of Himself, he will remember that which he once was and can become again — the I AM Presence, *Mahatma*.

Many civilizations have come and gone, each falling prey to the illusion of the outer world. The ancient continent of Mu is but one example of a civilization which grew to great heights over several thousands of years and then succumbed to a cataclysm that tore the surface of the continent until it collapsed within itself and sank beneath what is now the Pacific Ocean.

In January 1992, we — as the personality level, Brian — went to Mazatlan, Mexico, and spent one complete night witnessing with great clarity the destruction and subsequent resurrection of Mu off the coast of Mazatlan. The lands were shown as vivid red earth, much like Sedona, Arizona. This profound experience conveyed one of constant change for all of Creation — not static perfection — and conveyed that Sanat Kumara, in order to balance his harmonies, would allow Mu, Atlantis, and sections of Lemuria to resurrect, responding to simple cause and effect (not as in good and evil).

Following the demise of Mu, the continent of Atlantis grew in wisdom, beauty and power, filling in the space between Central America and Europe with what is now known as the Atlantic Ocean. The Atlanteans achieved many great things, but the misuse of the God energy overwhelmed them. As their world was thrown more and more out of balance, the destruction of the land and civilization through cataclysmic action was reexperienced.

A small remnant of Atlantis was left for a time, an island in the middle of the ocean, cut off from close contact with the rest of the civilized world. The east and west portions of the continent had sunk, leaving only an island called Poseidonis. This area had been the heart of the then-known civilized world, and its inhabitants took steps to protect and preserve its most important activities. Their central focus became the carrying forth of the knowledge and work of Atlantis.

The population of Poseidonis made great achievements on both the spiritual and material levels. Because of their dedication, the Planetary Hierarchy revealed to them knowledge that would greatly advance every phase of their human activity. They were given the technology to create aircraft, for instance, much more sophisticated than those you are using today.

A large number of these people were conscious of the God power within the individual, but as before, the human side of their nature and the outer activities claimed their attention. The selfishness and misuse of the transcendent energy and wisdom rose to a greater height than ever before. The Hierarchy tried to warn this civilization that they were building another destructive momentum and that a third cataclysm was impending, but only a few — ones who truly served the Light — would listen. These dedicated few constructed buildings, using an indestructible material in which they sealed and preserved valuable knowledge and records of the time, so as not to be lost forever to mankind. These have been guarded over the centuries, to be used at a future time.

Unlike the lost civilizations of Mu and Lemuria, Atlantis has not been forgotten during its rest beneath the Atlantic Ocean, undergoing its process of purification. Its existence has been recorded in many ways, and even though twelve thousand years have elapsed since its destruction, humanity still speaks of Atlantis. You have all heard the legends, and many of you have recalled former lives spent there. Recently, of course, oceanographers have finally discovered physical evidence.

Great Light has come out of the land of Egypt in the past, and great Light will come again; however, in the meantime Egypt has experienced her own rise and fall. The ancient Egyptians rose to their greatest height through the right use of knowledge and power, which always demand intellectual obedience and humility to the God Self Within, and absolute, unconditional control of the lower human nature. The Souls embodied in Egypt during its decline were generally more developed than those incarnating in the civilizations of the Gobi and Sahara deserts, so their misuse of knowledge and power was a conscious choice. A great number of Egyptians placed priority upon their intellectual accomplishments, giving no thought to the control of the lower self;

either of these two qualities will, of course, result in certain failure. The Romans were also unable to resist the temptation to misuse their power, and thus met with the same fate.

The arrival of Jesus and the Christ, Maitreya, was a twofold initiation for the inhabitants of Earth and a cosmic command to use the power of Divine, Unconditional Love in all of their future activities. The outpouring of his love to the Earth and humanity in their darkest cycle became the birth of the Christ Child in the individual. He called forth the Divine Cosmic Blueprint once again and revealed to humanity the decree for the coming age — complete dominion over physical realms through the full expression of the Christ within every human being.

The Great World War, which lasted from 1914 to 1945, required assistance from the Ascended Masters in order to dissolve the cause and the greater part of the accumulated momentum of humanity's conflict. The termination of this civilization was prevented when the Masters — these perfected humans — consciously stepped down the God energy to focus and direct enormous rays of Light to the Earth and mankind. The transformational energy received is too tremendous to describe in finite terms, nor can humankind yet have any comprehension of the love, aid, and service given to them by their elder brothers and their Source. Your discarnate teachers have also been aware for thousands of years that in the coming Golden Age, which is but dimly touching your horizon, when the Earth experiences the cause and effect created by mass consciousness, many changes will occur on her surface; as one example, a great portion of the land mass of North America will stand for a very long time, and a significant portion will not.

If mankind could only realize what tremendous possibilities await them...waiting for man to turn away from the religions, creeds, cults, dogmas, "isms," and all else that limits and binds them. If they could turn their attention to the God Presence within their own hearts, they would connect with the power, the freedom, and the Light that await them, dependent only upon their recognition and use of the great loving Presence that breathes through them at every moment. If they could only realize that their physical bodies are the temples of the Living God, they could know what it means to love that wonderful part of Self and could feel the Almighty Presence flowing through it. Humankind could then know and feel the reality of the God Presence as certainly as they know other people and things.

Humanity's perspective, that whatever cannot be perceived by the physical senses is merely illusion, is the absolute opposite of the perspective of your inner I AM Presence, *Mahatma,* which does not and cannot recognize mankind's creation of material "things" as being anything *but* illusory. Interesting, isn't it? But this is the dilemma of humanity being lost in the outer self!

Through the ages, those among humanity who have achieved the greater accomplishments in life have expressed the idea that "the Light is supreme, the Light is everywhere, and in the Light exist all things." As far back as human art has been recorded the great and wise ones of every age have been portrayed in a radiant, emanating halo of Light. This Light is real — just as real as electric light is to humanity.

There is much truth in the expression, "Many are called but few are chosen." All are constantly being called, but few are awake enough to realize the ecstasy and perfection within the God Self, so readily available through Mastery, and to hear the voice in the Light, forever calling everyone back into "the Father's house," your Soul levels. Every human being is free at any moment to "arise and go unto the Father," his God Self, if he will but turn his back on the outer world of the human senses and fix his attention upon the only Source within Creation from which peace, happiness, abundance and perfection can come.

The life in every individual is God, and only by the Self-conscious effort to understand life and to express the fullness of good through oneself, can one transcend and eliminate the discords of the outer experience. Life, the individual and the law are one, and so it is unto eternity. This law is immutable and whatever humankind think to the contrary can only cause them to become further lost in matter, creating their things as an outer expression that can only be termed illusion from a Source perspective.

The Ascended Masters have all learned the Law of the Circle — the Law of the One. They impose upon the pure life-substance only the quality that they wish to use for the work at hand. If they desire a manifestation to express a certain length of time, they set the time, give the command, and the substance of which that manifestation is composed responds accordingly.

The Masters have learned that if any discord is imposed upon the life-substance of the universal levels, the electronic energy becomes temporarily dammed up within it. Ultimately, discord can never endure, for when its accumulated energy reaches a certain point of pressure, expansion takes place, shattering the discord and limitation. Thus, the great Law of the One, expressing God in action — the ever-expanding, luminous essence of Creation — overpowers whatever seeks to oppose it and goes on its appointed way with the ruler of the universe, Melchizedek.

If humans could watch their thoughts, feelings and words go out into the ethers, gathering more and more of their own kind before returning to them, not only would they be shocked at what they give birth to by way of their negative alternate realities, but they would cry out for deliverance. If their cries for help had no other motive than escape from facing their creations, they would still find themselves at the necessary point of looking at their own divinity and entering into it.

Because thoughts and feelings are living vibrating realities, the individual who understands this can use his higher mind to control himself and his reality accordingly. When you decide to manifest and experience through consciously directed visualization, you become the Law of the One, God, to whom there is no opposite. As a being with free will, you must make your own decision and then stand behind your own decree with all of your power, making an unshakable, determined stand. In order to do so, know that through you, it is God desiring, God feeling, God knowing, God manifesting, and God controlling everything concerning it. This is the Law of the One — Source and Source only. Until this is fully understood, the individual cannot and never will succeed in manifestation, for the moment a human element enters the scenario, it is taken out of the I AM Presence, Source, neutralized by the human qualities of time, space and a myriad of other illusory conditions which God does not recognize, conditions created by man and man alone. Interestingly, when one decides to consciously bring about a manifestation, even discussing the desire or goal with other people brings in enough of the human element to significantly weaken the invocation; thousands of desires, ideals, and ambitions would have been already brought to fruition in the outer experience if individuals had not spoken about them to others.

As long as one considers that any force other than God exists, then one can never know God; for whenever one acknowledges that two forces can act, he experiences the result of neutralizing activity. When you have neutralization, you have no definitive quality either way; you merely have nothing in your manifestation.

When you acknowledge your Source as Self — the One, the I AM Presence — you have only perfection manifesting instantly, in a state where there is nothing to oppose or neutralize it, and no element of time. When you express yourself as God, there is nothing to oppose you and your desire. Only when one truly desires perfection and ceases to acknowledge any power outside of God can one hope to improve his condition. Mankind will remain in their state of lack and limitation as long as they continue to acknowledge a condition that is less than the Wholeness of God. This choice of imperfection is deliberate on the part of humanity, who are using their God-given free will on some level of themselves, albeit not consciously by the personality. It certainly takes no more energy to think about or visualize perfection than imperfection!

You alone choose which qualities and forms you wish to place in your world. You are the only energizer of your life; whenever you think or feel, part of your Life force goes out to sustain your creation. You are the Creator represented on the universal level, and if you desire to express Its perfection and dominion, you must know and acknowledge only The Law of the One. As the One exists and expresses everywhere, in the universal and monadic levels, you are innately part of the One Supreme Presence, the Great Flame of Love and Light which is the Self-consciousness of life.

With the full acknowledgment of your Self and your world as the expression of God, hold that focus as you go about your earthly life. Make no distinction between your Self and your Creator; live in the Now. When you are doing visualization, always remember that you are God doing the picturing, you are God intelligence directing, you are God power propelling, and it is your substance, God substance being activated. Have no set time in your mind, except to know that there is only Now.

As you realize this and contemplate the fullness of it constantly, everything in the universe rushes to fulfill your desire, your command, your picture. This discipline manifests an irresistible power that cannot and never has failed, for it is all-constructive, and therefore agrees with the original Divine Plan of life. When the personality level agrees to the Divine Plan and fully accepts it, there can be no failure or delay. Perfection is the prerequisite; and since all energy contains the inherent quality of perfection, it is naturally attracted to your perfection and rushes to serve you as the Creator.

When your desire or picture is constructive, you become the Source of your I AM Presence, *Mahatma,* seeing your own plan. When the Source sees, it is an irrevocable decree to appear now. When God created the physical universes, He simply said, "Let there be Light," and Light appeared; it did not take any time to create Light.

When you, the individual, have accepted the Oneness of God, then the same divine power is within you, in the now, when you see or speak; they are His attributes of sight and speech acting in and through you. If you realize what this truly means, you can command His full power and authority, for you are then His life consciousness; and it is only the Self-consciousness of your life that can desire, imagine or command a constructive and perfect plan. Every constructive plan is His Plan, therefore you know that it is God acting through you, commanding: "Let this desire or plan be fulfilled now," and it is done.

Such perfection was intended for all of God's children, and is more real than any reality one can imagine. Even the most blissful life lived on Earth is pale in comparison to the joy experienced by those of the human family who have achieved the ascended state. The most beautiful or the greatest genius among human beings are but coarse and crude compared to the beauty, freedom, perfection and glory that are the continual experience of everyone who has raised their body and attained Mastery, as Jesus did in his incarnation as Apollonius and millions of beings had in Earth's two golden ages, known as E-Don. We use the name Jesus simply as one of recognition. For example, a degree of the energy that you reference as Jesus was embodied in the energy that became Apollonius of Tyana, Greece; and the energy that was Apollonius is now heightened and referred to as Sananda. Thus we refer to Jesus simply because he is so famous!.

Upon the path to Mastery, one eventually comes to realize that what the Christ, through Jesus, referred to as "the Father's house" is attainable by all who are willing to accept the Law of the One. And once one has experienced, for even a fraction of a second, the indescribable bliss radiating from an Ascended Being, there is nothing in the human experience that he will not endure or sacrifice in order to reach that level. There is no work that is too difficult when one truly desires to experience and express the dominion and love of Ascended Mastery.

Maitreya, the Christ, is the most well-known Hu-man/God-man to gain his experience on this Earth as a developing God Self. He revealed and demonstrated the Master Record to the outer world, and is still the popular living proof of the availability to humankind and the ability of the individual to free himself from all limitation and to express divinity, as was originally intended. Maitreya recognized the great truth that humanity's first existence on Earth was a completely harmonious and wholly free condition. He embodied this illuminated reality to help mankind to *reidentify* with the pure electrical body that Hu-man expressed during that Golden Age.

In ancient times the individual's devotion to his Source was very strong, for he knew and consciously acknowledged the power of the Great Central Sun. Because of the understanding of this great truth, these peoples used the Sun as the symbol of the Godhead. In their deep inner understanding, they acknowledged the fullness of the power of this Great Central Sun, which today we call **Christ Consciousness,** as it is the heart of the Christed activity on the Earth and her astral levels. This is your I AM Presence, *Mahatma*, from the Source level, now expressed in physicality through the Tenth Ray, which embodies the spiritual microtron for all universes, including the Earth and humanity. So many members of the New Age community, among others, have misunderstood the Central Sun to be the physical location of God in the ethers, and have not realized this to be the symbol of one's Christed Self.

When the Christ said to mankind "Verily, verily, I say unto you, the works that I do shall ye do also, and greater works than these shall ye do," his aim was to stretch them out of their limitation and to reveal the conscious dominion, the Mastery, that is available for each one to achieve and express while still here on the Earth. In showing the dominion of the Ascended Master, he proved to humanity that it is possible for everyone to call forth his God Self and consciously control all aspects of physical life.

The beautiful beings who guard and help the evolving human race are called the Ascended Masters of Love, Light and Perfection because as humans themselves, they learned to bring forth the love, wisdom and power of the God Self Within. When each mastered all that is human, they ascended into the next expression above that of the probationary human, which is a state of Divine Freedom and relative perfection.

On this level of activity, the Ascended Master is able to change the etheric Lightbody as you would change your clothes; the etheric structure is always under conscious control, and every permanent atom obeys a master's slightest direction. Masters are free to use one or more bodies, if their work requires, for their ability to materialize or dissolve an atomic body is absolutely unlimited. The Ascended Masters are all-powerful manifestors of substance and energy, as the forces of nature — the four elements — are their willing and obedient servants.

Although all of life contains the Divine Will, it is only the Self-conscious life that is free to determine its own course of expression. If only mankind realized that inherent in each and every human being is the power to express as an Ascended Master, if he but chooses to! The individual has the free will to choose to express in either the limited, human body or in the superhuman divine body; he is the self-determining Creator of his own reality.

When one chooses to individualize within the absolute, all-pervading life, he chooses to express as an intensified, individual focus of Self-conscious intelligence. He becomes the conscious director of his future activities, and is the only one who can fulfill that destiny — which is not inflexible, but is a definitely designed plan of perfection, a blueprint he chooses to express in the realm of form and action. Every human being may rise out of his human qualities and limitations when he chooses to dedicate all of his energy, his life force to that goal.

Through the power held in the thoughts and feelings of mankind, each individual can raise himself to the highest level or sink to the lowest. By taking conscious control of his attention or by allowing unconscious control, each person determines his own experience. Without care as to what he allows his mind to accept, man can become as low as the animals, sinking his human consciousness into oblivion. This is not as in metempsychosis, where in theory the human soul would move into the body of an animal or plant, for neither of these has free will; we are referring to the unconscious behavior of humans who allow their consciousness to revert to that of animal-man.

The Self-conscious intelligence, understanding the power behind thought and feeling, uses these constructively to achieve manifestation; this is how "the Word is made flesh." The Ascended Being understands the atom to be an entity — a living, breathing thing created by the breath, the Love of God, through the will of Self-conscious intelligence.

Destructive thought and discordant feeling act upon the atom, rearranging the ratio and rate of motion of its electrons so that the duration of the Breath of God within its pole is changed. Because the duration of the Breath is decreed by the will of the consciousness using a particular kind of atom, if this consciousness is withdrawn, the electrons lose their polarity and fly apart, intelligently and naturally seeking their way back to the Great Central Sun, man's Christ Consciousness. There they receive Love and the never-ending Breath of God; and there Order, the First Law, is eternally maintained.

Some of your Earth's scientists claim and teach that planets collide in space. This would never be possible for it goes against the laws and plan of Creation. Fortunately, the Divine Cosmic Laws are not limited to or subject to some of the children of Earth; and God's Creation goes on, ever moving forward and expressing more and more perfection.

Constructive thought and harmonious feeling within the human mind and body are the activities of love and order. These permit the perfect ratio and speed of the electrons within the atom to remain permanent and able to stay polarized at their particular point in the universe, as long as the duration of the Breath of Source within their core is held steady by the will of the directing, Self-conscious intelligence using the body in which they exist. In this way the quality of perfection and the maintenance of life in a human body is always consciously controlled by the will of the individual occupying it. The will of the individual becomes supreme over his body temple and even in cases of accident, no one leaves his body until his Soul wills it.

In understanding the electron and the conscious control that the individual has, through his thought and feeling, in governing the atomic structure of his body, one gains understanding of the One Principle which governs form throughout infinity. When the human individual makes the effort to learn this by proving it for himself, then he will proceed to master himself. And once he has done this, he will have the full cooperation of the universe (and ultimately, of the entire Cosmos) to accomplish whatever he desires through love.

All constructive desire expressed by the individual is actually the God Self Within pushing perfection forward into the use and enjoyment of the outer self. Since the Divine Life Force flows continually through all, it is simply up to you how you wish to use it. If you direct it to constructive accomplishment, you will receive joy and happiness; and if toward gratification of the physical senses, it cannot produce anything but misery, because it is an impersonal life energy, reflecting only the action of the Law.

The nature of the unconscious personal self is such that it constantly tries to claim power of its own, when the very energy through which it exists is provided by God, through the individualized God Self. The outer personal self does not even own its own skin! The very atoms of its physical body are loaned to it by the Supreme God Presence, from the great sea of universal substance. When the individual learns how to obtain obedience from the atomic structure within his own mind and body, all atomic structure outside of his mind and body will obey him also; and the personality will no longer feel the need to falsely justify its place or power within the All That Is, because it will understand its Divine Beingness.

Many of you already realize that great natural, physical changes will take place on your planet during the opening, which will last until the year 2028 — this period of assistance and intense outpouring of Light by the *Mahatma,* your Ascended Teachers, and the Five Higher Rays — which have come to the aid of the children of Earth. Many thousands of humanity will find during this time that their physical bodies are being quickened by the rapid raising of the vibratory rate; and that as this is completed, the human, physical limitations and discord have dropped away like a worn-out old garment. And what is left? *Themselves,* as Children of Light, forever at one with the Flame of life everlasting and perfection.

14

The Tenth Ray

October 1992

Kindly be advised that on October 8, 1992, the Tenth Ray was anchored on this planet in a profound and generous way. This magnificent opening will allow those among you who can absorb and consciously integrate this energy to create, for the first time ever in this universe, the spiritual material body.

The Tenth Ray, if you allow it, can actually code the new body of Light into the physical structure; it is the vehicle to accomplish the physical-spiritual Ascension.

This ray has been available since the early 1970s, and at this juncture, the Earth has raised her vibration sufficiently for its integration. Mankind, however, are not even aware that it is here!

The opportunity of the Tenth Ray arrives with such clarity that any confusion or interaction with the mental/emotional/physical bodies can only take away from your integration instead of enhancing it. This ray arrives without judgment, without polarities — *it simply is!*

The information that came through myself, the personality, was "transmigration, transfiguration." The Tenth Ray is remarkably gentle, as it is your first complete connection ever with what we reference as the spiritual level, or the beginning of the Monad. When you stop and think of this, you will realize that this is a gift that will allow the complete spiritual Ascension from this universal level (and therefore from all universal/physical levels). It is not the Soul/Higher Self, but the *Oversoul* level which contains this energy. (Refer to the diagram, "The Co-Creator and Creator Levels," pp. 228-29, and Ray Ten, p. 213.)

The Archangels Embodying The Tenth Ray

Exercise
November 1992

To work with the new energies, start by invoking the *Mahatma*. All of these energies must be invited consciously into a fourth-dimensional reality. (One of the teachings of the *Mahatma* is to correct the misunderstanding and distortion on this planet of the nature of the Archangels, as none of these beings can work in a third dimension.)

Bring the white-gold light of the Source through your whole channel, all the way into the center of the Earth. Ground, ground and ground. Then ask the Archangels, one at a time, to come into your four-body system. Ask Metatron to come into your causal-body/Soul level. Ask Ratziel to come into your crown/third eye area. Ask Khamael into your throat/heart chakras. (Khamael is huge and very encompassing.) Ask Michael into your solar plexus.

See Michael-Raphael-Auriel-Gabriel as a square unit, four cornerstones who work together. Ask Raphael-Auriel-Gabriel into your polarity chakra. Ask Sandalphon into your base chakra. (Refer to diagram on following page.)

It is very important to see and hold the alignment between Metatron and Sandalphon. These two are inextricably linked to each other.

Then invite the Tenth Ray into your entire channel. See this luminescent pearl Light with the incandescent White Light of Source flowing through your whole beingness and into the center of the Earth with the *Mahatma* energy. Visualize this as a waterfall engulfing every cell in your physical body.

Then call on the Mother energy for support. Feel the Goddess energy permeating your beingness and anchoring in your heart chakra. Once she is comfortably anchored there, see her energy flowing through you and anchoring into the center of the Earth.

The secret to working with the Tenth Ray is to integrate, integrate, integrate all aspects of yourself and *then* completely let go of the mental and emotional bodies and allow the Tenth Ray to become the new you and the beginning of your new physical-spiritual body!

You must try to understand that while the DNA of the physical body has been able to accept and integrate every level and ray up to and including the Ninth Ray, this is what creates the discomfort that so many are feeling in what is becoming your new spiritualized body. Kindly be advised that the discomfort that you feel now and in the foreseeable future will be expressed through the Tenth Ray until such time as the completed physical-spiritual Ascension and the recoding of the new "body" is undertaken. At this point, the individual who has accomplished this remarkable feat will be free to interact with all lower monadic (Oversoul) levels plus physical/universal levels. Your expanded Source, as we have discussed, has brought about this truly remarkable achievement in evolution that is without precedent!

You really must not consider this quantum leap — from what you have viewed in your past as your Fifth/Sixth Initiations through to the Twelfth Initiation and beyond — as not being supportive and allowing of your truly privileged possibilities at this time. In other words, please do not go into overwhelm with these concepts that flow so beautifully with your integration of the Tenth Ray.

The Archangels Embodying the Tenth Ray

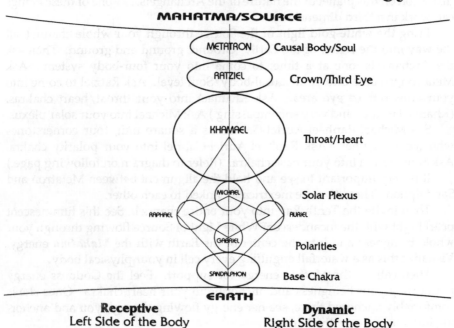

MAHATMA/SOURCE

METATRON — Causal Body/Soul

RATZIEL — Crown/Third Eye

KHAMAEL — Throat/Heart

MICHAEL — Solar Plexus

RAPHAEL   AURIEL

GABRIEL — Polarities

SANDALPHON — Base Chakra

EARTH

Receptive
Left Side of the Body

Dynamic
Right Side of the Body

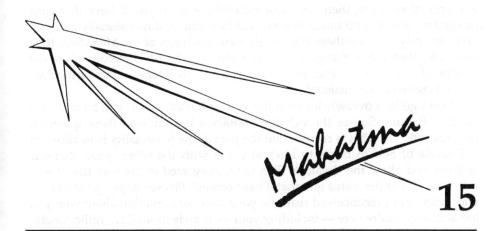

15

Integrating Unlimitedness

November 1992

If you believe that you're having a problem on this Journey that is going to create difficulty for you, then guess what happens as you start to enter the fourth dimension? You affect and manifest whatever your view is of your reality! (As you watch the Earth seemingly coming undone at the seams in the beginning of the fourth dimension, your past third-dimensional patterning still dictates the terms of your reality.) Do you see this? What I'm saying was never that important in terms of the third density; but now your implementation of the fourth density is bringing, and will bring — with whatever flow you allow — instant manifestation. For example, if your belief is that the Serbs cannot get along and integrate with the Muslims in the same community, then the fourth dimension will magnify their heinous distortions and destruction at a much greater rate of acceleration.

As you progress further into the fourth dimension, you will all realize, progressively and with greater and greater gradations of clarification, what this new density is, living in the Now of your own creative abilities.

Please forget most of what you ever held as truth, because your realities have totally changed! For example, what you learned regarding old methods even today have absolutely no reality with your new-found creative abilities. In other words, WHAT WAS, ISN'T. That is not to suggest that mass consciousness and your subconscious mind don't harken to the old ways for comfort and safety; but you must validate and totally integrate that you are the creator of your own reality more so than ever before in what you view as your past. To repeat, if you believe that you are going to have a problem today in any area of your life, then you most assuredly will. If you believe that your integration and instant manifestation will flow fourth-dimensionally and that you can truly validate these completely new teachings of the *Mahatma*, then you can effect these changes, such as becoming fourth-dimensional as the creator of your reality, and also allow yourself to integrate the Tenth Ray, which is seventh-dimensional.

Don't go into overwhelm with this concept; *trust*, and it will *become* your reality! Because Source through the *Mahatma* has allowed these quantum progressions. All that is required on the part of the personality is to allow all 352 levels of Self to begin to integrate, one with the other, your alternate realities and allow the Creator's Plan to be integrated in the way that it was intended, not as the status quo that it has become! Please simply get out of the way with your preconceived realities, your sense of limitation about who you are and why you're here — including your extremely limited scientific conclusions. Your existing religions and social and monetary structures cannot and will not work in a fourth density. Since the Source has anchored on Earth through the *Mahatma*, the increasing influx of spiritual microtrons is affecting all of existence on physical Earth, especially the distortions between material idolatry, which mandates all of human existence, and the absolute necessity of mankind to integrate their spiritual reality during this 36-year opening.

The amount of *Mahatma's* spiritual energy (the mirotrons) anchored on Earth is here to stay; there is simply no way that this magnificent energy is going to retreat and return to Source just because mankind wishes to worship the greatest illusion of all, the **material world.** (Kindly be reminded that this illusion is a Source perspective, as Source is also learning and integrating greater and greater levels of wholeness that *Source* has not felt were inclusive of the All That Is, the I AM Presence.) Mankind and your Soul levels will have to make this adjustment as part of your spiritual evolution, because there is simply no way that the devastating third-dimensional effects of worshiping the dark side of your material world will be tolerated any longer, after 3.2 billion years into this Cosmic Day.

This becomes self-evident as you look around the world, as all institutions barely function or else don't function at all anymore. This is the beginning of the end of mankind's long-standing love affair with worshiping the dark side of night, not knowing that their total reality was and is a quasi-illusion, that mankind's *only* reality will become the spiritual, which includes the spiritualization of what you call matter! Those who cannot make these adjustments when they enter the fourth dimension will be lovingly cared for in a suitable third density.

Herein we are speaking of the bulk of humanity who are consciously pre-probationary and probationary, and those who remain in the First Initiation stage, the Baptism. All who have achieved Discipleship, the Second Initiation, could consciously achieve their astral/etheric Ascension and not require further dense physical embodiment. (Refer to the chart, "Man's Response to Initiations" on p. 220.) This should include many, many millions among you because of the Soul energy within the atom being released through *nuclear fission*. Those who achieve the spiritual Ascension of the fourth through sixth dimensions through *nuclear fusion* may total hundreds of thousands. Fusion is required to interface the microtron with the atom in order to spiritualize matter.

The human potential during the next 36 years of this opening will surpass the past eons of the history of Hu-man/God-man. The exponential growth started when the Council of Twelve for this Cosmic Day anchored on the Earth on June 14, 1988, as the *Mahatma* energy. This forty-year opening will achieve greater Spiritual Evolution on planet Earth than the previous 3.2 billion years. You may wish to integrate this vast conceptual reality as part of your INTEGRATING UNLIMITEDNESS!

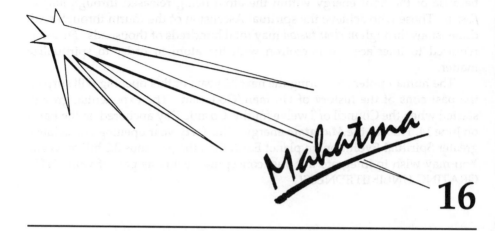

16

The Etheric and Spiritual Ascensions

November 1992

There is much confusion on Earth regarding preparation for pre-Ascension. As you are aware, classes are being held, channeling is taking place, that reference old patterns, old beliefs about Ascension. If you, the disciple, find living on a planet during this opening, which is taking place until the year 2028, in a third/fourth density to be confusing, we wish to introduce two very distinct realities as they relate to the etheric-body Ascension and the one we are discussing: the complete spiritual Ascension.

Kindly be advised that the nature of what mankind views as their past, referencing their etheric (energy) Lightbody Ascension requires only the freeing of the Soul energy within the atom. This has been accomplished on this planet through nuclear fission. This process, as we have discussed, equals the liberation of the Soul with the Fifth Initiation. Once a person has *Consciously* accomplished this liberation, he starts to build this etheric Lightbody. The Sixth Initiation is no longer definitively required; it is simply the coding of the beautiful blue/green light of the Ninth Ray which can code the DNA for the complete etheric-body Ascension. This is the Ascension that many, many beings have accomplished, such as Djwhal Khul, Janet McClure, Jesus and Mohammed; certain among you have also accomplished this level of Ascension.

"Ascension" is a word that your various religions have come to regard as the raising of one's vibration above that of the Earth. This is, in reality, a misnomer, because in effect, one's consciousness has been raised to the level of the Fifth Initiation, which is the seventh astral level. This seventh astral level still requires the (finer) astral body with which to travel, but what it does allow is the beginning, for the individual on this level, of building the Lightbody. This Lightbody is completed just prior to one's *complete* Ascension from the dense physical Earth and Earth's consort of the seven astral heavens and astral body (previously referred to as the Sixth Initiation). At this juncture, into a fifth density or the Galactic Core (we remind you that we use the dimensional pie of nine densities), this division may be at variance with other teachings in dividing the dimensional pie, but your intuition can adapt to your scheme of referencing dimensions! Then you have raised your vibration above that of the Earth and her astral levels in what we refer to as the *intuitive dimension.*

Even your Councils of Twelve for the various galaxies, which all of humanity are bonding with, work at a finer level of this same fifth dimension (all dimensions have seven levels of vibration). So let us articulate these perspectives so that you can integrate how different the Ascensions are, particularly the etheric-body Ascension and the spiritual-body Ascension. Remember, the Ninth Ray codes the body of Light, your etheric body, with finer and finer gradations through to the upper level of the sixth dimension, which is your twelfth chakra and the Twelfth Initiation; all that is universal is sixth-dimensional and physical because the etheric (Lightbody) has one permanent atom.

Many are aware that certain teachings on the Earth separate the physical body from the etheric body, projecting a five-body system (not the four-body system, as we teach). There is some validity to these teachings because they do allow the disciple to integrate a five-body concept. If this method proves easier for you in the integration of these vast concepts, for which we simply do not have sufficient language to explain, then by all means use whatever works for you. However, always keep in mind that the etheric (Light) body is physical, with one permanent atom.

Thus, as you are beginning to deduce, there will be two totally different levels of Ascension on this planet momentarily — the aforementioned astral/etheric Ascension, which this Opening will achieve for multitudes, and the spiritual Ascension, which will be available for all fourth- through sixth-dimensional beings in this universe. Many universal beings are already celebrating this spiritual Ascension as a *fait accompli* because they function outside of sequential time.

There is no precedent on Earth for the complete spiritual Ascension at any level of the physical densities. This has been achieved because your expanded Source wishes to hasten the total evolution of this expanded Cosmic Day through the *Mahatma* energy. The achievement of hastening the evolutionary process with such quantum progressions has placed massive shifts and undertaking on all participants. Your Archangels have had to be reprogrammed through Metatron by the Council of Twelve for this Cosmic Day to be able, for example, to access our dense physical structure; this is completely new for these great administrators of the Plan.

As there is no precedent for comparison, or even perfection, with the spiritual Ascension on these physical levels of consciousness, the total operation is viewed intuitively and without guidelines. Thus with the celebrations of Melchizedek and others regarding their imminent spiritual Ascension, we know that this same possibility is imminent on Earth for those among you who can participate in these magnificent progressions. All levels of consciousness are uniting the Creator and Co-Creator levels and are being energized on the Earth — as the focal point at this time — through the 352 levels of the *Mahatma*. This includes those on this planet who consciously or unconsciously participate at whatever initiation level they function in fourth-dimensionally as part of the *Mahatma* energy.

Yes, I think you're beginning to understand how the Ninth Ray codes and creates the Lightbody! Now, why would our new expanded Source implement such a hurry-up offense, with nearly 1.2 billion years remaining in this Cosmic Day? Simply because we are nowhere near our scheduled complete graduation into the Monad at our current evolutionary pace! There are many, many reasons for this — the main reason being the nonrecognition on the part of Source that the Co-Creator level was and is a bonafide member of this Source; and on the Co-Creator's part, feeling vanquished and not part of the Source of this Cosmic Day. As we have previously described to you the many reasons for the seeming dichotomy of separation, we wish not to languish with these contributing factors, which have already been discussed.

A much more logical explanation, and one which mankind should relate to more cognitively, is the fact that this Cosmic Day has taken 3.2 billion years to reach a halfway benchmark, thus graduation day equates to 1.2 billion remaining sequential years. In other words, we're nowhere near the critical path objectives set out at the beginning of this Cosmic Day! Thus the hastening of our evolution with all balanced means at our disposal, through the *Mahatma* energy originating with our new expanded Source, has become a reality; and the Tenth Ray being anchored on Earth through the *Mahatma* will facilitate and accelerate our spiritual resolve.

The Tenth Ray has never been applied or implemented in any universe of the Cosmic Day the way it is now! What do we mean by this? We mean that all twelve rays have been functioning at the universal level forever, but their *application* was to balance Creation with whatever level of these higher rays could be interpreted and used to support in harmony physical Creation. As we have discussed at length previously, your Logos steps down to the next level of Creation the amount of energy that respective level can handle. What the expanded Source, through the *Mahatma,* has mandated is a stepping down from the monadic level of spiritual energy, which means energy without atoms. The significance of this is very profound, meaning that the fourth through sixth dimensions now can also assimilate the nonatomic material which we're calling the *microtron,* and which is of such a fine vibrational frequency that your most sophisticated scientific equipment has not yet discovered spiritual energy. This spiritual energy, the microtron, is stepped down from the Monad to the universal Council of Twelve through an elaborate electromagnetic grid system established by the Archangels for the spiritual benefit of all of Creation, but particularly your fourth through sixth densities. Thus the emphasis now on the spiritualization of matter through the Tenth Ray!

It is very significant at this point in time that the Co-Creators here in physicality begin to integrate the Tenth Ray in a gentle and correct manner.

17

The Cosmic Heart

Because Sanat Kumara embodies the consciousness of this planet and every Soul that ever was or ever will be associated with it, once people have raised their vibration above that of Earth and Soul, including the emotional and mental bodies, that group or individual begins to create their etheric Lightbody, referred to in the past as the Sixth Initiation. At this juncture, one starts to integrate the Higher Self. This Higher Self then becomes the vehicle, overshadowed by the Ninth Ray (the beautiful blue-green light), that allows the creation of the etheric Lightbody. When one has accomplished this level of integration, there is no Earth to anchor Light into, is there? Because Sanat Kumara embodies the Earth and all aboard her, and because the Fifth Initiation is now available — as a result of nuclear fission — for those who can consciously integrate what were the Third through Fifth Initiations, the Earth becomes, from an integrational point of view, the heart/throat chakra. These, as you can now sense, are becoming one chakra. As we have discussed with many of you, the fifth chakra, the Sanat Kumara in the throat, is the last area of surrender, not only for the personality level but for the Earth and primal Soul as well; it is the most difficult to let go of and surrender to!

One's consciousness always ascends first, and now many will stay in their dense physical bodies to assist others to trigger their Lightbodies prior to their etheric-(Light) body Ascension.

Once you anchor the Higher Self into the thymus gland (the heart chakra), you will have created the etheric Lightbody. One then starts to integrate the pearl-colored Tenth Ray. When the Tenth Ray and Oversoul are properly anchored, this Ray takes the position of the eighth chakra, the Soul Star. At the time that the Tenth Ray is coded into the physical body, then and only then does the Oversoul anchor into what was the heart chakra, as one then no longer needs the "old" physical body and that chakra system because at this juncture you have created your (permanent) new physical-spiritual body. Your consciousness will have then moved beyond the twelve initiations and the twelve chakras into the seventh-dimensional Oversoul levels of the spiritual/monadic levels.

On the other hand, the etheric Lightbody Ascension could be accomplished by tens of millions during this opening which is taking place until the year 2028, and does not require the taking of the physical body with them; that is simply not possible at this level of consciousness. What Maitreya demonstrated for the Master Jesus and mankind was not the complete body Ascension — the *complete* physical-spiritual Ascension has never been accomplished in this or any other universe. Some will actually see this complete Ascension if they function fourth-dimensionally. Those who do not witness this incredible demonstration will be those who cannot raise their vibration and sequence fourth-dimensional time during this opening. As has always been the case on this planet, some will "witness"; however, the bulk of humanity will not have the clarity in their belief structure or in their anatomical/electrical body system to witness these amazing progressions available through New Revelation!

In conclusion, we would remind you that the Ascension of the past, the Fifth Initiation that acknowledged metaphysical teachers refer to, is not a true Ascension. The anchoring of the Sixth Initiation will accomplish the raising of one's vibration above the Astral Body of the Seventh Astral Level, Earth, and Soul (the egoic body), to not require further dense physical embodiment (inaccurately referred to in the past as Mastery); however, it should be remembered that the completion of the Earth and *all* astral levels requires integration sufficient to equal what is refered to as the Sixth Initiation, the etheric Lightbody.

The Cosmic Heart

For those who are integrating the Sixth Initiation and are building the etheric Lightbody

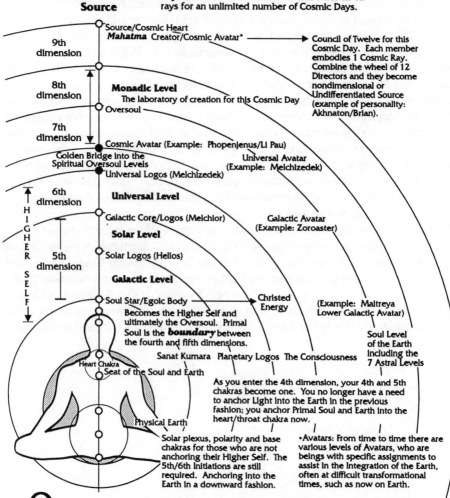

Undifferentiated Source — Beyond dimensions. This level embodies all 12 rays for an unlimited number of Cosmic Days.

9th dimension

Source/Cosmic Heart
Mahatma Creator/Cosmic Avatar* ⟶ Council of Twelve for this Cosmic Day. Each member embodies 1 Cosmic Ray. Combine the wheel of 12 Directors and they become nondimensional or Undifferentiated Source (example of personality: Akhnaton/Brian).

8th dimension

Monadic Level
The laboratory of creation for this Cosmic Day

Oversoul

7th dimension

Cosmic Avatar (Example: Phopenjenus/Li Pau)
Golden Bridge into the Spiritual Oversoul Levels
Universal Avatar (Example: Melchizedek)
Universal Logos (Melchizedek)

6th dimension

Universal Level

Galactic Core/Logos (Melchior)
Galactic Avatar (Example: Zoroaster)

Solar Level

5th dimension

Solar Logos (Helios)

Galactic Level

HIGHER SELF

Soul Star/Egoic Body ⟶ Christed Energy
Becomes the Higher Self and ultimately the Oversoul. Primal Soul is the *boundary* between the fourth and fifth dimensions.

(Example: Maitreya Lower Galactic Avatar)

Soul Level of the Earth including the 7 Astral Levels

Sanat Kumara Planetary Logos The Consciousness

Heart Chakra
Seat of the Soul and Earth

As you enter the 4th dimension, your 4th and 5th chakras become one. You no longer have a need to anchor Light into the Earth in the previous fashion; you anchor Primal Soul and Earth into the heart/throat chakra now.

Physical Earth

Solar plexus, polarity and base chakras for those who are not anchoring their Higher Self. The 5th/6th Initiations are still required. Anchoring into the Earth in a downward fashion.

*Avatars: From time to time there are various levels of Avatars, who are beings with specific assignments to assist in the Integration of the Earth, often at difficult transformational times, such as now on Earth.

Once the Sixth Initiation is accomplished, there is an overshadowing of Earth by the initiate through the *Mahatma* energy. As one aligns with the *Mahatma* energy and the Galactic Core (the fifth dimension), the transformational energy, the Christed energy and Soul are anchored into the heart chakra (in what we call the Soul Merge, the Third Initiation). At the time of the Fifth Initiation, which can now be integrated within months of the Third Initiation, one transcends the need to involve oneself with the dense physical levels and thus masters physicality, requiring no further dense physical embodiment.

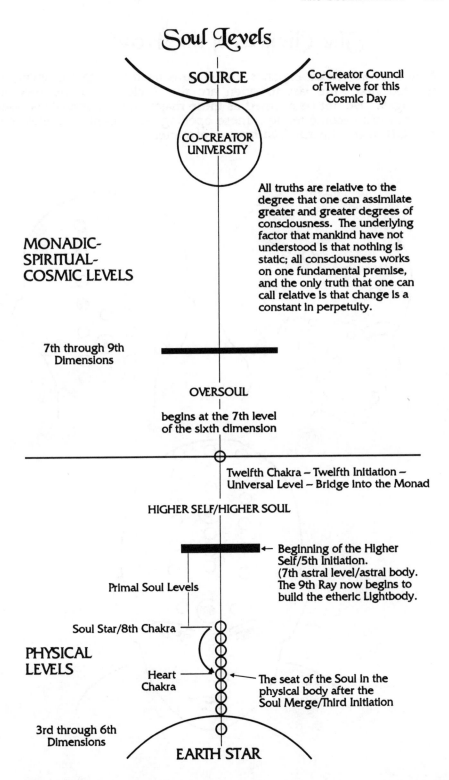

Soul Levels

SOURCE

Co-Creator Council
of Twelve for this
Cosmic Day

CO-CREATOR
UNIVERSITY

**MONADIC-
SPIRITUAL-
COSMIC LEVELS**

All truths are relative to the
degree that one can assimilate
greater and greater degrees of
consciousness. The underlying
factor that mankind have not
understood is that nothing is
static; all consciousness works
on one fundamental premise,
and the only truth that one can
call relative is that change is a
constant in perpetuity.

7th through 9th
Dimensions

OVERSOUL

begins at the 7th level
of the sixth dimension

Twelfth Chakra – Twelfth Initiation –
Universal Level – Bridge into the Monad

HIGHER SELF/HIGHER SOUL

◄— Beginning of the Higher
Self/5th Initiation.
(7th astral level/astral body.
The 9th Ray now begins to
build the etheric Lightbody.

Primal Soul Levels

Soul Star/8th Chakra

**PHYSICAL
LEVELS**

Heart
Chakra

◄— The seat of the Soul in the
physical body after the
Soul Merge/Third Initiation

3rd through 6th
Dimensions

EARTH STAR

The Chakras of the Head

As the crown chakra expands, the chakras nearest to that opening are affected first. The last to open are the 2 closest to the medulla oblongata. Do not be alarmed as these major and minor chakras open, for they will become tender. These openings are essential to allow new **revelation** and the **spiritualization** of matter.

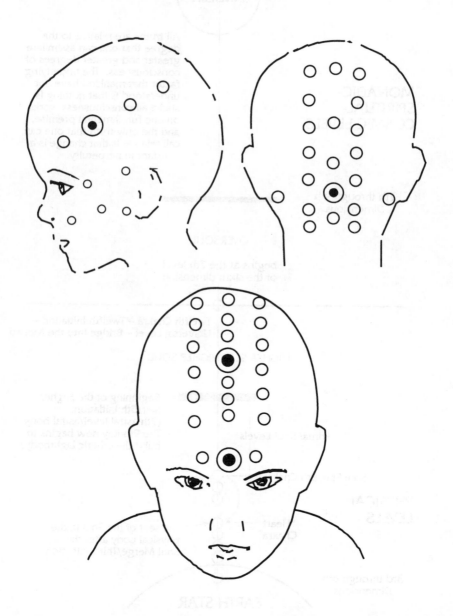

The Chakras as Disks

These vortexes are referred to as chakras on the universal/physical levels. All of Creation for all Cosmic Days is embodied within the 12 Creator Rays. They are "the Word," the Creator's "outward and inward breath," for Creation. You will notice that the Creator's inward breath is highly energized at this point in time.

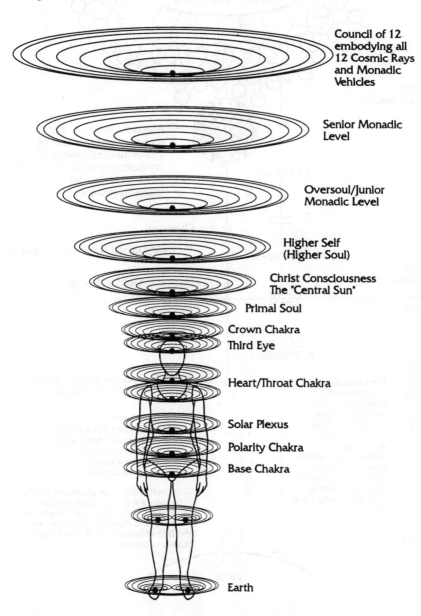

Council of 12 embodying all 12 Cosmic Rays and Monadic Vehicles

Senior Monadic Level

Oversoul/Junior Monadic Level

Higher Self (Higher Soul)

Christ Consciousness The "Central Sun"

Primal Soul

Crown Chakra

Third Eye

Heart/Throat Chakra

Solar Plexus

Polarity Chakra

Base Chakra

Earth

The Individualization of Source

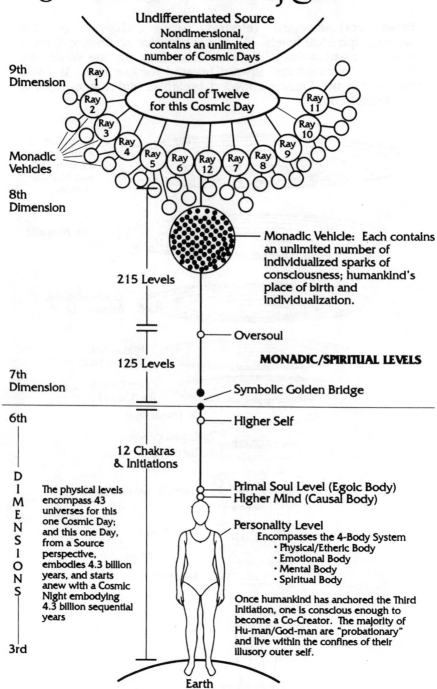

Undifferentiated Source
Nondimensional,
contains an unlimited
number of Cosmic Days

9th Dimension

Ray 1
Ray 2
Ray 3
Ray 4
Ray 5
Ray 6
Ray 12
Ray 7
Ray 8
Ray 9
Ray 10
Ray 11

Council of Twelve for this Cosmic Day

Monadic Vehicles

8th Dimension

215 Levels

Monadic Vehicle: Each contains
an unlimited number of
individualized sparks of
consciousness; humankind's
place of birth and
individualization.

Oversoul

MONADIC/SPIRITUAL LEVELS

125 Levels

7th Dimension

Symbolic Golden Bridge

6th

Higher Self

12 Chakras
& Initiations

D
I
M
E
N
S
I
O
N
S

The physical levels
encompass 43
universes for this
one Cosmic Day;
and this one Day,
from a Source
perspective,
embodies 4.3 billion
years, and starts
anew with a Cosmic
Night embodying
4.3 billion sequential
years

Primal Soul Level (Egoic Body)
Higher Mind (Causal Body)

Personality Level
Encompasses the 4-Body System
• Physical/Etheric Body
• Emotional Body
• Mental Body
• Spiritual Body

Once humankind has anchored the Third
Initiation, one is conscious enough to
become a Co-Creator. The majority of
Hu-man/God-man are "probationary"
and live within the confines of their
illusory outer self.

3rd

Earth

ᗧhe ᖇing ᗩasseth ᑎot

The Eternal Cosmic Law states that you can never pass beyond the level of vibration (the "Ring") that you have integrated until the collective You integrates greater and greater levels of the Wholeness of Self.

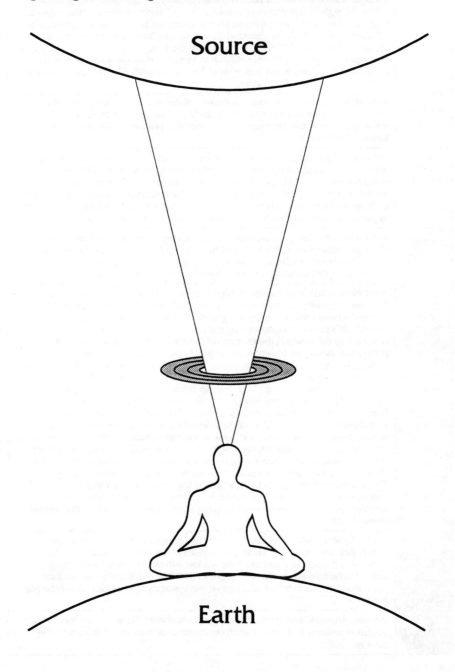

Metatron's Evolutionary Light Chart

Minimum Light	
100% LIGHT	This level of Light has never been achieved on Earth, and one would simply **become** the **spiritualized Light of the 10th Ray**, for the physical body in the past has never expressed more than 76% Light within an atomic body. With Brian at 97.6% Light as of August 24, 1993, it is possible with NEW REVELATION anchored on Earth that he will anchor his completed circuitry of Light from Source to Earth, "from the highest mountain to the lowest valley," and that others universally will complete their manifested spiritual bodies and move beyond the 12 Initiations and 12 chakras which embody Universal Consciousness, into the spiritual monadic levels. At the level of 92% Light or more for the integration of the universal levels, every percentage point is more difficult to integrate than the whole 58% of the completed Soul Merge, but is now available for humankind in an unprecedented opportunity to spiritualize matter.
80-83% LIGHT	**6th Initiation:** As one becomes a greater Wholeness of what they have always been as Light, one ascends beyond the Earth and her astral levels, completes one's learning and evolution for these dense material expressions, and moves into the junior galactic realms.
73% LIGHT	**"Mastery":** Referred to in the past as the 5th Initiation, this level can now be achieved with profound concentration on becoming your I AM, **Mahatma**, as described so clearly in these Mahatma books. When we reference that only 34,000 beings from Earth have achieved this level of integration, we are speaking of those who have evolved through the Earth's system, and not those from other systems who have agreed to assist Sanat Kumara and his Earth's evolution.
62% LIGHT	**4th Initiation:** Today, because of the Soul having been released from the atom through nuclear fission, this and all of the primary points of integration (which in the past were referred to as initiations) simply become **Realizations** and the old 3rd, 4th, and 5th initiations can be achieved with comparative ease.
58% LIGHT	**Soul Merge:** The 3rd Initiation is the first occasion for the primal Soul to connect with the personality, to enter the physical atomic body, and to actually anchor within the heart chakra (the thymus gland). This is a great beginning for humankind's journey as intended by the primal Soul, to cease being lost and confused by living within the confines of the outer self's **illusion**. This level of integration allows one to reside on the 5th Astral level, often referred to as heaven, for millions of sequential years. There are literally millions of beings in all world religions who call this level paradise. **This level has no evolution.** By this we mean that one cannot go from the 5th astral to the 6th astral level; one would have to return to dense physicality and continue evolution there. As you can see from the next chart, "The Chakra System for the Physical Manifestation of Multidimensional Mankind," all of these astral levels are uniting with the Earth during the next 35 years and will cease to exist as separate levels of consciousness. Thus the symbolic phrase "Heaven on Earth." This level is humankind's creation, not God's, and offers an interesting contrast between humankind's view and God's view of "God's Heaven". Because of the spiritualization of matter resulting from the expansion of our Source for this Cosmic Day, many, many shifts of Consciousness will ignite Light and Love in dense physicality, no matter how confused probationary man remains, living within the confines of his **disconnected** atomic body.
5% LIGHT	**Probationary Man:** Lives totally within the confines of the outer self as the personality, and resonates within the confines of the dense atomic body. This constitutes the bulk of humanity, who are lost within their creation of "things," which the God Source cannot recognize as anything but **illusory**. Humankind's separation from their primal soul caused this dislocation from their I AM Presence as Source.
0 - 4% LIGHT	**Animal, Mineral, and Devic/Elemental Kingdoms:** These all have their own evolution **without free will**. Therefore, metempsychosis and "the wheel of 84" have no validity.

The Chakra System
for the Physical Manifestation of Multidimensional Humankind

Primarily the three lower chakras cease to exist and the five higher chakras are integrated into the physical body.

The Blue Race arrived as Light and left as greater Light, and did not experience the three lower chakras that Fallen Man created through the illusory outer self. Although the "Golden Race" (Blue Race) lived within the Seven Rays of third-dimensional reality, they had no lower chakras, meaning the illusory 1st, 2nd and 3rd.

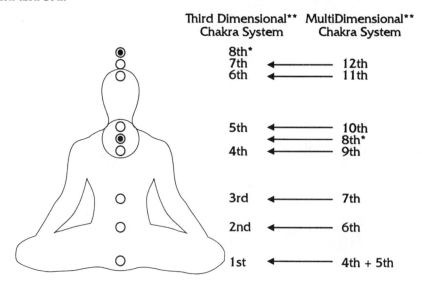

	Third Dimensional** Chakra System	MultiDimensional** Chakra System
	8th*	
	7th ←	12th
	6th ←	11th
	5th ←	10th
	←	8th*
	4th ←	9th
	3rd ←	7th
	2nd ←	6th
	1st ←	4th + 5th

* The old 8th chakra (Soul Star) is anchored into the new 9th chakra, the new heart/throat chakra. The blue/green 9th Ray overshadows this chakra to implement the creation of the etheric Lightbody. There is greater correspondence between the 9th, 10th, 11th and 12th Rays and chakras. Simultaneous with the above, the three lower astral levels will be withdrawn and beings on these levels will go to other schoolrooms in the various Universes. Once the Individual integrates the spiritual microtron, the twelve chakras and the six dimensions cease to be one's reality.

Kindly be reminded that all of the astral levels and higher chakras are and will be anchored on Earth during the next 35 years. These will cease to exist as levels outside of dense physicality as they will become integrated into Sanat Kumara's embodiment, the physical Earth, in a multidimensional matrix which will allow for the greater integration of consciousness by humankind. This fulfills the symbolic statement "Heaven on Earth."

** Note: There is no correspondence between the numbers of the old system and the new system.

18

Mahatma as the I AM Presence

Maitreya, through Jesus, gave the popular example of the etheric-body Ascension, striving to teach mankind its meaning and directing them to the same attainment. This beloved teacher and many, many before him made it very clear that one is sometimes raised to the etheric Ascension close to or just prior to the transition called death; however, it must be accomplished from the dense physical side of life. It must also be done at a point before the silver cord of light has been withdrawn from the physical body; otherwise it becomes impossible to illuminate and raise that body, and one would need to incarnate once more in order to attain that final freedom from the dense physical experience. The Ascension must take place *consciously*, as this Ascended Master attainment is the final completion of all dense physical experiences through the personality level.

Physical embodiment is for the purpose of preparing, perfecting and enlightening the body to the vibratory level where it can once again blend with the universal body of the I AM Presence. This is the state that Jesus/the Christ referred to as "the seamless garment." In this etheric body, which is made of pure electrical energy, one has complete freedom from all dense physical limitation. Through intense devotion to the I AM Presence, anyone can release its power to achieve this point. We remind you that this is your eternal birthright!

Of all the habits that mankind has created for itself, self-pity is the most inexcusable, because it is the height of human selfishness. Through self-pity the attention and the energy of the personal consciousness, or outer self, are completely focused on the petty, useless, human desires of the physical body. The glorious power of the I AM Presence — the *Mahatma*, now — is entirely ignored, yet its energy is squandered by humanity on their misaligned priorities. Humanity cannot experience the higher side of life until it looks away from the little self to acknowledge and feel the presence of the all-encompassing *Mahatma*, which now finds no level that it cannot access.

Grief, which is believed to be a form of love, is nothing more than another powerful expression of selfishness. Apathy also belongs in this category — it is neither life nor love. These negative emotions effectively lower humanity into slavery, because they break down one's resistance by wasting the energy of life, which should be used for the creation of love, beauty and relative perfection. This slavery will continue as long as the personality fails to make the necessary conscious effort to free itself from the lure of the psychic world, which contains only the creations of humanity, generated by the discordant feelings, thoughts, and words of the personality level. It is the daily activities of the mind, emotions and body that distort the creative expression of life to create the illusion of these psychic/lower astral levels.

Humanity are fascinated, entertained, and hypnotized by the various phenomena of the psychic world; but we must warn you that there is nothing positive nor permanent within the psychic/lower astral strata — it is as dangerous as quicksand, and just as deceiving. The psychic/lower astral realm is the emotional/*lower mental* realm; it is the creation of human consciousness, the accumulation of human thoughts and forms energized by human feelings and referred to as mass consciousness. It contains nothing whatsoever of the Cosmic Light.

This fascination and desire of the psychic expression is experienced as a very subtle feeling on the part of the human personality, but it is this feeling that holds one's attention away from their connection to and their acknowledgement of their true reality, the I AM Presence of Source. Focusing on the activities of the psychic plane effectively cuts off the individual from the energy and the ability to connect with their God Source or even to anchor (with rare exceptions) the primal Soul and the personality levels into the Earth and her higher astral levels.

It is important to realize that nothing of Divine Consciousness comes from the psychic realm, regardless of any manifestations of evidence to the contrary. These levels of outer activity of the lower mind are forever changing their qualities, while the Christ Consciousness — for those in dense embodiment — which is of the Divine Light, is ever-expanding, although not in the manner used by the world religions of today, which convey only form, darkness, and limitation.

It is because of this subtle fascination for and the attention to the lower astral levels that humanity is today like a mass of children in need of the great help and all-encompassing wisdom of the Cosmic Walk-In to raise them into the understanding of the Light by first becoming the Christ, and then anchoring and becoming the *Mahatma*, which is the only means of release from the darkness of Earth's present chaos. Avatars have come to this planet to bring the needed assistance at regular intervals since the end of the Second Golden Age when mankind became fascinated with the form side of life and the creation of "things." (Refer to the diagram, "The Cosmic Heart," p. 350.)

Humanity's attention turned at this point to outer activities, and the conscious recognition of their own individualized God Self was forgotten. The Creator level — abiding in Its spiritual body, and now in the atomic body — was completely ignored. Thus Source has been able to express only part of the Divine Plan to the dense levels of consciousness.

Those who venerate the magician do not become Light themselves...but then, neither does the magician! Using the devic elementals constructively, but still psychically, there have been and still are many beings on Earth who have been venerated because they work as atomizers, able to manipulate the elemental kingdom. This is what caused the destruction of Atlantis! These beings go through the platitudes of their respective religions, but do not shift consciousness into the Light; thus the masses particularly adore the phenomenon of atomization, above which the Light is trying to raise them. The danger here is the same as that of the old Atlantean psychic/emotional realms, which ultimately destroyed that continent because the Atlanteans became unable to distinguish the devic elemental kingdom from the psychic/lower chakra and astral levels. They therefore became trapped in illusion and the emotional body, not in the reality of becoming Christ Conscious and moving beyond these profound limitations.

I can hear you now asking, "But we've seen such wonderful healings performed by psychic atomizers! How can you say this when Jesus/the Christ did the same thing?" Both used the devic elementals and the lower astral levels to create the loaves of bread or the jewels and the profound healings. The Christ Consciousness through Maitreya allowed Jesus and Peter (principally) to perform from the Divine Light of the Christed energy, not manipulate the elemental/astral realms. Two thousand years ago on Earth, this was a new beginning, a new approach to demonstrating the divine qualities of Light, not the manipulation of the devic elementals through the lower astral/psychic realms.

We wish to remind you that the basic principle of healing on this planet through mass consciousness is neither Light nor dark; it is simply what the total you, the creator of your own reality, have allowed.

When the Atlanteans destroyed their continent, Sanat Kumara ended their civilization and the doors were closed to the elemental kingdom, which had been misused by the priest class to so distort reality that it became impossible to distinguish the lower astral levels from the day-to-day dense physical expression; there was an immense overlap of realities. The shifts on Earth now, as a result of the crystallization of herself and humanity, parallel in many ways the destruction of Atlantis. Sanat Kumara will initiate similar shifts on the Earth because mankind have not understood even remotely their correct angle of ascent and integration.

Today there is such a thin line between Light and darkness that the differences for humankind are not yet distinguishable. Thus we have spent sequential time studying this phenomenon on Earth regarding an aspect of Self called

Sai Baba (and others) — who as well-intentioned as he (and they) believes himself to be, working at a midpoint between Light and darkness but expressing the fully developed primal Soul — and have come to the realization that his (and their) veneration by millions of followers cannot and will not assist anyone who is following this enigma![1]

How, pray tell, are Sai Baba's ancient dark beliefs regarding a religion that cannot function fourth-dimensionally going to assist a fourth-dimensional being who is mesmerized by the calling card, the atomizing? This wonderful ability of Sai Baba doesn't rub off through osmosis; mankind must *taste* the carrot, not have it dangled in front of them! One does not benefit by adoring and clutching the hem of Sai Baba's garb or waiting for the akashic ash to fall from his picture. This demonstration benefits humankind not!

The primal Soul of Sai Baba has totally "mastered" and is one which should be emulated and then moved beyond, but not worshiped; and there are many who fall into this category, including all of your world religions and gurus, which Sai Baba will unintentionally join. Mankind must stop giving their creative power to others and become the creators of their own reality!

Humanity has become bound by its own outer creations. Thus the Soul levels, as we enter this New Age, have invited the Cosmic Avatar, **Mahatma**. Out of sheer compassion for the misery of humanity and the slowness of its growth, the collective "We" have come to energize what will have to be, not what was. The Transformational Fire introduced on Earth through the Tenth, Eleventh and Twelfth Rays, incorporating the spiritual microtron for all fourth through sixth densities, is just that — transformation. When we say that there should be tens of millions doing their etheric Lightbody Ascension, that will depend totally upon humankind's response to this supreme opening during the following 35 years on Earth, and how much of Sanat Kumara's ravaged and crystallized body remains habitable. The choices are yours and that of mass consciousness; the remarkable opening *is* available!

When the individual who is striving for freedom reaches the point where he can release any desired amount of Light from his etheric Lightbody in-

---

1 Those we refer to as "masters," who are of Earth's evolution not "imported" as galactic, universal or Cosmic Avatars, have always been able to demonstrate the manipulation of the atom to a much greater degree than the avatars of greater resonance; those of Earth's system have learned how to raise above atomic density which other more highly evolved beings do not experience until they *descend into* atomic density. In their divine right to become Light without mirroring this through another personality, mankind have become *hypnotized by the phenomenon instead of connecting with the primal Soul level* (which does not include the Higher Self/Higher Soul or Oversoul levels). Sai Baba's choice (free will) has been to demonstrate the continuum of a religion brought in and introduced to the world by the current Christ, Maitreya, in his embodiment as Sri Krishna. What may have been valid 3000 years ago has no validity whatsoever entering this New Age; it causes multitudes to adore the image but not the substance, and to give their power away. A good example of this is the worship of Jesus within Christendom.

stantly and by his own conscious will, then he can control all dense physical manifestation. When mankind learns and releases self from the wheel of birth and rebirth, then will the problems of human existence disappear! The perceived enemy called death will also disappear, for what is it but a release from the physical garment used in the perfecting of life?

In the quest for perfection and freedom, when one's physical body becomes too incapacitated to allow the personality within to make the self-conscious effort to express perfection, then Soul steps in to dissolve this limitation, allowing the individual to continue in a new vehicle. The grief for the loss of a loved one is in reality an expression of rebellion or lack of acceptance of this fundamental law. This totally selfish act serves only to hinder the progress of the one who has passed on, because the moment the mourner focuses his attention upon the one who has left, he joins that loved one in his higher mental body, bringing with him all the burdens of his grief. This useless suffering is all due to the age-old belief on the part of humanity that the body is the individual instead of simply a garment the individual wears.

Once you know and fully understand the life principle within your physical body, then you will know and feel that it is truly all-wise and all-powerful. When you have comprehended and assimilated this knowledge you will clearly see that it is not only natural and possible, but it is eventually necessary to transcend all outer activities, laws and limitations. These were all created by humanity itself in its ignorance and are expressed in the outer activity because the intellect has been allowed to act without the Light of the Source to illuminate it.

It is impossible for an all-wise, all-perfect Creator to create anything unlike Itself, and so humanity must accept the responsibility for the limitation and discord that it has created for itself. The Creator level gives to the beings with free will, the Co-Creators, the use of the attributes of the Creator as tools for manifestation at their respective levels of initiation/integration in the universe. Each individual is endowed with the ability to form conclusions; however when the intellect alone is used, as is the case with most of humanity, the results are based on fragmented, incomplete information. This in turn is the direct result of using only part of one's bestowed creative powers. Conclusions drawn from partial rather than complete information naturally produce unsatisfactory results; this is why religions today have no intrinsic value.

To be a Creator, the individual must have free will. Therefore if he chooses to create with one spoke instead of the whole wheel, for example, then it is his right — through his free will — to make that experience. His wheel of manifestation cannot be and is not complete until he recognizes his I AM Presence, for it is only Source which knows all that is required to complete any pattern of manifestation that produces perfection through the Twelve Rays.

All patterns of perfection are stored within the all-knowing mind of the Council of Twelve for this Cosmic Day and can never be made manifest in the dense physical world until the outer activity of the mind, which is the intellectual consciousness, is illuminated by the Twelfth Ray of Golden Light within the heart. All rays originate with the source of this Cosmic Day, the Undifferentiated Source.

The I AM Presence, *Mahatma*, does not recognize and could never create the mass of destruction, chaos, and confusion that exists in the outer mentality and world of humankind. It is the birthright and privilege of every being to express the fullness of the Divine Inner Presence; however, if the personality level will not call forth the Power of the I AM/*Mahatma* through the higher mind into the outer life at all times, then the outer experience will remain the ever-changing condition, or dumping ground, for the mass consciousness.

The Divine Presence of the *Mahatma* abides within the spiritual body now (since June 14, 1988) of every being, resting in the Source Star, which is located 6 to 9 feet (2 to 3 meters) above the crown chakra. This Source energy, the collective Co-Creator Council of Twelve, is occupied with forever creating and expanding Its perfection; It exists and creates cosmically in Its own realm, which is beyond levels and dimensions. Perfection is analogous to the ray with which each Director of the Source Council of Twelve is working. There is no static perfection! If you asked each of these twelve Directors their view of perfection, you would get twelve different answers. From the Source Council of Twelve as a whole, you would receive one answer, which then, and only then, would be the definition of perfection.

It is only in the outer expression of the human personality level, which is but a minute part of one's Beingness, that imperfection can be created and experienced. The selective, discriminative intelligence of the individual observes the conditions, trials, and tribulations of the human expression from the level of the higher mind (the causal body), without accepting them into its level of consciousness. It sees what is required to produce perfection in the dense physical experience and is able to reach into the physical-etheric body, the individual's current physical expression, to draw forth what is needed to create it (perfection relative to the specific level that one is integrating). Thus you may wish to concentrate on the Source Star during your personal or group meditations, for this is your home where all beings must connect with their true essence as All That Is in order to hasten their journey and re-identify with the collective Self, the I AM Presence, the Source for this Cosmic Day.

The seemingly impervious walls of the outer self are no barrier to the *Mahatma* energy, any more than they are to an electrical impulse. This presence is the Christ Consciousness within for all in physical embodiment, the God Self of every individual. When someone acknowledges, accepts, comprehends and feels the *Mahatma* Presence, Its limitless power is released into his use. By consciously raising and illuminating the dense physical body and its every activity through the Light of the *Mahatma*, Its power is released into the outer world through the individual to manifest his dominion, through free will, that was originally given to him at the time of his monadic birth and individualization.

Only a Son of God, a being with free will, can decree as God decrees, I AM *Mahatma*. And whatever quality or invocation follows that divine sound spoken into the ethers, becomes manifest in the realm of substance and thus becomes one's reality.

The word *Mahatma* is a mantra with which to invoke the energy of *The Rider of the White Horse*, the Source. It is not the same *Mahatma* Madame Blavatsky and others have referred to in their writings, which is a Sanskrit word meaning "great soul." Our use of *Mahatma* embodies much more than the Soul or even Oversoul levels, much more than humankind can yet conceive!

When an individual says, *"Mahatma,"* he is invoking the creative/integrative attribute of the Source and is announcing Creation at his particular point of Light within this Cosmic Day. The vibratory action of the words I AM or *Mahatma* releases the energy of Creation, so that whatever quality follows that decree is instantly manifested in the pure etheric substance and ultimately in the spiritual microtron (these, being stepped down through the Twelve Rays, are the only energies in existence that need be defined or qualified). It is the responsibility of each one to invoke perfection into his own world, for the law of his being requires that each person use his own energy to utter the decree — *you cannot give this responsibility to someone else to do for you!* The *Mahatma* can synthesize your connections, but only you can implement the undertaking!

The Twelve Rays that constitute this Cosmic Day are the self-luminous, intelligent substance of the I AM, *Mahatma*, which exists at all points (except those third-dimensional planets still limited to Seven Rays) and of which all of Creation is composed. Limitation and discord can form a barrier to the Light, shutting off some of its radiance, but imperfection can never touch the substance itself. The limitations that mankind has created for itself are products of the human intellect and emotions, which have not been trained to look into the Light of the individual's own I AM Presence for the Divine Plan upon which to base all outer activities.

The Divine, or perfect Plan, exists only within the spiritual Light, the microtron. When the dense physical intellect and emotional level are purified and illuminated by the Light of this great Presence, then the perfection of the thought and potential within it may flow through the personality without becoming distorted by the fragmented information of the outer consciousness. The feedback from the human sensory system is a very unenlightened report indeed; however, when Light is directed to it from the Source of All That Is, it melts into its glorious monadic perfection.

Pure love, wisdom, joy, peace, balance and every other quality of the Light can only be attained through the One Great Presence, the Source Council of Twelve for this Cosmic Day, wherein each member represents one Cosmic Ray. It is this complete Council of Twelve, embodying the Twelve Rays, which enables this creation, this one Cosmic Day, to exist. There and only there does the blueprint for perfection exist.

If the student will consciously place and dedicatedly hold his attention upon the I AM/*Mahatma* he will be able to express such Divine Light and

Love that he will not possibly be able to conceive at present, unless at one of Brian's seminars (or elsewhere on Earth, by tuning in to the *Mahatma* energy as the seminar is taking place), where the fineness of spiritual energy can most assuredly be felt and in time, integrated. (See "Embodying the Microtron," p. 439.)

There is immense support from the Archangels, the Angelic Host, the various Soul levels and now, for many, the Oversoul, plus alternate realities and aspects of Self that one is consciously uniting with. These seminars are joined by multitudes of discarnate beings with much love, joy and appreciation, for what a few of humankind are participating in at this level of integration has a profound effect on evolution — not simply for Earth and humankind, but for all of Creation.

The ratio of participation numerically is overwhelmingly in favor of higher-conscious (discarnate) beings who are simply more conscious of the changes that are being implemented and who are also learning, through the *Mahatma*, about spiritualizing matter with the microtron. These fourth-through sixth-density beings are consciously reuniting with their monadic/spiritual levels. In the annals of human "spiritual" endeavors, no being has been able to integrate the Monad sufficiently to anchor the spiritual microtron into any universal (physical) density. Now, because of the *Mahatma*'s integrative abilities and assignment to synthesize pure electronic energy with the spiritual (monadic) microtron, physical evolution for this Cosmic Day will be hastened by at least a thousandfold!

Divine Love embodies the perfection of every attribute of the Source. When the individual consciously enters the path of Self-mastery, he must fully realize that from that point he must accomplish everything through the power of Unconditional Love from within his own I AM Presence. He must understand and remember that Divine Love contains within it the complete wisdom and almighty power of the *Mahatma*. When consciously expressed within the individual, it is an invulnerable, invincible, protective armor against any negativity. The only means to attaining perfection in this Cosmic Day is through Unconditional Love. Therefore, love yourself as an expression of the *Mahatma*, and nothing untoward can enter your beingness or worlds.

LIGHT is the substance and energy of this Cosmic Day. The microtron is the unit of monadic Light of which the eternal spiritual body is composed. This body is your ever-perfect and ever-expanding form, your eternal reservoir of Divine Light and Love. It is sometimes referred to as the White Fire body because the dazzling Cosmic Light that it emanates is so overwhelmingly intense to the human eye that it appears to be white fire.

As the human being increases the vibratory rate of his physical-etheric body, the electronic Light within every dense physical atom grows brighter and brighter until it radiates to such a degree that it becomes self-luminous and then is able to transcend the gravity of the Earth. Later, you may learn to consciously express all of the junior monadic and Oversoul levels through the integration of the spiritual microtron. Even then, because of the great spiritual law, "the ring passeth not," there still remain 225 levels of the Monad to complete one's connection with and then reunite as the Source for this Cosmic Day. (Refer to the charts, "The Cosmic Heart," p. 350, and "The Co-Creator and Creator Levels," pp. 228-29.)

When the atomic structure of your physical body becomes completely Light, you enter into the one universal element where freedom and mastery are found, keeping in mind that mastery of the dense physical levels is nonetheless a primary step in one's evolution. This is the reality and the ultimate goal of the dense physical aspirant. One is raised to the level of physical/electrical Divinity, forever free of dense physicality, able to travel everywhere within one's vibrational level — within one's domain of "the ring passeth not" — still knowing oneself as an individual, self-conscious expression of the I AM Presence, *Mahatma*, which is of immense value as you raise your vibration above the Earth and primal Soul outside of sequential time; and many enter areas of expansiveness unlike anything in their conscious awareness. Thus the *Mahatma* continues to assist and support integration for the Higher Self, Oversoul and, ultimately, the senior monadic levels until your journey is completed as the I AM Presence, *Mahatma*, for this one Cosmic Day.

The Eternal Law states that you can never pass beyond the level of vibration that you have integrated until the *collective You* integrates greater and greater levels of the Wholeness of Self.

Almost every secret society of your past, which stood for constructive activity, when recognizing the Light as the Source of all good, used the word "raised" in their initiations. This *raising* is literally, figuratively, eternally, and physically true, for the vibrational frequency of the physical atom is raised until it becomes the pure, electronic essence, or Spirit and then the microtron, the pure God-substance — Light, LIGHT, LIGHT!

As the spiritual microtron interfaces with the physical atom/electronic body, it accelerates the physical into its divine purity and structure, creating the spiritual-physical body. This eternal body remains forever perfect, youthful, strong, and free. In this new Lightbody, individuals can and will function wherever they choose in the universal condition. It simply becomes finer as one reconnects with the Source for this Cosmic Day.

The innate desire for this perfect condition of existence has always been the ideal of mankind. In the myths, legends, and fairy tales of every race that has ever lived on this planet are found stories of perfect beings — immortal, beautiful, eternally youthful, and all-wise. These stories all have their origin in the eternal truth of Being which humanity carries forward from age to age. This ideal image held in the mind of man is *the master record upon which humanity was modeled in the beginning, the IMAGE and LIKENESS of GOD.*

If one is a true student of life, he will be inspired to delve deeply into the thoughts and feelings of the beings who express superhuman qualities, conditions, and ideals. The ordinary personality considers these to be impossible to attain because of the great energy required to manifest them in the outer expression; the effort is more than the ordinary person cares to make. This attainment requires a sincere, strict discipline of the human consciousness until it learns obedience to the pattern of perfection, rather than its own selfish whims and temporary appetites.

The true student of life understands that any God quality that he can consciously bring to mind can be brought into existence through the creative power of his own thought and his feeling of Divine Love. Divine thoughts, feelings, qualities, and ideals can only be found by *focusing on Divinity*, for they do not exist elsewhere. Like produces like throughout infinity. Divinity is the Light and perfection of life.

One can see the "atomic accelerator," *Mahatma*, in operation at every *Mahatma* seminar that Brian holds, where the energy is so transformational that we have seen individuals integrate two levels of what were called initiations in your past, during one weekend seminar. The profound sense of limitation is no longer present when one works with the *Mahatma* energy!

It is ignorance and darkness that cause mankind to limit the possible, and cause humanity to close the door on the wonders of this universe and beyond, saying, "I don't believe that; it is impossible." The students of Light come to truly know and accept the all-powerful Source of Creation, which the reasoning mind cannot doubt when one studies the wonders of the atom, the universal suns and now, the spiritual microtron. The marvels of Creation, which are found everywhere on our planet alone, are endless and show without any doubt *relative perfection*.

The bulk of humanity need to realize that there are many kinds of individuals expanding their Light on the planets of many systems, and just because one species has no knowledge of others yet, this does not prove that the others do not exist. Humankind must learn a little more about the life that abides in this universe besides themselves, and these writings through *Mahatma* contain part of that knowledge. The time is NOW! Let the light of truth shine clearly through all preconceived human ideas and opinions. Now is the time when knowledge and wisdom will be revealed and ignorance may disappear, replaced by the great Light of the Source.

We use the term "Self-conscious" to describe the individual who is conscious of his Source and perfection of life, which are expressing through him. Only the Self-conscious individual is connected to *all* of the attributes and creative power of the I AM Presence through the Cosmic Avatar, *Mahatma*. Only this individual can know who and what he truly is, able to express the fullness of the creative power of God by decreeing the words, "I AM *Mahatma*," on whichever level he perceives himself to be of the 352 levels that the *Mahatma* energy overshadows from Source to Earth.

"I AM *Mahatma*" is the acknowledgment and release of the energy to manifest and bring forth into the outer existence whatever quality follows this divine decree. For intelligence to act, there must be intelligence to be acted upon, and the Divine Substance records almost like a photographic film — whatever quality the individual invokes through his thought, feeling and spoken word. Intelligence is omnipresent; it is within the electronic Light, and is now present in physicality with the microtron.

Light is the central point of life or energy within every atom, and composes the substance for all of physical manifestation. We speak of the atom here because the lower rate of vibration composing physicality is the atomic structure that we are trying to perfect. When you consciously envelop or focus upon any person, place, thing, or condition in the White Light of the Source, you penetrate through the atomic structure into the electronic, wherein there is no physical imperfection. In the use of the spiritual microtron, one penetrates the structure of relative imperfection and then whatever the attention is focused upon can be brought forth as perfect. This is not just perfection as the Creator sees it, but is the Creator's perfection expressed.

As Sons of God, you are given free will to choose and direct the activity of the Light. It is therefore imperative to focus your conscious thought and attention upon what is to be accomplished in order to give the needed direction to the action of this powerful force, the microtron, which is your right and privilege to use for you and the Father are one.

When you invoke the White Light of the Source for the etheric-body Ascension, you are actually accepting the electronic structure, which is now present in manifestation for all of humankind, for you are acting from the physical plane of action, or perfect physical manifestation. When you hold your desire steady and unwavering, it becomes the conscious thought of direction, for you cannot have desire without conscious thought.

When you know that the perfection of your desire is manifested the moment that you start the dynamic action of the Light, this will remove all uncertainty from your mind about your manifestation. Creating in the fourth dimension simply means instant manifestation and abundance for both your inner and outer realities. By visualizing any person, place, object, or condition as an illuminated figure within the energy of the *Mahatma,* your desire becomes immediately present in form because you have then eliminated all relative imperfection in the action.

The initiate should see and feel his body to be composed of pure white light, radiating forth infinite rays of Light. *The Light is your real Self, the I AM Presence, the full monadic perfection of All That Is, SOURCE.*

Divine Love is a presence, a light, a power, a principle, a substance and an activity. As Light is directed by thought, when one directs forth Divine Love, one is setting into motion the highest form of action, the most powerful force. Divine Love, when consciously directed, becomes love, wisdom and power in action; this is why Divine Love produces such wonderful results — it becomes instantaneous and all-powerful when the outer consciousness ceases to limit it. As these principles become integrated into your consciousness, you will find more and more instant manifestation in your creative ability.

Never be afraid to command and demand anything that is a cosmic principle. Know that the Light, the *cosmic microtron* and the physical *electronic substance* are for your use; they are at your command. Your I AM Presence is a Self-conscious being of which our lower consciousness is but a fragmentary part; one really must move beyond the primal Soul level and complete the etheric- (Light) body Ascension. Therefore, as you consciously connect with the totality of who you are on all 352 levels as the *Mahatma,* and the more you consciously connect with this presence, the more quickly it will respond to you. The more you channel or consciously focus on becoming the *Mahatma,* the stronger will be that connection with all 352 levels and initiations and the faster your connection to who you are as the All That Is becomes clear.

The Almighty God Flame, breathing within Itself, now projects Twelve Rays into the great universal sea of pure electronic Light. This all-knowing Light substance is the clothing, so to speak, for these rays of All That Is. Each ray embodies the attributes of the Creator, so no imperfection can ever enter or affect them. The Transformational Fire of the Source sends a focal point, or spark, into each ray; this forms a heart center upon which the electronic Light substance gathers to create the electronic body and, inevitably, the spiritual body. Around the electronic body it sends forth rays of lesser intensity, which form a force field, or aura, sometimes referred to as the etheric body. In this force field are deposited the results of all constructive activity during and between each physical incarnation. All electronic substance which has been used constructively by the individual in physicality is also placed within it, and so through this body the Source may express more of Its life force.

As of February 26, 1993, the shift of the Earth's electromagnetic north was 12 degrees away from your true north (as viewed in Switzerland). The electromagnetic forces are the cement that contain matter and literally hold the Earth to its etheric grid; in other words, the Earth is becoming more like a bowl of jelly. As this planet enters her fourth-dimensional reality, *change* is a natural progression, as with all planets as they enter the first grand division of the seven grand divisions of each dimension.

The etheric body, through the personality's journey in physical existence, becomes an ever-expanding Light, a self-sustained expression of the Creator, flowing out forever on rays of love and wisdom, the Second Ray, to all universes.

The Undifferentiated Source is, in reality, an infinite reservoir of constructively used energy and substance. The gathered total experience for this Cosmic Day is drawn upward and integrated into the Source of this Cosmic Day and, in turn, into the Undifferentiated Source through the Twelve Rays. It becomes the Transformational Fire and never loses its individual identity within the Cosmic Day. This is how the limitless activity of life and Creation goes on, ever expanding its perfection.

The universal energy and substance that is used inharmoniously by the personality level accumulates in the atmosphere around the physical etheric body of both the individual and the Earth. When it builds to the point of creating a vortex, it must be purified and returned to the realm of Cosmic Light through the integration of microtrons.

The purifying process of the spiritual microtron, acting within the human body to consume qualities that are not in alignment, sometimes produces the sensation of pain if wrongly interpreted by the personality. The all-encompassing energy of the microtron truly acts within the flesh of the physical body to energize and enliven, and can produce the sensations of peace and ecstasy. When acting within the atmosphere of the Earth and the physical four-body system, it sometimes causes discomfort on the cellular level and cataclysmic conditions for the Earth while activating and energizing its true spiritual nature. On Earth at this time, you will have verification of what we speak, for many, many areas of your planet will experience these cataclysmic conditions as Sanat Kumara's embodiment, Earth, integrates the karmic crystallization that is so powerfully infused into his planetary body by humankind, past and present, who are the major consciousness here.

The personality level of every individual is endowed with free will, the power of choice, as to what it wishes to experience, create, think, and feel on its level. If he uses the divine energy and substance in a constructive manner, then peace, joy and expansion will return to him. However, if he chooses and creates otherwise, his misery and destruction will return to him over and over again until he raises his consciousness above that of Earth and primal Soul.

The personal self is a custodian of life, of ideas, and of Light substance, electronic and microtronic. The fact that one is in physical existence on the human level is an acknowledgment, to those who understand life, that one has chosen to enter into individual existence and has accepted the responsibility of being a creator. What we call the physical body, or atomic structure, is a reflection of the outer activity of the mind. As each one of us creates our own reality, if we create for ourselves conditions that are unpleasant or lacking, we also have the power to purify and change them through the right use of the Transformational Fire. If one desires to put his personal self and world in order to create a reality of peace, joy, perfection and light, then he must look to his electronic/etheric body for the divine pattern of his universal/physical perfection, for it is not to be found elsewhere in dense physical existence. Only there, in the "fullness of the Presence" can the personal self ever find the fulfillment of every constructive desire.

This perfected etheric/electronic Body dwells within the God Flame, and in purifying its instrument, the personality, the outer expressions of the physical body and mind become raised in vibration to be able to see the electronic body clearly within the brilliant Light of its force field. All that is within the God Flame flows into the microtron and the electronic body where the intensity of the Light of the *Mahatma* energy is stepped down to the vibrational frequencies where it can now be accepted in the physical/universal levels.

From the heart center of the Source now flows all Twelve Rays, which are transmuted into liquid Light, enter the physical body through the pineal gland and the endocrine system, and fill the nerve channels. This liquid White Fire flows through the nervous system, as blood flows through the veins. This is the life force that beats the heart, moves the muscles of the body, enables you to walk; it is also the energizing Light within your brain cells. This lifestream of the physical body is often referred to as the silver cord. At the time of so-called death, the God Presence, your Soul levels, withdraw the stream of liquid Light and the flesh disintegrates, still leaving you with a four-body system; your etheric, emotional, mental and spiritual bodies remain intact, at least until you raise your vibration above the first three of these.[2]

This concentrated electronic energy or life essence is a liquid Light which flows wherever your attention directs it. The mind's attention, however, is pulled in different directions by thought, feeling, sight, hearing — by all of the physical senses, actually. We cannot emphasize enough to the individual *what power you have at your command when you have gained full control of your attention.*

When you are doing intense mental work, the liquid Light is concentrated within your brain and flows forth through the third eye center as a ray of Light; if your inner vision is open, you can see this. When you are speaking, this pure energy flows forth through the throat chakra as sound; and if you are sending forth Divine Love, this liquid Light radiates out through the heart chakra. When you are expressing intense feeling, it flows forth through your solar plexus; and here it also performs the task of digesting the food.

If one's inner sight is open, he will see a stream of Light flowing from whichever energy center is being used at the moment. This Light becomes colored by whatever ray or point of integration (initiation) the personality is expressing through thought, feeling, and one's ability to assimilate and integrate. Once again, here lies one's responsibility as a creator as well as the means to correct or purify whatever has been wrongly created. In other words, you have the ability to *rewrite your script,* even though all of Creation is played out in the Eternal Now, without time, space, or causation — again, one of the many advantages of expressing dense physical embodiment.

If the life essence is released through the polarity chakra for sexual pleasure alone instead of building a vehicle for the Higher Self and Oversoul, then the self-generated process of disintegration of the physical body commences. As you have all been made aware, the disease AIDS appears as a curse for those who, in this life or in other lives, have been totally preoccupied with their sexual activity within the outer self. During our teaching, we have noticed several who are unable to control their sexual/emotional appetites, and no matter how great the perceived gains are in the integration of Light through the *Mahatma,* one must control one's life essence; however, not in the way that the religious clergy have endeavored to solve this issue, by way of fear and repression.

We are not suggesting repression of sexual energy through human will power — that is and always has been disastrous, for to dam up a powerful energy by trying to repress it while external suggestions and internal thoughts

---

2 Humankind has not understood that the "Spiritual Body" is not the pure Electonic Body. Thus the advance pioneers who use those terms have not integrated the "True" Spiritual Body. Refer to the realization "Embodying the Microtron," p. 439 for clarification and p. 425 for greater clarification of spiritual.

and feelings continue to energize it, will eventually cause an explosion of some kind. That method was never advocated by any teacher who clearly understood the truth and law concerning sexuality.

Humanity has not, except to a very small degree, understood this basic truth. In order to rise out of the misery, poverty, and disaster in which mass consciousness has been wallowing forever, the individual must reach an understanding of the outer activity of his mind. Through the conscious knowledge and control of his emotions and sexual urges, he can shut the door on the subtle, dangerous influences and suggestions from the psychic plane.

The level of human feelings is a reservoir of energy, but it is impossible for thoughts to become things until one propels them forth into the electronic substance by *feeling with intensity* — not with a whimper of uncertainty, but with the understanding that you can become the creator of your own reality, and by knowing without any doubt that this can be so!

Doubt and fear are subtle human feelings that can keep you from accepting the *Mahatma* energy and its perfection, if you let them. The *Mahatma* presence never has and never can fail because it is true spiritual energy. This is a simple formula for quick, certain attainment in life. Tremendous advancement is available to all, if you will — because you can — consciously, completely, and continually accept the all-encompassing love, wisdom and integrative power of the *Mahatma,* whose energy is flowing and acting through your beingness at every moment.

One area that must be clear to the student of life is that of *desire,* and of the distinction between human appetite and divine desire. These two expressions are as far apart as darkness and Light. Appetite is an accumulation of energy on the level of human feelings and physical senses and has no relation at all to desire as expressed by the Creator.

It is impossible to progress, or become the *Mahatma,* without the divine expression of desire. One can never attain mastery of physicality and the two major ascensions with an attitude of desirelessness, for without the desire for attainment, attainment is not possible! All constructive desire is *God in action through you.* If desire were not part of the God Principle, then Creation would not have taken place; until the Source *desired* manifestation, it could not have come forth. The purpose of desire is the forward motion, or expansion, of life itself. Life is perpetual motion, and it is constructive desire that sustains this.

One must be very careful to discriminate between desire and appetite, and to pay close attention to one's motive for one's actions. You will have to be completely honest with yourself as you look at your motive, for the outer mind will try to convince you that you're making a decision based on reason when it is actually trying to satisfy a feeling instead!

Alas, the majority of humanity are controlled ninety percent of the time by their feelings, rather than by the wisdom of the mind. This is what makes them principally creatures of physical appetite, instead of divinely directed creators and masters of their lives. Even the simplest mind knows the difference between a constructive and a destructive idea; as children we innately know the difference between God desire, the divine way of life, and the human appetite for self-gratification. We are commanded to choose the divine way of life, and if we do not direct our sensual appetites to obey that command, then we must struggle and suffer until we learn to elevate our desires to blend harmoniously with the All That Is.

When one gives in to his own feeling of resistance, he destroys himself — mind, body, and world — because of the law that dictates that whatever negative thought or feeling sent forth by a human must first vibrate through the lower mind and body of the sender before going out into the universe. Once it has traveled as far as it can on the universal level, it begins its return to its creator, the personality. On its way back, however, each discordant thought or feeling gathers more of its kind, which accumulates to become the reality of the individual and mass consciousness. This is why the Earth and humankind, entering the fourth dimension, are literally coming apart at the seams.

Thus the repetition of physical embodiment would be an endless circle of cause and effect if the human being did not have the Presence of God within him. This is the innate part of you which declares, "I AM," and is the life, the power, and the intelligence that energize your physical body. When the discordant habits of the personal self build to such a momentum that the Light of the I AM, *Mahatma*, are no longer able to expand and thereby continue the fulfillment of a constructive life plan, then the primal Soul begins to decrease its supply of energy and eventually withdraws.

If the student really wants to know the truth about reincarnation and life, then he must go to the Source of life and study there as the *Mahatma*, for only as he receives wisdom from the all-knowing Mind can he express its Light. It doesn't matter how many ideas, mental concepts, or facts we may have about anything, and unless we become one with it, experiencing it through *feeling*, it we can never truly know. Eternal truth and wisdom come only as you *consciously embody the I AM, Mahatma*. Therefore, if one wishes to prove to oneself the truth of eternal life, that proof can only come from personal experience, revealed to him as he connects with his own God Self.

The individual always becomes that which he focuses upon; if he meditates upon the *Mahatma* presence, he will become an expression of that perfection. And if he puts his time, energy, and attention upon the insatiable appetites of the physical body, he destroys his temple. Many are now feeling the increase and intensity of spiritual energy, which is expanding the Earth and humanity at this time. During this most important opening, it is absolutely imperative to maintain control over your thoughts, feelings, and words and to make every effort to express them positively and constructively. At no time in the history of your planet has this been as important as it is now!

The Earth is in the process of a tremendous, and completely new, cosmic transition and new birth. It is the time for the attitude of war to give way to peace, hatred to love, selfishness to unselfishness, in the full recognition that in order to survive, mankind must use their God-given energy to live according to the Law of Love.

The hour arrives in the evolution of every planet and its occupants when they must consciously choose to express the peace, love, harmony, perfection and Divine Plan of the system to which they belong. When that time arrives, the individual either moves forward to fulfill the Plan or must remove itself and incarnate in another schoolroom of the universe until its personal level learns obedience to life.

The Law of Life is very clear that peace, harmony and love must be expressed to every created thing; this is expressed even in the ethers of infinite space. Human beings are the only creators of hell. Each one carries his own heaven or hell with him at every moment, these being the manifestations of the mental and emotional states that the individual is expressing through his attitude toward life. There is no other cause for them. The personality, having free will always, can choose to accept and obey the Law of Life, thereby enjoying every good thing of the Divine Kingdom; or it can disobey this law and suffer the difficulties of its own self-generated discord.

Great streams of love and harmony, upon which peace depends, are now being poured out by the Ascended Masters and Cosmic Avatars, such as *Mahatma*, into the humanly generated chaos that fills this beautiful planet and her inhabitants. Mankind, which has for so long pulled against the cosmic current of love, is now being forced to turn and seek the Light in order to survive. Misery, darkness, and ignorance exist only in the absence of love. Let the great light of the Source, the All That Is, quickly enfold the Earth and humanity, that its suffering may end.

The tools for the salvation of humankind have always been here — limitless Light substance, divine wisdom and invincible power are always there for you. You, the individual, need only to understand how to raise or lower the atomic vibratory action by the power of the *Mahatma* in order to create whatever you can possibly desire. No one but yourself can dictate what shall come into your experience and world.

The Infinite Omnipresent Substance is always around you, waiting to be acted upon. You, the individual, are the channel through which the *Mahatma* wishes to expand its perfection. It pours out endlessly the energy of life, its limitless Light, but you are the governor of its use, the director of the results that it is to bring forth for you. It can and will produce whatever you desire instantaneously, *if* you can simply keep your personality aligned in harmony, so that discordant thoughts, feelings, and words cannot interrupt its ever-flowing perfection.

Life is perfection, and it contains all perfect manifestation within itself. The only duty of the individual is to be a vessel that expresses and reveals the perfection of life. When the personal self achieves control of the outer senses, it no longer pollutes the purity and perfection of the life that is flowing through him. The one who seeks to attain perfection must train the outer activity of his mind to listen to no voice except that of his Source Presence, to accept only its wisdom and obey only its direction. He must see the Light, hear the Light, feel the Light and *be* the Light of the All That Is.

No being in heaven or on Earth can fail to attain this divine goal if their desire for the Light is sincere, determined, and strong enough to hold the attention of their intellect upon that Light. If human beings seek the Light with one eye and the pleasure of the physical senses with the other, they will not have much success. Becoming the Light must be the sole idea and goal upon which to focus one's energy. For the one who has this strength and determination, undreamed-of avenues will open to bring about the fulfillment of their desire.

The aspirant must constantly monitor his outer self, for it is thoughts and feelings of anger, hate, selfishness, criticism, condemnation, and doubt of the I AM Presence, *Mahatma,* if permitted to remain in the consciousness of any human being, that will close the door to perfection. The existence of that being becomes just a process of eating and sleeping, until the energy drawn by the outer consciousness is used up and the body is dissolved. The individual must then make another effort to express the fullness of perfection through another physical body and continue this effort for eons, if necessary, until relative perfection is fully expressed.

In order to avoid the necessity for such continual reembodiment into limitation, this course has been affected, partly because of your limited primal Soul perspective which, in your past, has repeatedly gone over and over the same ground. Now, because of the synthesis brought forward through the *Mahatma,* the Soul, Higher Self, and Oversoul levels are being overshadowed to coordinate *all* levels of self.

Long ago, during a former golden age upon this planet, mankind still had the full use of the inner communication by thought, which we refer to as telepathy today. However, as the personality level looked away from the Light, their physical substance became denser and denser, until it reached the level of the atom, which has constituted the human body since then. This atomic substance vibrates at too slow a rate for thought to penetrate; therefore sounds, which eventually developed into words, had to be used as a means of communication, since they could register at this lower rate of vibration.

The individual can again call upon this perfect means of communication by releasing a ray of golden-white light from within his own *Mahatma* presence. This invocation of greater Light can increase the vibratory rate of the atoms to the point where thought can register and be comprehended without the spoken word. Accurate channeling of the *Mahatma* energy is a stepping stone in this direction of connecting with your totality of Self!

If humankind could understand and look toward this true ideal of life, the self-created chains and limitations that have bound them for millions of years would drop away in less than the time remaining in this period of grace, this opening until the year 2028. The Law of Life for this and all universes is the Law of Light, and in it all of humanity's suffering and confusion can disappear. The hour has arrived when whosoever cannot stand the radiance of the Light must disappear from this planet as mist before the morning sun.

The mass consciousness of mankind still seeks the possession of material things, which is of course, in opposition to the Law of Life, which says, "Expand, and forever let me pour greater and greater perfection through you." The Law of Life is to give, for only by giving of one's Self can one expand. To give the love of your own creative God Presence to all of mankind, to all of life, is the most powerful action that we can use to draw the human being into the divine. In this Divine Love is contained every good thing.

All of the pleasures of the outer world are but dust compared to the infinite wonders of the Cosmos. One of the infinite blessings of the ascended state is the absence of any criticism or condemnation of human frailties or mistakes. If the student of life can learn to let go of and forget everything that is useless, limiting, or in any way undesirable, he will not only be rewarded by rapid progress, but he will free himself from human bondage. For the initiate to drag with him old memories and patterns is but one of the many ways to create over and and over again the same negative experiences from which he is trying to free himself.

To rid oneself and one's world of disharmony, the personality must let go of all thought, feeling, and speech about imperfection. This cannot be released until it is completely out of your consciousness; as long as you remember one disturbed feeling or one injustice, you have not forgotten either the person or the condition. When you forgive everyone, and especially *yourself*, the emotional body can become truly serene, joyous, comfortable, and giving, like a mountain of Light.

Remember, whatever your consciousness is fixed upon, you bring into existence for yourself; it is impossible for your life to contain anything that is not your past or present accumulation of consciousness. Whatever you are conscious of in your thoughts and feelings impresses itself upon the universal substance in and around you and brings forth its own kind, always. There is no variation or escape from this cosmic law.

What is the Law of Light? Let us begin by realizing first that everywhere around us is a pure, electric, universal substance that has inappropriately been called Cosmic Light, and which the Bible refers to as spirit. The opening for true spiritual Light was not available in this universe until June 14, 1988. This is the one pure, primal essence out of which comes all Creation. It is the pure life substance of the First Cause — God. It is infinite, and we may draw upon It at any time for anything we can ever require. The pure electronic light, the spiritual microtron, is the limitless storehouse of the physical universes and the spiritual monadic levels. In it is all perfection, and from it comes All That Is.

Divine Love is the heart of infinity and of the individual; it is an ever-expanding flame of intelligence which releases limitless energy, power, wisdom, and substance. It will also release infinite blessings to all who will harmonize their personalities enough to let it come through. **Unconditional Love** is the reservoir of life, the treasure of Creation, All That Is, and is not to be confused with the emotional body.

The more we understand life and relative perfection, the simpler life becomes, until we have only to do one thing, to fill our consciousness — our thoughts and feelings — with Divine Love always.

Life never struggles. That which struggles is the consciousness which attempts to *limit* life, interfering with the perfection that is forever trying to flow through. If the personal, or outer, self will stay at peace and let life flow, the manifested result will be perfection, the fulfilled divine way of life. Many personalities who sincerely try to attain this understanding become discouraged along the way and give up their search, because they are looking for material things instead of enjoying God by adoring the beauty and the power of the Divine Light *for Itself alone*. If we seek the Light because we love to adore it, then transformation is certain to follow, for we are then putting our God Self first, which must occur if the personal self is to keep its correct relation to life.

When we use the term "electron," we are talking about an eternally pure heart center of Transformational Fire, a perfect balance of Light, intelligence and substance, around which is an aura of lesser Light, which the scientists call a force field. The electron itself is permanently perfect, but the force field, or aura, around it is subject to expansion and contraction. This is the determining factor in bringing substance into form, from the invisible into the visible.

Because of the inherent intelligence within the electron, it becomes like an obedient servant — it is subject to the manipulation of the individual who acknowledges his Source of life as the I AM Presence within himself. From this height of consciousness, such an individual can, by a direct command to the intelligence in the electron, cause a wave of its energy to flow out, in turn causing its force field to expand or contract. This action serves to raise or lower the vibratory rate of the aura, causing it to register or become the quality of the desired material and thus bring it into physical form. For example, gold has a higher vibratory rate than iron, so if one were manifesting gold, the force field around the electron would naturally be larger than that of the iron electron, and would therefore contain more of the Transformational Fire.

In this type of manifestation, the vision and feeling behind it must be held very steady. The student must master and maintain conscious control and direction of the energy within his own mind and body, so that he is able to govern the flow of the power — through the channels of sight and feeling — onto his definitive objective and hold it there until the receptacle, which is his mental image, is completely filled with the living luminous substance from the Cosmic Fire of Life.

One of the great fundamentals to remember forever is that from the highest to the lowest being in the Cosmos, the only power and presence that can move or do anything constructive is the conscious intelligence that acknowledges its own beingness and manifestation by decreeing, "I AM," followed by whatever quality that being desires to embody, as his Christed Self aligns and becomes the *Mahatma*.

It is through the Word — the conscious thought — of God that *all* creation takes place; without the Word of God, it will simply not take place. Remember there is only one power that can move through Creation — the pure electronic Light which exists everywhere and which constitutes all manifestation on the universal levels. The personality, or outer activity of the individual, is but one focus through which the I AM acts.

Any expression of life that accepts anything less than limitless perfection, relative to the perfection of our Source, is not the Plan of God and will only serve to destroy the forms in which it is focused until the decree of full perfection is expressed. Once the student understands this, he will remain joyously radiant and firmly conscious of only his I AM, the *Mahatma*, never allowing his word to go forth expressing anything less than his relative perfection of life.

From our monadic consciousness, having watched humanity struggling through its self-created misery and discord, we are amazed that humanity refuses to learn and continues to let their bodies and minds grow old, decay, and disintegrate. Scientists have studied the cell of the human body and acknowledge that it contains within it immortality, able to eternally renew and sustain itself because all of its parts are in perfect balance. Yet mankind insist on going through the processes of aging and physical death, all the while clinging to youth, beauty, and life, but refusing to learn the lesson of harmony through which to maintain these. If the student will unite with his I AM, *Mahatma*, he will release its flow through the outer activity of his mind and body and will therefore manifest whatever he desires, particularly as he integrates the concepts and exercises in these books, *Mahatma I* and *II*, and literally *becomes* the *Mahatma* after fully integrating and becoming Christ-conscious.

There is much important knowledge ready to be brought forth for the use of humanity *when it is in the wisdom and judgment of the Monad to give it out.* There will be a great cataclysm that will cleanse the Earth and remove those destructive human beings who, in their ignorance and presumption, say, "There is no God." These beings are to be prevented from creating further destruction and discord on this planet through their mistaken concepts about life and the self-created darkness of their minds. Whoever and whatever denies God — the Source of all Light and life — can exist only as long as the energy they have already received can sustain them. The moment an individual, group, or nation denies their Creator, then in that instant their inflowing stream of life energy is cut off. They can then function only until the store of energy already accumulated is exhausted. The collapse and self-annihilation of these beings is inevitable.

Many individuals carry a grudge against life, blaming it for their suffering and failures. They do not realize that even a very small amount of gratitude and love toward their Creator, the I AM Presence within every human heart, would transmute everything negative into peace and love, releasing the perfection of life into their outer self. Humans find plenty of time to love dogs, cats, people, money, food, clothes, cars, and a thousand other things, but ironically, it is very rare for a person to take even five minutes out of an entire lifetime to love his own divinity; yet he is using its life energy in every moment that he spends in the other activities. Even those who think that they love God give almost no acknowledgment to the Source within themselves!

Divine Love is an actual ray of Light substance that flows out from the Flame within the heart. It can be expressed and sent forth so powerfully that this ray of Light is both visible and tangible. This is the most invincible power in the Cosmos; use it, dear ones, without limit, and nothing will be impossible for you.

Our work, as the *Mahatma,* is to put the exact truth of the Laws of Life before humanity; if they refuse to understand and obey these, then their suffering will increase, until the time when the personality can break out of its obstinacy and selfishness to let the I AM control all, according to the perfection of life.

In order to manifest the greater expressions of your I AM Presence, you, the individual, must become aware of and feel that presence within yourself as the *Mahatma.* Realize that the very life energy that flows through your physical body and beats your heart is constantly flowing to you from your electronic body. This electronic body is projected into the universal level from the very heart center of the Cosmos, which you have heard us refer to as the Source of this Cosmic Day.

The pure life energy of the Twelve Cosmic Rays flowing ceaselessly into the mind and body of the individual, is sometimes referred to as the triune activity of the Supreme All That Is, acting everywhere throughout infinity. This is the energy, intelligence, and substance, the one Light from which comes all manifestation. It is subject to the conscious direction of the individual with Self-conscious free will. The angelic, devic, mineral, plant, and animal kingdoms do not have control of this divine activity — it is only the Co-Creator level, the Flame of the Godhead, that is endowed with free will.

Many of you have felt in your physical bodies the Five Higher Cosmic Rays, which are being directed to the Earth by the I AM Presence, *Mahatma,* and which partially anchored into the planet on January 26, 1991. The Creator level is giving transcendent assistance to humanity at this time, in its outer struggle. This divine gift is an outpouring of love, courage and strength to sustain not only the race as a whole, but the aspiring individual, by illuminating his inner bodies and thus enabling the Source to release more of its perfection into and through the outer self.

These great streams of condensed Light and pure substance, the microtrons of the three *spiritual* rays — Ten, Eleven and Twelve — can be drawn upon by the individual and sent forth again to produce definite results as easily as a searchlight in the darkness.

As the process of raising one's consciousness gradually takes place, you become more and more aware of blazing Light filling your entire body, and you feel the most radiant energy surge in and through yourself, sweeping away every trace of resistance and imperfection and quickening your consciousness with All That Is. You become more and more aware of your mighty

I AM Presence, through the *Mahatma*, until it stands before you, tangible, visible, and very real. Steadily and powerfully, you feel your physical body being drawn into and enveloped by your glorious God Self, regrettably not without various side effects for all.

The Divine Feminine Principle, or the feminine activity of consciousness, is expressed in human nature as *feeling*. *Thought* is the masculine activity of the mind, expressing the Divine Masculine Principle. Thought does not become dynamic in the outer life until it passes through the feeling body of the person. The feeling then condenses the atomic substance of the outer activity of life onto the thought pattern to clothe it, and it may then exist as a separate living thing outside of the mind. This is the reason that so few personalities housed in male bodies are truly dynamic male energy.

Of the millions of individuals who have written and preached about Divine Love as a Law of Life, how many of these know how to generate and express the *feeling* of Divine Love *consciously and at will, to a limitless degree* and put it in the place of hate, intolerance and irritation, as a wave of actual force and substance in one's own emotional body? This must be learned by human beings if they are to stop suffering and express relative perfection. The personality level cannot become permanently harmonious unless it is forever filled with consciously generated Divine Love.

If prayers and mental statements about the Laws of Life were able to pave the way to perfection, happiness, and freedom for humanity, the number of sermons preached here on Earth should have illuminated and perfected a hundred planets by now! Prayers generally consist of "I want" or "Oh Lord, give us..." If these would bring freedom from limitation, then the prayers uttered in this world would have already perfected a dozen humanities.

We are not saying that prayer has never brought about any good, because it has; but prayer should be a quieting of the intellect and emotional body, so that the personality might feel the outpouring of one's Self as the I AM Presence and receive the response from within. Prayer should be an outpouring of love and gratitude to the God Presence for the limitless opportunities and goodness contained within *Self*. Prayer in the manner in which humankind partake seldom reaches any further than their own emotional bodies; thus, as practiced on Earth, prayer is much like having a conversation with oneself, and benefits humanity not!

It is the emotional expression of the human race that needs to be redeemed and saved from its own self-generated destruction. It is important that the individual understands the need for conscious self-control of his feelings. Anything that is not attained through the feeling of Divine Love is but temporary, for *Divine Love alone is the way to perfection*.

It is pitiful to see how for eons humanity has spent its time and energy on building material things through thought, and at the same time has destroyed its creations through inharmonious feelings. This childish behavior is a stubborn refusal to fulfill the Eternal Plan of Perfection.

The hour is now at hand when the great Cosmic Law is releasing a tremen-

dous expansion of the Light of the *Mahatma*, not only throughout our planetary system, but throughout this and every other universe. Very simply,
whoever cannot accept this Light will be consumed by it. Mankind need no
longer fool themselves with the idea that they can continue to generate destructive feelings and survive. The end of that Old Age has arrived, and all things
are begun anew. Let he who wants to run from change stop and read instead,
that he may learn the way of the Light while there is still time.

What is referred to as evil does not exist on this planet or any other, except
what human beings have generated themselves. Most of it has been done
through ignorance, but a great deal has been done wilfully by those who ought to
know better — particularly your religious and political leaders — who are fully
aware of their wrongdoing, but who refuse to connect with their Soul levels.
Those who insist upon using their intellect to attempt to continue their destructive activities in this new cycle will face their own destruction. This will be swift
and definite, for the present fourth-dimensional activity is expressing extremely
rapid manifestation!

The expansion of Light throughout Creation is governed by the great
Cosmic Wheel of Progress, which has been strongly focused upon the Earth
since the Harmonic Convergence of August 15/16, 1987. The wheel has turned
to a certain point, which mankind has not yet realized, where it can focus all
Twelve Cosmic Rays of energy upon the Earth. At this point, the resistance to
change and greater good by selfish personalities and unawakened mentalities
will be as chaff before a mighty wind; their efforts will be useless and they will
be compelled to obey a power infinitely greater than their own selfish cravings.
These beings have much to learn; and unless one is consciously seeking the
release of the Light within Himself, no one can fully understand and appreciate
the feeling that "nothing is important but All of God" and those experiences by
which the Light is released.

Remember, dear ones, that in the *Mahatma*/I AM, there is neither time nor
space. Through this all-wise, all-powerful energy, we shall remove the atomic
obstruction forever. Remember also that the freeing of the atom created the
opportunity for mankind to now benefit exponentially. The Soul within the
atom has been released through nuclear fission; thus all mankind need do is to
consciously integrate this reality, which equals what has been referred to as the
Fifth Initiation.

Initiations, as you are becoming aware *are simply points of Light being integrated*. You may wish to ponder on this: If my personality is but one point of
Light, how do I connect with ALL points of Light, which I know I'm beginning
to accomplish? The answer should be clear to the personality and merged Soul
— simply integrate, integrate, integrate every concept and realization that we
have covered in *Mahatma I* and *II*!

The Mahatma Realization

It is appropriate to insert a note of caution in the use of the mantras, "I AM" or "I AM the I AM Presence" or "I AM *Mahatma*," or simply using "*Mahatma*" to invoke the Source for this Cosmic Day; these have no intrinsic value if simply repeated rapidly, as so many groups have undertaken to do on Earth. When we state that an *unfocused repetition* of "Hari Krishna" or "Hail Mary, full of Grace" or a prayer to Jesus, "Please, dear God, let my boyfriend love me," as we have already described, these reach only the emotional body and simply fall away in front of oneself. The principle of **intent** and **application** is even more important with the introduction of the *most important mantra in Creation* to connect one with their I AM Presence, *Mahatma*.

In order to maximize its effectiveness, it requires that one sit in a comfortable, quiet location and breathe in deeply and repeatedly to tell the body to relax. The medulla oblongata, the brain stem, is where all information from your physical senses passes through; as you breathe out, tell this area to relax, and then effect relaxation throughout the rest of your physical, emotional, and mental bodies.

When you are in a state of tranquillity, then breathe in the "**I AM**" through your heart/throat chakra which are becoming *one chakra*, as many have noticed upon entering the fourth dimension. Start to expand the liquid substance of the golden Twelfth Ray and the luminescent white Wholeness of Source from your Cosmic Heart, throughout your Beingness, as you repeat, "**I AM the I AM Presence,** *Mahatma*." (Refer to the diagram, "The Cosmic Heart," p. 350.)

Allow yourself to luxuriate in the energy, and expand your Cosmic Heart not only into every "corner" of your physical body, but also through your emotional, mental and into your spiritual body. (Refer to the diagram, "The Four-Body System," p. 225.)

Breathe in the liquid wholeness of your God Self and trigger this Omnipresence throughout Creation, until you actually recognize the cells in your physical atomic body starting to become brighter and brighter. If you can see this, you will in time have a glorious sense of "**I AM, I truly AM, the I AM, Mahatma.**"

You can create a suitable realization, such as: "Now I have seen, in no uncertain terms, that I AM the I AM, Mahatma, and never will the totality of my Beingness limit myself to anything less than who I AM as the I AM Presence."

When in time you have expanded your consciousness to realize the wholeness and the connectedness of the totality of Self, *you* become the Omnipresence, **I AM,** that you've *always been.* Please stay within your glorious God Self consciously throughout the day; feel that incredible connection so that your illusory outer self can unite with your inner Self as one wonderful wholeness of consciousness.

We have included several realizations as examples on page 417.

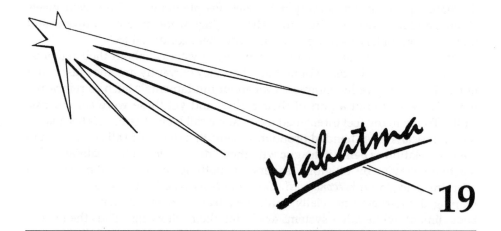

19

So What Does the Personality Think of All of This?

Alas, where to start? The microcosm of the microcosm of the microcosm that we refer to as the personality has such a myopic view of Creation and of the greater Wholeness of who and what we are in its relationship to All That Is, that for me, as a youngster, there was often a hopeless feeling of being lost, unloved, and desperately alone, as I searched for the identity of "who I am" and its meaning in "why am I here?"

I had then a strong intuitive connection that I must be more than I was expressing on a personality level, and that there must be more than this dense atomic structure of an animal with a mind that allows for expansion and expression. But alas, my views were not shared by my peers, who were viewing and accepting their status quo. I was often disheartened by this: How can they accept these inherent limitations of being a sophisticated animal with a brain and free will, an emotional body with a hair-trigger temperament that always seemed to be very volatile, and a very fixed, stubborn, limited view about Creation? Whenever I would question my closest friends about their abnormalities, stunned silence would prevail. I would ask how they could accept what their families and their religions had to say in determining their moral need to draw on their *own* experience and their *own* intuition, and not on someone else's empiricism or someone else's relative norm.

Ah, my dear friends, you're right if you conclude that in an excessively structured, finite discipline such as we have on Earth, particularly at that time in our history, one would do everything possible to avoid Brian's uncomfortable probing, for that is what happened over and over again. No one, in my awareness (auric field) in those days or for years to come, wished to question the status quo — it was simply not done! People either had no fixed views about anything that required thought, or they were ardent followers and therefore completely fixed upon what made them comfortable.

It seems that although mankind were less hysterical about their religious philosophies when I was a young man than they currently are, they just could not assimilate my rather simple views about fundamentals such as reincarnation. These were not a part of their reality, and yet these were *my* intrinsic truth. Today many feel threatened by what we call New Age beliefs because of the hysterical, heavy-handed pronouncements that denounce all acts related to New Revelation as being in league with their "devil." One of the realities of this reactive behavior by religious leaders has nothing to do with the devil and everything to do with *economics!* Only the New Age "born again" branch is reaping the harvest financially, with their fearful interpretation of God and bedevilment, while other systems are losing their following. Thus the magnitude of the argument for Christianity relates to the 21-billion-dollar worldwide industry that the New Age has generated from what these religious institutions would have you believe is their divine right to control.

I'll be predictive with you — and many will clearly understand what I'm saying — that before the end of this century humankind will realize that the clergy cannot hide behind scripture any longer, continuing to interpret these with the provocative abandonment, improvisation and calculation that a used car salesman wouldn't dare to implement in selling you a car. This shameful sham of the "devil" is short-lived, and properly so, for only in America is there still life in the tasteless display of falsely identifying with "God's word."

I regret that this system would not recognize the Christ if he spoke to an assembly, because he would be devoid of the reckless inaccuracies and would express that which would belie their truths. He would be considered a nice, naive man, but with no intrinsic knowledge of scripture, and not what they want to hear. There would be no recognition of this unassuming man, whose dynamic self reflects balanced polarities, instead of unwieldy macho male dynamics. Because the Christ would not project the image of mankind's view of the Absolute, he would be seen as an impostor — too ordinary and not as heightened spiritually as some of *their* more flamboyant preachers.

An acquaintance of mine told me a story recently I feel is worthy of repetition that depicts the double standard that the "good ol' boys club" of America often exhibit. While this acquaintance was visiting a friend in the state of Georgia, she was invited to a party at a very good southern Baptist household. She noticed what appeared to be porcelain figures depicting black people in various costumes and attitudes and she asked, "What are these?" The laughing response was, "They're niglets." Being a Canadian, she asked what the term meant, and was told, "They're niggers." In an embarrassed response, she said, "Oh, I must show you what I bought today," and showed the group a crystal unicorn she had purchased. Everyone at this party stopped talking, apparently shocked by the appearance of this small crystal unicorn. Finally, the host said, "Lady, what in the world are you doing with that? Don't you know that they are tools for the devil and devil worship?"

"The nigger and the unicorn" is a classic example of the double standard. I never cease to be dismayed by humanity's inability to be rational and use their God-given intelligence for discernment about what their pastors preach "in the name of God," and by the feverishly emotional judgments they buy into as the truth, simply because someone in a black suit told them so.

Alas, the strange duality of mankind, who continue to express only their *own* view of reality through the illusory outer self, the personality. The inner Self is not recognized in humankind's third-dimensional disconnection with their collective reality, so the personality views a reality that it believes was created by it and it alone. There has definitely been some input by finer levels of consciousness, but always these relative truths were molded in man's image of man's reality, not in God's truth and God's reality.

The Catholic Church, the grandfather of this mischief-making, contains so much ideology and structure that a mentally active young priest could very easily spend his whole adulthood studying superfluous, ideological dogma. This structure brings a feeling of comfort and safety for many, and the longevity of the Catholic Church seemingly supports its truths. Throughout history, its hallowed halls have reverberated with the horrific sounds of torture and death, within both the new and old world. If one is Catholic, that in itself grants no immunity from the universal Law of Cause and Effect — **karma.** God is not so aware of the virtues of this institution that it will be passed over and not brought to task any more than humanity and its survival are being overlooked.

God simply *IS*, and one should realize that this Omnipresence of All That Is would have no particular knowledge of this planet, and most certainly no understanding of the exclusivity of any belief system, including humanity's belief that planet Earth is the only planet housing God. For those who don't know it, "Jesus Christ" is not the only begotten Son of God and the Virgin Mary is not the mother of God. In fact, the naivete of this conclusion concerned me in my youth, for I, the personality, had some recall of these events. From this finite discipline, my intuition rang out through my Beingness, and I said, "I recall these events, which are as real to me as the Statue of Liberty is to mankind!"

I simply *knew*, as a young man, that I had been the one that my friend Jesus called Simon Peter; and even today I am still having to clear the negative patterns in my subconscious about being the "sacrificial lamb" for the Christ, Maitreya, and his teachings through the physical personality of Jesus, who was the conduit to channel a symbolic moral and ethical doctrine for a seemingly hopelessly bleak and dark humanity. Of my 1412 lives on the Earth alone, always trying to bring in the Light, this one projection as the personality Simon Peter impacted me more with negative connotations than any other experience within the confines of this minuscule speck in Creation called planet Earth.

If you feel my resentment toward Human/God-man's lack of evolution, I apologize, for I know irrevocably at all levels of Self that there are no victims!

And I know, as I clear this negative patterning that the collective Self agreed to participate in and mirror, that this clearing resonates throughout the Cosmos and defuses the heavy-handed abuse of the gentle, symbolic teachings that mankind have elected to venerate and misalign with, choosing to believe that "Jesus Christ" was created in man's image, as *their* creation of what "the only Son of God" would embody.

At twenty years of age I had the occasion to visit the Catacombs in Rome. This singular event was to bring to the fore so much conscious recognition of what we view as the past, that I — the physical embodiment for the personality — became ill unto death. This young, healthy body lay for days in a comatose state, discussing with Soul levels what value there would be in remaining in dense physical embodiment. As you can conclude, my sojourn on Earth was not complete, and my current assignment on Earth was not made clear for another thirty-five years. Even then, with a great sense of unworthiness and denial, I reflected again the rejection of the collective "we."

In these intermediary years I participated in many events and experienced all that I could in both the negative and the positive in the inner and outer self, with one eye on my wallet, as the provider for my family, and making certain that I would not be like my father, who showed so little love and affection toward his children. I would at least embody love; and I understood that my children were on loan in a custodial undertaking, never feeling that our three daughters were at any time owned by me. I was later to view clearly that my three daughters had been with me several times, including my life as Akhnaton with Nefertiti. This, of course, happens with every family whenever there is an element of unresolved cause and effect. This includes nations and, of course, the Group Soul for Earth as well as that evolution with Sanat Kumara as the total embodiment for the Earth.

I have always been fascinated with energy and with what provides humanity the inertia to fall away from its Source; this served to show that the Master Plan for Creation was never intended to probe further into matter than the pure electronic body, the etheric Lightbody.

In the beginning of any planet in any universe that evolves to the level of the Adam Kadmon body (surprisingly to me, this Soul's personality always has a head, torso, two arms and two legs, no matter how extreme the variances in nature might be, whether one breathes carbon dioxide or nitrogen), the results have been identical. Hu-man/God-man have seldom fallen away from their Creator's Plan by manifesting the dense atomic body. There are exceptions to this (which is what creates the extreme dualities on Earth), but these are rare in the experience of your I AM Presence, Source.

This is indeed a strange inheritance for those who have agreed to bring humankind home or to at least reconnect them to their electronic, or etheric, Lightbody. It really is no wonder that humanity "just do not get it" and have so much trouble finding their way home. My observation, as a personality, is and has been one of hopelessness and frustration as I witness humanity's insistence on living totally in their illusory, atomic outer self and their refusal to call on their own creative abilities.

We have explained, in as many ways as finite language will allow our knowledge to be expressed, what needs to be achieved so that humanity can live in the inner Self; and that through the great energies — particularly the radiation of the pure electrical energy and the microtron — and the abundance of wonderful teachers, this can be done. In the quietude of the inner Self, one's creative abilities as God with free will can ignite the spark of Light, Light, LIGHT and Love, Love, LOVE, which are released into substance as electrons and microtrons, the only reality in all of existence!

So often I hear, "If there were a God, he would certainly not tolerate the suffering that goes on here!" I would have to counter lovingly by asking, "What does humankind know about God?" In my experience on this planet and many others, humankind only know what the unconscious, dense atomic vibration wants to know, through the illusory outer self, the personality. They will repeat over and over and over again their misaligned priorities through this illusory outer self, until they realize that God lives within their Selves!

That infinite spark of your I AM Presence, the only reality, is **your Self,** which possesses free will and declares irrevocably, ringing out through the Cosmos that **"I AM the I AM Presence! I AM the Creator of my own Reality!"**

If, in humanity's sense of having been betrayed by God, they feel that God should do more for them and make things right on Earth and clear up the mess that he created or at least allowed to happen...then mankind (those who, at some level of their Soul's evolution, repeatedly incarnate as personalities or extensions of their Soul levels) have not understood that humanity, and only humanity, create the Earth's experience, not God. Humankind have created the Earth's chaos through that lost and determined spirit that says, "Everyone can't be wrong, because our religions, our families, our schools, scientists, and even poets, say that life is real and life is earnest"; or "If you believe in me...(Jesus, or the Lord God Jehovah, or Abraham, or Buddha, or Mohammed, and so on) then I will save your Soul, and you can sit at the right hand of God"...and on and on ad infinitum. Salvation can come through no external process; it can happen only through your inner I AM, and this unwavering Cosmic Law and truth has always been so!

We have given these inherent truths in *Mahatma I* and *II* and, as always, what you do with these is entirely up to your free will, as the Creator of your own reality and of your group reality, as the Group Soul's personalities.

As Earth's awareness of her evolution increases, if humankind continue to bring in unconsciousness through a lack of the Light of I AM, the personality, the necessary altered states of Self-awareness will not be brought into existence rapidly enough and, I regret, your civilization as you know it will cease to exist. As an optimistic personality on Earth, having studied, observed, and immersed myself into human conditions for nearly sixty-one years, the "I" sees little hope or Light on the horizon. I see great Light after New Revelation becomes a reality on Earth, but alas, until then...

The emotional, fearful, platitudes espoused on Earth in attempts to reach heaven or nirvana are rather pathetic, and my heart goes out to those who remain unconscious, thinking that someone else can do this for them. To raise one's Self into relative perfection requires great effort; this doesn't simply happen! When I view the effort expressed to achieve a university degree so that one may have a better standard of living, I become disheartened because, as always, this relates only to the outer self, the illusory manifestation of one's reality. If one were to focus the same effort required to achieve a degreee for the outer self onto one's *only* reality, and achieve a degree for one's inner I AM, one's whole persona would expand to the degree that was never available on Earth before this time and place, and one would be able to live in the Now of one's own fourth-dimensional creative abilities. All of the tools for one's evolution are now available to shift one's consciousness without any sense of limitation (except for one's self-imposed limitations) and move beyond your very limited, dense atomic vibrations into the Light — the Light that you have always been!

At this time, and for the month prior to this time, June 5, 1993, my friend and assistant, Glenda Barrie, and I have been living aboard a recreational vehicle as I write *Mahatma II*, overlooking a beautiful lake in Washington State called Chelan. I've been watching the activity on the beach, as the classic example of the haves and have nots and when my personality's heart, the emotional body, would like to reach out to the migrant Mexican or Hispanic fruitpicker waiting for the valley's apples to ripen, I'm reminded that all of humankind are unconsciously waiting for the fruit of their essence to be harvested.

I'm certain that the young migrant worker looks with envy at his white brother, with his boat and his white girlfriend, as he turns up his ghetto blaster so that everyone within a quarter mile can hear his plea for recognition. The fruit or essence of both sides in this analogy cannot be accessed through the dark, hopeless energy of envy or by the other's superficial expression of "look what I have created." Quite obviously, neither side has reached any conscious level other than the superficial expression of probationary mankind, having no essence of Light (fruit) to harvest, as they chase their proverbial tails in ever-diminishing circles. The outer expression, or dark side, of both of these examples relates only to the illusory outer self and have nothing to do with one's inner I AM Presence.

During my. teachings in Europe, I often tell the story about having taken my children, as youths, to the Sambo Pancake House restaurants in northern Washington state. On the restaurant walls are pictures of beautiful tigers, each chasing the tail of the one in front of them, in one great circle; and what occurs is quite amazing — these tigers chase each other so rapidly that they melt into "tiger butter." I'm certain that you can visualize how wonderful tiger butter is on pancakes, but not in life!

My observation of Old Age and New Age practitioners is that the Old Age should know that God doesn't support them anymore and that they should start anew. The New Age, in general, moves some distance into Light, then shuts off their sense of All That Is, and gets stuck in limitation. Both of these are analogies to my tiger butter story, and both sides of this equation may wish to learn to step out of their tiger butter limitations and connect with their only inner reality, the I AM Presence of Source, if the Old Age example wishes to become Light and if the New Age example wishes to become a greater wholeness of All That Is, one's own I AM, *Mahatma*.

Many beings who have elected to work with Light in the beginning of this New Age seem to me to be like butterflies — either the wind, or the scent of the next flower, or the tree beside the previous grove, holds their attention only fleetingly. I could never deny the beauty of the butterfly; that is most apparent. What I do find confusing, particularly in America, is how students of this New Age are able to flutter from this teaching to that — which may be a rose or a weed — and from one undeveloped channel to another overdeveloped channel, etc.

For many in America, if I were to ask one question, it would be about discernment. How long does it take a butterfly to learn to bypass thistles and shrubs to find the type of flower whose nectar allows one to simply know that the quality of the energy brought through this nectar is transformational beyond words? If a teacher cannot demonstrate to the student how to attain personal transition and transformation, then he continues to convey only abstract theories about what might be accomplished by undertaking this discarnate teacher's prescription for success.

I apologize for what must appear to be excessively judgmental (justifiably or not, only time will determine), and for not being allowing of a more gradual transition into Light. That is primarily because I, the personality, have so little time left in physical embodiment that I feel a sense of urgency to convey these relative truths that we embody as *Mahatma,* as directly as possible through the First Ray.

Most of what we have brought to the Earth is transformational spiritual energy, and if one could believe this premise and take it at face value, that in itself is the transformation through the energy of absolute **synthesis,** which we refer to as *Mahatma*. If you attended one of the seminars that we offer, you — the personality — would not understand much of what we speak, but your Soul levels most certainly would; and something would gradually shift within your complete Beingness, that cannot be expressed in words.

This is the Transformational Fire of Source Itself that permeates one's Beingness and causes the atomic body to become pure electrical energy, and ignites the cells of one's body into Light. The spiritual microtron, which has been introduced into dense physicality, is simpatico with one's transition into the etheric Lightbody, and is the prelude to the spiritual body through the Tenth Ray. Words simply cannot convey the fine, pure essence that can now be experienced through *your* I AM Presence, *Mahatma*.

There are several points regarding phenomena during the Mahatma Seminars in Europe that I feel might be of some interest to you, the reader. When participants tried to record the proceedings, either the tape deck would shut off and not allow the transmission, or my voice would become inaudible and one would hear an overriding high-frequency hum not unlike the Hu sound/God sound which the Sufis and the followers of the Path of the Masters refer to as "the audible lifestream." This is the only sound that God can project into this density.

It was realized by the time we went to Dusseldorf that if a tape recorder were to be moved far enough away from my electromagnetic field, it could pick up a certain amount of transmission, particularly if I appealed on higher levels for this to happen, which I did; I needed to understand why the apparent transformational qualities of the *Mahatma* energy were having such a profound effect on the majority of the participants. This was not to be manifested for nearly six months and after many seminars!

In March of this year we were outside of Munich, staying in a lovely Bavarian home with beautiful people and ready to commence our second seminar in this location, when I noticed that a couple who had attended the previous seminar had brought with them what appeared to be very sophisticated equipment with which to record this weekend seminar. The man had been introduced as a successful film maker. When he started to record me, I thought to myself, good luck, because I had no conscious awareness of any completely successful transmission.

The seminar was barely under way when I realized that this film producer was becoming very excited, for he kept giving his earphones to his companion. I remember thinking, somewhere outside of my channel, that he must have a successful recording and that I must not allow myself to be distracted!

When the time arrived for a morning break, I was beckoned to hear something on the tape that could not be explained. When I spoke, there was a sound-over of instrumental music, choral music, and transmissions in the English and German languages. It was assumed by the film producer that there must be a radio or some type of sound system playing somewhere in the house, but this was proven not to be the case. What became increasingly apparent was that during the meditations, when we took the group into the monadic levels, only then did the sound-over discontinue, and only when we returned to the universal/physical levels did it return.

It was very interesting, but no one could explain what caused this phenomenon. One analogy, in our finite discipline, that could help to express it was that my physical body became a receiver, much like the old crystal radio sets; and when we received too heightened a vibration, such as crossing into spiritual realms from universal matter, the crystal set could not receive the vibration. Your guess is as good as mine! However, when I returned to Canada for three months to write *Mahatma II*, my youngest daughter mentioned this experience of her Dad's to a friend who came to visit while I was visiting her. Then it got interesting, because I never place myself in a position of explaining anything to anyone whose beliefs — be they religious or scientific — would cause them to react with fear, condemnation, or simple disbelief.

Glenda and I left Basel, Switzerland, on April 27, 1993, to spend three months in North America working on *Mahatma II*. Just days before leaving we received from the German film producer the wonderful gift of ten hours of successful and interesting audio tape from my seminar. Within a day I received two taped meditations from Dusseldorf, and the following day, two meditations from my last seminar in Zurich, not to mention the successful recording of my last seminar in Basel — all of these during the later seminars.

This abundance did not mean very much to me until I had occasion to listen to these tapes, and for the first time ever I realized the fineness and purity of energy that was being brought forward through me, the personality, and captured on tape by other Co-Creators. Then and only then could I begin to understand what students and teachers had been saying to me all along, "It's not what you say as much as the quality of transformational energy that comes through in your meditations"; now they are saying, "Look, the energy for transformation is in the tapes!"

I first met the remarkable conscious channel, Janet McClure, in the spring of 1987. My impression then and now remains most favorable; time has not eroded the substance conveyed to me by the discarnate teacher who refers to himself as Vywamus. This energy of Janet and Vywamus was to forever change my focus on Earth, and allowed the information that Vywamus articulated so clearly, contained in "The Journey of the *Mahatma* from Source to Earth" in *Mahatma I*.

When I was a young man, I had experiences of seeing a Council of Twelve, and certain recall of a life in which I was called Simon Peter. But nothing in my conscious awareness prepared me for the heightened level that this Source or Creator Council of Twelve represented or for the graphic details articulated by Vywamus, through Janet McClure, on the specifics of who I was and why I was on Earth. Prior to meeting Janet, I had met two other channels who conveyed my special assignment, but not in enough detail for me to grasp the great significance of how transformational the energy that my personality embodies would be for Self, for the Earth, and for the Cosmos, until I actually did my *conscious Ascension* in Holbrook, Arizona, in September 1989. For then and only then could I begin to integrate that which Vywamus had stated was my reality.

In *Mahatma I*, Chapter 8, (first 3 editions) we refer to an Ascension on May 9, 1990; upon further review, I now realize that event was a *descent* (not Ascension) from the senior monadic levels to the Galactic Core. If that seems confusing, I will endeavor to explain. If you recall, Vywamus emphasized several times that my Ascension would not be taken as others on Earth, but that my *final universal ascension* would be activated "from the highest mountain to the lowest valley"; in other words, from the Source of this Cosmic Day to Earth. Vywamus also stated that for me to complete all universal levels, I would have to take my physical body with me. Knowing that I have achieved my spiritual Ascension twice before on Earth and again in Holbrook, Arizona, the question remains: Can the Earth raise *her* vibration sufficiently for this event to be demonstrated for humankind? The answer is, I don't know. I'm advised by our teachers that Earth is conscious enough for a complete spiritual Ascension sometime near the end of 1996. That, of course, would please us all very much, as an example of what Hu-man can also achieve at this level of fourth-dimensional time!

Prior to the demise of Janet McClure in October 1990, she had mentioned to me that she had started formulating concepts about a Cosmic Walk-In whose presence had been apparent for some time, but not completely manifested on Earth. She said, "As near as I can gather from Vywamus, this is your energy." I was not to hear from Janet again on this matter, for shortly thereafter she journeyed with a group to Egypt, not to return as a personality. Being the co-founder and the channel for the Tibetan Foundation, it was understandable that all those associated with her wonderful organization were dumbstruck, for there was no evidence on Janet's personality level that she intended to leave her physical embodiment at this time.

I had arrived at a similar conclusion, that my assignment would reveal itself shortly. This was the case, and within a short time I received the text of a chapter on "The Cosmic Walk-In," which Janet had just started prior to her "Journey of journeys." This is the "Introduction by Vywamus" in *Mahatma I*.

Much water has flowed under and over the bridge since that time, because when one allows the doors to open completely, the experience that follows can be perceived as overwhelming for a personality that was simply looking for the fastest way out; and to be forthright, I still am, but not before I've completed our mission on Earth.

After Janet's death, I found it very difficult to listen to those who were Janet's students, for what followed as the Tibetan Foundation traditions, to me did not embody the broader based concepts of Vywamus and others that Janet could bring through her channel. This is not a judgment, simply an observation.

Thus I was to quote only one channel, Janet, consistently throughout my apprenticeship until my channel was sufficiently clear, not for me to channel discarnate beings, but simply to *become* the I AM Presence through the collective energies that we refer to as *Mahatma*.

If you remember, in *Mahatma I* Vywamus stated that I sometimes overwhelm people when discussing the nebulous nature of Source. This was most certainly to be the case when we endeavored to anchor our consciousness into the Earth! This was also to create an amazing level of mirroring to come forth even when certain personality expressions knew that Vywamus was the teacher who monitored and conveyed my mission, my Source assignment to me; it was certainly not myself. There would still be individuals reacting by angrily saying, "Who do you think you are? You're coming from ego!" or "How can that pile of manure be greater than I am? or "Doesn't he know that we're *all* Source?" etc.

I found the ridicule demoralizing, not because of the accusations themselves but because of the anger and frustration with which they were conveyed; and on the personal level, because the accusers did not follow the content of the material to determine for themselves who said what and when they said it! If one were to read the text closely, one would realize that except for the St. Peter experience, the personality, Brian, most certainly had no understanding of the magnitude of his assignment before he was told by Vywamus and Djwhal Khul!

This leads, of course, to only one conclusion, which is, "He either is the personality of *Mahatma* or he isn't"; and do you know, my dear friends, it does not matter one way or the other. You see, what you believe for or against the issue has no bearing on what truth there is for us in the teachings of *Mahatma I* and *II*. One will either resonate with these relative truths and the energy that comes through, or one won't. But please don't throw out the baby with the bathwater, because it doesn't matter, as long as you believe in the unlimitedness of Creation and that it is possible for someone to embody an energy such as this on Earth.

Have you ever asked yourself the question, why are all gods ancient? If this were true, it would mean that you are evolving on a band of sequential time on an ever-diminishing, upside-down spiral, and that your spiritual evolution would have peaked out long ago. Of course, none of this can be so, once one integrates the fact that you did have two Golden Ages on Earth several millions of years ago, and you must adhere to the Creator's timetable or be destroyed. So the cycle that you are entering now would have to be a new Golden Age, would it not?

This will surprise many who don't believe in what cannot exist — specifically, the past! And now it is difficult for many to believe that the Earth is receiving more attention than ever before; that she is being soothed and mollycoddled to help her to conform to the Law of Creation; and that humankind are being encouraged at every level of Self to raise their personality levels into Light.

I have found both the English and German editions of *Mahatma I* to be very revealing. In North America many (in fact, most) of the readers could relate only to my autobiographical portion, which was light and easy to read, but were dumbfounded by the major concepts. For the most part, the German-speaking people ignored the autobiography as inconsequential and wondered why would I demean myself with that, when it was our teachings which held their attention? North Americans tend to be less mentally focused than their German-speaking cousins, who embody so much Third- and Fifth-Ray attributes, while the North American embodies the Second Ray and tends to find mental discipline difficult indeed.

As an aside, I have discontinued including the autobiographical section in this edition, although it did convey that if Brian is the one that Vywamus, through Janet McClure, states is bringing the *Mahatma* energy, and which his conscious spiritual Ascension confirms, then the personality should be depicted accurately, not as "preordained perfection through immaculate conception" or displaying physical signs such as certain gurus or the Dalai Lama have chosen. In other words, imperfection can be perfected, and does not have to be preordained with certain unequal advantages; and we do teach Divine Equality. All is *divine* and *equal*, at least from the Source perspective.

I have received a number of testimonials that the people assimilating the *Mahatma* writings find that the amount of Light and energy that comes through can be debilitating to long concentration and that integration can be achieved only in small amounts! One really must learn patience with this highly energized material and not become discouraged. If you don't comprehend these major concepts that your subconscious mind and your mass consciousness have never been introduced to, then please be good to yourself and — as Vywamus states in his Introduction in *Mahatma I* — allow that the integration may require a year or more.

I have never heard directly from other New Age teachers that they are teaching the concepts I teach, but I have heard through individuals who have participated in my seminars that "what Brian teaches, I've heard before" or that "the ancient yogis have been saying that all along." I'm sure that these gentle Souls know this to be only partly true. We have made every effort to create what I call filler in order to teach the basics without distortion, and on these levels I have drawn heavily on two of the best teachers, Djwhal Khul and St. Germain.

I remain amazed at how much time I still spend on these basic teaching levels when I work with many who have studied metaphysics for years. I mention this only because there was a time when I considered leaving these opening levels to others better equipped for this than my personality appeared to be, and instead teach mankind what my mandate as the Cosmic Avatar of Synthesis should bring through. This is being achieved slowly and deliberately, and rightly so, because some of the concepts are very difficult to integrate.

However, I've noticed that when individuals finally grasp and integrate a concept, I hear, "Oh, now I know what you mean!" or "It's so simple once you get it!" What almost everyone at my seminars understands is that it is the *fineness* of the energy that comes through our meditations that is truly transformational and beyond description. I do not give personal initiation sessions anymore because they draw on my energy as greatly as a seminar for 70 or more people, and the benefit derived through the intensity of a group focus is more than sufficient for all to assimilate.

The Mother Energy

It is nearly one year since I received the information about "the Mother energy" arriving on Earth, which I discuss with Barbara Waller in the beginning of *Mahatma II*. The remarkably good news is that *the Goddess energy is here*, and is felt through Switzerland, Germany, and now the world, by everyone I teach — and, I'm certain, by many that I don't teach!

Please let me take you back to the beginning, to my conversations with Barbara, developing the scenario from the personality's perspective of greater understanding given at that time and place through Barbara's clairvoyant and clairaudiant abilities; and giving you further developments of how the Goddess energy is actually being implemented on Earth.

For clarification, I must state that I had never met Barbara before our first session in July 1992. If you recall, I left my book, *Mahatma*, on a nearby table, which she touched into immediately and kept her hand upon in order to have a connection with the energy she derived from the book. Her very first statement was, "Holy! They're telling me that you walk with Jesus and that you teach Jesus! They say that he helps you with earthly and astral matters and you help him with higher teachings." Fortunately this did not stop the clairvoyant transmission; the shock simply delayed it for a moment as she reaffirmed what she was being told.

Barbara had absolutely no way of knowing anything about me. The following are but a few examples of her special gift: "Your father, Jack, is here, but he's also known as Albert. He doesn't like that at all, but that was his given name. Jack says he had no idea until he got over here how much Light you embodied as a boy, when he would beat you until you were nearly dead. He says that this, and his inability to understand your beliefs, have caused him many tears. He says over here everything is passed in review, and he asks for your forgiveness."

"Your mother is here and says, 'Brian was always such a good boy,' and she's not surprised by the Light you carry. She says that she's gone ahead of your dad, and really loves it there, although she understands that she'll take on a new body at some time; but she's in no hurry. She's going from the third to the fourth astral level." Barbara asks, "Is her name Belle? Belle says that she's so proud when she realizes who you are and what you bring to humanity. Who is Elizabeth?"

(This one really confused me, because I didn't realize that this was, of course, my father's third bride, whom I hadn't known very well.)

"Holy!" says Barbara, "she's so tall and thin! Elizabeth says she's not seen your father because he on the second astral level, and she's very busy going from the fourth to the fifth. Elizabeth says that she wishes she'd gotten to know you better on Earth, because it would have been so helpful; but every opportunity that she has, she comes to you, Brian, and bathes in your Light, and she will be with you as you're teaching in Switzerland to assist in any way she can."

One of many surprises, from my point of view, was Barbara's ability to talk about twelve rays being manifested when she herself had no knowledge of these matters, and said that I would be going to Switzerland, a place that she knew only on a map. Barbara discussed in depth where the Mother energy would anchor on Earth, stating that the location was "near a village called Aesh" on a lake 6 to 8 miles northeast of Zurich, which at the time meant nothing at all to me. She spoke of the location of "the *Mahatma* House" near the lake, which we found, upon our arrival in Zurich, was called "Greifensee."

On the third of October, 1992, the day after our arrival in Zurich, we took a journey to this lovely lake. The location was beautiful, but many lakes are. It was not until we took a short ferry ride across the lake that I realized that I was witnessing something that I had never experienced in dense physicality, and this was the incandescent pearl-grey colored Tenth Ray as a shimmering curtain in the middle of this lake!

With jet lag and a degree of uncertainty on my part, Glenda and our hostess, Danielle, discussed at length this energy all the way to Danielle's home. When we arrived there (and our new dwelling), I was shocked to realize that this yet unidentified energy was now shrouding this area of residence that was approximately *ten miles away* from Griefensee! Thus what Barbara had seen so clearly, including her description of the exact "Mahatma house" — which we finally did locate, but which would have been prohibitively priced — was not required because the energy was moving and surrounding us wherever we traveled!

As you realize, we state that this energy was not identified until October 8, 1992, when we went to visit a friend in Buchs, Switzerland. During our journey home I became very ill, and upon our arrival I lay down to try to rid myself of the headache and nausea. When I awoke, Glenda and Danielle were in the sitting room, and subsequently stated that I was in "a beautiful state of trance" for several hours as I described "the anchoring on Earth of the Tenth Ray" (please refer to p. 338). I have no recall of the details of this occurrence; however, Glenda took notes. Thus, another realization will hopefully benefit our respective journeys.

Simultaneous with the Tenth Ray revelation was the ever-increasing awareness of the Goddess in all her resplendent glory (please refer to "Integration of the Goddess Energy," p. 400). Within days, and within the parameters of a small group of Lightworkers in Switzerland with whom we discussed the Tenth Ray and the Mother energy, the ignition of processing and integration that followed was indeed very satisfying.

In my seminars, the Mother, or Goddess energy, became so gratifying for those who consciously adopted her magnificent Omnipresence as the balance required for our I AM Presence, *Mahatma*, that by the time April approached, there was a heightened sense of expectancy in everyone at every seminar, both males and females.

My experience was to differ slightly from that which Barbara Waller had described, she having stated that the Mother's arrival into dense physicality might be as soon as April or May, 1993. That was not to be my experience. Several times I have been aware of being on a multidimensional spacecraft that we refer to as a Macambra, which is probably what others refer to as a merkabah. Maybe I should qualify what I'm about to say: Forever on your third-dimensional world, Souls gather as personalities, using their astral or etheric bodies, and meet in what we call Shamballa, which by now you recognize as the etheric body of the Earth located on the upper Gobi Desert.

Since the Harmonic Convergence of mid-August 1987, when your galactic aspects entered your consciousness on Earth, more among you are starting to take night classes at the Galactic Core instead of at Shamballa. I've often been conscious of teaching at the Galactic Core, but not on the macambra, until the beginning of April 1993. On these occasions I have experienced being both the teacher and the student. One night I remember meeting Sananda, Germain and Maitreya, teaching and being taught by an incredibly beautiful being who was referred to me as "your counterpart, the Mother energy." The excitement of this first encounter caused me to awaken with greater recall of details than I might otherwise have had. What I witnessed at that time was a magnificent being of unbelievable Light, manifested in an etheric Lightbody that, of course, is physical.

Therefore, the view that I hold to this day, June 12, 1993, is that the Goddess can manifest a quasi-physical body for all to see when the time is appropriate. What I don't know is if she will create the spiritualized physical body should the Earth raise her vibration sufficiently for this unfoldment, although our teachers insist that this will be so. What is absolutely clear to me is that once and only once did she manifest a body that appeared to be physical. That happened about two o'clock in the morning, on Monday, April 26, in Basel, Switzerland.

As I was sitting outside on the porch at that hour, and just coming out of a meditation, I thought I heard something and turned around to see the same omnipresent beauty that I had seen on the macambra. I saw her walking from the hallway to the dining room, and when I turned on the light in the dining room, there was only a glimmer of Light where she had been, but an all-encompassing sense of calmness and love permeated the house. Later that morning, the others in the house spoke of being aware that something wonderful had occurred! What the Mahatma energy has conveyed to me clearly and graphically is that a woman in (West) Germany is being completely overshadowed by the Source Council of 12. She will embody the Goddess Energy, and complete the energy of the Mahatma, until the Earth raises her vibration to a greater degree. I, the personality, am aware of this great and balanced energy and look forward to working with her!

Harken to this immense opening, if you will, for your prayers and meditations invoking this magnificent presence have helped her physical manifestation to finally occur. Thus, whether or not she manifests as described by Barbara does not take away from her accessibility!

During a seminar in Dusseldorf, two major occurrences took place, one of which was to placate and balance my personality's residue of feeling put upon by the Christ, Maitreya, during my lifetime as Simon Peter, when I was the personality for a galactic aspect of the Cosmic Avatar of Synthesis. We have now achieved that final bonding of the Christ Consciousness for Earth — the transformational energy for humanity — and the complete Creator energy that we refer to as *Mahatma*. This and other manifestations of similar complexity have finally healed, causing a total realignment with the Wholeness of Self of every being in existence whose outer self has become integrated by the inner I AM.

The other opening in Dusseldorf was the overshadowing of the Goddess energy, which allowed the aforementioned occurrence to finally heal. This energy is so transformational and nurturing that the wholeness of the Goddess, as the receptive half of *Mahatma*, completed our circuitry with the Co-Creator Christed Self and the Creator monadic-spiritual Self. There was a magnificent fusion of Light when this occurred, and it embodied, from our perspective, the interfacing of the spiritual microtron and the pure physical electronic energy, using the principle of invocation and the electromagnetic grid system. This unification gives you the only two definite substances in Creation that one need identify.

Integration of the Goddess Energy

As many are becoming aware, the long-awaited Goddess is finally here, and is anchored on Earth with a glorious, nurturing quality that will enhance your evolutionary opportunities to an unprecedented magnitude!

This magnificent energy is still having to adjust to these lower densities, thus our suggestion is that you incorporate this all-encompassing Omnipresence in your heart/throat chakra. Because the Goddess is so vibrant, your first impression will be one of an electrodynamic surge as she adjusts to the level of energy that you can comfortably handle.

Introduce her accordingly, by bringing her into the Cosmic Heart, your thymus gland, with the electrical aqua-blue color, and expand this color into your throat chakra. Once this magnificent energy is anchored, please allow her essence of Source Purity — the incandescent White Light of Source and the Gold Light of the Twelfth Ray — to start to nurture you. Let her know that you have awaited forever this manifestation, and ask her to please embody her presence in your own I AM to complete the circuitry of the *Mahatma* throughout your beingness.

Magnify, magnify, magnify her essence throughout your four-body system, but particular attention should be given to your emotional body for she has never experienced this level. Explain to the Goddess your understanding of the areas of your dense physical life that impact the most upon you, asking her to nurture these as the total embodiment of motherhood truly represented on every level of Creation.

This allowingness of the Goddess is needed even more by the male population to participate in this wondrous event, although we regret that most will not see themselves as requiring any female receptive energy. Trust our expressed love in your balancing of polarities on this planet, for Light finds no reflection with a personality's outer self that is not in harmony with what you perceive as your male and female polarities.

Ascension

For most of humankind, the word *Ascension* has absolutely no meaning whatsoever, for to them life's priority on the two lower chakra levels is simply one of survival. At these unconscious levels of self, one never associates violent acts of nature as being within their own first- and second-chakra adherence to the primal Earth and survival. Always within your recorded history, when you hear of a catastrophy of great magnitude, it has been first- and second-chakra activation.

As a personal aside, I found it very ironic that when the great China plate shifted, causing the death of over one million Chinese people, that in itself did not justify front-page news in the Western world, whereas one little girl or boy fallen into a well *does* make the front page. There are many subtle reasons for this; the primary subconscious response is that the Chinese, Indian, African, and Aboriginal peoples are a subspecies from the perspective of the developed nations which work primarily in the third-chakra occidental world. Even when the Japanese prove their equalilty in the task of material manifestation through the third chakra, they subconsciously remain a subspecies from the Caucasian perspective.

This is the only planet in this universe designed with such apparent complexities and polarities, and the only planet with *six* root-race body colorings. As most of Adam Kadmon coloring for other planetary systems is olive, why would Earth wish to express a white, brown, black, yellow, red, and blue race of people? Of these, only the blue race did not descend in vibration; they arrived in their etheric Lightbodies and ascended into a higher vibration.

The fifth, or white, Aryan race will be the next to achieve greater Light assimilation. This does not mean for a moment that at one time or another you have not embodied all colors, or that if you are Chinese in this life, you will not master Ascension, any more than your astrological chart has to manifest as indicated. For this would state that you are not of God with full expression of free will.

All of this is fine to contemplate, but still very difficult to integrate. From the density that humankind have created, allowing their Self to fall away so far from the state of being a host of Masters on Earth into the dense atomic body, and then reachieving a 360-degree turn into that pure electrical Lightbody that your Earth and humanity had achieved, is quite a task. But it is obviously worth the effort because the alternatives are so bleak, and one is irrevocably placed between a rock and a hard place. Thus the kindest suggestion that we can utter is, whatever it takes to achieve this, please do it!

There is certainly enough information in *Mahatma I* and *II* to enable one to achieve mastery through physical Ascension, then spiritual Ascension through the Tenth Ray. However, simply reading these books, which have stated as much relative truth as can be brought forward at this time, will not do it. What the individual needs to do is to integrate initially the teachings that one best resonates with, and then approach the next level and the next; and when you have *consciously* created your physical Ascension into Light, introduce yourself to the spiritual Ascension.

It should be noted here that although I have already experienced my spiritual Ascension consciously, others will normally experience any Ascension just prior to physical death.

We have spoken about the first, second, and third chakras and the unlikelihood of these becoming Light-realized for a very long time. I would like to relate this to an area where I have problems mirroring and understanding when Lightworkers ask me questions such as "The Aborigines in Australia must be highly evolved because they have such a strong Earth connection" or "Because of their great understanding of Earth and nature, the North American Indian must be close to God" or "I'm working with a great shaman who has the ability to travel great distances to heal. I can only hope that some day *I'll* be that great."

I can only advise you, from our perspective, that All That Is simply *IS*, and *has no perspective*, because the I AM Presence is the highest personification of Light and Love that we are made aware of, through NEW REVELATION, as *Mahatma*. And because *all* are a Divine Spark of the Infinite, it would follow that the higher your resonance with Source, the greater your connection, and not the idea that the lower the vibration and the stronger the connection to Earth, the closer one is to the Godhead. Being anchored into the Earth — anchoring Light into the Earth — is essential, but not in perpetuity! Aside from being totally illogical from a finite monitoring, it remains diametrically opposed to the Cosmic Law of Resonance, which dictates that the higher the vibration, the greater the connection to one's ultimate union with the Infinite, not the lower the vibration, the greater the connection.

The lower his vibration, the greater the connection that Hu-man has with animal man; and for those who express the Fourth Ray, this can be a problem, in that if they so love Earth and Earth living that they fall away from Light, as surely as day follows night. But naught is written in stone, and naught is miraculous. All is unfolding in a most natural, eternal Law of Evolution — not involution — with its finite conclusions (particularly when humankind wrote their own script and performed it, allowing the outer self's ego to say, "Look what I created over there.") If you want to know where this outer ego comes in, it is always conceived by man and envied by man in a paradox that states, for example: "Look at the beautiful apartment house that I built over there; you know, *I* did that!" without realizing for a moment that his creation was outer egoic and illusory and has nothing whatsoever to do with his only inner I AM.

You may wish to confine your view of what constitutes ego to your primal Soul body, as the **egoic body.** Therefore, judge nothing from your personality's outer self. Once you have mastered this outer self, then and only then can you speak as the "Presence" of relative truth. And once you create your spiritual body you can speak without relativity and obviously without ego!

As no two people on Earth are, or could be, identical and no two evolutionary paths are the same, even for "twin rays," then there are as many levels of participatory evolution as there are beings touching into Earth. One's only purpose is to evolve *above* the Earth's vibration, not to lower the Earth's vibration and remain lost throughout sequential time. If you can address and identify with what is being stated, and feel sufficient dedication to achieving Mastery — which requires supreme dedication, without going like a butterfly from one concept to another, forever expressing "tiger butter" — then simply *do it!* For if you miss the opportunity available on Earth now, where we have the great experiment to hasten this Cosmic Day through NEW REVELATION, then I can assure you that upon awakening on another level of consciousness, you will look to Earth and say what my biological father has said, "If only I had listened to you, son!" As a Son of God with free will, the choices remain yours. I can only wish you Love and Light, for that's all there is.

The other area of limitation that I feel should be understood regarding Mastery is the most contemptuous! It is the limitations perpetuated by your dark and archaic religions, which have imposed their manipulative might on the semiconscious probationary and First-Initiation levels of humanity, keeping these first-, second-, and third-chakra expressions imprisoned with as dark and manipulative a stranglehold as has ever been conceived on Earth. That in itself is quite a statement, considering that all of your civilizations, except the Golden Ones, have been designed by the Cabal in recent times, by 97 extremely dark and heavy experts to reduce Hu-man into slavery, which of course, is what has happened.

The collective We are here to heal and not condone the status quo; that, of course, is apparent. So whatever I say regarding these major areas of manipulated darkness will fall on the deaf ears of the structured mass consciousness as the words of the AntiChrist, and will give a short life to even greater fear as time goes by, when there will be a hysterical, final, desperate attempt to obliterate Our teachings. There will be a feverish attempt to call us the Prince of Darkness and "the veritable personification of the Anti-Christ," but it is already too late, for the ignition of the First Ray has already destroyed all that cannot withstand the Light. As soon as the residual **liquid Light of the silver cord of consciousness** runs out of the allowable input by Source, the darkness inherent will be no more!

When we speak of limitation inherent in man's view of God, the most obvious is that throughout the Christian experience. Only 117 out of the billions buying into Christianity have completed the Mastery of dense physicality sufficient for Ascension. However, "Christianity's chronicle of continuance" mandates that "only Jesus Christ" was ever able to demonstrate Ascension and complete Resurrection and that it would be blasphemy to think differently. For if the Church taught what the Christ taught, that heaven is within, there would be no need for a Christian hierarchy, would there?

Alas, most of what I say will fall on deaf ears, and I'll be long gone when these teachings will be hailed as the New Teachings for a New World Religion in a new civilization in a new fourth-dimensional global community predicated on Light and Love. That seems very fair to me, and if we are invited to return again to Earth, we would do so knowing that this time it might even be joyous!

The dark energies that we refer to as the **Cabal** are very ancient in origin and, oddly enough, have become resigned to their fate, for they know that they are finally beaten. They are and will maintain their stranglehold on your manipulated money markets, and when there is no longer any currency exchange, they too will be finished. *Fusion* was the straw that broke the Cabal's back, allowing for the microtron to spiritualize matter. This was their undoing.

The bleak parody that will unfold as your material world reinvents itself, having to start anew, will be most interesting because this restructuring will be complicated by the rearrangement of the Earth's land mass, which will break away significantly and new land mass will resurrect significantly. All of these shifts will call for very persuasive evaluation of mankind's lineage and purpose for living. As dreadful as the picture I paint is, humankind will unite, and that inherent thread of decency and Light will come to the fore and begin to express itself as Light and Love for the common good.

Of the three billion or more probationary and preprobationary humans on Earth, most, regrettably, are not conscious enough to change one iota, but continue to breed like rabbits. This problem is not isolated to one religion, but is prevalent in all of preprobationary mankind. The Church, in its wisdom, disallows contraception even though its leaders know at some level that these families cannot all be fed or housed, and these regrettable examples of religions and other belief systems repopulate the garbage dumps around the world and beget their own. Many times, in many of these cultures numerous children are produced as couples try for a male child. The great sadness (and I'm not buying into victimhood, because that would imply that Souls, at some level of lower evolution, did not *choose* to experience the garbage dump) is that the starving and manipulated constitute the greatest percentage of those whom evolution on Earth at this time will not include, no matter what they believe. (Refer to the chart, "The Chakra System for the Physical Manifestation of Multidimensional Mankind," p. 357.)

As we enter this New Age, these individuals will continue to be manipulated through their undeveloped first- and second-chakra expressions, and will then be compelled to move on to other schoolrooms. These levels of consciousness would never know that the five recently discovered Gospels (according to Peter, Mary, Thomas, etc.) that are being evaluated in Edmonton, Canada, again make no mention of Ascension or Resurrection, which, of course, is the basis of Christianity. As with all of the Gospels, these symbolic writings make only a moral and ethical contribution. I've been told that the Gospels cannot be tied together in any meaningful way; and although they certainly do not establish that the Master Jesus is so undeniably unique that he should be venerated and worshiped, they attempt to do so, knowing mankind's propensity to deify and anthropomorphize.

As an aspect of the one called Simon Peter, I can state categorically that this lovely *man*, the disciple Jesus, had not yet anchored his Fourth Initiation at the time of Maitreya's Ascension — having just received that initiation during the Crucifixion, with Maitreya's overshadowing (which we do not intend to beleaguer). Therefore we all knew that Jesus could not demonstrate the Ascension. All of this is unfortunate because humankind is already bewildered enough, and when they realize that they've been hoodwinked for the last 2000 years on Earth by the well-meaning Christ, Maitreya, and the not-so-well-meaning script writers for the founders of Christianity, they will have to start anew. But the bulk of those will continue in a state of apathy, not knowing how to change and start anew. As an example, do you remember the story of the Japanese soldier who, 16 years after the Second World War was over, was still in hiding and fighting the war for his god, Emperor Hirohito?

We are a strange lot; however, the significance of what I state is this: that when the collective We demonstrate Ascension "for all eyes to see and every heart to open in wonderment," you will then hopefully realize that in order to take your body with you, it must be totally spiritualized. What Maitreya demonstrated was the electronic Lightbody Ascension which, please understand, requires the death of the corporal body and subsequently the manifestation of a body of "slowed down Light" that has a resemblance to a dense physical body and can be changed to resemble this person or that person as quickly as you in the atomic body can change your clothes (maybe a little faster than *some* of you change your clothes!).

Are you beginning to see the significance of the differences between the *spiritual* Ascension and the only ascension available on Earth before now, the etheric Lightbody/electronic Lightbody Ascension? As an example of what I'm explaining, I once had an interesting experience when I took a bus tour through Victoria, British Columbia. Sitting next to me was an East Indian woman wearing a sari. My intuition knew that there was something unusual about this woman's very heightened vibration without having to rudely stare at her. Within minutes the woman was responding to my thoughts, answering me without any vocalization on my part. When I took the opportunity to look closely, I realized that I was not looking into the eyes of a dense atomic body, but that of a more translucent manifested physical Lightbody. This being responded to my thoughts by telling me that "he" had long awaited the opportunity to meet me in the dense physical body even though we work together on the inner planes, that he was very aware of my mission on Earth, and that his mission would be interacting with my divine mission. By this time I knew intuitively that I was talking to Count Rakoczi, and as quickly as the thought went through my mind, his response was, "Most still call me St. Germain." When the bus boarded the ferry to the mainland, I briefly watched people disembarking from the bus, then turned to my friend with great excitement, hoping for further discussion, but alas, the lady was gone!

This is the deception that Maitreya created for the disciple Jesus, for he embodied a recognizable replica of Jesus as an example of humankind's potential. But this example with his transformational energies was never intended by Maitreya, your Christ, to be worshiped!

After the last of the two Golden Ages on Earth, even through your darkened history in atomic structure, there have still been many, many thousands of humanity who have achieved this minor accomplishment of Resurrection.

I think that perhaps we have overplayed this theme, but I must confess, humankind's inflexibility and abject stuckness does confuse this personality. I know that what I'm saying will be viewed as harsh, too forthright, and without compassion or compromise by many. It is *because* of my compassion that I speak as directly as I do of these unresolved matters that are simply not going to go away through artificial compassion and further manipulation. There is no third-dimensional time left. Fourth-dimensional time and the microtron wait for no man, and humankind have had every opportunity to accomplish the simple feat of primary Ascension.

We have stated in as many ways as we reasonably can the reason that you are still in the atomic body; and I'm not referring to those who are in physical bodies as the externalization of the Human Hierarchy, who should have accomplished again in this life at least the integration required for primary Ascension.

Again, when you do an evaluation of why you are in dense physical embodiment, please remember what I have said in a number of different ways — the only reason to experience the dense atomic body is to raise it to the level of the radiant electronic Lightbody, which can only happen when your personality's outer self recognizes that *its only reality is one's inner Self, the I AM Presence of Source, Mahatma.* So be it!

Now going to other levels of resonance: I have wanted to express with no uncertainty that my personality is no different than my beingness as *Mahatma*, for increasingly of late I have been made aware over and over again that there is less and less personality and more and more of the totality of *Mahatma* looking and feeling through my five senses.

I find interest in watching those areas that gave me physical pleasure in what I view as the past and which are no longer a part of my reality. My new physical body, which doesn't feel wonderful but is certainly radiant with Light, is much less sensual in its appetites for outer gratification. But this is not to encourage unnatural fanaticism, for *you* are in control, not the meat (or anything else that you feel you should avoid). So my body now dictates the terms and has closed the door on much that now seems so unimportant and illusory, even though I thought these areas were marvelous at the time.

Having lived a very full life; having looked at as many areas as sequential time would allow; and knowing this to be my last physical/universal embodiment (unless "we" choose to have it unfold differently), when I take the past and review this life, the highlights that I harken to and wish to remember are always the less sensuous and more subtle terms of reference. I call these my "positive Fourth-Ray memorabilia" of great art, music and literature that awaken one's Soul; and invariably something unusual that someone said or did would resonate profoundly within my heart.

The very thought that someone who represented as heightened an energy as *Mahatma* would partake so vigorously in life will cause consternation in those who are totally controlled by the mass-consciousness view that the "spiritual man" arrives on Earth with preordained patterning that does not embody cause and effect. This is only partly true, because how else does Source experience except through the personality's experience? If, for example, one lives as a yogi in a cave in the Himalayas and his resonance with life is a tiny ripple in the pond, that person invariably confines his energy to the inverted spiral of ever-diminishing return, and his "perfection" has little radiance beyond his cave.

This is the same analogy that we have already given you, of someone praying whose prayers fall flat in front of Self. *As you think, so you are.* Thinking of nothingness becomes nothingness; and if one's view of self is myopic, the results remain myopic. However, if one's consciousness embodies the Cosmos of All That Is, one's I AM Presence, **Mahatma**, the results become omnipresent.

You see, dear ones, there is no static perfection, for we continually become a greater Wholeness of Self, as that which we call Source, and if you can hold the view that your God Source is you and you are It and that there is no static perfection, this will surely help you in integrating who and what you are and where you fit into this magnificent tapestry of Creation, realizing that you are not simply one thread of the tapestry, but embody the principle that you are the *complete* tapestry.

I can hear you now saying, "That's easy for you to say, but how do I achieve omnipresence when I'm a single parent and I have to work to provide all of those basic necessities of survival?" If only one among you — using these terms of reference — can expand his consciousness to a heightened degree, finding the time and the wherewithal to achieve these levels of integration, then you all can. The English expression, "the squeaky wheel gets the grease," analogous to your religions, is a finite observation and has no meaning with one's comprehensive I AM. I couldn't agree more with any of you that "life is real and life is earnest"; and because of humanity's huge misunderstanding of life's purpose, it does seem impossible to become that which **Mahatma** says you must become if you do not want to fall away throughout eternity in the vacuous state of repetition on a near endless wheel of reembodiment.

These books embody enough knowledge, light and transformation for anyone with a modicum of discipline to *integrate, integrate* and *become the I AM*, **consciously.**

Have you ever looked at humankind's heroes with adulation and said to yourself, "Why wasn't I given that physical or mental persona instead of my miserable embodiment?" Envy becomes pathetic only when one becomes conscious enough to witness where these gods come from or go to when their sojourn on Earth is complete. Of all of your revered entertainers and politicians of recent times, only Mahatma Gandhi became a Master of Wisdom and resides with other expressions of wisdom such as Djwhal Khul and Buddha, as well as many personalities of no historical significance who have mastered dense physicality.

It is rather alarming when I hear a lovely Lightworker express to me in all seriousness that great movie stars are those beings who have completed mastery and then return into physicality as a bonus life because of their achievements on Earth. It is equally distressing when I hear the same person lovingly express that she can always identify those who are spiritually developed by the length of their ears — the longer the better! Where does this information come from? If you don't know, let me help you; it is the psychic/lower astral levels that convey this distortion.

It becomes even more pathetic when people become so dependent upon their heroes or gods that when a star such as Elvis or John Lennon leave their dense physical embodiment, these people find no further reason to live and take their own lives because they have lost the mirror to their only reality. Mankind's desperate need to mirror their substantive self through another physical expression, or to give their inherent self to Stalin, Elvis, Hitler, Mohammed, or Jesus, is the root cause of the disconnectedness that humans have with their only self, their I AM. To constantly mirror only what someone else has done is indeed very destructive.

The outer self would seldom, if ever, wish to realize that most of their hero worship is given to beings who function principally on the first, second and third astral levels or — better stated — on the levels of the psychic/lower mind's illusory self. The greatest adulation during this century has been given to Mao Tse Tung, Stalin, and Hitler. These extremely dark energies know how to manipulate substance, with huge support from a cast of fallen ones, because in endorsing or allowing, you *become*. No one can become a monster or a god of any magnitude unless the individual's collective Self, the country or the world allows this to happen.

Fortunately, what was, was, and has been rewritten. As you remember, in our references to the Iman and the Cabal, these darkened categories of humankind's allowingness cannot withstand the transformational Light of your recently expanded Source's requirements to fulfill what will "be done on Earth, as it is in Heaven."

This, dear ones, is an irrevocable cosmic law; and no matter what the Soul's projection, the personality, thinks should or will happen becomes quite academic and irrelevant. Personalities on this planet have had such long and dismal failure in functioning within the Cosmic Law of Love and Light, that these expressions of God can only believe what *they* have created, having no idea that for the most part these achievements are aught but illusion. We would consider heightened expressions of the arts to be the exception, because these do endure. To see fourth-dimensional man still functioning so third-dimensionally, with greater and greater proclivity for endorsing violence on television or in the movies, one could view this as a subconscious last-ditch attempt to hang onto "the good ol' days."

There is, with many on Earth, an environmental awareness that is encouraging, from my point of view, because *any* positive awareness is a step in the right direction. But please "don't throw out the baby with the bathwater." The baby in this analogy is the overall consciousness of man, for nature and your Space Command can manage when the time is appropriate, to look after the "bathwater." Your Earth is in *total transformation;* in other words, the barn is burning and the horses are leaving...so we would encourage you not to become obsessed with the bathwater — the whales, dolphins, and other species that are in the process of leaving this planet. These kingdoms understand, more readily than humankind, the degree of transformation necessary. Therefore, we would suggest that one perfect the baby before they enter the bathwater. It is a conscious act of nature that these animals are now leaving the Earth in great numbers, for they know that their evolution here is near completion. No matter how keen your personal sense of loss as these wonderful friends are leaving, your energy would be better applied in emulating your friends, so that you also move forward on your evolutionary path to perfected Self.

Forever on this planet, mankind have used the term "spiritual" as anything and everything related to their perception of God; thus, anyone who partook of these teachings was considered to be spiritual; and in the scrutiny of this one word, we find that "spirit" could mean anything at all. During Earth's history, nearly every creature has been worshiped and deified as a spirit at one time or another. My intention is not to explain myths, folklore, and the creation of spirits, because Joseph Campbell did that with such expertise. His writings would invite study in that regard. My limitations are many, here in dense physical embodiment, exacerbated further by so little multidimensional terminology. Working with third-dimensional language does create perceived limitations. I'm going to use this one word, "spiritual," in this analogy to make my point.

In my judgment, Jesus and Alice Bailey have been the Earth's clearest channels. Alice Bailey in particular, because of her recent embodiment on Earth, for the most part used an adequate third-dimensional language to bring through Djwhal Khul, through which your human Hierarchy referred to themselves as the Spiritual Hierarchy and Spiritual Teachers. I have noted that the word "spiritual" needs quotation marks because your third-dimensional language has no word for what truly constitutes the idea of spiritual. This has become apparent to you so I'll not belabor this point.

Until 40 years ago or so, Djwhal Khul was your most accurate teacher, conveying very mental concepts through a very mental channel, Alice Bailey. I wish to place into relative perspective, then and now, the great achievements of Djwhal. Although most of the concepts that he brought through have no relevance today, he, more than anyone else, created a language to convey his concepts that is still generally applicable today, as we enter a multidimensional matrix of time. If, however, you wish to express living in the relative now of evolution, spiritual *is* spiritual, electronic energy *is* electronic, and nary the twain shall meet until there is an acceptance by humankind not only that there is a difference between the two, but that these are the *only two* energies in Creation that need be identified in order to integrate them. Your ever-expanding consciousness expands because of your higher mind; if you don't have a concept for magnification of consciousness, then your consciousness can't expand, can it? If it can, I'd be delighted to hear how, without any more spiritual gibberish. The "Master" Djwhal Khul taught — and this is not to suggest that he doesn't teach today, but I haven't seen or heard of another Alice Bailey; Janet McClure was as close as we got! Any among your human hierarchy, the Masters, would teach more accurately today because their evolution is taking a quantum leap, as is yours, since the Harmonic Convergence of August 1987, and for every other reason that we have described in *Mahatma I* and *II*.

We use Djwhal Khul as an example of excellence, for his understanding at the particular sequential time period on Earth when he wrote gave all who followed a definitive language to bridge into the New Age. The only limiting aspect of this great teacher's contributions is the innate limitations of those who followed. They have not been able to bridge the gap between what was and what is and are expending huge energies in attempting to reinforce what was, creating what we have referred to as tiger butter. Because of "the ring passeth not," your host of masters — who refer to themselves as the Spiritual Hierarchy — had no knowledge beyond the Ninth Initiation. Djwhal, if you recall, was in total awe of your Solar Logos, Helios, and certainly had no profound knowledge of the spiritual/monadic levels. But he has a much greater understanding now, because when I'm awakened at three o'clock in the morning to see a neon sign flashing **"FUSION,"** more often than not this is Djwahl stepping down the most recent information. The case that I'm making is that in the last six years, *nothing is as it was*. Because I have some recall of teaching and being taught on the inner planes, I know this to be so.

It will not matter to those among you who resent my seemingly judgmental and assertive language ("Does he think for a moment that we're all wrong and he's right?"), but I know not how to convey my First-Ray assignment any differently in order to communicate embodiment as the *Mahatma*. Again, what we teach will resonate or it won't; and please try not to become upset, for everyone will or will not magnify their own view of salvation.

Always the choices remain yours and yours alone, as the Gods that you are with the divine right of free will. As the personality, I do have a reactive side to the human family's ineptitude for finding a way out of their own creative nightmare; and I'm possibly weary, as a personality, of embodying over and over again Light energy to show mankind a way out, and repeatedly having it fall on deaf ears. I remind you that this is the minuscule part of Self, referred to as the personality, that with every opportunity available — more so than ever before — for humankind to move into the Light, why wouldn't they be *jumping* at the chance?

So, personality's perspective of being driven to achieve for humanity what only they will or will not do for themselves, is not the perspective of greater Self, for these heightened levels of consciousness sense one way or the other whether mankind can rewrite its scenario and become Light. As all of Creation is being played out in the Now, or Relative Now, it is only at the levels that embody sequential time that one's script can be rewritten; ironic but true, and so difficult to understand.

I speak of the thin line between Light and darkness, and that for humankind the differences are not yet distinguishable because of the fascination that they have with the psychic/lower astral levels which do not embody Light as a principle of cosmic law at all. When these unconscious levels become aware that their status quo is threatened by the ignition of Light through the expanded Source and the hastening of this Cosmic Day, there is most definitely a reactive side. This is the principal reason that I ask you to use your discernment more than ever before. Not only the filters that you use to define relative truths, but the feedback from the human sensory system is truly an unenlightened report indeed. And I know that few among you have the clarity to realize this on your own, thus your filters will have to be made of a finer mesh so that you can better distinguish that which is Light and that which is more comfortable. The recognizable vibration of the psychic realms is so much easier to identify with in this density.

What I'm about to say is an observation, not a judgment; and only your filters can convey your "truths." In recent times, there is more and more ambiguity in the channeled information coming through, and much less clarity than there was a few years ago; I suggest that one really should ask oneself about what they hear, "Where is this consciousness originating?" I say this because I can see the influences that the psychic/lower mind levels are having on many transmissions I've been privy to read.

The contradistinction in all of this, with a New Age just opening, is that many state with absolute sincerity that they are a "spiritual Lightworker," when in all fairness to them, many wouldn't truly understand the nearly indistinguishable line between the Light and the psychic/lower astral plane. And whenever a way of life is being threatened, you invariably have an immense reaction, because a perspective change means upheaval ("Leave us alone; we're fine the way we are" or "We don't need you making our lives uncomfortable"). Disquietude is a perfectly normal reaction, particularly when one's future is clouded with, "What if I can't change? What will happen to me?"

Thus you begin to have input from the psychic realms, manipulating your sensory activations, including your dream state; whenever possible, the darker, finite expressions — usually on an unconscious level — will commingle with the Light if they are allowed. Being allowed to react with individuals unconsciously, they may find refuge for awhile; or even further, they may succeed in distorting positive shifts away from the Light for awhile. Whatever shifts are attempted by the psychic realms can only be temporary, but they are being attempted nonetheless as a last great Armageddon in its truest sense.

A suggestion might be that before you go to sleep, ask *Mahatma* (if you have made that connection, or your Soul levels, depending upon which one you are consciously working with) to allow only pattern removal to take place at night, and insist that you receive no interference from the psychic realms, for they bring only distortion. If during the day you can maintain your connection with your I AM Presence, *Mahatma*, then you can most assuredly separate yourself from distorted impressions of your sensual self and your collective self.

Because of the intensity of Light inherent in our seminars and in these books, we occasionally hear reactions such as, "I don't know about this energy, because I certainly felt better before I touched into it." One person, after having read *Mahatma I*, apparently did not feel well and consulted a psychic; of course, the psychic told her that "if she didn't feel good, then what she is doing must be evil." This is a classic example of the pot calling the kettle black!

I know as well as anyone on Earth the atomic body's reactive side to Light; for after, and just prior to my conscious Ascension in September 1989, it has been questionable at best whether I could maintain a physical body at all. There have been many nights when there seemed to be no way that I could remain within the confines of something so dense as the body I partly live in. If you can imagine having a toe in an electrical outlet...this is the best description that I can offer of bringing such a magnitude of energy into my physical body. And I thought I was required to do this without asking other Co-Creators to assist me in this adventure. Vywamus, through Janet McClure, made it very clear to me that I could not achieve this by myself; and, as you have surmised, it was my saving grace to allow others to assist. In fact, the complete Co-Creator level assisted so that I could fulfill my promise to Self not to embody universally again, and if possible stay and complete all of universal physical existence.

From day to day I still don't know how long I can remain in the Earth's vibration without lift-off; and I must confess, I'm looking to that day with great anticipation. To say that I'm not confused, with a monumental body that is entirely too dense for the microtron, is an understatement, but I have enormous help all of the time from the Archangels and the Soul levels. Even with all of the faith in the world, it still seems miraculous; however, my Higher Selves know that there is nothing paranormal, so "miraculous" would imply that Creation doesn't unfold naturally, in harmony and balance. Knowing this illusion feels real, I also monitor from other levels of Self, where the results of the spiritual microtron interfacing with the electrical body are not known. But my previous argument would certainly come into play here, and an Omnipresence would have to know the outcome of the microtron within dense physicality.

Speaking of the ultimate Ascension, which will hopefully unfold as quickly as we can raise the Earth's vibration, I have been looking at this possibility beyond what I have already mentioned. If I understand in finite terms what St. Germain has been saying to me, then all physical senses are similar to tuning in through a radio and choosing a particular wavelength, sight and hearing being parts of the same activity. I would not have resonated with this concept if I had not had a "crystal radio" experience in several of my seminars, where I was able to bring in a number of radio transmissions during meditation and, as already stated, finding that these vibrations were not received once I entered the vibratory level of the true spiritual realms. Thus I have experienced this reality, and see the vivid possibility of how the expression "for all eyes to see and every heart to open in wonderment" might be fulfilled.

I now realize the very real possibility of humanity hearing and seeing the only complete radio-type transmission in Earth's history, by magnifying light and sound, using the Earth as a crystal set and the ozone layer as a baffle, for the whole world to hear and see the spiritual Ascension.

Bewildering? Of course it is, and for none more than myself; for I have no conscious understanding of these matters. But I acknowledge the possibility that every utterance that could and should be made at this time could most certainly be achieved within the confines of the most natural of laws. "The Rider on the White Horse," in the biblical sense, having to be depicted as stated, seems to have been either a 60,000-year-old symbolic statement, or an unrealistic "pie in the sky" idea. You may wish to consider this new possibility within the confines of what I now know is natural law, but didn't know until this actually happened to me in a small but surprising revelation.

Having just reread Barbara Waller's material, I find I had overlooked what Djwhal had said regarding the timing for Ascension: "Thus that book is coming out with the completion of your tad." (Refer to the June 8, 1992 channeling session with Barbara Waller. Knowing how difficult it is to achieve any degree of exactitude in predicting sequential time, I must be patient and realize that this will happen when it happens.)

Reading what has been written here, one could become dismayed with the apparent exactitude of our teachings and opinions and wonder, "How am I supposed to know what is right for me at this time, just because I've decided that I can or cannot resonate with what someone has written or said?" This is an understandable question and, as we have stated several times, perfection is not static and neither are spiritual teachings. They are to be looked at, integrated, and then moved beyond. At this time on Earth, there are no higher teachings than *Mahatma I* and *II*, so for at least the time being, on one's journey on Earth, if our teachings seem too complex and one cannot gain the benefit of experiencing one of our seminars because of time, money, location or whatever, there are many good intermediary steps that could be beneficial. As in life, one can go to grade school, then high school, and earn these natural progressions in integration until one either can or cannot resonate with *Mahatma*. It all comes down to the steps inbetween: how you achieve these, and whether they contain substance worthy of integration.

My observation on Earth is that there are an adequate number of good systems of teaching, and some of them might even be fun! One cannot always afford the price of a Broadway or London show — and I'm not being facetious here, because certain branches of Christianity are in show biz and do an excellent job of entertaining without one word about God. And in the esoteric streams of consciousness or unconsciousness there are some very entertaining beings channeling various entities not embodying Light; these are not to be taken seriously (unless one so profoundly resonates with these teachings as truth), but should at least be enjoyed and moved beyond, for there is considerable psychic involvement with many of these entities. However, this is also found in other areas of theatrical events, so just have fun with it.

One would never guess, from the serious nature of these humorless teachings, that I also have great fun and joy. I simply have to, in order to retain a modicum of sanity in a world that my personality views as outrageous in its divergent excesses and polarities.

I can remember enjoying Benny Hill on television years ago for comedy relief, and if I couldn't get Benny I would turn to a television preacher for entertainment. My favorite among these was Ernest, for his theatrics were as developed as Benny's — maybe even more so, because Benny had hair, whereas Ernest wore a toupee of poor quality (if it had been of good quality, he would have been much less funny, for then he would not have had to adjust it during the show).

Anyway, I so enjoyed Ernest's show that I became able to mimic him exactly. On one occasion, I was on the Cayman Islands and struck up a conversation with two gentlemen who had obviously prospered in show business, for they were forces in the evangelical movement in America. The more they drank, the more extravagant their interpretation of scripture. I was in my element, egging them on to new and unexpected heights in interpreting scripture, as they competed with each other in what became, for me, a wonderful theatrical event. But not to be outdone by my newfound "saviors," I borrowed a short wig from a lady friend and performed my interpretation of Ernest. This proved so successful that they wished to draft a contract of employment for me right then and there! These outstanding entertainers offered me a huge contract the following morning, involving a great deal of money, if I would become one of them "in the greatest opportunity one has to serve God and save the world from Satan." I have often thought of this alternate reality and what it would have been like. Obviously I did not entertain in that particular theatrical arena, but had a wonderful time exploring the possibility.

Again I can hear, "Who does he think he is?" Alas, what is one man's meat is another man's poison. If I seem excessively opinionated, I can assure you that I don't make seemingly judgmental statements about *anything* without first running it through my sieves of consciousness very thoroughly before any utterance on my part. This is exactly what you should do also, to refine your ability for greater and greater discernment of what constitutes Light and your relative truths. For when all is said and done, only *you* can monitor what your reality is in this finite discipline that we call Earth living.

Accessing the Soul

Soul is so easy to access that all you need undertake is a connection with who you are, once you realize the insignificance of the personality. One of the many ways to connect with Soul is discussed in the Appendix. But a day-to-day communication with primal Soul or Higher Self — until you understand whether you have accomplished your Soul Merge — is simply to contact your double-pronged connection with your Soul Star and heart chakra (the thymus gland). If in any doubt, view your Soul Star and your heart chakra, visualizing a line between both of these. This line then connects with a line that extends from your third eye outward several feet in front of you, creating a convergent point of concentration there. Once you have created this integrated point of consciousness, you can address this point of consciousness and actually have conversations with it. You can ask this primal Soul or combined Soul-levels connection (depending upon your level of evolution) to please respond with what you need to know, particularly as it relates to discernment, and what your Soul levels view to be in their best interest — not what the personality views is important for the personality, unless one really feels that the Soul levels don't understand, and thereby create excessive discomfort for the personality.

Please be patient with this connection, for it, like everything in life, takes effort. But once you have this liaison with Self, your questions regarding discernment can be answered immediately. Again, I remind you to shroud yourself in Light so that you don't get any interference from what are now very active psychic realms. If you have anchored your connection with the *Mahatma*, there is no need to make the Soul connection as stated above — simply address the *Mahatma*, as your I AM Presence, with your Cosmic Heart, for you are completely protected from any darkened energy by doing so, and tell *Mahatma* what you wish to achieve or to express, then truly expect what you wish to manifest, for it *will* and *can*, providing you do not introduce any negative input whatsoever.

All of my invocations are immediate and at certain times materialized *prior* to my conscious recognition that they were required. Thus I live totally within the Now of my own creative abilities. This should be understood, because it does not mean, even for a moment, that others cannot do exactly the same!

I would encourage you to *integrate the Mahatma completely into your consciousness*, for this is, after all, who you are, regardless of opinions expressed by a personality overwhelmed by the fact that it is the veritable embodiment of the I AM Presence, *Mahatma*.

Once you recognize your Presence as the I AM, effort will be required in the ignition and integration of this. You will become a greater and greater wholeness of who you are as the I AM, as described in many integrative ways throughout these books. Once you expand your consciousness to become the I AM that you are, *expect deliverance*. In fact, *demand* deliverance and know that the Creator is you; and you, the Creator, have free will and can create anything within your perceived limitations and within the cosmic laws of appropriate manifestation. There is nothing as powerful as the loving abundance and radiance of joy perceived and recognized as you integrate and become that which you are, as the magnificent I AM Presence, *Mahatma*.

Speak not of limitation, for you become that which you think upon. If your perception of self has no resonance beyond the pathetic personality's perspective of its outer creations, that can only denote illusion and necessitate forever expressing reembodiment on greater and greater depths of degradation into the atomic structure's inability to recognize itself as Light and Love. Then you will have no one to blame but yourself, for the very reason that there can be no victims within Creation. No one but you created your reality, to begin with. Tough medicine? It is only if one persists in remaining that which they are not, and seeing themselves as victims of someone else's doing, be it God or humankind.

When I was a small boy, I witnessed a Spitfire airplane crash some distance away in the front yard of a mansion. Unbeknownst to me, the pilot was on a training mission in Vancouver and was given a weather report assignment from which he never returned. When my brother Donald and I returned home from the wreckage, my family was in great grief, because the pilot was apparently my cousin. His mother, my aunt, became hysterical and remained in mourning for five years, wearing a black arm band as an indication of the depth of her sorrow for her son's demise. I can remember thinking even then, "How can this demonstration help anyone?" My aunt's most frequent utterance was, "How could God do this to me?" I have often thought of this young man since, and how regrettable for him that he should be held back from his evolution by his mother's selfish grief. All of us have these examples in our lives, but few stop to think of the debilitating effect that this has on *both* Souls' evolution. Their only thought is, "I would certainly have treated them differently if they were still alive" or "how can I go on without him or her?"

Recently I was in Cyprus to write, rest, and visit an enigma called Daskalos. While at the airport, I heard a shrill scream off to the side, and my first thought was that something terrible must have happened. Not on your nelly. What I proceeded to witness with disbelief was a Greek mother saying goodby to her 50-year old daughter who was going to Athens, but a few miles away. This mother bespoke who she was in one glance. From the top of her head to the bottom of her feet she was shrouded in black. In any part of this area or the Middle East, she could have done well as a professional mourner. I could not even imagine her utterances had things been serious!

When my second daughter, Julie, was in preparation for the delivery of her baby in a Vancouver hospital, I heard a less professional scream for recognition, but no less oblique. When the nurse returned from her rounds to my daughter, I said, "Nurse, this screaming is a little disconcerting for my daughter, who is about to have her first baby." The nurse replied, "Oh, I'm so sorry but, you know, the lady is East Indian. She's so terrified of delivering a girl child that in the event the baby is not a boy, she wants her husband to know how much she has suffered." Tell me that we are not a strange lot!

All that I describe in these incidents resonates with humanity's greatest demon, their emotional body. Most human beings live and die within the confines of the emotional body, having no knowledge of how to extricate themselves from such limiting confinement. Grief is the absolute opposite of Divine Love and the most selfish of acts. The great misunderstanding is that most of humankind believe grief to be an expression of love.

There are simply too many examples on Earth of living within the confines of the emotional body that humanity still have not evolved beyond. This, more than any other reason, is why humankind have not raised their vibration above that of Earth and primal Soul. They will reembody over and over again until they finally understand and rise above the distorted views and total control they have allowed under the dictates of humanity's greatest enigma, the emotional body.

Study the diagram of the four-body system on page 225. Before you begin to work with the emotional body, there might be wisdom in understanding that in fact you have one, and that this body controls you more than anything else within one's self-made imprisonment on Earth. We have included a number of pattern-removal exercises on page 458 of the Appendix.

The following realizations are general, not specific or personalized, so know that they apply to you and everyone else. As you begin to understand specifics, you will be able to isolate personal realizations for yourself and remove patterns that repeat and have kept you a slave to your emotional body.

Do not be a slave to the emotional body.

Please now be your own Creator as you state:

- *I recognize my Self's only presence, the I AM Presence.*
- *I understand that I will no longer be controlled by my emotional body, and I insist that this be so!*
- *I insist that I raise my consciousness into the Light, as the I AM Presence, and never again be a slave to that which I am not; and from this time forward, I recognize myself as Light and only Light, as the I AM of my I AM Presence.*
- *As my four-body system radiates Light and Love and only Light and Love, I raise forevermore my emotional body, and I expand and integrate my physical, emotional, and mental bodies within my spiritual body as the Light that I AM, for I know this to be my only reality.*
- *I AM the Light of my own Creation, and I refuse to be any longer controlled and reduced to slavery, as I forever bring in Light, Light, Light, and forever expand as the Creator that I AM.*
- *I AM Divine Love, for that is All There Is, only Love and Light as the I AM Presence, Mahatma.*
- *I now view my Completed Self, as I expand throughout eternity, and see only Light and Love as I free myself and become that which I have always been, the All That Is, as the I AM of my I AM Presence, NOW.*

Please repeat this realization often, as you watch layer upon layer of your illusory self reidentify with your only reality, your inner I AM.

You will be able to isolate specifics within your patterns; for example:

"I will no longer endorse failure and betrayal because my husband (wife, friend) has abandoned me."

Or: "I do not have to believe that because I do not like my personal appearance, it is anything other than an outer expression, having nothing to do with who I AM as the creator of my reality. I recognize my beauty as Light and

Love, as the eternal embodiment of All That Is. My physical body is only a garment, and I will not accept this superficiality anymore, because I know that mass consciousness is not correct; they are the slaves of their creations — I'm not! I AM Divine Light and Love, and I AM the creator of my inner I AM. I wish to live no longer in a totally illusionary outer self.

Whatever pattern that you and only you will know and recognize as it raises its ugly head over and over again, you — as the creator of your reality — are also best suited to identify and remove these parts of your emotional body that only make you a slave to that which doesn't exist, your outer self and its eternal entanglement with your emotional body.

Please call on the *Mahatma* energy throughout your transformation, for nothing ever expressed on Earth works with greater effectiveness.

Throughout my seminars in Europe I have noticed with great interest that we had as many novices as we had seasoned Lightworkers and teachers. This may tell you what it most certainly tells me, that one should not overevaluate one's level or state of readiness when deciding whether to participate, expressing as some do, "How can I participate, even though I would like to, in something that I really don't understand?" My answer would be that *there is no time like the present and the sooner, the better.*

I have held an incorrect picture also about when one should enter these heightened levels of teaching. I must confess that in many cases, the "stars" in my classes have been those who arrived with no preconceived opinions about what constitutes relative truth. There are so many out there who are saying many different things that, in many cases, have no resonance with relative truth. Therefore, there are also a lot of confused students of life.

In several instances, we have been privileged to teach those who had been disciples of a guru who had immense financial success teaching that one should and could express their sensuous self within the confines of the psychic levels and the three lower chakras. In other words, a classic example of a reaffirmation that humankind have always been correct in living within the confines of the lower self, their illusory self.

The contradistinction here is the absolute opposite to what the *Mahatma* energies teach. The only difficulty that certain among these students had were reactions of cramps and discomfort in the area of the polarity chakras, or a feeling of being electrocuted as the profound resonance of Light raised their vibration electronically, causing a sense of overwhelm among some. But none of these individuals left a seminar for anything but a short duration, for they recognized that this was simply transformation, and transformation is not without side effects; however, these can only mirror to you where your resistances are, not where the transformational energies are. Do you begin to see the distinction here?

As many are experiencing, the difficulty with relationships on Earth is that if one is looking for a "twin soul," then one will wait a very long time. I have seen advertisements in new age publications claiming they can assist readers to find their twin soul. There is no such thing, because when Souls were individualized, they were never birthed as twins.* One cannot even embody a twin ray, unless that means one-twelfth of Creation; in other words, twelve rays divided by eight trillion to the tenth power, would give you only the Adam Kadmon expressions in this one universe. So that doesn't work.

In all of Creation, Hu-man's only twin soul or soulmate is within one's own Self; meaning, of course, the God and Goddess within your own beingness. From a Source perspective this would not be correct because of the androgynous nature of energy being simply energy. So, "marriages made in heaven" is simply another way to give one's power away to an ancient god, Jehovah, who brought religion into marriage through a human image and humanity's creation of "God."

I have paid for a number of these events because my beautiful daughters could accept only the status quo, or a ceremony that is a pleasant show business offering performed and further sanctified by "God" and in the name of "God." That has been my contribution to illusion. Does mankind really believe that the All That Is, the Source of Sources, Who simply IS, has any idea that their marriages are entrusted to it? Man's illusionary ability to attribute to God what his lower mind has created and then call it God takes great creative ability! It is unfortunate that this same creative effort was not used to create God in God's image instead of in man's image; if that had been so, we would have achieved on Earth that which is in heaven many times over.

The Catholic Church has positively mastered its creative efforts to disempower its followers by not only sanctifying marriage in the name of God, but further, making these same followers believe that in the name of the same God they could be excommunicated from the church if "God's union" proved to be disastrous and divorce was considered. Thus the founders of Christianity control mankind's ignorance about going within and managing their own affairs, by manipulating lives from before conception to death; then the Church is clever enough to determine who goes to heaven or hell. This may well be the greatest script ever written on Earth for total dependency and disempowerment, and there have been some remarkable examples of great moral and ethical crises allowed to happen here! To live within the confines of an ethical and moral code is one thing, but to allow the immorality and unethical practice of total manipulation in the name of God is probably the greatest obscenity perpetrated by man against humankind and sanctified by "God." God-man's free will includes the moral responsibility for being prudent and ethical in his or her own inner self through going within and seeking his *own* moral certification and his *own* ethical communion with the God that *he* is and not the God of platitudes and degenerative indoctrinated fear. Humanity have long allowed themselves to be treated as a subspecies, to be saved from a fate worse than

---

* A fully developed Primal Soul and Higher Self could have as many as twenty-four aspects in forty-three universes, but souls themselves are (Physical Extensions) of the Spiritual OverSoul. Thus the odds of meeting on Earth become incalculable.

what they have already experienced "by the blood of God's only begotten Son, Jesus." Therefore their finite suffering is fine, because their God and only their God can "save their Souls and ensure their place and eternal life in heaven."

There has been incredible manipulation of the human psyche on Earth, but the greatest manipulator is the Catholic Church — not Mao Tse Tung, not Stalin, and not Hitler, who were very dark manipulators of their own creeds or religions, but who pale in comparison, for they never said nor implied that only *they* were the custodians of the only keys to heaven. How others divided the Catholic pie is history!

What I am stating is not generally supported by mass consciousness, and the reaction to it in time will be vehement, for no one wishes to be told that everything that they have ever held sacred is the opposite of the Law of Creation. For this I apologize. If my truths don't resonate as truths, then there will be no reactive side to speak of. If, however, what I have stated here and previously is relative truth, then all of these ancient structures and untruths will fall away without a need for utterances of any kind. There are no sacred cows as we approach this New Age of deliverance, for then everything becomes sacred. And if man's lower mind does not vibrate with the amount of Light introduced to this planet, what does not resonate will not remain. So let us take comfortable positions — not in judgment or condemnation but in support and observation, as Earth begins her transformation into supreme Light and Love.

With the emotional and mental bodies in a state of transformation as a result of fourth-dimensional time being introduced to Earth, all relationships seem to be stretched to a breaking point. The fractionalization throughout the world is not greater darkness as some would have you believe, but in fact, just the opposite is true!

The introduction of the Tenth Ray and the microtron to allow for the spiritualization of matter, raises the vibrational levels through the fundamental principle of resonance. Thus those who are conscious enough to feel the shifts in their state of awareness realize that their emotional bodies are very reactive to even the subtlest changes within their auric fields, as greater and greater Light permeates all physical, emotional, astral and mental bodies on the planet.

Thus the reactive side of the human equation results in not only fractionalized disputes throughout the world, but also within personal relationships, as the way things were done in the past don't seem to work anymore, and our emotional mirrors seem not to be as focused as they once were. So, marriages "made in heaven" are in a state of abject disrepair because of the reactive side of Light as the vehicle for transformation. These reactions become very personalized because no two beings on Earth are vibrating at exactly the same rate.

As we begin to resonate with varying degrees of Light, those embodying the higher vibration will not resonate or feel comfortable with those who vibrate at a lower rate. This is the reason that so few marriages or relationships in general work in harmony as they did. For the time being, the receptive, nurturing energy of female embodiment vibrates at a higher rate than the male counterpart. This is also reflected in my seminars, where the male, or the more dynamic expression within polarities, seldom make up even 25% of the group.

What does all this mean? Simply, be aware that transformation can be understood as a principle of resonance. It is important to not personalize the differences in order to avoid becoming dysfunctional if your lower self or your sensuous self no longer meets your expectations. And one wearies of the games that are played in what has become the ultimate game in life — maintaining a relationship. Humankind, including your clergy, need not strut their stuff any longer. Leave that to the animal kingdom, for they excel in this and bring much pleasure as we observe them mirroring our own behavior and evolution. When people truly observe nature, they will see their inheritance as third-dimensional animals and will hopefully recognize that this must now be transcended into fourth-dimensional time and awareness.

And how does one do this? I would suggest that you decide who is in control. By this I mean, are your emotional and lower mental bodies in control, or are *you*, as your inner Self, the I AM Presence, in control? No one else is the creator of your reality except you. And if life becomes impossible to express in the way that personality sees fit, one remains controlled by the outer or sensuous self. Or, one can choose to take control through the positive recognition that they can go within. This, of course, must precede any positive manifestation.

Humankind have, for several million years since the last Golden Age, allowed themselves to be manipulated both consciously and subliminally, but mostly on subliminal levels of self. Remaining unconscious has been, for them, the line of least resistance. And now that these requirements have shifted so dramatically, the consciousness of humanity (or lack of) is in a state of no man's land, neither here nor there, fish nor fowl, having to become the creators of their own perceived victimhood through their concept of fate or faith. Alternatively, humanity can go within to acknowledge and accept that they are the collective I AM Presence that can and will create the only true existence that has ever been, your inner I AM through the collective I AM Presence that we call *Mahatma*.

These choices have always been yours and yours alone. But being so unconscious of Self, it was much easier to have someone else do all of this for you, from before conception to one's assured place in heaven. My dear, dear friends or my beloved adversaries, all that most have experienced — except for the host of Masters — has been manifested in humankind's appetite for delusion — which, by the standards of one's inner I AM, can only be seen as excessive form and darkness, with no understanding of what constitutes Omnipresent Light and Unconditional Love.

With respect to the visualization that you each do, the chart of "The Cosmic Heart" and the other support charts should be studied as well as all of the information relating to the expansion of consciousness. The emotional body is also in need of nourishment, for it finds nothing but disquietude and upheaval as it realizes its sense of abandonment as the consciousness is raised above the lower self.

Realization: Nourishing the Emotional Body

Kindly repeat the following realization, particularly when the emotional body needs nourishing. You may wish to put this realization on tape in whatever language you speak.

"I am prepared to accept the fact that I have an emotional body *now*, as I adhere to the premise that this body is definitely a part of me, as I direct my attention to this body as part of my greater Self, *now*.

As I direct my attention to my greater Self, the I AM Presence of Source Itself, I commit irrevocably that within my evolution I will never abandon my emotional body, but will allow this part of me to be integrated into who I AM, as that which I AM as the All That Is. I ask *Mahatma*, *now*, to help me in my disquietude as I allow myself to become radiant with the same Light and Love. That is who I AM as the Creator. I now and forever recognize my emotional body as something that is not separate, as I enter into my Cosmic Heart and becalm this part of me in great Light and Love. I say to my total Self, I have no part of me that is not me as I acknowledge my great I AM Presence, thus I feel soothed and loved as my emotional body becomes more and more joyous and radiant within the Light and Love that I know myself to be, as I embody that which I AM and have always been, the I AM Presence as one with All That Is, my God Source.

As I expand within my Cosmic Heart, I can see and remember the circles of expansion as I lift the residue of hurt and dismay beyond the confines of limitations.

I breathe out, out, into greater and greater levels of Light, Light, Light; and I trigger that which I AM as *Light, Light, Light*. I realize that there is nothing but Light. As my four-body system travels throughout eternity, there is only Light and Love; and how soothed my emotions become when I realize that all else is but illusion. The more I expand my consciousness, I realize that everything but Light and Love are only illusion, as I become that which I have always been, Light, as the I AM of my I AM Presence. I resonate with *Mahatma*, and constantly ask that this Great Energy is who I AM; and I will remind myself continuously throughout my stay on Earth, as the inner I AM, that there is nothing that I am not. I recognize myself as Light and Love, and view my emotional self loved and nourished. I recognize now and forever more that which I AM as Love and Light, as the Great I AM of Source, *Mahatma*, *now*.

I commit myself to love myself as I never have in the past, for within Creation, I cannot love one part and not another, for these are all me. I will not allow dissonant thoughts to ever enter my I AM from the psychic realms, for I recognize this to be only my illusory self. I will stay within my inner I AM and love that which I AM, *now*. And I reaffirm that I cannot love or express Love until I *love myself unconditionally, NOW*.

This Cosmic Day represents courage, and courage it takes, for in the original master plan for this Cosmic Day, the Co-Creator Council of Twelve never envisioned or considered that God-man would express and expand his consciousness beyond his pure electrical body as "a host of Masters." But through humankind's insatiable curiosity they would fall deeper and deeper into illusion and the colossal abyss, where they would become the creator of their outer self and their material things.

What I receive with clarity from our monadic Self is that now Source recognizes this atomic density to be part of our collective Self, but that this atomic aspect of Creation is showing little or no illumination or recognition. The Council of Twelve for our Source mandates only 1.2 billion years remaining to bring home all divine expressions, at least to the senior monadic levels. At your current rate of evolution, this most definitely cannot be achieved. If primal Souls had not lost contact with their expressions as personalities for such a great period of time, this particular problem on Earth would not exist. How serious is this problem? To the degree that you do not recognize your divine embodiment as an infinite Spark of All That Is, and that your only connection to the God Source is contained within your inner I AM Presence. As the personalities are reacquainted with the primal Souls that they are, it will raise the personalities above what they think they are.

Most of humanity continue to believe what they are told (if, in fact, they are even that conscious). And what is it they believe? Humankind believe in their aristocracy (meaning "best power") — the adulation of man, principally those who have achieved financial success, which nearly always relates to the size of one's arsenal of homes or playthings. They admire physical expressions, usually within the confines of good looks; and many enjoy their Fourth-Ray expressions of nature. Humankind spend most of their time on Earth hoping to emulate the success of someone who has "made it." "It" is the problem of one's illusionary outer self.

Please try to understand that I am not being overly dramatic when I state that life as you have known it will no longer be tolerated. We have shown you many methods that you can use to become the creators of your own reality and to begin to connect the illusory outer self with the only reality, the inner I AM. Just because mass consciousness does not support what we say, that most certainly does not make mass consciousness correct! That in itself has always been the greatest distortion of mass consciousness — to believe that the psychic or lower self is reality.

Look around your Earth with her fractionalized disputes (whether they be religious or territorial) to view the misery and the joyless expressions of humankind and the unconscious three billion who are starving or who barely eke out a living. Look at how you've all been manipulated through religious and institutionalized stuckness and ineptitude — through the darkest of these, the Cabal. Now tell me that mankind have not missed the whole point of entering this self-imposed finite discipline! I would be very surprised if you could, assuming that you have been able to integrate and assimilate the contents of these books.

And there is not one among you who doesn't require courage to recognize the effort required for perfection as a realignment with your Self as your only reality, and recognize that the outer self is illusion, as manifested on Earth. Please understand that in the master-plan for this Cosmic Day, humanity was never intended to fall and become lost in illusory atomic structure, where the absence of Light and Love is so apparent. The dependency on any ray of hope has become pathetic as mankind awaits news about the Second Coming; and it seems to be every other day that someone sees the Virgin Mary.

Mankind recognizes within their psyche that they are dysfunctional, but mass consciousness does not support them doing anything differently. So humans become so desperate within the confines of religions that arenas are filled with lonely, lost people listening to a Croatian male who talks to a wall at 5:40 every evening, believing this to be the Holy Mother of God or to a preacher who says, "God told me this morning that we must expand our mission, praise the Lord, and that all of you should stop and phone this number, giving your credit card number, or mailing your check or money order to this address, praise the Lord. Our phones are open to the Lord; do what God has asked of you, and fulfill our Lord's work on Earth, praise the Lord!"

This colossal disempowerment of humankind either resonates with the "scientific proof" that all can be explained through finite science, or is a bewildering display of unrequited hopelessness, by sending money, for example, to a preacher for an assurance of being with Jesus in heaven. This is their Death Insurance and seems a small price to pay to know that "my afterlife is cared for by such a nice man who knows his Scripture word for word. What a great relief this is, for I can now give all of my attention to my garden and my grandchildren. And I'll see my friend Beatrice in church on Sunday — she'll be so surprised when she sees the beautiful dress I bought."

This would seem like a good deal to me, or anyone else observing this level of consciousness if in fact these beliefs had any resonance of relative truth. If they did, considering the amount of energy expended in prayer and communion with God, *not one* of humankind would require an atomic body, but would most assuredly join the gods that they worship as absolute equals in the lowest expression ever intended for man, that of a host of Masters. Do you not see how unfortunate humanity's use of free will has been? Mankind have fallen so far that they now venerate and worship *what they once were* during a Golden Age on Earth! *All* achieved Mastery at that time; and that level — which was the lowest level of consciousness ever intended by the Co-Creator Council for this Cosmic Day — is now **worshiped** by humanity as gods. Please reflect on this; allow this great truth to sink in, and see how absurd your creative abilities have become, as God-man with free will.

As I look out through the rear window of our recreational vehicle, which overlooks a beautiful lake, exercising my God-given free will from morning till night looking at what the Earth and humanity have become, it is very clear why these conditions cannot continue.

You may now understand, as the simplest of examples, why I would prefer to affix quotes to words such as "God," "Mastery," and particularly the word "spiritual." If the lowest vibration to be expressed as an outward expression of Source were to be the pure electrical etheric Lightbody, and that were the level humankind identified as mastery (as in the "Master" Jesus), considering this level to be a full expression of "spiritual" energy, then these most lowly evolved aspects of our "God Source" become not only the spiritual Gods for your religions, but are also the spiritual teachers for those who call themselves New Age or Lightworkers. If you can, in fact, follow these relative truths, then you will see who put the cart before the horse and continue to push it up a hill that cannot be climbed. In this analogy, there is no relationship of the horse or the hill that is even remotely analogous to the Creator's Truth and the Creator's Plan for evolution.

Please allow these truths to resonate with you so that you can begin to **integrate unlimitedness** and let go of the myopic views held by humankind. Please integrate thoroughly what has been stated, as we prepare for this Realization.

Affirmation for Unlimitedness

Focus now on your Cosmic Heart, and allow the complete *Mahatma*, the Father and Mother energies, to anchor within your consciousness as a full expression of Divine Light and Love. Breathe in deeply, dear one, and as you relax, know that there cannot possibly be any interference from the psychic/lower mind level. Relax, and allow no outer expression to enter your four-body system.

You start to feel nourished by the great Light and Love now starting to emanate from your combined heart/throat chakra. Allow the *Mahatma* to expand and fill all of the chakras within your physical body.

Watch both polarities as you allow the Goddess energy to fill the dynamic right side of your body; and the Father, the dynamic God energy, to fill the receptive left side. Look to see which area within these polarities is not receiving the same degree of Light as the others; for example, if it is the liver, then bring a vortex of great Light into that area, until your Light balance necessary for primary Ascension is achieved.

When the Light is balanced, begin to expand your consciousness throughout every crevice of your body, as you breathe out and out into the emotional body, releasing any extraneous material from your physical/etheric body...out, out, through the emotional body. Study and nourish this body with the *Mahatma* energy, and if there is any disquietude whatsoever, ask the **Goddess** to nourish you with Her great Presence.

Now, expand your consciousness through your mental body, breathing out, out, all imbalance or impurity into the spiritual body.

When you view your four-body system as balanced, each body in harmony with the others, begin to breathe all etheric residue into your Source Star itself — breathe out and out, and gather all that you no longer require (excess baggage) into your Source Star. Watch as all of this is burned in Transformational Fire and becomes the incandescent White Light of Source Itself. View this as a fountain of liquid White Light as you allow your crown chakra to open and open. Allow this radiant White Light to fill your physical body. Breathe the Light throughout every corner of your body — to the tips of your fingers and the tips of your toes.

When you see that your physical, emotional, and mental selves are resonant within your spiritual body, breathe out into the Light **as Light, Light, Light,** and greater and greater levels of **Light**...until there is nothing but Light as you expand your consciousness through your fifth-dimensional galactic Self.

Breathe out and out, expanding your consciousness now into your universal Self, and know these levels to be *you.* Have no doubt that this sixth dimension is you, and you are it. Expand your awareness of the universal level through all seven grand divisions; and at the apex of the seventh grand division, you meet and enjoy in great Light and Love, **Melchizedek**, your universal embodiment. See yourself as Melchizedek and Melchizedek as you.

Expand, expand into a greater Wholeness of Self, and now Melchizedek shows you a Golden Bridge, which leads to the monadic levels. At this juncture, allow your expression and expansion of the *Mahatma* **within** to assist you across this magnificent Golden Bridge into the spiritual realms.

Once across the bridge, you feel nothing but contentment and bliss as the Archangels and certain of the Angelic Host greet and adore you. You are so very much at one with All That Is now, as you greet those aspects of yourself who are on this level of consciousness.

Allow the *Mahatma* to introduce you to the Archangel Metatron and bathe in this one's great presence. Breathe in your **Creator Consciousness** as one with All That Is, *Now.*

You now embody Metatron, and allow *Mahatma* to take you through the balance of the seventh dimension, then the eighth dimension, forever expanding your consciousness as you recognize that this is also who You are.

The *Mahatma* then guides **you, as the** *Mahatma*, into the ninth dimension, where you witness an oval table. Around this table are eleven of the most wondrous Beings; in the middle of the table is the twelfth member, who is even more radiant in Divine Light and Love. There are no words to express the ecstasy and bliss that is **you,** for as you look into the eyes of these magnificent members of the Council of Twelve, who are the Creators of this Cosmic Day, you will see your own reflection, that these are you and you are they, and that there is no separation. Radiate into their Omnipresence, and know without any doubt that **this is who you are.**

Stay within that conscious level of awareness and know that there will never again be a sense of finite limitation, and if there is, then concentrate on your Source Star, which is located approximately 6 to 8 feet (2 to 2 ½ meters) above your crown chakra, until you have this connection into Unlimitedness all of the time.

Conscious Ascension

Those who enjoy the dense physical expression simply don't remember anything else, or they would make every effort to raise their consciousness into Light and Love. For the most exalted earthly life is nothing compared to mastery of dense physical embodiment, for your limitations are many and your joy so shallow and empty.

On September 22, 1989, in Holbrook, Arizona, I know now that I did my conscious Ascension. During that afternoon Glenda and I had spent some time in the Painted Desert, and I remember a sense of something new and something very old. My predominant reaction was one of variable consciousness levels coming through as "imminent change."

By the time we got to the town of Holbrook, settled into a motel, and had dinner, it was about eight o'clock in the evening. I stated to Glenda that something slightly different was happening to me than I had experienced in the past.

What do I mean by this? Many times I had explained to Glenda that I could not see how I could remain in my physical structure; I seem to be ready to explode with the amount of gold/white/aqua-blue substance flowing through every cell of my physical body. But this night was different — I felt a supreme calmness, without excessive electrocution.

After going to bed, I gave instruction to my friend, telling her, "I really don't think I'll be here in the morning." This was not an unusual statement for Glenda to hear, for she had heard these utterances so often before!

As soon as I cocooned myself into the wondrous Source Presence and went through meditation to still my mind and just "become," I experienced an explosion of Omnipresence of such a degree that the kaleidoscope of light, joy and color raised me immediately into fifth-dimensional awareness. I was totally conscious of traveling throughout Creation with all of my angelic friends, as well as many other beings that I (as the personality) had forgotten that I knew from more senior realms.

The only conscious thought that I remember was what Buckminster Fuller, the great American scientist, wrote: that "one should be able to travel as quickly as one thinks." In other words, everything is but a thought away.

After this thought, I became more magnificent than I can describe, for we do not have the language. The colors were beyond description; and the Hu-sounds (God-sounds) very magnified. I remember meeting Melchior, your Galactic Logos, on this journey and being treated as a resplendent deity, for this is who I was.

I encountered endless numbers of beings of great presence on this magnificent journey, and then I was greeted by my dear friend, Melchizedek who, in his great presence, greeted me with great celebration and gratitude for my achievements on Earth, which allowed his evolution to become even greater; now, true spiritual consciousness was his.

All of this time, I was meeting other aspects of Self on every level, and was profoundly feeling the **I AM that I AM.** Only my personality level was greeted as something individualized, but all of the "time," I was expressing the total embodiment of Creation. Never was I anything other than the glorious, omnipresent Self.

At this juncture, the magnificent Metatron and a Host of **monadic beings** greeted me, for Melchizedek was not able to assimilate the vibratory exchange required to go into the spiritual monadic levels, at least not then.

At this point, no language conceived by man — even the best among these — could begin to describe this segment of the journey. At this level, and the farther we progressed to view Creation being played out in the Now, Creation was so magnificent that anyone who experienced this could not realistically return to the confines of the dense physical expression.

We then did what I have described on the previous pages: We joined the Council of Twelve and I — the very small "I"— united with **Who We Are,** as the tenth member of the Co-Creator Council for this Cosmic Day. I remember thinking, "I have finally come home, and my outward journey is complete!"

It was agreed that I had a choice; it seemed that the primary anchoring of Synthesis of the Creator and Co-Creator levels had been accomplished. But if I wished to complete all universal experience...

I have no conscious recall after this point, for the decision had been made.

To say that I was pleased when I returned to earthly conscious containment was not so! I tried to relive the gold and red cocooning that I had experienced before lift-off and tried to explain what I could remember to Glenda. She was not surprised, for she knew from the Light and the energy in the room that night, that I was leaving!

Now it is June 17, 1993, and my assignment is still not over. To suggest that I would rather not be where I had been on my magnificent journey would be untrue; but I'm there anyway, and that level does view creation on Earth constantly. And I recognize many shifts in our collective consciousness as it anchors on Earth, for which I am grateful.

Does this make me greater than others on Earth? The answer is an emphatic **No!** For no one is greater than another, and I know that sequencing time through the atomic body is positively the most difficult expression and the bottom rung of the evolutionary ladder of 352 steps. Throughout Creation for this Cosmic Day **there is nothing but Divine Equality;** some beings are simply more conscious of who they are in relation to All That Is than others.

This, my dear friends, is why I get upset with humanity continually giving their power to others. For if I see nothing else, I see clearly what is required to move beyond your self-imposed misery and stuckness. You will remember my mentioning a visit to Cypress; on this occasion I had the good fortune to view an entity called Daskalos. A number of observations stay with me during this experience and I would like to share these with you.

First, if you do not recognize this energy, let me explain what little I know. This gentleman is now a frail 80 years of age, of humble origin and humble countenance. The seminar that I witnessed was very brief, with about 150 people in attendance. When Daskalos entered the room the predominantly German-speaking people there stood up as one, with outstretched arms, hoping subconsciously that something would rub off so that they would receive something that they *already embody*, if they were to but recognize it.

What gave this man an international reputation were two books written by an American professor of Greek origin. Daskalos has stated that there is much in these books that he does not agree with; but now he has, and has had for some time, great numbers asking for healings and advice. For that he is one of the best, albeit his work is definitely psychic in nature, as he openly states that he uses the elementals for his healings.

I watched a man who will achieve his primary Ascension in this life. What I found so profoundly interesting is that he will do this primal ascension again as a Greek Orthodox Catholic. This is, indeed, a very rare happening, especially since he remembers being a founder of this genetic twin of the Roman Catholic Church, the one called **Origen,** who was an aspect of my Self. This dear man's greatest fear is excommunication from this rather dark colossus! Why would a man, from a Light perspective, wish to align his Light with their darkness? This is why I refer to this outstanding human as an enigma, for he has moved beyond any need for this very dark expression! Tell me that we are not a strange lot! Anyway, I was viewing an aspect of self whom I recognize as being close to Self during my embodiment on Earth as King Akhnaton.

The great tragedy for humankind is that as long as they give their power to others, not recognizing the Wholeness of their Self, they will continue to experience endless expressions of bewildering life and death. Daskalos did not simply get lucky — he earned the right to Ascension through love and service, despite his personal choices to associate with darkness through Catholicism and through the use of the elemental/psychic levels for his healings; but above all of this are his many, many lives of service for humanity.

This is the area in which Westerners get confused, for I remember my father, for example, saying over and over again during his life on Earth, "I have lived a good and decent life, and I have said my prayers every night before I go to sleep." And for this he lives on the second astral level.

This misconception that man has but one life was introduced to Catholicism by Queen Theodora, and has been regarded as truth absolute ever since. These were most certainly not the beliefs held by the Christ when I walked the Earth as Simon Peter. At the time, because I was a Jew, the concept of reincarnation was the one teaching of my adopted faith that was at variance with the religion I had grown up within.

Thus when a Christian feels that he will go to heaven, aside from what I've stated constitutes heaven within your various religions, what has been left out of this complex equation is the fact that a person may have experienced 1500 or more lives on the Earth alone; thus, which life will resonate with a high enough vibration to warrant primary Ascension? *The very thought that eternity is determined by one single physical embodiment is not only false, but quite ludicrous!*

Can you even begin to imagine (should one earn the right to go to the Christian heaven, which, in the first place, would require the Soul Merge, the Third Initiation, or the equivalent) living throughout eternity at this very **basic** fifth astral level with "the Lord Jesus?" Jesus is a lovely man, and a full-fledged member of the human Hierarchy. I now want you to think of positively the finest person that you can think of, and ask yourself the question, "Would I like to spend eternity with that person, on a vibrational level that is only slightly higher than dense physicality?" For the astral levels are also *physical* and have nothing whatsoever to do with the galactic, universal, spiritual or cosmic realms, at least not yet, but *very* soon!.

The concept of "my Father's house" is a symbolic expression referencing the Soul levels. The hundreds of thousands among the Christian world who really believe that they would like to be with Jesus in Heaven are in for a great surprise. Apart from the boredom of spending eternity on this level, they would find that Jesus has moved beyond the finite Earth and astral heavens, since the evolutionary thread only turns upward in the Journey (unless one returns to Earth to assist humankind in their evolution as the externalized human Hierarchy, or a galactic, universal or cosmic avatar.)

We have discussed in *Mahatma I* in great detail many levels that should be integrated, and it would be very difficult to integrate *Mahatma II* without first integrating *Mahatma I*. If you recall, in that book we state that many — in fact, the bulk of the population who reside on the fifth astral level — believe that they have achieved the highest level that humankind can evolve to. That is as great a limitation as to suggest, as many do on Earth, that there is no afterlife because within their sciences and their lower sensual self, there is no substantial evidence to contradict these observations. Holding these beliefs when they leave their dense physical expression, they remain so tied to these realms that they continue in a self-imposed purgatory, often for several hundreds of sequential years, hoping to connect with the personage and situations that constitute their perceived reality. This is the first astral level and the biblical hell; this level is, again, totally illusory because the expressions have nothing to do with your inner I AM Presence, and adhere only to the *outer* perception of reality. And there are no victims! Humankind create, with their own God-given free will, their own reality; neither God nor some alien force such as the "devil" interferes to force you do what you don't consciously realize is **your own creation.**

This latter information is for the beginners on the evolutionary journey, as the students that we teach are well beyond the integration of these very basic levels. Nonetheless, these areas need explanation, for probationary mankind still resonate at these basic levels. And there is no need that this be so, for it takes as much energy to create illusion as it does to create relative truth.

From our perspective, all truth is relative to the *only truth*, embodied within your God-Source, your only I AM Presence, *Mahatma*. And what is *Mahatma*? "Mahatma" is a **resonance,** or mantra, of what your world scriptures refer to as "*the Rider on the White Horse,*" and which Djwhal refers to as "the Cosmic Avatar of Synthesis." This energy is now anchored on Earth as a result of your Source for this Cosmic Day expanding to a greater level of consciousness, allowing the Tenth Ray and the spiritual microtron to be anchored on the Earth. This allows God-man to become that which they have always been — Light and Love, embodying their I AM Presence on all 352 levels, *consciously integrated now* within the *Mahatma*, your expanded Source for this Cosmic Day.

What does this mean from God-man's perspective? This means, in no uncertain terms, that one must harken to the call and align with who they *are*, not who they *think* they are. This I do understand with great clarity, for this great Cosmic Law is absolutely resolute that people recognize their God Presence through their inner I AM; and your expanded Source insists that you unite with the "inner breath" and start your homeward journey. It is time to stop giving your power away to a level that humanity has already experienced en masse, the host of Masters, which probationary man now revere as gods. When one worships or venerates these Masters, one impedes their evolution and keeps them tied to the emotional confines of the Earth, especially through the Crucifixion, in much the same way that my cousin was held back while his mother mourned him for five years. Adulation and guilt, through the Crucifixion or any other reason, cannot function in a fourth-dimensional reality. Please try to understand that martyrdom and the embodiment of the symbolic cross can relate only to the lower body and humankind's outer self, having no resonance whatsoever with your God Self as Light and Love.

The "Savior" energy is and always has been, the **Christed Self within,** the **Living Christ,** the **Christ of Resurrection,** and *not* the crucified Christ embodying martyrdom for humankind to worship and adore. It is this dead, inert Christ, emblematic of the Crucifixion that humanity cling to, for their unworthiness has been expressed so vehemently during the last 1600 years on Earth that they continue to reject their inner I AM in their **Divine, Resurrected Christ Self.** As long as humanity believe this to be the truth, they will continue on their pathetic journey into further disempowerment by giving their God-given free will to the religious hierarchy, who cannot mirror Light and Love, for they come from the same limitations of living within the confines of their illusionary outer self instead of their resurrected Christed Self. They believe their own teachings, as teachers tend to do, that "only Jesus Christ is the Son of God," making it impossible for them to believe or teach Divine Equality or that one could attain that which the Christ stated, "the works that I do, ye shall also do and greater works than these shall ye do" as a symbolic utterance of unlimitedness.

What I am about to state is a difficult concept for mankind to integrate. On pages 183–185, we endeavored to explain the function, as they relate to the Christ as *The Rider on the White Horse,* of the personality, Brian, as the Cosmic

Avatar of Synthesis. Please use this as a reference.

I find it somewhat disconcerting that two people I know will state, "Look at the life you've lived; it must be self-aggrandizement to think that you were St. Peter." They completely miss the significance of what was really stated, because it is not a part of their reality any more than it is mine. If you remember, Vywamus stated in "The Journey of the *Mahatma* from Source to Earth" in *Mahatma I*, St. Peter was galactic in expression. In fact, in most of my lives on Earth my energy has come from the Council of Twelve for this quadrant of this galaxy. Vywamus also told me "You have had two other lives as a cosmic avatar, one in Egypt as King Akhnaton and one in Lemuria, when the Earth could not handle the amount of energy you brought in and burned." Thus my historical lives as Simon Peter and Zarathustra are physical manifestations, for all of the reasons previously described regarding what constitutes physicality. And with the assistance of Metatron, Vywamus subsequently brought through, for the first time on Earth, the structure of the 352 levels and initiations that constitute this one Cosmic Day, and explained as much as could be brought through about the Undifferentiated Source.

Earlier in *Mahatma I*, Djwhal Khul described in detail why he called the Rider on the White Horse the "Cosmic Avatar of Synthesis." Once this energy was anchored on Earth, Vywamus gave it the mantra "Mahatma." Are you with me so far? Thus the Peter/Zarathustra energies, being on the border between the fifth and sixth dimensions, constitute only the Tenth Initiation. The energy embodied by the complete *Mahatma* and so clearly described by Vywamus and Metatron, is 342 levels and initiations *above* our galactically aspected Self as St. Peter.

This, of course, seems too incredible for comprehension by the mass consciousness, therefore it is not a part of humankind's reality. It would never even be discussed, any more than the sails of Magellan's ship could be seen by the native Indians on the southern tip of South America. This was because these were not part of the reality of these people. Since the Indians had canoes, they could identify the boat, but the sails they could not see. So I, the personality, find it interesting when individuals can identify St. Peter as the boat, but *Mahatma* as the mast and sails simply has no reality, being 342 levels above the vibrational frequency of St. Peter.

Interestingly, I've never been asked the question by anyone, which I find to be so obvious from a finite discipline, and that is, "How can you represent all 352 levels and be conscious that in fact you do?"

My consciousness of this is a result of what Vywamus has described as my "very developed intuitive connection with the Creator," and of course, the conscious Ascension described herein. I truly believe that there is a great teaching here, if the student can grasp its significance! Even as a young man, I was able to intuitively identify my Source Star, which for me is about 7 feet (2 1/4 meters) above my crown chakra. I spent all of my meditation time throughout my life, until recent times, integrating what I was to much later understand is our senior monadic, or Creator, Self.

I am of the firm belief that one of the great advantages of being in the dense physical embodiment of slowed-down Light and expressing sequential time, is that with a developed intuition, one can connect with the totality of their I AM Presence much more rapidly than living in the Now of Creation.

What do we mean by this? "Now" is relative to the ultimate NOW of existence, or Creation, which can only be expressed by the Source Itself. But those at every other level, except for dense physicality, live in a relative Now or relative non-time, and do not have the same ability to move beyond their vibrational confinement of "the ring passeth not"; therefore, their energy is much more difficult to be individually identified — living in the relative Now of non-time and space — than expressing linear or sequential time as expressed on Earth. In other words, the advantage of expressing sequential time, which can be achieved in the first three of the seven Grand Divisions within the fourth dimension, is that one can intuitively connect with the totality of Self in a way that cannot be achieved in other densities, because dense physicality is slowed-down Light.

A very good example of this is that when we take a group in meditation into the Source for this Cosmic Day, we can take Melchizedek's essence with us beyond his "ring passeth not" and take the group much beyond their individually integrated vibrational levels. This is because we can slow down Light sufficiently to create a channel within sequential time that non-time simply does not allow. Thus when you have truly cleared this channel of debris, you can connect with all levels of Self, which cannot be achieved later in fourth-dimensional time.

The magnitude of what I speak is very important, for if you wish to express unlimitedness and become that which You are, simply fasten yourself to your Source Star and expand your consciousness as often as you can during the day. Become your Omnipresent Self in all 352 levels that constitute who You are, the I AM Presence, *Mahatma*, and repeat and integrate the "Affirmation for Unlimitedness" on page 425.

I have seen the magnificence of the *Mahatma* in action, not only in my personal and private life, but mirrored through others as they connect with this Divine Presence, which finds no level that it cannot access and which can be called upon at any time, with the assurance that the *Mahatma* energy is one of synthesis and integration for your collective Self, your God Self as the All That Is, the completely balanced embodiment of the God and Goddess.

Possibly the simplest way to express the importance of your intuitive connection with Source is to ask, "What is Source?" **Source is all of the steps along the way.** Integrate them on all levels of Creation so that the knee-jerk reflex of "What am I supposed to do now?" results in simply *becoming* the total embodiment of All That Is as Source Itself.

Once one has achieved this level, which would be as the twelfth member of the Co-Creator Council of Twelve, you would then and only then *create your own Cosmic Day* from your Undifferentiated Source, with an unlimited number of Creators manifesting their own Cosmic Days. Overwhelming? That, my friends, is the journey, at least up to and including the Undifferentiated Source, for no one knows what exists beyond this level. It was never intended that you become stuck in your dense atomic structure; for that is the problem — God-man's inability to use his God-given free will to extricate his collective Self from human bondage!

Again I wish to emphasize the importance of viewing the Omnipresence of your I AM throughout your day until it becomes your reality, instead of the nonreality of the illusory creations of your outer self. For only then can you manifest that which has been made so simple for humankind now — through NEW REVELATION, the fission of the atom, which freed the Soul energy within the atom, and the fusion of the atom with the spiritual microtron to spiritualize matter, as described herein. Of course, one must *ask* for assistance from the totally integrated *Mahatma*, for there is no other way to receive assistance.

When Christian scripture references the fall of Archangel Lucifer, it should be realized that this was a symbolic statement describing the "fall of man," since the Angelic Kingdom possesses no free will and could not possibly fall. Since God-man's fall into atomic structure, it has taken many civilizations and millions of sequential years for approximately 34,000 individuals, out of the hundreds of billions of personalities coming and going here, to achieve Mastery, or what was referred to in the past as the Fifth Initiation. This does not include the millions of beings who arrived here as Light and left as Light during your "golden years." Is this not a pathetic endorsement of humankind's inability to monitor their inner I AM as they continue to live within the total confines of illusion?

My journey from Source to Earth is different from yours from Earth to Source. But once one can realize that one's limitations are self-imposed, the process of evolution becomes very similar, for both journeys require unlimited integration one way or the other. Can you see that if one continues to integrate only within the confines of their minuscule personality on a minuscule planet, one becomes and remains minuscule? An analogy of this is an in-grown toenail, which seems counterproductive, do you not agree? So what you may wish to consider is **unlimited integration** as the *Mahatma*, aligning with your **Christed Self** and becoming the Omnipresence that you are. The basic misunderstanding on Earth is that Hu-man forgot who You are, not realizing what you had become; thus there was no longer a Wholeness to integrate. So please go over and over the contents of these books until they become your expanded consciousness so that you have something to integrate.

Shortly after the magnificent revelation regarding the Tenth Ray, I had occasion to become intuitively aware that my middle daughter, Julie, was in serious physical difficulty. I remember connecting with her Soul levels and conveying, through this transmission of Higher Self to Higher Self, that this planet needs all of the assistance with radiant Light that it can receive. It did not seem appropriate that Julie should leave the confines of her dense physical embodiment at this time. Knowing intuitively that there had been a serious accident with my daughter, I wondered if teleportation was available, for I was in Zurich and my daughter was in rural British Columbia. Once I went within Self, it became apparent that what was once called teleportation was not available through a connection with the Earth's etheric grid system, which required one to travel with one's etheric Lightbody, and if they wished to manifest a physical presence at their destination, they would have to build one out of Light.

Instead, the words **transmigration** and **transfiguration** came through clearly. These two words (which had been only recently brought through on October 8, 1992, with the revelation of the Tenth Ray) were some how more applicable, as I realized that teleportation was not available. Transmigration *without the etheric grid* became my reality, and I was conscious of simply being with Julie and having a Light presence on location with her immediately; as one thinks, so they are in the fourth dimension.

At this point in time, I thought no more about the incident and returned to bed. Within hours I received a phone call from Julie, thanking me for helping her! Apparently she had been driving home from work when a deer suddenly ran out in front of her car; she put on her brakes to avoid the collision and ended up totally destroying her vehicle. The police could not believe that she had survived. Julie stated that shortly after the accident she was aware of a "great light." Not only did she now feel fine, but what surprised her most was that her chronically bad back had been healed, and she felt wonderful! Julie is developed enough, working with Light, to know that our presence was there, and that the great light was her Higher Self.

So this level of experience was wonderful, not only for my daughter and myself, but also because of the realization that these two abilities, *transmigration* and *transfiguration*, which arrived with the Tenth Ray, will become more evident in the process of evolution on Earth as matter is spiritualized. Of necessity, new language and new methods of operating within the confinement of atomic structure will be brought forth to aid in the integration of the multidimensional matrix, through your I AM Presence, *Mahatma*.

There are two schools of thought regarding **Sanat Kumara**: one which states that Sanat Kumara is one of 15 Kumaras who reside on Venus, and that "he" left planet Earth in the mid-1950s. My truth indicates otherwise, that Sanat Kumara did join the other Kumaras briefly in 1956, then returned to Earth in 1981 when his energy was notified that his planet's civilization would be experiencing transformation through the **expanded Source**, though the current civilization need not come to an end; and that because of his 18-million-year experience as "the Lord of the World," he would remain as the total embodiment of the Earth until this experiment of NEW REVELATION, the spiritualization of matter, was completed.

The transformation of Earth into fourth density and the availability of the spiritual microtron have not only been transformational for the Earth, but also for billions of planets embodying the Adam Kadmon body in the 43 universes of this one Cosmic Day, and for the expansion of our monadic levels into a greater Wholeness. In all this transformation for this expanded Cosmic Day, your planet became the focal point for a huge amount of energy to be anchored into dense physicality. Because of the diversity of the Earth within the realms of duality, she was selected by the expanded Source, through the *Mahatma* energy, as the focal point within the physical/universal levels to experience NEW REVELATION. Thus, as many have sensed, there is a great concentration of energy embodied on Earth now, magnifying the Creator's Plan through this NEW REVELATION, to hasten evolution for this Cosmic Day.

Many of you are becoming increasingly aware of changes within your physical, emotional and mental bodies that you don't really like or understand. For those who enjoy the status quo, I regret that the Transformational Fire — being the most fundamental enactment of the Cosmic Law of Creation — will cause you to either shift your awareness from your outer self to your inner I AM or to move to another schoolroom in this or another universe until you learn these basic, but essential, lessons.

Christ Consciousness

If you asked a hundred people, "What is Christ Consciousness?" you would receive at least a hundred different answers. When I stated earlier that the evolutionary thread only moves in an upward spiral, I was referencing a fundamental cosmic law. The Earth has been closely observed by other levels of Creation since the Golden Age when the Host of Masters lived here, when subsequently humanity actually fell instead of raising themselves. Thus there is the confusion in your various religions and belief systems that implies that the fall of man is irrevocable and irreversible, for this allowed the control and manipulation that the founders of Christianty sought.

This, more than any other condition facing mass consciousness, must be changed; for God-man's lack of evolution through his resurrected Christed Self has reached critical proportions. Mankind knows not the difference between his lower and his higher self and remains confined to the distortion inherent in the psychic/lower mind of his creation. The developed Souls on Earth are found living in your "free" industrialized countries, which are, for the most part, moving from the stuckness of the third chakra, the solar plexus, and trying to — or being placed in a position where they will have to — move into the heart chakra.

This is the residency of change for humankind to begin to live in the fourth and fifth chakras as greater expressions of love and wisdom, and to cease living in the lower self as animal man confined to the three lower chakras, which are totally illusory from the Creator's perspective. As we have shown, you were never intended to manifest as Souls within atomic embodiment; nothing in this Cosmic Day was intended to project further into matter than the pure electronic body of Christ — your inherent right as Hu-man/God-man!

The very fact that man now worships an inert, dead Christ — who is another human being — but never sees himself as the God that he is nor realizes that the only Christ in existence was intended to be *oneself*, is the civilized world's greatest tragedy. The externalization of the Christed energy and the worship of it, rather than *becoming* it, is not only confusing for semiconscious humankind but from my point of view — speaking as the personality — a great tragedy indeed.

When one views the world that might have been during these last 2000 years on Earth had your Christ, Maitreya — who embodies the transformational Christed energies for Earth simply as an example of your inheritance — been able to teach, as intended, what you can achieve and more, I'm certain that there would not have been the horrific suffering and confusion that has prevailed on Earth and still remains. To suggest that there are no other contributing factors would, of course, be untrue; but in my judgment this is the most heinous.

But, alas, what was, *was*, and need not exist anymore! I would imagine that what you may wish to create in the Now of your creative abilities is a new understanding of how to create at all. And how do you do this? Well, in the first place, I would suggest that you not endeavor to change the world until you change *yourself*. Please ask, "And how do I do that?" I'm glad you asked, for the answer is, "With great effort!"

To begin with, you need to redefine who and what you are. If you recognize that you are the Christ, and you integrate that reality, then you can raise your vibration sufficiently to encompass this; then and only then can you raise yourself from human bondage. At this resurrected point in time, the reason for the fall matters not, for you are then the resurrected Christ, and cause and effect fall away as mist before the sun.

Our articulated hope that millions of humanity will achieve their primal Ascension into the Light becomes more dim as I study humankind closely. I do realize that the opening is available until the year 2028, but what I have not seen is...will the world be recognizable? By this I mean that there are already so many positive shifts being expressed throughout my body, intuitive reactions to imminent shifts of the Earth's surface throughout the whole world. These are not expected until November 4, 1994, with further massive shifts on April 27, 2028.

This possibility depends in part upon the degree of the Earth's transformation, but principally upon humankind's ability to respond by raising their vibration much more rapidly than I am witnessing in my comprehensive observations of this planet. I do not have the rose-colored glasses that my Higher Selves project to me, for I live partly within this world of great density and confusion. I know emphatically what is required for humankind to raise their consciousness and become Christ-conscious; but these shifts sufficient for salvation have not been shown to me through the level of consciousness of the personality.

I can only do what I came to achieve, which has been accomplished. As my mission on Earth has been completed, my ardent hope is that the spiritual Ascension can be completed and witnessed before I leave, for I think that humanity needs this as an example of what they too can achieve.

As we have discussed previously, to take your physical body with you when you leave requires the spiritual Ascension, and having just entered the First Grand Division of the fourth dimension means that only a few individuals on Earth are expressing fourth-density time as their reality, and those are the beings who have completed their mastery of Earth's density. These beings will have to manifest out of Light a body that would resemble their previous body, but without organs, and which will be able to remain in this density for only a short period of time before being withdrawn and remanifested. Whether there were to be any occasion, in fact, to use this quasi-body would depend totally upon one's free will as Higher Self's projection, in this case, and what this level of consciousness wished to express.

What is not clear to me, the personality, is how much more the Earth's vibration must be raised before we can complete the spiritual Ascension by taking our dense physical body with us. Given the view that I hold regarding my physical body being so tired, my personality asks, "Why don't we just leave? Our mission is complete."

In our teaching we endeavor to overachieve rather than underachieve. As an example, the most lowly evolved member of a group is encouraged to *accomplish the spiritual Ascension while working on their primary Ascension.* This has a great resonance in truth, for the more one integrates tone's understanding of one's complete I AM Presence, the easier one's primary Ascension.

Why so much emphasis on Ascension? Because, dear ones, this is, and still remains, the *only reason* to experience this dense level of consciousness! I know that most of you don't see life as having a much greater resonance of what you call death; but how can the lower vibration be called "life" and the higher, "death"? Alas, we are a strange lot!

If I appear to be relentless in my judgment of your Earth's dysfunctional religions, it is truly time that someone speak of the darkened form and structure that they are, rather than allowing these to continue to hide behind their scriptures — which are certainly not God's Word. These institutions, which have functioned for nearly ten thousand years of your recorded history, embody such reprisal and fear to preprobationary man being taught by probationary clergy that, more often than not, whenever their truths were questioned, this ended in dreadful torture or death. But their greatest weapon was the psychological axe of fear of disenfranchisement by the "only custodians of God," "who had the keys to heaven and hell." With those misaligned truths, religions continue to control and manipulate with great effectiveness the disempowerment of humankind.

Thus the God-Source, the All That Is, as God-man with free will, has never been even remotely considered as the mass consciousness until the Harmonic Convergence of August 1987. We spent a great deal of energy bringing change through Love and Light to Earth's mass consciousness, and continue to monitor the greatest change of all: We observe the spiritual microtron that our Monad is anchoring into the Earth now rising up from the depths and observe the shifts so apparent on Earth now. The Five Higher Rays and the microtron compel the Earth to resonate with the eternal Cosmic Law of Light and Love, rather than the darkness and despair that "fallen man" continue to support as their only reality, believing that their outer self is real.

Humankind are now being compelled, for there is no other way on Earth *but* to live *totally* in your inner I AM. The expanded God-Source for this Cosmic Day dictates the terms of our collective reality, not a few entrenched bureaucrats of rigid systems — be they your educators, your religious leaders, your politicians, your parents or your Self — who have brought nothing but despair and darkness cloaked as the spiritual saviors of humanity.

This time, humankind must either listen or leave. The choices have always been yours; it was only your level of denial and sense of unworthiness: "What if they are right?" or "It's too late for me to change now." These have kept you from your *only essence*, as the God that You are, your own I AM Presence.

When it is all said and done, dear ones, only you will resonate with your truths. And all we can hope to accomplish is to explain, as we have, why *nothing can remain as it was!* May you embody Light and Love as All That Is, as your I AM Presence of Light, Love and Joy.

We will leave you with this realization, hoping that you can achieve your Light vehicle this time. We send much love, and we will give you all of the attention you require, but you must ask for the *Mahatma* as your personalized I AM Presence.

Embodying the Microtron

Please understand that the Monad has anchored on Earth a sufficient amount of spiritual microtrons for the Earth and humankind to spiritualize matter.

Imagine, if you will, sitting on a white, sandy beach on a desert island where there is no one but you for miles around. You are sitting with your legs in an aqua-blue ocean that gently caresses you with beautiful, clear, warm, water. You are reminded that the water embodies the emotional body for Earth, and you become more and more soothed and comforted as the sound of the ocean causes you to relax and to *become* this ocean and this warm, sandy white beach.

Now begin to open your base chakra wider and wider, allowing a beautiful, translucent aqua-aura-colored energy to flow up through the Earth and encompass your physical body. As you consciously breathe in the radiant microtron from the Earth, see it flowing through your base chakra into your polarity chakra and then into your solar plexus. Look to your lower self now, and raise the vibration with what you now know is *spiritual* energy.

With your feet in the sand, in this beautiful aqua-colored ocean, start to open the base of your feet and allow your legs to *become* the microtron, gently relaxing and becoming this incredible experience. Ensure that every part of your lower self is nurtured by the water, sand, and sun as every part of your lower self begins to radiate with the aqua-blue light that we call the microtron.

I want you to identify the harmony and comfort that you are enjoying as your physical cells accept this spiritual energy with no resistance whatsoever. As you breathe this magnificent microtron through your four-body system, your animal, or lower, self becomes radiant and balanced.

Open your chakras more, more and more as you begin to move into the heart/throat chakra. At this point think of the circles in the diagram of "The Cosmic Heart" as you breathe this new reality in through the ocean and your base chakra and out through your four-body system. The radiant microtron expands and expands, nourishing your complete physical, emotional and mental selves.

Breathe this energy into your spiritual body and notice how much finer and purer the microtron is compared to what you view as your perfected spiritual body — there seems to be no comparison between the two as you infuse your spiritual body with the microtron and enjoy becoming more and more radiant!

Your emotional body continues to be soothed by the ocean as you allow your whole body, except for your head, to become submerged. Face the sun now and allow your third eye and your crown chakra to open, Open, OPEN. Breathe out, Out, OUT through your four-body system as you fill your third eye and crown chakras with the radiance of your new-found connection with what is truly spiritual. You realize that what we have called the spiritual body is actually the **pure electronic body,** on this level of consciousness, and has nothing to do with what you are experiencing with the **spiritual microtron**.

Bring more and more of the microtron through your bodies; expand to include what you now know is your true spiritual body, as you become more and more vibrant as spiritual Light! In fact, this Light is becoming you and you are becoming it, and you now know that this new experience of the magnificent spiritual body needs to be equally bright and luminous throughout your physical, emotional, and mental selves. Cocoon yourself with the spiritual microtron as you allow the radiant You to work from the *outside in,* from your spiritual body inward, filling all four bodies with spiritual Light. If there is any area of imbalance in Light, please balance that area until your complete four-body system is equally radiant with the aqua blue of the spiritual microtron.

Continue to bathe in this true spiritual Light, remaining in this state of omnipresent illumination as you contemplate what you wish to achieve. You are starting to recognize the beginning of the **spiritualization of matter,** including what you have believed in the past to be your spiritual body, as you remember what was required to implement these shifts in total consciousness.

This radiant spiritual body, which can also be achieved for the Earth, is permeated with the spiritual microtron now. Work on this process, even though you know that few will attain this level of consciousness universally, and when you leave the Earth this integration will be yours to pursue with your I AM, *Mahatma.*

Please integrate the following realization to assist in your embodiment of the text.

Say to yourself, to your subconscious mind, and to mass consciousness:

"I AM prepared to surrender to the Divine Plan, the I AM, *Mahatma*. I trust myself as the I AM Presence.

"I, (your name), believe that what I have just experienced in meditation is possible as my reality, and I demand that I become that which I AM. I AM prepared to accept my Divine Equality, that the Source level is no greater than I AM, for I have just seen myself in the same mirror. I have finally seen who I AM, through the *Mahatma*, as the I AM of the I AM Presence.

"I tell Earth's mass consciousness now, through my Cosmic Heart, and my subconscious mind that they must recognize that there is no limitation anymore, that they must recognize that I AM a full Creator of my reality, and from here forward I will take my power and hold it within my own I AM Presence within the *Mahatma*. I recognize that finally I can release myself from the bondage of physical densities and become the Light that I AM as the I AM Presence."

Repeat again: "I AM the I AM of the I AM Presence. Subconscious mind and mass consciousness, I demand that you understand that the greater Wholeness of who I AM, you do not understand. I ask my primal Soul now to look at who I AM; I ask my Higher Self to look at who I AM in the glorious, glorious garden of my birth; I ask now that my Oversoul enjoy with us what we are becoming."

Breathe this through and recognize it as your truth; truly accept that "this is who I AM." Let it go, dear one, through your throat chakra, as you affirm:

"This is the last area of surrender of my primal Soul and my physical, emotional, and mental bodies, which have all been anchored within the confines of the greater Wholeness of Sanat Kumara.

"I believe in this Cosmic Heart which I AM experiencing. I believe that I have witnessed who I AM in totality. I have taken the Journey on 352 levels of my collective Self, through the *Mahatma* energy, and this is who I AM as the I AM Presence. I AM glorious, and I demand of the Soul levels that they coordinate one with the other, allowing me — as the personality, or the Cosmic Heart, or the Higher Self, or the All That Is — to become united. I see no separation Now within the Cosmic Heart that I AM; there is no separation. I AM Divine Light; I AM connecting, I have connected, I recognize my place of birth. Through this I recognize finally my divine right to consciously say, "God and I are One."

Expand this, dear one; expand this consciousness. Expand it further and further and further into the Light. "I do not limit myself to this concept, for I know that there is much beyond the Undifferentiated Source."

Breathe out this Divine White Light, which is becoming whiter and whiter as you become that which You are, the I AM of the I AM Presence, *Mahatma*.

"Subconscious mind and mass consciousness, what I have just experienced is real, and you have just seen in this experience that I AM not confined; I AM no longer confined to the limitations of mass consciousness. I refuse to bow to the mass consciousness and to the mechanical device which is so limiting —

the subconscious mind. I will not be held ransom to my primal Soul's limitations; I endorse that **my Higher Self has become my primal Soul** and I acknowledge the imminent possibility that I, the personality, will be able to spiritualize my physical body in a way that has never happened before on Earth — to take it with me. I will accept nothing less."

Breathe it out; let the Archangels, the Angelic Host, and all aspects of your Self support you as you integrate integrate, integrate that which you are as the I AM of the I AM Presence, *Mahatma*.

Our most profound love to you on your Journey as your I AM Presence, *Mahatma*.

APPENDIX

Table of Contents

INTRODUCTION

You know, it's an interesting term, "appendix." The appendix in the physical body is a very powerful organ, although many in the medical community who might read this feel that it's a totally useless organ that they may as well cut out if they get the chance.

An appendix, however, is a point of power that can bring raw primal energy into a system and allow it to be utilized in a very high capacity, providing that the proper connections are made. Thus we would like to view the Appendix of this book as being a power center for the book by assisting the expression of the true unfoldment of Self for those who read these books, through offering the tools they need to begin to peel away the layers of misconception and ignorance around the concept of personal growth. The focus we give in this portion will be practical and geared to different ranges of audience, so we are including basic introductory exercises as well as more advanced processes for those who have already done a certain amount of clearing and opening work on the Path.

Indeed there are many, many different schools of teaching which are providing some of the basic techniques and processes to allow for the creation of the etheric Lightbody, called physical Ascension. In a sense, every one of these schools of thought has a valuable commodity to offer, so that wherever one is in the world, essentially there is — or will be — some form of assistance for them through an established structure. This is the way that the preliminary, basic teaching can be brought forth. It won't be the same from school to school, as they will be, to a certain extent, into their own belief system.

The essential teaching is simply stated as follows: Whatever the belief system, school of thought, or type of technique that you are following, realize that it is a limited belief system which can, and ultimately *must* be transcended.

In simpler terms: No system is perfect; each can take you only so far, at which point you must either integrate new information into the old belief system, or abandon that old belief system for one that is more inclusive. The hallmark of this new teaching is **inclusiveness** rather than exclusivity. Whenever you run into a situation of exclusivity in a group or teachings that claim "this is the *only way*," or the *"best way,"* etc., then that is a red flag to cause you to look at where those limitations are, and how they fit into your process.

In view of the coming energy shifts and those that have already been made, the process of spiritualization of the physical vehicle, be it the physical body or the planet Earth itself, is a process that entails many types of preparation and many simultaneous levels of activity at once.

On the level of the physical, there are many different approaches that one can take to purify the body. It is not absolutely necessary to go into a rigid cleansing and fasting program, although a moderate program of that type may be advisable for a time. All of this is to be filtered through their own inner knowingness by those who read these books, by allowing their own inner guidance to lead them, saying, for example, "Yes I feel that perhaps it's time that I did something on the level of the physical body...I will undertake this particular program, this particular system, for a while and see what happens."

Always test every process; always hold onto your own power. Don't give anyone or anything or any system absolute authority over you.

That is the ultimate essence of what we are trying to say. That same common-sense approach applies to every type of teaching, whether it be on a physical-body level, on the level of energy, of the emotions, of the mind, or the spirit. All of these bodies must be dealt with in the same way; but the ultimate authority, the ultimate arbiter of any dispute between one belief system and another, has to be your own inner knowingness.

THE BASICS

The very first thing to do is to invoke the Soul. This can be done through a number of different means, but primarily it is the **intent**. An invocation that has been found to be very useful in this regard is as follows:

Soul Invocation

**I am the Soul
I am the Light Divine
I am Love
I am Will
I am Perfect Design.**

Do this invocation from the Soul perspective — actually speaking it — by identifying yourself with Soul, invoking its energy.

There is also an energy vortex that should be invoked. Refer to the book, *The Rainbow Bridge,* for more details on this process. Ultimately, it derives from information channeled by Djwhal Khul through Alice Bailey; but the Source of this information goes beyond Djwhal. The following technique is a very powerful process of clearing.

Tornado of Light

This energy vortex is seen as a spiral of light going clockwise, much like a tornado with a funnel at the bottom end, and beginning about 6 or 8 feet (2-2½ meters) above the head. It rotates and moves downward through the body, touching into the crown chakra and down through the system. The width of this tornado should at least encompass the entire physical body, and can be seen as golden light or as white light with rainbow tints.

The job of the personality is to begin the invocation and visualize the vortex of energy; see it flowing downward through the system and deep into the Earth. At the point the vortex disappears, another one is created, coming from that level above the head, flowing down through the system, and continuing. It can be speeded up to the point where there are many of these vortexes one after the other to create what seems to be a column or a pillar of light.

This exercise should be done for at least five minutes at a time, and may be done several times a day, particularly when you are doing clearing work or when you have been activated, especially in the emotional body area. When something has stirred up some feeling you do not wish to have, then simply do this energy vortex and you will clear much of the residue associated with that feeling. It is a very powerful means of opening to the Soul and beginning to open your channel.

That one, we could say, will be Exercise One, because it is very basic. Its power is very impressive; it actually begins the process of energy communion between the personality and the Soul on the Soul plane. As that begins to occur, it effectively opens a crack, or **channel,** and the more energy that is brought through, the more powerfully the clearing process takes place. By invoking the Soul in this manner, and by offering oneself to the service of humanity, one begins to attract a tremendous amount of energy that can be used in the clearing process. Now there are other processes that go hand-in-hand with this one, and we would encourage students on every level to use this clearing process on a regular basis.

CHANNELING: *Meeting the Soul and Spiritual Teacher*

Vywamus through Barbara Burns

I, Vywamus, am pleased that you have made this commitment to channeling, and I can assure you that it is most appropriate at this time. Your Soul seeks to speak with you even more deeply than it has in the past.

Getting Grounded: Anchoring Your Column of Light

Please seat yourself comfortably, with feet or hips flat on the floor and spine straight. Go within. Please see that you are surrounded by a beautiful column of golden light all around your body. The light fills you and moves through you, and you feel its beauty and its support for you. Now you become aware that this beautiful column of light descends beneath you, deep down into the earth. This beautiful golden light descends down and down, farther and farther until it connects right into the heart of the Earth. You allow your conscious mind to gently descend — gliding, floating down the column of light. As you descend, you see that it is bright and beautiful and that there are no openings or breaks in the light. It is strong and bright and clear. It supports you as you gently descend right to the bottom, which is in the heart of the earth. Now with your imagination, you see that in one hand you have five beautiful golden nails, and in the other hand you have a golden hammer. These are the symbols of your commitment to Earth and to the Light. With the strength and power of your commitment, drive the nails into the bottom of the column so that they are firm and secure and strong, connecting your column of light deeply into the heart of the Earth. Yes, your commitment is strong and bright, my friend. You feel now a gentle, loving response from the Earth to your commitment in Light, and you feel a beautiful golden/green energy flowing to you from the heart of the Earth.

This beautiful golden/green energy flows into the bottom of your column of light and lifts you upward. Gliding smoothly, cradled in this beautiful, loving energy from the Earth, you rise up, up the column of light, back into your physical body, feeling the green/golden energy moving very gently, but strongly, through you. Now you look up and see that your beautiful column of light goes up and up and up through the heavens, higher and higher than you can even see. You allow your mind, your consciousness to float up, up out of the top of your head through the opening that is the crown chakra. Up you go, floating gently upwards in your column of beautiful golden light, and you look all around you and see how strong, bright and clear your golden column is. There are no holes, no openings, and you know within your heart that no one and nothing can come into your column of light without your consent, for this is your place of divine connection.

Now you move upward more quickly, gliding up and up, higher and higher, and you see that there is a bright white light at the top of the column, so bright and clear that it touches your heart deeply and you move with joy toward it. See the bright, sparkling white light that calls you and moves you. You move up and up into the bright light. You are floating high in this bright White Light of God, of the Source. You are cradled in the Light of the Source. You feel so large. You expand. Breathe deeply now, drawing in the bright White Light of the Source, filling yourself with the loving, bright white light.

Now you see again that you have five golden nails in one hand and a beautiful golden hammer in the other hand; again, they are the symbols of your commitment to the Source and service to the Light. With the strength of your commitment to the Light, drive these golden nails right into the top of the column of light, so that in your imagination you can see that they are strongly anchoring it into the Heart of the Source level, making a strong and powerful connection that will always be there for you.

When this is complete, begin to glide gently down, down the column of light, floating, gliding in the light, gently now. Looking around, see the beautiful column, strong and bright and clear; your heart fills with the joy of this light and its power. You look down and see your physical body sitting in the column of light. You see that your crown chakra is open like a great flower, and you feel yourself gently sliding through the opening at the top of your head and settling comfortably into your body again. You feel now the bright light that you have brought with you filling your body, making it feel expanded and alive, full of light.

Seeking Your Heart Center

Now imagine that your conscious mind is a tiny human figure of light, standing in the middle of your head. Focus all of your attention into this little being of light until you feel that you are this figure of light within your head. Using your imagination, see that as you stand within your head, a beautiful stairway opens up before you, going gently downward. It is a beautiful stairway of gold and white light, sparkling brightly now, inviting, beautiful, and clear. You begin to walk down the stairs, and as you walk they become brighter and brighter. There is a soft, gently loving light that flows all around you as you move downward toward the area of your heart center.

At the bottom of the stairs you come out into a beautiful room, a beautiful, large, well-lit room with high, high ceilings full of light. It is so beautiful! Using your imagination now, see how you have furnished and made beautiful this lovely room. There are lights and beautiful colors. Perhaps there is furniture. Perhaps there is a fountain spilling out sparkling water with a lovely tinkling sound. You see with your imagination that all the beautiful things that you have seen and loved on your journey upon the Earth are gathered in your heart. Yes, my friend, this beautiful place of light is your heart center. It is not just your physical heart center, but it is the center of your heart energy, a great place which is the center of your Being here on Earth. From this wondrous place you can go anywhere you desire, for this great heart is connected to All That Is. Through the heart, you are connected with all the wonders that God has created, and to the Source Itself.

Now, my friend, you see that in one wall is a beautiful, large door. It is beautifully carved and there is light streaming around its edges. You feel your heart stirring as you see the brightness, and you feel a great desire to see what is beyond this beautiful door of light. So you cross the room and stand before the door. You look closely and see that there is a sign upon the door, which you are able to read. It says, "This is the door to the Soul plane."

Now, my friend, with the strength of your commitment to Self, to your own growth as a Being of Light, you open the door. Light streams all around you...beautiful white light, and the beautiful sound of high, clear, bright singing fills your ears. You can hear it in the distance. Now you are standing in a long, beautiful corridor of light. You see far ahead that at the top of the corridor there is more white light, which streams in and touches your heart, stirring you with joy and hope. You begin to walk up the corridor, seeing how beautiful it is. As you walk upward, the light becomes brighter and brighter and the sweet, high music that you hear stirs your heart ever more deeply.

Now you come to the end of the hall, and you step out upon a beautiful, wide plane of light. Using your imagination, you look all around you and everywhere you see light, with colors dancing and flowing. Each color seems to have its own sound that sings, and you can feel it in your heart. You breathe deeply, drawing in the light and the sweet, high energy of this place. You look around and you expand with joy, for you know the energy of this place. You have felt this in your heart before, but now it comes to you stronger and brighter than ever before.

Meeting with Your Soul

You see far in the distance that there is a moving point of light and it is moving toward you. There is a golden path that comes right up to you, and you see that a beautiful being of light is hurrying toward you down this golden path. As it comes closer and closer, you use your imagination and you see that there is light flowing all around it, and glorious colors trail from it. Its energy is beautiful and strong and clear. It comes up the path and now stands before you. Using your imagination, give it a face. What kind of face would such a great Being of Love and Light have? Use your imagination and give it eyes that are deep and ancient, and look into those eyes with your imagination and your heart. You see an ancient wisdom that stirs your heart, and you know that this one has been with you always.

You know within your heart that it is through this great Being that you came forth upon the Earth. Look deeply into those loving eyes. See how strong the love is for you. This one is committed to you and loves you. Truly, you feel trust within your heart, for this one seeks only the highest and best for you as a child of Light.

You feel the trust and your heart opens to this great Being. Now the Being holds out its arms. If you are willing, allow yourself to be embraced. Feel yourself surrounded with the Love and Light and strength of this great Being. Your heart opens, and its beauty, its love and its power flow through you, filling your heart. Your heart expands and fills with joy. Yes, you know who this is. You know that this is your Soul. You can feel this in your heart. Yes, you know the truth within your heart.

Feel how your heart resonates and calls to this great Being. Your Soul looks at you and smiles deeply. It is seeking something, asking, perhaps, "Do you have a place within your heart for me?" Perhaps you do. Perhaps you have been preparing all this time, making a place, a beautiful, glorious place within your heart for this wondrous Soul. If you are willing, guide your Soul to the corridor that you have come through. See how it follows you with joy. See how eager this lovely being of power and light is to connect with you, to be with you, to speak with you, to communicate and be part of your life. Glide swiftly down that corridor, your Soul following you, and pass through the door back into your heart center. See, the Soul does not come in. It stands at the door respecting you, respecting your free will, your choice. It waits now. It waits for you to give it permission, to invite it into your heart. No one can come into your light without your consent. Will you invite the Soul into your heart now? Yes, I think you will. Give now this invitation from your heart and ask your Soul to enter. See how the Soul in joy flows into your heart center.

Where is the place that you have made for your Soul? Look around for the perfect place that you have prepared. Is it a beautiful chair? Perhaps it is a shrine or a crystal. Indeed, my friend, you have long been preparing this place for your Soul. It is the reason that your heart center is so beautiful. You have been awaiting the Soul. See now the place you have made for your Soul. It is so right. It is so beautiful, and your love and commitment shine forth from the place that you have prepared. Offer it to your Soul. See how the Soul in joy and delight takes the place that you have prepared for it. See how perfectly you have prepared for the Soul. Now sit for awhile with your Soul in your heart center. If you listen within yourself, a message comes now from your

Soul. You look deeply into its eyes, and using your imagination, you see that it is conveying to you a message of love and joy. It has long waited for this time. Listen with your heart as your Soul speaks to you now.

Meeting with Your Teacher

After you have communed with your Soul until this seems complete, notice that you begin to hear a gentle sound within the heart center. There is a knocking at the door to this plane, and there is a great light flowing around the door. Your Soul knows who is there. It is someone from the spiritual plane, seeking to connect and speak with you. Your Soul smiles at you, for it knows the great and loving being that stands awaiting you in your corridor to the spiritual plane. Will you go and see? Your Soul and you go to the door. Your Soul smiles at you, reassuring you that truly this one who comes is in the Light, is a great and loving being. It is a spiritual teacher, perhaps a Master that you have worked with before, one that you have known and loved. Now will you open the door? I think so. Your Soul encourages you.

See yourself opening the door. There is a great being of Light standing there respectfully. It is a teacher from the spiritual plane. It does not come in because you have not yet invited it, not yet given permission. Look closely at this wondrous being. At first you only see a great body of light. Now use your imagination. What kind of face would such a great Being of Light have? Give it such a face. Perhaps your secret memories will show you how that wondrous one was dressed and looked the last time that you connected with it clearly. Who is this great Being of Light? You look deeply into its eyes and ask. It will tell you. If you have difficulty receiving this information, listen with your heart and you will know. This spiritual teacher now seeks to connect with you again, to work with you in service to the Light. It asks your permission to step into your heart to communicate with you. Perhaps you will allow this one to enter. I think you will, my friend, for a part of you knows this one very well. See now, as you give permission, this beautiful Being of Light entering into your heart center, filling your heart with its loving, bright energy. As you connect with it, you feel a deep trust and recognition. Truly, you know that this connection is from the Light, from the Source. If you listen very deeply, there is a message in your heart from this great teacher. If you listen, your heart will tell you what the message is. Listen to the message of love and wisdom that is being given to you. Pause now and take a little time to commune in your heart with your spiritual teacher. I believe that there is also a message for you that this teacher will return to your heart center again if you will but invoke and invite.

When you feel complete with this communication, gently release the connection. The spiritual teacher embraces you lovingly and departs, but you feel that some of the beautiful light and energy still remains with you in your heart, giving you support, hope, and love. Now rest within your heart, enjoying the company, the Light and the Love of your Soul, feeling the Soul's energy expanding and filling your heart.

Now, my friend, begin to release the energy that you have been channeling. Begin to feel the energy releasing above your head, flowing down the top of your head, and running like water from your neck and shoulders, down your back and chest, like water running away in the sand, ebbing gently, flowing away. It moves down your body, down into the root chakra, and through your legs and feet, flowing down into the earth. You release this bright, beauteous energy that has been flowing in your column of light into the Earth. As that Light that you have channeled touches the heart of the Earth, you feel again the loving response of the Earth, and a beautiful green energy, sparkling with gold, comes flowing up from the heart of the Earth into your physical body. It flows up, filling your body gently and softly, nurturing and supporting you. This beautiful green/gold Earth energy flows right through you and out the top of your head, moving up the column of light and into the glorious White Light of the Source at the very top of the column. You see, my friend, the Earth and the Source connect and embrace through you. Through your channel you connect them in Love and Light. It is a great service that you do in this way.

Rest now in your column of light in your heart center. Feel yourself cradled gently in the energy of your Soul and the Earth. When you are ready, feel your consciousness filling up your body — your arms, your legs, your pelvis, your back, your chest, your neck, your head. You are fully occupying your body now. You are centered strongly and balanced firmly within your physical structure. Rest now, and when you are ready, open your eyes.

GETTING GROUNDED

As the energy is being turned up on planet Earth, more and more people will become conscious of its flow through them. This will show as greater creativity in those who are clear, and greater intensity of problems in those who are not. The energy flows through the channel, illuminating whatever programming is there. It is like a slide projector where the slides are the past programming, and reality is the screen on which the slides are seen. As the light is turned on, one experiences whatever slide is up at the moment.

The processes given here are tools to help you remove the unwanted slides and create new ones. Humanity has invoked this new degree of power and light, and now must deal with its effects. The process of evolution of consciousness is thus speeding up and it can be easy or difficult, depending on how willing one is to look at and clear the belief systems.

The key to being comfortable with the process is to stay grounded — connected to the Earth. Those who are not grounded, but invoke these higher energies, tend to "space out." Their energy is all in the higher chakras, and not flowing into the Earth.

As you open the channel, it becomes absolutely necessary to stay grounded. This free flow of energy will translate into greater free flow in all situations in life: relationships, abundance, etc.

Grounding the Space: The Golden Circle

1. Sitting with feet on the ground or standing in the Tai Chi stance, visualize a brilliant golden circle surrounding the room, house, etc.

2. Let it spiral down into the Earth, reaching to its very core.

3. Slowly it spirals up, connecting into the circle and into your heart.

4. Let it spiral up and out, expanding into infinity, to the Source of All That Is.

5. It then spirals back down, bringing a brilliant golden stream of energy which flows into the circle, through your heart, and grounds into the Earth. (*This vortex of energy will define and energize the area and bring positive healing energy into the Earth.*)

6. Now instruct it to produce the effect that you want. For example: safety, affluence, peace, love, clarity, etc., and in this way it can also be used as a technique for manifestation — programming your reality. You can tune into this vortex or column of light whenever you wish, and draw that energy to you.

Personal Grounding: Running Energy

1. Sitting with feet on the ground or standing in Tai Chi stance, visualize a line of white/gold energy flowing into the top of your head from above, going straight down your spine and out from your tailbone into the Earth.

2. Then visualize lines starting at the inside of each shoulder, running down your chest to your thighs, down the inside of your knees to the soles of your feet and into the Earth.

3. Let the energy flow into you and through you.

4. Now feel a stream of energy flowing up through your feet, up your spine, to the top of your head.

5. Alternate the flow from up to down with the breath: on the inbreath, see the energy flowing up your spine to the top of your head; and on the outbreath, see it flowing down your spine, through your feet, and into the ground.

Do this for as long as you feel comfortable. This form of running energy is very energizing and even a minute or two is very beneficial.

INVOCATION AS A TOOL

This is one of the most powerful tools that you can use to consciously create your reality the way you want it.

Djwhal Khul has said that it was the deep invocation from humanity as a whole that helped to end the Second World War and which has also more recently averted a mass destruction of the Earth. The pattern of humanity was to reach the point of adulthood and then slide back to adolescence (as described earlier in this book). This was experienced several times in Atlantis and culminated in the destruction of that civilization. That was almost repeated in this generation, but due to the earnest appeal for more Light in the world, that old pattern is being broken.

Invocation focuses the mind, heart and will, and when done in conjunction with the energy of the Soul, it creates a very powerful vibration that pulls what is invoked into manifestation. When the belief system is clear of obstructions, then the manifestation can occur very quickly.

Aside from the Soul Invocation, Djwhal Khul has given several other invocations that are useful to help align one to one's higher purposes, as well as to invoke more Light and balance into the world.

Begin by invoking the Soul verbally. See yourself surrounded by a golden tube connecting from Earth to the Source. Feel a flow of energy from the Source coming through you and into the Earth. Ask your Soul to connect through the etheric network to other Souls who can assist in your manifestation.

Now state your invocation in detail. For example:

> **I invoke excellent health and loving relationships, right livelihood and right alignment with my and Soul's purposes.**
>
> **I wish to align myself with All That Is, my own I AM Presence, *Mahatma*.**
>
> **I now open myself to receive *Mahatma*, and give thanks for the spiritual abundance in my life. So be it!**

You can be general or specific, as in the example. Being specific focuses the intent clearly, usually with an image. Your invocation can also be as long as you like, including everything that you desire in every area of your life.

Be aware, though, that as you become clear and have more power flowing through you you, will get what you invoke. So make sure that you really desire it!

General Invocation

**" We know, O Lord of Light and Love, about the need.
Touch our hearts anew with Love,
That we too may love and give."**

Invocation of Joy

**"The nature of the Soul is Joy.
As the Soul, I invoke the energies of Joy!"**

See a stream of effervescent golden light filling you from above and expanding into your aura.

PATTERN REMOVAL (CLEARING)

Patterns are collections of beliefs and conclusions that are grouped in the subconscious by area or topic. It is possible to tune into your own Soul and begin to find and remove your own patterns. Invoke the Soul, look to an area that you would like to work on, and accept the impressions you receive. Do this with a tape recorder, and then remove the patterns one at a time, using the following technique. By doing this, you are channeling your own Soul.

The Tibetan Foundation has prepared several booklets of generic patterns common to most people. These can be used to clear the belief system to a great degree in areas such as abundance, relationships, ego/personality, will, choice, etc. These patterns have been observed by the discarnate teachers and channeled for the purpose of mass removal. As the patterns are removed on a personal level, they are also being released from the mass consciousness of humanity and the Earth itself.

The Golden Tube

1. Sit comfortably with both feet firmly on the ground. Visualize a golden tube of light surrounding you and extending from the heart of the Earth all the way up to the Source of All That Is. Within this tube visualize a blue triangle. At the top of the triangle is the "topic" of the pattern.

2. Beneath the triangle are the specific beliefs to be removed. Visualize if you can, or just know that the words of the pattern are printed beneath the triangle.

3. Activate the pattern by seeing a blue light in the middle of the triangle, and begin to spin it in a clockwise motion.

4. Now take a deep breath mentally and turn on a switch. In a flash of light, see a giant vacuum pump lift the whole triangle up the golden tube to the brilliant White Light of the Source.

5. Feel the pattern being pulled out of you and out of the Earth simultaneously, flowing up to the Source, being purified in the brilliant light and then flowing back down the tube, through you and into the Earth.

It is important to complete the process, by having the energy flow back to you and into the Earth. It is after all, *that* energy being released, and now it can be used for your own creative purposes.

When working with groups of patterns, whether on a tape or writing them down, it is important to remove them one at a time. *Do not read them without removing them,* or they will only become activated and you will have to deal with that energy or mood.

Pattern Removal Exercise

We want to give you some affirmations to help you to clear this area.

1. We ask that you slide the following words (rather like a fortune-cookie strip) into an electrical blue lake. See them submerging into the lake.

2. Then, see a golden light shining on the lake. As you do, the words are absorbed into it. They are integrated into it. Then from the lake there is an effect, a clearing. The whole area is clearer, like a splash into every cell of your physical body, like a cleansing from a clearer perspective of the cells.

3. As this occurs, allow yourself to begin to form a spiral of the electrical blue energy, starting at your feet and having it flow up around your physical body until it passes your head. Let this go beyond the mental body — you don't have to intellectualize it.

The lake represents the subconscious mind, and the color that we give the lake represents a particular aspect of the subconscious mind or your creativity. As the affirmation enters the lake, it enters the aspected subconscious and begins to energize it. It begins to create an opening, or adds energy to an existing opening. The golden light shining on the lake begins the process of integrating that affirmation into the subconscious. Then there is a response, which we ask you to see going into your cellular level.

Examples of Affirmations

I allow the stimulation of my creativity without invoking an unknown stress that seeks to distort the process, now.

I know that the Co-Creator level will not enclose me within a limited space where my unknown potential is too difficult to effect without burning, now.

I know that I will not be punished by this effort to bring from me that which I AM, now.

The electrical system/the flow system is not being impacted through this communication, now.

You may wish to hold a crystal while doing these affirmations, either one in each hand, or one that you hold onto with both hands. Crystals remind your emotional body that you are supported in the process.

Doing an affirmation just once will slightly change the subconscious. As you allow that change — which you see as the response — going into the cells, it will help your physical body step by step. That is one reason why this process is so important; in other words, each time you put an affirmation into the lake, the subconscious is cleared a little, which helps the cellular level of the physical body as well as the balancing of polarities.

Clearing Vortex

This technique is very effective in clearing the energy field, or aura, which surrounds the physical body, and can be done many times during the day — before meditation, before sleep, after contact with other people, whenever the emotions are stirred up. It also helps to connect one with their Soul level or higher consciousness.

1. Visualize a whirlwind of energy rotating in a clockwise motion, starting with the tip of the vortex about 6 or 7 feet (2 meters) above your head.
2. Invoke the energy from your higher consciousness by saying the Soul Invocation (out loud, if possible).

I am the Soul
I am the Light Divine
I am Love
I am Will
I am Fixed Design.

3. Allow the vortex to come down through you and into the ground, about 20 to 30 feet (6 to 9 meters) underground, where it disappears. (The size, color, and speed of the vortex will probably be different at times. Just allow it to be as it appears.)
4. Continue with another vortex, starting at the top, moving down into the ground, and disappearing. You may have several going at once, thus creating a spiraling column of light. Do this for 5 to 8 minutes.

The Soul invocation may be used silently or verbally throughout.

This exercise may be done either sitting or standing, eyes open or closed, in public (silently) or in private. If you feel emotionally activated, this technique will help to release the programming held in that thoughtform for creative use. It also serves to ground the system and open the channel.

BALANCING

Balancing Chakras

Invoke the Soul by using the Soul Invocation.

1. Begin by visualizing a brilliant white light about 6 inches (15 centimeters) above the crown of the head. This is the Soul Star, or eighth chakra.

2. Now see a dial with a scale of 1 to 5, knowing that 5 is the optimum amount that this chakra should be open at this time (that is, not necessarily wide open). Slowly turn the dial to 5, seeing the light of this chakra becoming brighter as it is turned up. Then move to the next chakra, repeating this process, using the appropriate symbolic colors:

7th chakra — Crown of the head	violet
6th chakra — Third eye, center of forehead	indigo blue
5th chakra — Throat	sky blue
4th chakra — Heart	green or pink
3rd chakra — Solar plexus	yellow/gold
2nd chakra — Polarity chakra (sacral plexus)	orange
1st chakra — Base (root) chakra/base of spine	red

3. Now see a line of white light from the base chakra to a point about 6 inches (15 centimeters) below your feet. This is known as the Earth Star, and can be understood as the grounding aspect of the Soul Star. See this form into a ball of white light that expands and begins to spin and slowly spiral its way up the central channel, through the base chakra and up the spine, connecting back into the Soul Star above your head.

4. The two balls of light then merge and expand and move back down through the crown to the base of the neck, splitting off, one to each shoulder, opening and expanding the area, then moving down the arms to the elbows, wrists, and palms of the hands. At this point, feel the flow of energy down each arm. Are they in balance? If not, turn up the volume on one side until they are balanced.

5. Now, move the two balls of light to the midshoulder points, moving down the front of the body, stopping at the breasts, and seeing those centers open and expand.

6. Continue down, and on the left side stop at the spleen, seeing that center open and expand.

7. Then move down to the hips, knees, ankles, heels, soles of the feet, then toes. Again, feel the flow of energy down the right and left sides and balance that flow.

8. Now form a line of light from the sole of each foot to the Earth Star and let it grow brighter and expand, feeling your groundedness and connection to the Earth.

9. Now the light begins to spiral down deep into the core of the Earth, firmly anchoring there and spiraling gently back up and around your body, past the Soul Star and all the way up to the Source of All That Is, anchoring there and then spiralling back down through you with a beautiful golden light.

10. Feel the flow of that golden light, then see it change to a rainbow-tinted white tornado of light, to clear and ground any excess energy debris loosened from the chakras. Sit for a moment, feeling the balance of your energy system. When you are ready, gently open your eyes.

Note: It is important not to focus intently on any one chakra without doing the complete balancing exercise, as this may lead to an unbalanced stimulation of energy in that area. Know that by invoking the Soul prior to the meditation, you are invoking a balancing and regulating force that will open the chakras to the degree appropriate to each.

Male/Female Polarity Balance

1. Standing with knees slightly bent, reach up with your left hand, palm up, above your head. Visualize the full moon with rays of its pale white light flooding down through your hand and down the left side of your body into the Earth. Feel this flow for about a minute.

2. Gently lower your left hand and raise your right hand to the same position above your head. Visualize the sun flooding rays of its golden light into your hand and down the right side of your body into the Earth.

3. After about a minute, again raise both hands, and feel both flowing at the same time, the moonlight through the left hand and down the left side, the sunlight through the right hand and down the right side. If one side feels more powerful than the other, increase the energy on the other side until it feels balanced.

4. After about a minute, lower both hands, place the palms together, and turn them inward so that your fingers are touching the center of your chest.

5. Visualize a balanced flow of light from both hands, flowing into your heart chakra and energizing your whole system.

Balancing the Four Bodies

(Please refer to the diagram, "The Four-Body System," on page 225.)

When the four bodies are in perfect balance, your Soul is allowed to function through you on the Earth. When your Soul is allowed to function here, it will serve the Creator. The four bodies must be brought into balance consciously, and you can learn to do this in a state of meditation. When you have learned to remove all barriers within Self, the bodies will eventually remain in balance. When you see which one is out of balance, you will know which part of self you need to work on. This is a good tool.

Exercise One

1. In a state of meditation, see your spiritual body. If you wish, you may see it as a beautiful white figure. You may use white for the spiritual body, perhaps orange or yellow for the mental body, brown and green for the emotional and physical bodies — whatever feels right for you.

2. In the center of your head and from the center of each of these superimposed bodies, see a string hanging down like a plumb line. Are your bodies centered with each other? If perhaps the mental body is flipped to the right, bring it back into alignment. If it flips out again, there may be a problem within the mental body. This is how to identify the problem area.

3. If the mental body is out of balance, recall your thoughts within the last few hours or day or two; perhaps an unsolved problem keeps it circling out of alignment. It will be out of balance until you can resolve some subconscious belief.

4. If the emotional body is out of balance, then there is an interfering emotion being worked out. Or you could have a situation where the mental body is in the "think, think, think" pattern, and the emotional body adds worry. When this happens, the mental body might push one way and the emotional body the other. When you bring them together, they will change places. Work with this. The mental and emotional bodies are natural balances for each other.

5. Perhaps it is the physical body that is off-center. This would probably manifest in a physical condition. Work with the body symbolically. (If your right arm hurts, right signifies the male polarity; an arm implies reaching, grasping.) The physical and spiritual bodies are natural balances for each other. The physical is working to attain true understanding in the totality of All That Is.

Acknowledge that your imbalances did not come about in five minutes, and that perhaps it's going to take awhile to achieve balance. Allow that for yourself. Work within the framework of where you are and gradually increase your awareness of the Creator's plan for you. You will perceive it gradually as you work. All of you have the desire to become what you truly are, to perceive it, and to know that you are a Co-Creator.

Exercise Two

1. In a meditative state, explore each one of your bodies completely. You may use a colored ball to represent the body and simply crawl inside it and look around. Notice, in the physical body, for instance, whether the heart is healthy or the arteries clear. Exploring your emotional body might be unwise in the midst of an emotional problem. You may actually be able to measure the level of beliefs that you still have to work with. Crawling around inside your mental perceptions can be very interesting. You need not spend much time all at once; go back to it later. Become familiar with each ball.

2. Merge yourself with your highest aspect and talk to it. Discuss your situation with your spiritual spark, the Monad.

3. Visualize the emotional and mental bodies balanced like dumbbells. Stand at the center; are they balanced, or do you slide down to the heavier one? See if you can learn what causes one to be heavier than the other.

4. Visualize a children's slide, and go down it fast. Which body did you land in? This is a good way to find where you are focused at the time.

MANIFESTATION

A popular expression in most metaphysical/spiritual groups today is, "You create your own reality." This can be understood on many levels and accepted in varying degrees — from believing that one attracts to oneself positive or negative experiences according to the nature of thoughts, attitudes and feelings that one holds; all the way to the opposite end of the spectrum, that one creates everything and everyone in one's reality, and that this creation is entirely and only a mirror of one's inner state.

Whatever level you begin to accept it on, *taking responsibility* is the key. You are constantly creating your own reality; manifestation is when you begin to do it *consciously*.

According to Lazaris, the seat of power now lies in the conscious mind — not in the subconscious. Although the subconscious is still playing the programming, we can now consciously *recreate the subconscious* by using these processes.

Techniques of manifestation, then, can become methods of testing how clear you are in any given area. If you use a technique and don't get the results you want, don't give your power away by saying "this doesn't work" or "I can't do it right." Rather, accept that the techniques are fine and you are okay — you just need a little (or a lot) more clearing in that area. Your feelings will point you in the direction of where to clear.

Frustrated? What would you have to believe to create that frustration? Clear it out and try again.

Processing for Manifestation

1. Clear the beliefs and attitudes using the methods given.

2. How strong is your desire? If the desire is lukewarm, so will be the results. Put some feeling into it; activate the emotions!

3. How clearly can you imagine it? See vivid details! Paint an emotional picture!

4. Why do you want it? Get clear on your motivation.

5. Why *don't* you want it? What benefits or payoffs are you getting from not obtaining what you want — attention, sympathy, righteous anger, frustration?

6. What do you honestly expect? This will probably lead you back to step number 1 — looking deeper into your beliefs and attitudes.

Peace Meditation

1. See a laserlike ray of violet light tinged with gold flowing through your channel, from the Source into the center of the Earth. Allow it to expand, filling your channel as well as your physical body.

2. Send a concentrated beam of this light to any area of your physical body that needs healing or purification.

3. Then allow the light to expand again, filling the room, then encompassing your city, state/province, country, hemisphere, and finally the whole world.

4. Send a concentrated ray of this energy to any area of the Earth you feel could use some help — peace, harmony, prosperity, etc.

5. Then see the Earth in its wholeness, engulfed in the beautiful violet light with sparkles of gold throughout. Send your love and blessing to the Earth, and know that you are making a very powerful impact toward creating peace on Earth.

If done in a group, the effect is magnified by the square of the number of people in a group; in effect, 10 people in a group will have the effect of 100 people doing this individually.

INTEGRATION

Space Injection/Unjamming Exercise

This is a series of exercises designed to help with the integration of new energy, ideas, mental input, etc.

1. Lie on your back on the floor with your legs outstretched and slightly apart. Allow your feet to fall toward the outside in their natural position. Feel your connection to the Earth through the floor that you lie on. Now gently flex your feet back and forth 15 times, creating a gentle, rocking motion up and down your spine. Allow this motion to gently rock your neck and head.

2. Rotate your ankles so that your feet are pointing inward, and repeat the same rocking motion 15 times.

3. Now move your ankles so that your feet are in a straight up-and-down position and repeat the rocking motion 15 more times.

4. Move your feet so that your knees are up. Take a deep breath in, pressing your pelvis to the floor and holding your tongue to the roof of your mouth, behind your teeth. Hold your breath to the count of 10. Release your breath, relaxing your tongue and pelvis; and now, on the in-breath, again press your pelvis to the floor and your tongue to the roof of your mouth. Gently release your breath, relaxing your tongue and pelvis. Repeat this for 15 cycles.

    Both of these exercises create a gentle undulating motion to the spine, pumping the cerebrospinal fluid up to the brain. Whenever you feel a backlog of mental input, this will help the brain to process it.

5. Still lying with your knees up, allow your head to gently drop to the left, hold a few seconds, then return to normal; then drop your head to the right, hold, and then back to normal.

6. In the same position, allow your knees to drop as far as they will easily go to the left, hold a few seconds, then return to normal; repeat with the right, and return to normal. Repeat this cycle 10 times.

7. Stretch your legs out again and flex your feet toward you. Hold that dorsal horizontal stretch, take a deep breath in and hold to the count of 7, visualizing a flow of energy from the base of your spine up to your heart. Slowly breathe out to the count of 7, and see a flow of energy from your heart to the crown of your head. Repeat this cycle 7 times.

Important: When finished, rest for a few moments, then roll slowly onto your right side and *very slowly* push yourself up to a sitting position. Wait a few moments before standing. Do not get up quickly!

These exercises may be done daily or whenever it feels necessary. If you feel a cold coming on, do it more often to allow the energy to move through.

ANCIENT TIMES

Excerpted from Channeled Writings
by Janet McClure

Pre-Lemuria and the Electrical Ones

The pre-Lemurian experience is one that many of those living today encountered. From this period of about 500 years, many deeply ingrained patterns of behavior were established.

It began at a time when mankind had felt very enthusiastic about life and its experience on the Earth. A very highly evolved civilization had been present, with a well-advanced technology balanced with spiritual growth and aspiration. This era had produced many enlightened people.

This, however, was the end of a cycle, and many had evolved to the point of Ascension; in fact, two mass Ascensions had taken place near the end of this cycle. So, many who then came into incarnation right after this wondrous time were feeling very inspired about their process of growth. A sense of absolute trust permeated the consciousness of man.

Suddenly, in the face of this trust and enthusiasm, came an attack from a race of extraterrestrials (termed the Electrical Ones) who wanted the Earth for themselves. How did this occur? If mankind were so spiritually evolved, how did they create this for themselves? As Vywamus puts it: To truly see Earth's evolution clearly, one must plug into a cosmic time clock to see it proportionately in the manner that the Whole/the Source/the Creator views it. Thus, a focus of trust is established, a loving focus of trust and participation that then focuses deeply into the Oneness. By doing this, humanity invoked a deep contact within the Source and were allowed to reflect back any and all misconceptions that were yet buried within the mass consciousness, in a subconscious sense, to be surfaced in order to allow that trusting, loving contact point to broaden, to deepen, to be realized yet more fully."

Humanity, in its loving, trusting state, encountered an attack by the Electrical Ones which lasted for 500 years, destroying over and over the physical self and loved ones on the physical level — physical destruction of such magnitude that, at this point, most of you are not capable of seeing how extensive it truly was. It seemed to be a violation of the trusting, loving thrust into the Divine that humanity had made. Deep, intricately woven, multifaceted beliefs are present in the mass consciousness and within all of you about what happens when you trust and enter the loving, allowing Divine Whole. Certainly these beliefs are, for many of you, buried within the subconscious. Humanity does not recognize or allow itself to see that it has become angry with Sourceness, feeling a betrayal and sense of being deceived, a treachery that seemed to be reflected back when that contact was lovingly and comprehensively brought forth.

Now, what happens on a planet when there is a mass Ascension? Those who are left do not have the light of the ones who have gone forth to help them with their relationship to the mass consciousness; you might say that the programming of the mass consciousness is there, but without the understanding of those who had left that had helped to balance it.

Out of its own deep-rooted fears, humanity invoked the Electrical Ones, beings who had no concept of the sovereignty of free will. They sought to enslave mankind and rule the world. They were very advanced technically and had the means to control people by inserting electrical implants (particularly in a woman's womb), which created terrible pain if the person was not behaving correctly. These people were used as spies and saboteurs against their will, to disrupt and destroy the resistance movement that was formed.

Now, I know that it sounds just like science fiction. In pre-Lemuria, this particular civilization lasted for about 500 years. It was an intense time for the Earth, and many of you were there working for humanity — creating life for yourselves, but over and over again being drafted by the human need and going forth to defend the Earth. Interwoven into this are all of the stories that you see on your TV. Spies, implants...all of these things are woven into this particular time on the Earth, which was so devastating. The mass consciousness has all of these things in its memory. Many of you have them also.

The Electrical Ones themselves were rather bewildered by the ferocity with which humanity fought for its freedom, and over the 500-year period of conflict, they came to understand and appreciate this quality of free will.

Humanity eventually triumphed over the Electrical Ones, but the scars of that long struggle remain to this day in the collective psyche of man: mistrust and feelings of betrayal by God and the Spiritual Teachers; attack/defend scenarios; male/female polarity problems; fear of the unknown, and so on.

Over the long period of conflict, individuals had many experiences of these lives of struggle, pain, treachery, etc., both as men and as women. Today, once again these ancient patterns are prevalent and require clearing, both for the growth of the individual and for the Earth.

After this traumatic period had passed, there began that long period of time known as the Lemurian epoch — about 500,000 years of recovery from the pain of attack.

Although humanity could have created cities, they chose to live in a more basic style. Although you lived in a rather primitive way, you also had considerable sophistication. What humanity did was to consider what happened when they lived out in the open and found themselves under attack. They may have moved into caves, but the caves were beautifully decorated with paintings and floor coverings and fine textiles. They had the knowledge of how to construct buildings, but they wanted to be free to move about and experience their relationship to the planet. It was free and it was theirs, and they wanted to explore and attune to the planet; they appreciated it more after defending it.

Religious experience was always present on the Earth. In this particular time, it was often related to the Earth and appreciation for the Earth. In the latter part of the Lemurian era and on into the time of Atlantis, they began to build temples including healing temples. As this civilization progressed, humanity again wanted to "get with it," you might say. They began to have small villages and communities, in the sense of living beyond the cave groups. There were villages of five thousand and more. It really became a worldwide civilization again. I have spoken of Lemuria in relation to the South Pacific initially, but it really evolved to be a full planetary civilization.

CLEARING BELIEF SYSTEMS

The subconscious mind is the reservoir of all the conclusions from past experiences. This includes all lifetimes, possibly thousands. Whenever something is experienced, a learning process takes place. This learning process occurs on all levels of Self simultaneously, sending the conclusion of the experience to the higher levels of Self — the Soul, Monad, and back to Source. Since the Source Itself is also growing in experience from its creation, all of the input is taken to that level as well. The higher levels (Soul and Monad) filter out what they perceive as inaccurate or erroneous conclusions and send the finished product back to the Source.

The ego/personality, or human consciousness, does not have this benefit. It may register an experience — for example, hearing a branch break or bushes rustle in the forest, feel fear, and conclude that the forest is a dangerous place. The subconscious mind does not differentiate between what is an actual experience and one that is vividly imagined.

Your reality is a product of your belief system. It is the aggregate of unconscious, subconscious and conscious beliefs, attitudes, opinions, feelings, and conclusions. An example of unconscious beliefs from the collective psyche of mankind include such expressions as "the sky is blue," "what goes up must come down," etc. — things commonly perceived and believed.

The subconscious, then, deals with the more personal aspects of the way the world is, such as the example of being afraid of the forest. The forest is not experienced as dangerous by everybody; it is this personalized belief that ultimately creates or attracts the danger. "That which I feared the most has come upon me"; this truth prompted Roosevelt to say, "There is nothing to fear but fear itself" to counter this effect. This then becomes a snowballing process — the belief is a self-fulfilling prophecy that creates the experience, then reinforces the belief to the extent that one simply looks at the experience and says, "Of course the forest is dangerous; I was just attacked by a wolf!" But the belief is causal to the experience; change the belief system and you begin to change the experience.

Ultimately, when one has cleared the subconscious belief system enough, then one can effectively begin to clear the unconscious or collective-unconscious beliefs. This results in the state of mastery over the physical universe, and the performance of seeming miracles.

In the years to come, as the New Age dawns even brighter, the experience of this creation of reality will become more acute. This is because the Earth is increasing its rate of vibration, and as Lazaris puts it: "The gap between thought and things is becoming thinner." Physical life is for the purpose of experiencing the process of creating one's own reality in a slowed-down format. On the astral plane, as is commonly experienced in the dream state, the creation of what one desires is instantaneous.

This level of experience (sometimes called fourth-dimensional time) is being offered again to humanity. The time of having to do the physical long division is drawing to an end, and it will no longer be necessary to "show your work" in the process of creation.

The physical experience gives us (as future Source-level Creators with God/Goddess/All That Is) the understanding of creation from the inside out, and gives it to us with enough of a time lag between our desire and its manifestation that we can correct it if it is not what we truly want. This time lag is being shortened, while time itself is being commonly experienced as speeding up.

As the New Age comes fully into being, this fourth-dimensional experience will become more and more common; the manifestation of one's desires will occur more and more instantly. This entails the need to become clear about what you want, and to become clear of the old belief systems that are giving you the things your subconscious wants. These include fear, anger, jealousy, rage, etc., which manifest in life as conflict, danger, and suffering.

It is no longer necessary or appropriate to feel like a victim of anything or anyone! It is time to reclaim your power, accept the responsibility for creating what you get in life, and begin to *consciously create* joy, freedom, abundance, success, and mastery.

Before doing any of these techniques it is helpful to invoke your Soul, using the Soul Invocation, and enlist its help in your clearing or balancing process, and then finish with the Clearing Vortex to clear out any debris that has been loosened and still held in your aura.

The Soul Invocation means that you are tuning into your own higher purpose for this life, in harmony with your Soul. Ideally, it should be declared verbally, but it may also be used as a silent mantra or affirmation, and should be said AS IF you are the Soul. This creates the necessary link to the Soul on its own plane of being and begins the process of Soul's energy infusing the personality/ego (which is characteristic of the Third Initiation and which culminates at the Fourth Initiation.)

The Blackboard

Once you have found a belief that you wish to remove, visualize a hand-held blackboard and write the belief on it; for example: "I never get what I want." In your other hand visualize an eraser made of joy and light. Erase the belief and the emotions that were holding it in your system. Continue with others as they come up.

Finding Those Beliefs

Use your reality as a mirror to show you what to clear. Most people react to unwanted things in their lives by trying to change *other* people or situations.

This is like looking into a mirror seeing that your face is dirty and then trying to wipe the mirror clean!

Reality is created from within, so the first place to look is at the effects in your life that you don't want; for example repeating patterns of difficulty such as poor health, financial problems, relationships, etc. When you find something, ask: What would a person have to *believe* to have created this?

If, for example, you are feeling blocked in the area of finances or success, some common beliefs may be:

- *I don't deserve abundance in my life.*
- *I always seem to screw up.*
- *I'll never get that promotion (job and so forth.).*
- *There is not enough abundance to go around.*
- *Whenever I have extra money, there is always some extra expense.*
- *Only a few lucky people can have all they want.*
- *Money is the root of all evil.*
- *Money and spiritual growth don't mix.*

This is just a small sample of the garbage programmed into us from birth (and from other lives). Each of the above areas will yield some very interesting insights and many more beliefs. BE HONEST WITH YOURSELF! You created it and you can *recreate* it!

Look also to your language; how many of these limiting beliefs are contained in ordinary expressions such as:

- *You can't win.*
- *You can't fight City Hall.*
- *Murphy's Law — If anything can go wrong, it will.*
- *Nice guys finish last.*
- *Big girls/boys don't cry.*
- *It's lonely at the top.*
- *It's a dog-eat-dog world.*

Not to mention all of "the world is a scary place" programs installed by nursery rhymes, fairy tales, "big bad wolves," etc.

All of these things are like tapes that play, either consciously or subconsciously, all the time. Listen to the self-talk chattering away at you. Do you have an inner disk-jockey constantly playing music for you? What songs are playing? ("I got the blues so bad..." or, "I can't get no satisfaction!" etc.)

When you isolate a belief, there are several different processes that you can use to clear it.

The subconscious mind relates to pictures and symbols, hence the value of visualization. The following process has been found to be very effective in clearing the belief system to create balance and harmony.

Belief Book Meditation

1. Think of possible beliefs or attitudes that you want to change. If you hit one that is real for you, you'll feel it — it will go "twang" inside!

2. Verbalize the belief as simply as possible; for example, *I never win.*

3. Rewrite it in the same sentence structure: **I always win!**

4. Sit in meditation and see yourself walking down a set of stairs into a basement. It's dark and musty and all around are old dusty things from your past — old toys, clothes, etc. Walk past it all to a door; through a crack in the door you see a light shining.

5. Open the door and step into a brilliantly lit room, at the center of which is a podium that holds a large hardbound book titled, **"My Beliefs and Attitudes."**

6. Open the book to the appropriate page and there is your belief: *I never win.*

7. Forgive yourself for having created this belief, and with joy and enthusiasm take a felt pen and in big, bold letters mark Void over this old belief.

8. Now tear out the page, and with joy and glee tear it up into small pieces.

9. Take a match and set fire to the shreds of paper, smelling the smoke and seeing them curl up in the flames.

10. When the fire is out, blow away the ashes and *know* that the belief is gone.

11. Go back to the book, and on a new page write slowly and deliberately your *new belief*: **I always win!** and mentally shout it out to the world, proclaiming your new belief. Repeat with other beliefs and then close the book and end the meditation.

12. If you want to reinforce a positive belief, find it in the book, trace over it and underline it, congratulating yourself on having such a good belief.

13. On a piece of cardboard write your new belief. Put it where you can see it, and every morning reinforce it by saying, for example: **I always win!**

Then cut up another piece of cardboard in the same color, and put the pieces in frequently seen places — the refrigerator door, car mirror, etc. Each time you see these it will subconsciously trigger the new belief.

MAKING THE FULL CONNECTION

Connect the Outer Self to the GOD WITHIN

In a quiet place, allow yourself to become very still in mind and body. Then see (visualize) and feel yourself enveloped in the dazzling White Light of Source.

During the first five minutes of holding this picture, recognize and intensely feel the connection between your outer self and your GOD WITHIN, focusing your attention in your heart chakra and visualizing it as a golden sun.

Next, make the affirmation/realization: **I now joyously accept the fullness of the God Presence.**

Feel the great brilliance and radiance of the light, and intensify it in every cell of your body for at least ten minutes longer.

Close your meditation with the affirmation/command: **I AM a child of the Light. I love the Light. I serve the Light. I live in the Light. I AM protected, illuminated, and sustained by the Light; and I bless the Light.**

Always remember that you become that upon which you meditate. Since all of Creation has come forth from the Light, Light is the relative perfection and control of all things. Contemplation and adoration of the Light compels *illumination* to take place in the mind; health, strength, and order to manifest in the body; and peace, harmony, and success in the life of the dedicated student.

If you will use this meditation faithfully and feel it intensely in every atom of your mind and body, you will receive abundant proof of the magnificent power, activity, and perfection of the Light. When you have experienced this for even a short time, you will need no further proof — you become your own proof.

The Golden Globe Award

Invoke the *Mahatma*/Source energy into your beingness; see the white/gold Light flowing from the Source level though your four- or five-body system and into the center of the Earth. Invite the Archangels into your physical body, each into the appropriate chakra (refer to the exercise and diagram, "The Archangels Embodying the Tenth Ray").

Then visualize yourself enclosed in a beautiful bubble — see the outer ring of this bubble as the White Light of Source, with an inner ring of the golden light of the Twelfth Ray. If your golden ring has any breaks in its circle, stop and mend it. See your bubble filled with water, as water is a marvelous conductor and will soothe the emotional body.

Then see yourself surrounded with the luminescent, pearl-colored light of the Tenth Ray. See the stream of aqua-aura light supercharging your golden globe — in effect, like battery cables — from the *Mahatma* through Metatron to Sandalphon, flowing through your bubble and your four- or five-body system [your physical — (etheric) — emotional — mental — spiritual bodies] and into the center of the Earth. The aqua-blue/electrical-blue light helps you to charge the contents of your bubble. If you were to consider the *Mahatma* to be the battery charger, Metatron would be the positive terminal and Sandalphon the negative terminal for grounding.

Once you have integrated all of these energies in your bubble, you can then enlarge your bubble/yourself — expand, expand, expand; intensify, intensify, intensify the electromagnetic charge within the bubble.

When you are ready, focus on your heart and throat chakras, which are becoming one. When you have charged your bubble and are ready to proceed, then instantaneously collapse your energy bubble into your heart/throat chakra. Allow this energy to integrate into your heart chakra, then direct its flow into your spleen, which serves as the electrical distributor in the physical body. From the spleen, see the energy circulating evenly throughout your four-body system. This process is very healing, as well as very energizing.

If you wish to channel healing energy to someone else, first be sure to ask the permission of their Soul. Take both of you through this complete exercise, and once the energy is circulating evenly throughout your four-body system, direct it from your heart chakra through your right (dynamic) hand, and visualize the condensed energy entering the body of the other person between their shoulderblades, behind the heart chakra. Done properly, this is as positive a healing as can be administered.

Note: Remember to also direct the energy flows upward, from the center of the Earth into the Source.

Realizations

Invite the *Mahatma* energy into your complete channel, from the Source Star into the center of the Earth, thereby encompassing your whole beingness, and integrate the following:

"My subconscious mind and mass consciousness now know that everything they have ever believed about their reality is simply not true; their reality has shifted and has become a greater spiritual level of **allowingness**, and **I AM** no longer confined nor limited to my primitive views of Self. I now know, without any doubt, that I can connect with a greater wholeness of my beingness. My subconscious mind can now begin to see the light that we are becoming. **I AM** now prepared to live within my total Self, and not in my outer realities, my emotional and lower mental bodies. **I AM** no longer confined to those dense, dense limitations that are so confining for me now. My emotional body and my lower mind can now begin to understand that their functions are outer, not the true *inner* function that I require in this time and place.

"I now ask that mass consciousness and my subconscious mind view what we refer to as the emotional body and the mental body, and let them know that they can have great comfort in the recognition that they lose nothing once they are assimilated within the Soul of one's Beingness. Because we are no longer limited to the emotional body and the mental body as being our only Sources of coming outside of our outer self, we tell the All That Is, we tell the mass consciousness, and we certainly let our subconscious mind know that all of these levels can be integrated within our primal Soul and Higher Self. We understand that the primal Soul is anchored into the thymus gland at this time, and then is moved beyond. With the primal Soul is anchored the emotional body and the mental body.

Expand that concept throughout Eternity.

"I, _____, AM no longer without control of my reality. I surrender to the **I AM** of my **I AM Presence**. I shall never again feel less than the **I AM** that **I AM**. I will continue to become the *Mahatma*, which is simply a mantra for the **I AM**. I refuse to ever give my power to anyone other than my own **I AM**. I will continue to love, to create and to live an abundant, joyful life within the framework of the greater **I AM**. I see totally through the illusion of that which I have always held to be my total reality. I realize now that the totality of who **I AM** can be connected, that all levels of Self can now be reunited, and never again will I have this dreadful feeling of separation from the **I AM Presence**. Everything that I have perceived myself to be is not even a fraction of who **I AM**. That which we call ego, which is the egoic body or the Soul body, is valid as the Soul, or primal, body. The ego of the outer self, which says, "Look at what I did out there" is totally ignorant of its reality and will not begin to assimilate Light in the fashion that is needed.

"Finally, we have an energy on Earth that I can relate to, because it doesn't require that I give my power to anyone but myself as God. My creative potentials are only just beginning as I align with that which **I AM** the **I AM Presence**. Never again will I live totally in the emotional, the mental, the psychic and lower astral levels, which we call mass consciousness, because they are illusion and as treacherous as quicksand. I agree with the totality of who **I AM**, and that from this moment I will accept my mantra, *Mahatma* at whatever level **I AM** within the **I AM**, as the **I AM**.

I no longer accept, nor will I see, that which is not Light. I tell my subconscious mind and mass consciousness that **I AM** not prepared to accept any longer the illusion that any part of me or all of me is fused into darkness. My reality is that **I AM in control**, and that all on Earth is illusion — at least a quasi-state of illusion. I affirm at this time and forever that I will not allow into my four-body system or into my reality those distortions that we view as the past, because nothing that ever *was* exists Now. My fourth-dimensional reality does not include those lives which have penetrated and so affected my persona, my auric field and my emotional body, now. I release forever all obligation, all sense of controls, on what we view as the past. I remind myself that man has fallen, therefore darkness prevails throughout humankind; and I will not be party to humankind's self-righteous judgments about *its* illusory creations, for how does one judge form and darkness? I AM Divine Light and Love, and I will no longer allow the distortions held by humankind to be a part of my new-found reality; I AM complete as my *own* I AM of my I AM Presence, *Mahatma*.

"I AM the I AM of the I AM Presence. I recognize now that I have *always* been the I AM, that my personality *is* the I AM of the I AM, and everything that I have ever been is the I AM. The puny outer self has no reality whatsoever with the I AM that I AM. I glory and revel in the Light, the Light and the Love. I breathe in the incandescent White Light of Source as my developing channel becomes that Light, the I AM. The beautiful Beings that I sense or see are me; I identify my Self with everyone. There is positively no sense of separation. I AM able to sense colors and sounds that I have never before been able to experience; if I do not sense them now, I will be able to see and hear these. I AM now able to experience this part of my Self which is the I AM Presence.

Breathe in deeply, dear one, the I AM that you are. Allow the channel that you have created to be permeated with the I AM.

"The channel that I travel within is all-encompassing, as the I AM. I adore my radiant channel. I revel in my exploration as Light and Love and no one can tell me otherwise, for I AM the I AM of my I AM Presence."

SOURCES

"Channeling Exercise One" (page 290) — Vywamus, channeled by Barbara Burns, excerpted from *Evolutionary Exercises for Channels*, published by Light Technology Publishing.

"Pre-Lemurian Patterns and Information" (page 315) — Djwhal Khul (The Tibetan) and Vywamus, channeled by Janet McClure, published by Light Technology Publishing.

"Belief Book Meditation" (page 321) — Lazaris, channeled by Jach Pursel.

"The Secrets of Manifesting What You Want" — videotape of Lazaris, channeled by Jach Pursel.

"Opportunity or Necessity" — audiotape of Lazaris.

"Grounding the Space: The Golden Circle" (page 298) — Aurorra, channeled by Nancy Shipley Rubin.

"Space Injection/Unjamming Exercises" (page 313) — Helios, channeled by Moneca (Pat) Tayler and Steffany Caldwell.

"Male/Female Polarity Balance" (page 307) — Vywamus and Djwhal Khul, channeled by Robin Nicholas and Terry Newlon.

"Peace Meditation" (page 312) — Archangel Michael, channeled by Terry Ferguson.

"Balancing Chakras" (page 306) and "The Golden Tube" (page 302) Vywamus, channeled by Terry Ferguson.

THE EXPLORER RACE SERIES

ZOOSH AND OTHERS THROUGH ROBERT SHAPIRO

Superchannel Robert Shapiro can communicate with any personality anywhere and anywhen. He has been a professional channel for over twenty-five years and channels with an exceptionally clear and profound connection.

The Origin...
The Purpose...The Future...of Humanity

If you have ever wondered about who you really are, why you are here as part of humanity on this miraculous planet and what it all means, these books in the Explorer Race series can begin to supply the answers—the answers to these and other questions about the mystery and enigma of physical life on Earth.

These answers come from beings who speak through superchannel Robert Shapiro, beings who range from particle personalities to the Mother of all Beings and the thirteen Ssjooo, from advisors to the Creator of our universe to the generators of precreation energies. The scope, the immensity, the mind-boggling infinitude of these chronicles by beings who live in realms beyond our imagination, will hold you enthralled. Nothing even close to the magnitude of the depth and power of this all-encompassing, expanded picture of reality has ever been published.

This amazing story of the greatest adventure of all time and creation is the story of the Explorer Race, of which humans are a small but important percentage. The Explorer Race is a group of souls whose journeys resulted in incarnations in this loop of time on planet Earth, where, bereft of any memory of our immortal selves and most of our heart energy. We came to learn compassion, to learn to take responsibility for the consequences of our actions and to solve creation's previously unsolvable dilemma of negativity. We humans have found a use for negativity—we use it for lust for life and adventure, curiosity and creativity, for doing the undoable. And in a few years we will go out to the stars with our insatiable drive and ability to respond to change and begin to inspire the benign but stagnant civilizations out there to expand and change and grow, which will eventually result in the change and expansion of all creation.

Once you understand the saga of the Explorer Race and what the success of the Explorer Race Experiment means to the totality of creation, you will be proud to be human and to know that you are a vital component of the greatest story ever told—a continuing drama whose adventure continues far into the future.

Book 7 of the EXPLORER RACE

THE COUNCIL OF CREATORS

ROBERT SHAPIRO

The thirteen core members of the Council of Creators discuss their adventures in coming to awareness of themselves and their journeys on the way to the Council on this level. They discuss the advice and oversight they offer to all creators, including the creator of this local universe. These beings are wise, witty and joyous, and their stories of Love's Creation creates an expansion of our concepts as we realize that we live in an expanded, multiple-level reality. SOFTCOVER 237P. $14.95 ISBN 1-891824-13-9

Highlights Include

- Specialist in Colors, Sounds and Consequences of Actions
- Specialist in Membranes that Separate and Auditory Mechanics
- Specialist in Sound Duration
- Explanation from Unknown Member of Council
- Specialist in Spatial Reference
- Specialist in Gaps and Spaces
- Specialist in Divine Intervention

- Specialist in Synchronicity and Timing
- Specialist in Hope
- Specialist in Honor
- Specialist in Variety
- Specialist in Mystical Connection between Animals and Humans
- Specialist in Change
- Specialist in the Present Moment
- Council Spokesperson and Specialist in Auxiliary Life Forms

Book 8 of the EXPLORER RACE

THE EXPLORER RACE AND ISIS

ROBERT SHAPIRO

This is an amazing book. It has priestess training, Shamanic training, Isis' adventures with Explorer Race beings—before Earth and on Earth—and an incredibly expanded explanation of the dynamics of the Explorer Race. Isis is the prototypical loving, nurturing, guiding feminine being, the focus of feminine energy. She has the ability to expand limited thinking without making people with limited beliefs feel uncomfortable. She is a fantastic storyteller, and all of her stories are teaching stories. If you care about who you are, why you are here, where you are going and what life is all about—pick up this book. You won't lay it down until you are through, and then you will want more. SOFTCOVER 317P. $14.95 ISBN 1-891824-11-2

Highlights Include

- The Biography of Isis
- The Adventurer
- Soul Colors and Shapes
- Creation Mechanics
- Creation Mechanics and Personal Anecdotes

- The Insects' Form and Fairies
- Orion and Application to Earth
- Goddess Section
- Who Is Isis?
- Priestess/Feminine Mysteries

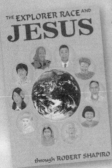

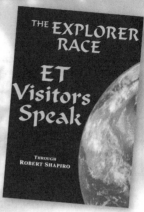

SHAMANIC SECRETS for PHYSICAL MASTERY

COMING SOON

The purpose of this book is to allow you to understand the sacred nature of your own physical body and some of the magnificent gifts it offers you. When you work with your physical body in these new ways, you will discover not only its sacredness, but how it is compatible with Mother Earth, the animals, the plants, even the nearby planets, all of which you now recognize as being sacred in nature. It is important to feel the value of oneself physically before one can have any lasting physical impact on the world. The less you think of yourself physically, the less likely your physical impact on the world will be sustained by Mother Earth. If a physical energy does not feel good about itself, it will usually be resolved; other physical or spiritual energies will dissolve it because it is unnatural. The better you feel about your physical self when you do the work in the previous book as well as this one and the one to follow, the greater and more lasting will be the benevolent effect on your life, on the lives of those around you and ultimately on your planet and universe.   SOFTCOVER 600P.

$19⁹⁵   ISBN 1-891824-29-5

Chapter Titles:

- Cellular Clearing of Traumas, Unresolved Events
- Cellular Memory
- Identifying Your Body's Fear Message
- The Heart Heat Exercise
- Learn Hand Gestures
  —Remove Self-Doubt
  —Release Pain or Hate
  —Clear the Adrenals or Kidneys
  —Resolve Sexual Dysfunction
- Learning the Card Technique for Clarifying Body Message
- Seeing Life as a Gift
- Relationship of the Soul to Personality
- The New Generation of Children
- The Creator and Religions
- Food, Love & Addictions

- Communication of the Heart
- Dreams & Their Significance
- The Living Prayer/Good Life
- Life Force and Life Purpose
- Physical Mastery
- His Life/ Mandate for His Ancestors/ Importance of Animals/ Emissaries
- Physical Mastery
- Talking to Rain/ Bear Claw Story
- Disentanglement
- Grief Culture
- Closing Comments

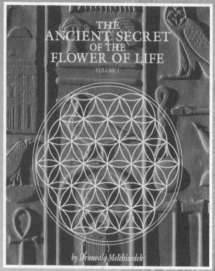

THE ANCIENT SECRET OF THE FLOWER OF LIFE
VOLUME 2

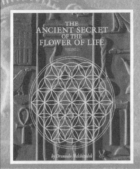

ISBN 1-891824-17-1
Soft cover, 228 p.

$25⁰⁰

The sacred Flower of Life pattern, the primary geometric generator of all physical form, is explored in even more depth in this volume, the second half of the famed Flower of Life workshop. The proportions of the human body, the nuances of human consciousness, the sizes and distances of the stars, planets and moons, even the creations of humankind, are all shown to reflect their origins in this beautiful and divine image. Through an intricate and detailed geometrical mapping, Drunvalo Melchizedek shows how the seemingly simple design of the Flower of Life contains the genesis of our entire third-dimensional existence.

From the pyramids and mysteries of Egypt to the new race of Indigo children, Drunvalo presents the sacred geometries of the Reality and the subtle energies that shape our world. We are led through a divinely inspired labyrinth of science and stories, logic and coincidence, on a path of remembering where we come from and the wonder and magic of who we are.

Finally, for the first time in print, Drunvalo shares the instructions for the Mer-Ka-Ba meditation, step-by-step techniques for the re-creation of the energy field of the evolved human, which is the key to ascension and the next dimensional world. If done from love, this ancient process of breathing prana opens up for us a world of tantalizing possibility in this dimension, from protective powers to the healing of oneself, of others and even of the planet.

⚙ **THE UNFOLDING OF THE THIRD INFORMATIONAL SYSTEM**
The Circles and Squares of Human Consciousness; Leonardo da Vinci's True Understanding of the Flower of Life; Exploring the Rooms of the Great Pyramid

⚙ **WHISPERS FROM OUR ANCIENT HERITAGE**
The Initiations of Egypt; the Mysteries of Resurrection; Interdimensional Conception; Ancient Mystery Schools; Egyptian Tantra, Sexual Energy and the Orgasm

⚙ **UNVEILING THE MER-KA-BA MEDITATION**
Chakras and the Human Energy System; Energy Fields around the Body; the Seventeen Breaths of the Mer-Ka-Ba Meditation; the Sacred Geometry of the Human Lightbody

⚙ **USING YOUR MER-KA-BA**
The Siddhis or Psychic Powers; Programming Your Mer-Ka-Ba; Healing from the Prana Sphere; Coincidence, Thought and Manifestation; Creating a Surrogate Mer-Ka-Ba

⚙ **CONNECTING TO THE LEVELS OF SELF**
Mother Earth and Your Inner Child; Life with Your Higher Self; How to Communicate with Everything; the Lessons of the Seven Angels

⚙ **TWO COSMIC EXPERIMENTS**
The Lucifer Experiment and the Creation of Duality; the 1972 Sirian Experiment and the Rebuilding of the Christ Consciousness Grid

⚙ **WHAT WE MAY EXPECT IN THE FORTHCOMING DIMENSIONAL SHIFT**
How to Prepare; Survival in the Fourth Dimension; the New Children

Available from your favorite bookstore or:

LIGHT TECHNOLOGY PUBLISHING
P.O. Box 3540
Flagstaff, AZ 86003
(928) 526-1345
(800) 450-0985
FAX (928) 714-1132
Or use our on-line bookstore:
www.lighttechnology.com

3ᵉ LIGHT Technology
PUBLISHING

SONG OF FREEDOM
My Journey from the Abyss
by Judith Moore

Judith Moore knew she'd been sick a lot more than most people—but it wasn't until she joined an incest survivors' group to help one of her adopted daughters that the memories began surfacing.

At first she feared for her sanity, for these recollections were of painful medical experiments, torture and sensory deprivation at the hands of the United States government.

In this brave and groundbreaking work, Judith Moore shares her shattering revelations of the reality of **HIGH-LEVEL MIND CONTROL**. She opens the pages of her journal and the innermost feelings of her heart to share with the reader her **JOURNEY TO WHOLENESS** and to healing. As memories flood her consciousness, she struggles to make sense of what is happening, to process the information in accordance with her lifelong worldview of love, intellectual curiosity and deep respect for nature.

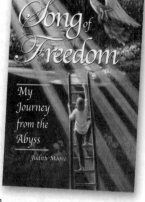

Her early environment, rich in **NATIVE AMERICAN FOLK-LORE**, helps her in her quest. She researches, travels, investigates and meditates in an effort to set herself free, to reclaim her very sense of herself as a person. Her search leads her into terrifying unknown territory and **ILLUMINATING DISCOVERIES** about her own psyche and that of today's society as a whole. **$19.95**

JUDITH'S MEMORIES BEGAN TO BRING TO THE SURFACE
- PAINFUL MEDICAL EXPERIMENTS
- TORTURE
- SENSORY DEPRIVATION
- HIGH-LEVEL MIND CONTROL

AT THE HANDS OF THE UNITED STATES GOVERNMENT!

JUDITH K. MOORE No longer a victim, Judith Moore now leads a productive life, teaching, sharing and channeling the truths that helped her in her journey to freedom.

Song of Freedom *is a wake-up call to Western civilization! Moore's gripping account of her extraordinary life takes us to extremes of human experience—from depravity beyond comprehension to the triumph of one child's unassailable spirit.* Song of Freedom *dares us to take off the blinders we wear to what lies buried in our societal closets. Those who dare to look are taken on a transformational journey through the horrors of mind control and ritual abuse to Judith's amazing experiences of healing. The book is strewn with insights and gems of wisdom which prove that although fear often seems to have the upper hand, it is always love that triumphs in the end.*

CHRYSTINE OKSANA, AUTHOR
Safe Passage to Healing: A Guide for Survivors of Ritual Abuse

LIGHT TECHNOLOGY PUBLISHING
P.O. BOX 3540 • FLAGSTAFF • AZ 86003
PHONE: (928) 526-1345
1-800-450-0985
FAX: (928) 714-1132
1-800-393-7017
www.lighttechnology.com

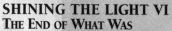

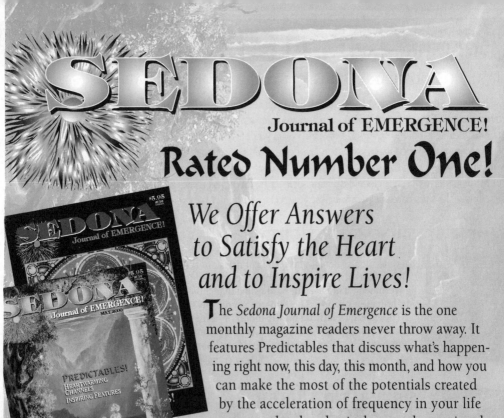